THE CASE OF THE
MISSING MEN

A HOBTOWN MYSTERY

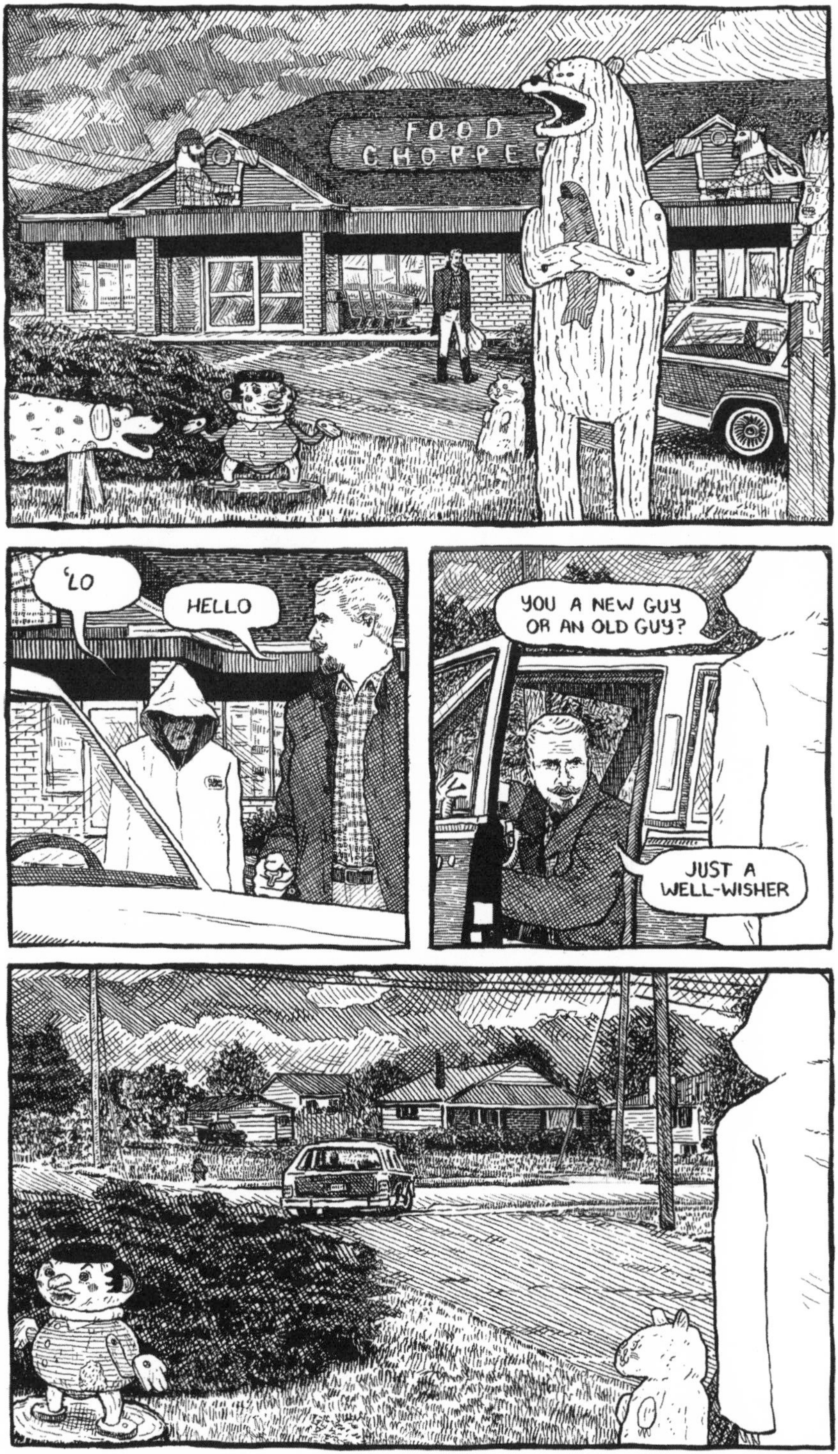
FOOD CHOPPE
'LO
HELLO
YOU A NEW GUY OR AN OLD GUY?
JUST A WELL-WISHER

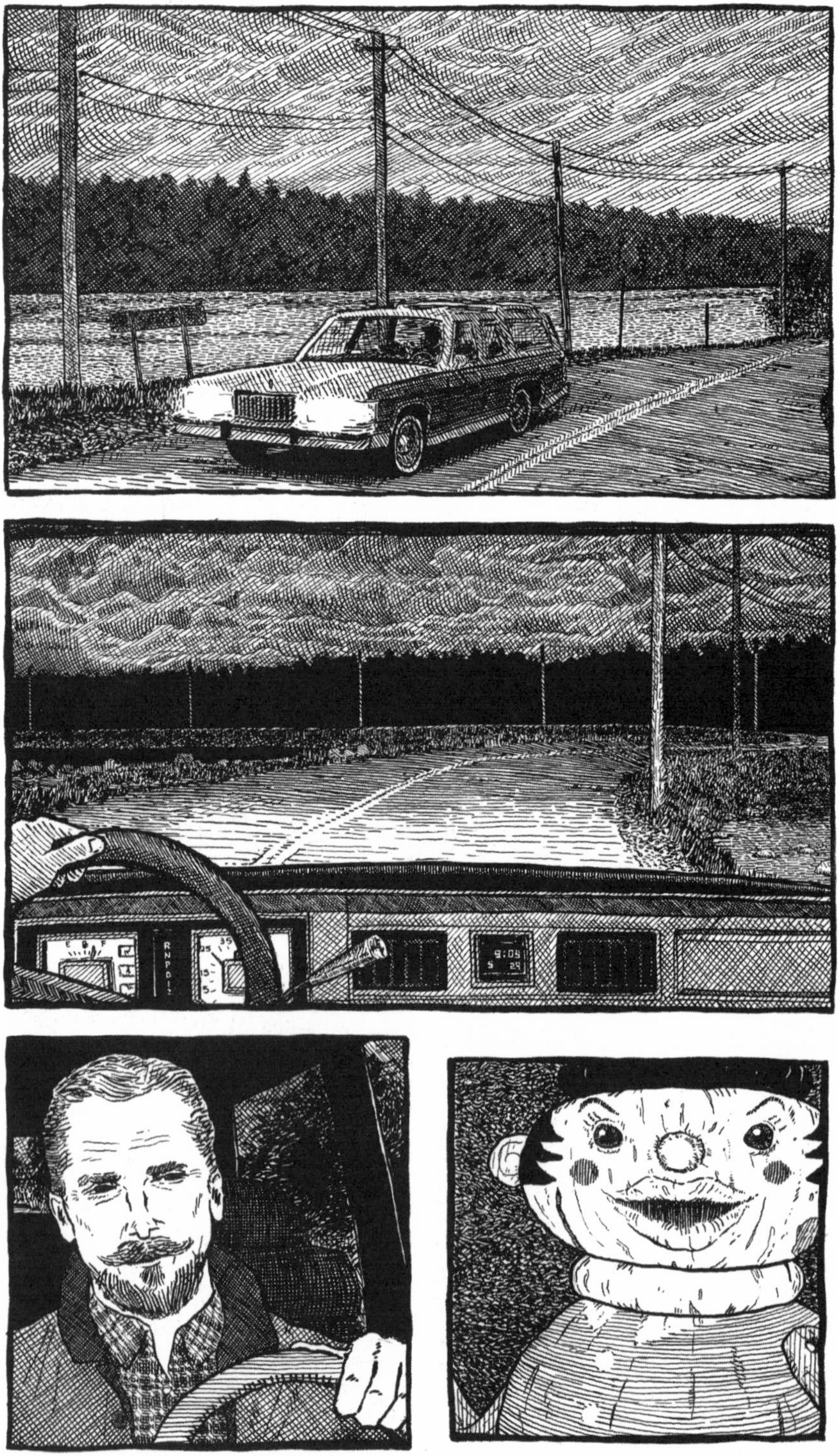

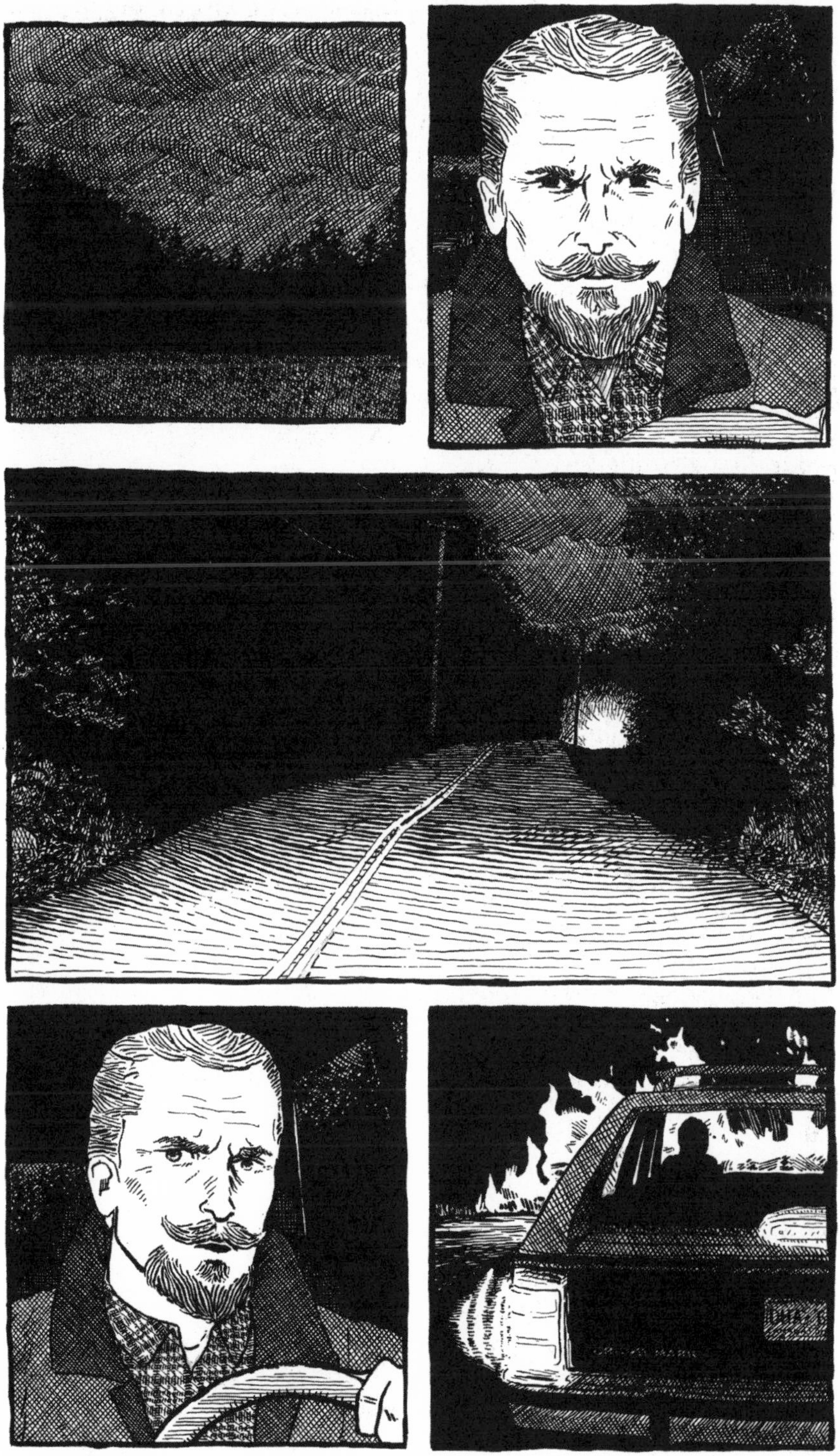

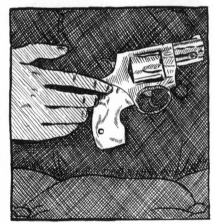

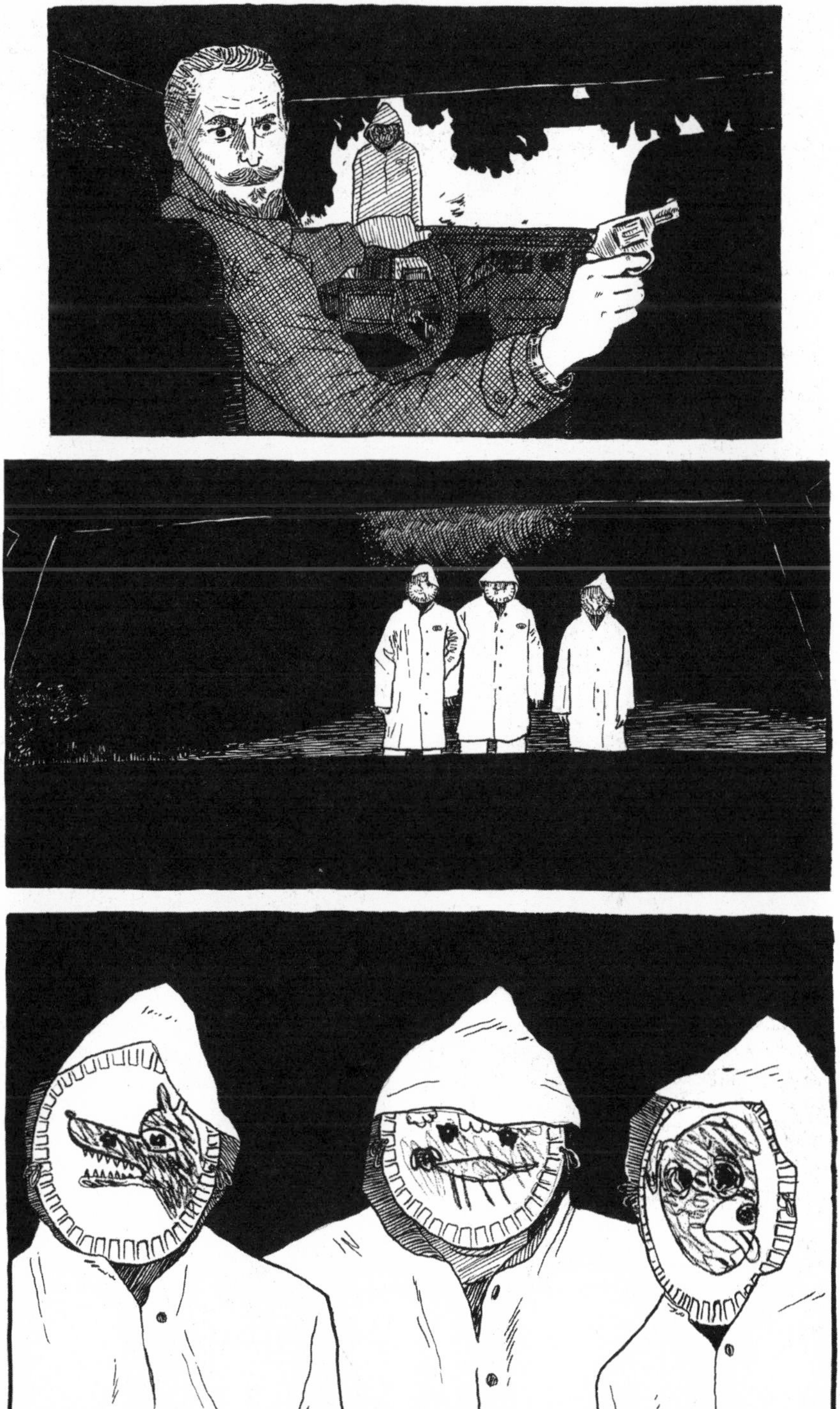

THE CASE OF THE
MISSING MEN

A HOBTOWN MYSTERY

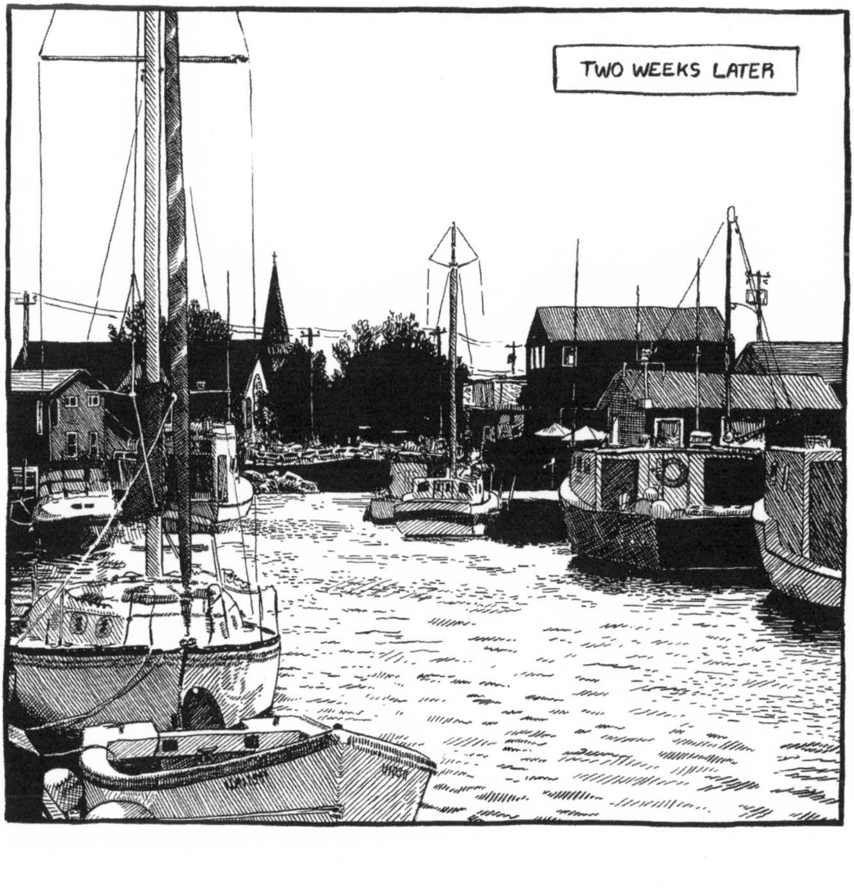
TWO WEEKS LATER

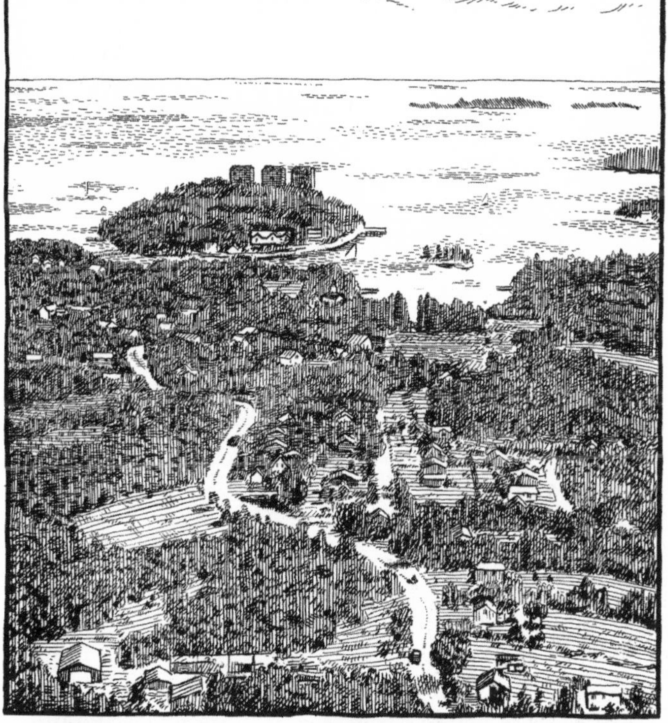

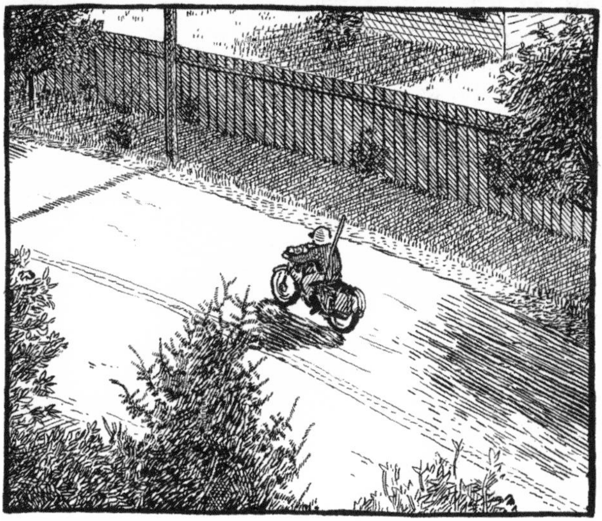

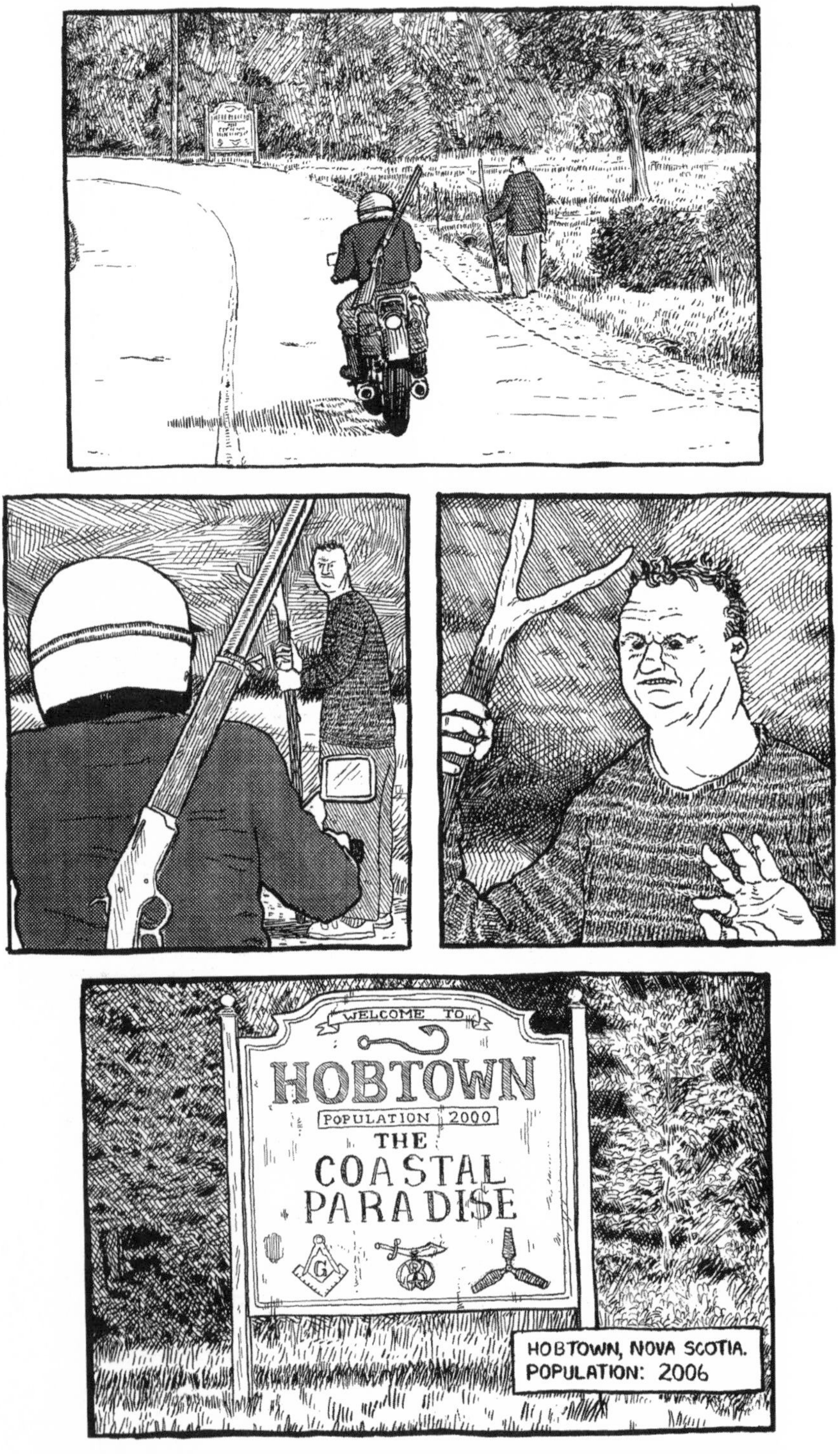
WELCOME TO
HOBTOWN
POPULATION 2000
THE COASTAL PARADISE
HOBTOWN, NOVA SCOTIA.
POPULATION: 2006

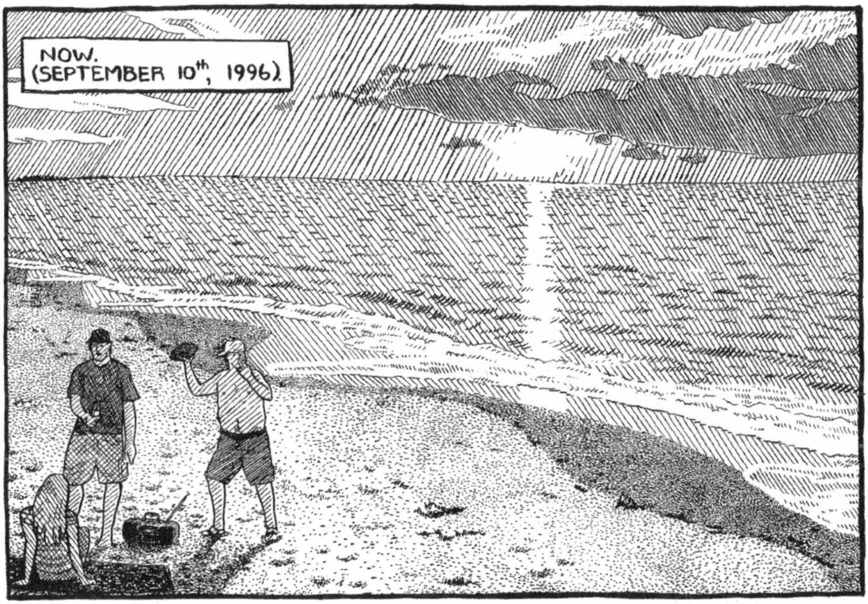
NOW.
(SEPTEMBER 10th, 1996).

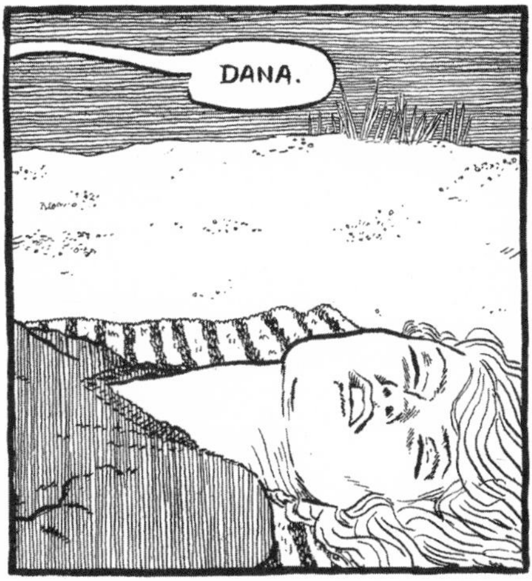
DANA.

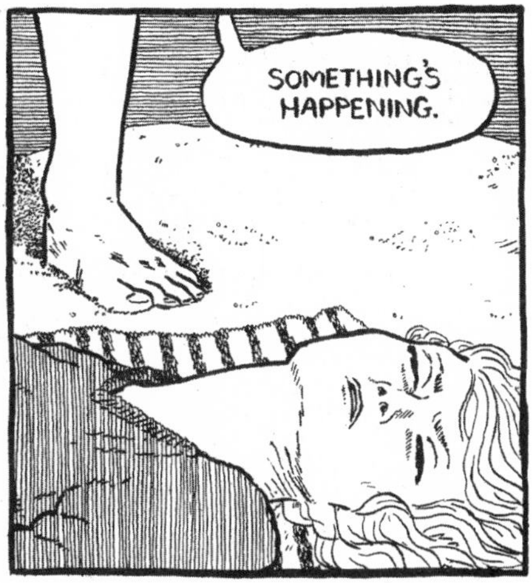
SOMETHING'S
HAPPENING.

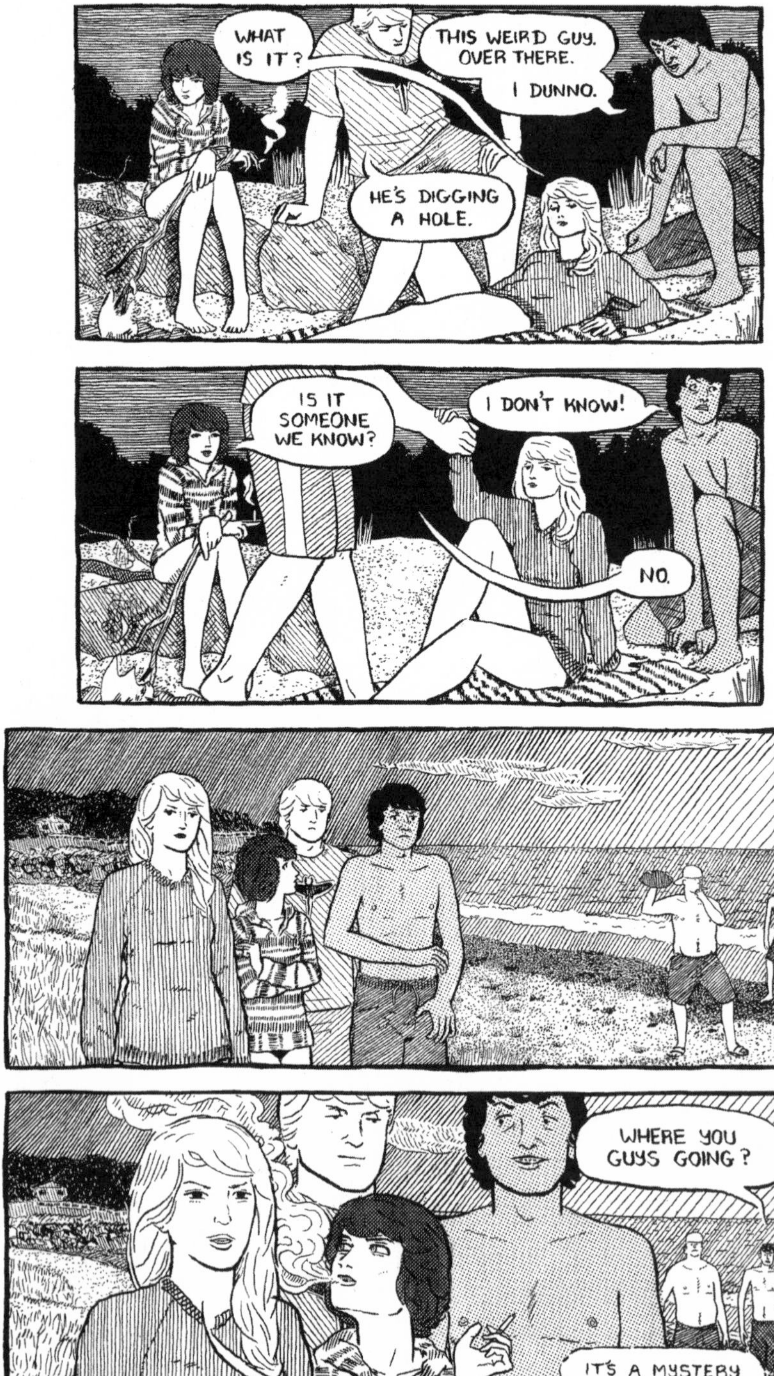
WHAT IS IT?
THIS WEIRD GUY. OVER THERE.
I DUNNO.
HE'S DIGGING A HOLE.
IS IT SOMEONE WE KNOW?
I DON'T KNOW!
NO.
WHERE YOU GUYS GOING?
IT'S A MYSTERY

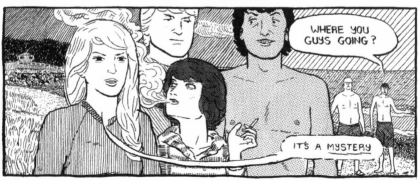

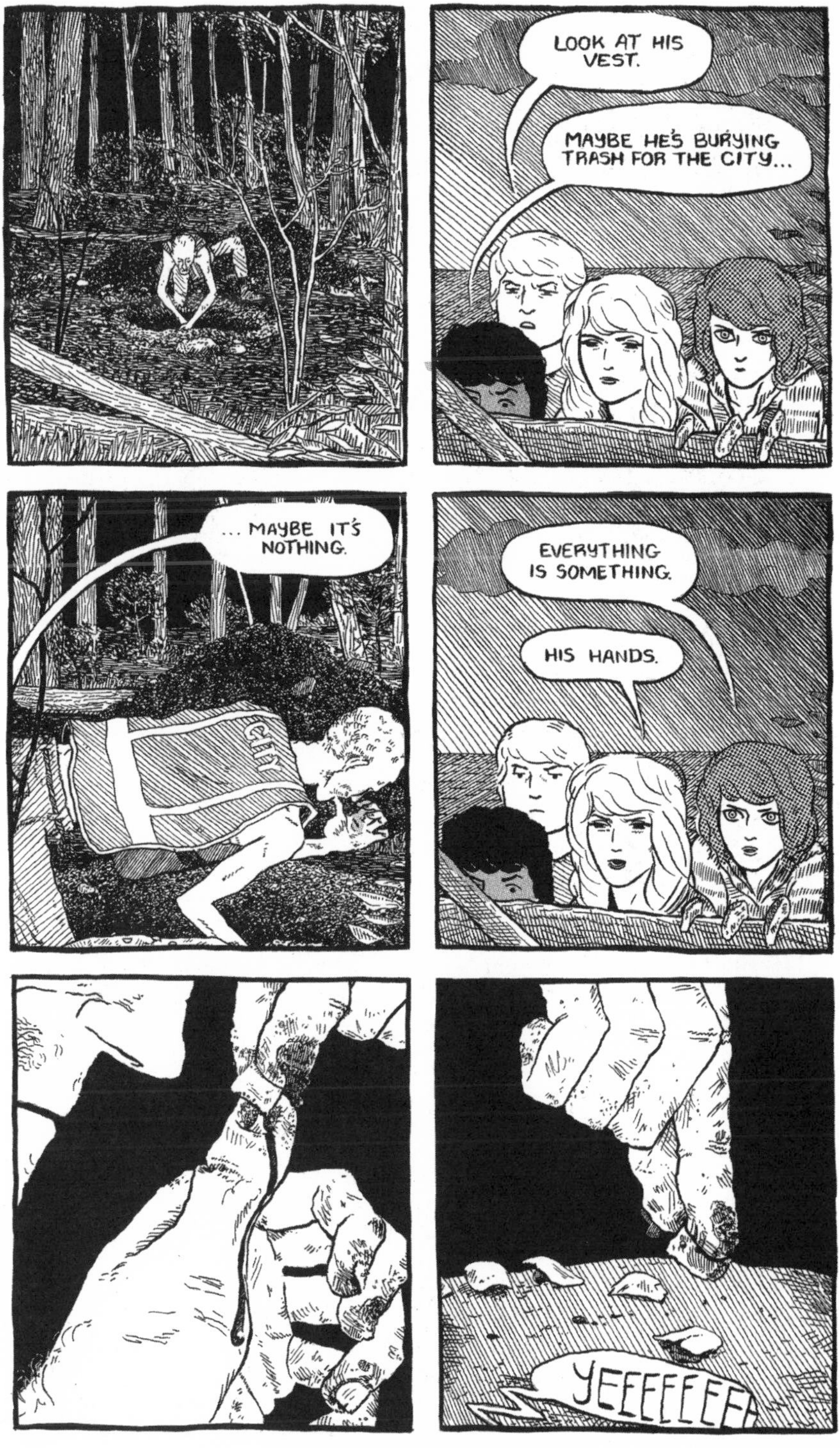
LOOK AT HIS VEST.
MAYBE HE'S BURYING TRASH FOR THE CITY...
... MAYBE IT'S NOTHING.
CITY
EVERYTHING IS SOMETHING.
HIS HANDS.
YEEEEEEEH

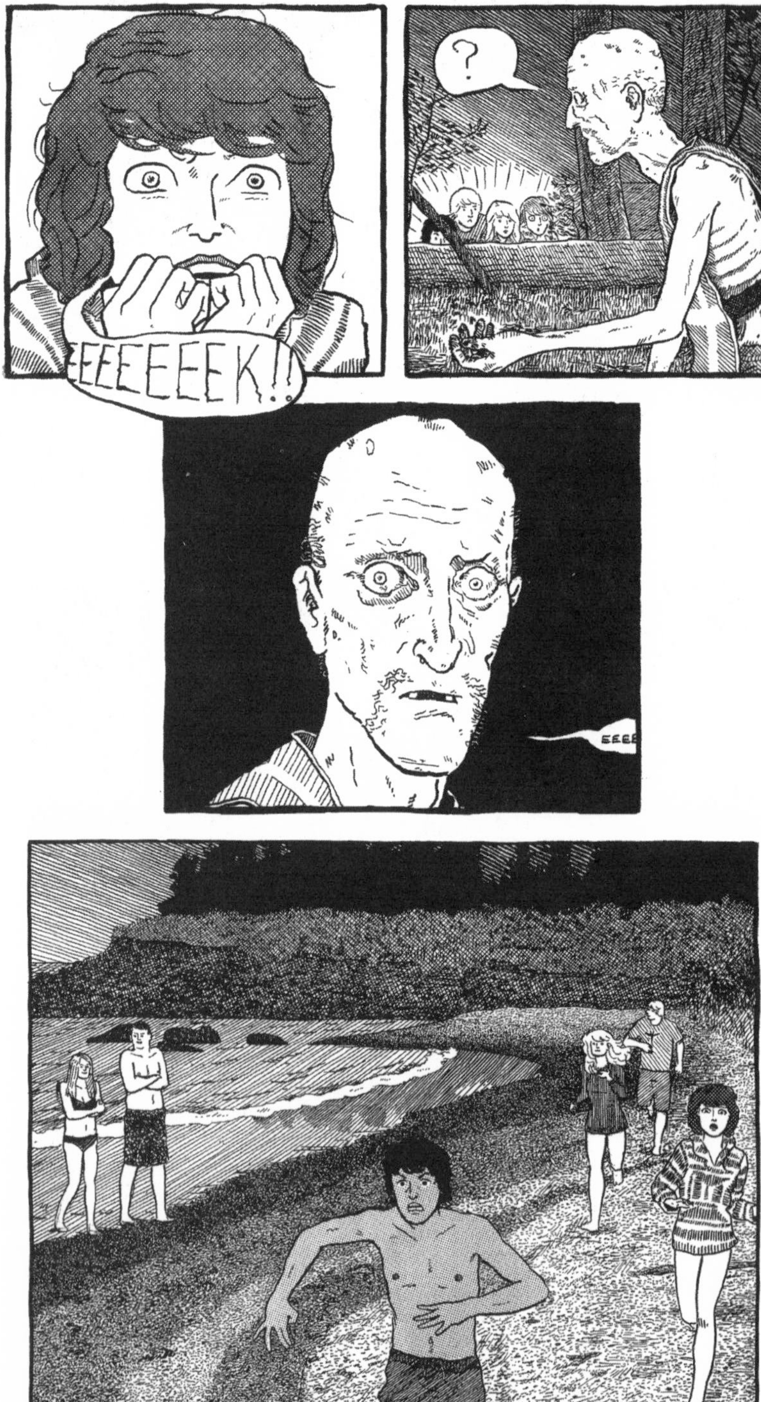
EEEEEEEK!!
?
EEEE

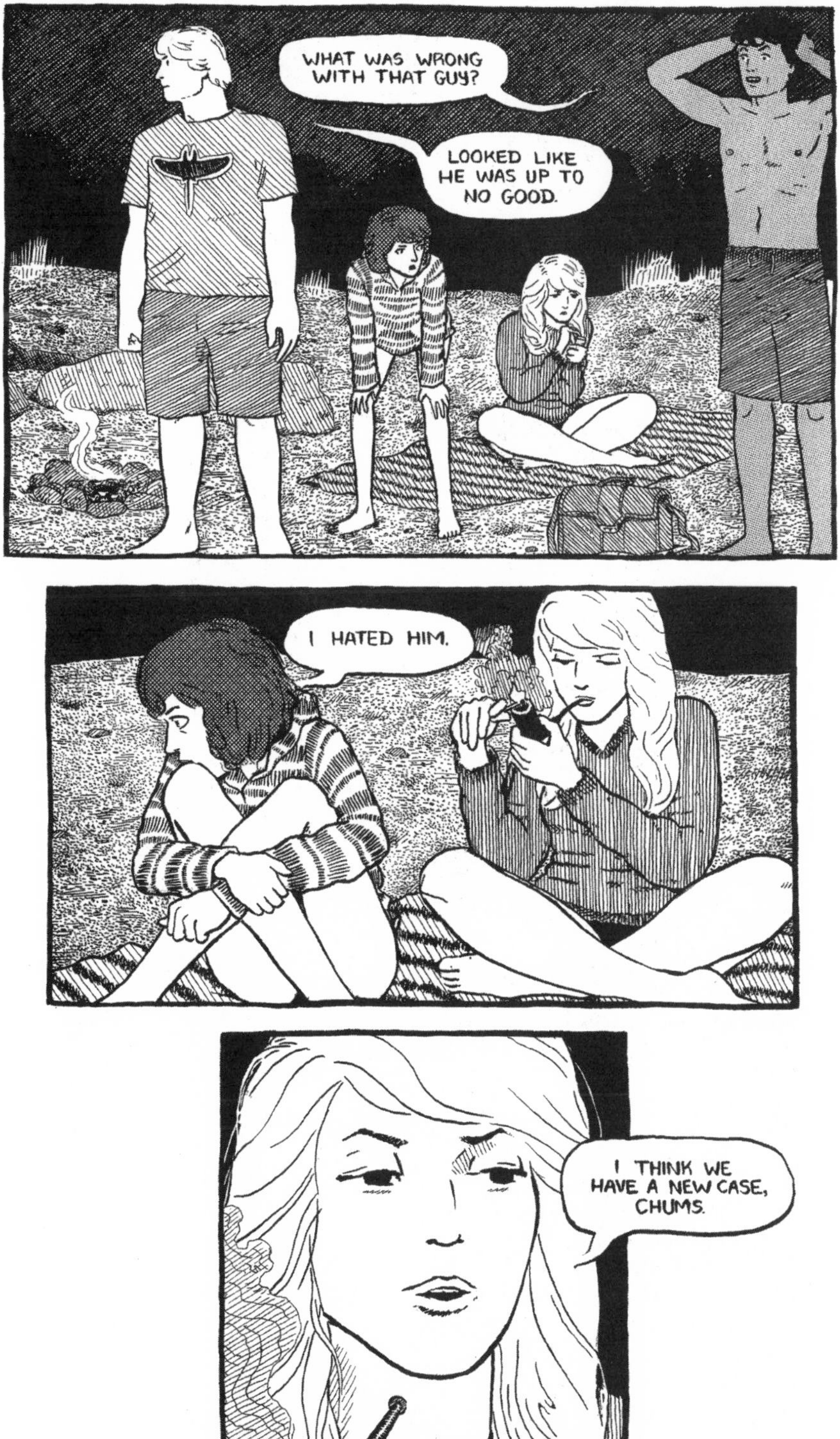
WHAT WAS WRONG WITH THAT GUY?
LOOKED LIKE HE WAS UP TO NO GOOD.
I HATED HIM.
I THINK WE HAVE A NEW CASE, CHUMS.

CHAPTER ONE

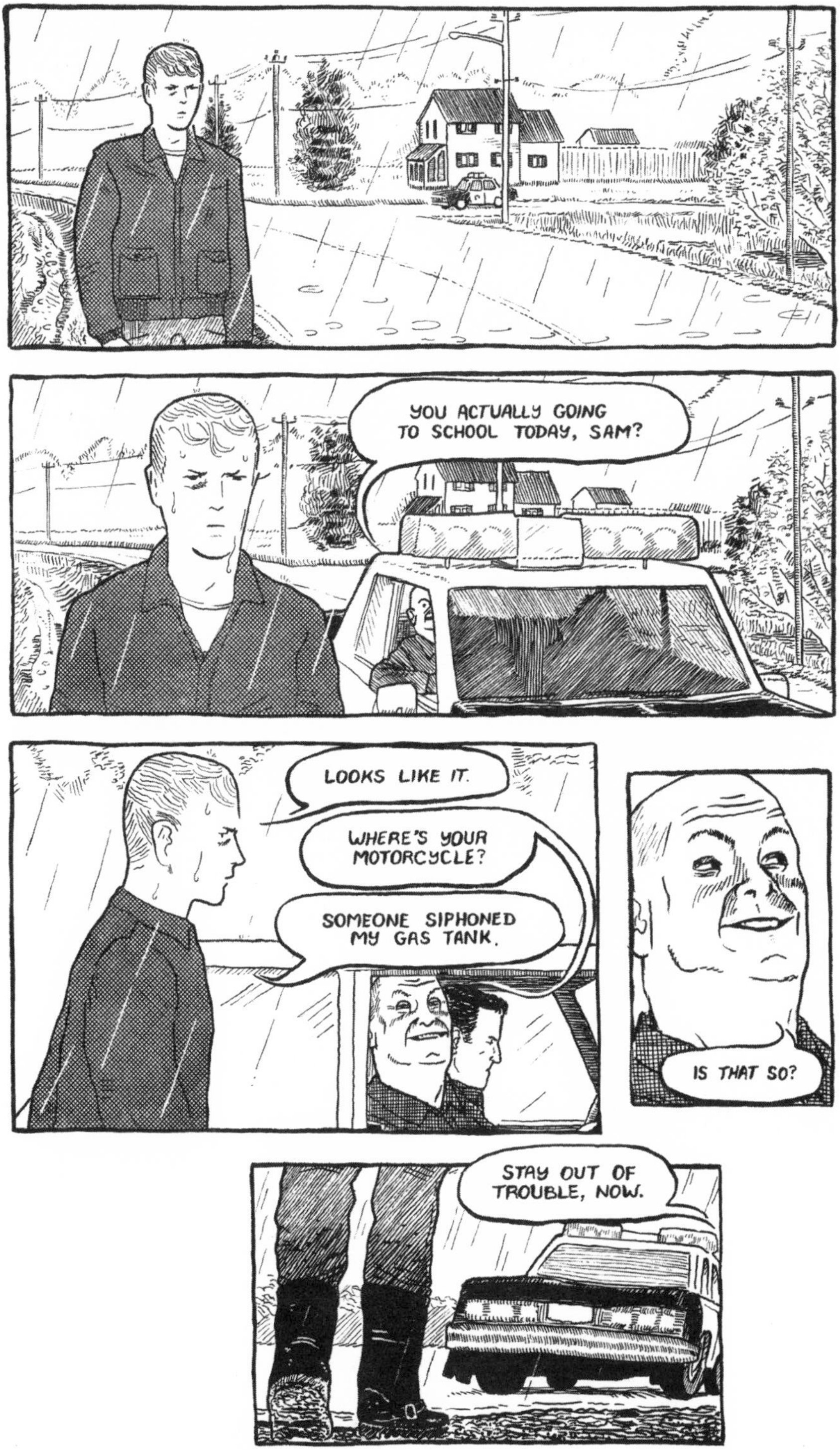
YOU ACTUALLY GOING TO SCHOOL TODAY, SAM?
LOOKS LIKE IT.
WHERE'S YOUR MOTORCYCLE?
SOMEONE SIPHONED MY GAS TANK.
IS THAT SO?
STAY OUT OF TROUBLE, NOW.

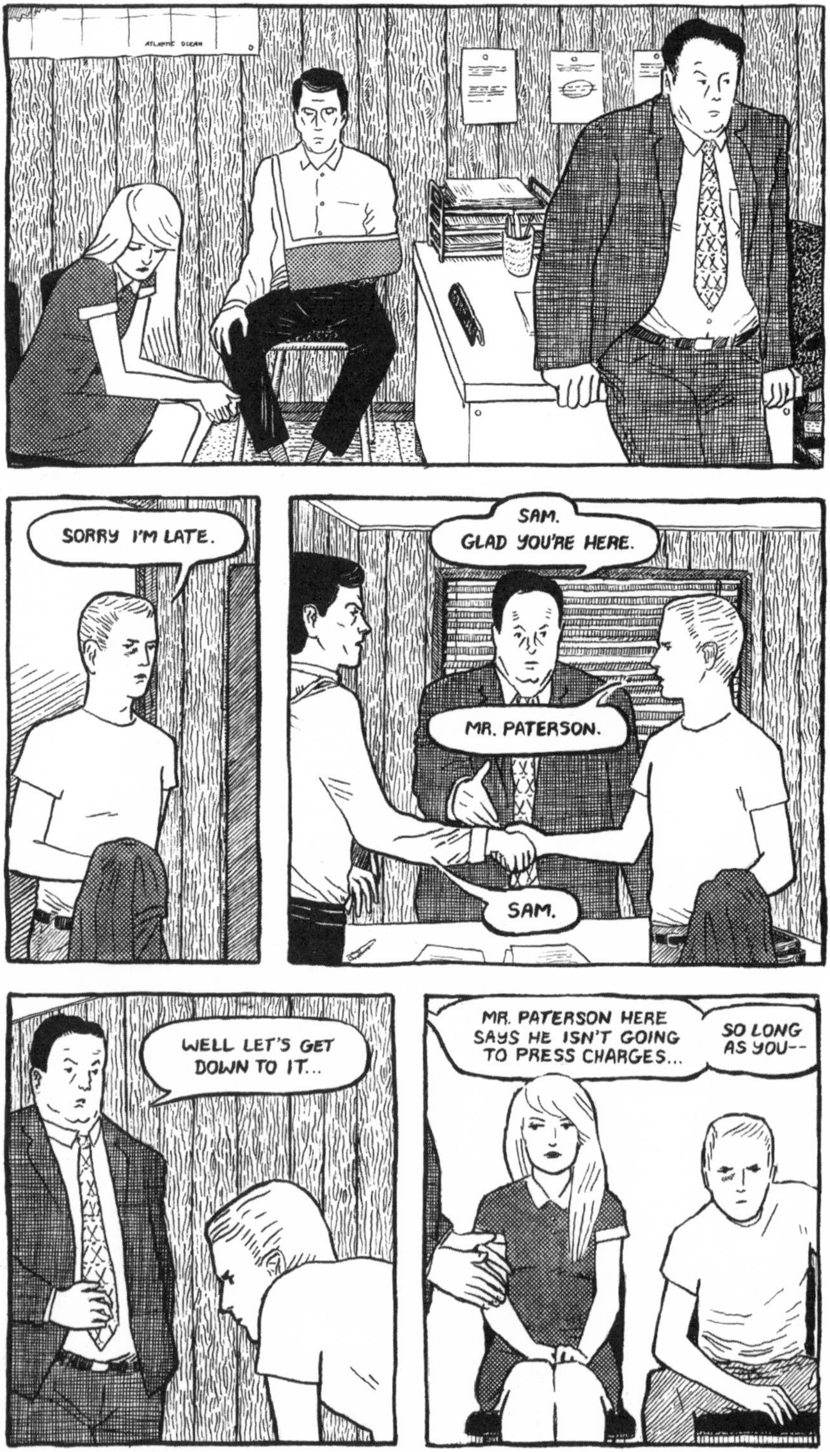
ATLANTIC OCEAN
SORRY I'M LATE.
SAM.
GLAD YOU'RE HERE.
MR. PATERSON.
SAM.
WELL LET'S GET DOWN TO IT...
MR. PATERSON HERE SAYS HE ISN'T GOING TO PRESS CHARGES...
SO LONG AS YOU--

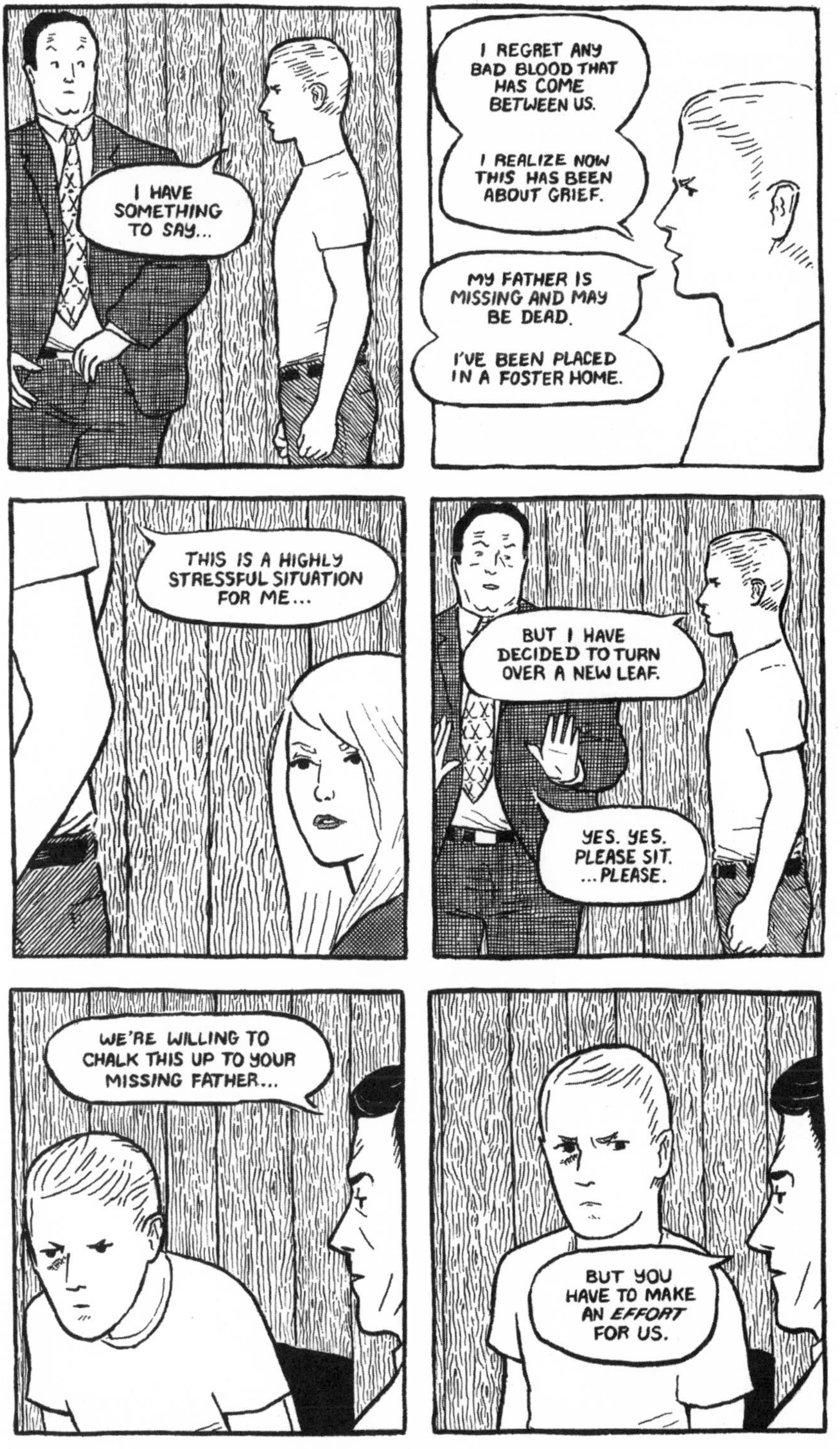
I HAVE SOMETHING TO SAY...
I REGRET ANY BAD BLOOD THAT HAS COME BETWEEN US.
I REALIZE NOW THIS HAS BEEN ABOUT GRIEF.
MY FATHER IS MISSING AND MAY BE DEAD.
I'VE BEEN PLACED IN A FOSTER HOME.
THIS IS A HIGHLY STRESSFUL SITUATION FOR ME...
BUT I HAVE DECIDED TO TURN OVER A NEW LEAF.
YES. YES. PLEASE SIT. ...PLEASE.
WE'RE WILLING TO CHALK THIS UP TO YOUR MISSING FATHER...
BUT YOU HAVE TO MAKE AN *EFFORT* FOR US.

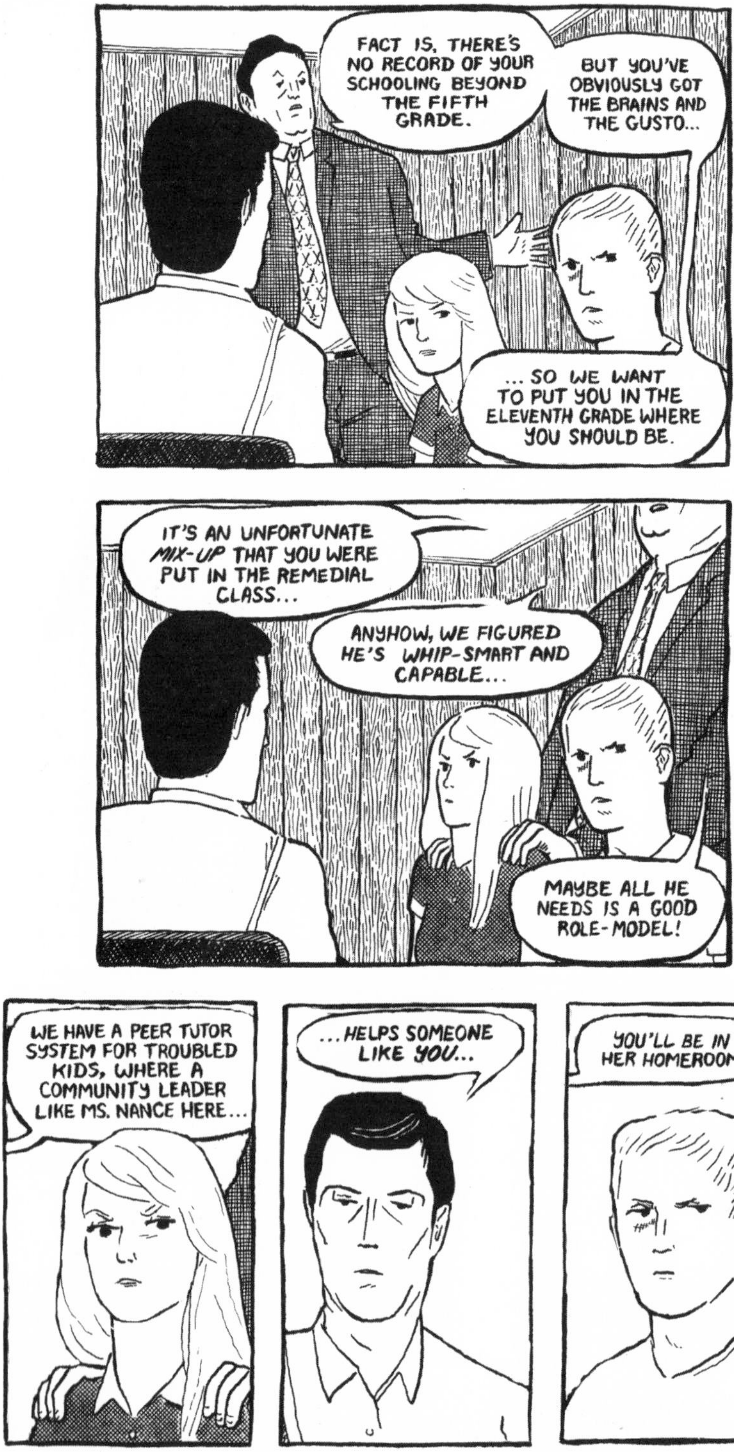
FACT IS, THERE'S NO RECORD OF YOUR SCHOOLING BEYOND THE FIFTH GRADE.
BUT YOU'VE OBVIOUSLY GOT THE BRAINS AND THE GUSTO...
... SO WE WANT TO PUT YOU IN THE ELEVENTH GRADE WHERE YOU SHOULD BE.
IT'S AN UNFORTUNATE MIX-UP THAT YOU WERE PUT IN THE REMEDIAL CLASS...
ANYHOW, WE FIGURED HE'S WHIP-SMART AND CAPABLE...
MAYBE ALL HE NEEDS IS A GOOD ROLE-MODEL!
WE HAVE A PEER TUTOR SYSTEM FOR TROUBLED KIDS, WHERE A COMMUNITY LEADER LIKE MS. NANCE HERE...
...HELPS SOMEONE LIKE YOU...
YOU'LL BE IN HER HOMEROOM.
YES

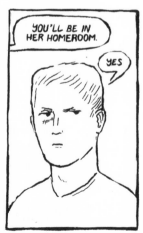

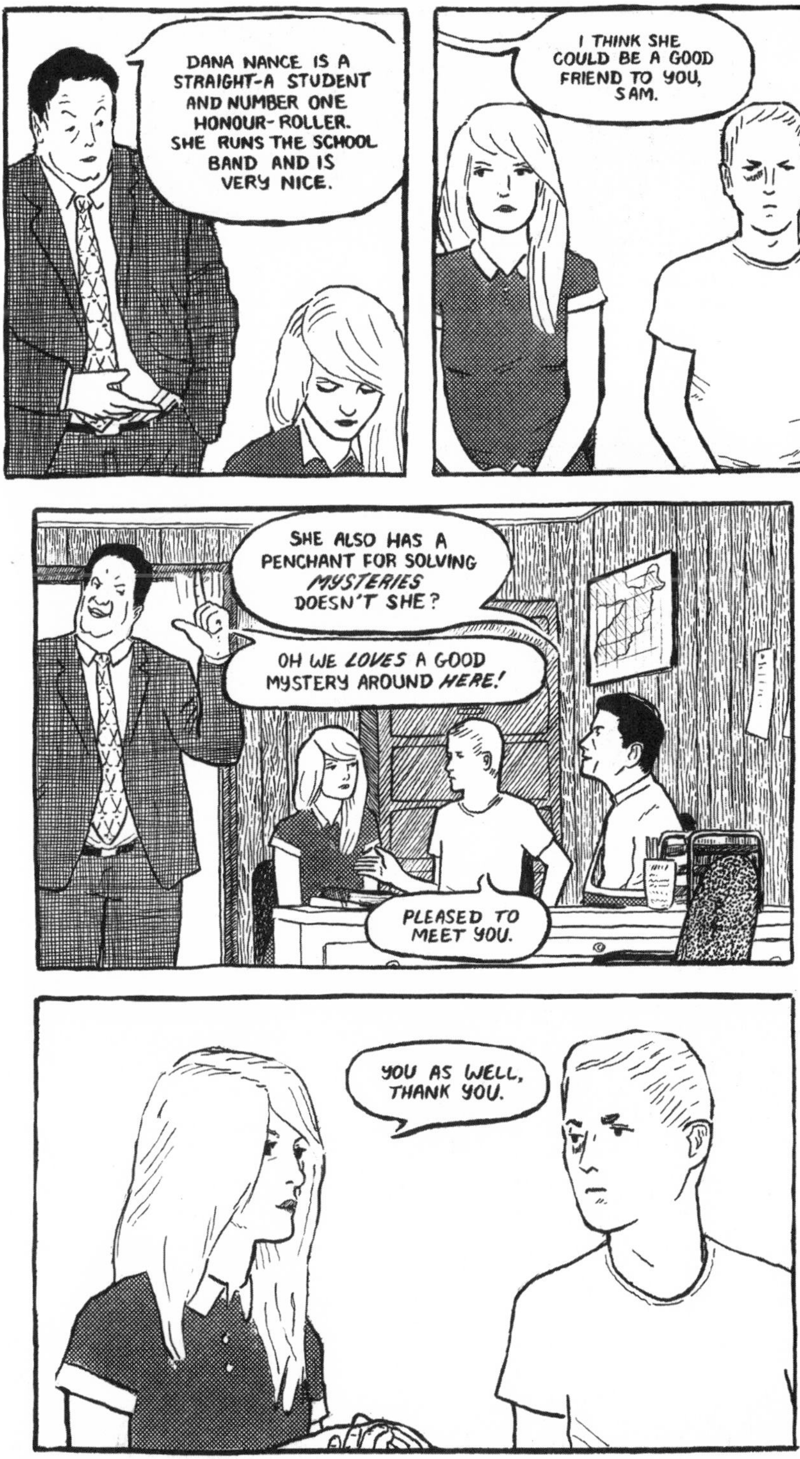
DANA NANCE IS A STRAIGHT-A STUDENT AND NUMBER ONE HONOUR-ROLLER. SHE RUNS THE SCHOOL BAND AND IS VERY NICE.
I THINK SHE COULD BE A GOOD FRIEND TO YOU, SAM.
SHE ALSO HAS A PENCHANT FOR SOLVING *MYSTERIES* DOESN'T SHE?
OH WE *LOVES* A GOOD MYSTERY AROUND *HERE!*
PLEASED TO MEET YOU.
YOU AS WELL, THANK YOU.

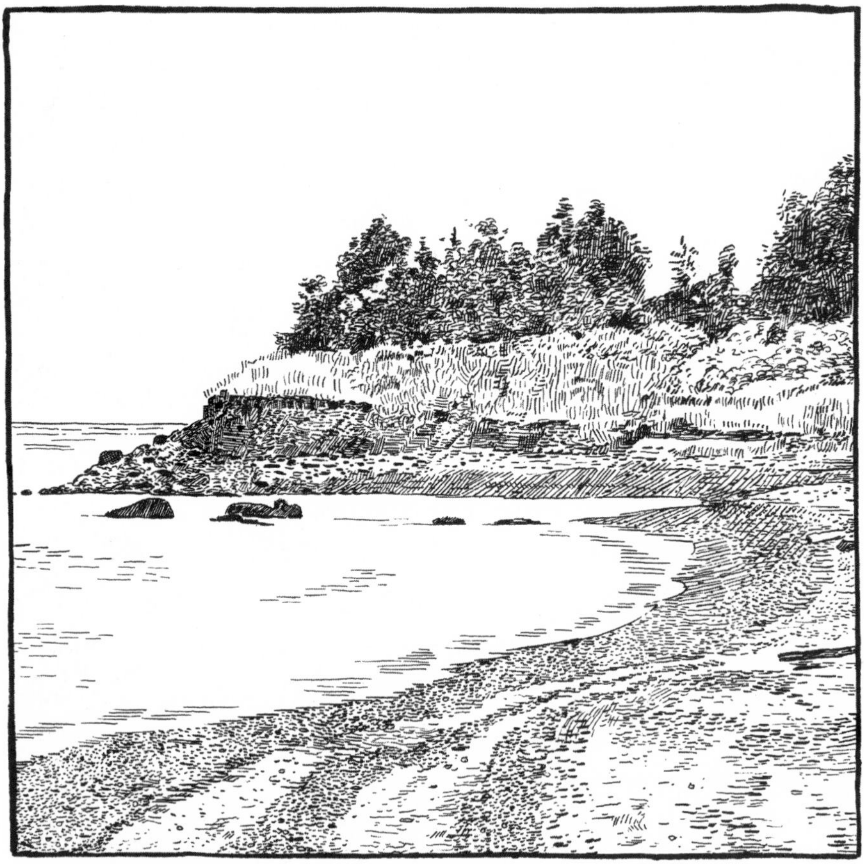

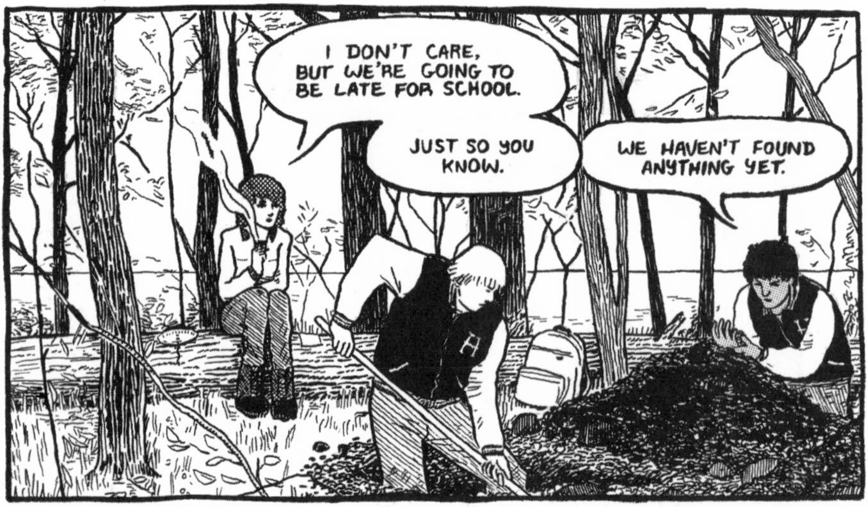
I DON'T CARE, BUT WE'RE GOING TO BE LATE FOR SCHOOL.
JUST SO YOU KNOW.
WE HAVEN'T FOUND ANYTHING YET.

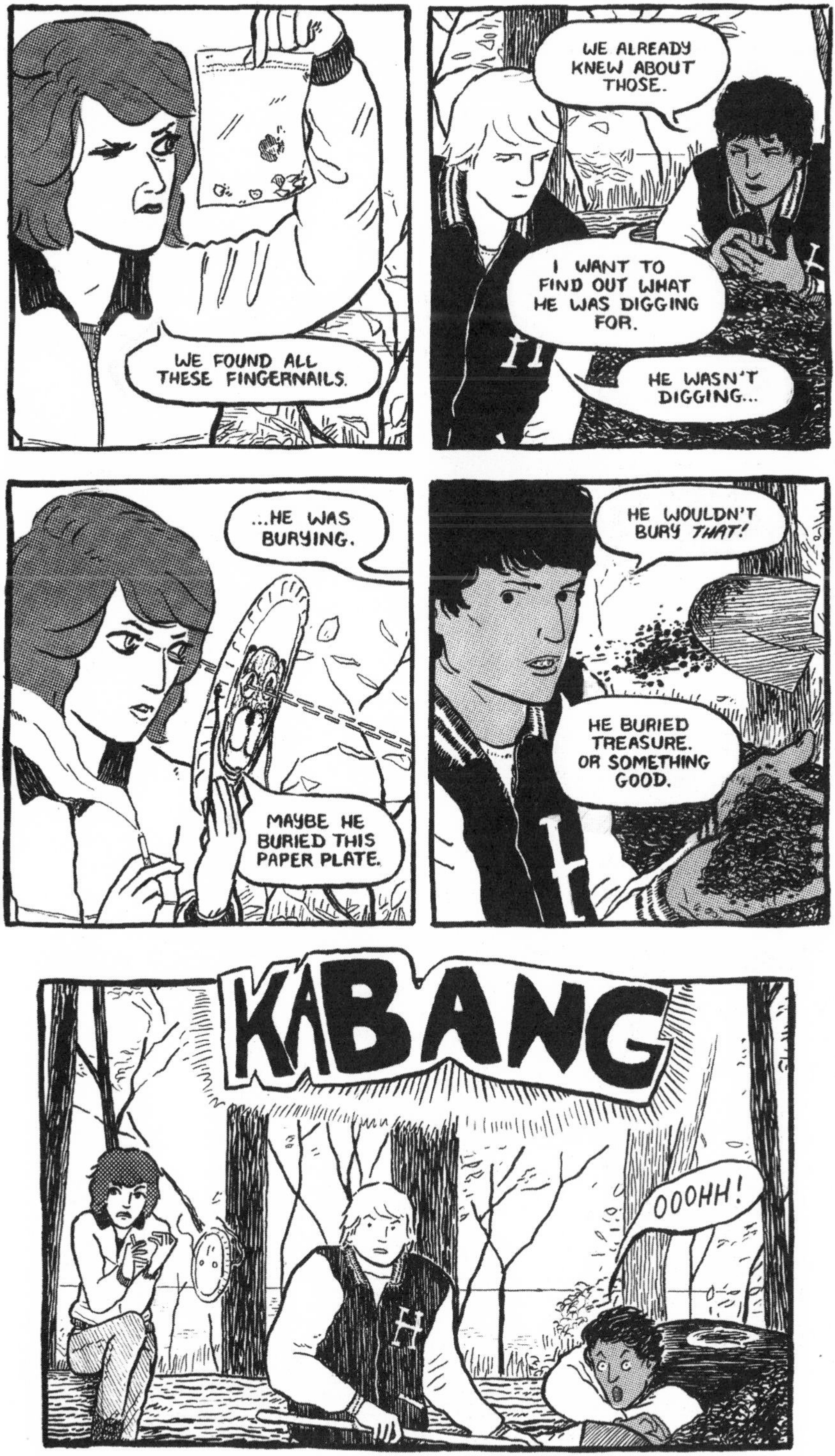
WE FOUND ALL THESE FINGERNAILS.
WE ALREADY KNEW ABOUT THOSE.
I WANT TO FIND OUT WHAT HE WAS DIGGING FOR.
HE WASN'T DIGGING...
...HE WAS BURYING.
MAYBE HE BURIED THIS PAPER PLATE.
HE WOULDN'T BURY *THAT!*
HE BURIED TREASURE. OR SOMETHING GOOD.
KABANG
OOOHH!

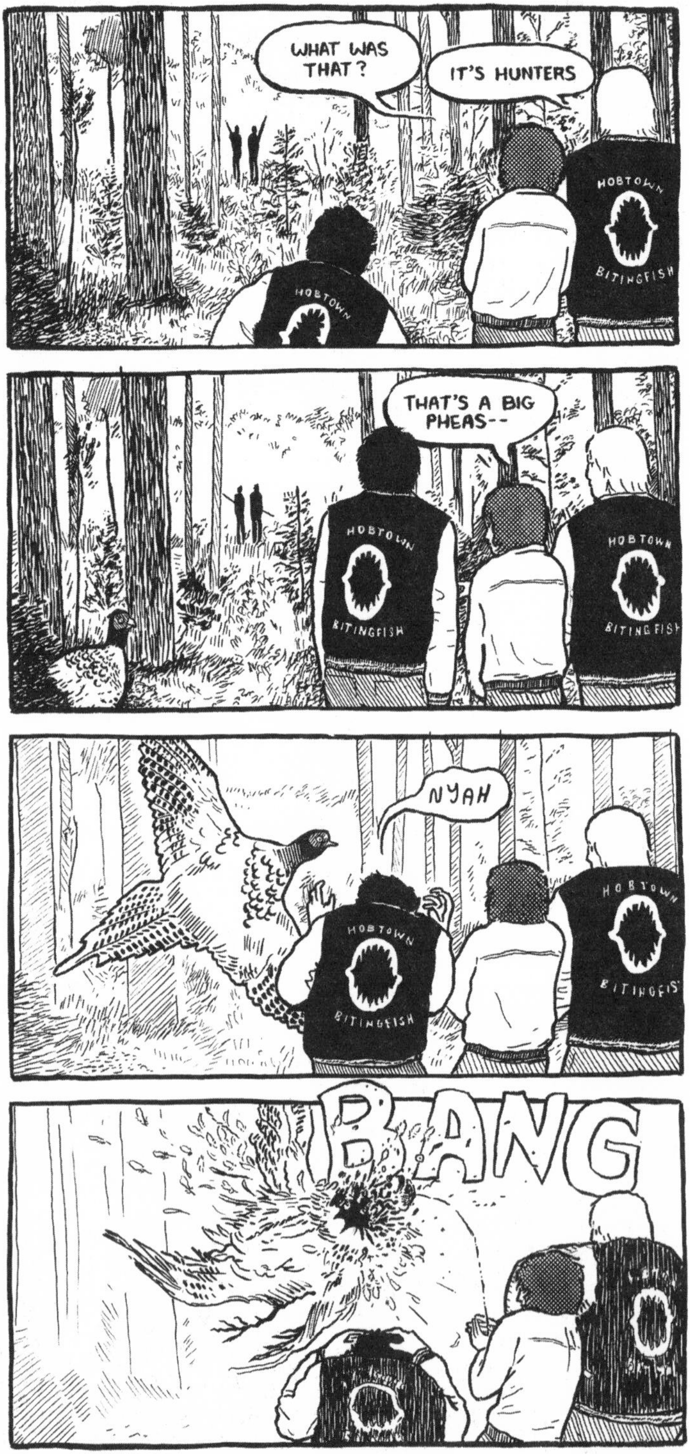
WHAT WAS THAT?
IT'S HUNTERS
HOBTOWN
HOBTOWN
BITINGFISH
THAT'S A BIG PHEAS--
HOBTOWN
BITINGFISH
HOBTOWN
BITING FISH
NYAH
HOBTOWN
BITINGFISH
HOBTOWN
BITINGFIS
BANG

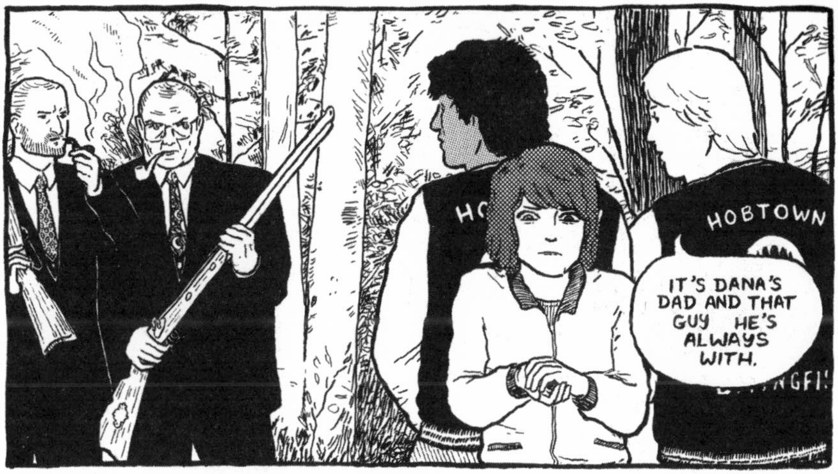
HOBTOWN
IT'S DANA'S DAD AND THAT GUY HE'S ALWAYS WITH.

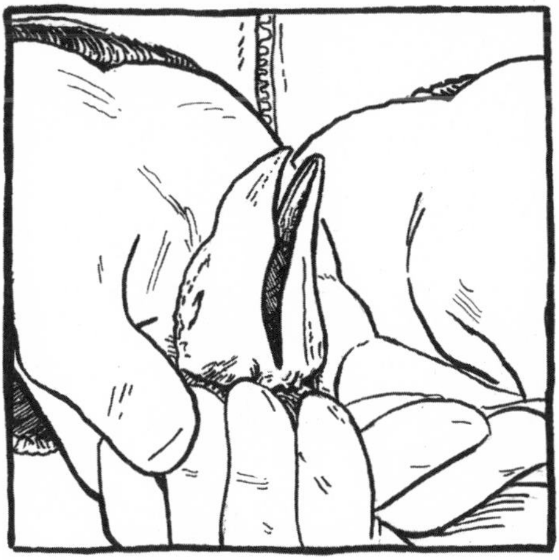

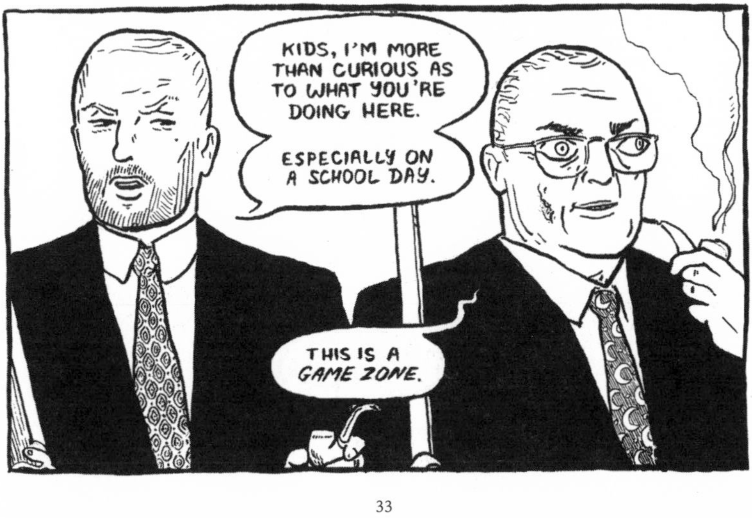
KIDS, I'M MORE THAN CURIOUS AS TO WHAT YOU'RE DOING HERE.
ESPECIALLY ON A SCHOOL DAY.
THIS IS A *GAME ZONE*.

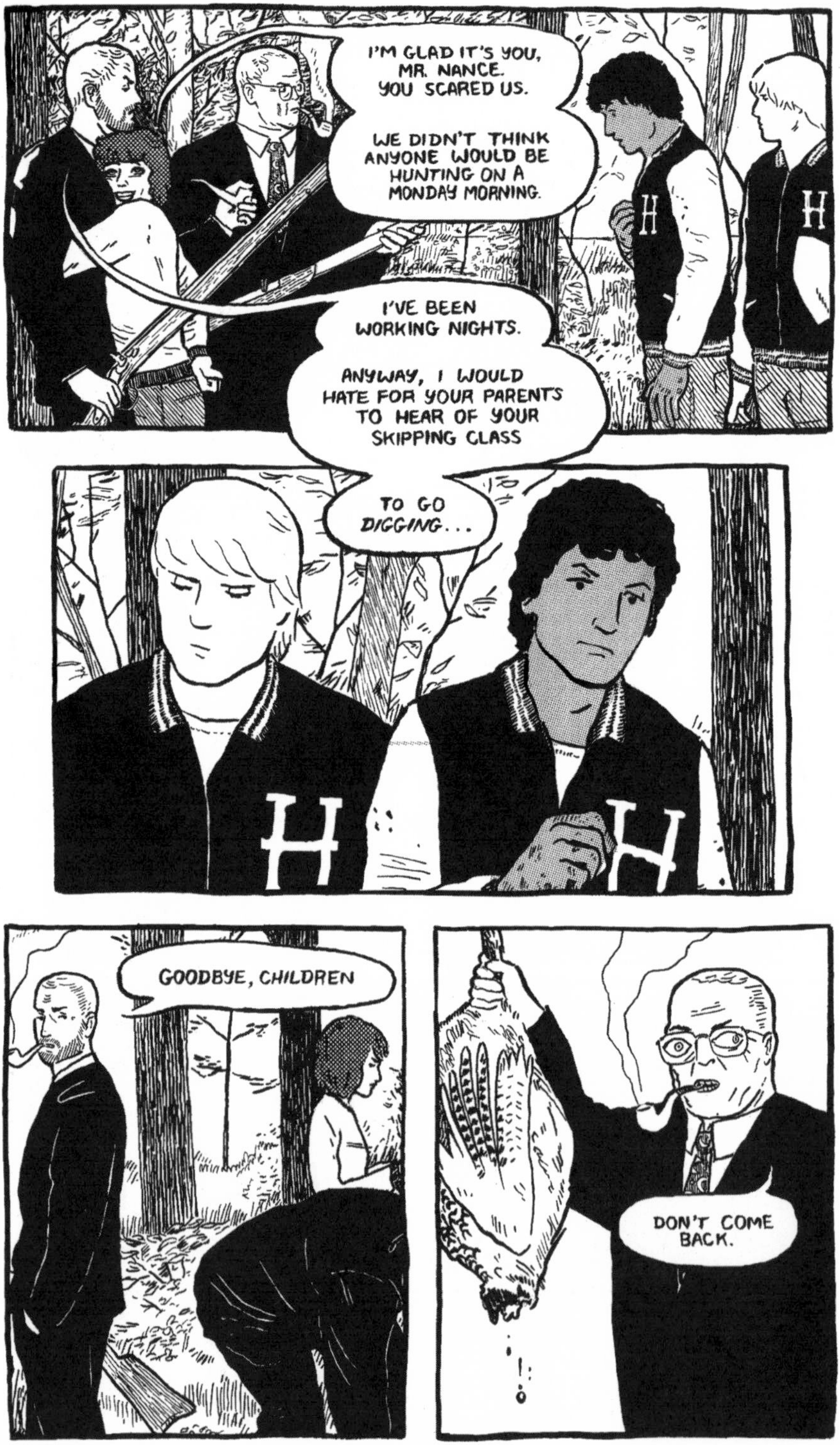
I'M GLAD IT'S YOU, MR. NANCE. YOU SCARED US.
WE DIDN'T THINK ANYONE WOULD BE HUNTING ON A MONDAY MORNING.
I'VE BEEN WORKING NIGHTS.
ANYWAY, I WOULD HATE FOR YOUR PARENTS TO HEAR OF YOUR SKIPPING CLASS
TO GO *DIGGING*...
GOODBYE, CHILDREN
DON'T COME BACK.

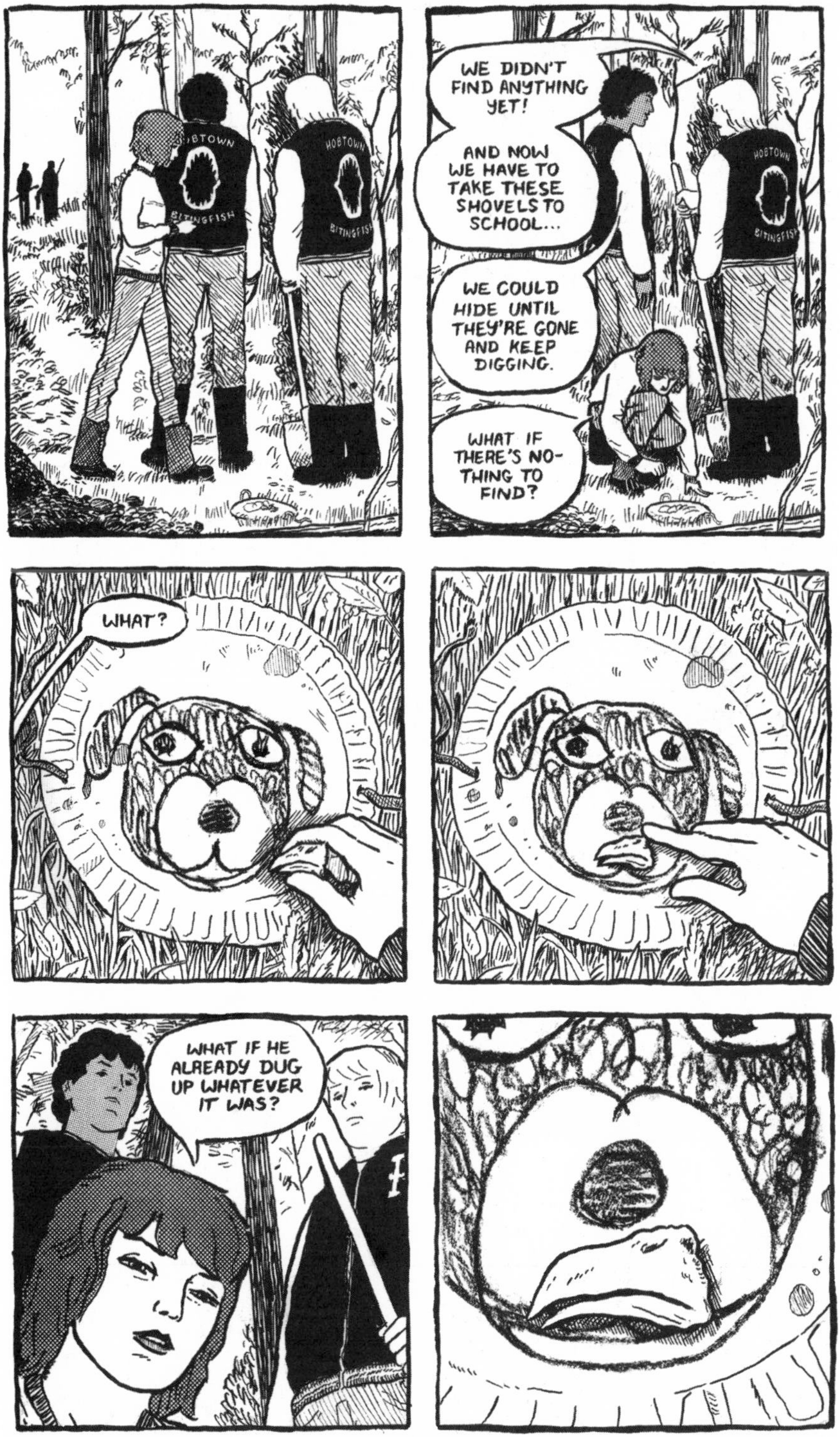
HOBTOWN
BITINGFISH
WE DIDN'T FIND ANYTHING YET!
AND NOW WE HAVE TO TAKE THESE SHOVELS TO SCHOOL...
WE COULD HIDE UNTIL THEY'RE GONE AND KEEP DIGGING.
WHAT IF THERE'S NOTHING TO FIND?
WHAT?
WHAT IF HE ALREADY DUG UP WHATEVER IT WAS?

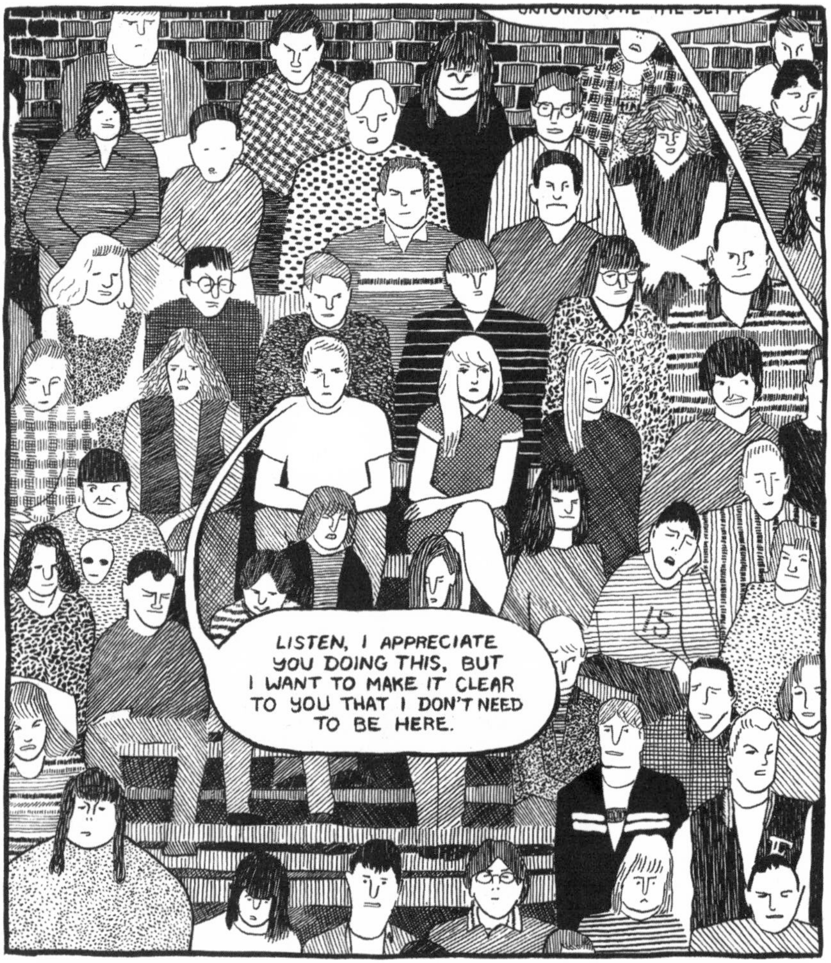
LISTEN, I APPRECIATE YOU DOING THIS, BUT I WANT TO MAKE IT CLEAR TO YOU THAT I DON'T NEED TO BE HERE.

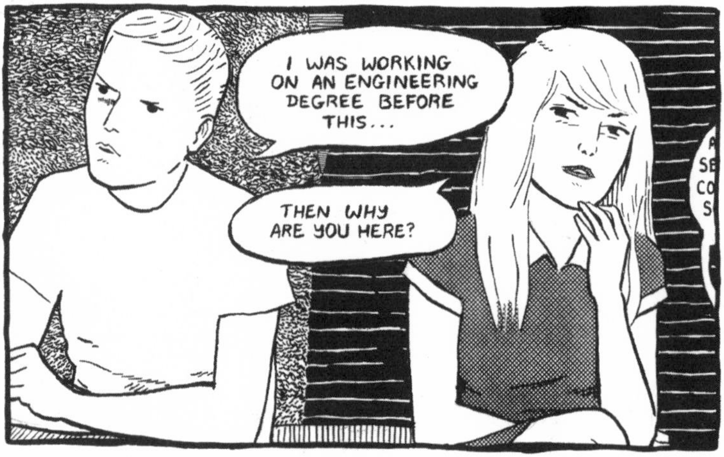
I WAS WORKING ON AN ENGINEERING DEGREE BEFORE THIS...
THEN WHY ARE YOU HERE?

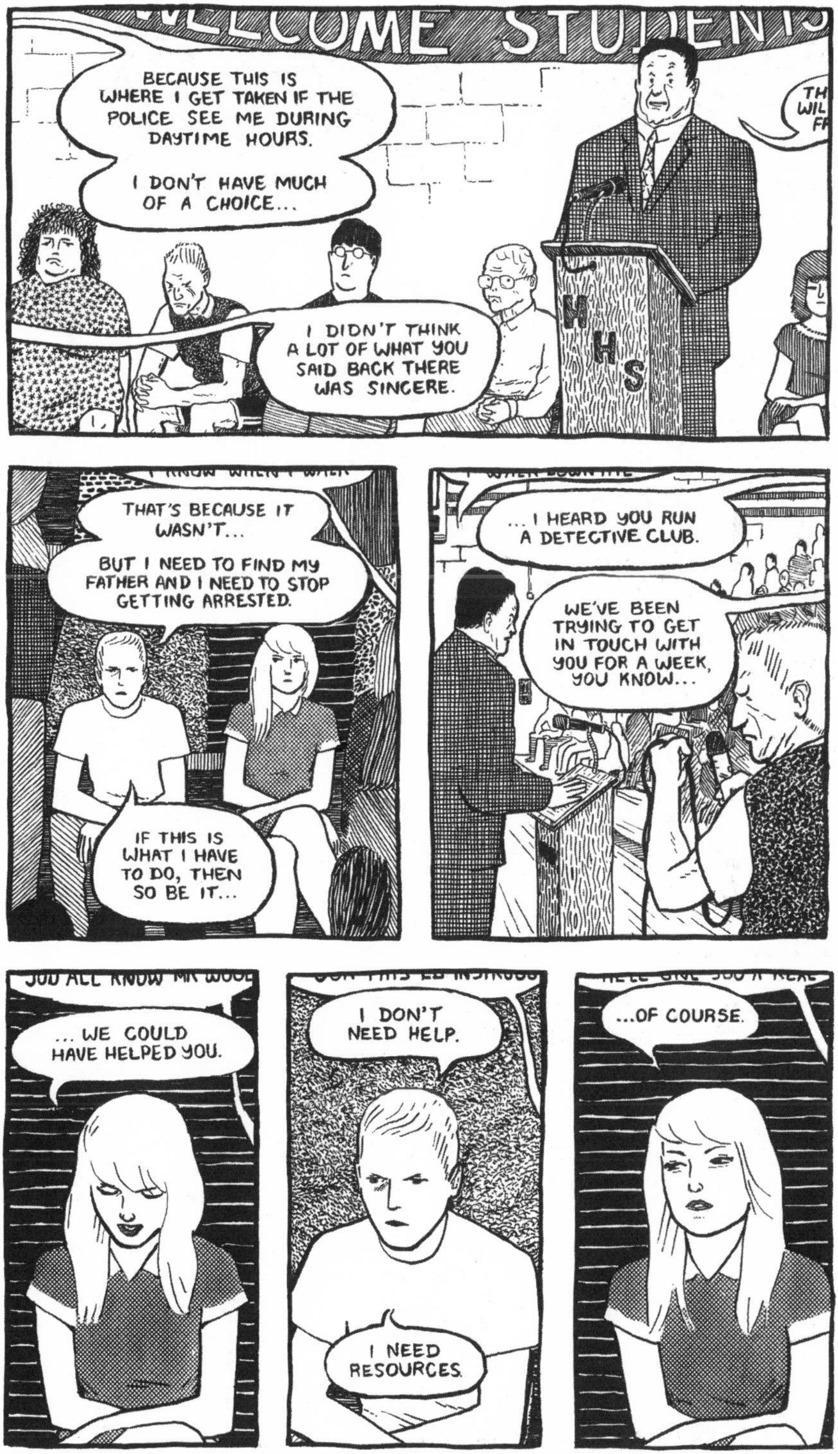
BECAUSE THIS IS WHERE I GET TAKEN IF THE POLICE SEE ME DURING DAYTIME HOURS.
I DON'T HAVE MUCH OF A CHOICE...
I DIDN'T THINK A LOT OF WHAT YOU SAID BACK THERE WAS SINCERE.
THAT'S BECAUSE IT WASN'T...
BUT I NEED TO FIND MY FATHER AND I NEED TO STOP GETTING ARRESTED.
IF THIS IS WHAT I HAVE TO DO, THEN SO BE IT...
...I HEARD YOU RUN A DETECTIVE CLUB.
WE'VE BEEN TRYING TO GET IN TOUCH WITH YOU FOR A WEEK, YOU KNOW...
... WE COULD HAVE HELPED YOU.
I DON'T NEED HELP.
I NEED RESOURCES.
...OF COURSE.

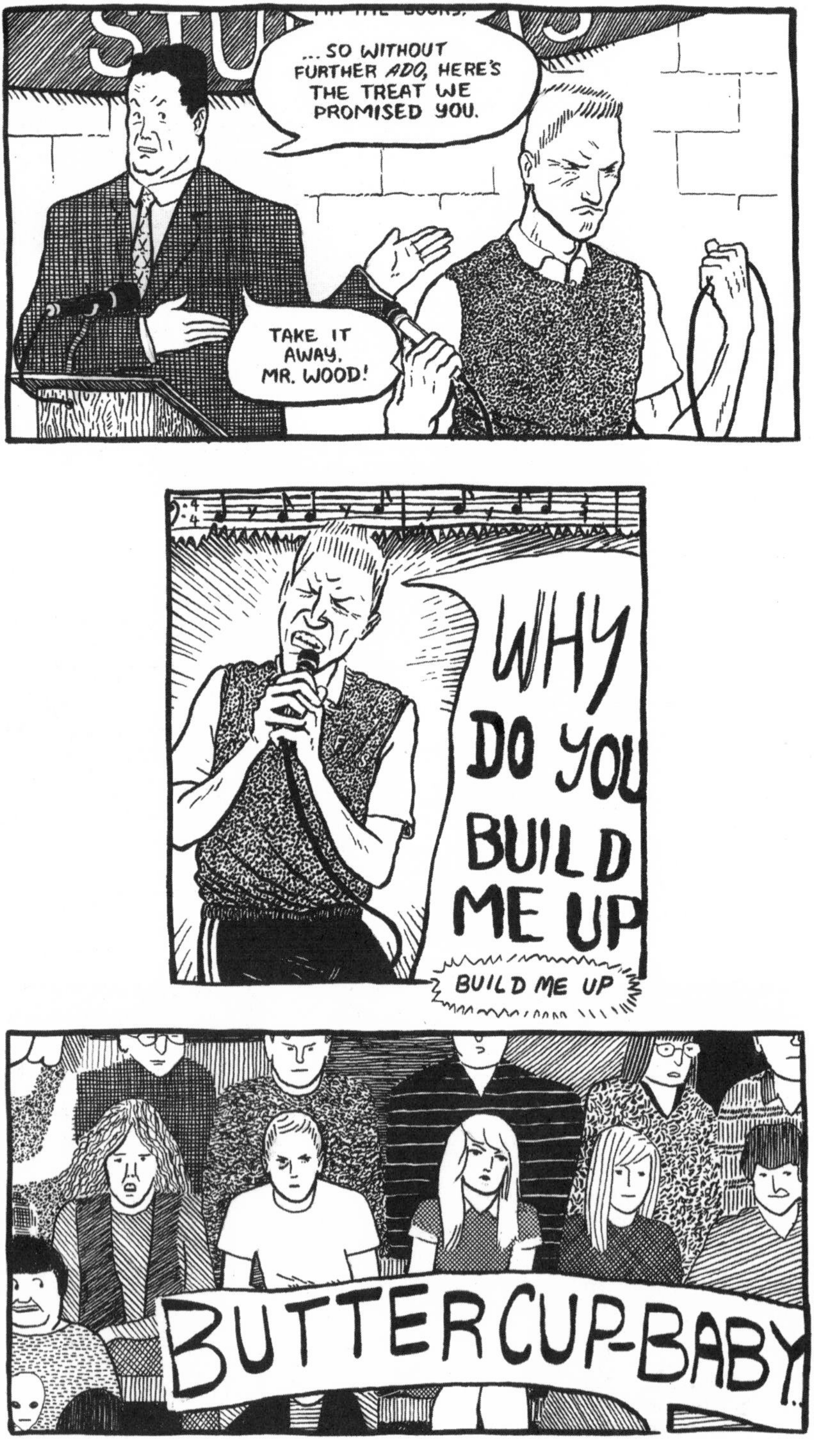
...SO WITHOUT FURTHER ADO, HERE'S THE TREAT WE PROMISED YOU.
TAKE IT AWAY, MR. WOOD!
WHY DO YOU BUILD ME UP
BUILD ME UP
BUTTERCUP-BABY...

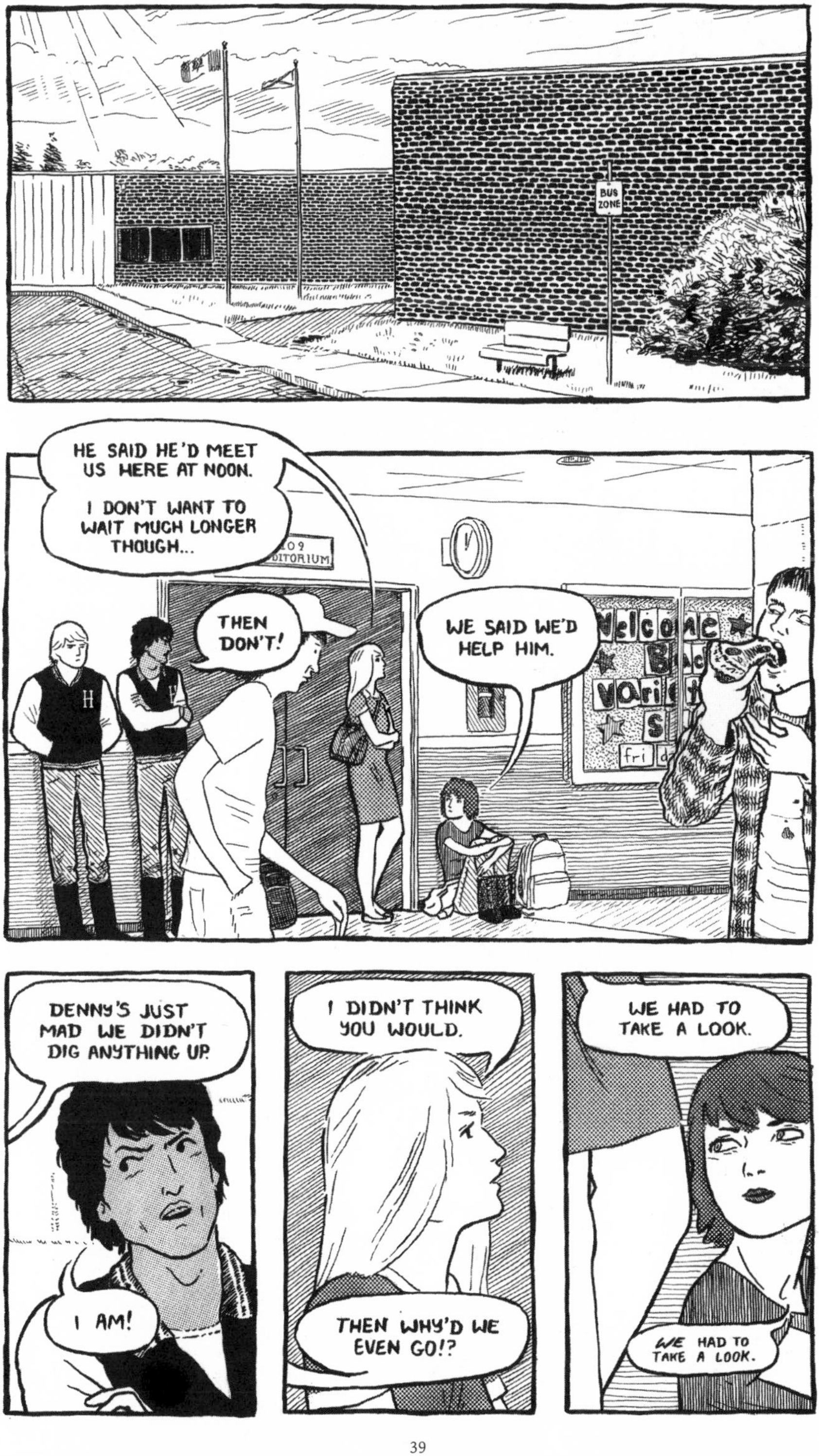
BUS ZONE
HE SAID HE'D MEET US HERE AT NOON.
I DON'T WANT TO WAIT MUCH LONGER THOUGH...
THEN DON'T!
WE SAID WE'D HELP HIM.
DENNY'S JUST MAD WE DIDN'T DIG ANYTHING UP.
I AM!
I DIDN'T THINK YOU WOULD.
THEN WHY'D WE EVEN GO!?
WE HAD TO TAKE A LOOK.
WE HAD TO TAKE A LOOK.

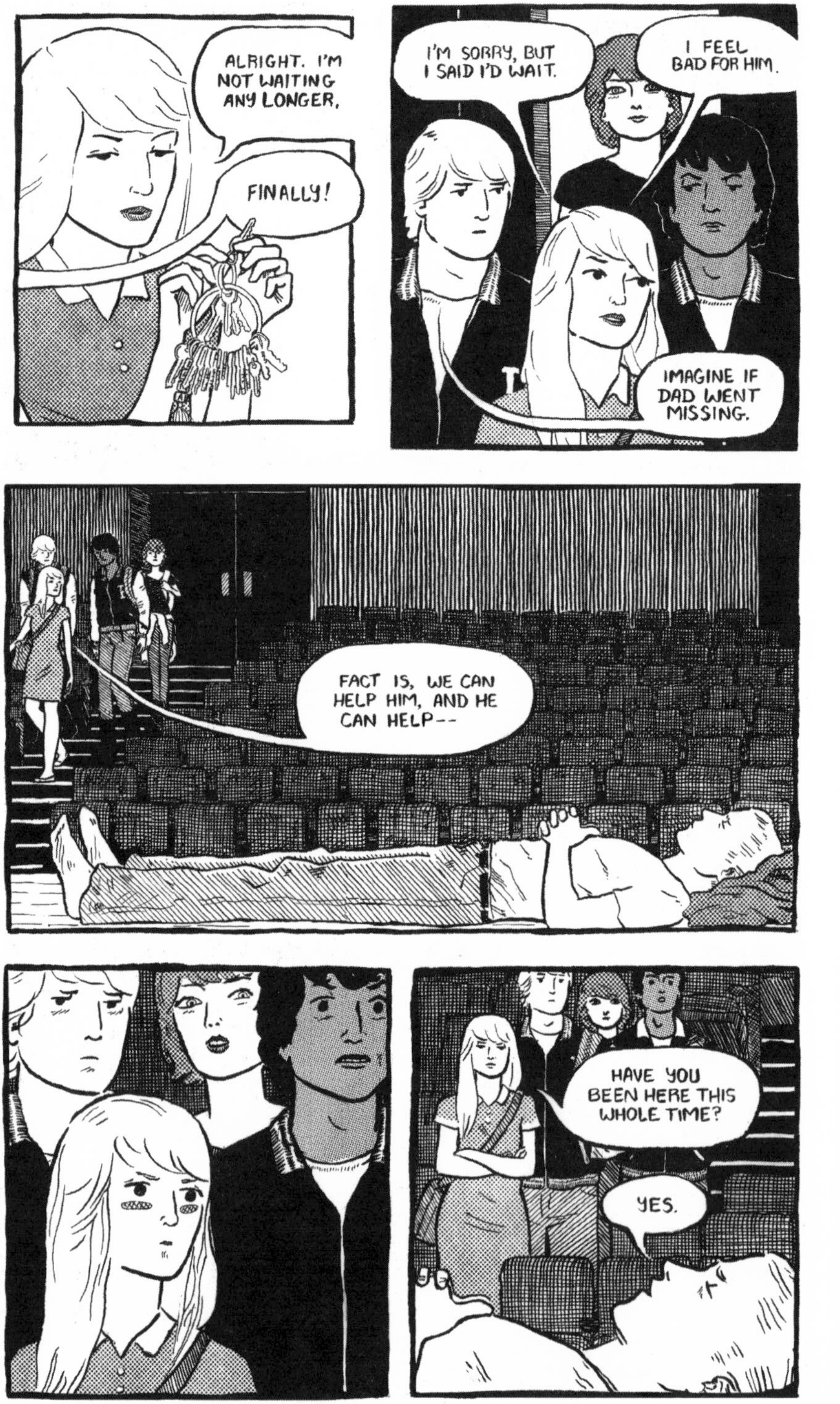
ALRIGHT. I'M NOT WAITING ANY LONGER.
FINALLY!
I'M SORRY, BUT I SAID I'D WAIT.
I FEEL BAD FOR HIM.
IMAGINE IF DAD WENT MISSING.
FACT IS, WE CAN HELP HIM, AND HE CAN HELP--
HAVE YOU BEEN HERE THIS WHOLE TIME?
YES.

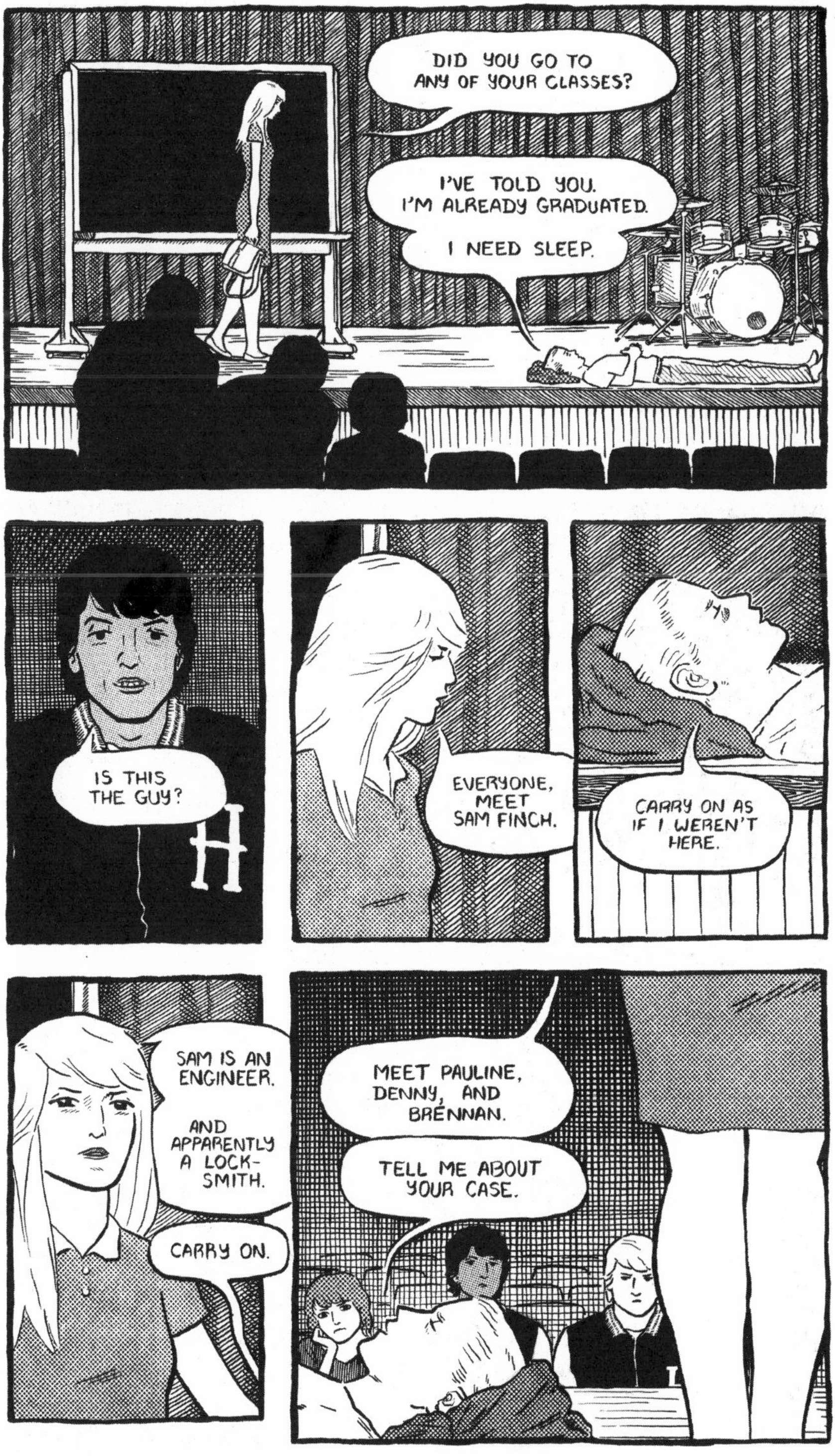
DID YOU GO TO ANY OF YOUR CLASSES?
I'VE TOLD YOU. I'M ALREADY GRADUATED.
I NEED SLEEP.
IS THIS THE GUY?
EVERYONE, MEET SAM FINCH.
CARRY ON AS IF I WEREN'T HERE.
SAM IS AN ENGINEER.
AND APPARENTLY A LOCK-SMITH.
CARRY ON.
MEET PAULINE, DENNY, AND BRENNAN.
TELL ME ABOUT YOUR CASE.

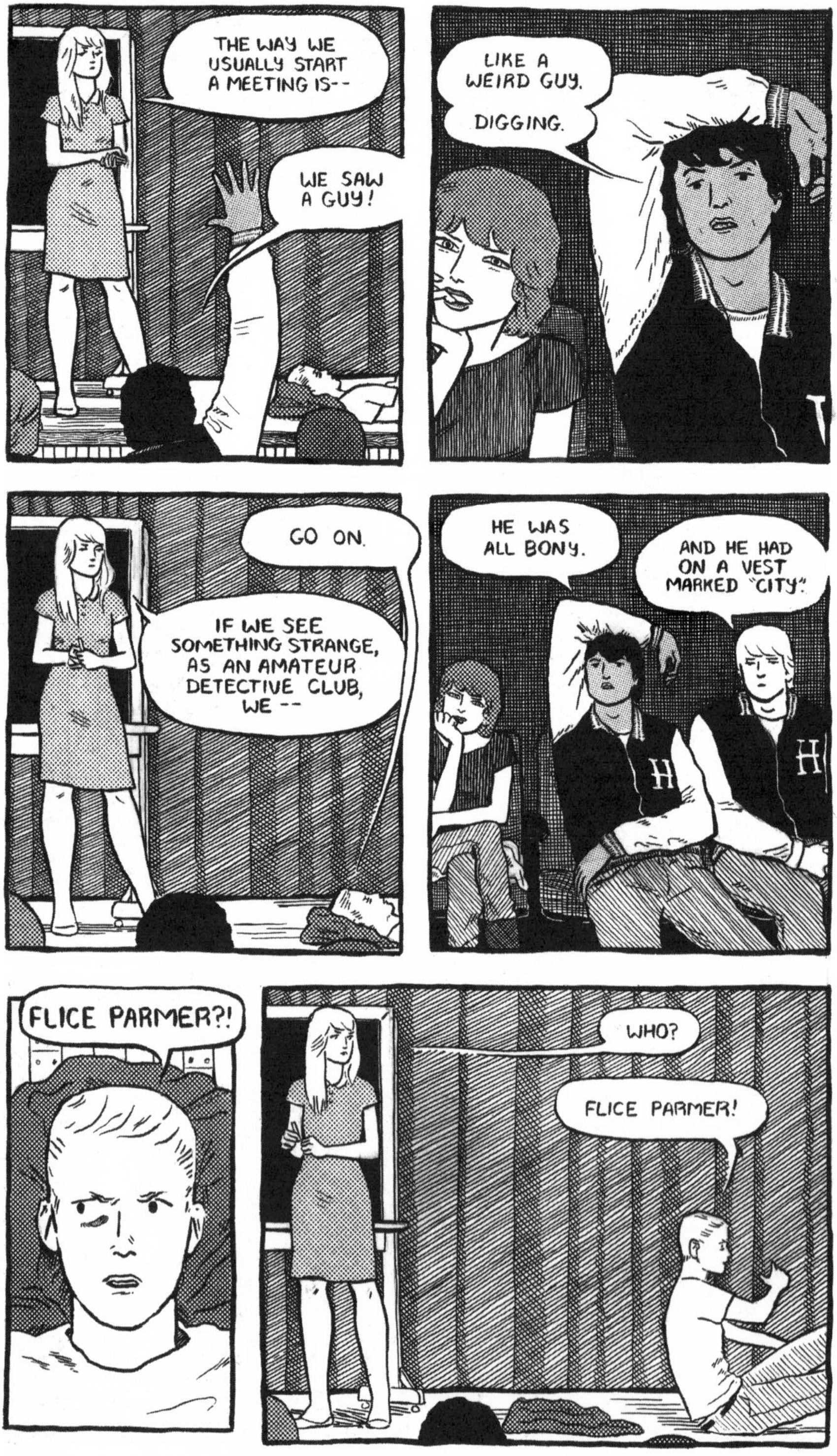
THE WAY WE USUALLY START A MEETING IS--
WE SAW A GUY!
LIKE A WEIRD GUY.
DIGGING.
GO ON.
IF WE SEE SOMETHING STRANGE, AS AN AMATEUR DETECTIVE CLUB, WE --
HE WAS ALL BONY.
AND HE HAD ON A VEST MARKED "CITY".
FLICE PARMER?!
WHO?
FLICE PARMER!

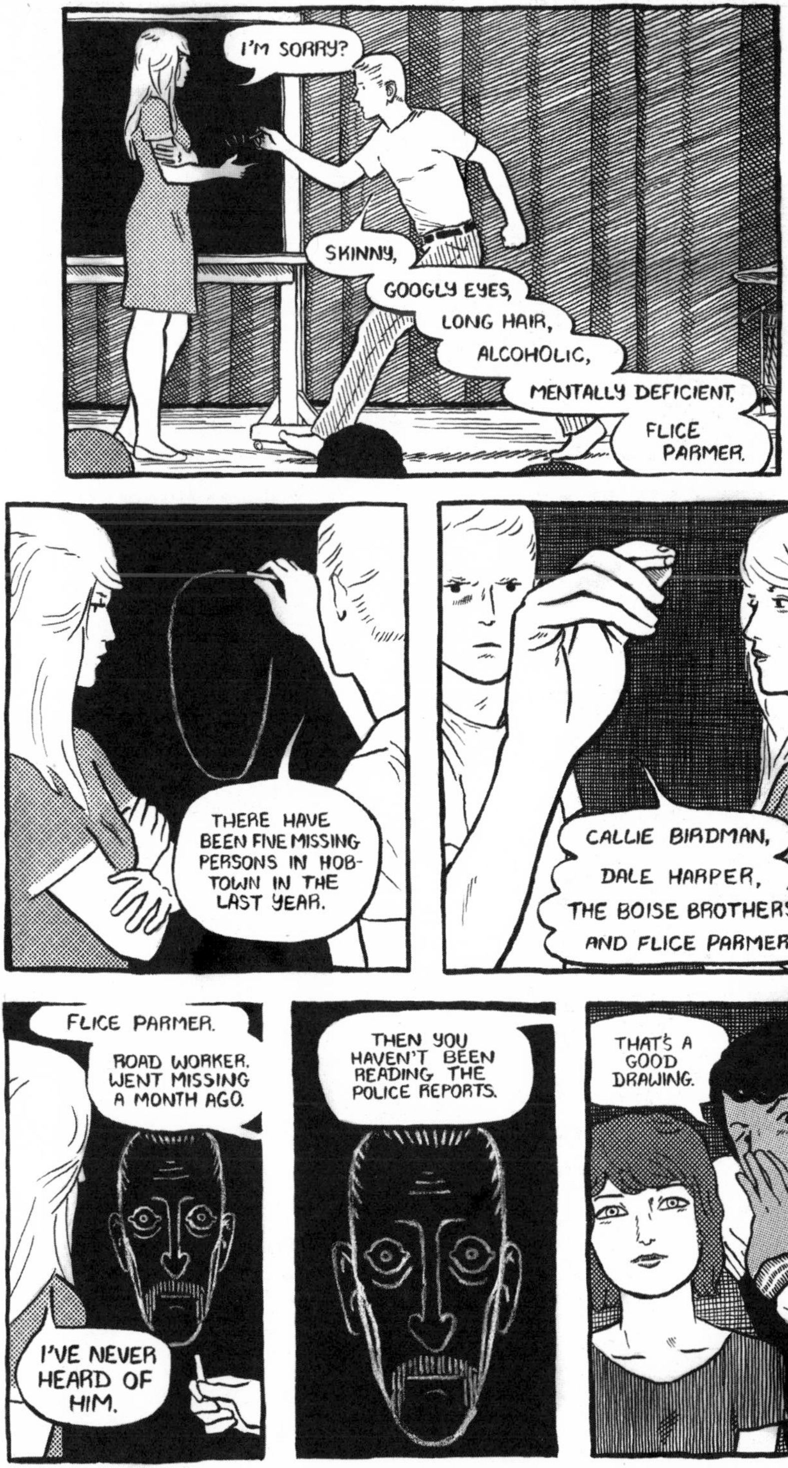
I'M SORRY?
SKINNY,
GOOGLY EYES,
LONG HAIR,
ALCOHOLIC,
MENTALLY DEFICIENT,
FLICE PARMER.
THERE HAVE BEEN FIVE MISSING PERSONS IN HOB-TOWN IN THE LAST YEAR.
CALLIE BIRDMAN,
DALE HARPER,
THE BOISE BROTHERS,
AND FLICE PARMER.
FLICE PARMER.
ROAD WORKER. WENT MISSING A MONTH AGO.
I'VE NEVER HEARD OF HIM.
THEN YOU HAVEN'T BEEN READING THE POLICE REPORTS.
THAT'S A GOOD DRAWING.

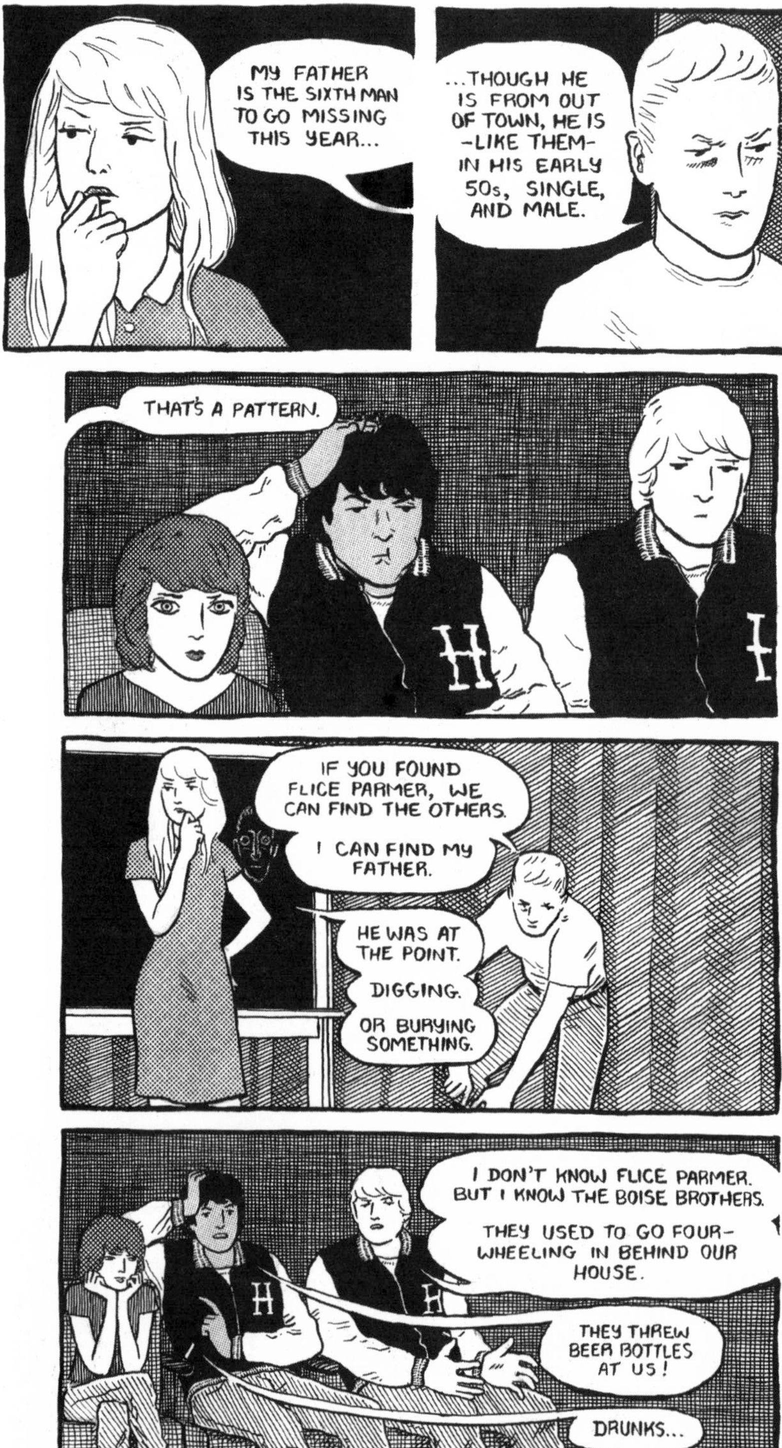
MY FATHER IS THE SIXTH MAN TO GO MISSING THIS YEAR...
...THOUGH HE IS FROM OUT OF TOWN, HE IS -LIKE THEM- IN HIS EARLY 50s, SINGLE, AND MALE.
THAT'S A PATTERN.
IF YOU FOUND FLICE PARMER, WE CAN FIND THE OTHERS.
I CAN FIND MY FATHER.
HE WAS AT THE POINT.
DIGGING.
OR BURYING SOMETHING.
I DON'T KNOW FLICE PARMER. BUT I KNOW THE BOISE BROTHERS.
THEY USED TO GO FOUR-WHEELING IN BEHIND OUR HOUSE.
THEY THREW BEER BOTTLES AT US!
DRUNKS...

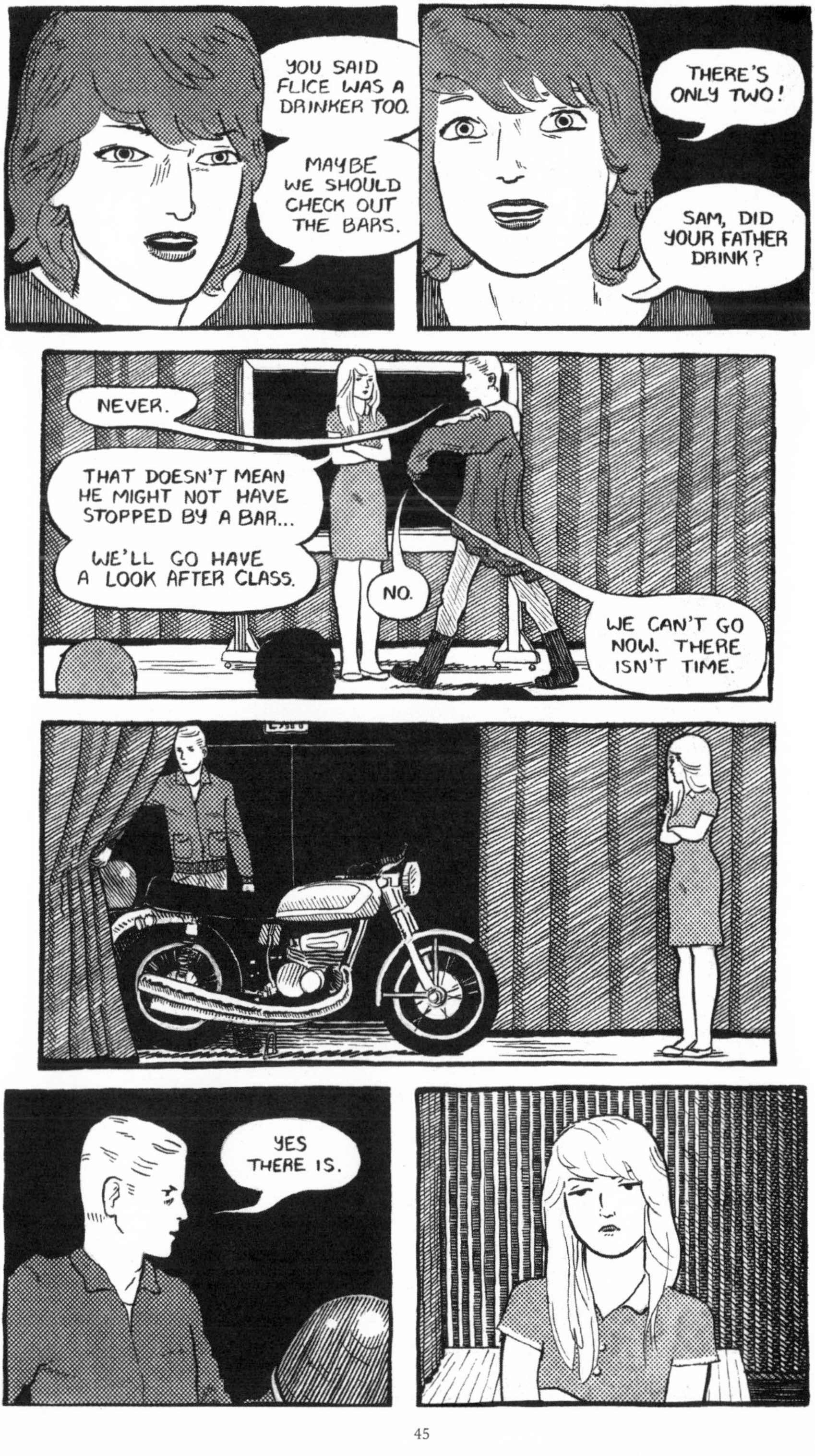

YOU SAID FLICE WAS A DRINKER TOO.
MAYBE WE SHOULD CHECK OUT THE BARS.
THERE'S ONLY TWO!
SAM, DID YOUR FATHER DRINK?
NEVER.
THAT DOESN'T MEAN HE MIGHT NOT HAVE STOPPED BY A BAR...
WE'LL GO HAVE A LOOK AFTER CLASS.
NO.
WE CAN'T GO NOW. THERE ISN'T TIME.
YES THERE IS.

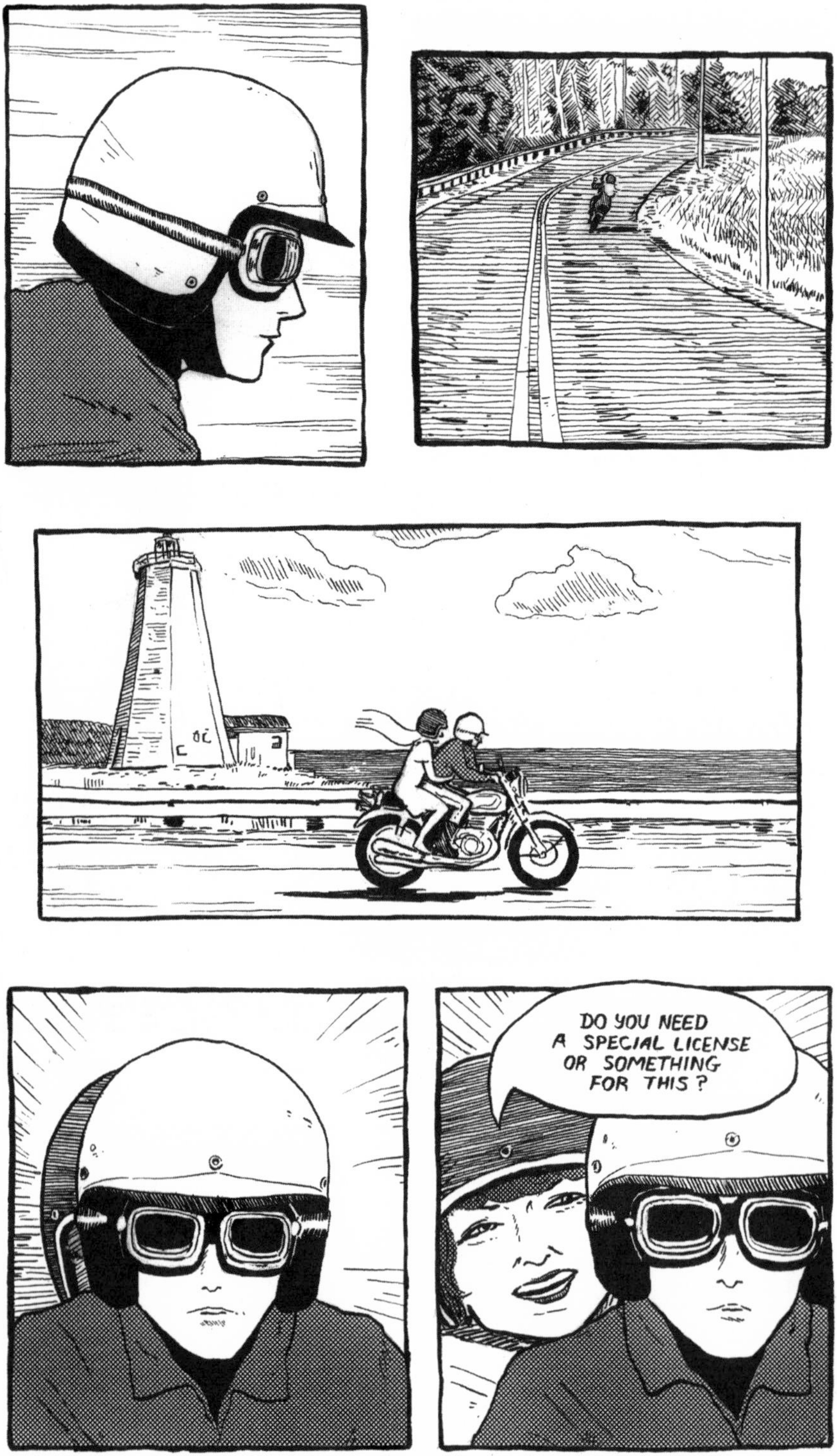
DO YOU NEED
A SPECIAL LICENSE
OR SOMETHING
FOR THIS?

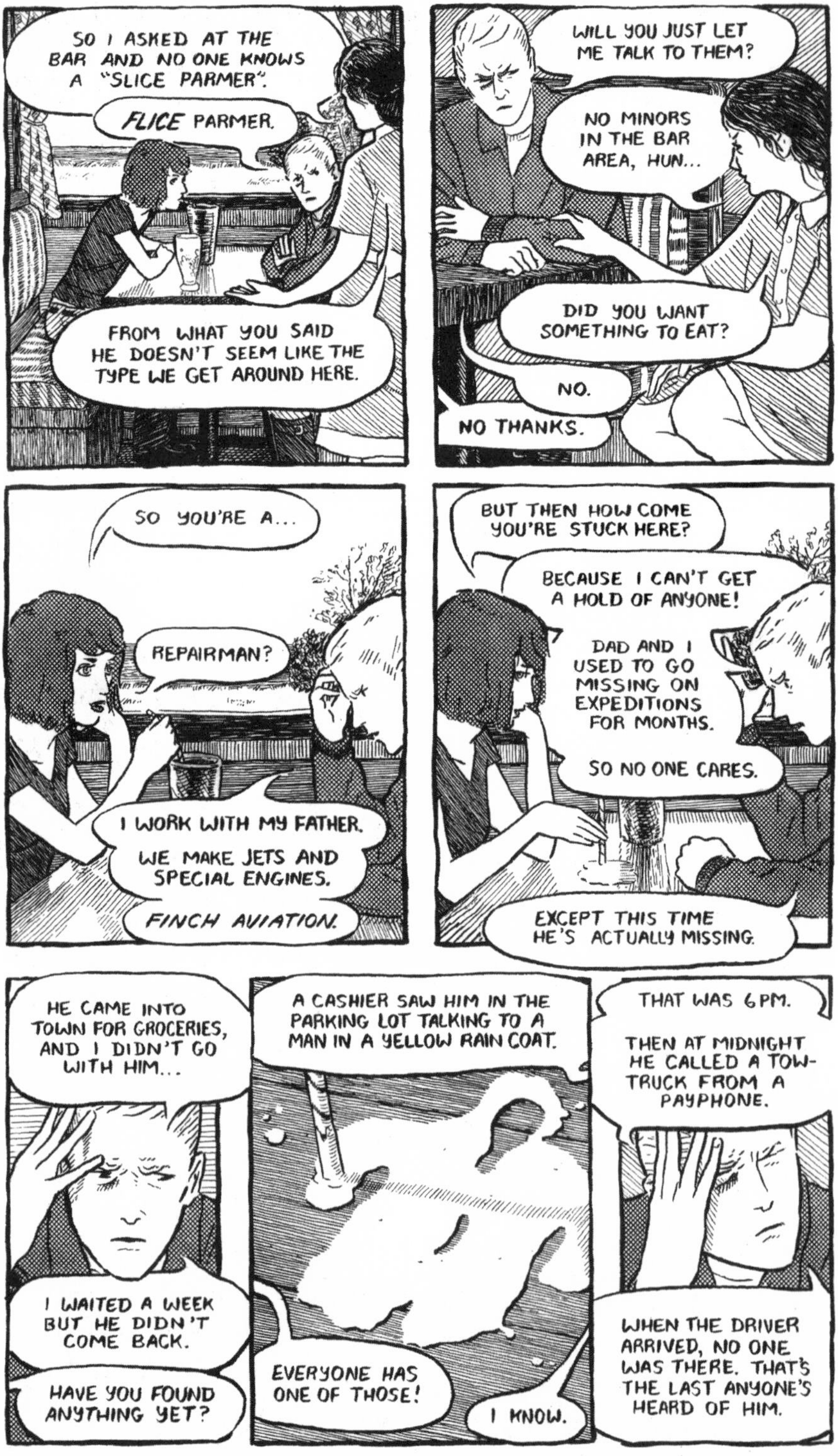

SO I ASKED AT THE BAR AND NO ONE KNOWS A "SLICE PARMER".
FLICE PARMER.
FROM WHAT YOU SAID HE DOESN'T SEEM LIKE THE TYPE WE GET AROUND HERE.
WILL YOU JUST LET ME TALK TO THEM?
NO MINORS IN THE BAR AREA, HUN...
DID YOU WANT SOMETHING TO EAT?
NO.
NO THANKS.
SO YOU'RE A...
REPAIRMAN?
I WORK WITH MY FATHER.
WE MAKE JETS AND SPECIAL ENGINES.
FINCH AVIATION.
BUT THEN HOW COME YOU'RE STUCK HERE?
BECAUSE I CAN'T GET A HOLD OF ANYONE!
DAD AND I USED TO GO MISSING ON EXPEDITIONS FOR MONTHS.
SO NO ONE CARES.
EXCEPT THIS TIME HE'S ACTUALLY MISSING.
HE CAME INTO TOWN FOR GROCERIES, AND I DIDN'T GO WITH HIM...
I WAITED A WEEK BUT HE DIDN'T COME BACK.
HAVE YOU FOUND ANYTHING YET?
A CASHIER SAW HIM IN THE PARKING LOT TALKING TO A MAN IN A YELLOW RAIN COAT.
EVERYONE HAS ONE OF THOSE!
I KNOW.
THAT WAS 6PM.
THEN AT MIDNIGHT HE CALLED A TOW-TRUCK FROM A PAYPHONE.
WHEN THE DRIVER ARRIVED, NO ONE WAS THERE. THAT'S THE LAST ANYONE'S HEARD OF HIM.

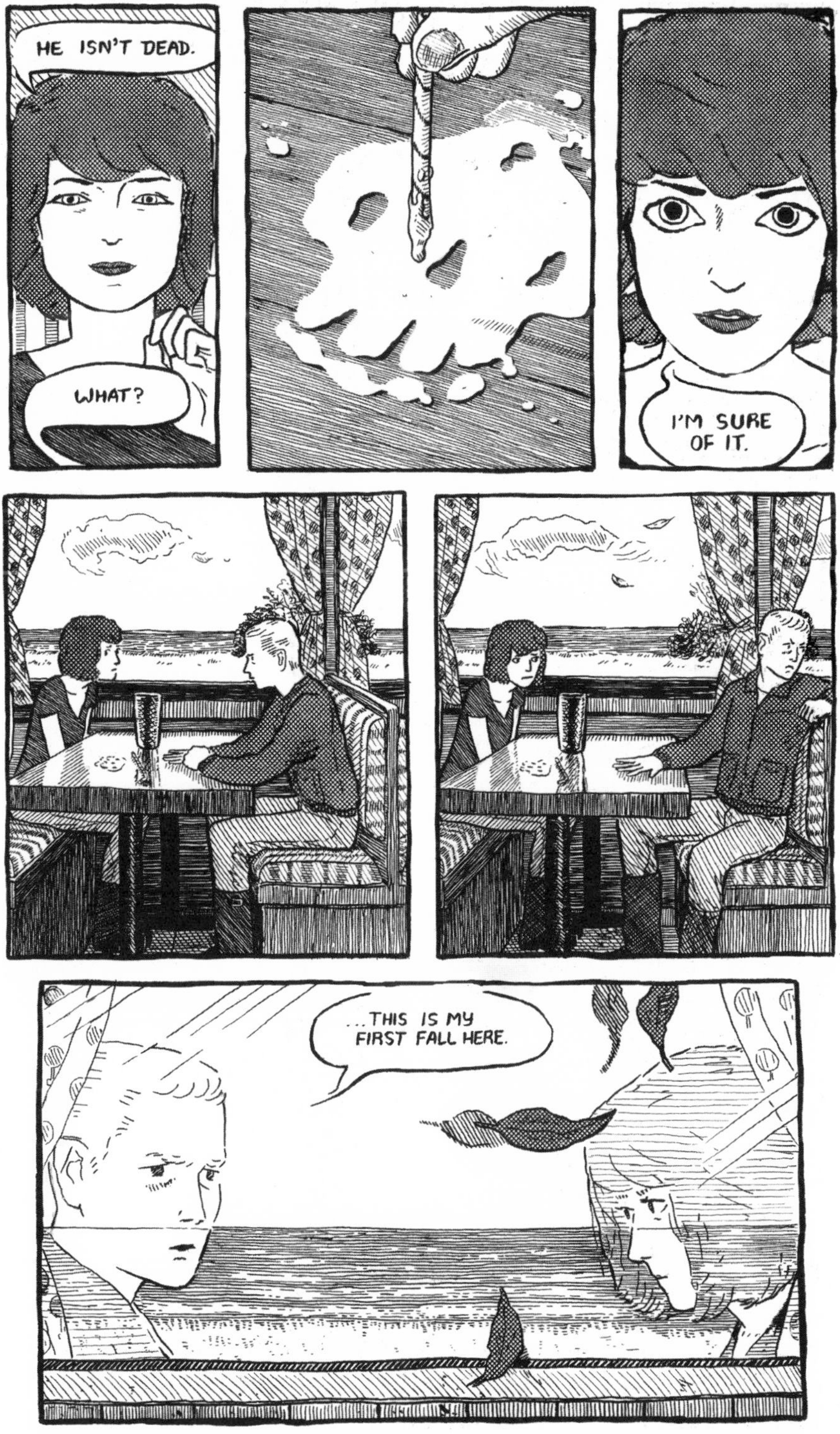
HE ISN'T DEAD.
WHAT?
I'M SURE OF IT.
...THIS IS MY FIRST FALL HERE.

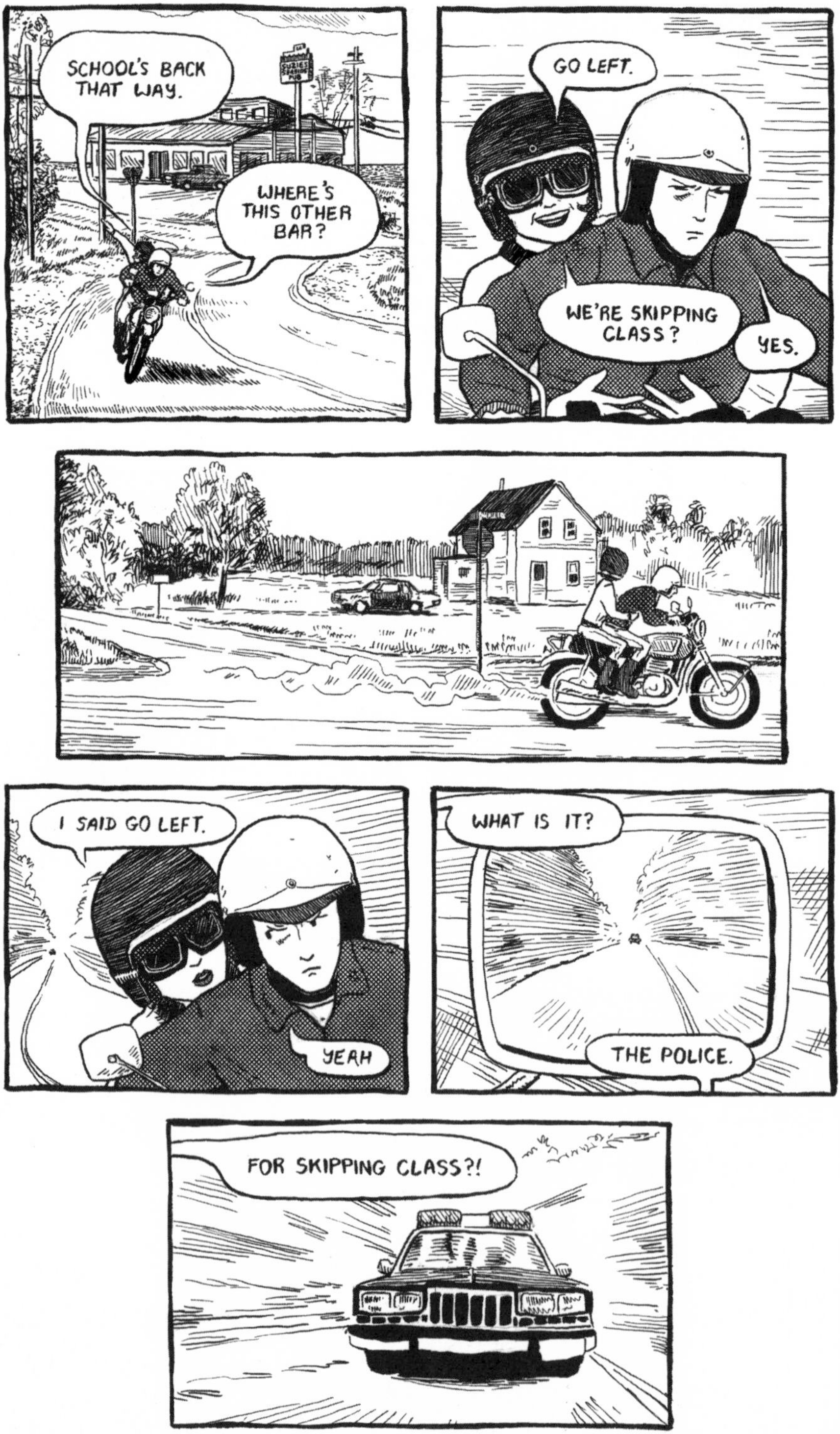
SCHOOL'S BACK THAT WAY.
WHERE'S THIS OTHER BAR?
GO LEFT.
WE'RE SKIPPING CLASS?
YES.
I SAID GO LEFT.
YEAH
WHAT IS IT?
THE POLICE.
FOR SKIPPING CLASS?!

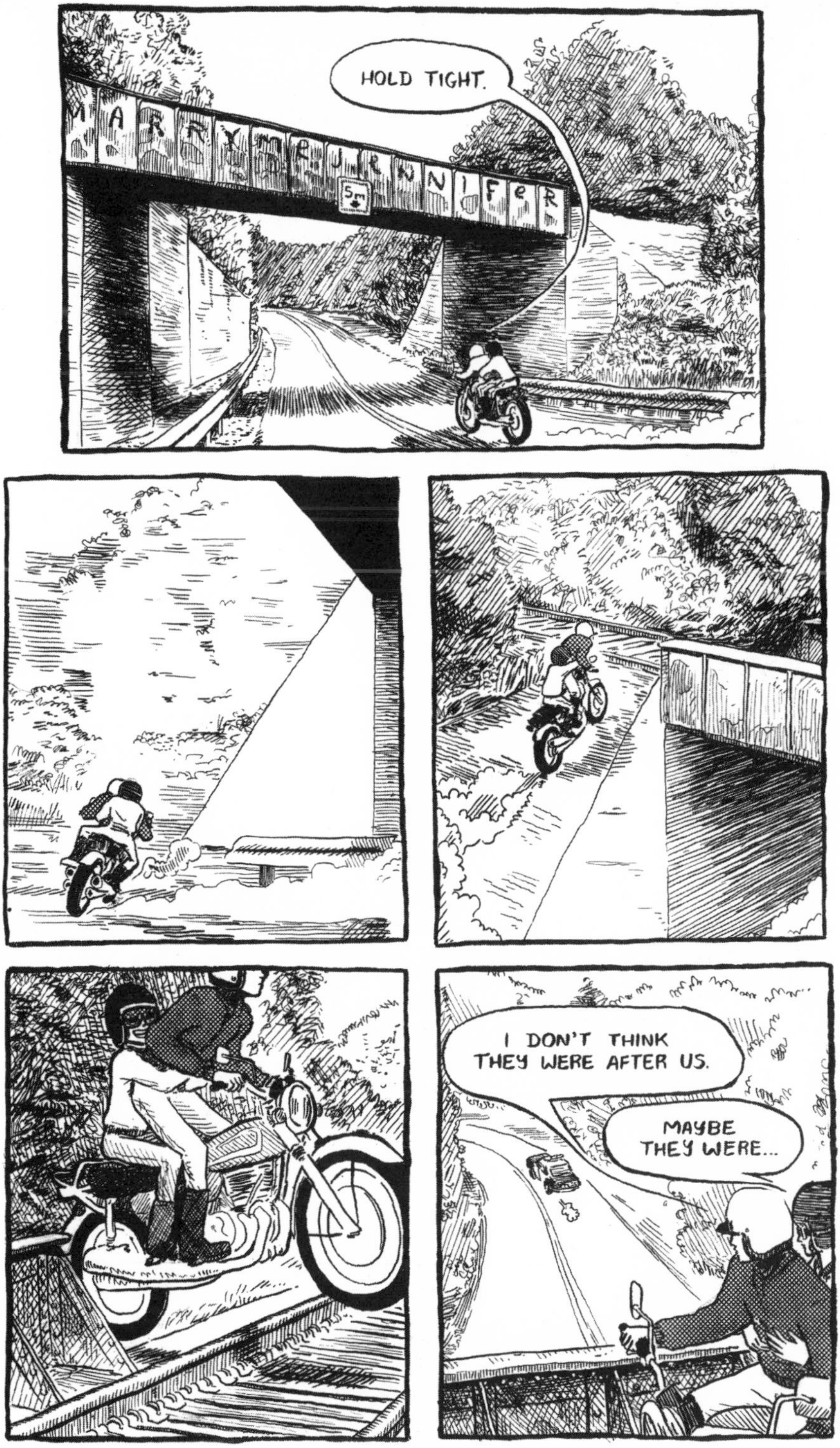
HOLD TIGHT.
5m
I DON'T THINK THEY WERE AFTER US.
MAYBE THEY WERE...

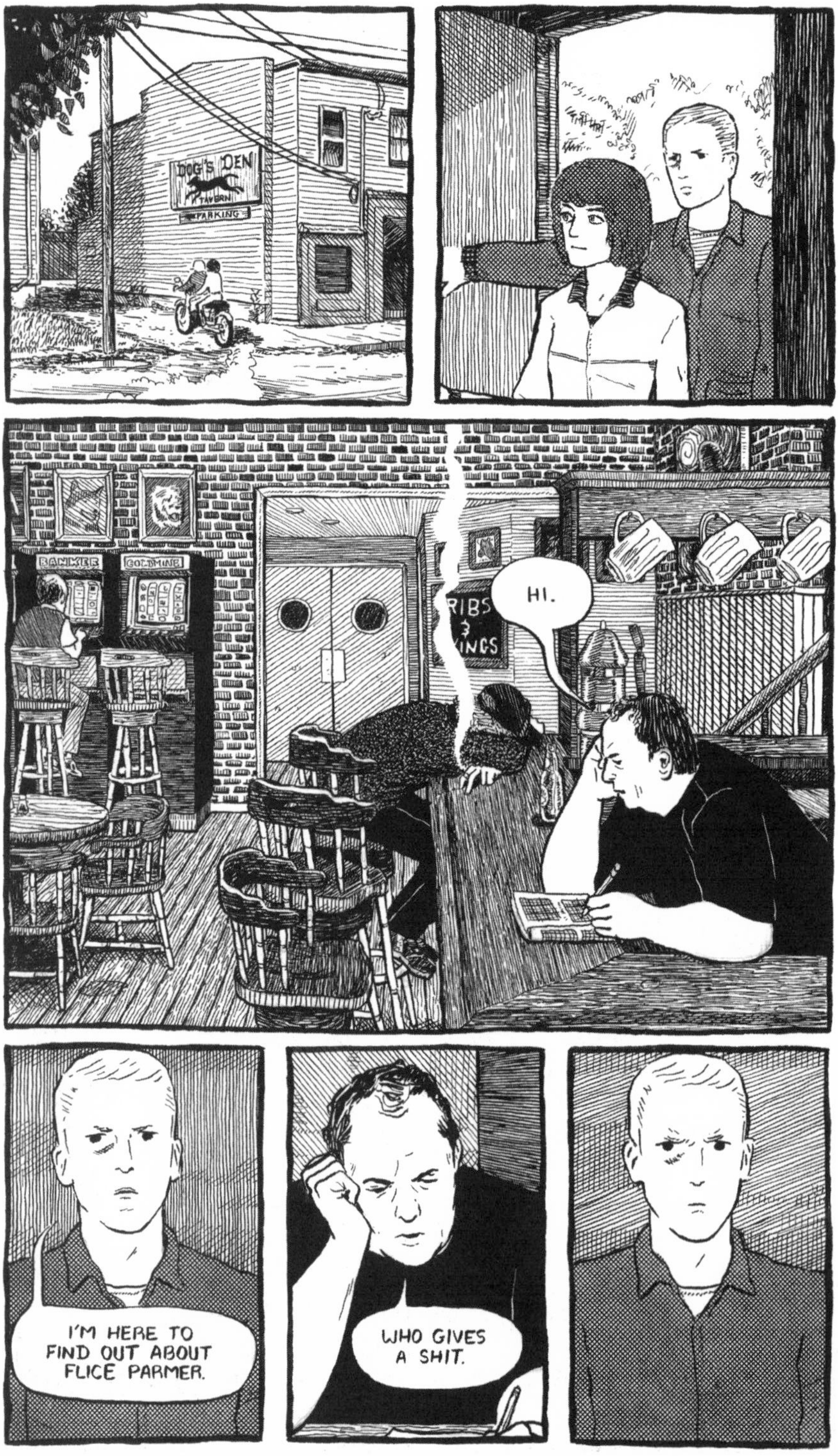
DOG'S DEN
TAVERN
PARKING
BANKER
GOLDMINE
RIBS
HI.
I'M HERE TO FIND OUT ABOUT FLICE PARMER.
WHO GIVES A SHIT.

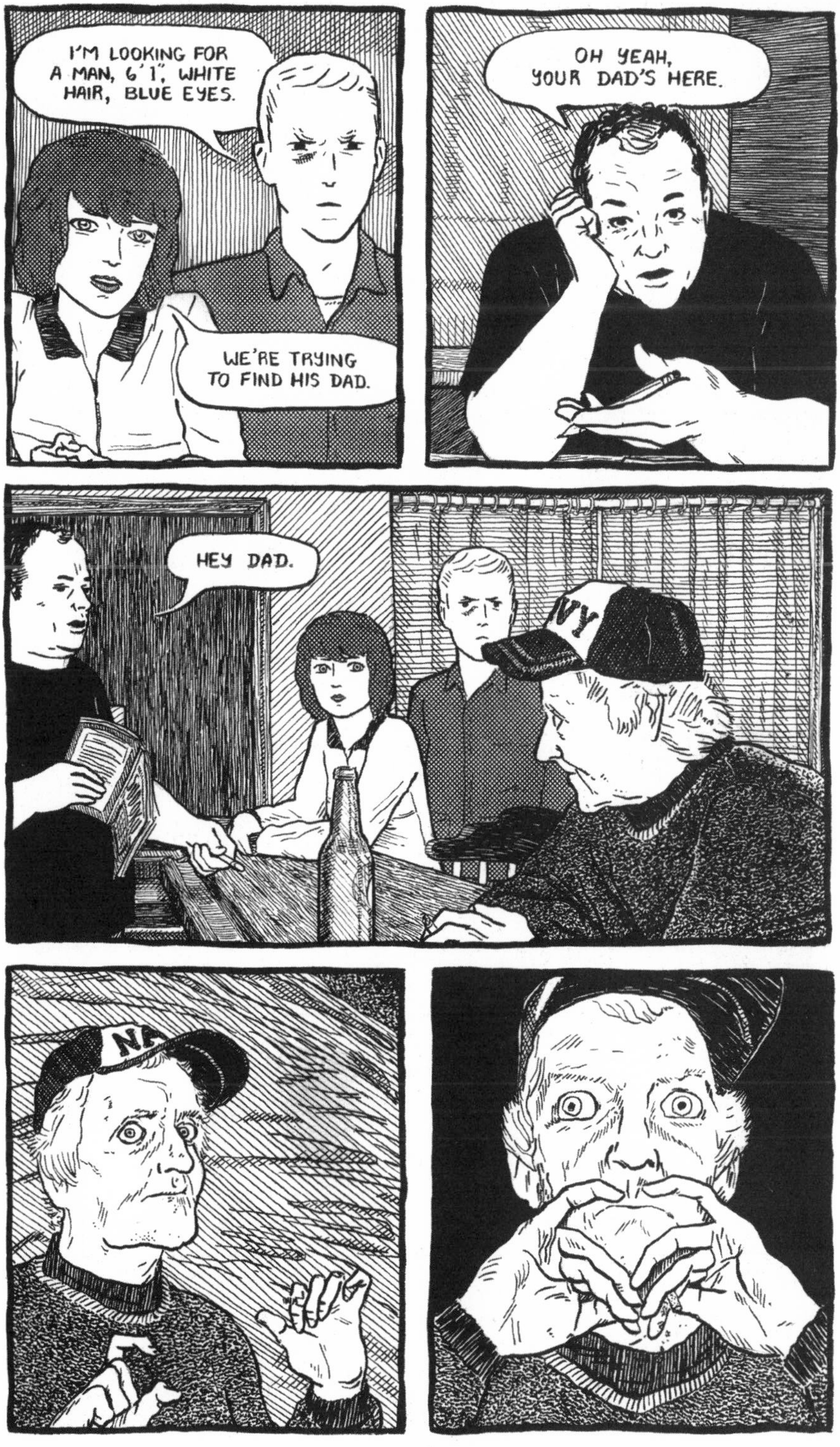
I'M LOOKING FOR A MAN, 6'1", WHITE HAIR, BLUE EYES.
WE'RE TRYING TO FIND HIS DAD.
OH YEAH, YOUR DAD'S HERE.
HEY DAD.
NAVY
NA

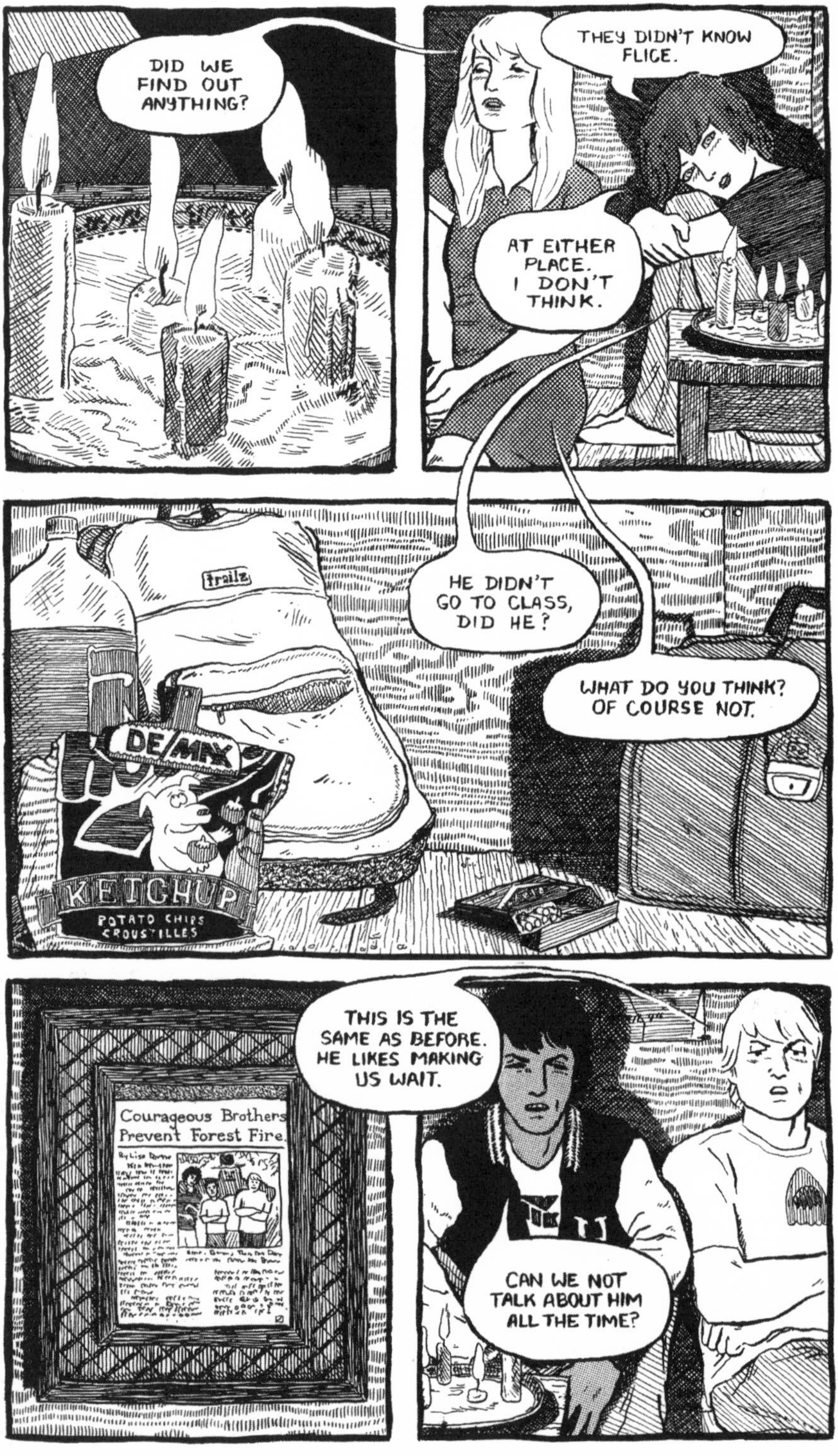
DID WE FIND OUT ANYTHING?
THEY DIDN'T KNOW FLICE.
AT EITHER PLACE. I DON'T THINK.
HE DIDN'T GO TO CLASS, DID HE?
WHAT DO YOU THINK? OF COURSE NOT.
trailz
DE/MAX
KETCHUP
POTATO CHIPS
CROUSTILLES
THIS IS THE SAME AS BEFORE. HE LIKES MAKING US WAIT.
Courageous Brothers Prevent Forest Fire.
CAN WE NOT TALK ABOUT HIM ALL THE TIME?

CHILD HOCKEY TEAM
He's a coach.
OOHMAMA MAGAZINE
...LIKE MAYBE TALK ABOUT THE MYSTERY FOR CHRISSAKES?
I THINK YOU'RE RIGHT, ACTUALLY.
WE'LL START WITHOUT HIM.
NO GREAT MISCHIEF
FRANKENSTEIN
HE'S COMING. HE'S HERE.
THIS IS EXACTLY THE SAME AS BEFORE.

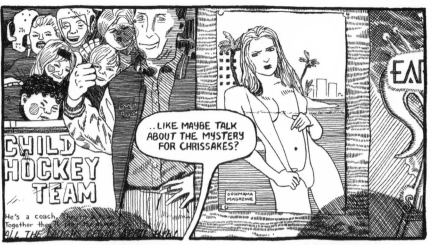

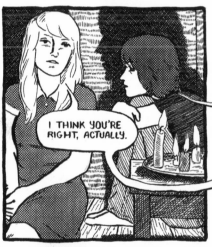

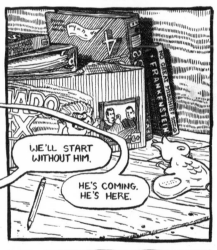

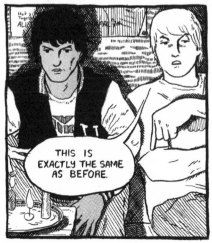

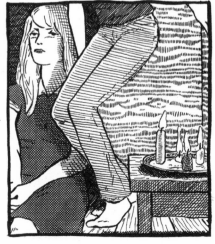

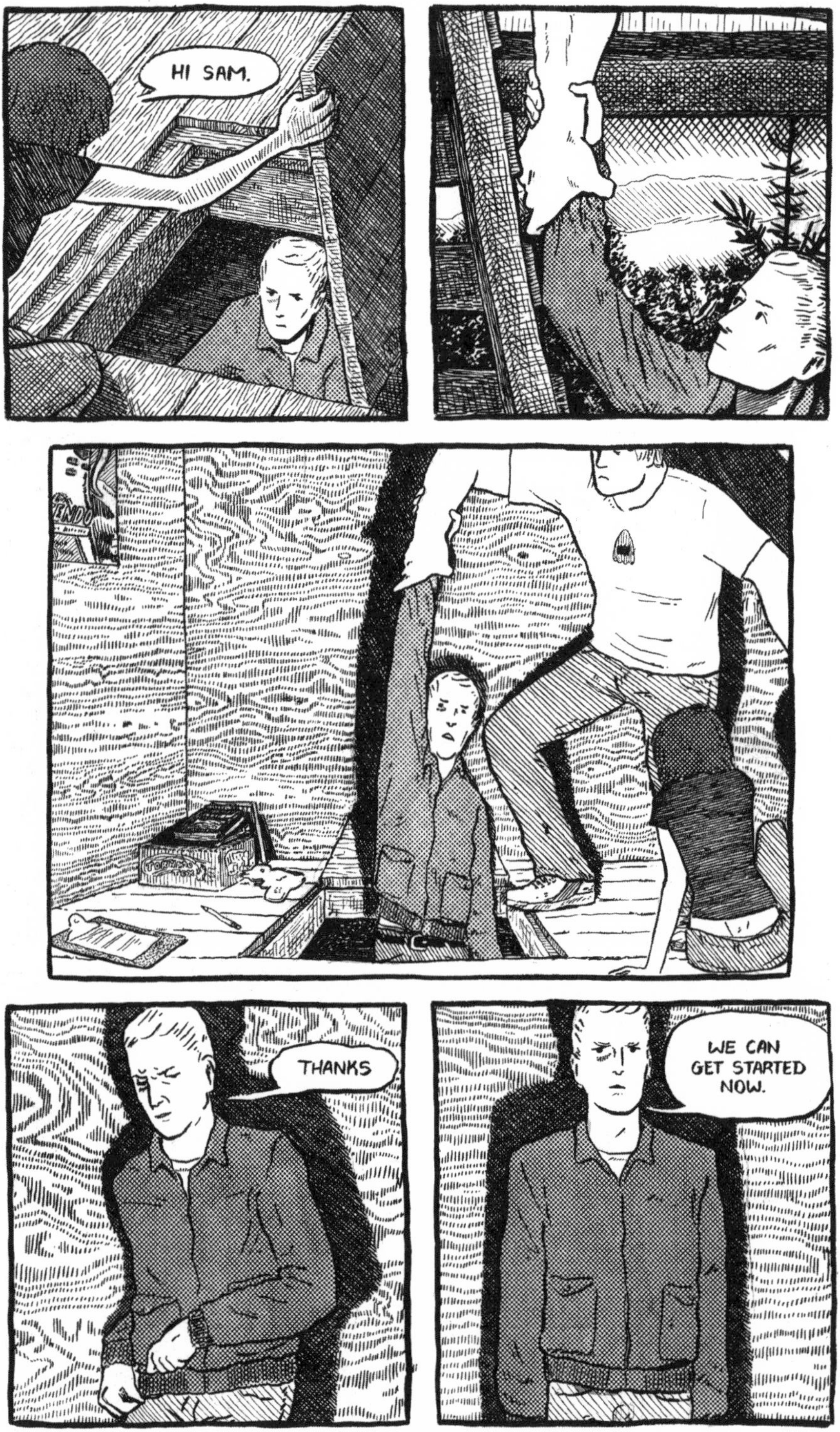
HI SAM.
THANKS
WE CAN GET STARTED NOW.

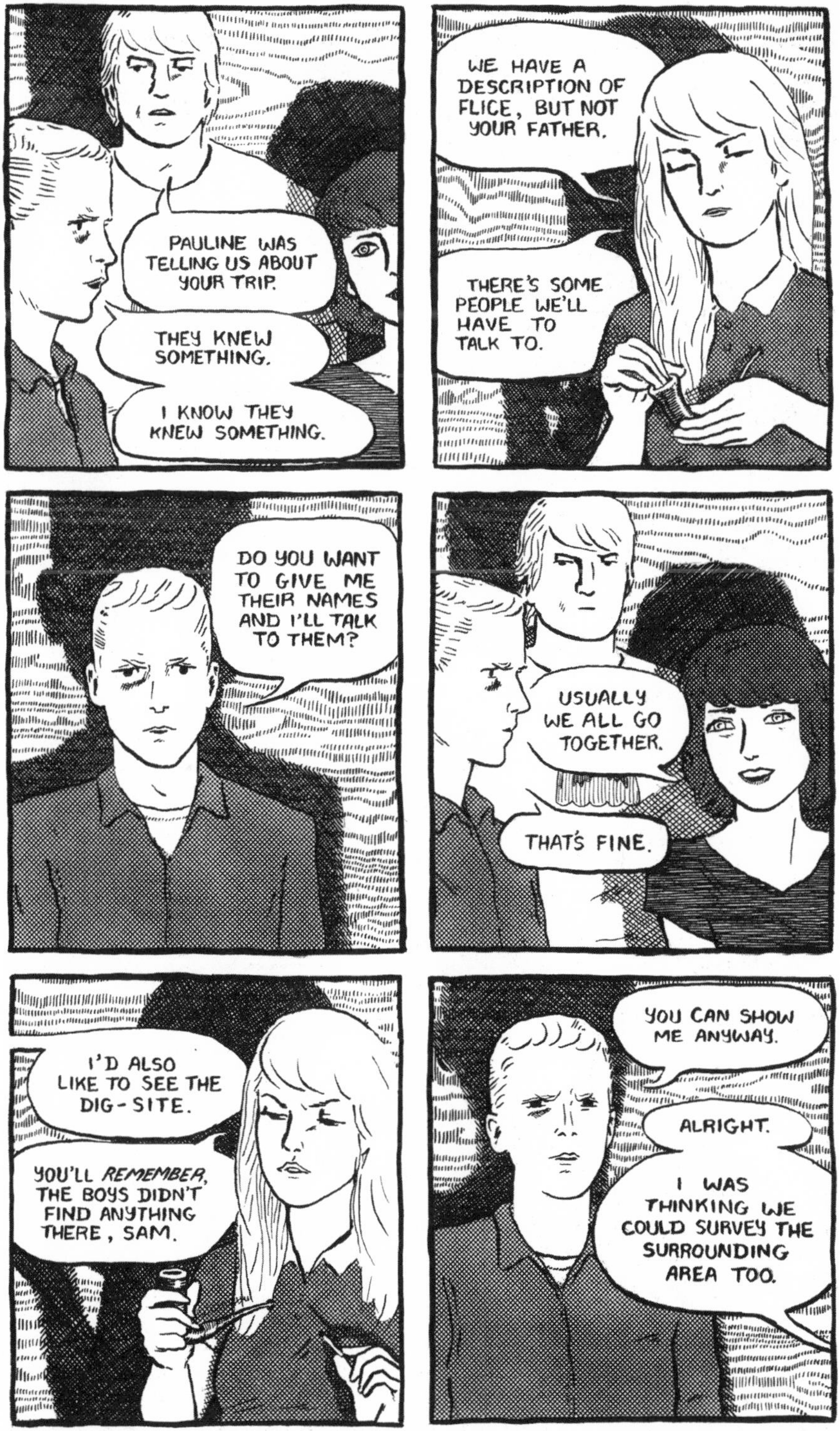
PAULINE WAS TELLING US ABOUT YOUR TRIP.
THEY KNEW SOMETHING.
I KNOW THEY KNEW SOMETHING.
WE HAVE A DESCRIPTION OF FLICE, BUT NOT YOUR FATHER.
THERE'S SOME PEOPLE WE'LL HAVE TO TALK TO.
DO YOU WANT TO GIVE ME THEIR NAMES AND I'LL TALK TO THEM?
USUALLY WE ALL GO TOGETHER.
THAT'S FINE.
I'D ALSO LIKE TO SEE THE DIG-SITE.
YOU'LL *REMEMBER*, THE BOYS DIDN'T FIND ANYTHING THERE, SAM.
YOU CAN SHOW ME ANYWAY.
ALRIGHT.
I WAS THINKING WE COULD SURVEY THE SURROUNDING AREA TOO.

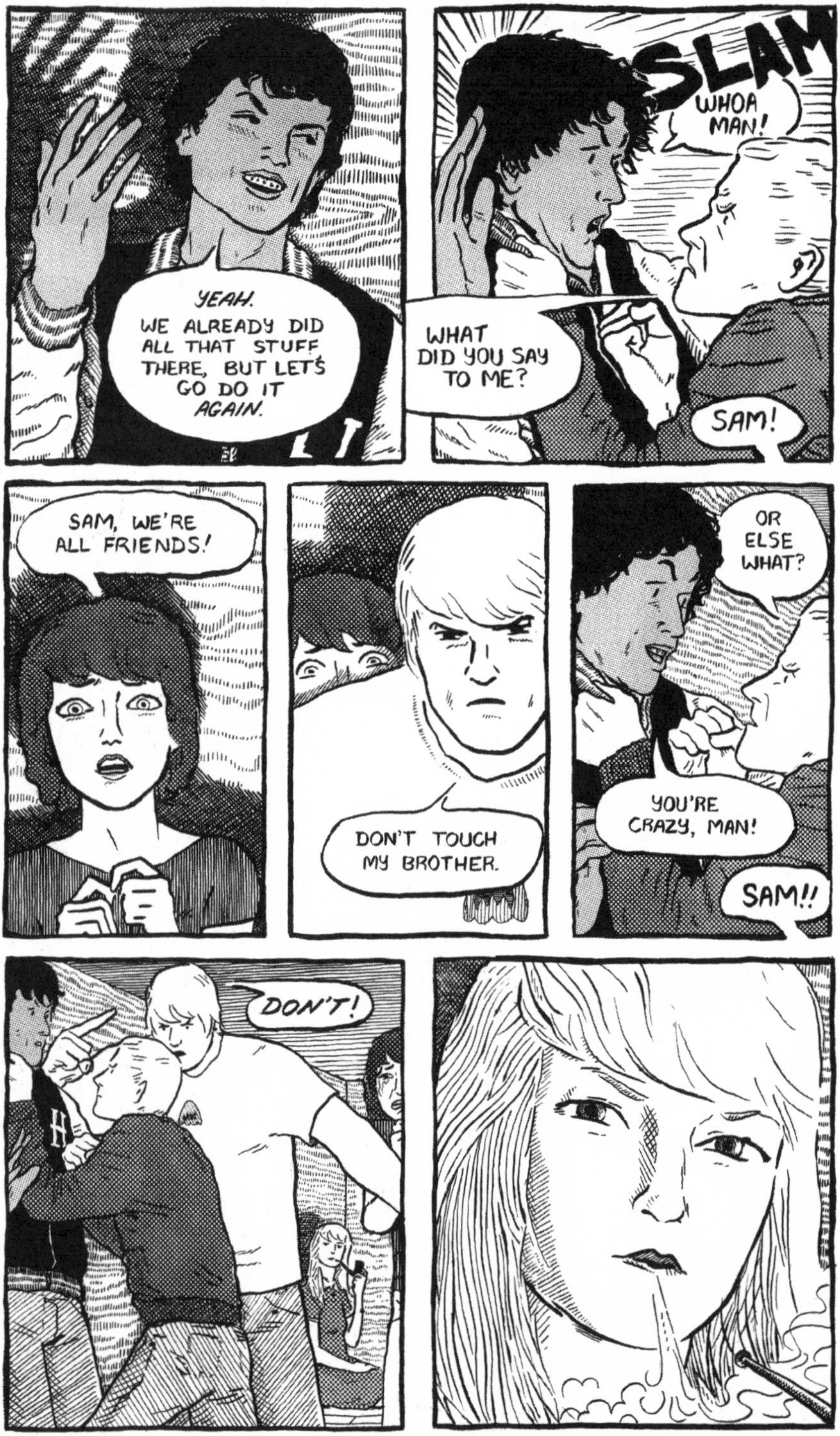
YEAH. WE ALREADY DID ALL THAT STUFF THERE, BUT LET'S GO DO IT AGAIN.
SLAM
WHOA MAN!
WHAT DID YOU SAY TO ME?
SAM!
SAM, WE'RE ALL FRIENDS!
DON'T TOUCH MY BROTHER.
OR ELSE WHAT?
YOU'RE CRAZY, MAN!
SAM!!
DON'T!

CHAPTER TWO

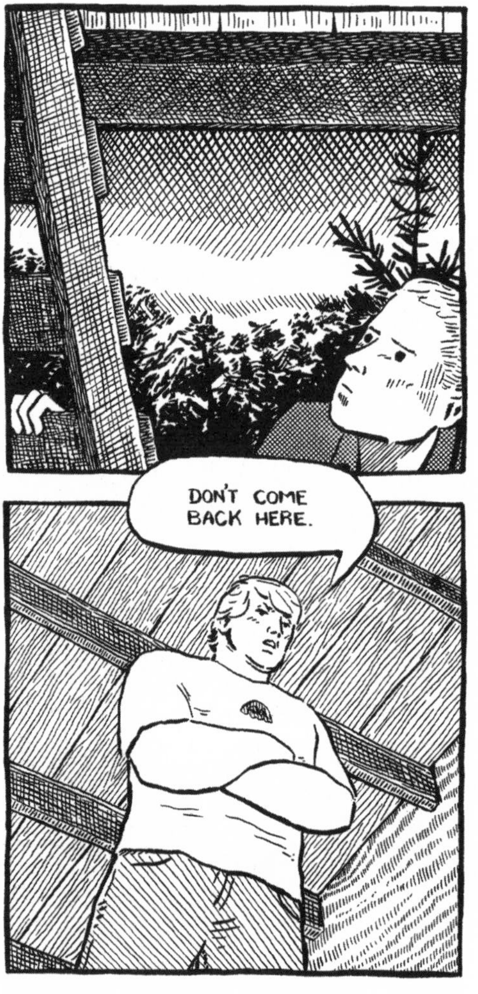
DON'T COME BACK HERE.

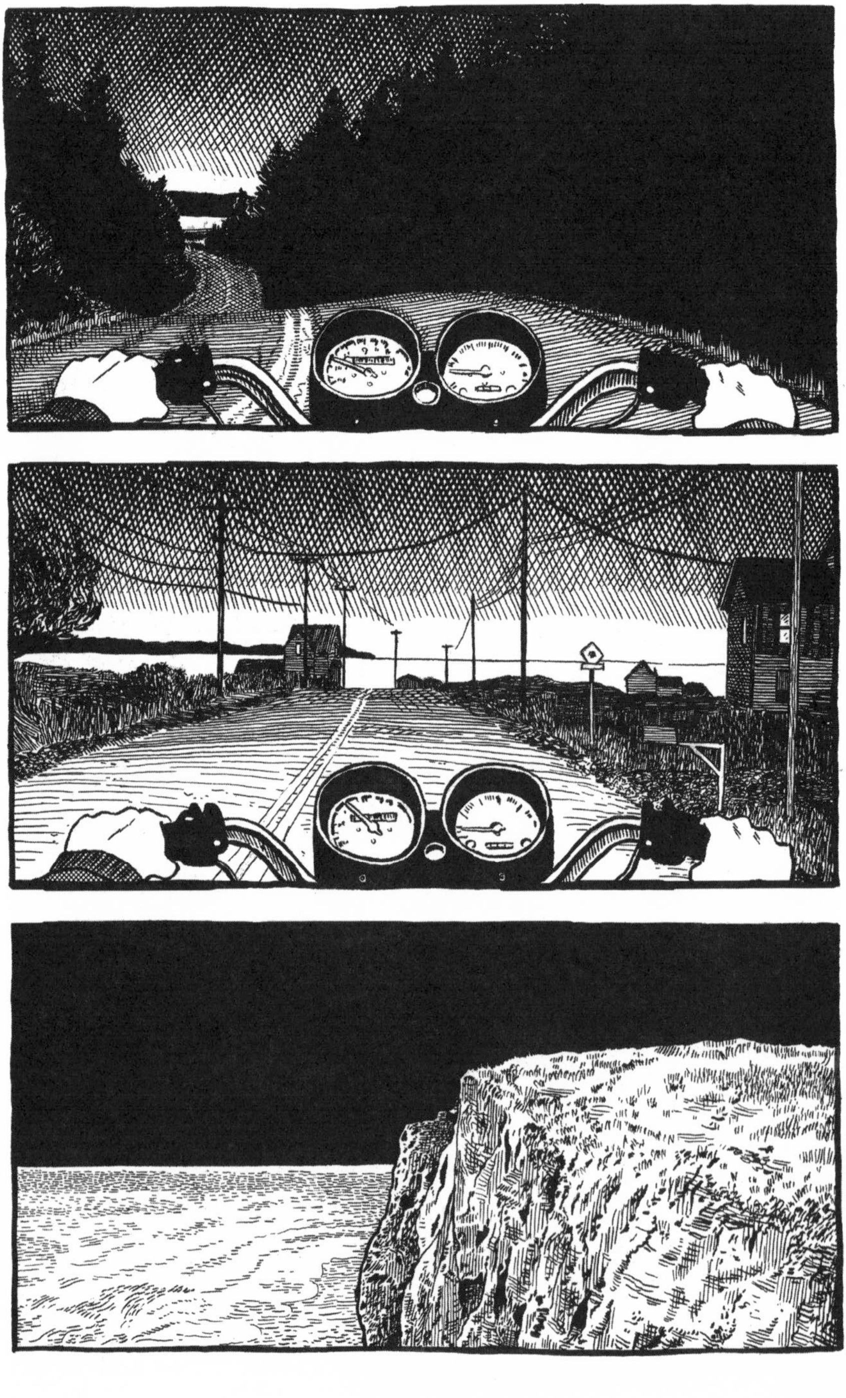

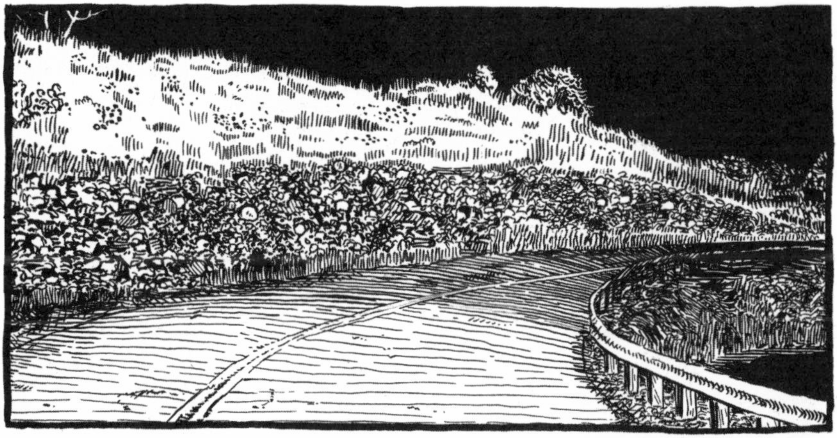
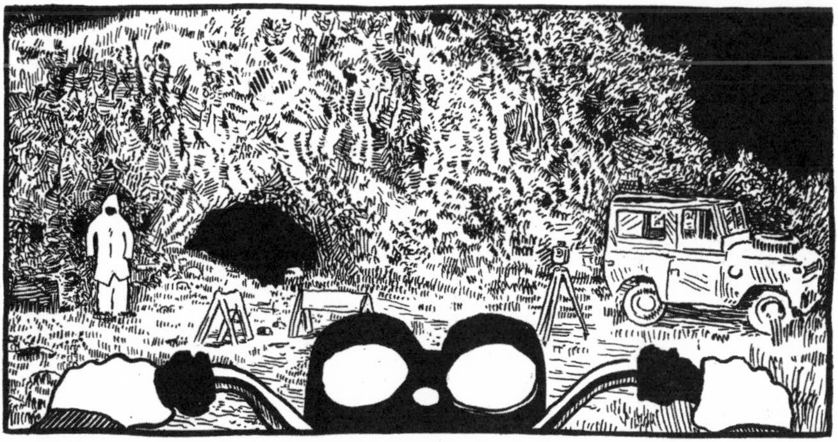
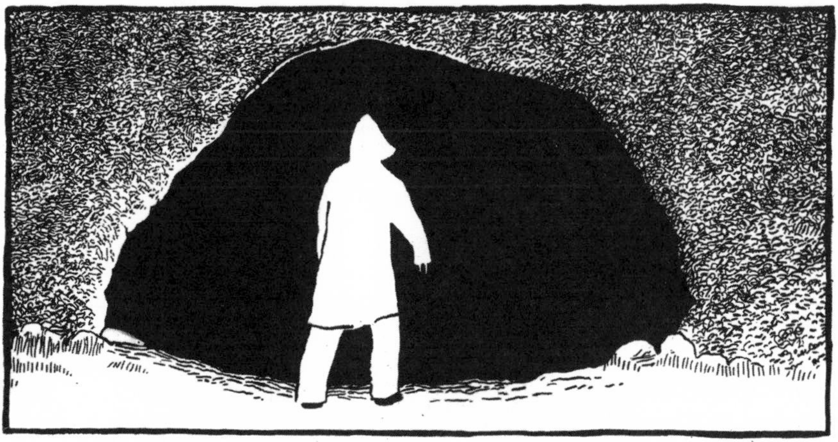

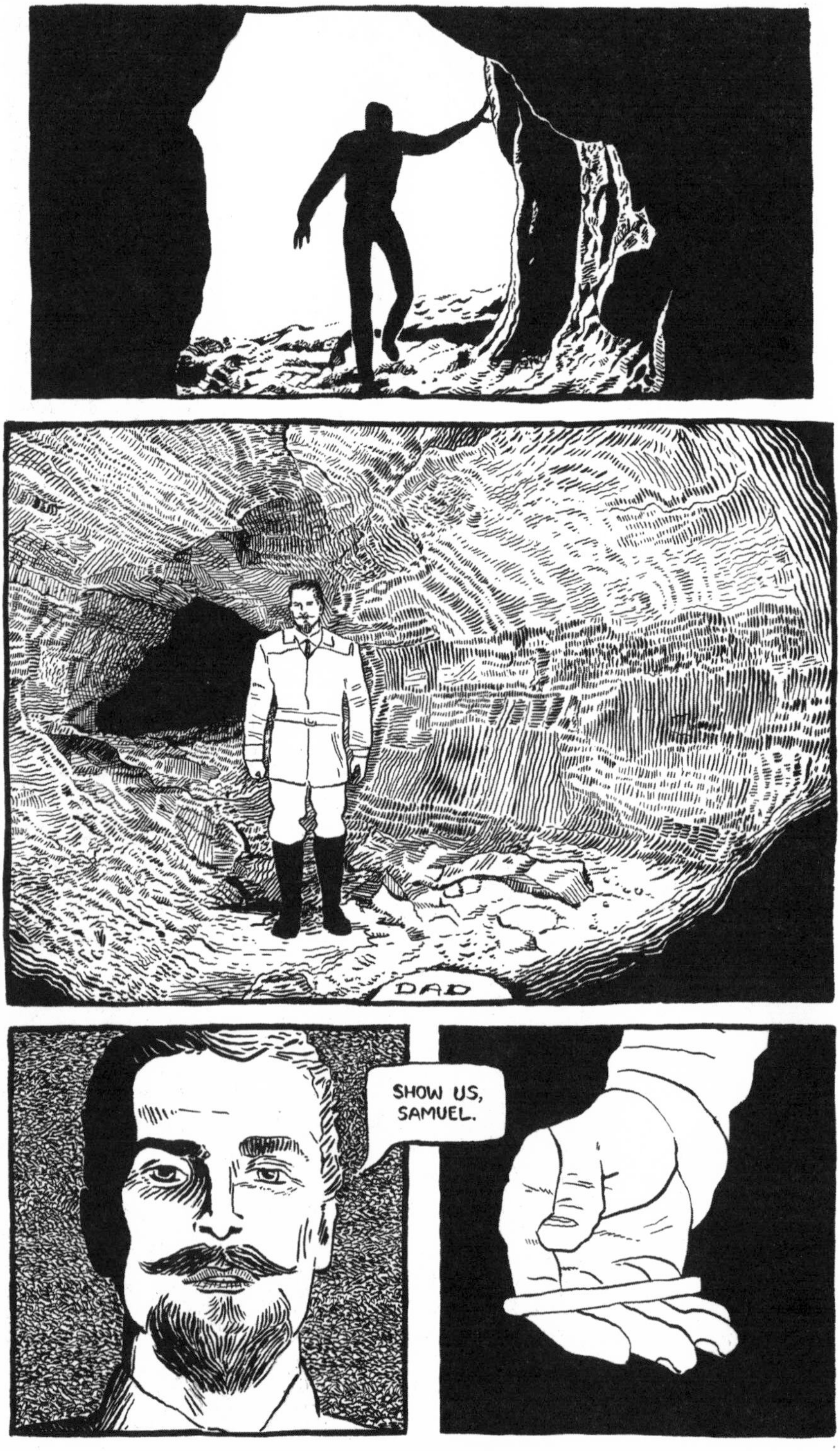
DAD
SHOW US, SAMUEL.

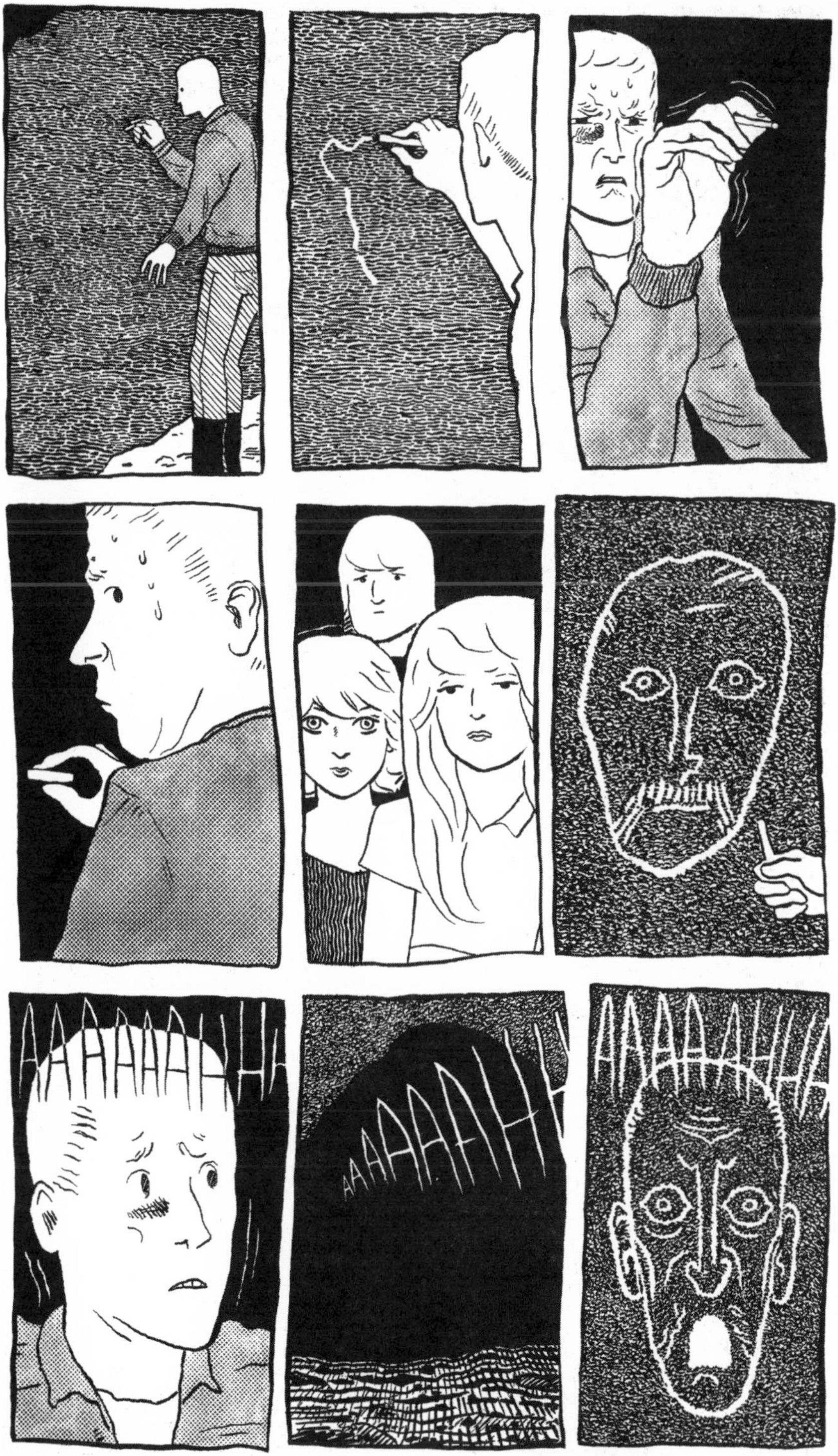
AAAAAAAHHA
AAAAAAAHH
AAAAAAHHHA

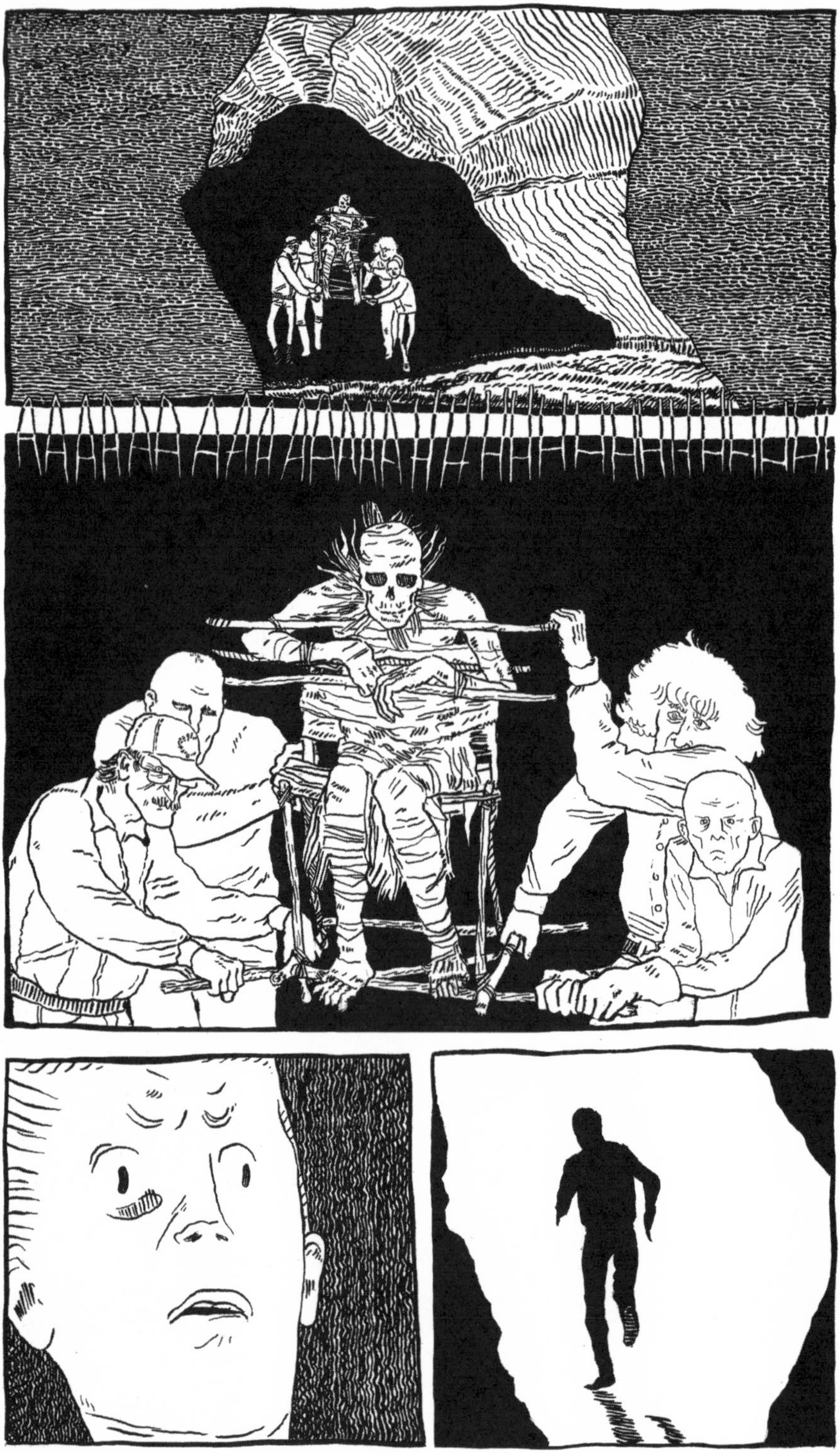
AAAAAA AAA AAAAAAHH HHAAAAAARRRRRUGH!

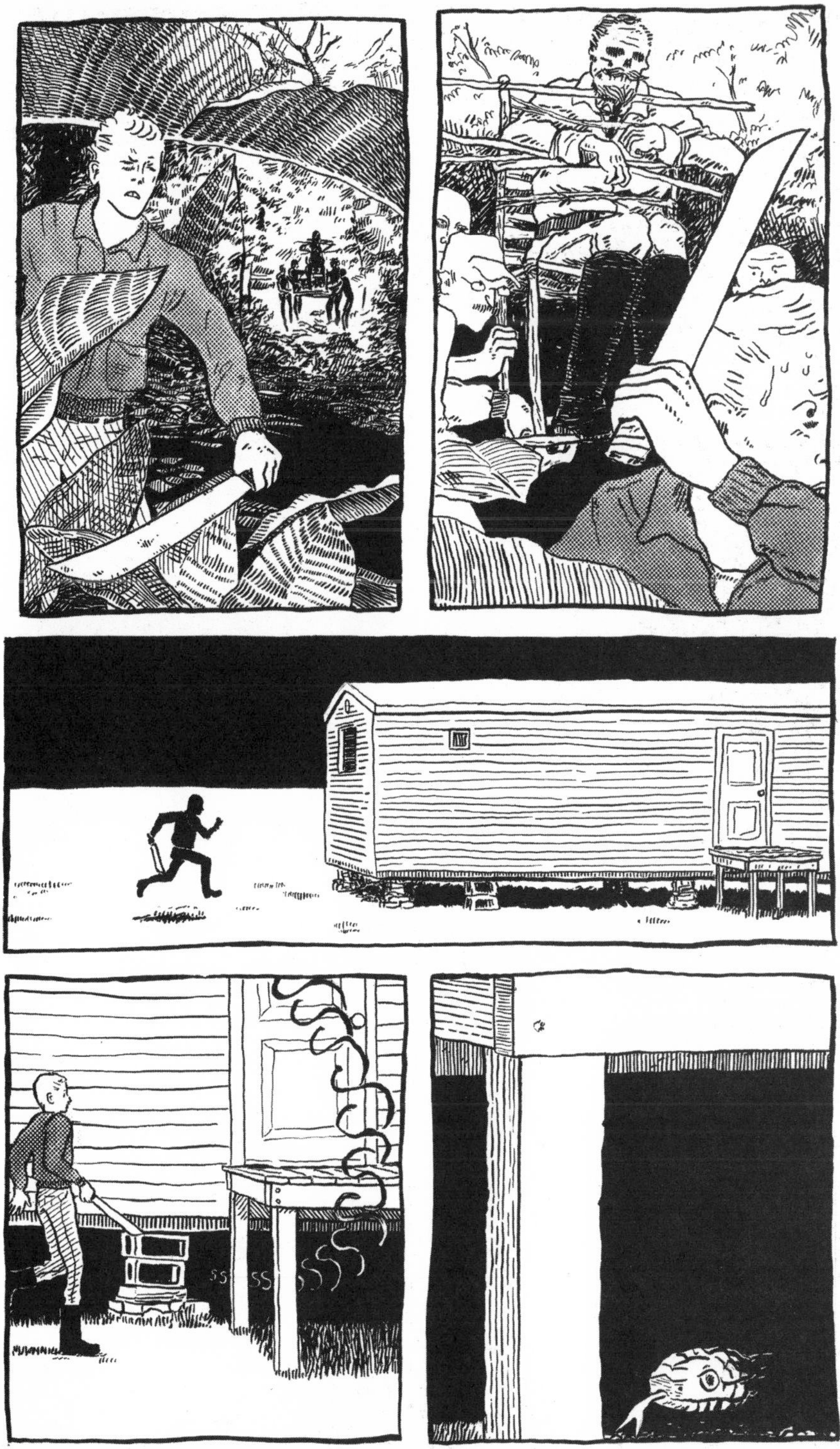

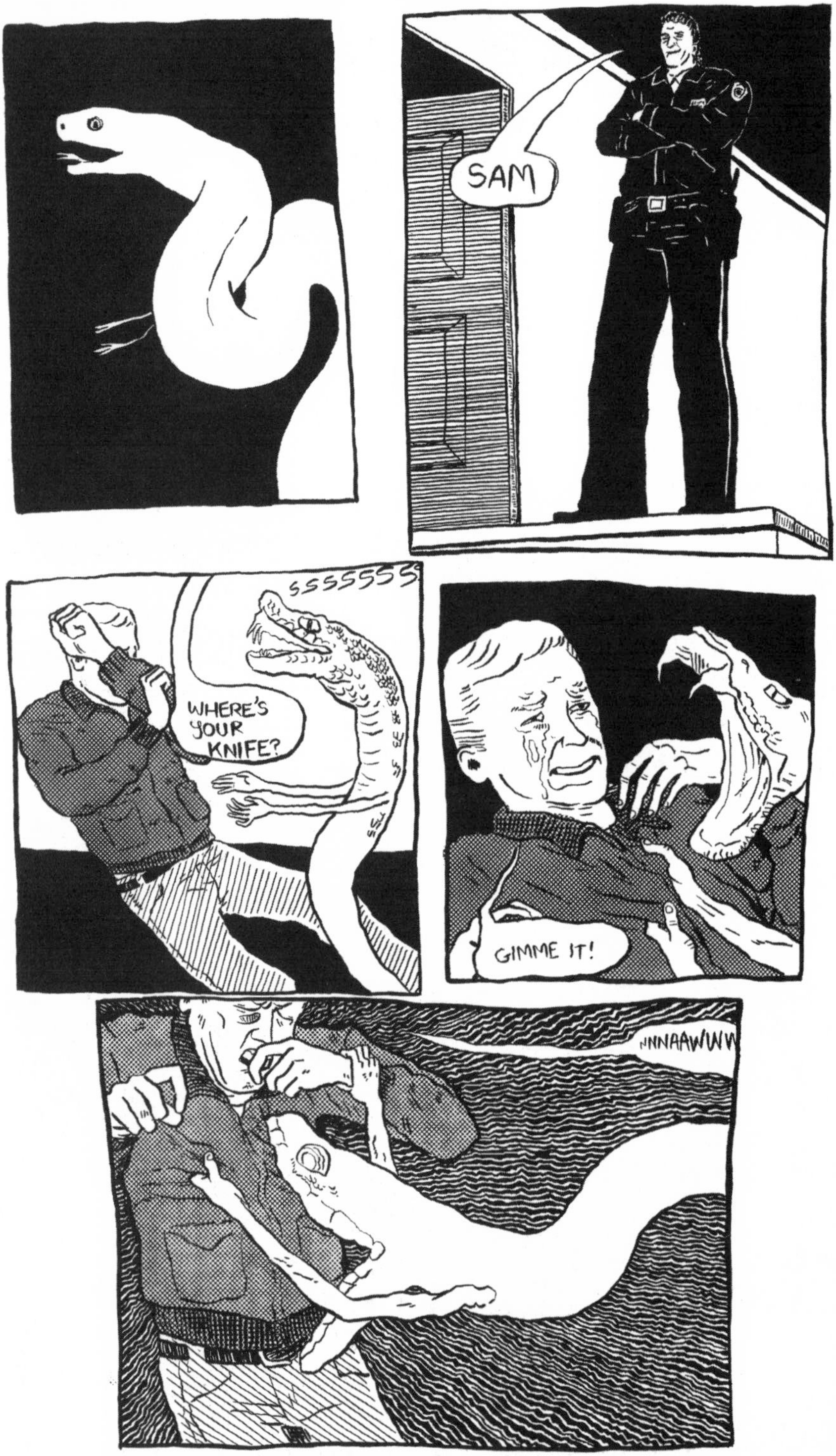
SAM
SSSSSSS
WHERE'S YOUR KNIFE?
GIMME IT!
NNNAAWWW

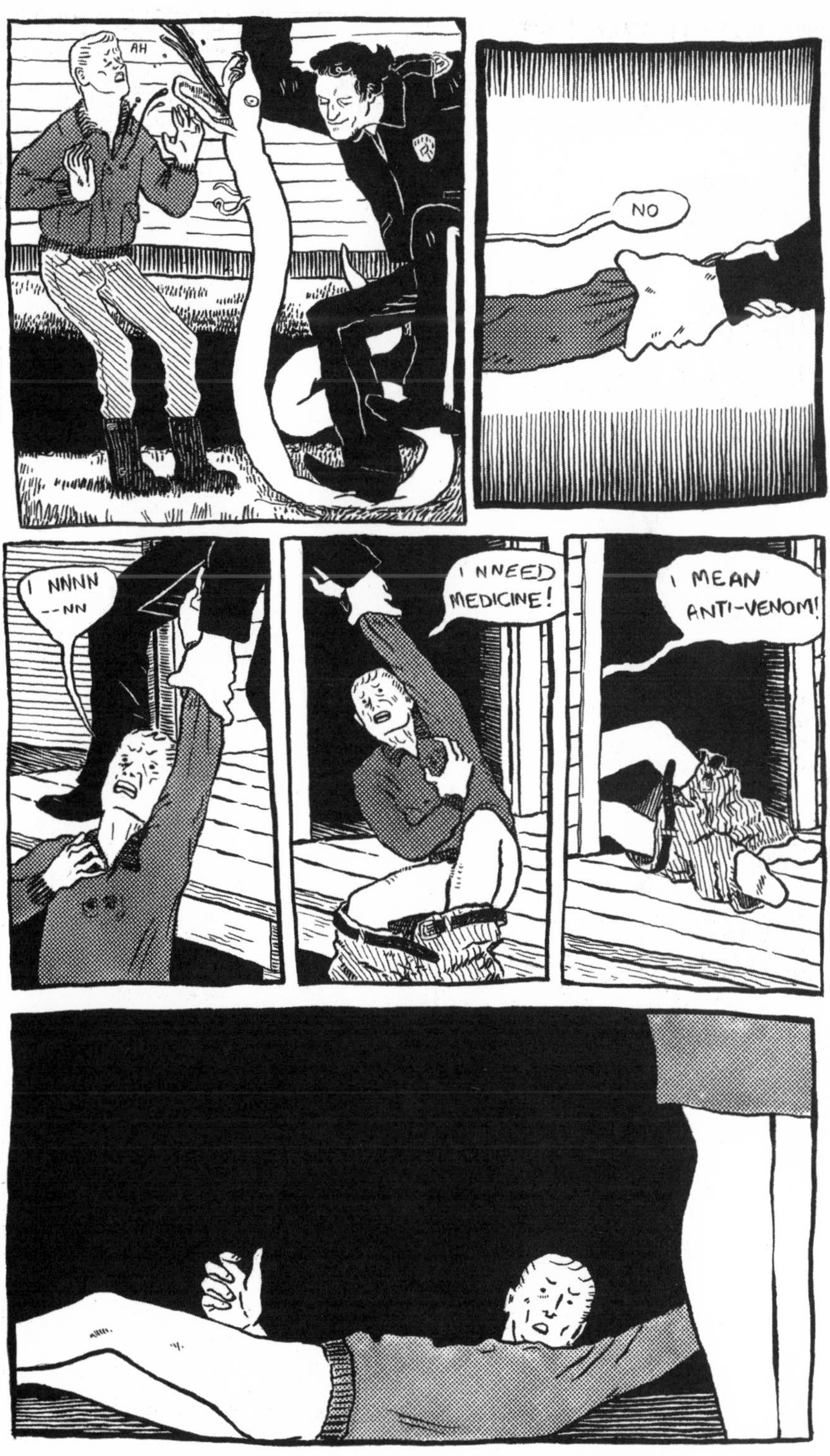
AH
NO
I NNNN
--NN
I NNEED MEDICINE!
I MEAN ANTI-VENOM!

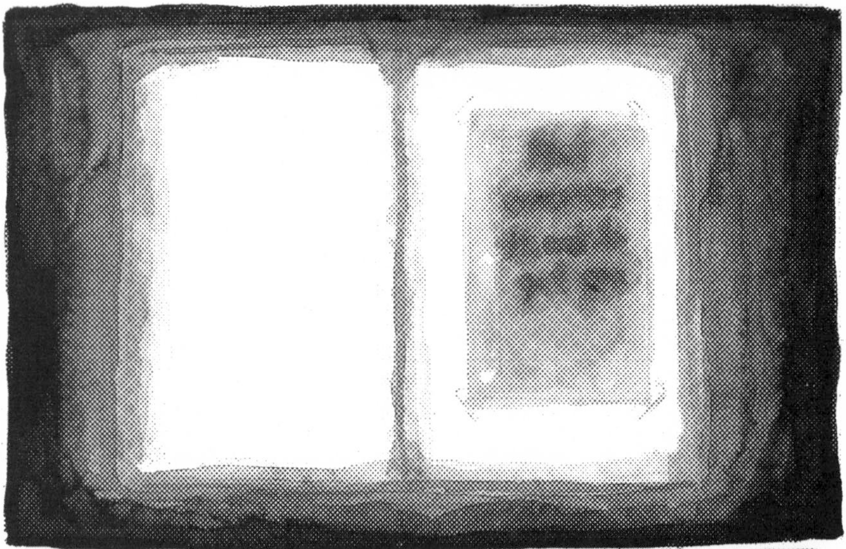

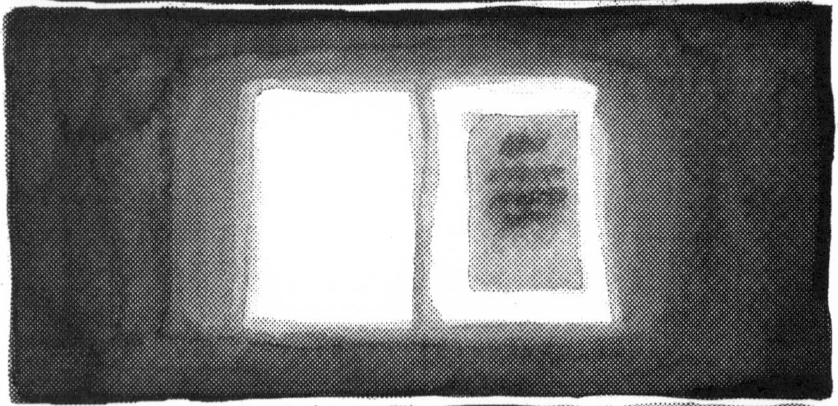

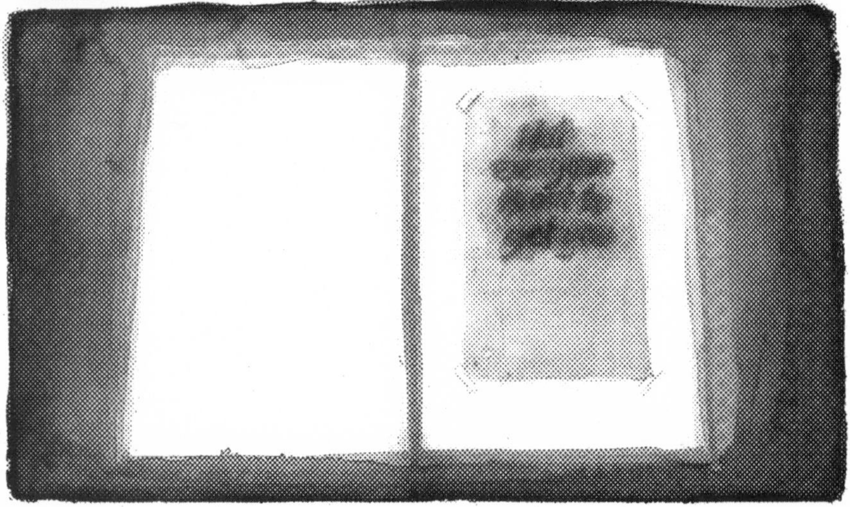

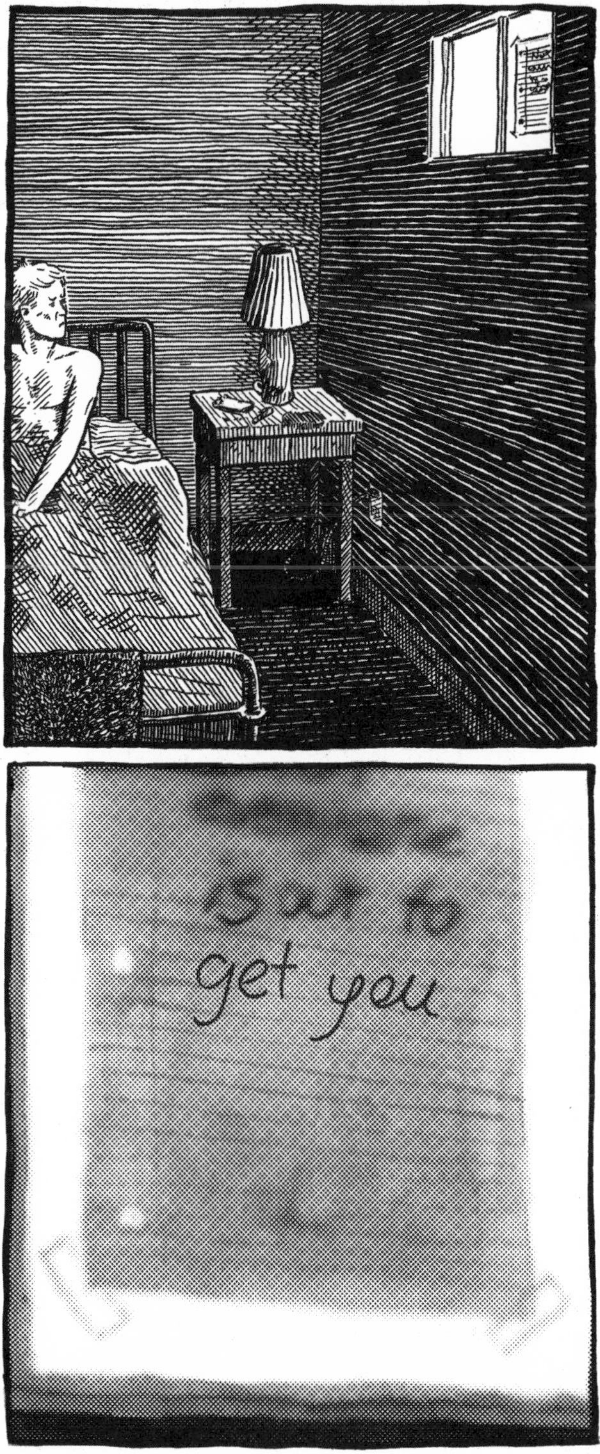
get you

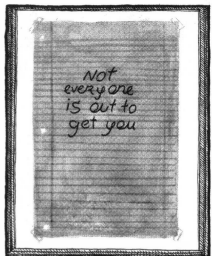

Not everyone is out to get you

BOY.

ARE YOU UP?

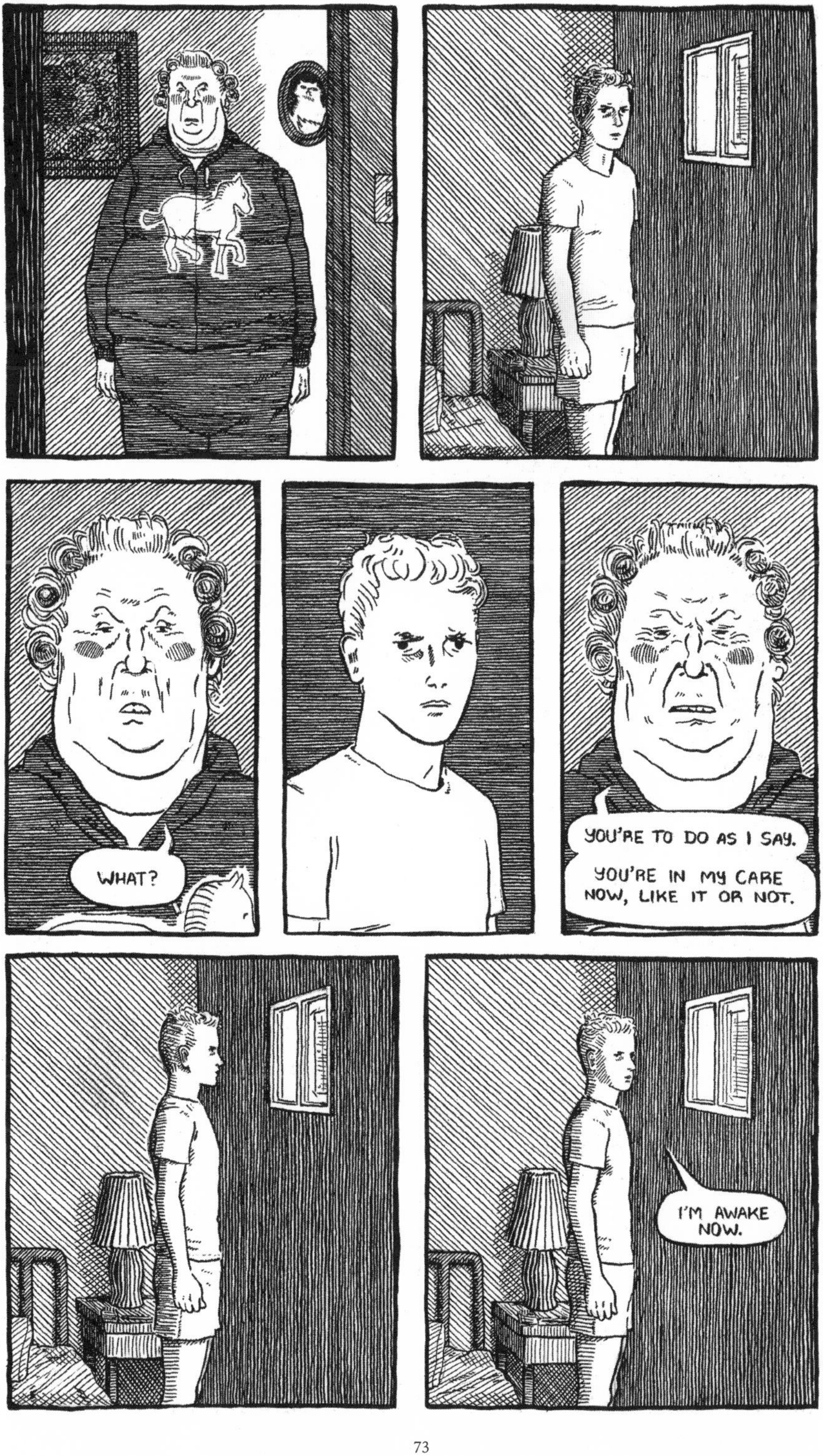
WHAT?
YOU'RE TO DO AS I SAY.
YOU'RE IN MY CARE NOW, LIKE IT OR NOT.
I'M AWAKE NOW.

CHAPTER THREE

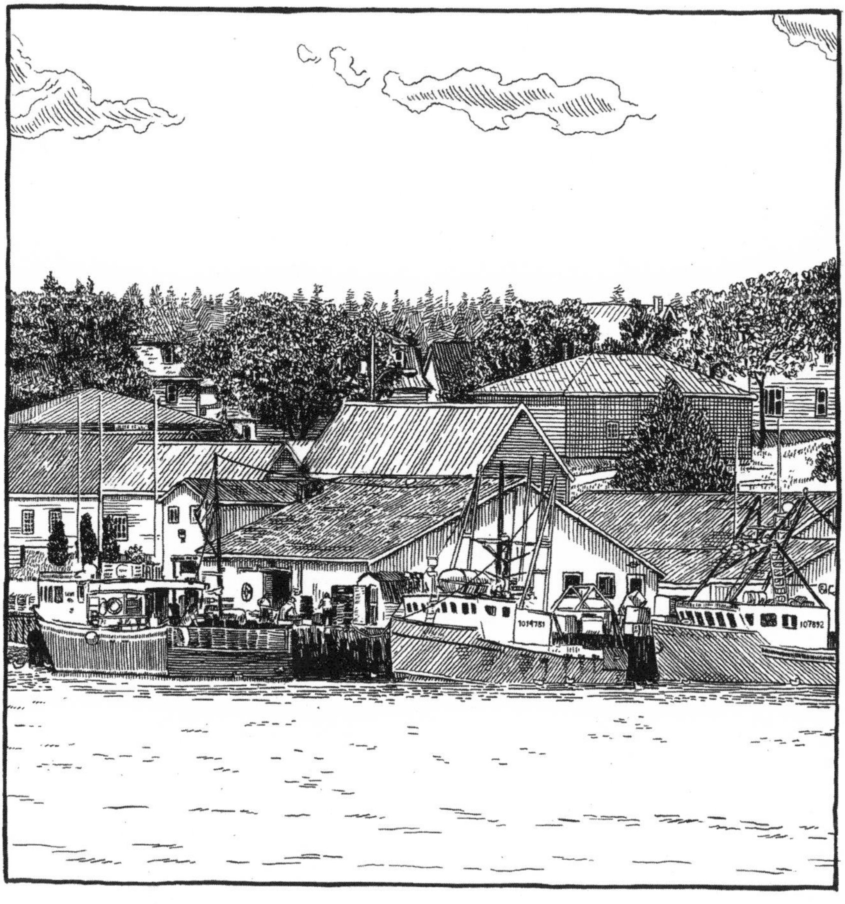

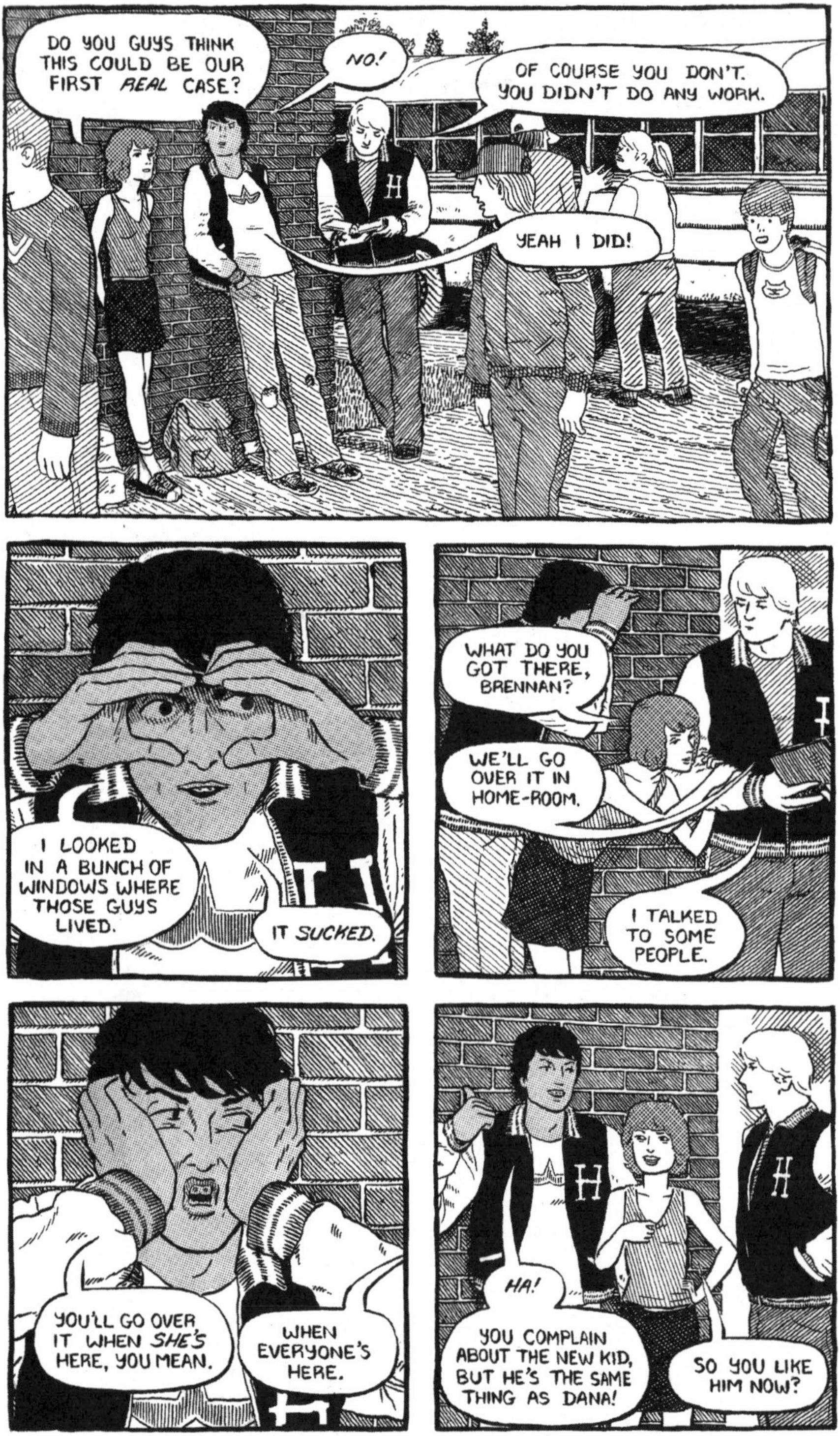
DO YOU GUYS THINK THIS COULD BE OUR FIRST *REAL* CASE?
NO!
OF COURSE YOU DON'T. YOU DIDN'T DO ANY WORK.
YEAH I DID!
I LOOKED IN A BUNCH OF WINDOWS WHERE THOSE GUYS LIVED.
IT *SUCKED.*
WHAT DO YOU GOT THERE, BRENNAN?
WE'LL GO OVER IT IN HOME-ROOM.
I TALKED TO SOME PEOPLE.
YOU'LL GO OVER IT WHEN *SHE'S* HERE, YOU MEAN.
WHEN EVERYONE'S HERE.
HA!
YOU COMPLAIN ABOUT THE NEW KID, BUT HE'S THE SAME THING AS DANA!
SO YOU LIKE HIM NOW?

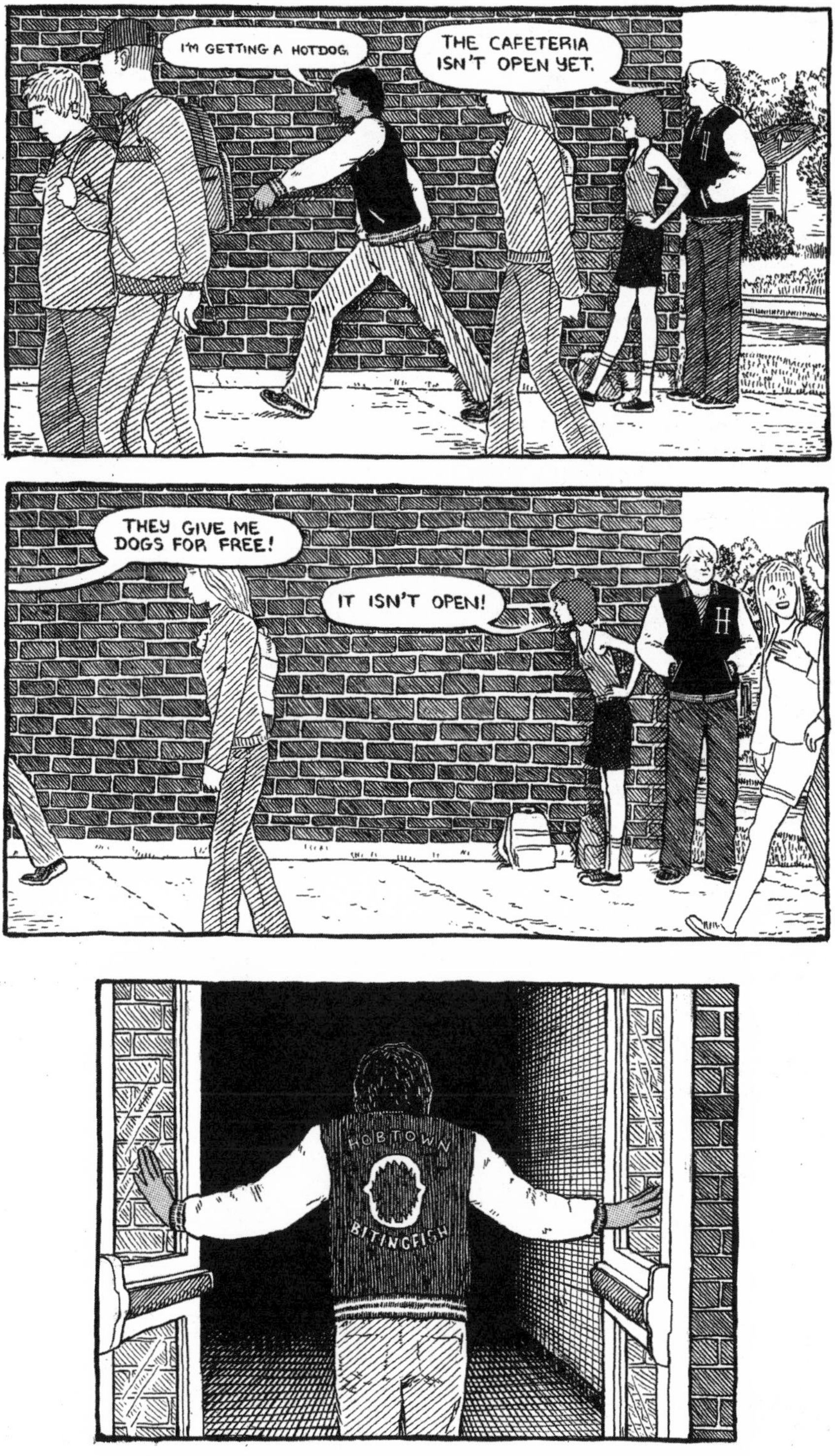
I'M GETTING A HOTDOG.
THE CAFETERIA ISN'T OPEN YET.
THEY GIVE ME DOGS FOR FREE!
IT ISN'T OPEN!
HOBTOWN
BITINGFISH

HEY.
YO.
NAVANA
HOBTOWN
BITINGFISH
DENNY.
YO.
SMELL THOSE DOGS...

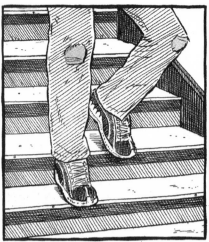

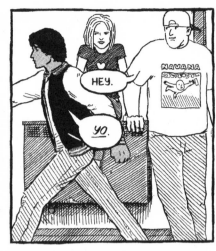

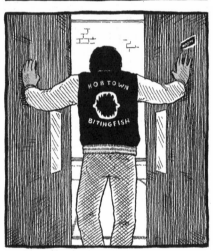

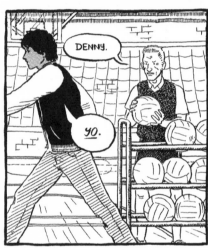

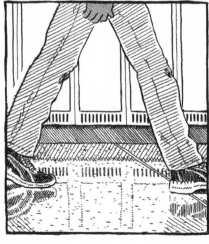

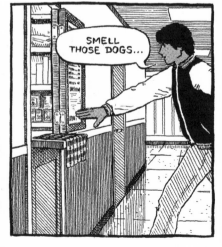

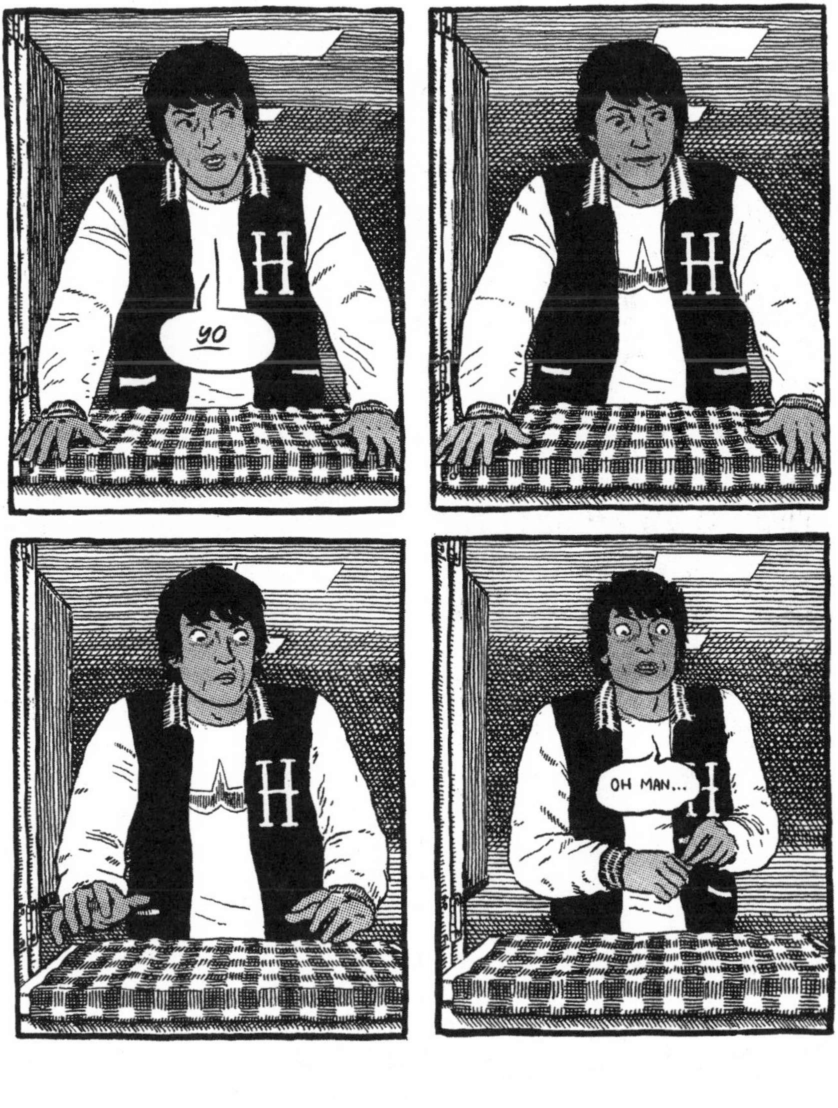
YO
OH MAN...

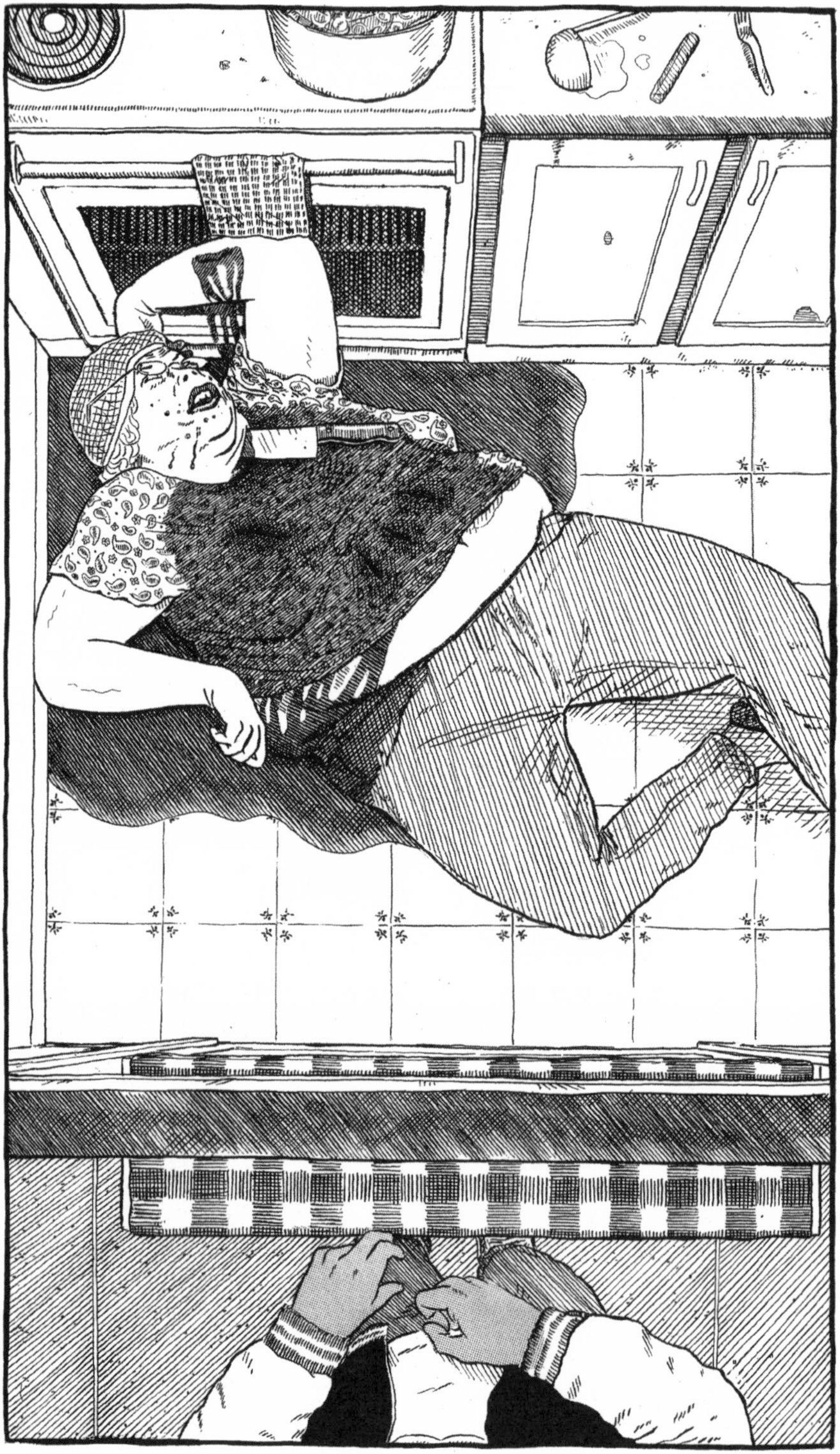

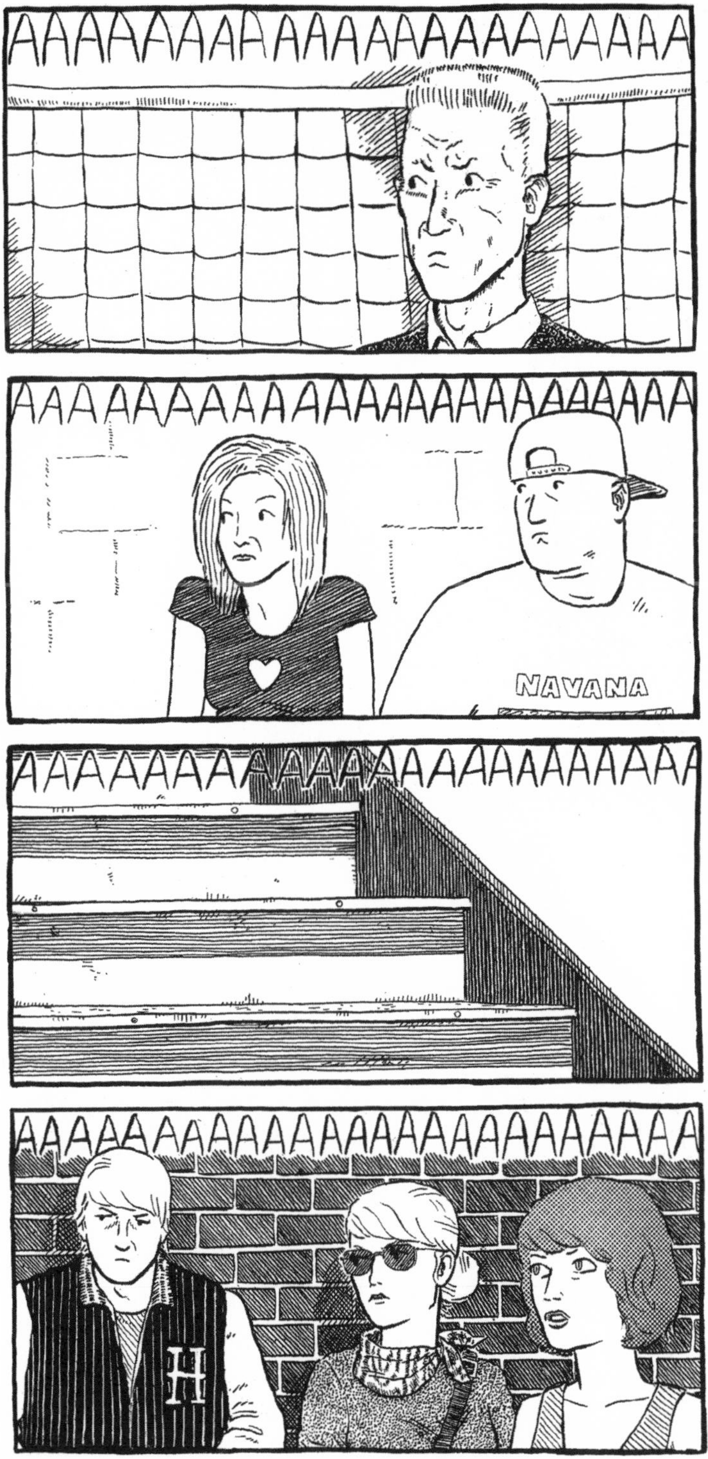
AAAAAAAAAAAAAAAAAAAAAA
AAAAAAAAAAAAAAAAAAAAAAAA
NAVANA
AAAAAAAAAAAAAAAAAAAAAA
AAAAAAAAAAAAAAAAAAAAAAAAA
H

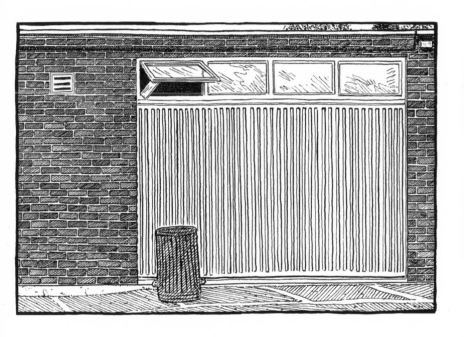

ACCURACY...
I NEED ACCURACY

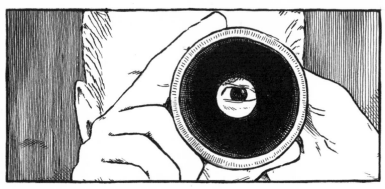

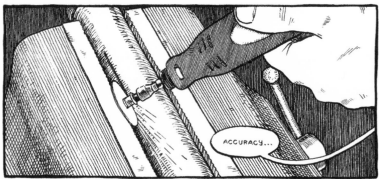

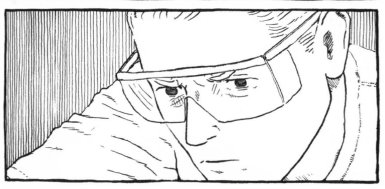

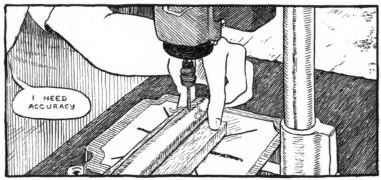

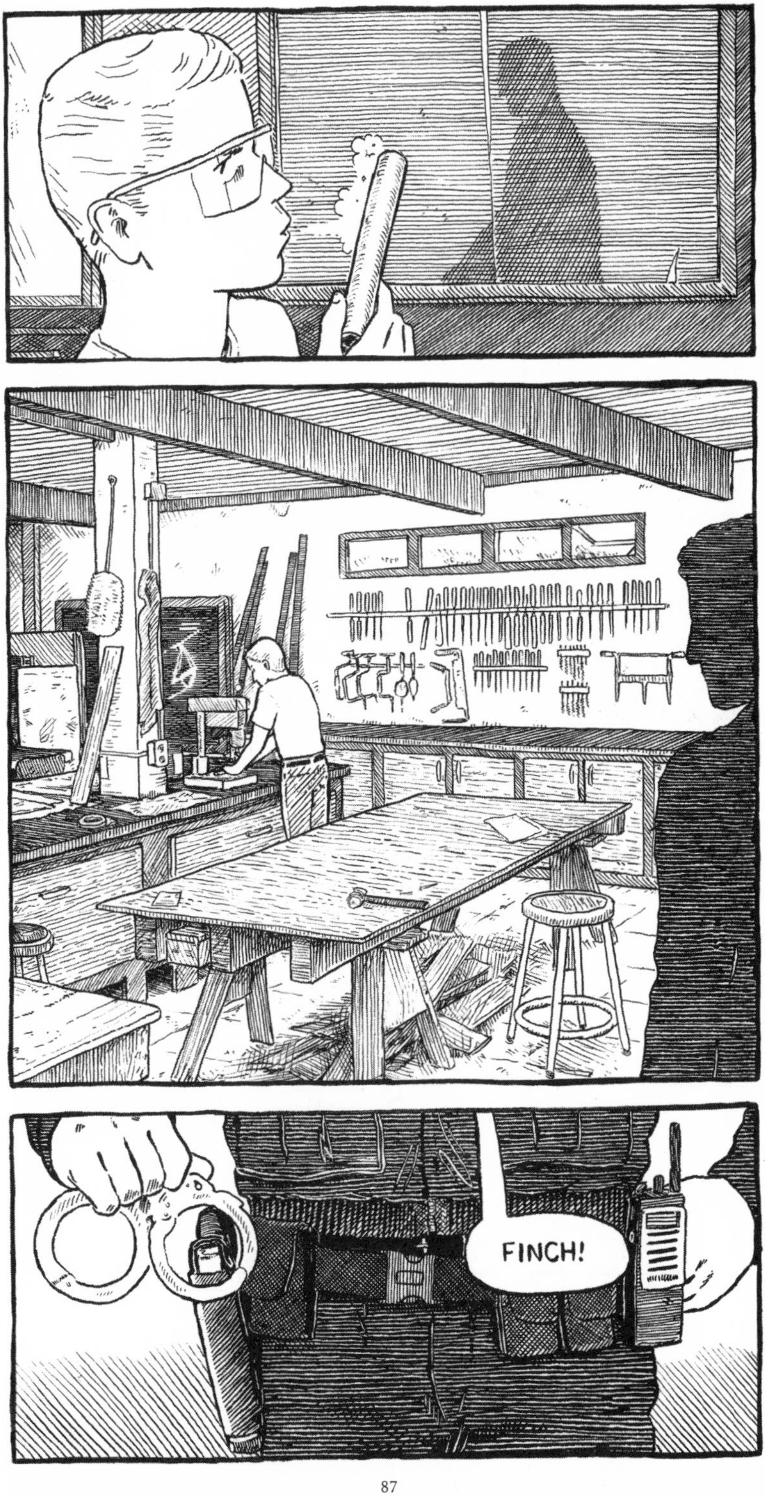
FINCH!

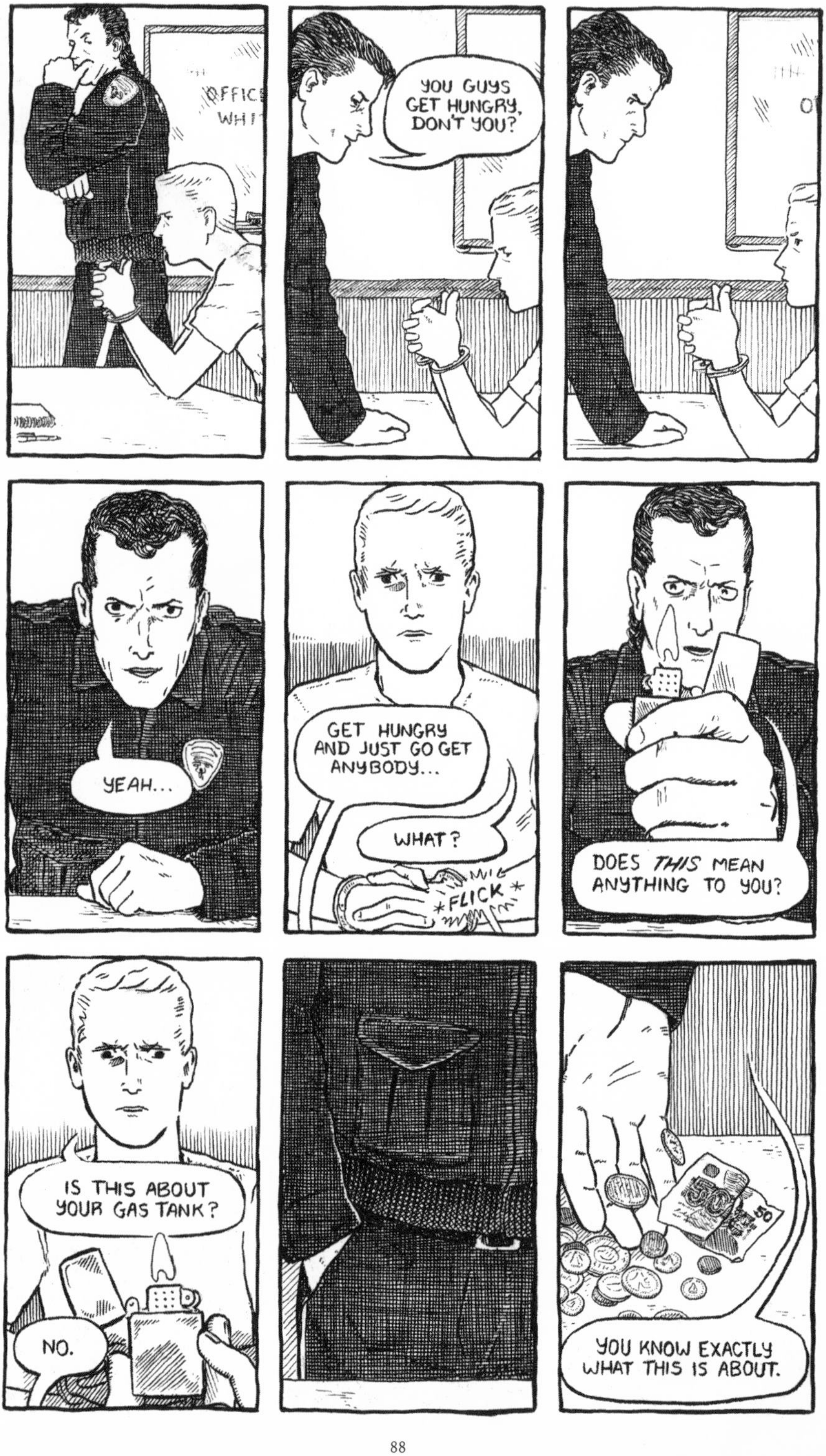
OFFIC
WHI
YOU GUYS GET HUNGRY, DON'T YOU?
YEAH...
GET HUNGRY AND JUST GO GET ANYBODY...
WHAT?
FLICK
DOES THIS MEAN ANYTHING TO YOU?
IS THIS ABOUT YOUR GAS TANK?
NO.
YOU KNOW EXACTLY WHAT THIS IS ABOUT.

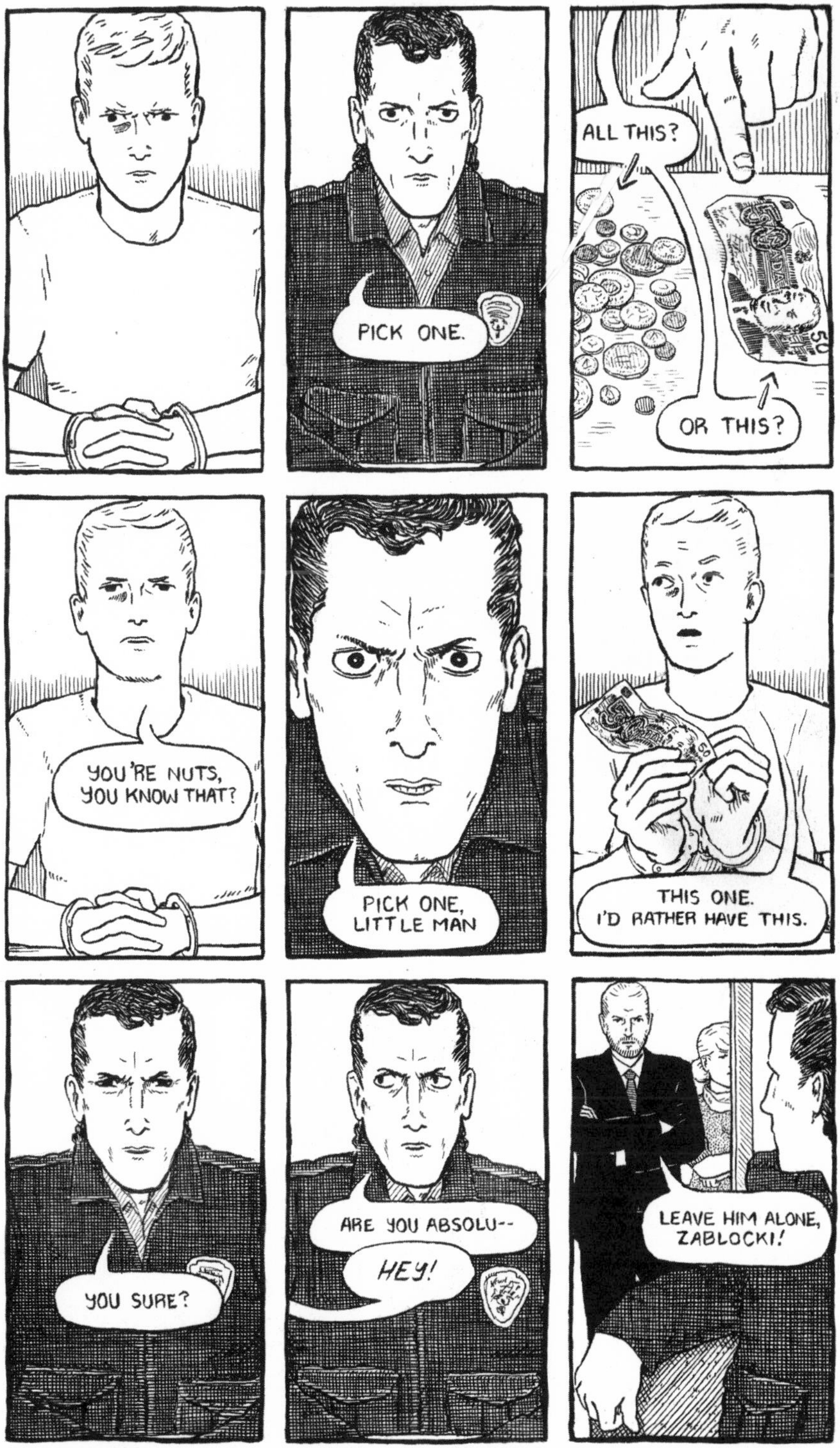
PICK ONE.
ALL THIS?
OR THIS?
YOU'RE NUTS, YOU KNOW THAT?
PICK ONE, LITTLE MAN
THIS ONE. I'D RATHER HAVE THIS.
YOU SURE?
ARE YOU ABSOLU--
HEY!
LEAVE HIM ALONE, ZABLOCKI!

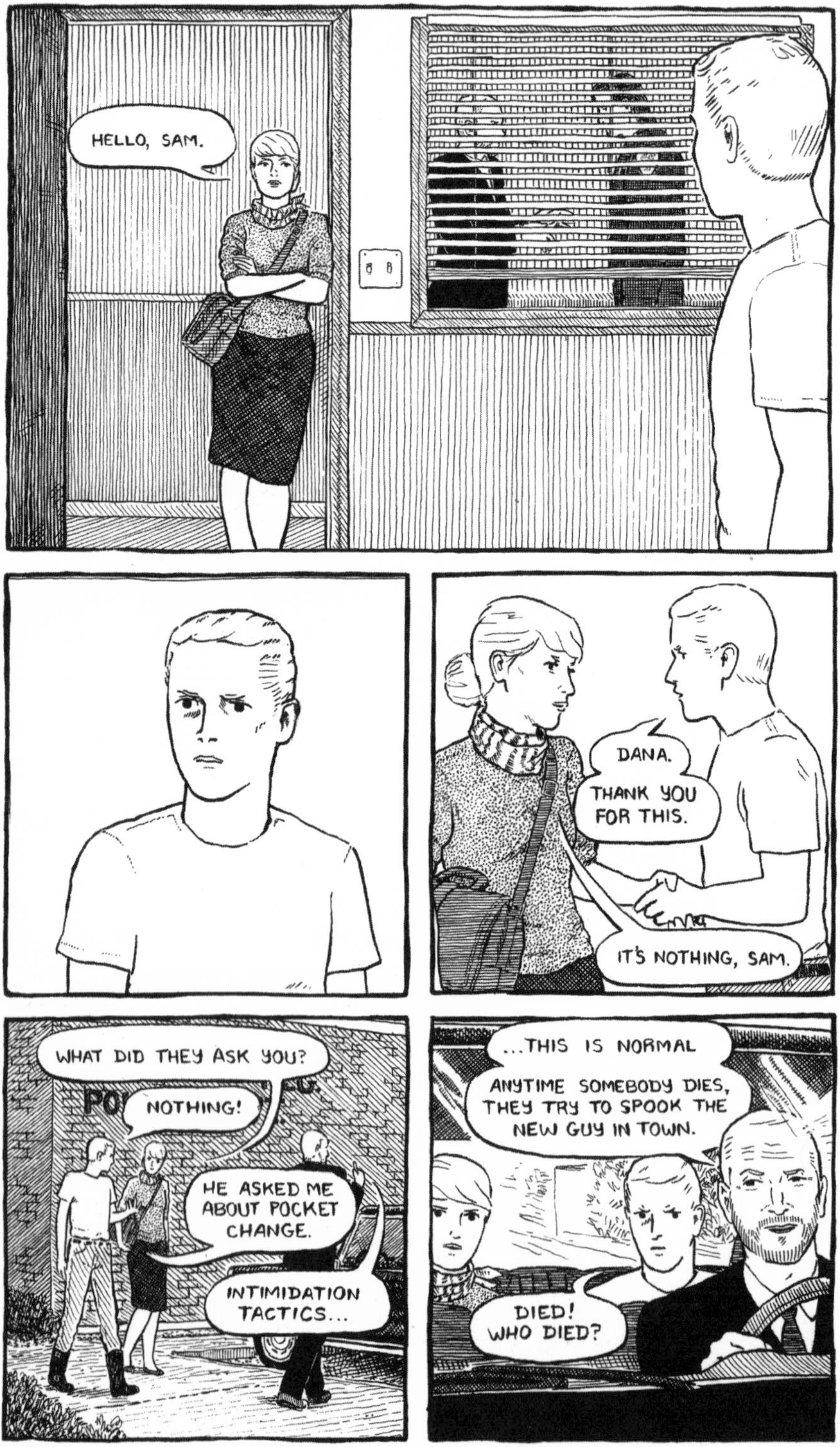
HELLO, SAM.
DANA.
THANK YOU FOR THIS.
IT'S NOTHING, SAM.
WHAT DID THEY ASK YOU?
NOTHING!
HE ASKED ME ABOUT POCKET CHANGE.
INTIMIDATION TACTICS...
...THIS IS NORMAL
ANYTIME SOMEBODY DIES, THEY TRY TO SPOOK THE NEW GUY IN TOWN.
DIED! WHO DIED?

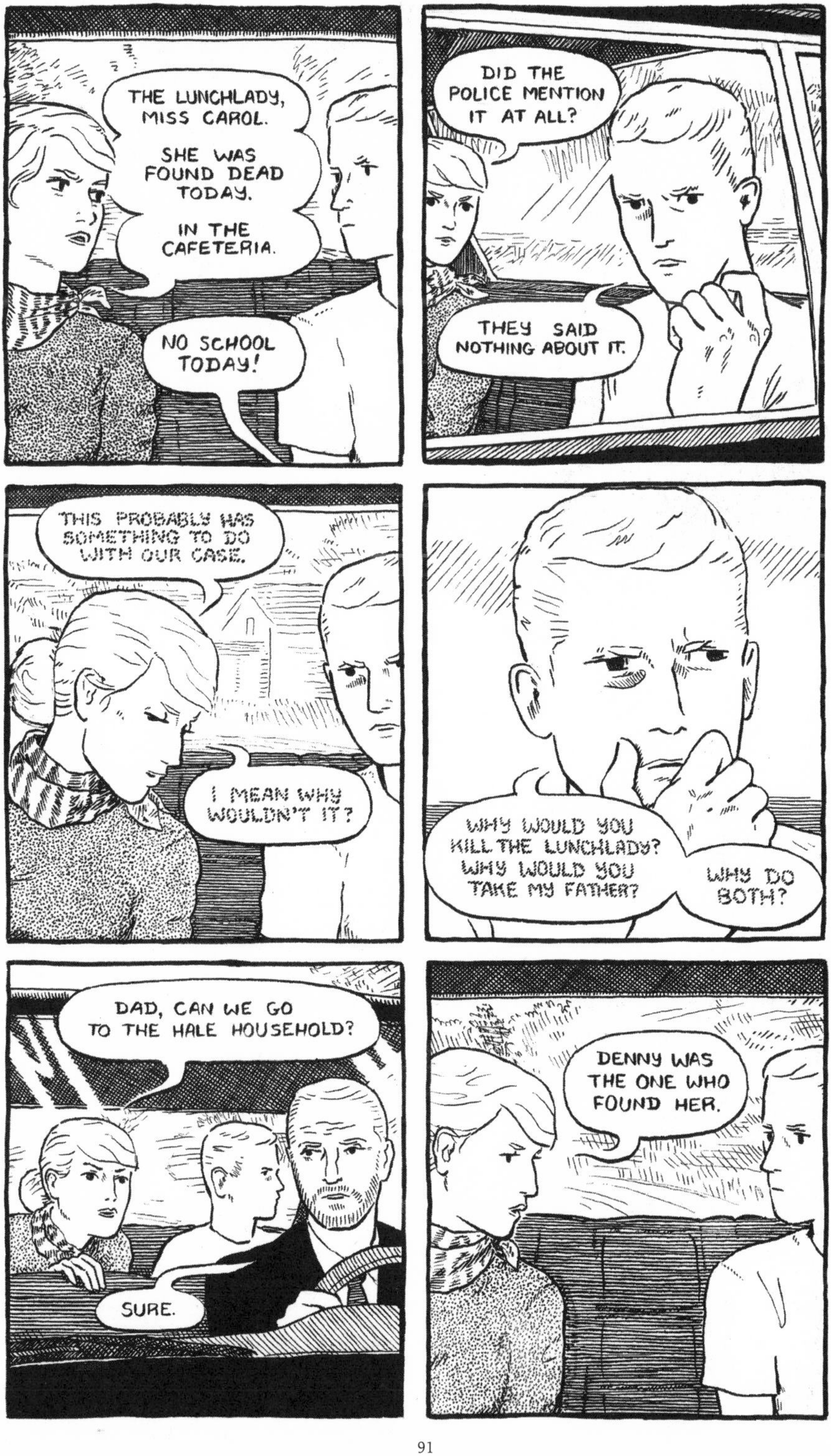
THE LUNCHLADY, MISS CAROL.
SHE WAS FOUND DEAD TODAY.
IN THE CAFETERIA.
NO SCHOOL TODAY!
DID THE POLICE MENTION IT AT ALL?
THEY SAID NOTHING ABOUT IT.
THIS PROBABLY HAS SOMETHING TO DO WITH OUR CASE.
I MEAN WHY WOULDN'T IT?
WHY WOULD YOU KILL THE LUNCHLADY? WHY WOULD YOU TAKE MY FATHER?
WHY DO BOTH?
DAD, CAN WE GO TO THE HALE HOUSEHOLD?
SURE.
DENNY WAS THE ONE WHO FOUND HER.

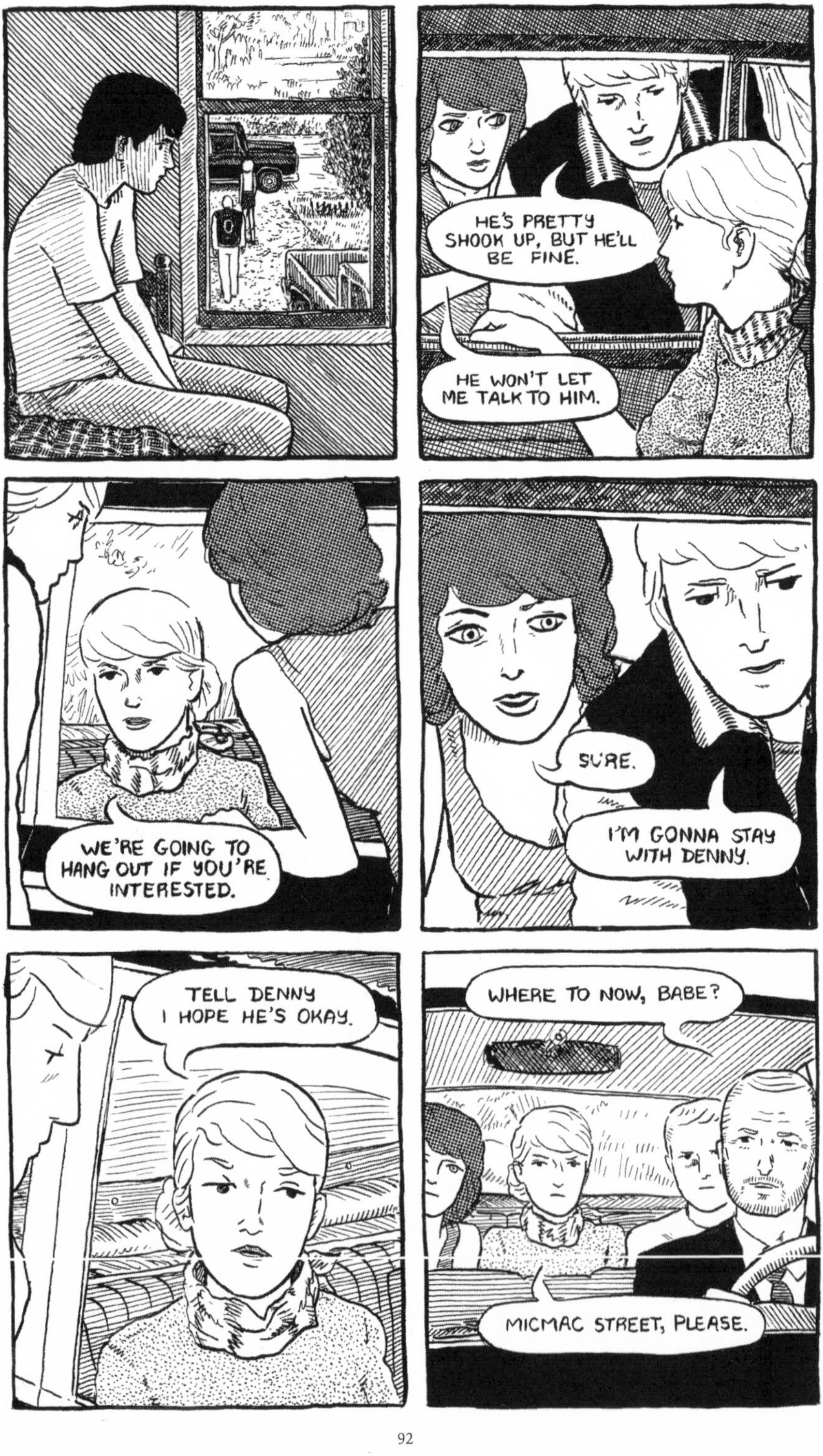
HE'S PRETTY SHOOK UP, BUT HE'LL BE FINE.
HE WON'T LET ME TALK TO HIM.
WE'RE GOING TO HANG OUT IF YOU'RE INTERESTED.
SURE.
I'M GONNA STAY WITH DENNY.
TELL DENNY I HOPE HE'S OKAY.
WHERE TO NOW, BABE?
MICMAC STREET, PLEASE.

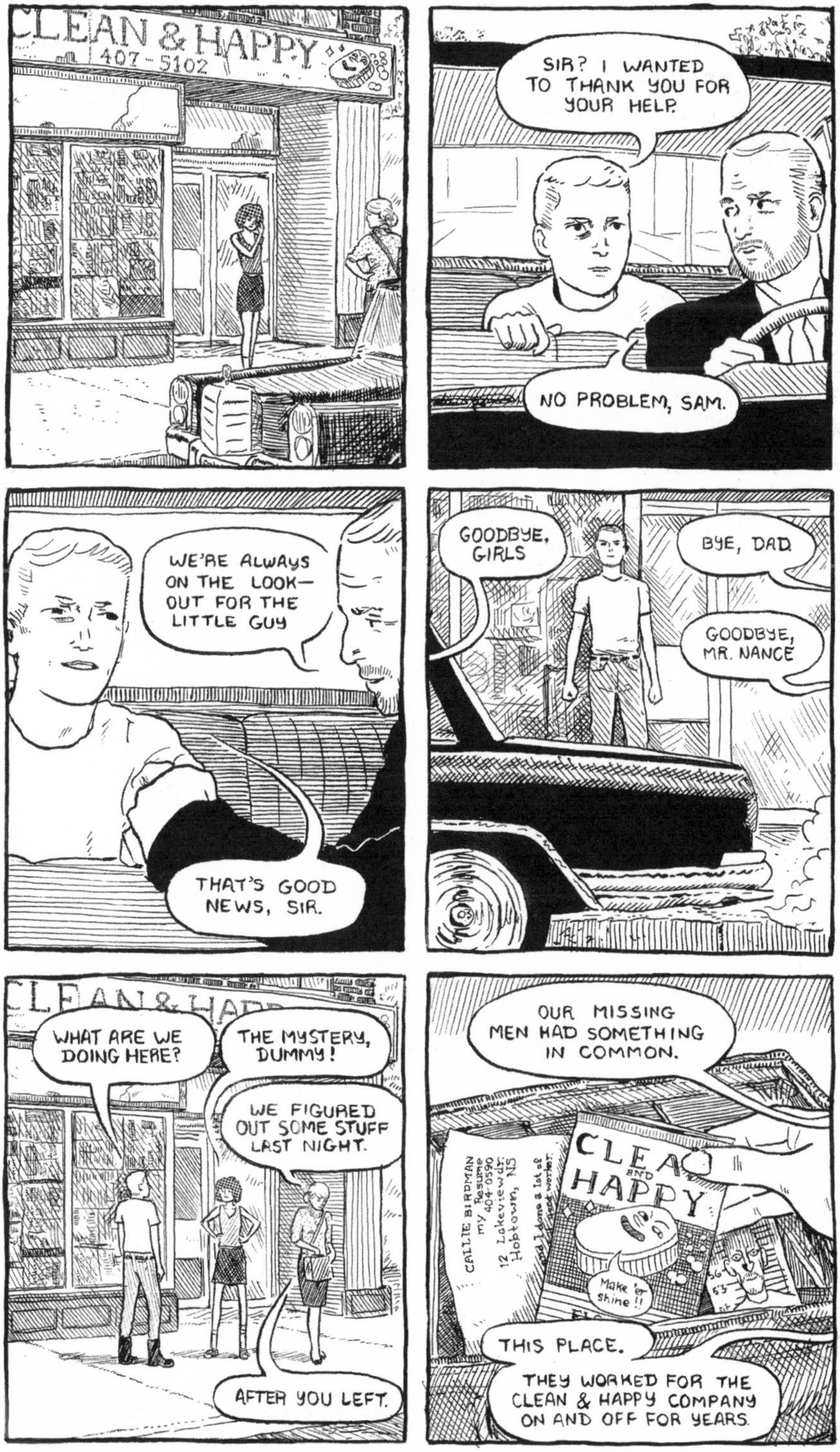
CLEAN & HAPPY
407-5102
SIR? I WANTED TO THANK YOU FOR YOUR HELP.
NO PROBLEM, SAM.
WE'RE ALWAYS ON THE LOOK-OUT FOR THE LITTLE GUY
THAT'S GOOD NEWS, SIR.
GOODBYE, GIRLS
BYE, DAD.
GOODBYE, MR. NANCE
WHAT ARE WE DOING HERE?
THE MYSTERY, DUMMY!
WE FIGURED OUT SOME STUFF LAST NIGHT.
AFTER YOU LEFT.
OUR MISSING MEN HAD SOMETHING IN COMMON.
CALLIE BIRDMAN
my Resume
404-0590
12 Lakeview dr.
Hobtown, NS
CLEAN AND HAPPY
Make 'er shine!!
THIS PLACE.
THEY WORKED FOR THE CLEAN & HAPPY COMPANY ON AND OFF FOR YEARS.

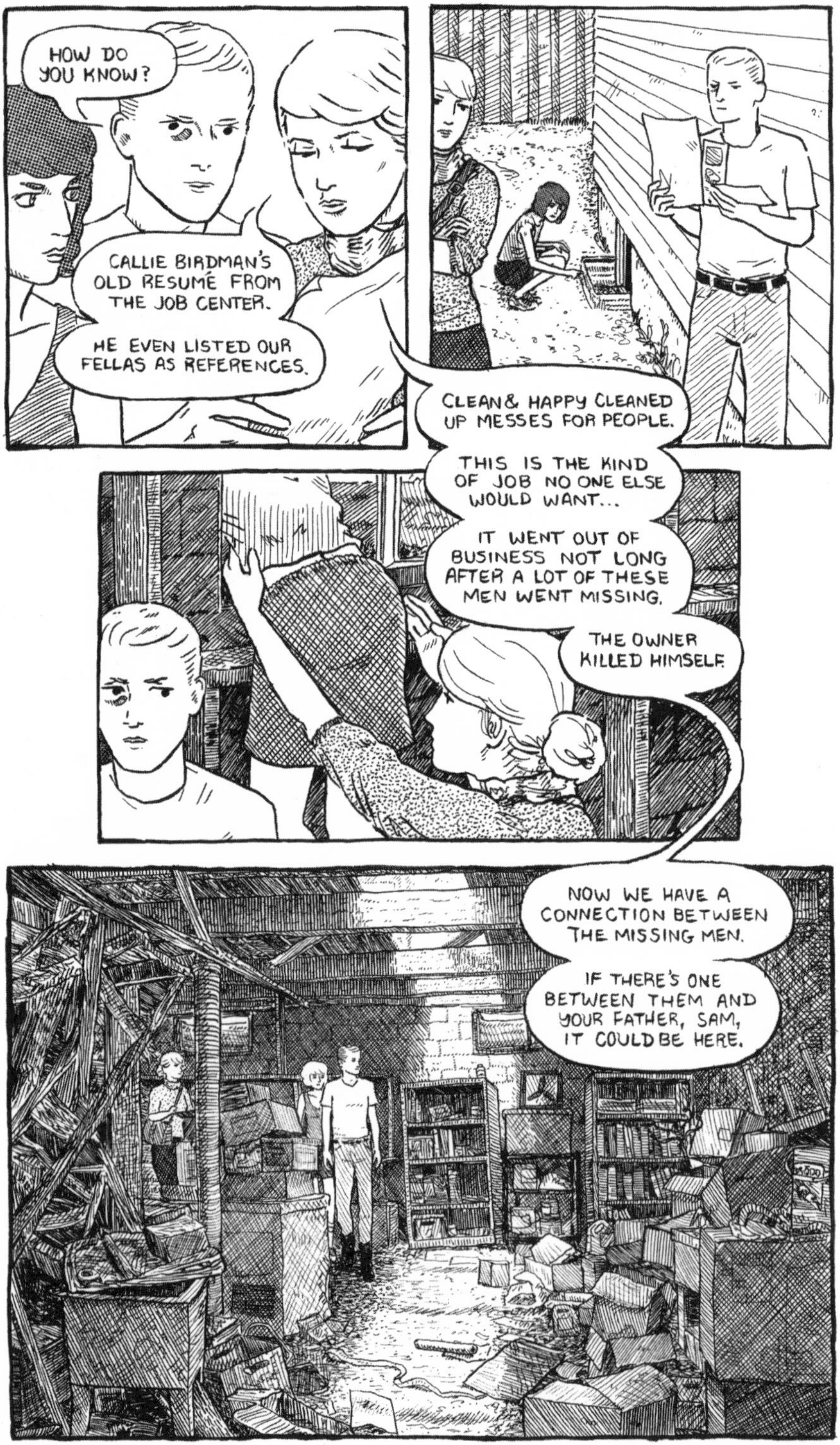
HOW DO YOU KNOW?
CALLIE BIRDMAN'S OLD RESUMÉ FROM THE JOB CENTER.
HE EVEN LISTED OUR FELLAS AS REFERENCES.
CLEAN & HAPPY CLEANED UP MESSES FOR PEOPLE.
THIS IS THE KIND OF JOB NO ONE ELSE WOULD WANT...
IT WENT OUT OF BUSINESS NOT LONG AFTER A LOT OF THESE MEN WENT MISSING.
THE OWNER KILLED HIMSELF.
NOW WE HAVE A CONNECTION BETWEEN THE MISSING MEN.
IF THERE'S ONE BETWEEN THEM AND YOUR FATHER, SAM, IT COULD BE HERE.

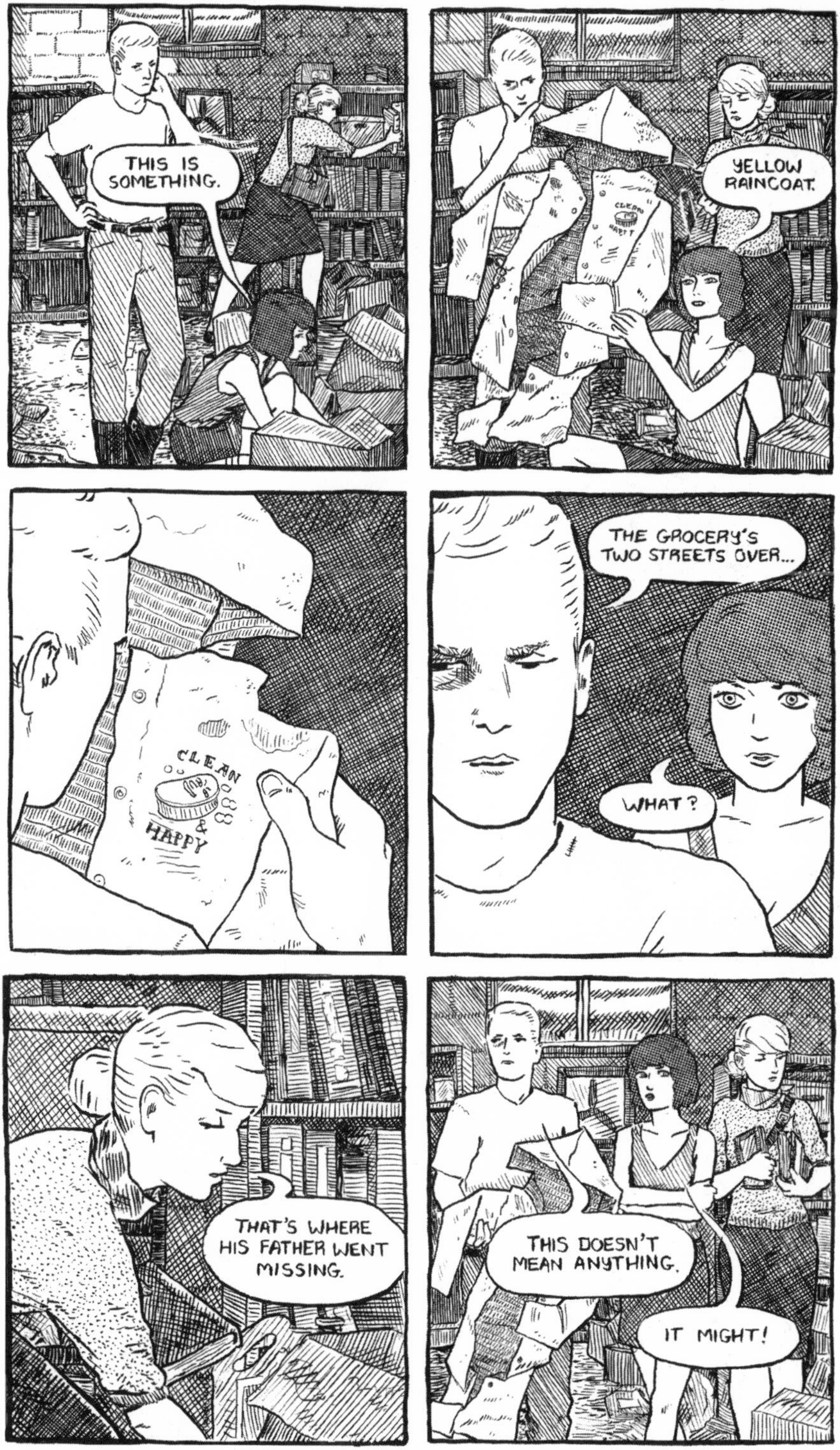
THIS IS SOMETHING.
YELLOW RAINCOAT.
CLEAN & HAPPY
THE GROCERY'S TWO STREETS OVER...
WHAT?
THAT'S WHERE HIS FATHER WENT MISSING.
THIS DOESN'T MEAN ANYTHING.
IT MIGHT!

IF IT DOES, IT DOESN'T CHANGE ANYTHING.

WELL, THIS MIGHT.

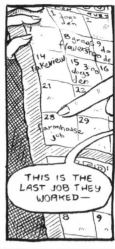

THIS IS THE LAST JOB THEY WORKED—

-- AND OUR CLEANERS WERE REPORTED MISSING NOT LONG AFTER...

BY THE OWNER OF THE CLEAN & HAPPY...

WHO KILLED HIMSELF.

WHAT WAS THAT?

LOOK!

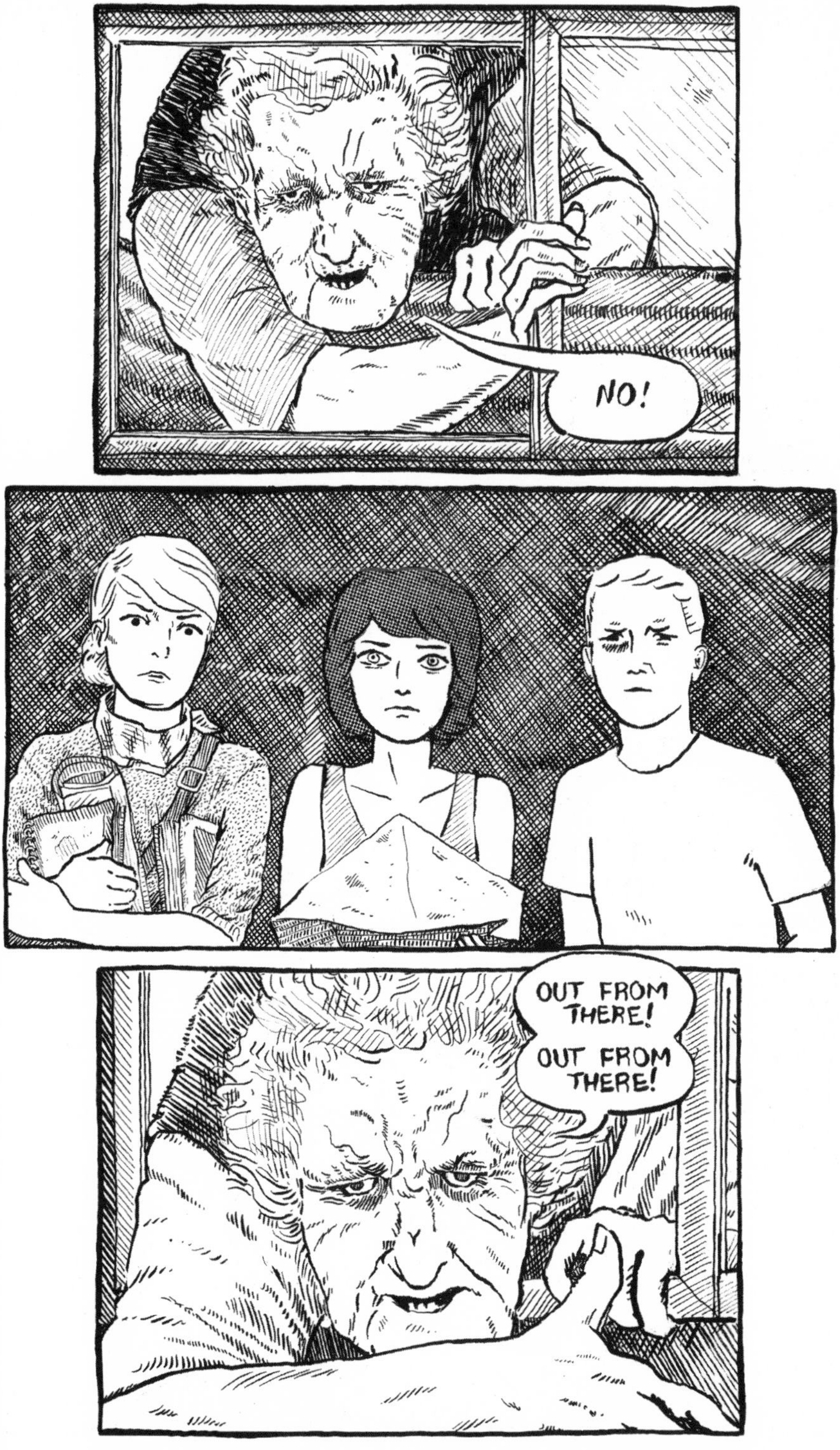
NO!
OUT FROM THERE!
OUT FROM THERE!

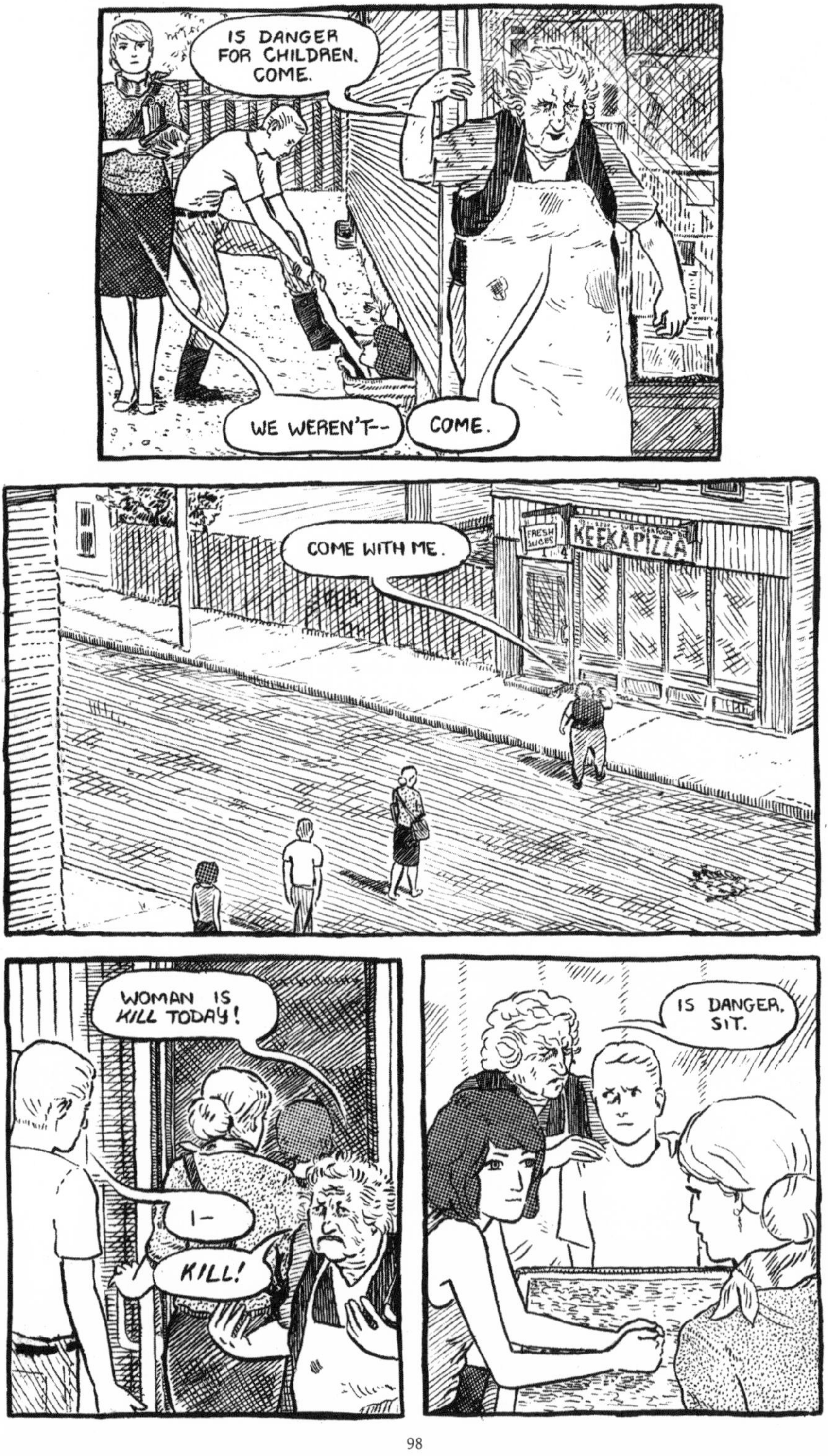
IS DANGER FOR CHILDREN. COME.
WE WEREN'T--
COME.
FRESH SUBS
KEEKAPIZZA
COME WITH ME.
WOMAN IS KILL TODAY!
I-
KILL!
IS DANGER. SIT.

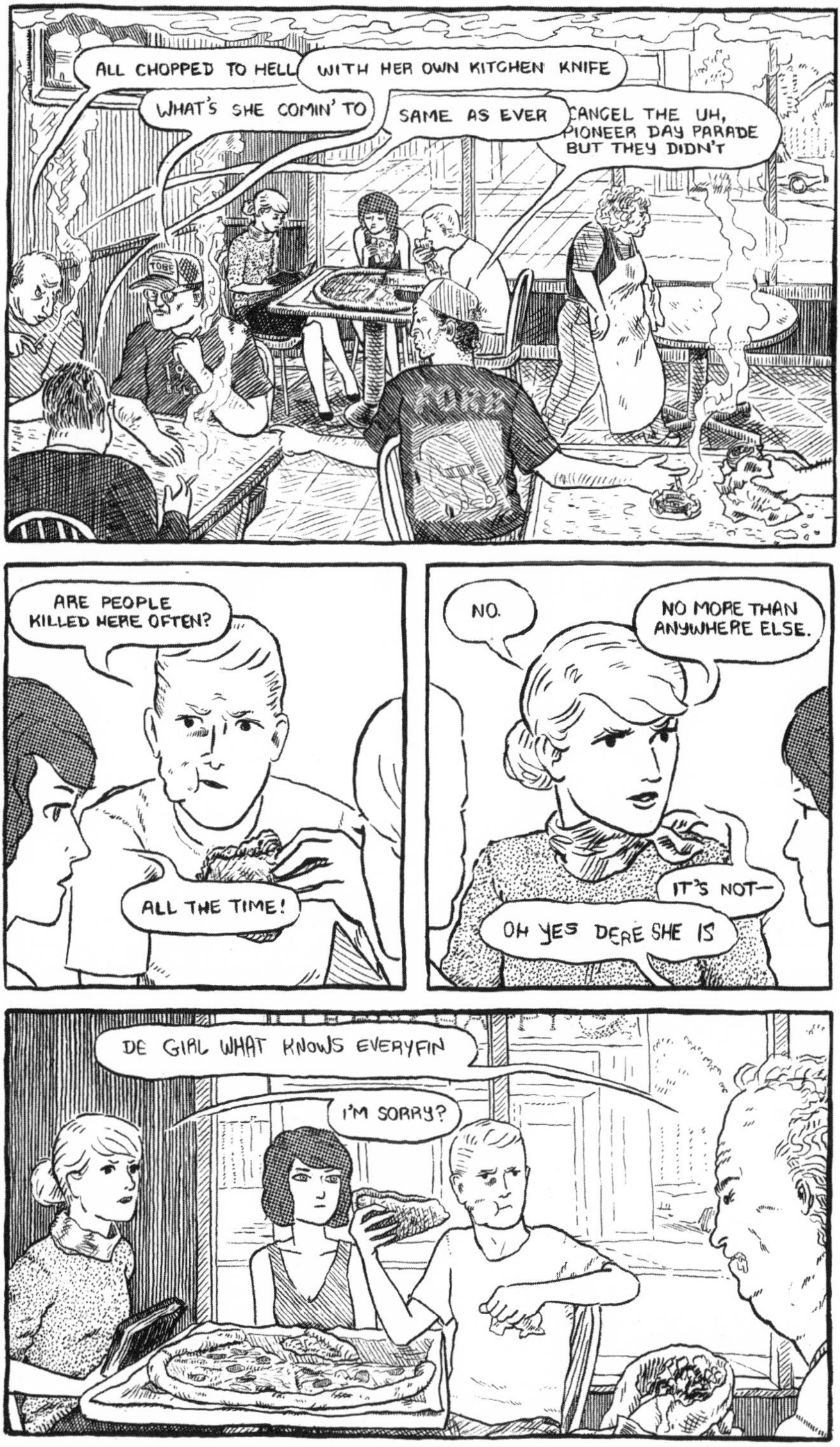
ALL CHOPPED TO HELL
WITH HER OWN KITCHEN KNIFE
WHAT'S SHE COMIN' TO
SAME AS EVER
CANCEL THE UH, PIONEER DAY PARADE BUT THEY DIDN'T
ARE PEOPLE KILLED HERE OFTEN?
ALL THE TIME!
NO.
NO MORE THAN ANYWHERE ELSE.
IT'S NOT—
OH YES DERE SHE IS
DE GIRL WHAT KNOWS EVERYFIN
I'M SORRY?

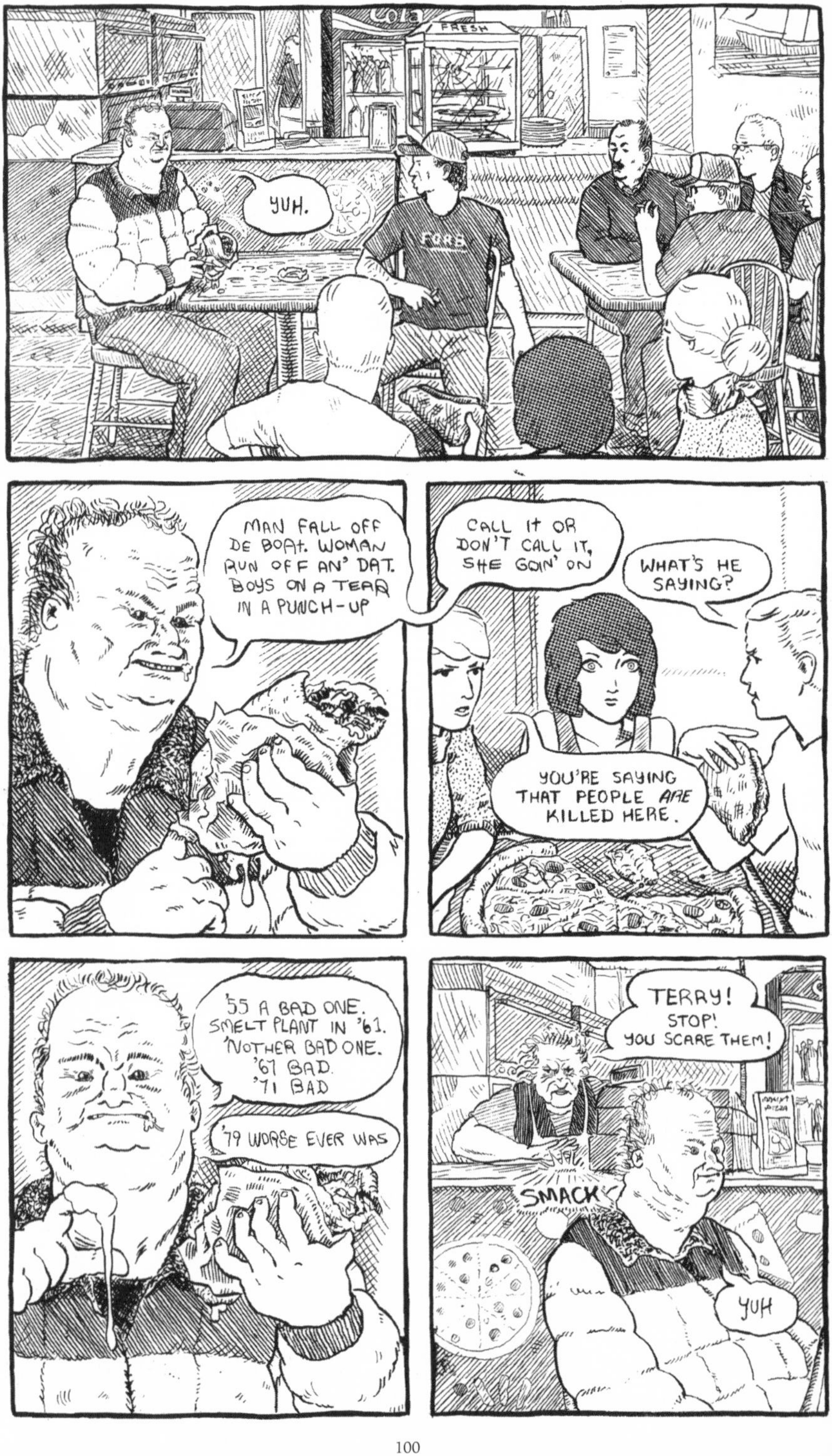

YUH.
MAN FALL OFF DE BOAT. WOMAN RUN OFF AN' DAT. BOYS ON A TEAR IN A PUNCH-UP
CALL IT OR DON'T CALL IT, SHE GOIN' ON
WHAT'S HE SAYING?
YOU'RE SAYING THAT PEOPLE *ARE* KILLED HERE.
'55 A BAD ONE. SMELT PLANT IN '61. 'NOTHER BAD ONE. '67 BAD. '71 BAD
'79 WORSE EVER WAS
TERRY! STOP! YOU SCARE THEM!
SMACK
YUH

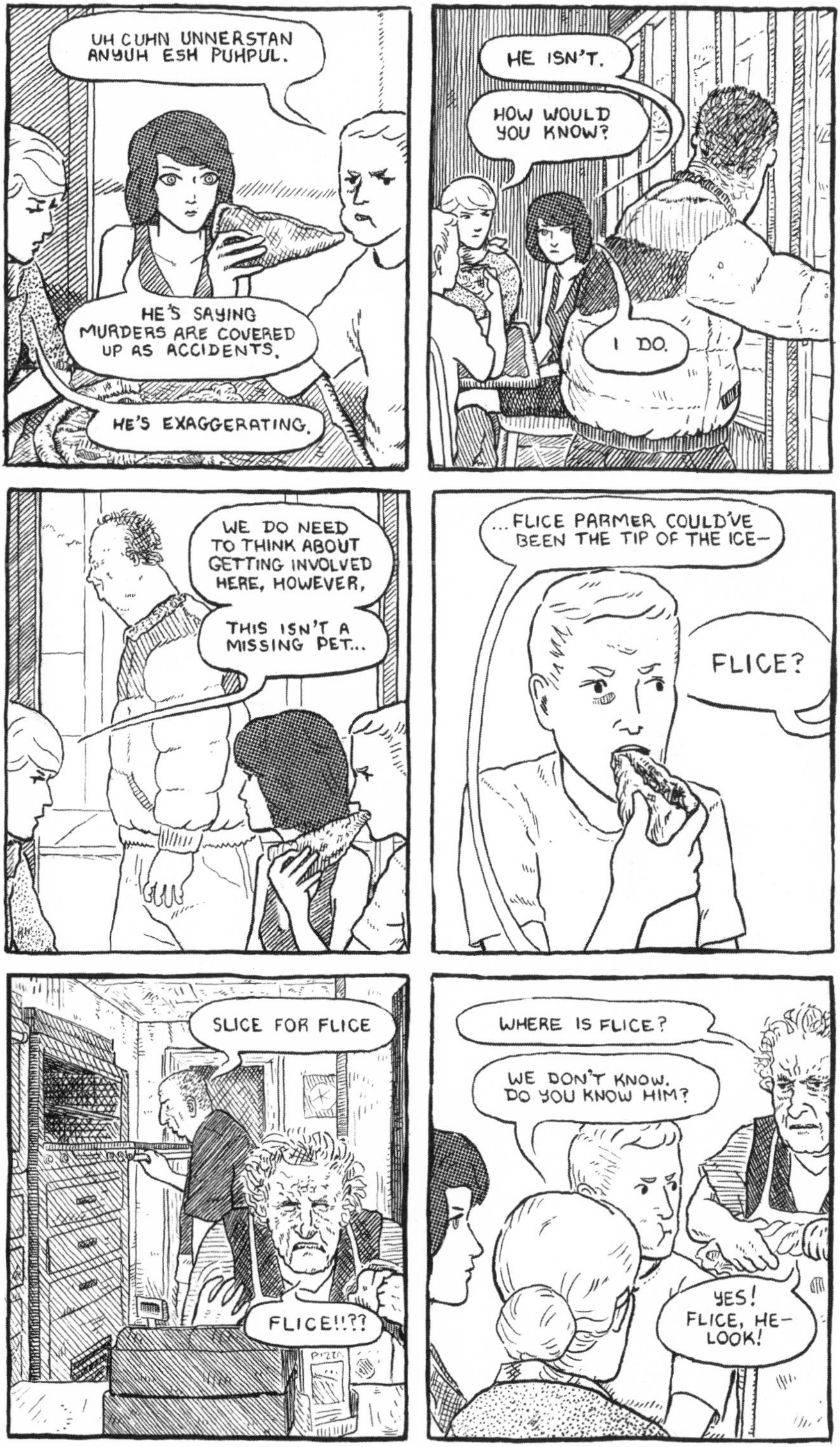
UH CUHN UNNERSTAN ANYUH ESH PUHPUL.
HE'S SAYING MURDERS ARE COVERED UP AS ACCIDENTS.
HE'S EXAGGERATING.
HE ISN'T.
HOW WOULD YOU KNOW?
I DO.
WE DO NEED TO THINK ABOUT GETTING INVOLVED HERE, HOWEVER,
THIS ISN'T A MISSING PET...
...FLICE PARMER COULD'VE BEEN THE TIP OF THE ICE—
FLICE?
SLICE FOR FLICE
FLICE!!??
WHERE IS FLICE?
WE DON'T KNOW. DO YOU KNOW HIM?
YES! FLICE, HE— LOOK!

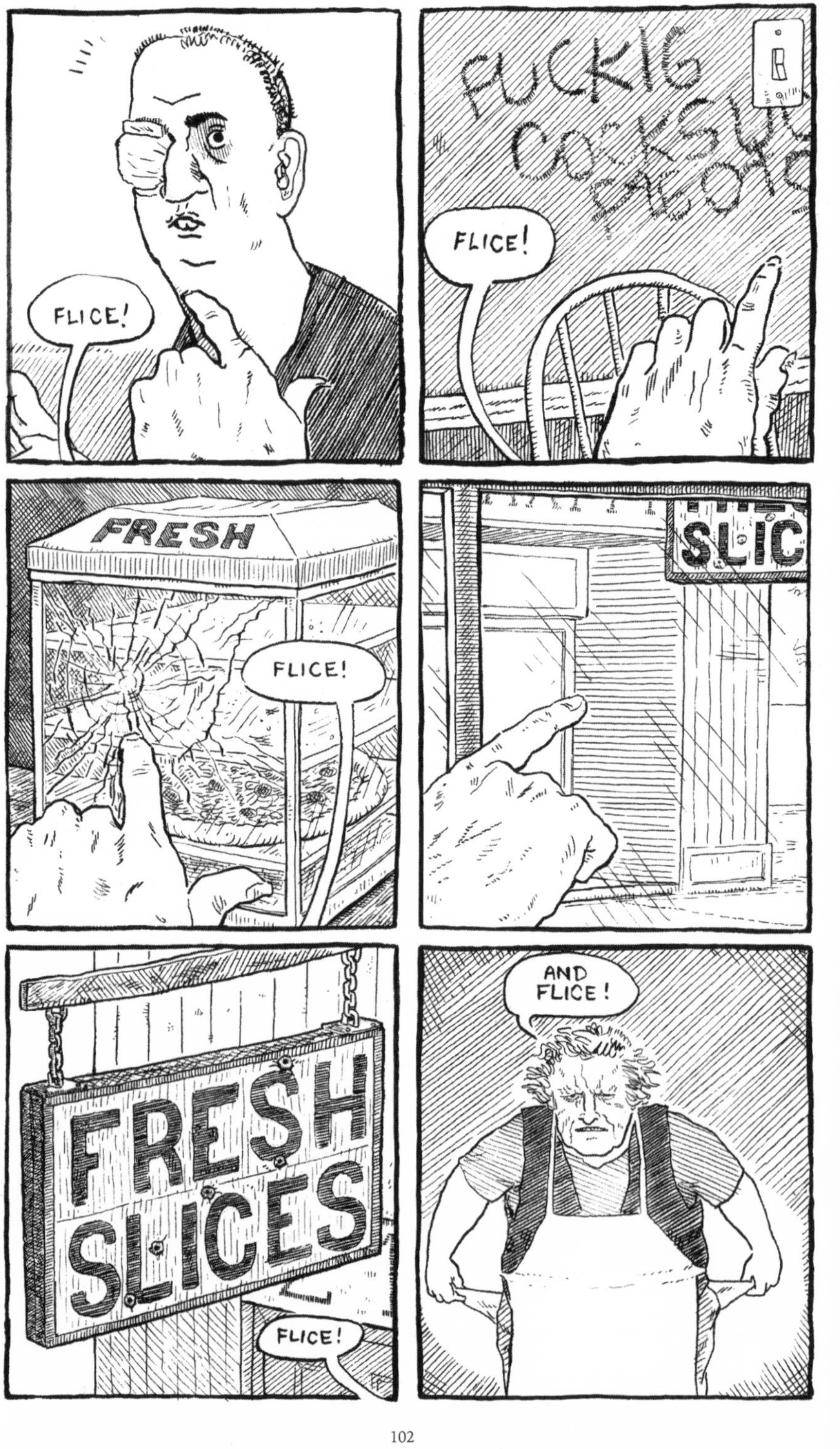
FLICE!
FUCKIG
FLICE!
FRESH
FLICE!
FLICE!
FRESH SLICES
FLICE!
AND FLICE!

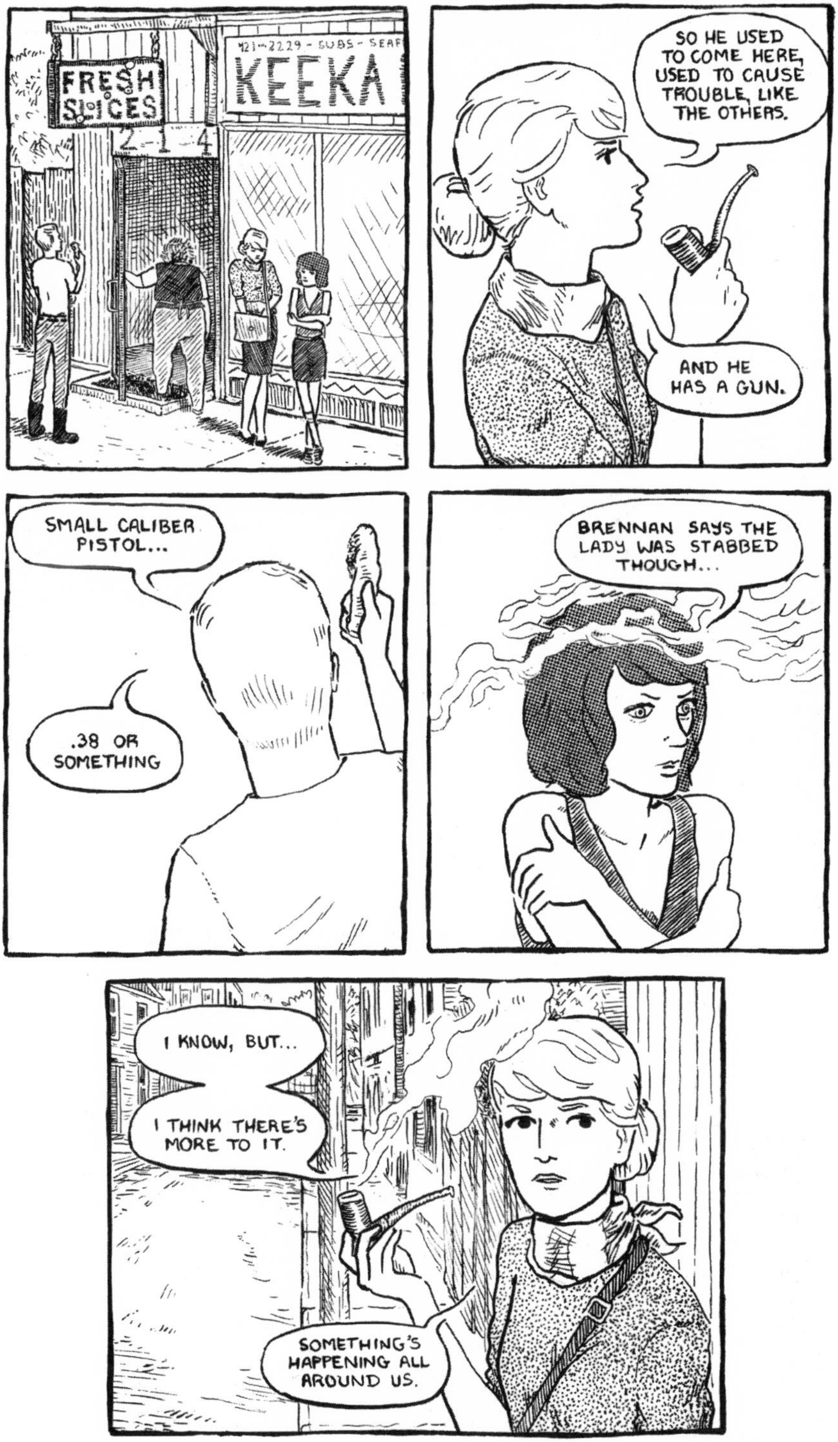
FRESH SLICES
421-2229 - SUBS - SEAF
KEEKA
2-1-4
SO HE USED TO COME HERE, USED TO CAUSE TROUBLE, LIKE THE OTHERS.
AND HE HAS A GUN.
SMALL CALIBER PISTOL...
.38 OR SOMETHING
BRENNAN SAYS THE LADY WAS STABBED THOUGH...
I KNOW, BUT...
I THINK THERE'S MORE TO IT.
SOMETHING'S HAPPENING ALL AROUND US.

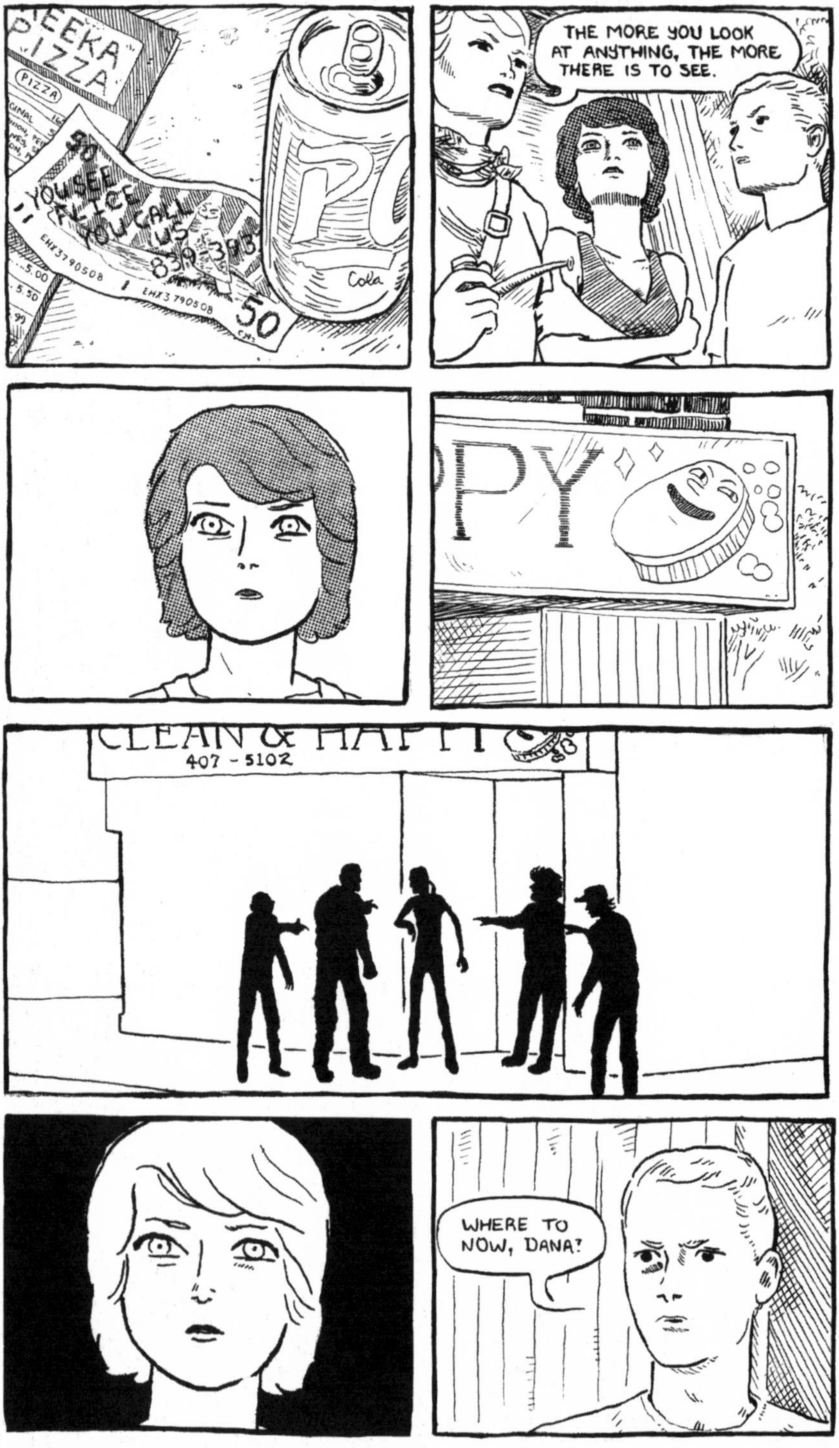
PIZZA
YOU SEE A SLICE YOU CALL US
Cola
THE MORE YOU LOOK AT ANYTHING, THE MORE THERE IS TO SEE.
PPY
CLEAN & HAPPY
407 - 5102
WHERE TO NOW, DANA?

CHAPTER
FOUR

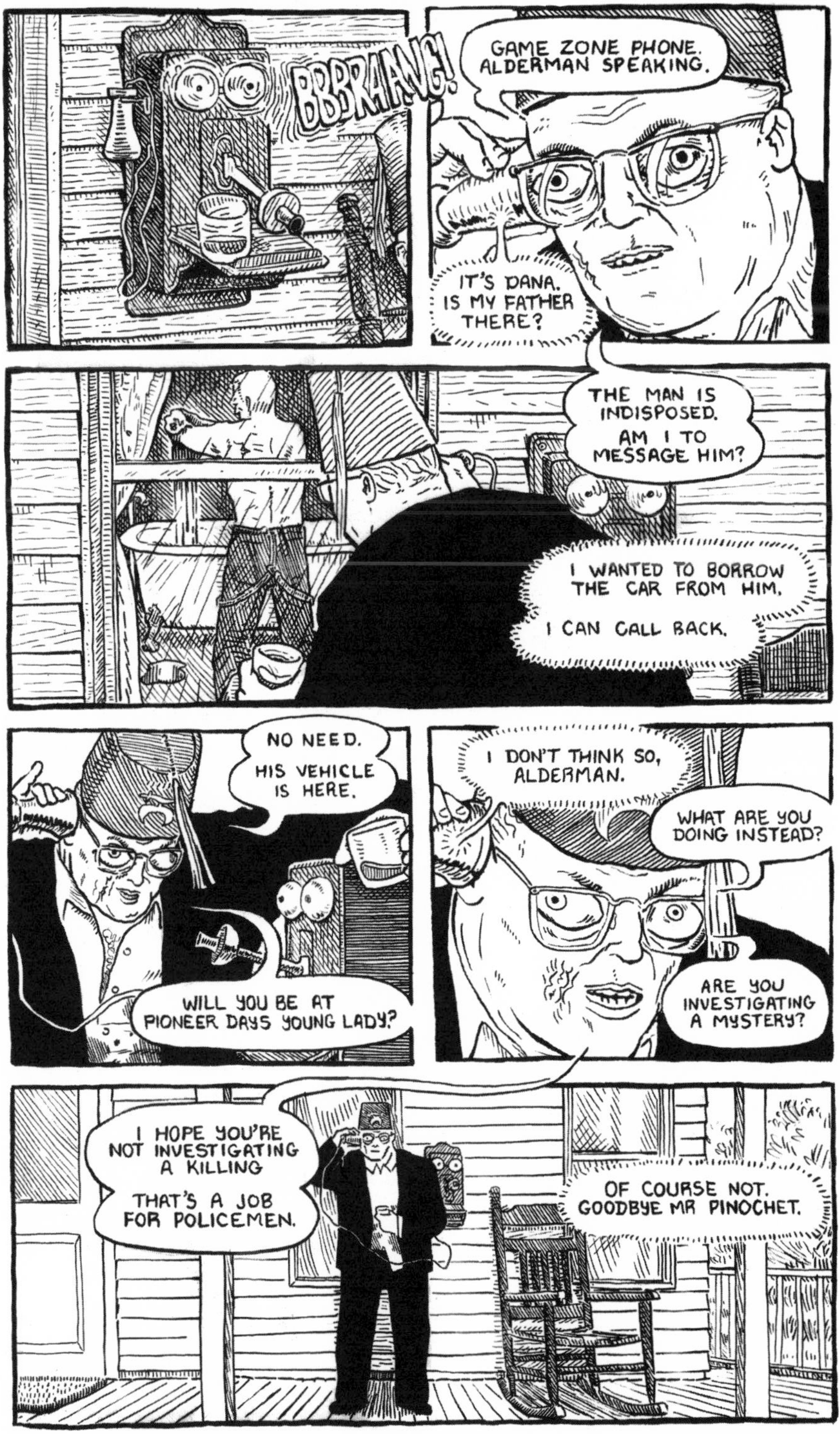
BBBRAANG!
GAME ZONE PHONE. ALDERMAN SPEAKING.
IT'S DANA. IS MY FATHER THERE?
THE MAN IS INDISPOSED.
AM I TO MESSAGE HIM?
I WANTED TO BORROW THE CAR FROM HIM.
I CAN CALL BACK.
NO NEED.
HIS VEHICLE IS HERE.
WILL YOU BE AT PIONEER DAYS YOUNG LADY?
I DON'T THINK SO, ALDERMAN.
WHAT ARE YOU DOING INSTEAD?
ARE YOU INVESTIGATING A MYSTERY?
I HOPE YOU'RE NOT INVESTIGATING A KILLING
THAT'S A JOB FOR POLICEMEN.
OF COURSE NOT. GOODBYE MR PINOCHET.

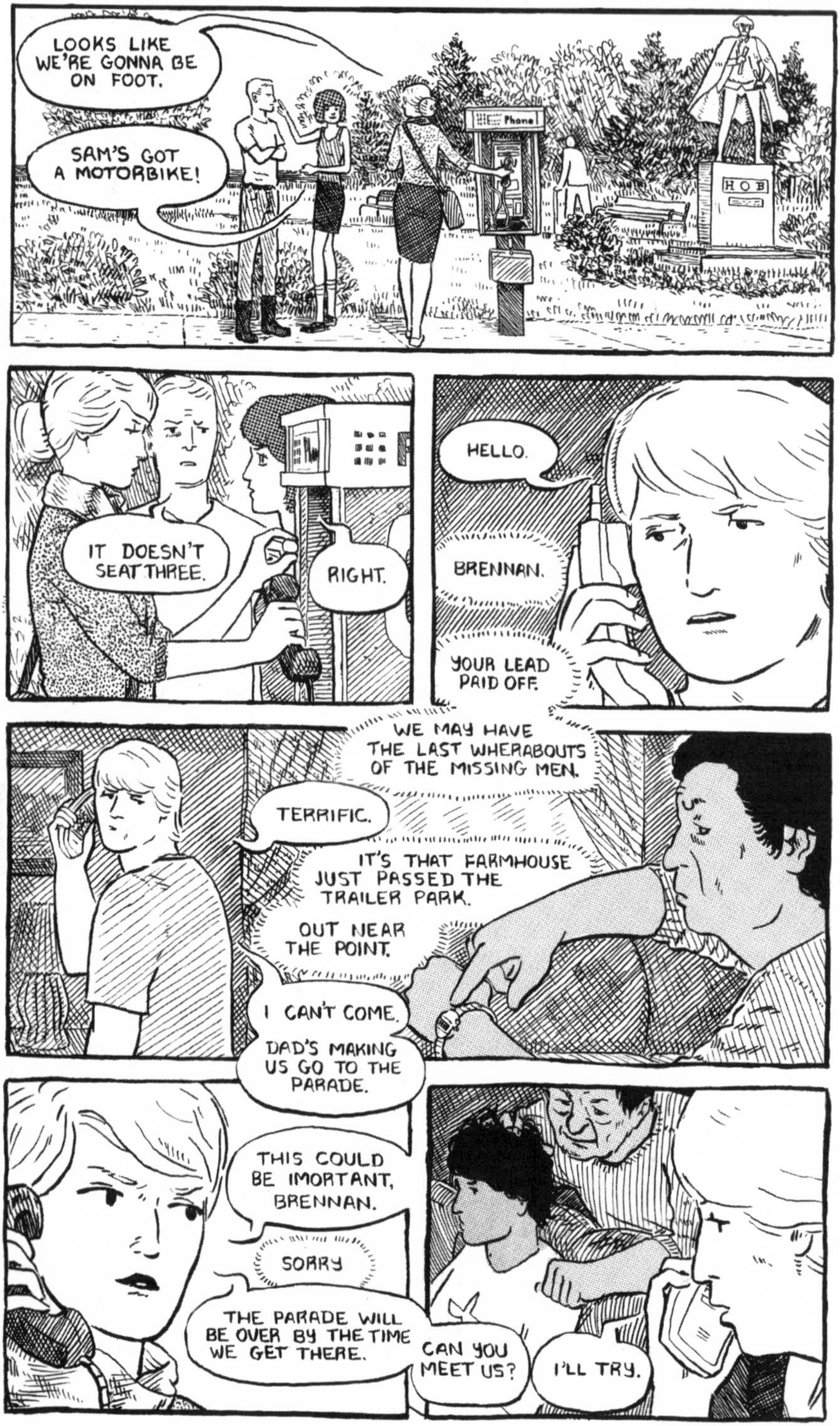

LOOKS LIKE WE'RE GONNA BE ON FOOT.
SAM'S GOT A MOTORBIKE!
Phone
H O B
IT DOESN'T SEAT THREE.
RIGHT.
HELLO.
BRENNAN.
YOUR LEAD PAID OFF.
WE MAY HAVE THE LAST WHERABOUTS OF THE MISSING MEN.
TERRIFIC.
IT'S THAT FARMHOUSE JUST PASSED THE TRAILER PARK.
OUT NEAR THE POINT.
I CAN'T COME.
DAD'S MAKING US GO TO THE PARADE.
THIS COULD BE IMORTANT, BRENNAN.
SORRY
THE PARADE WILL BE OVER BY THE TIME WE GET THERE.
CAN YOU MEET US?
I'LL TRY.

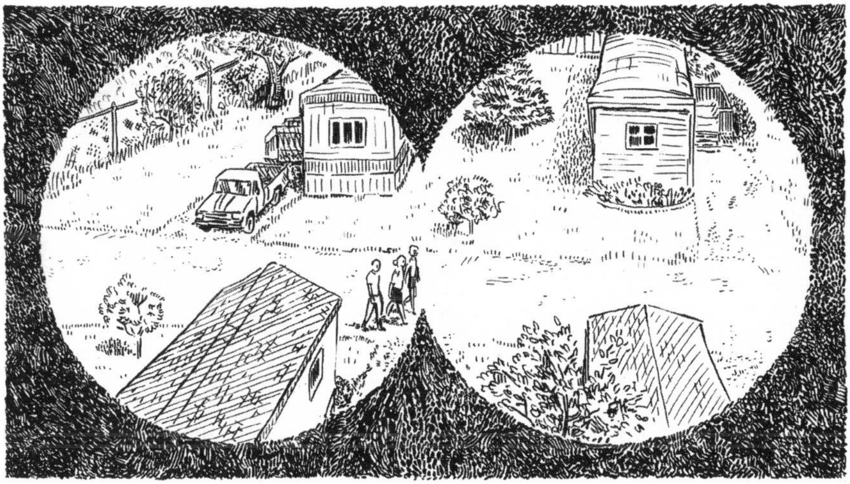

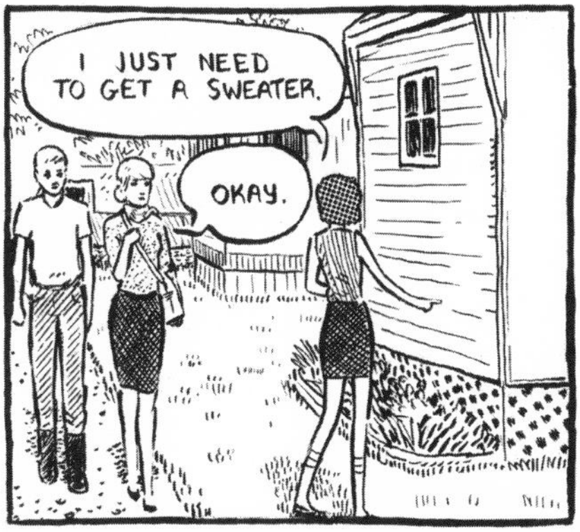
I JUST NEED TO GET A SWEATER.
OKAY.

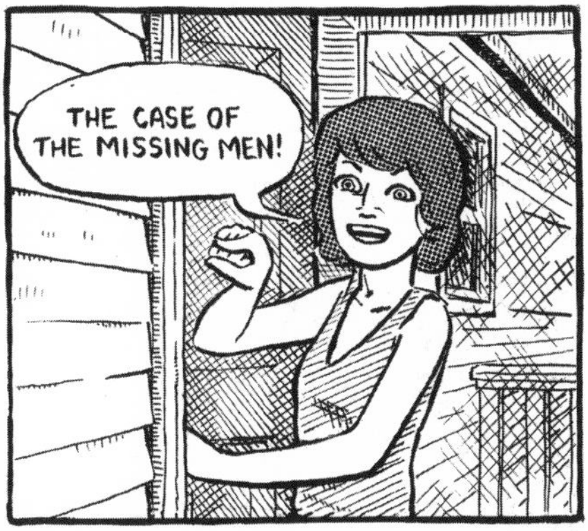
THE CASE OF THE MISSING MEN!

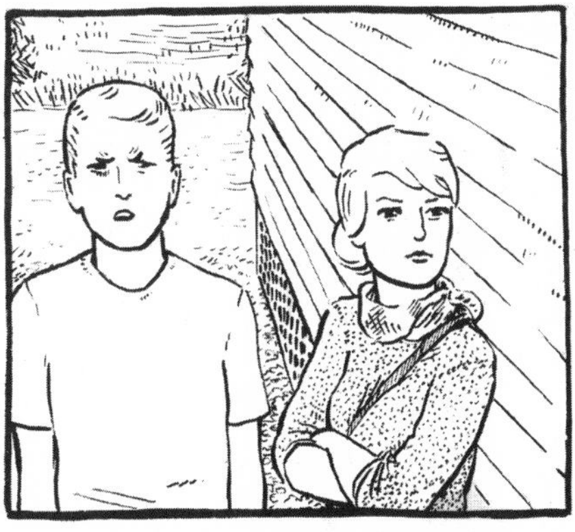

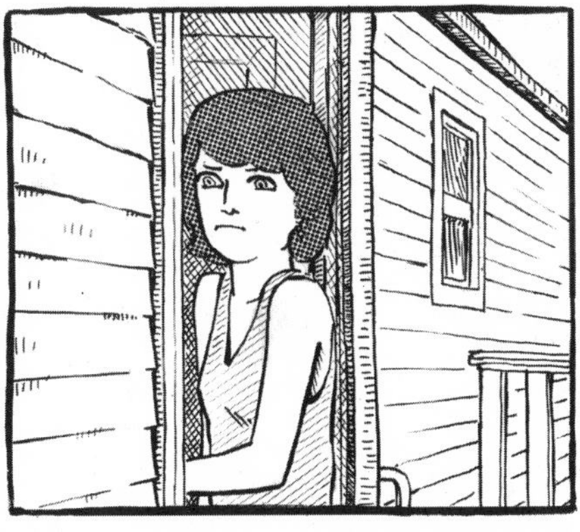

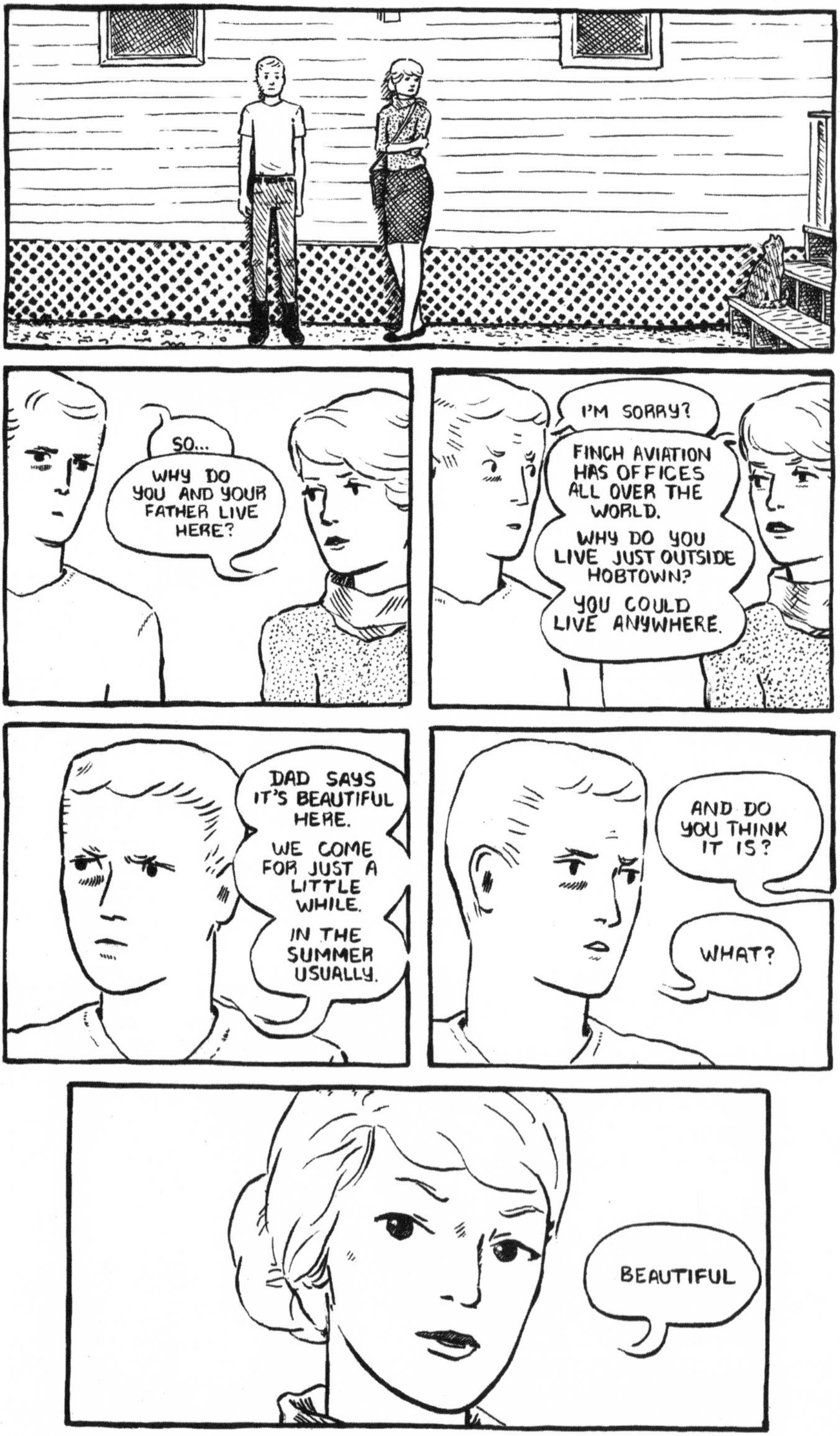
SO...
WHY DO YOU AND YOUR FATHER LIVE HERE?
I'M SORRY?
FINCH AVIATION HAS OFFICES ALL OVER THE WORLD.
WHY DO YOU LIVE JUST OUTSIDE HOBTOWN?
YOU COULD LIVE ANYWHERE.
DAD SAYS IT'S BEAUTIFUL HERE.
WE COME FOR JUST A LITTLE WHILE.
IN THE SUMMER USUALLY.
AND DO YOU THINK IT IS?
WHAT?
BEAUTIFUL

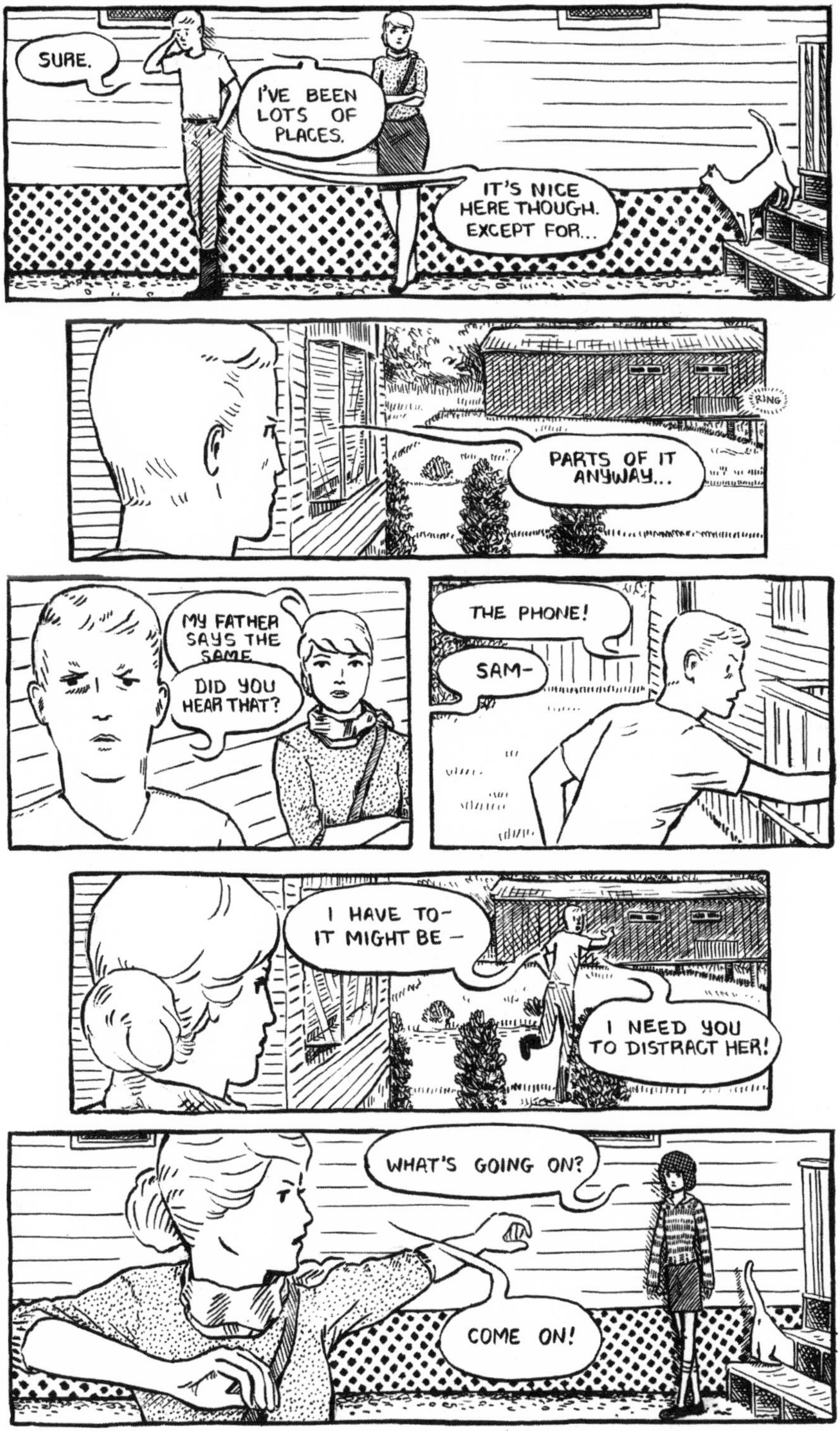

SURE.
I'VE BEEN LOTS OF PLACES.
IT'S NICE HERE THOUGH. EXCEPT FOR...
RING
PARTS OF IT ANYWAY...
MY FATHER SAYS THE SAME.
DID YOU HEAR THAT?
THE PHONE!
SAM-
I HAVE TO- IT MIGHT BE -
I NEED YOU TO DISTRACT HER!
WHAT'S GOING ON?
COME ON!

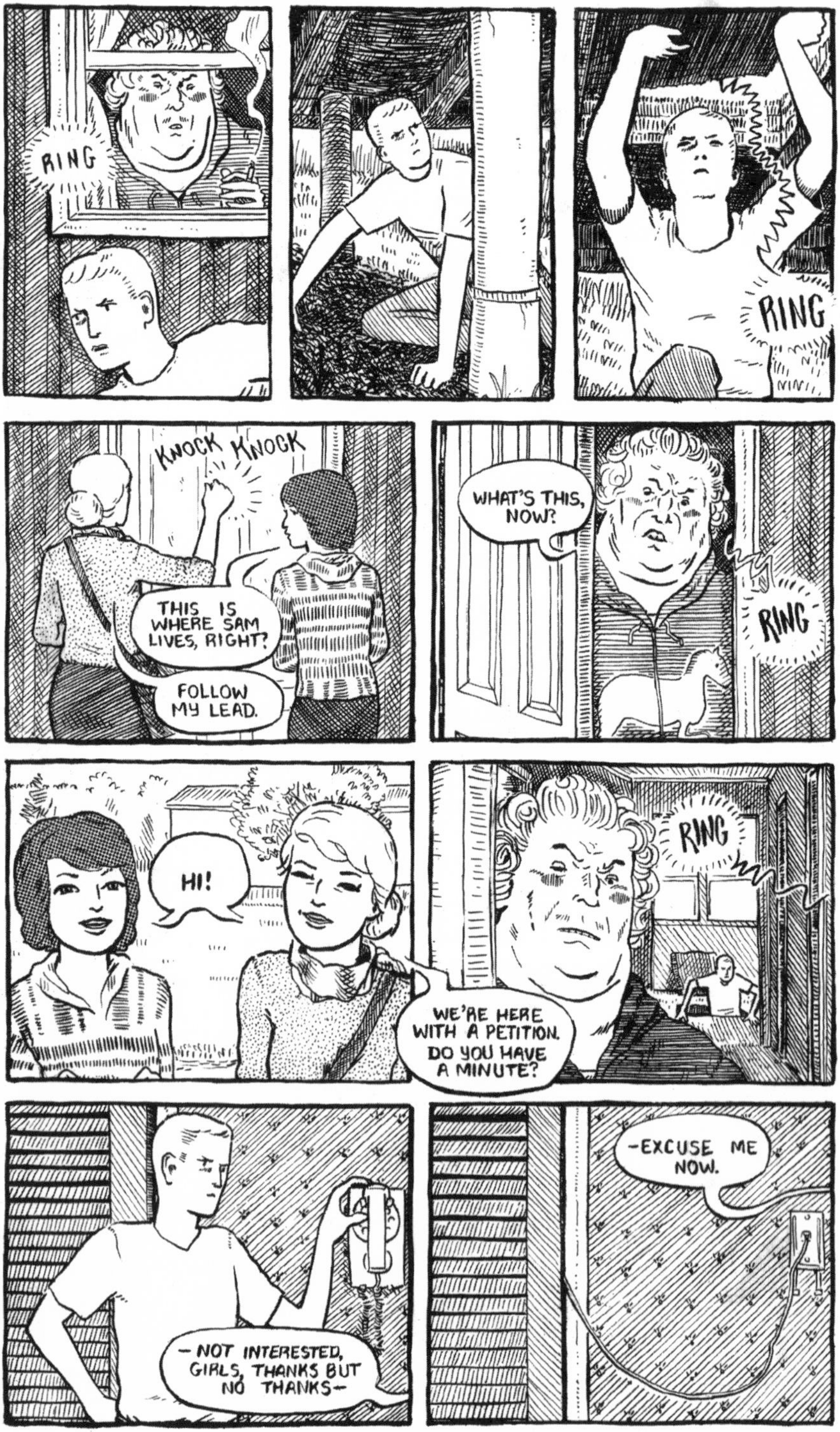
RING
RING
KNOCK KNOCK
THIS IS WHERE SAM LIVES, RIGHT?
FOLLOW MY LEAD.
WHAT'S THIS, NOW?
RING
HI!
RING
WE'RE HERE WITH A PETITION. DO YOU HAVE A MINUTE?
—NOT INTERESTED, GIRLS, THANKS BUT NO THANKS—
—EXCUSE ME NOW.

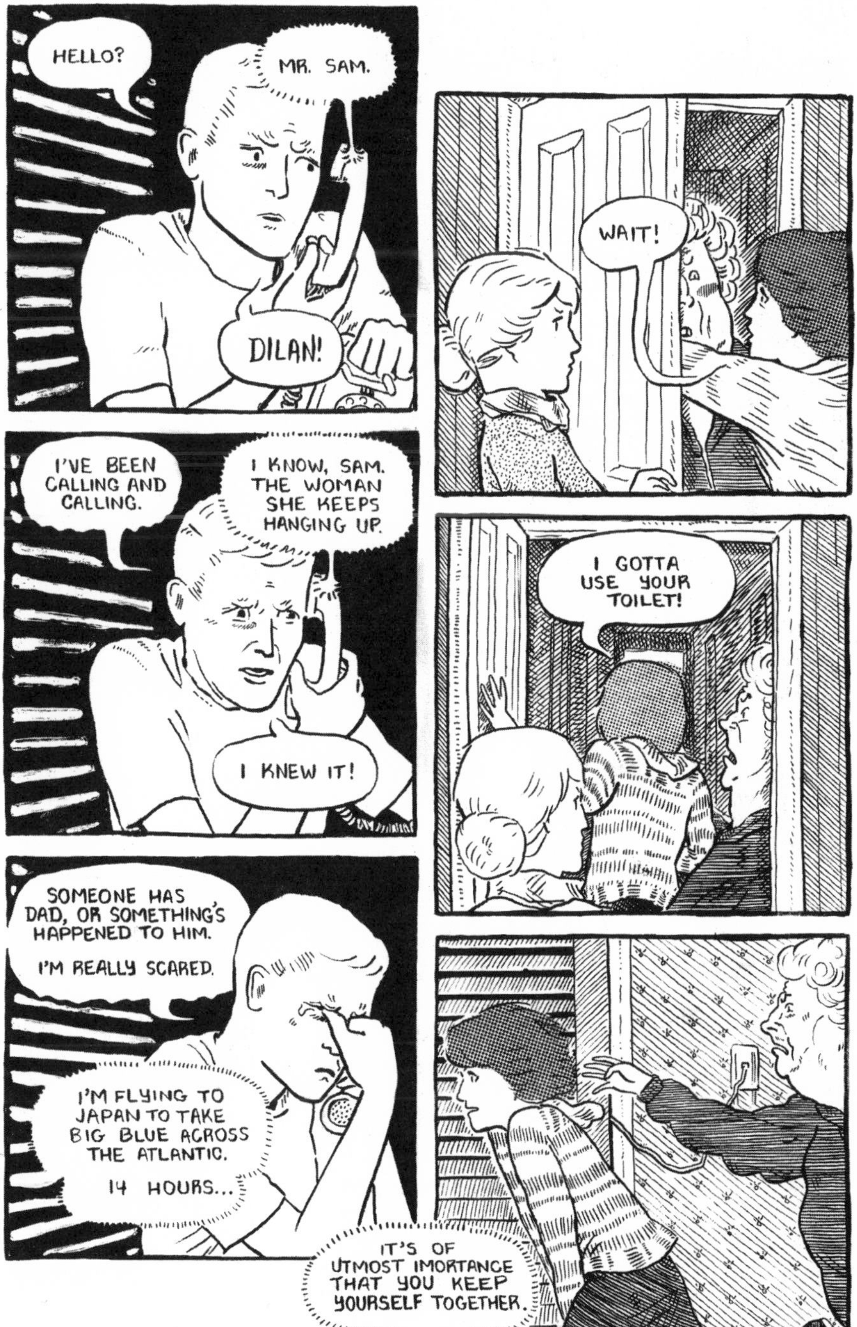
HELLO?
MR. SAM.
DILAN!
WAIT!
I'VE BEEN CALLING AND CALLING.
I KNOW, SAM. THE WOMAN SHE KEEPS HANGING UP.
I KNEW IT!
I GOTTA USE YOUR TOILET!
SOMEONE HAS DAD, OR SOMETHING'S HAPPENED TO HIM.
I'M REALLY SCARED.
I'M FLYING TO JAPAN TO TAKE BIG BLUE ACROSS THE ATLANTIC.
14 HOURS...
IT'S OF UTMOST IMORTANCE THAT YOU KEEP YOURSELF TOGETHER.

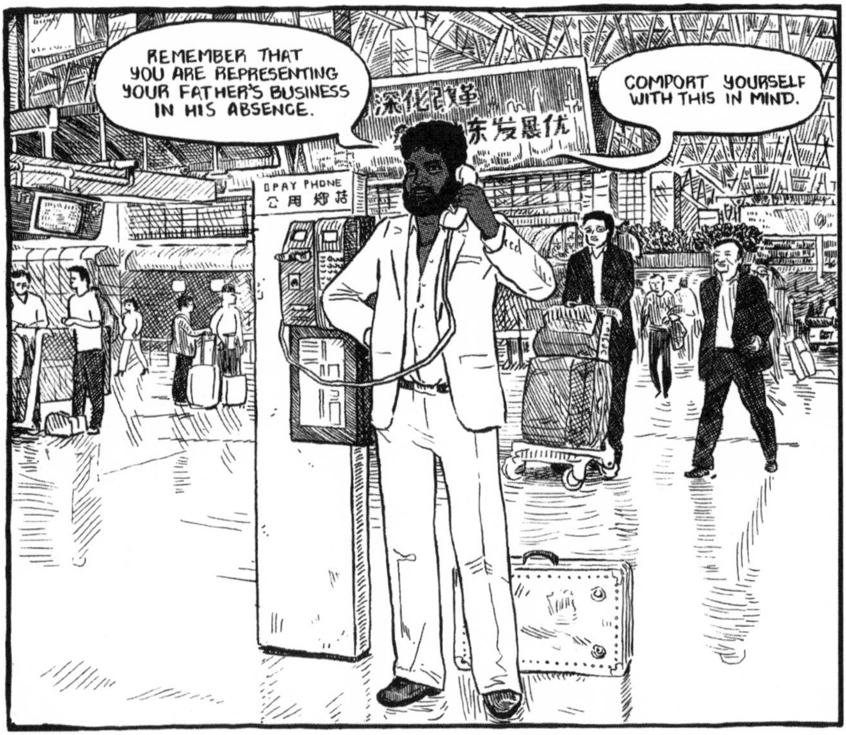
REMEMBER THAT YOU ARE REPRESENTING YOUR FATHER'S BUSINESS IN HIS ABSENCE.
COMPORT YOURSELF WITH THIS IN MIND.
PAY PHONE
公用电話

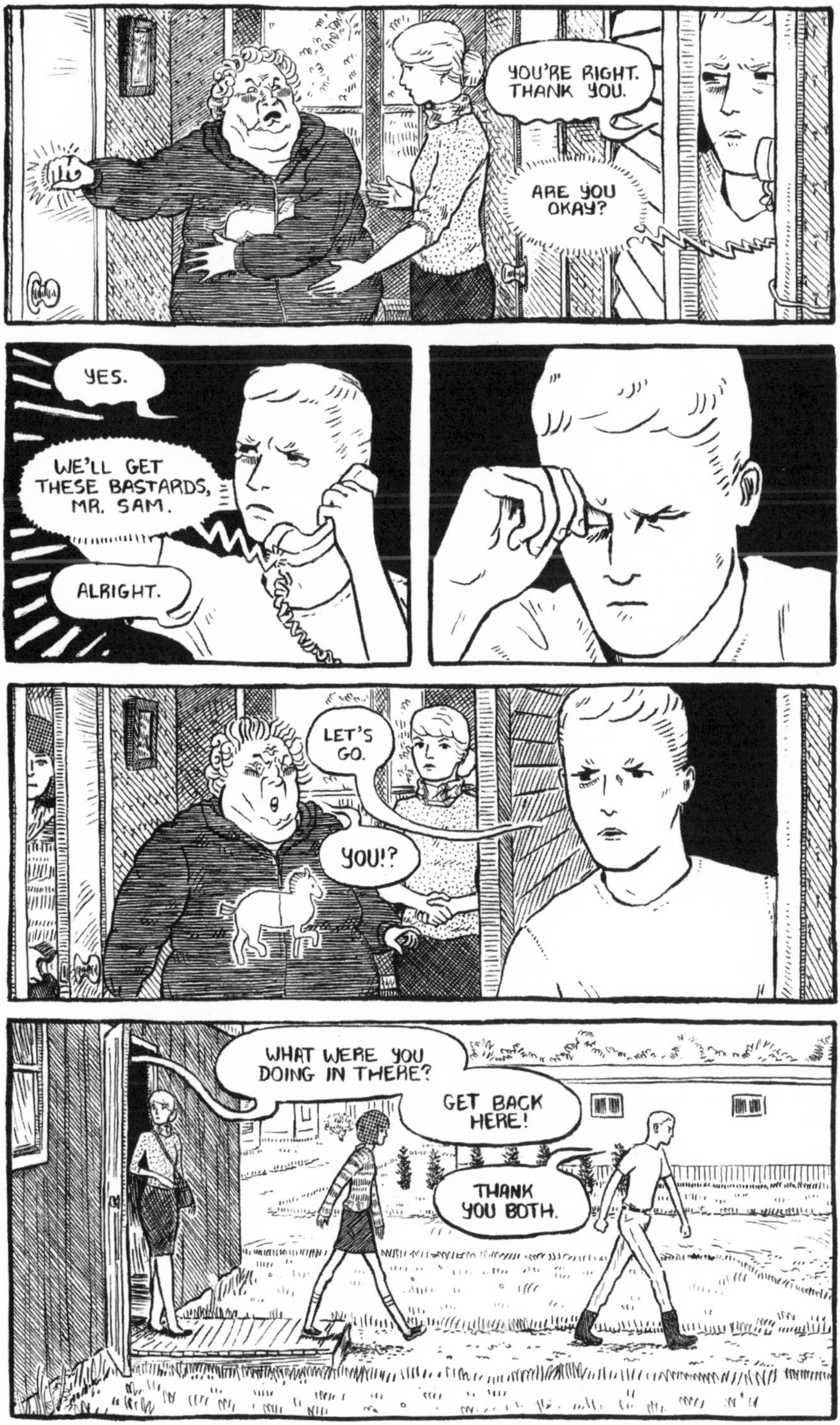
YOU'RE RIGHT. THANK YOU.
ARE YOU OKAY?
YES.
WE'LL GET THESE BASTARDS, MR. SAM.
ALRIGHT.
LET'S GO.
YOU!?
WHAT WERE YOU DOING IN THERE?
GET BACK HERE!
THANK YOU BOTH.

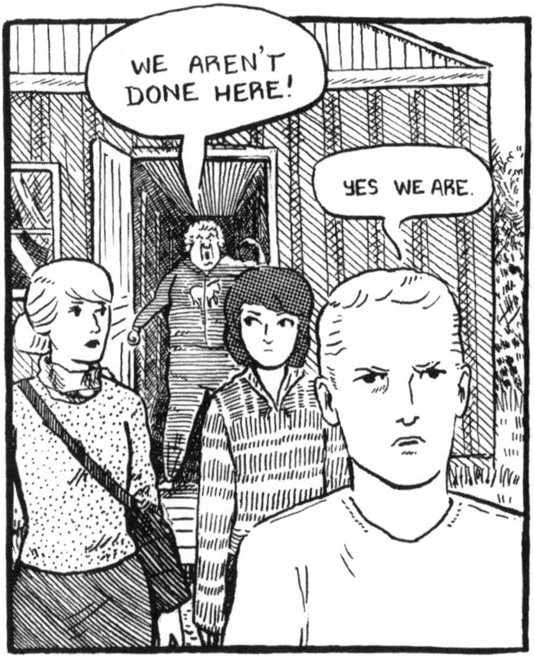
WE AREN'T DONE HERE!
YES WE ARE.

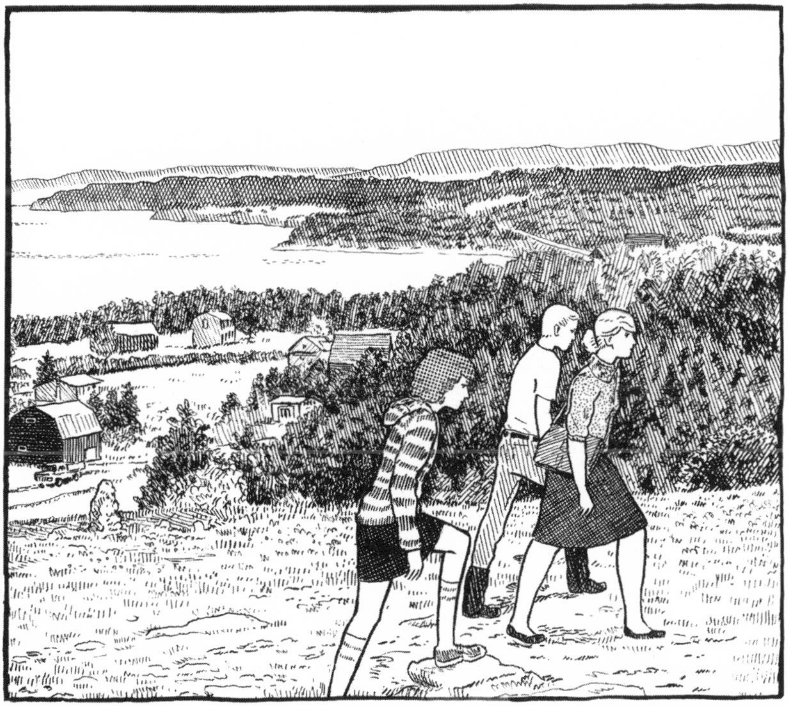

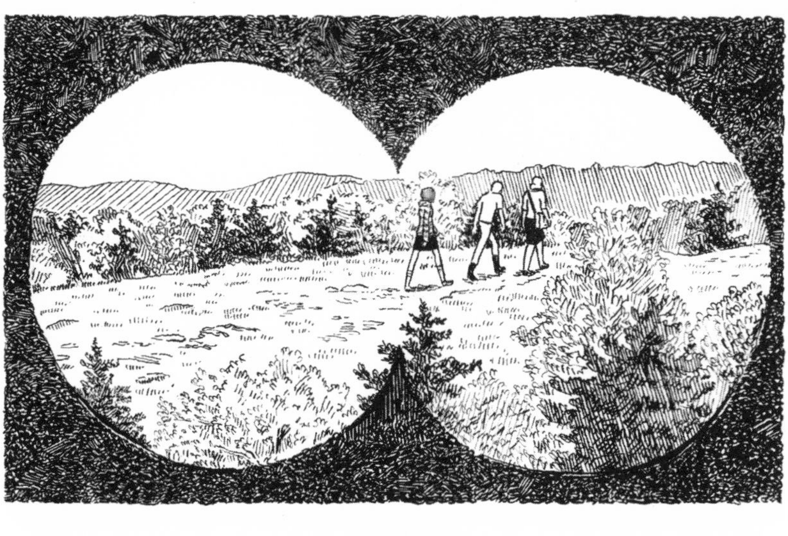

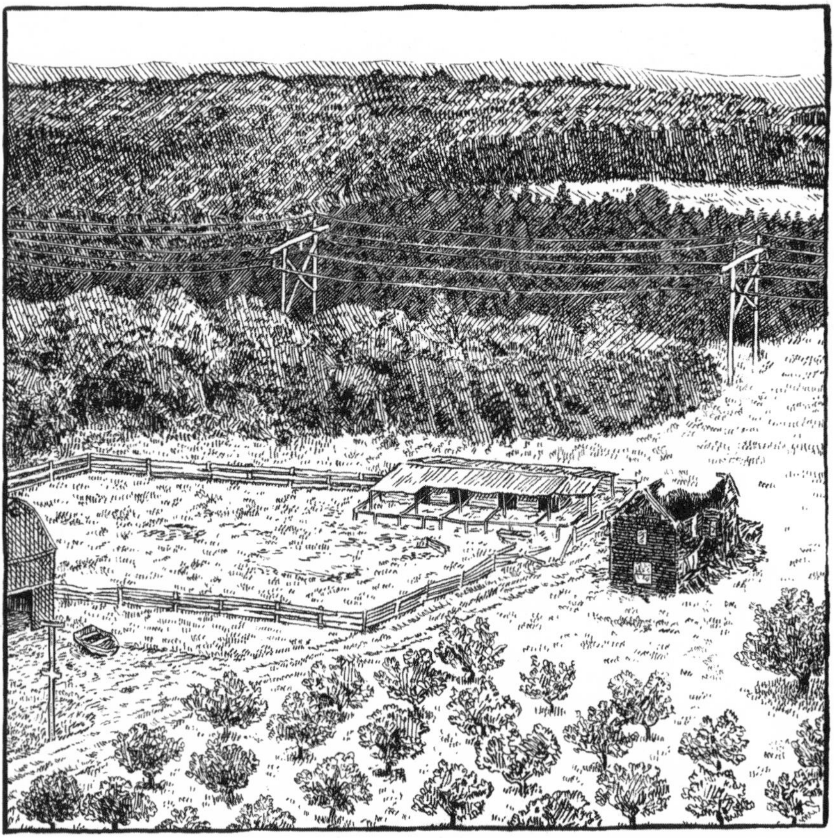

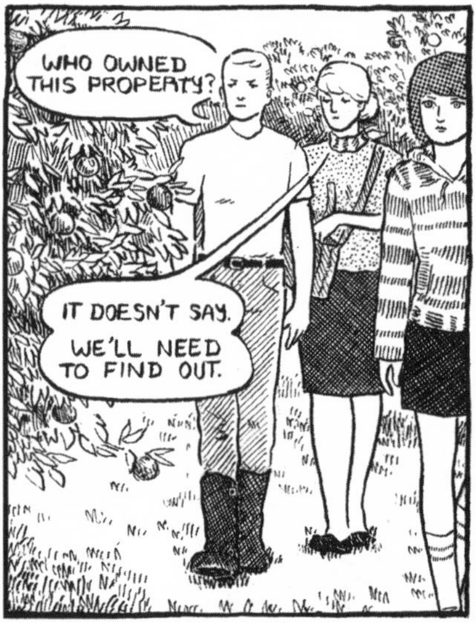
WHO OWNED THIS PROPERTY?
IT DOESN'T SAY. WE'LL NEED TO FIND OUT.

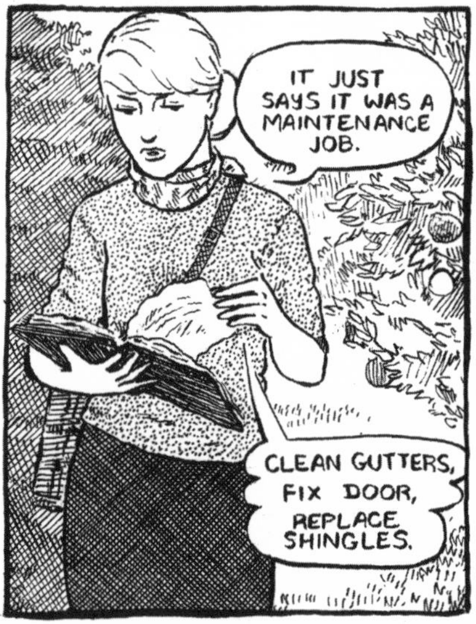
IT JUST SAYS IT WAS A MAINTENANCE JOB.
CLEAN GUTTERS, FIX DOOR, REPLACE SHINGLES.

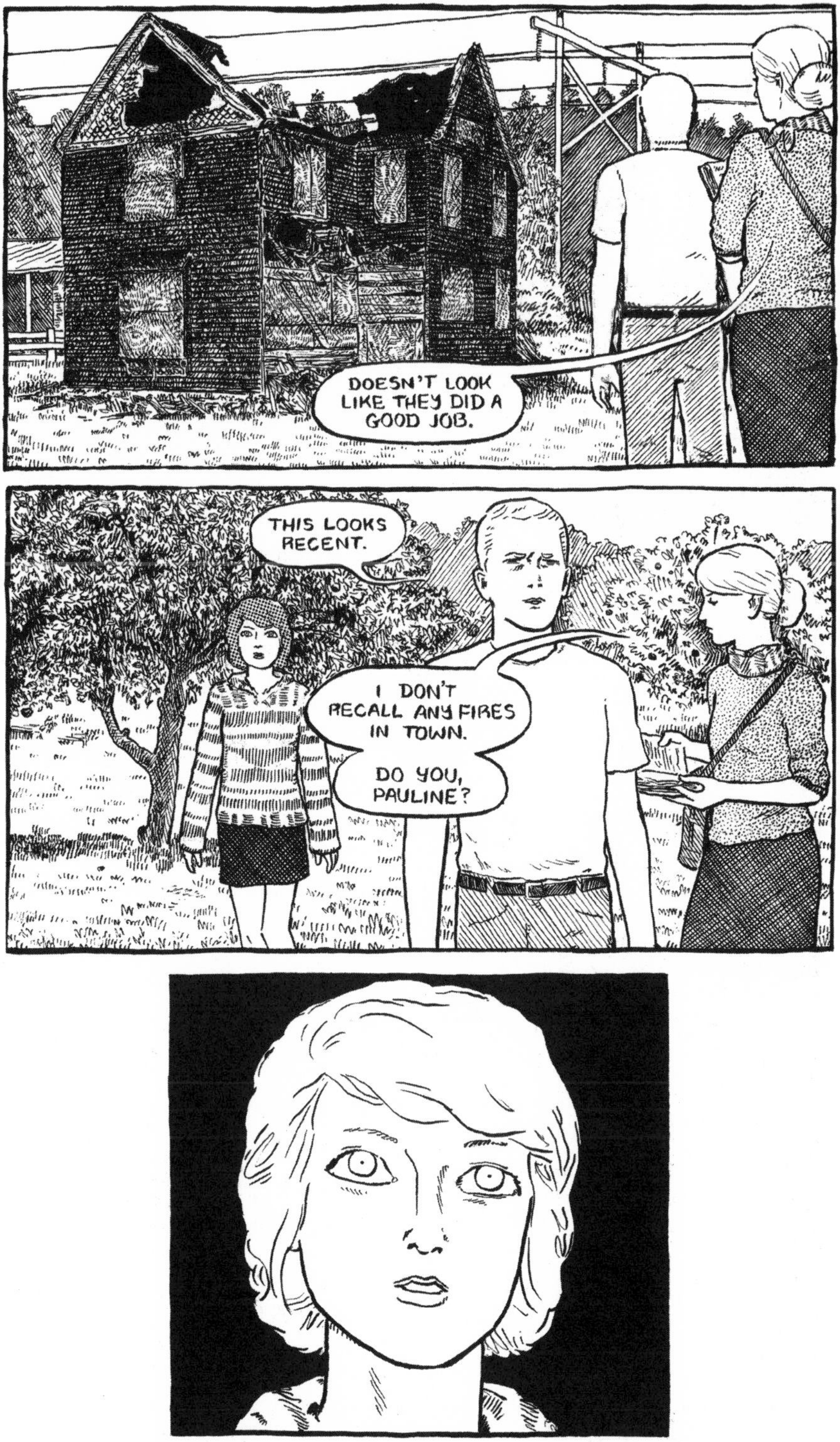
DOESN'T LOOK LIKE THEY DID A GOOD JOB.
THIS LOOKS RECENT.
I DON'T RECALL ANY FIRES IN TOWN.
DO YOU, PAULINE?

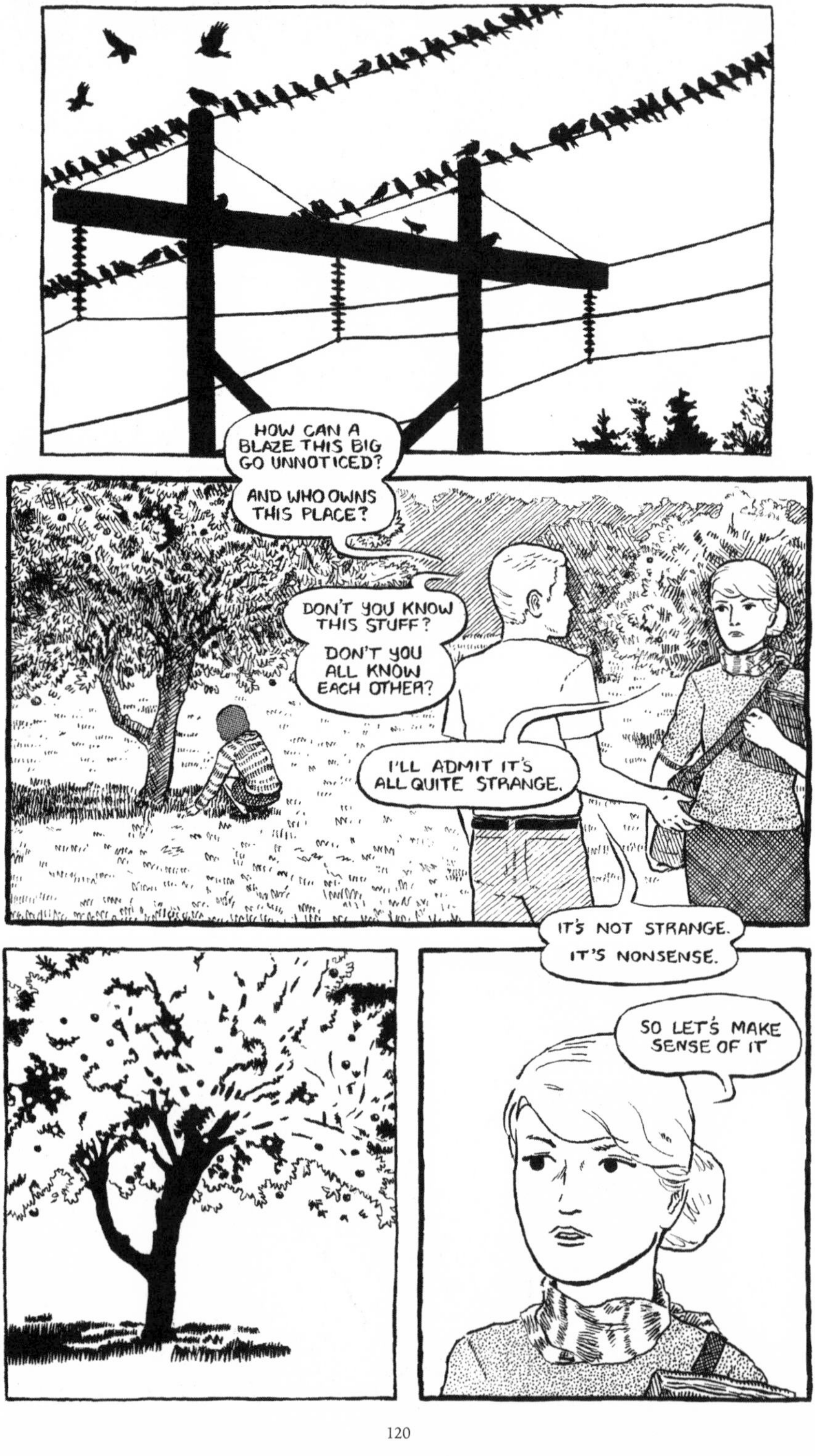
HOW CAN A BLAZE THIS BIG GO UNNOTICED?
AND WHO OWNS THIS PLACE?
DON'T YOU KNOW THIS STUFF?
DON'T YOU ALL KNOW EACH OTHER?
I'LL ADMIT IT'S ALL QUITE STRANGE.
IT'S NOT STRANGE.
IT'S NONSENSE.
SO LET'S MAKE SENSE OF IT

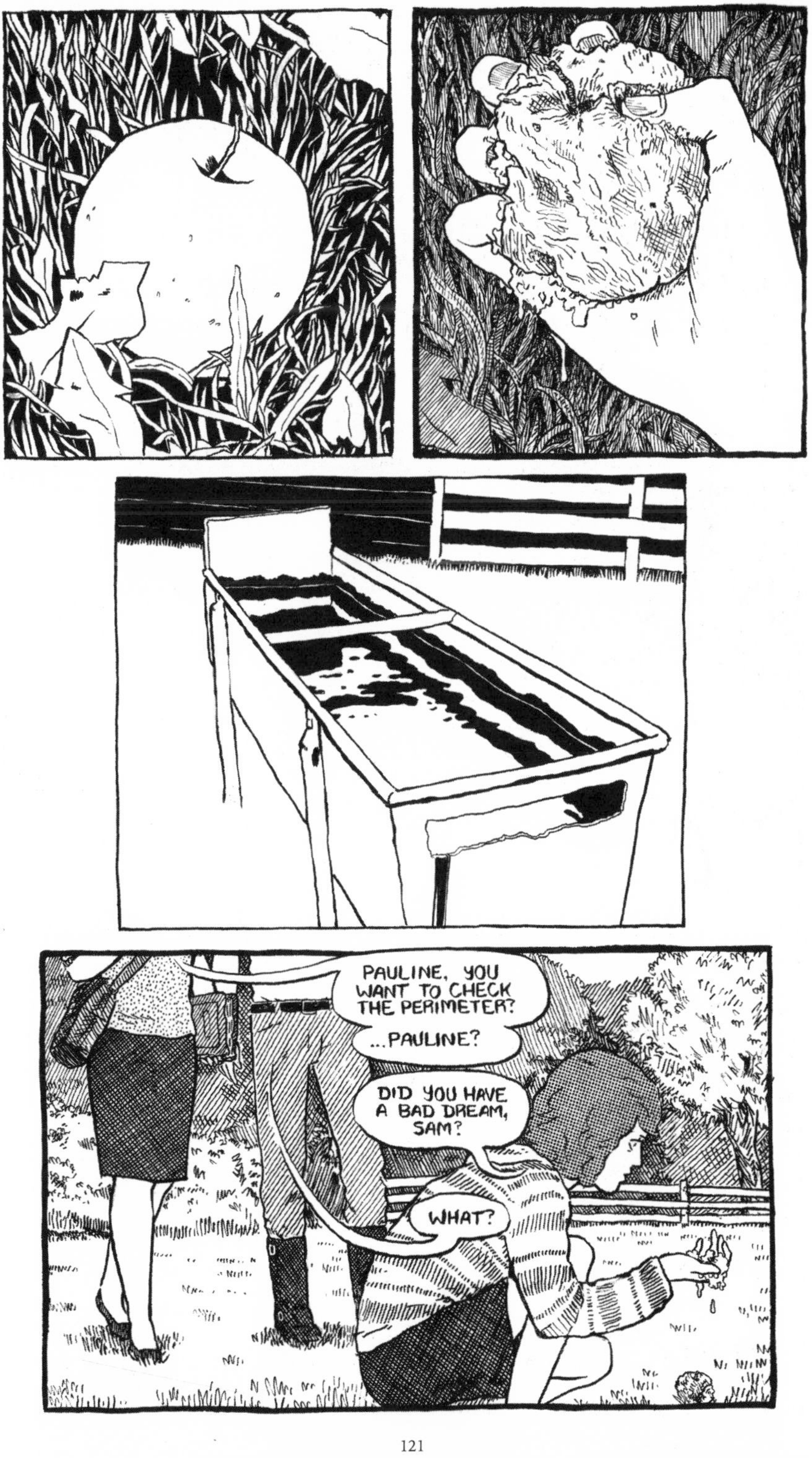
PAULINE, YOU WANT TO CHECK THE PERIMETER?
...PAULINE?
DID YOU HAVE A BAD DREAM, SAM?
WHAT?

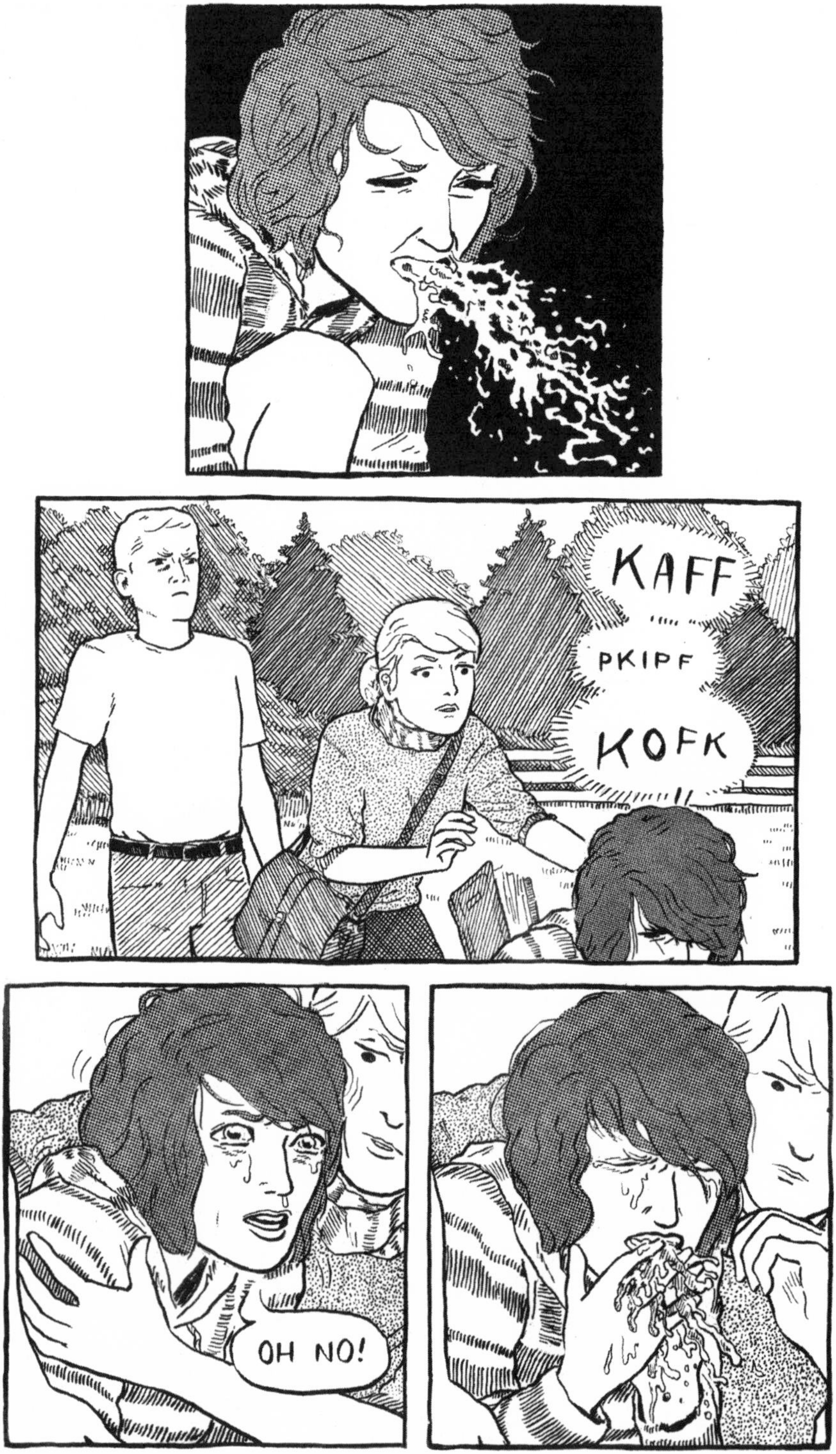
KAFF
PKIPF
KOFK
OH NO!

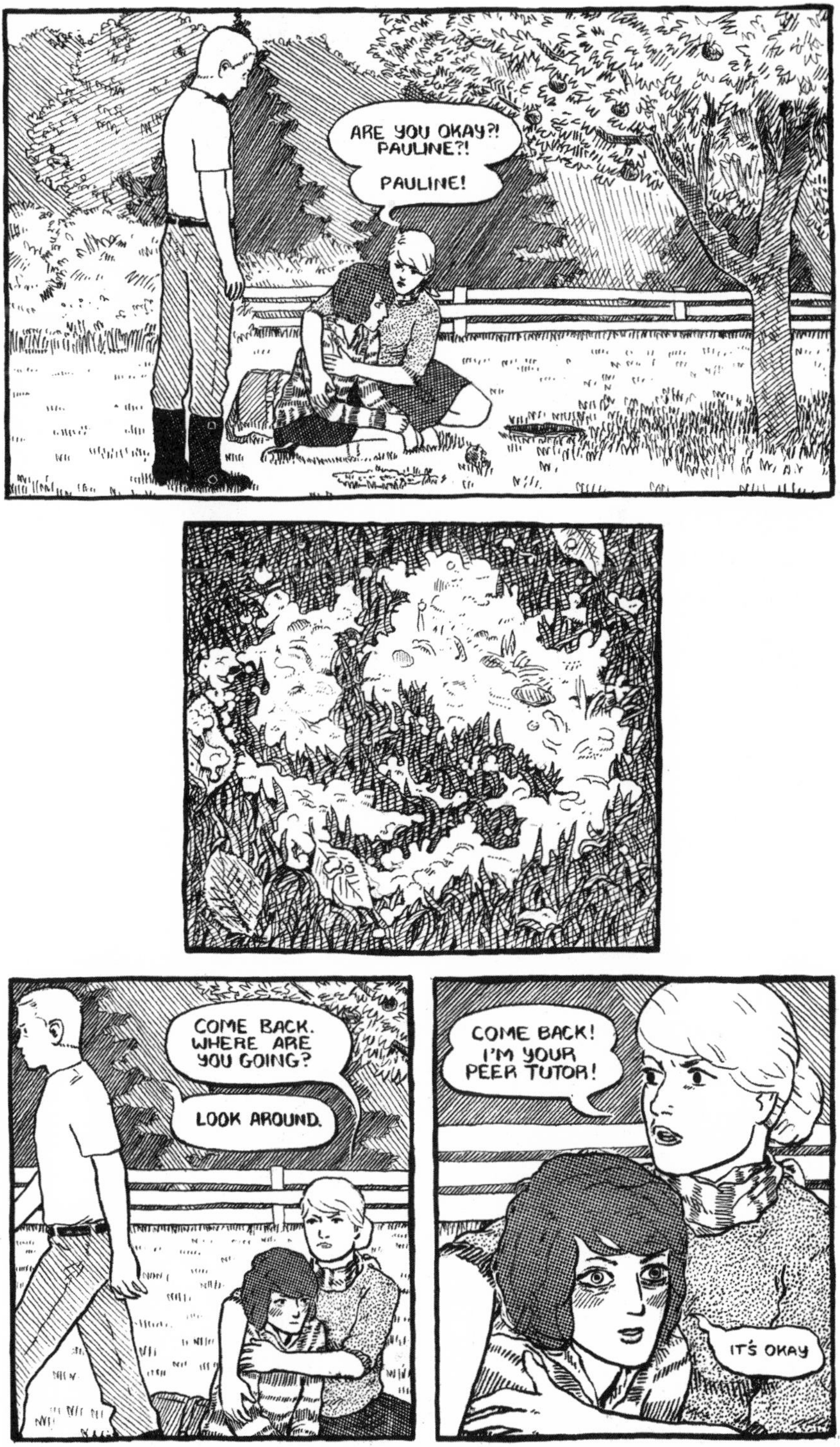
ARE YOU OKAY?! PAULINE?!
PAULINE!
COME BACK. WHERE ARE YOU GOING?
LOOK AROUND.
COME BACK! I'M YOUR PEER TUTOR!
IT'S OKAY

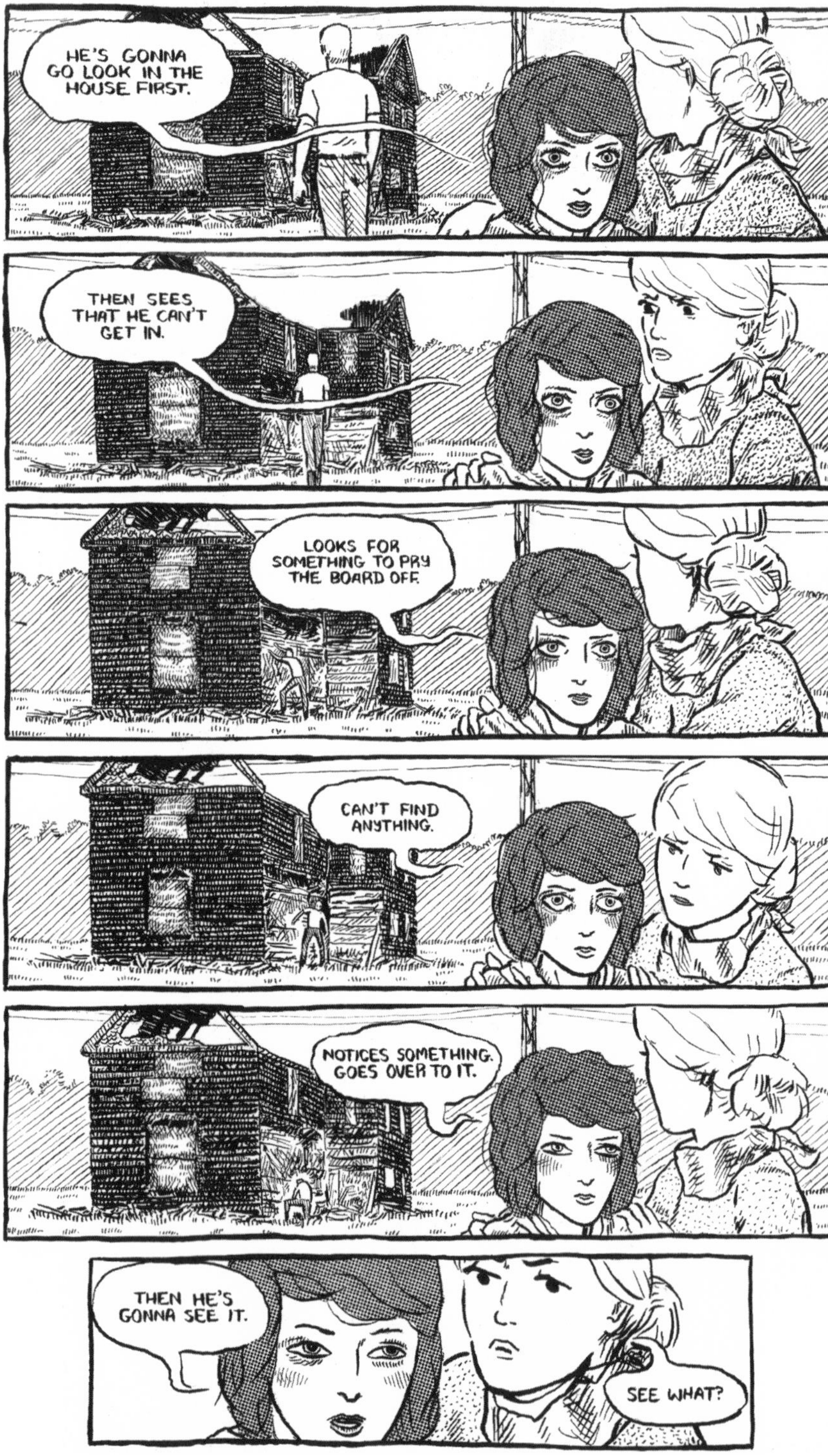
HE'S GONNA GO LOOK IN THE HOUSE FIRST.
THEN SEES THAT HE CAN'T GET IN.
LOOKS FOR SOMETHING TO PRY THE BOARD OFF.
CAN'T FIND ANYTHING.
NOTICES SOMETHING. GOES OVER TO IT.
THEN HE'S GONNA SEE IT.
SEE WHAT?

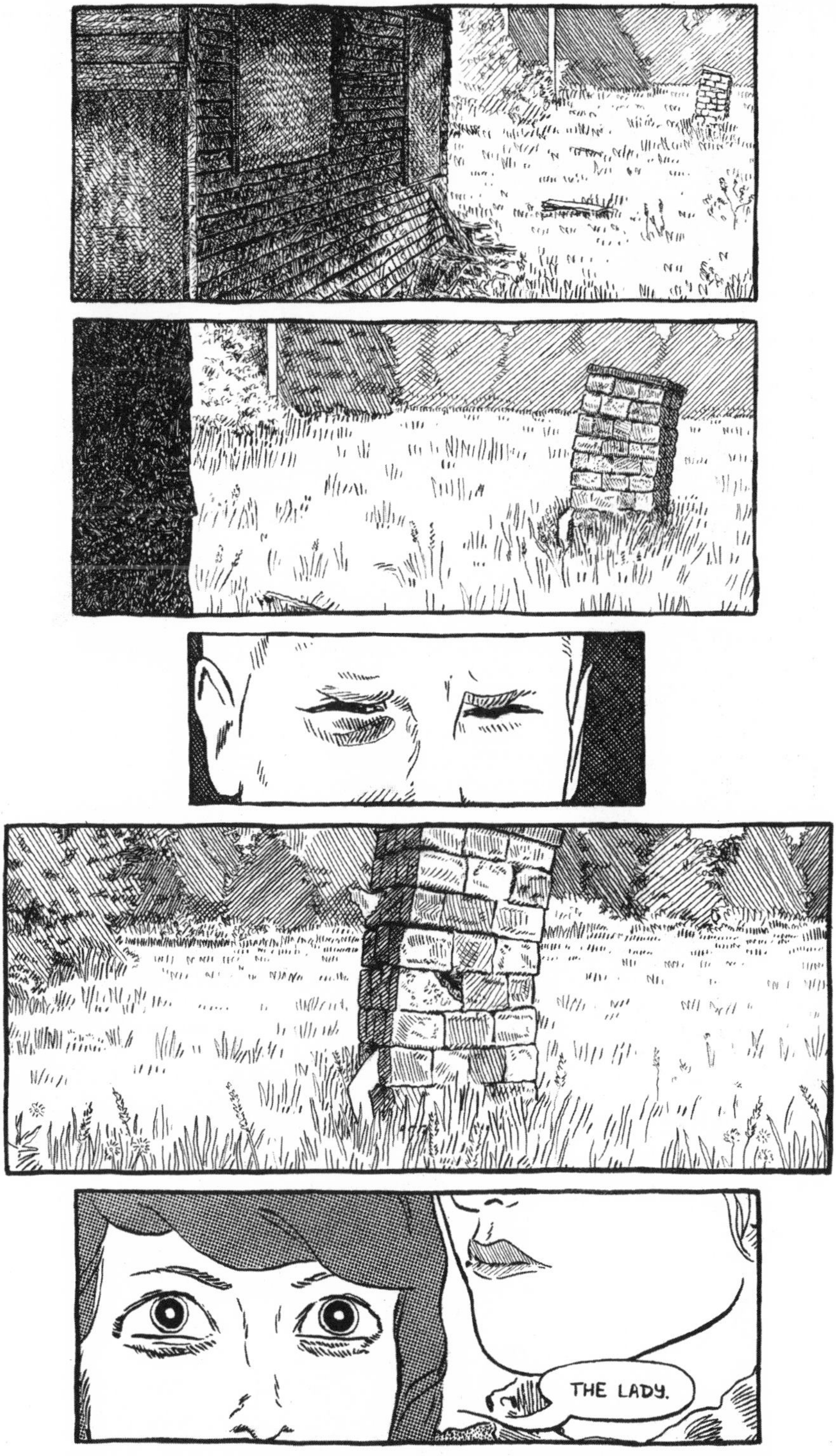
THE LADY.

CHAPTER FIVE

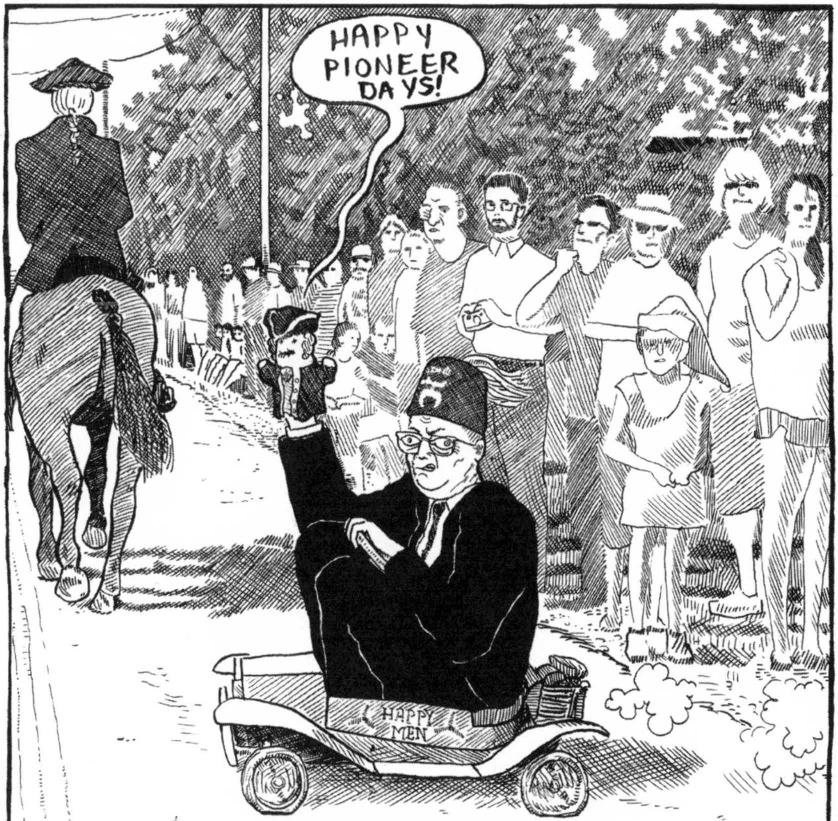
HAPPY PIONEER DAYS!
HAPPY MEN

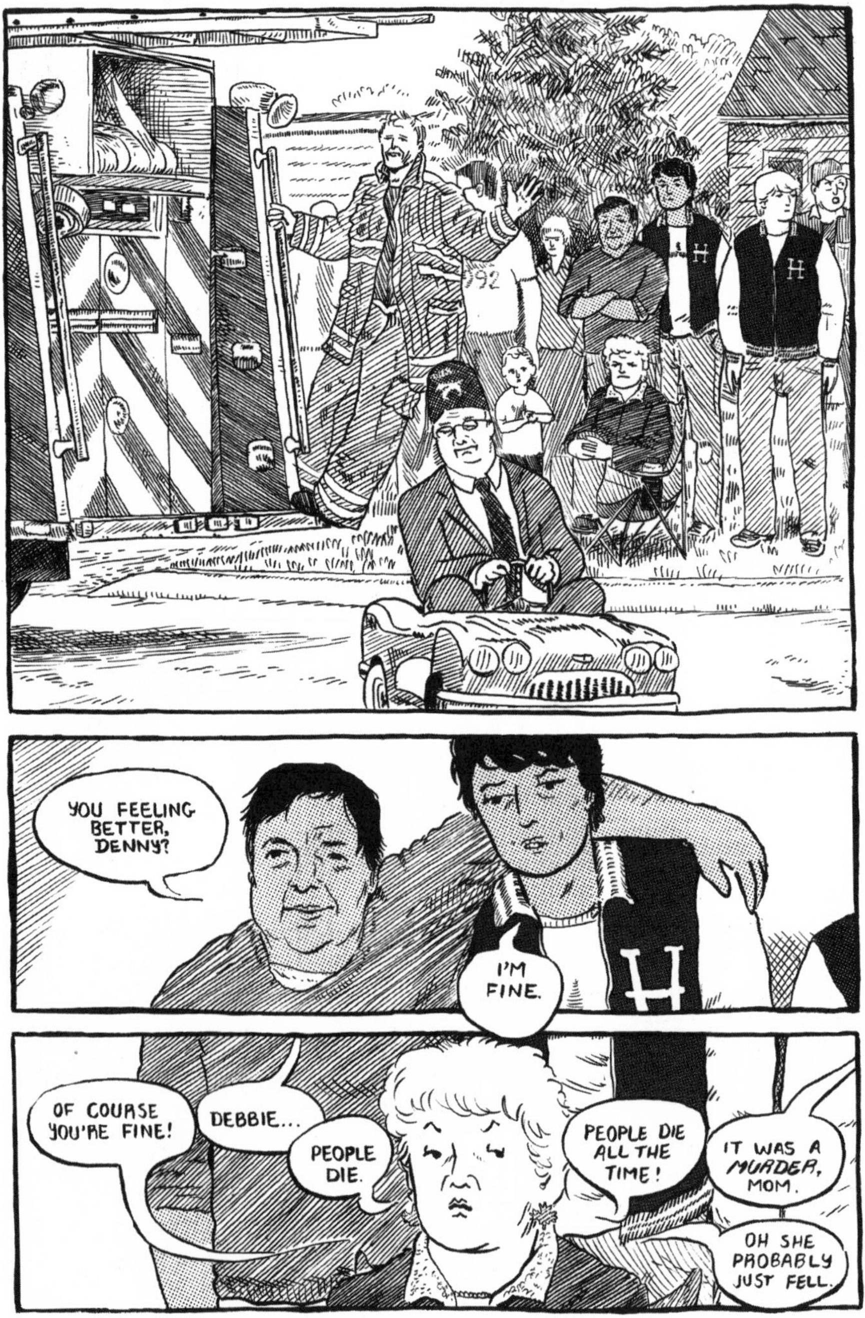
YOU FEELING BETTER, DENNY?
I'M FINE.
OF COURSE YOU'RE FINE!
DEBBIE...
PEOPLE DIE.
PEOPLE DIE ALL THE TIME!
IT WAS A *MURDER*, MOM.
OH SHE PROBABLY JUST FELL.

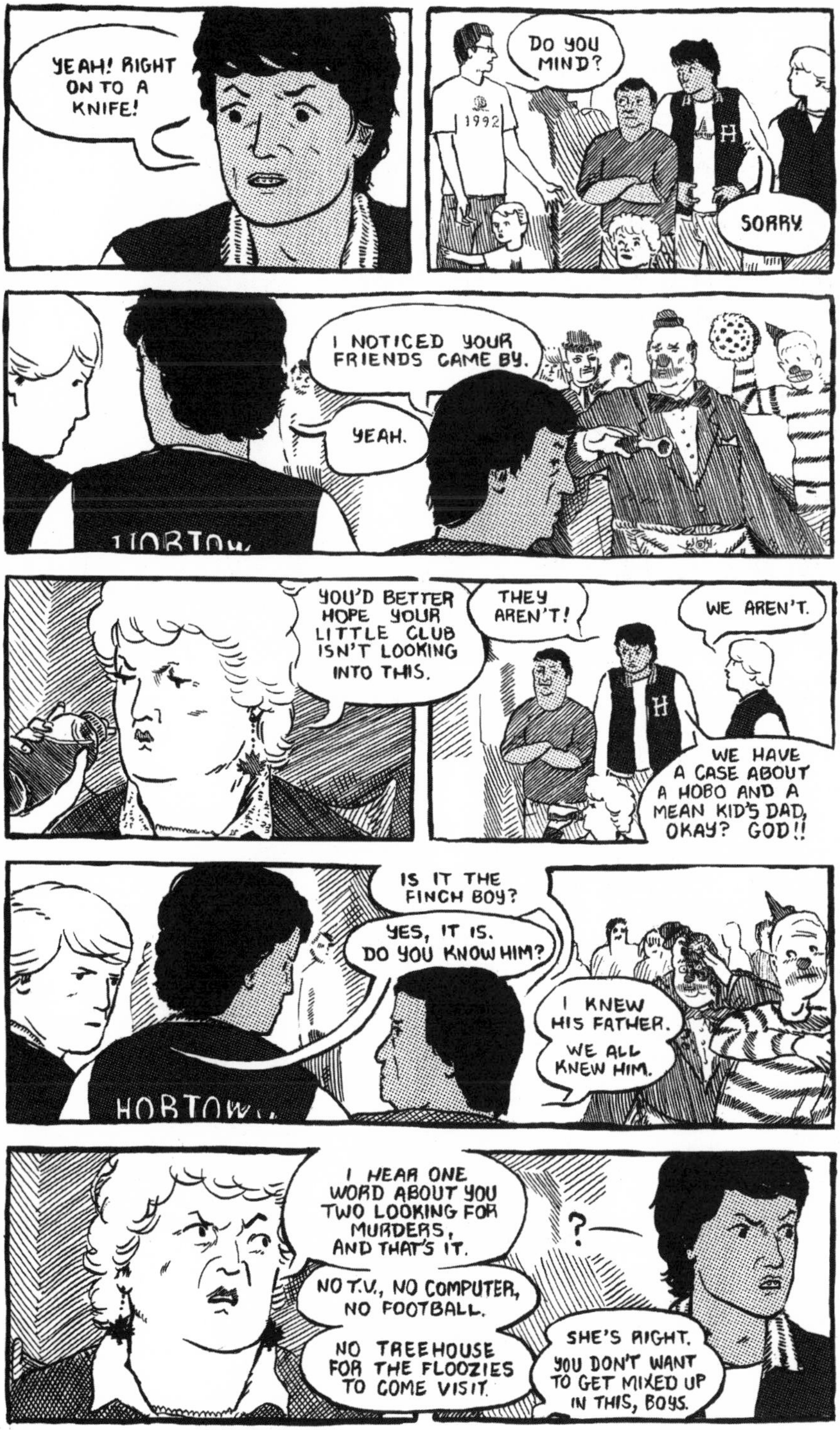
YEAH! RIGHT ON TO A KNIFE!
DO YOU MIND?
1992
SORRY.
I NOTICED YOUR FRIENDS CAME BY.
YEAH.
HOBTOW
YOU'D BETTER HOPE YOUR LITTLE CLUB ISN'T LOOKING INTO THIS.
THEY AREN'T!
WE AREN'T.
WE HAVE A CASE ABOUT A HOBO AND A MEAN KID'S DAD, OKAY? GOD!!
IS IT THE FINCH BOY?
YES, IT IS. DO YOU KNOW HIM?
I KNEW HIS FATHER.
WE ALL KNEW HIM.
HOBTOW
I HEAR ONE WORD ABOUT YOU TWO LOOKING FOR MURDERS, AND THAT'S IT.
NO T.V., NO COMPUTER, NO FOOTBALL.
NO TREEHOUSE FOR THE FLOOZIES TO COME VISIT.
?
SHE'S RIGHT. YOU DON'T WANT TO GET MIXED UP IN THIS, BOYS.

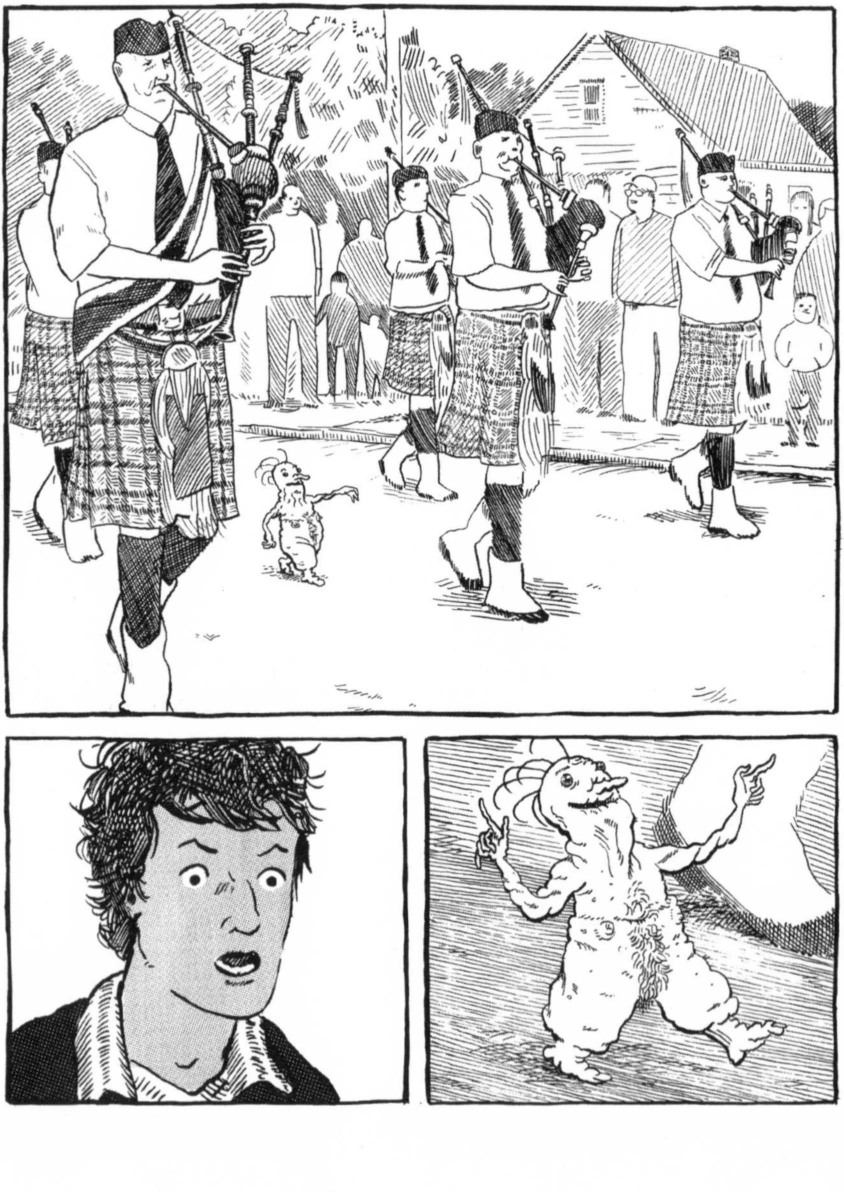

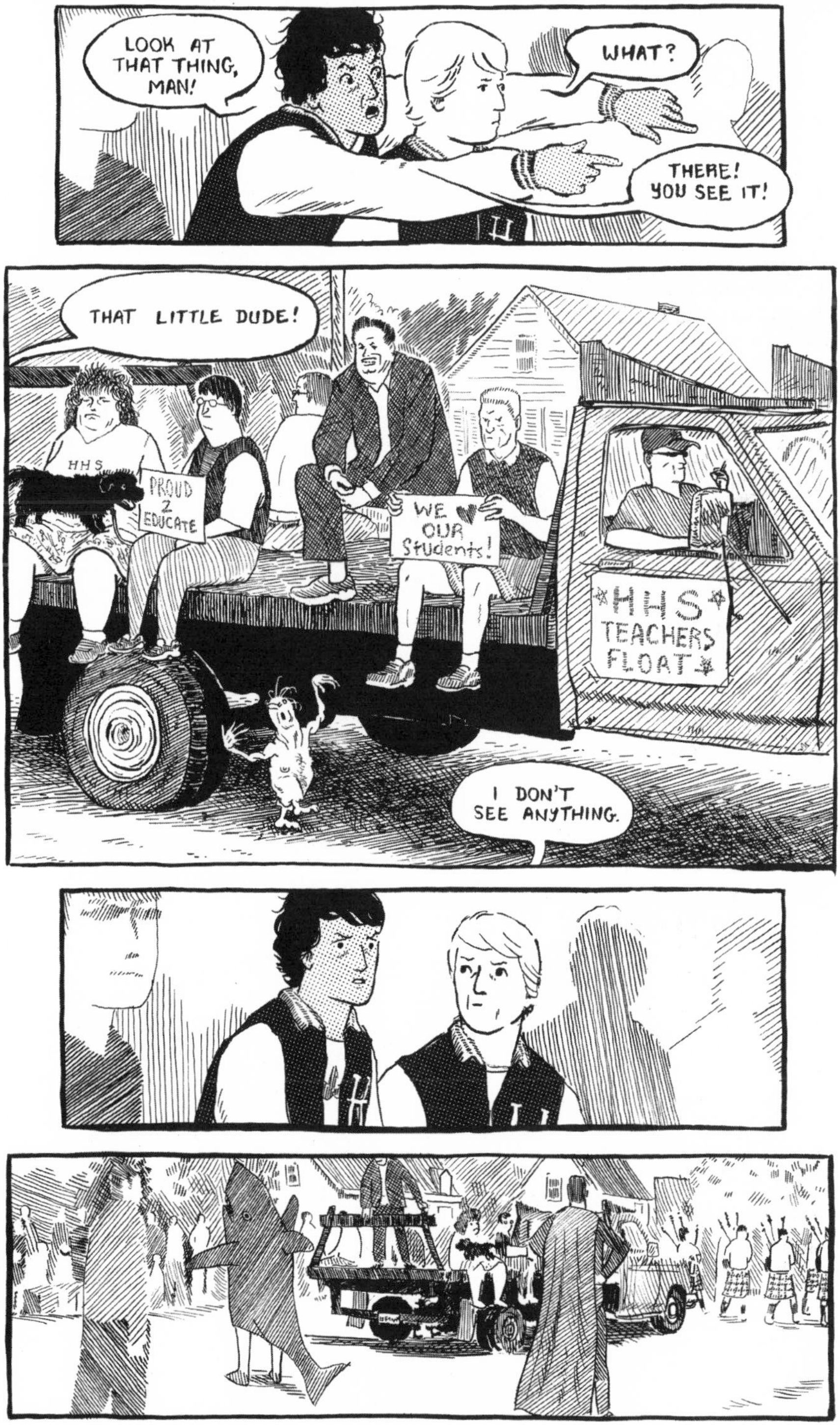
LOOK AT THAT THING, MAN!
WHAT?
THERE! YOU SEE IT!
THAT LITTLE DUDE!
HHS
PROUD 2 EDUCATE
WE ♥ OUR Students!
HHS TEACHERS FLOAT
I DON'T SEE ANYTHING.

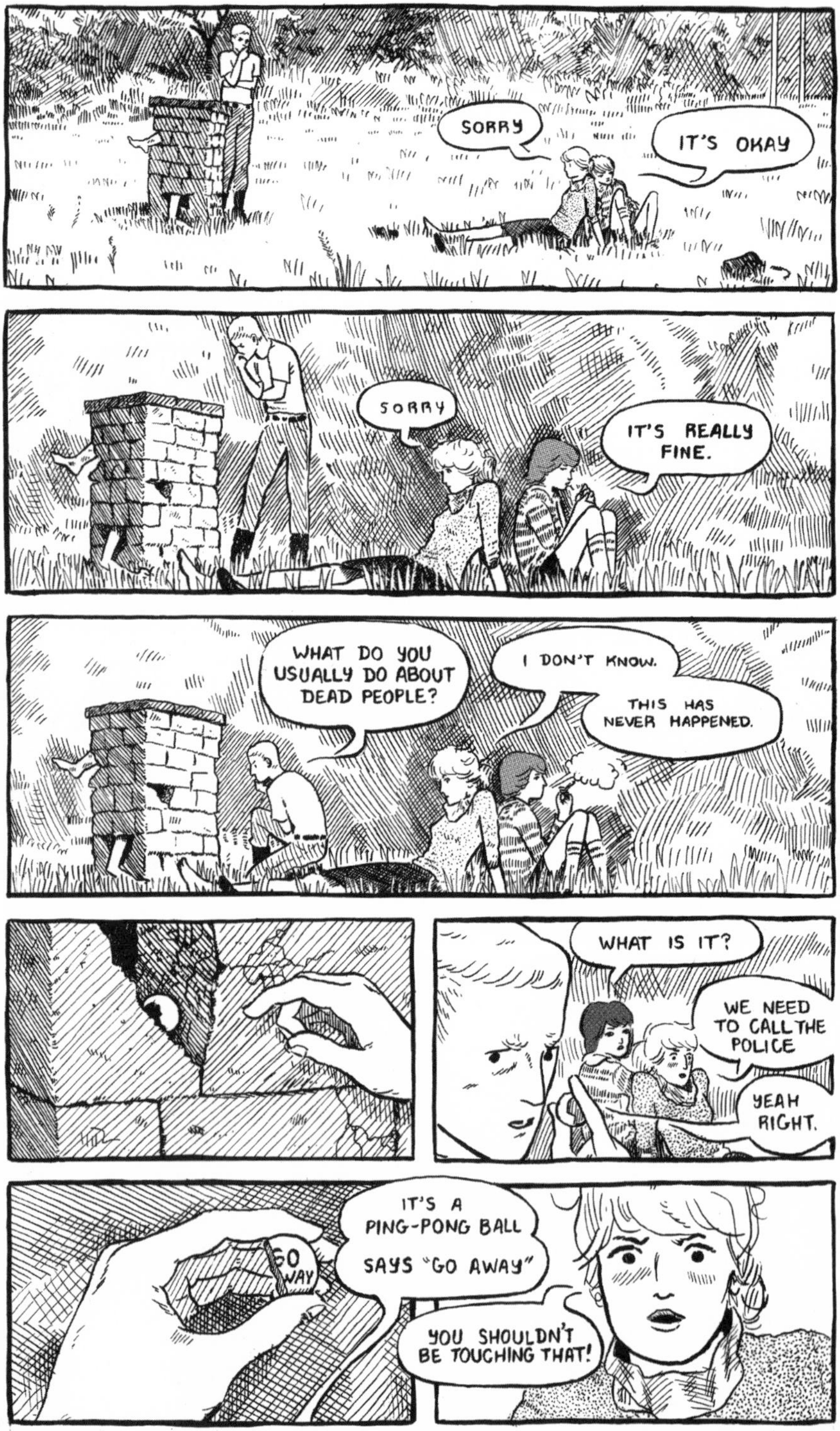
SORRY
IT'S OKAY
SORRY
IT'S REALLY FINE.
WHAT DO YOU USUALLY DO ABOUT DEAD PEOPLE?
I DON'T KNOW.
THIS HAS NEVER HAPPENED.
WHAT IS IT?
WE NEED TO CALL THE POLICE
YEAH RIGHT.
GO AWAY
IT'S A PING-PONG BALL
SAYS "GO AWAY"
YOU SHOULDN'T BE TOUCHING THAT!

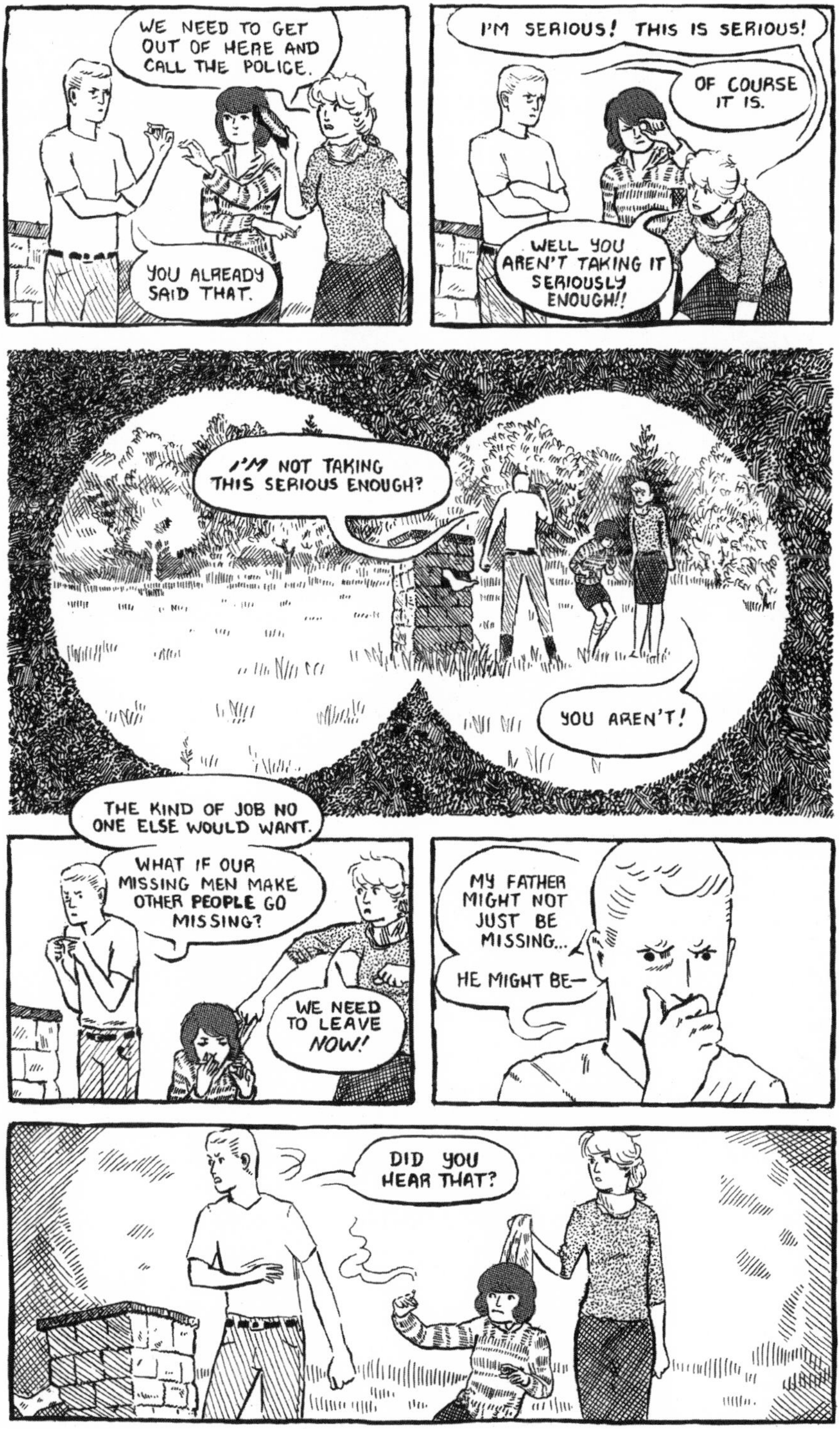
WE NEED TO GET OUT OF HERE AND CALL THE POLICE.
YOU ALREADY SAID THAT.
I'M SERIOUS! THIS IS SERIOUS!
OF COURSE IT IS.
WELL YOU AREN'T TAKING IT SERIOUSLY ENOUGH!!
I'M NOT TAKING THIS SERIOUS ENOUGH?
YOU AREN'T!
THE KIND OF JOB NO ONE ELSE WOULD WANT.
WHAT IF OUR MISSING MEN MAKE OTHER PEOPLE GO MISSING?
WE NEED TO LEAVE NOW!
MY FATHER MIGHT NOT JUST BE MISSING...
HE MIGHT BE—
DID YOU HEAR THAT?

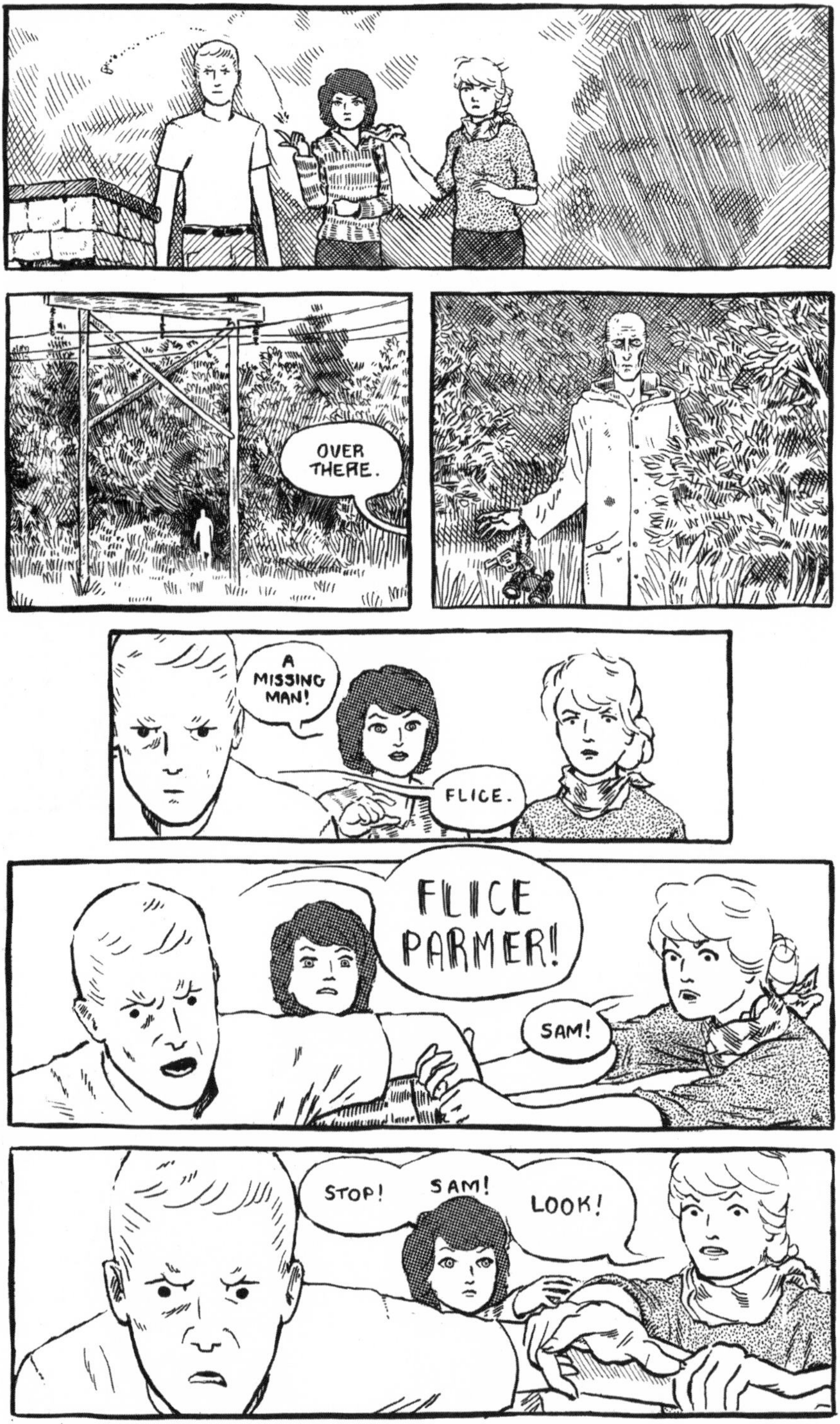
OVER THERE.
A MISSING MAN!
FLICE.
FLICE PARMER!
SAM!
STOP! SAM! LOOK!

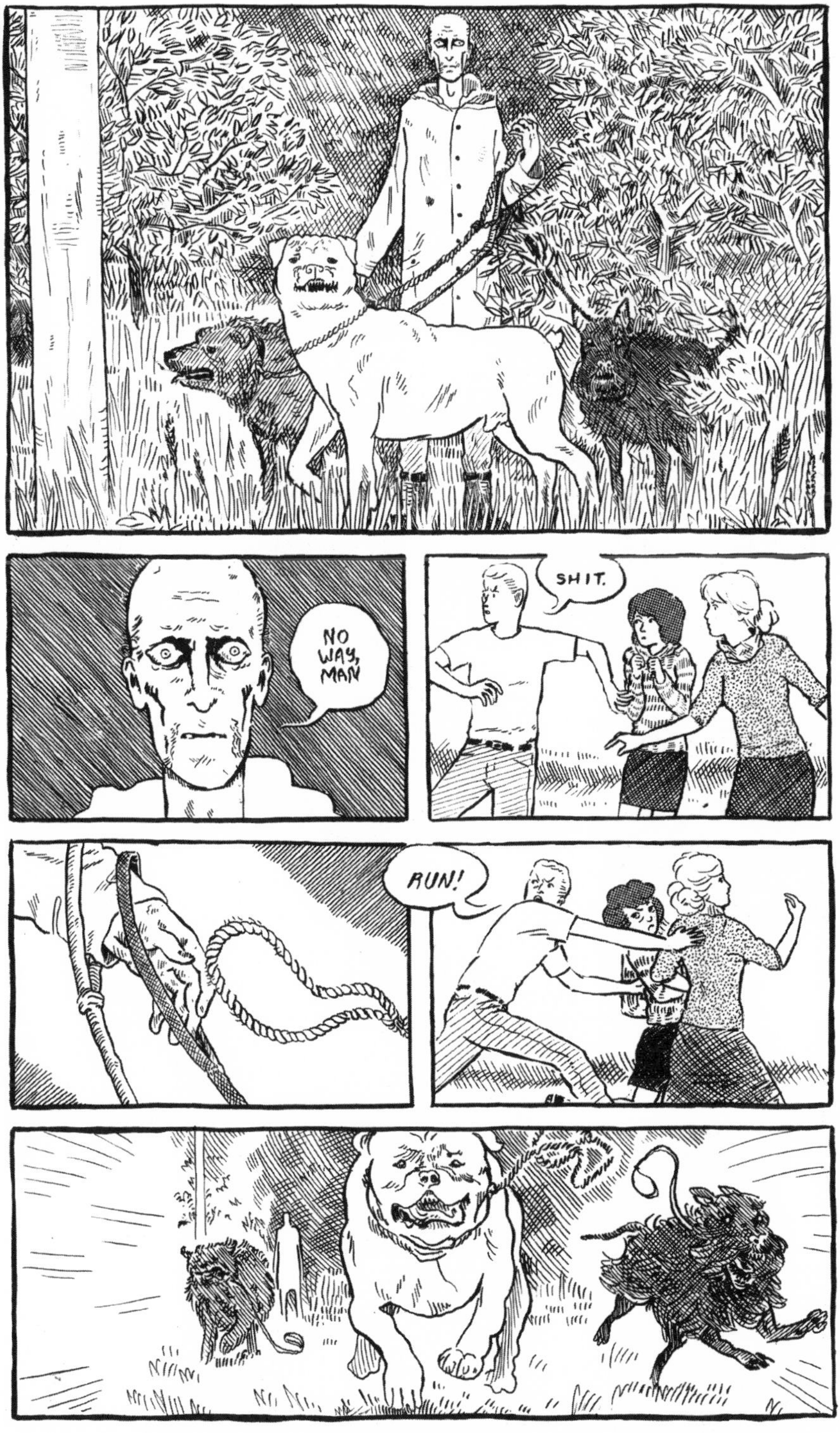
NO WAY, MAN
SHIT.
RUN!

CHAPTER SIX

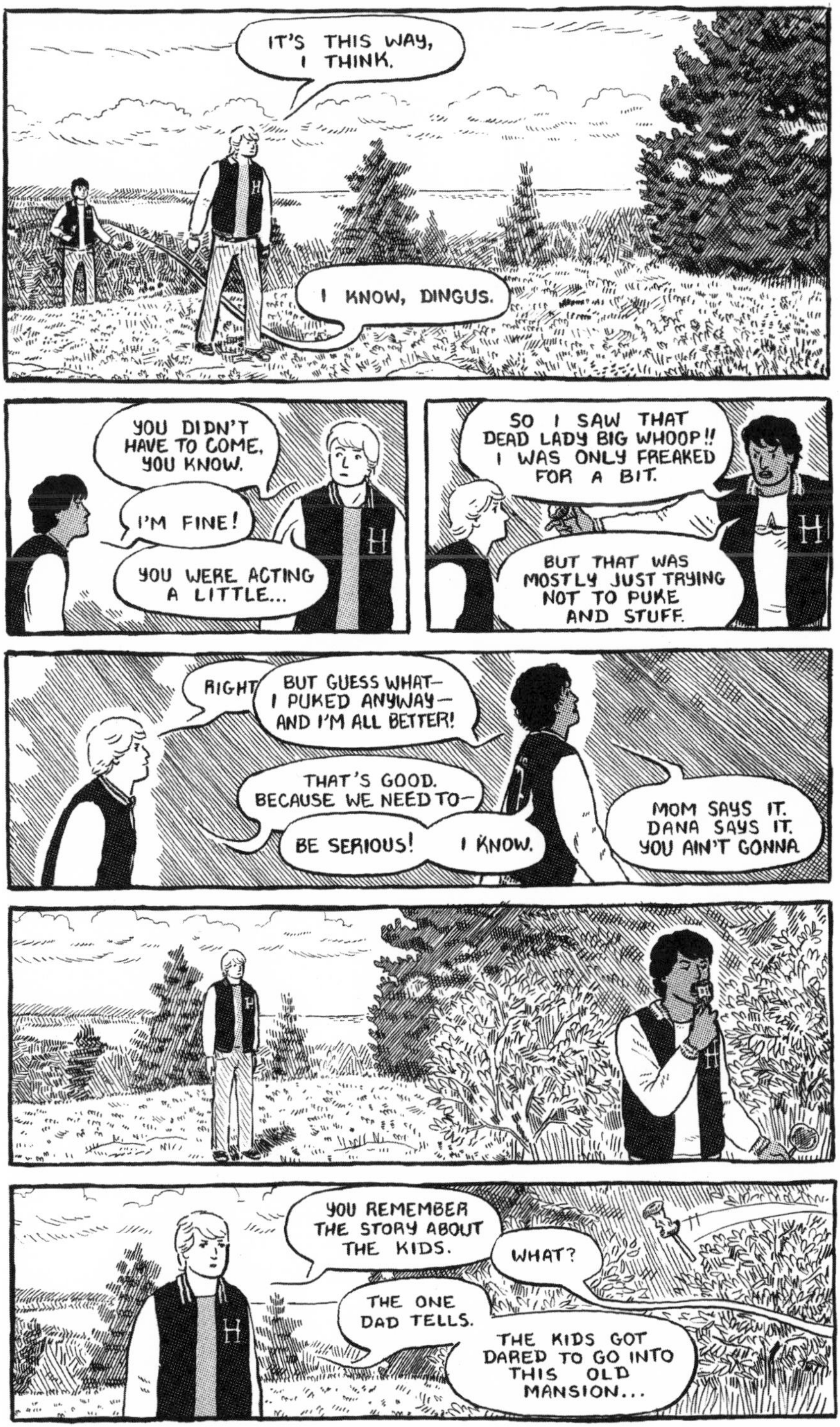
IT'S THIS WAY, I THINK.
I KNOW, DINGUS.
YOU DIDN'T HAVE TO COME, YOU KNOW.
I'M FINE!
YOU WERE ACTING A LITTLE...
SO I SAW THAT DEAD LADY BIG WHOOP!! I WAS ONLY FREAKED FOR A BIT.
BUT THAT WAS MOSTLY JUST TRYING NOT TO PUKE AND STUFF.
RIGHT
BUT GUESS WHAT— I PUKED ANYWAY— AND I'M ALL BETTER!
THAT'S GOOD. BECAUSE WE NEED TO—
BE SERIOUS!
I KNOW.
MOM SAYS IT. DANA SAYS IT. YOU AIN'T GONNA
YOU REMEMBER THE STORY ABOUT THE KIDS.
WHAT?
THE ONE DAD TELLS.
THE KIDS GOT DARED TO GO INTO THIS OLD MANSION...

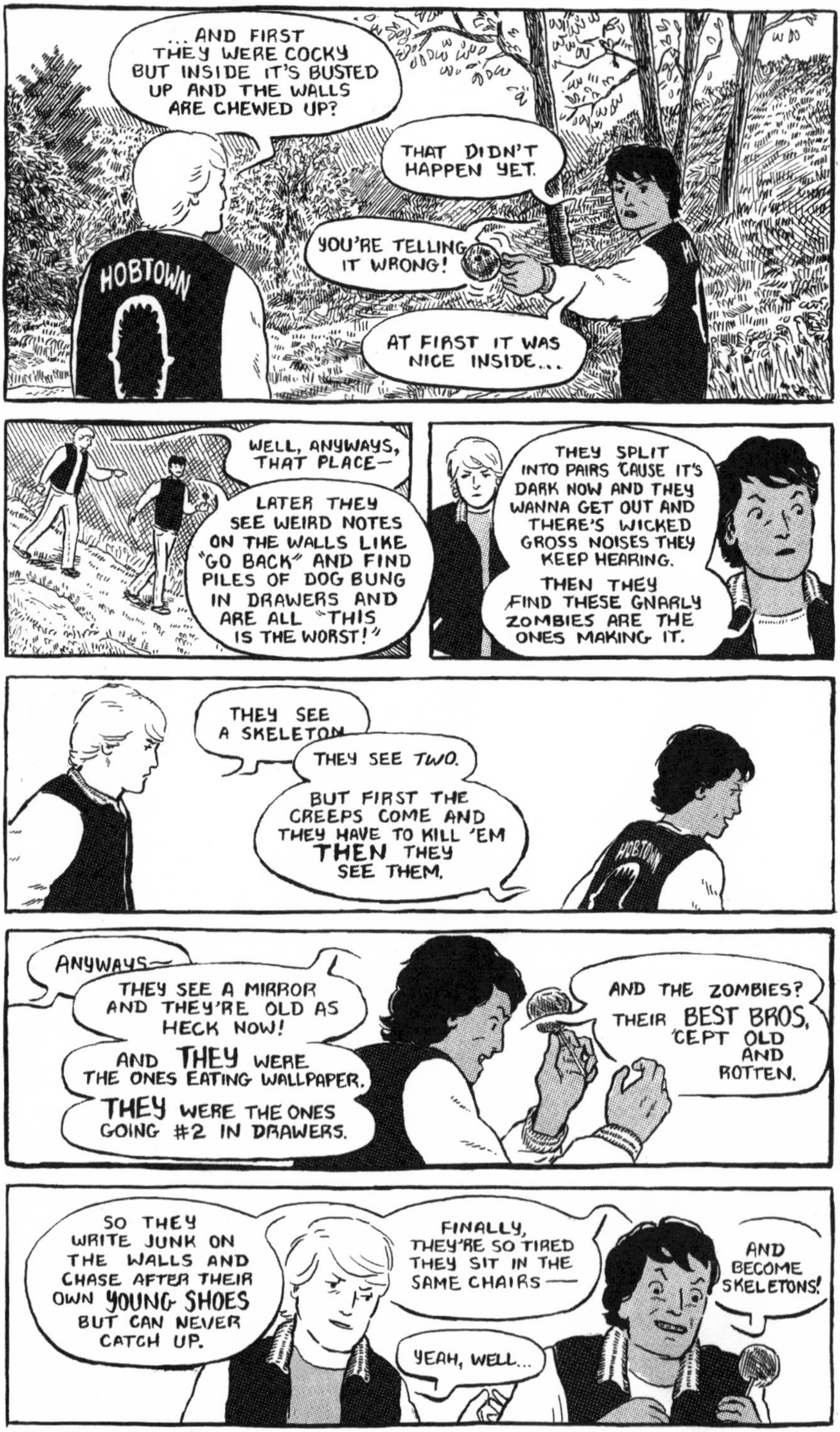
... AND FIRST THEY WERE COCKY BUT INSIDE IT'S BUSTED UP AND THE WALLS ARE CHEWED UP?
THAT DIDN'T HAPPEN YET.
YOU'RE TELLING IT WRONG!
AT FIRST IT WAS NICE INSIDE...
WELL, ANYWAYS, THAT PLACE—
LATER THEY SEE WEIRD NOTES ON THE WALLS LIKE "GO BACK" AND FIND PILES OF DOG BUNG IN DRAWERS AND ARE ALL "THIS IS THE WORST!"
THEY SPLIT INTO PAIRS 'CAUSE IT'S DARK NOW AND THEY WANNA GET OUT AND THERE'S WICKED GROSS NOISES THEY KEEP HEARING.
THEN THEY FIND THESE GNARLY ZOMBIES ARE THE ONES MAKING IT.
THEY SEE A SKELETON
THEY SEE *TWO.*
BUT FIRST THE CREEPS COME AND THEY HAVE TO KILL 'EM **THEN** THEY SEE THEM.
HOBTOWN
ANYWAYS—
THEY SEE A MIRROR AND THEY'RE OLD AS HECK NOW!
AND **THEY** WERE THE ONES EATING WALLPAPER.
THEY WERE THE ONES GOING #2 IN DRAWERS.
AND THE ZOMBIES? THEIR **BEST BROS,** 'CEPT OLD AND ROTTEN.
SO THEY WRITE JUNK ON THE WALLS AND CHASE AFTER THEIR OWN **YOUNG SHOES** BUT CAN NEVER CATCH UP.
FINALLY, THEY'RE SO TIRED THEY SIT IN THE SAME CHAIRS—
AND BECOME SKELETONS!
YEAH, WELL...

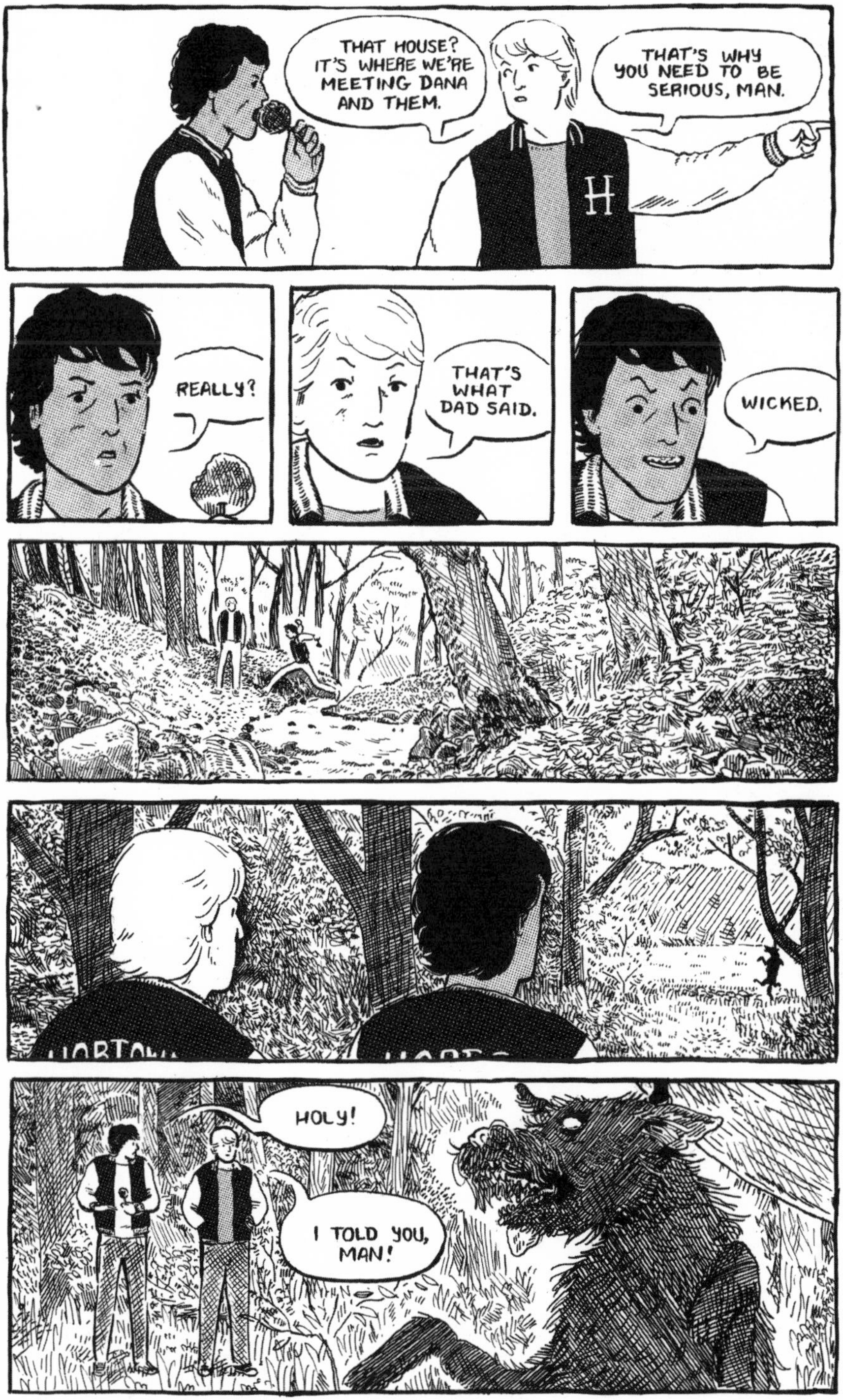
THAT HOUSE? IT'S WHERE WE'RE MEETING DANA AND THEM.
THAT'S WHY YOU NEED TO BE SERIOUS, MAN.
REALLY?
THAT'S WHAT DAD SAID.
WICKED.
HOLY!
I TOLD YOU, MAN!

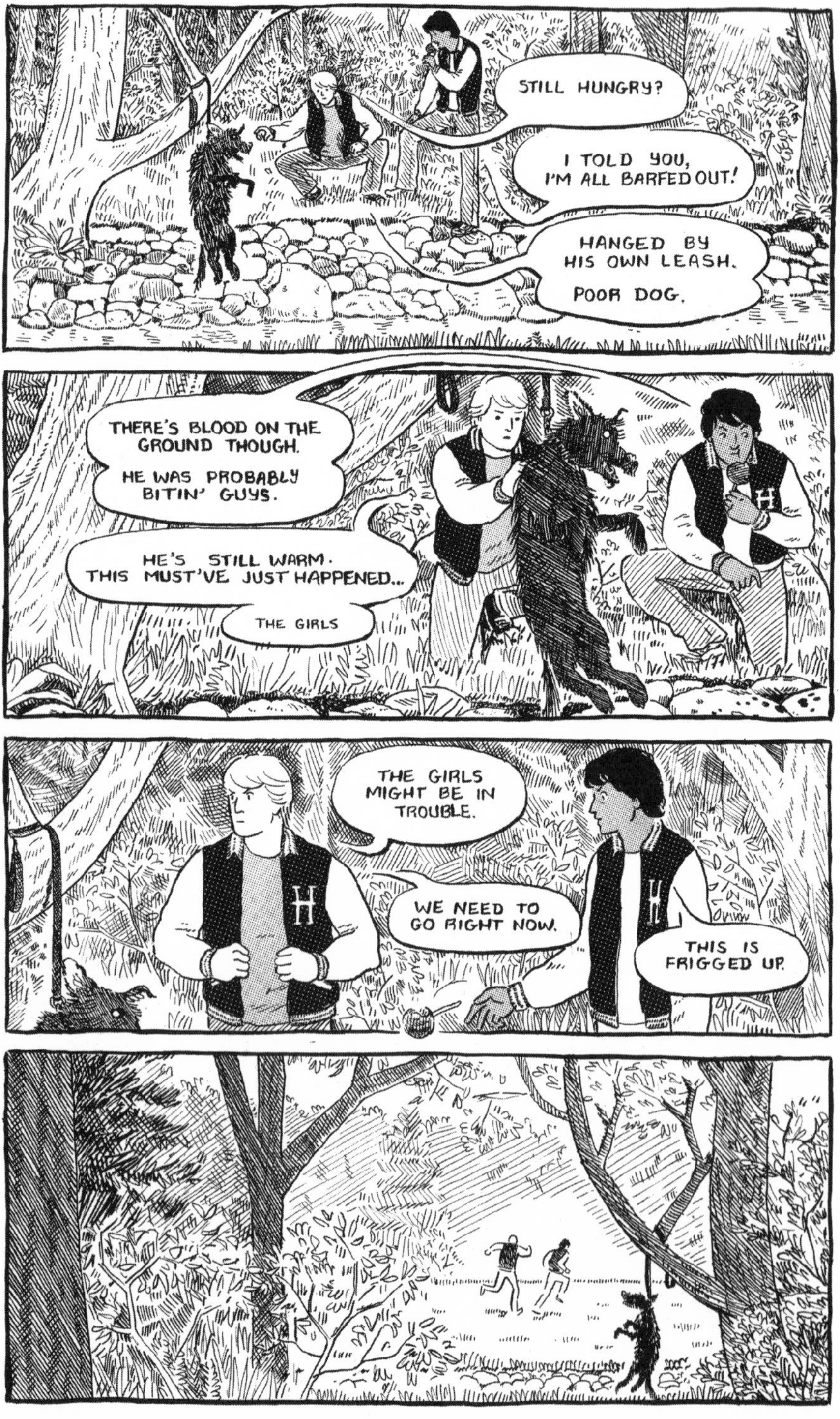
STILL HUNGRY?
I TOLD YOU, I'M ALL BARFED OUT!
HANGED BY HIS OWN LEASH.
POOR DOG.
THERE'S BLOOD ON THE GROUND THOUGH.
HE WAS PROBABLY BITIN' GUYS.
HE'S STILL WARM. THIS MUST'VE JUST HAPPENED...
THE GIRLS
THE GIRLS MIGHT BE IN TROUBLE.
WE NEED TO GO RIGHT NOW.
THIS IS FRIGGED UP.

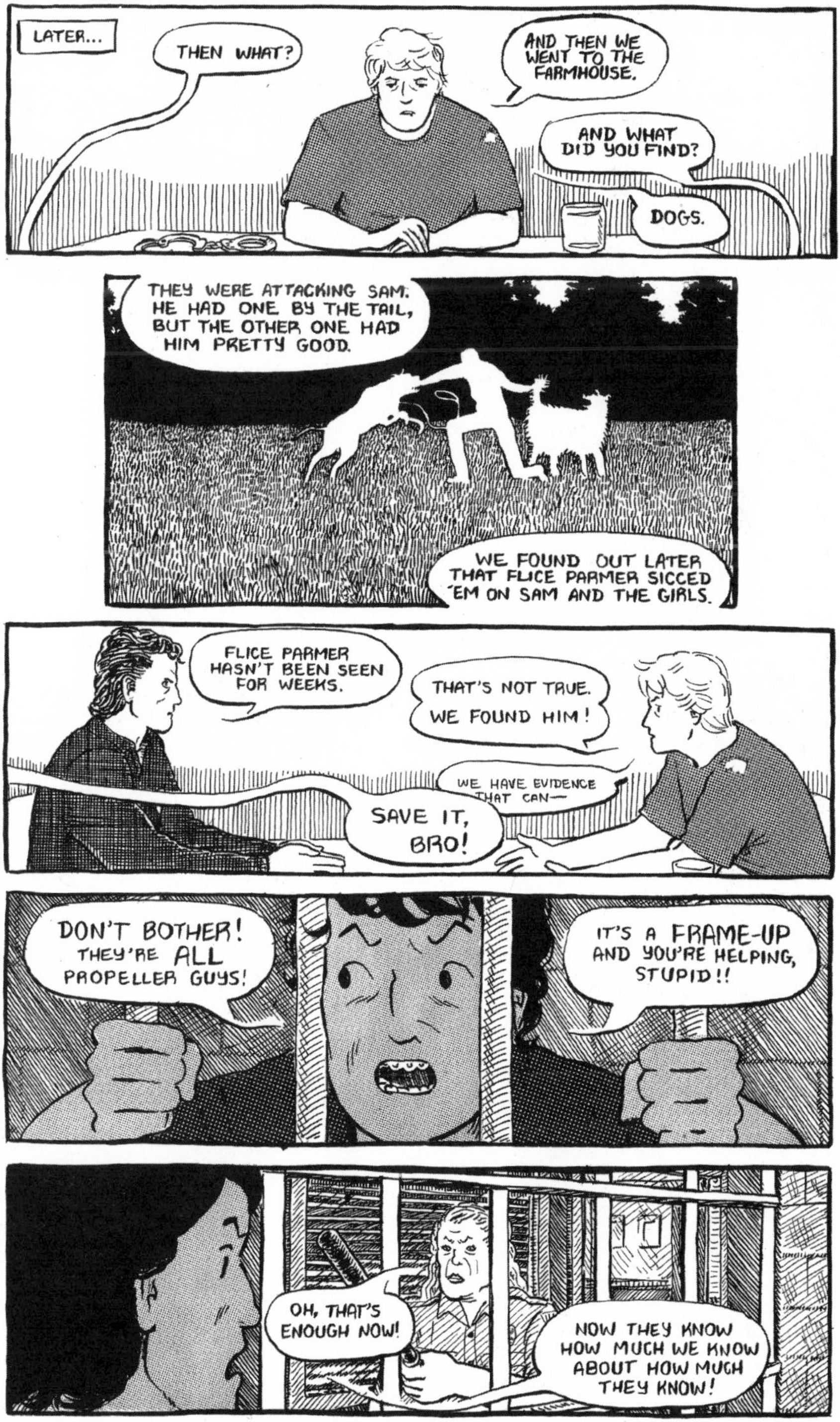
LATER...
THEN WHAT?
AND THEN WE WENT TO THE FARMHOUSE.
AND WHAT DID YOU FIND?
DOGS.
THEY WERE ATTACKING SAM. HE HAD ONE BY THE TAIL, BUT THE OTHER ONE HAD HIM PRETTY GOOD.
WE FOUND OUT LATER THAT FLICE PARMER SICCED 'EM ON SAM AND THE GIRLS.
FLICE PARMER HASN'T BEEN SEEN FOR WEEKS.
THAT'S NOT TRUE. WE FOUND HIM!
WE HAVE EVIDENCE THAT CAN—
SAVE IT, BRO!
DON'T BOTHER! THEY'RE ALL PROPELLER GUYS!
IT'S A FRAME-UP AND YOU'RE HELPING, STUPID!!
OH, THAT'S ENOUGH NOW!
NOW THEY KNOW HOW MUCH WE KNOW ABOUT HOW MUCH THEY KNOW!

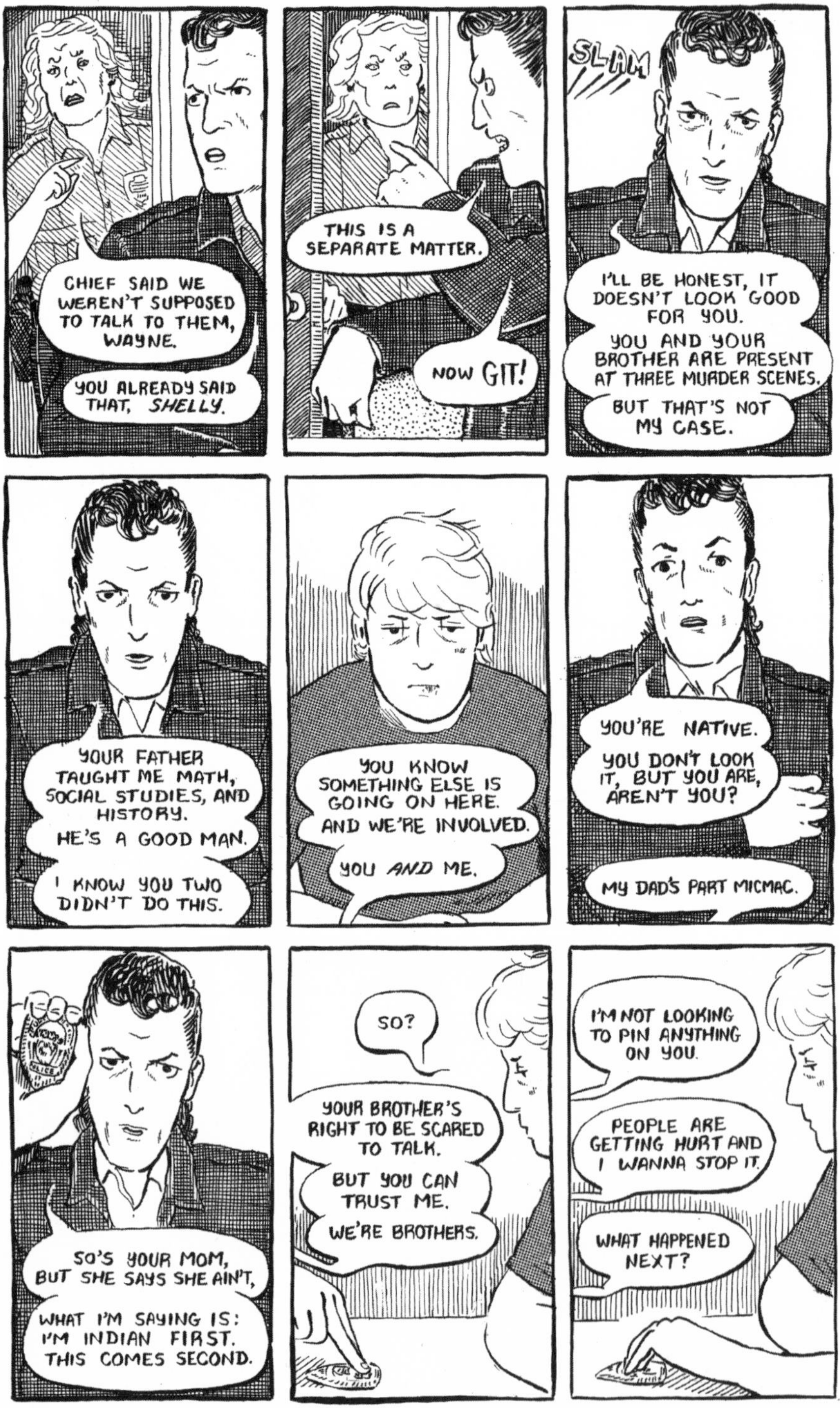
CHIEF SAID WE WEREN'T SUPPOSED TO TALK TO THEM, WAYNE.
YOU ALREADY SAID THAT, *SHELLY*.
THIS IS A SEPARATE MATTER.
NOW GIT!
SLAM
I'LL BE HONEST, IT DOESN'T LOOK GOOD FOR YOU.
YOU AND YOUR BROTHER ARE PRESENT AT THREE MURDER SCENES.
BUT THAT'S NOT MY CASE.
YOUR FATHER TAUGHT ME MATH, SOCIAL STUDIES, AND HISTORY.
HE'S A GOOD MAN.
I KNOW YOU TWO DIDN'T DO THIS.
YOU KNOW SOMETHING ELSE IS GOING ON HERE. AND WE'RE INVOLVED.
YOU *AND* ME.
YOU'RE NATIVE.
YOU DON'T LOOK IT, BUT YOU ARE, AREN'T YOU?
MY DAD'S PART MICMAC.
SO'S YOUR MOM, BUT SHE SAYS SHE AIN'T.
WHAT I'M SAYING IS: I'M INDIAN FIRST. THIS COMES SECOND.
SO?
YOUR BROTHER'S RIGHT TO BE SCARED TO TALK.
BUT YOU CAN TRUST ME.
WE'RE BROTHERS.
I'M NOT LOOKING TO PIN ANYTHING ON YOU.
PEOPLE ARE GETTING HURT AND I WANNA STOP IT.
WHAT HAPPENED NEXT?

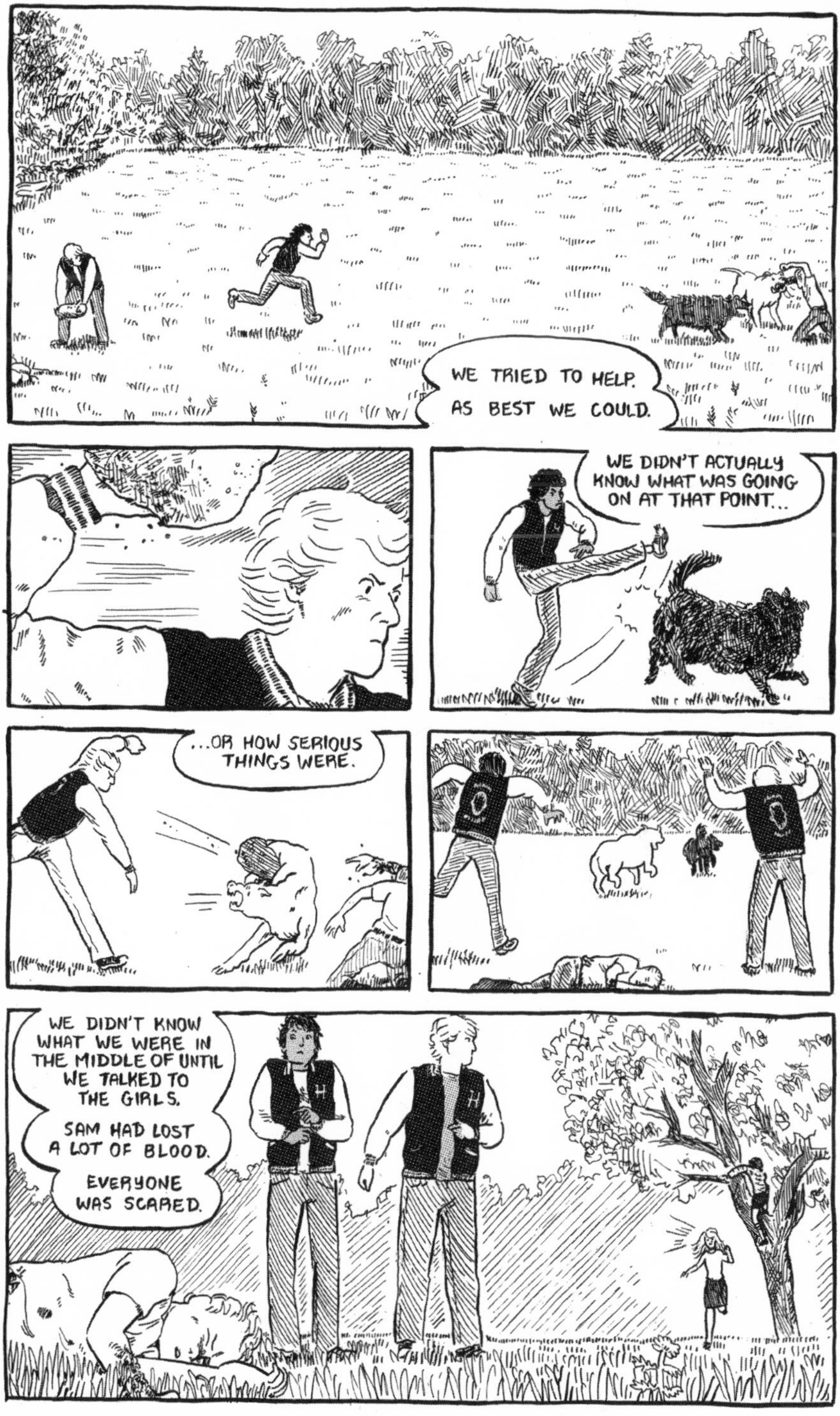
WE TRIED TO HELP. AS BEST WE COULD.
WE DIDN'T ACTUALLY KNOW WHAT WAS GOING ON AT THAT POINT...
...OR HOW SERIOUS THINGS WERE.
WE DIDN'T KNOW WHAT WE WERE IN THE MIDDLE OF UNTIL WE TALKED TO THE GIRLS.
SAM HAD LOST A LOT OF BLOOD.
EVERYONE WAS SCARED.

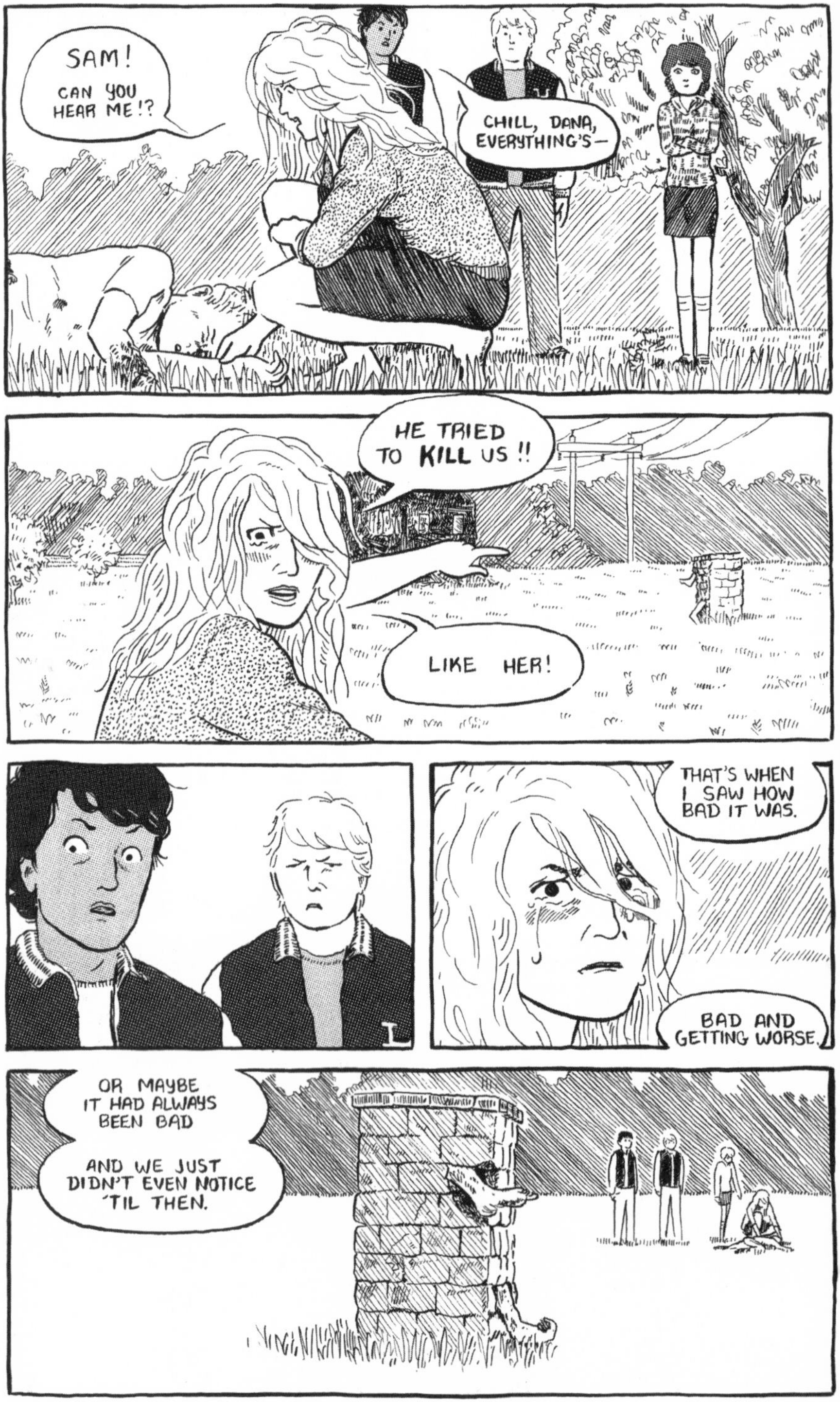
SAM! CAN YOU HEAR ME!?
CHILL, DANA, EVERYTHING'S—
HE TRIED TO KILL US !!
LIKE HER!
THAT'S WHEN I SAW HOW BAD IT WAS.
BAD AND GETTING WORSE.
OR MAYBE IT HAD ALWAYS BEEN BAD
AND WE JUST DIDN'T EVEN NOTICE 'TIL THEN.

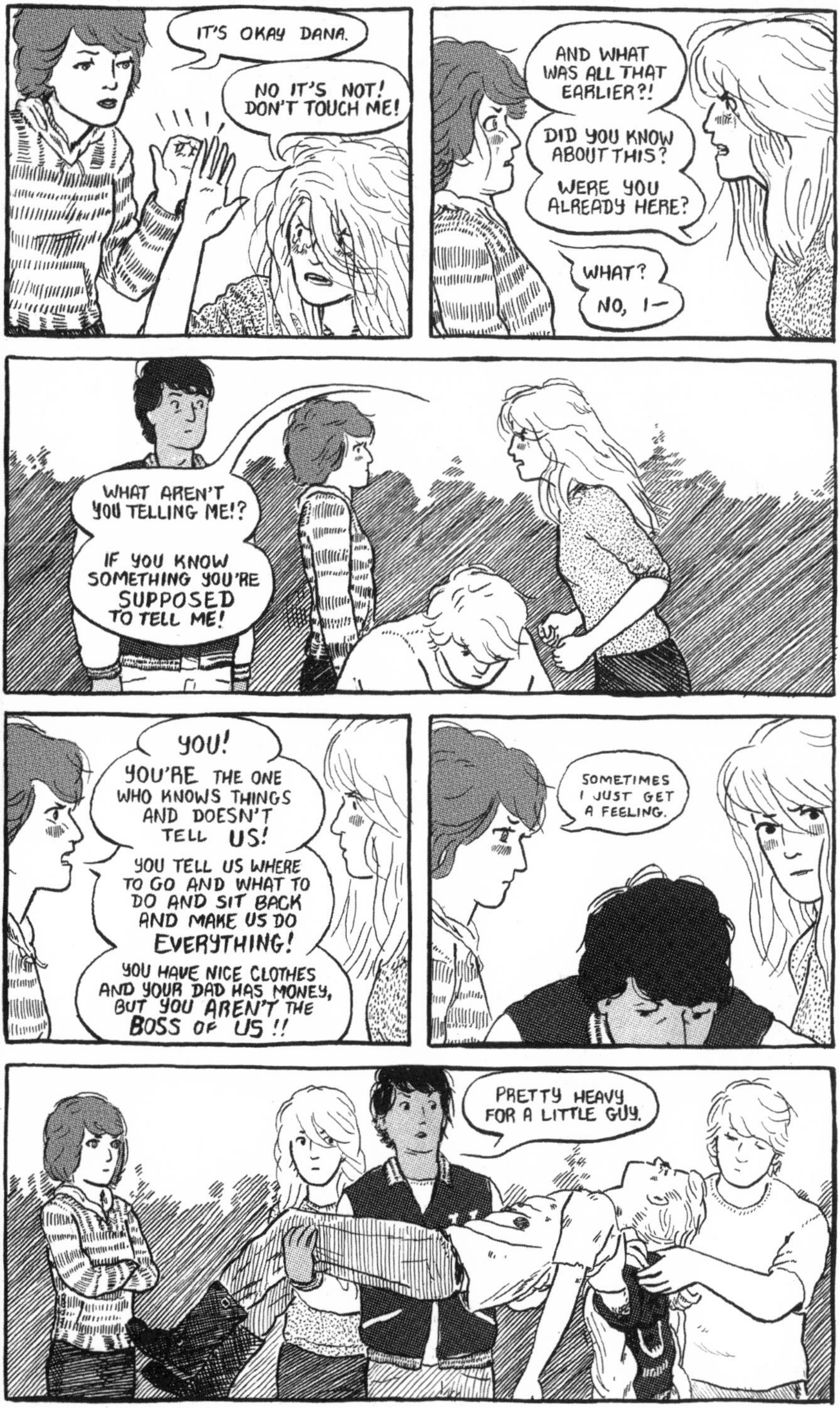
IT'S OKAY DANA.
NO IT'S NOT! DON'T TOUCH ME!
AND WHAT WAS ALL THAT EARLIER?!
DID YOU KNOW ABOUT THIS?
WERE YOU ALREADY HERE?
WHAT?
NO, I—
WHAT AREN'T YOU TELLING ME!?
IF YOU KNOW SOMETHING YOU'RE SUPPOSED TO TELL ME!
YOU!
YOU'RE THE ONE WHO KNOWS THINGS AND DOESN'T TELL US!
YOU TELL US WHERE TO GO AND WHAT TO DO AND SIT BACK AND MAKE US DO EVERYTHING!
YOU HAVE NICE CLOTHES AND YOUR DAD HAS MONEY, BUT YOU AREN'T THE BOSS OF US!!
SOMETIMES I JUST GET A FEELING.
PRETTY HEAVY FOR A LITTLE GUY.

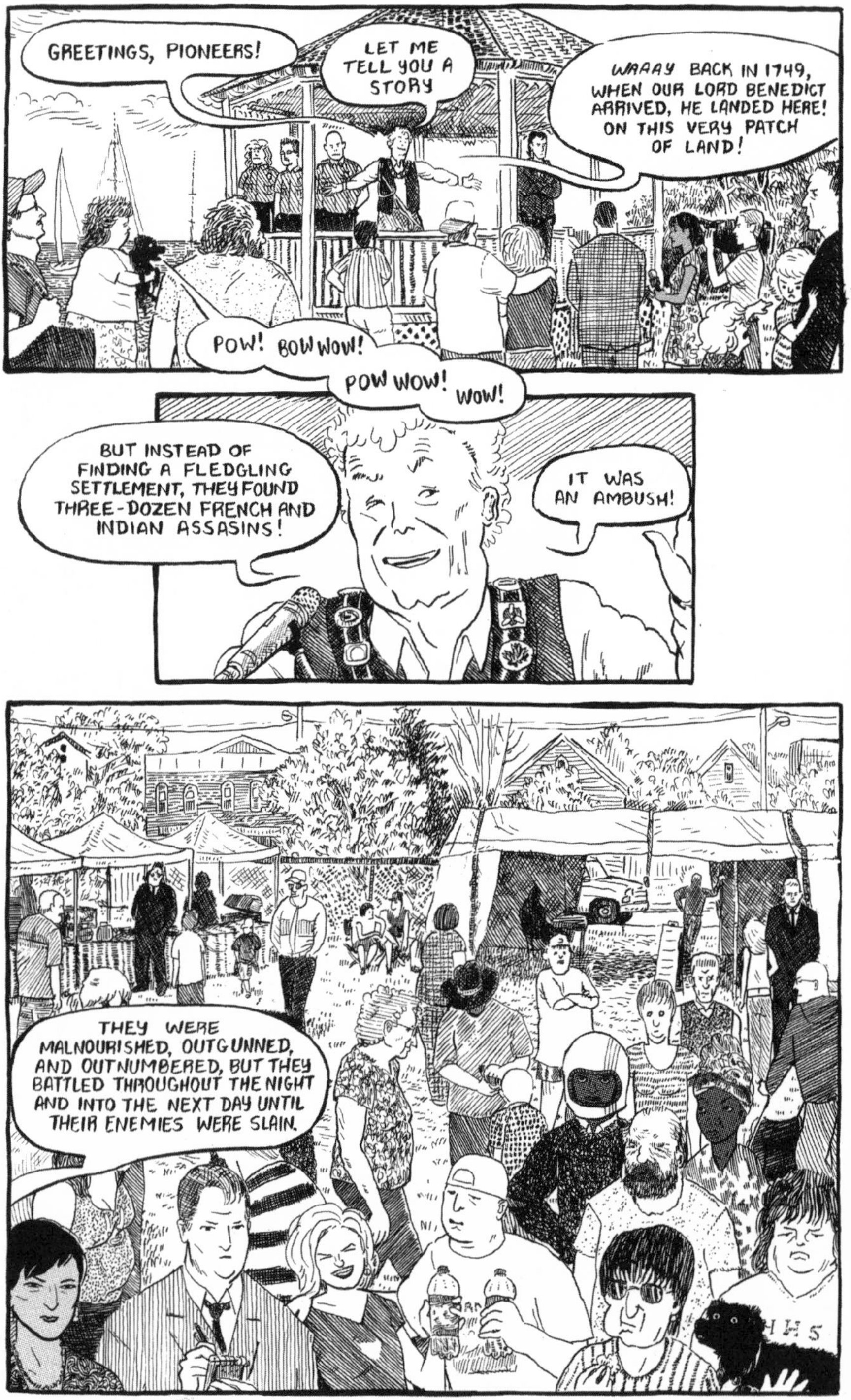
GREETINGS, PIONEERS!
LET ME TELL YOU A STORY
WAAAY BACK IN 1749, WHEN OUR LORD BENEDICT ARRIVED, HE LANDED HERE! ON THIS VERY PATCH OF LAND!
POW! BOW WOW! POW WOW! WOW!
BUT INSTEAD OF FINDING A FLEDGLING SETTLEMENT, THEY FOUND THREE-DOZEN FRENCH AND INDIAN ASSASINS!
IT WAS AN AMBUSH!
THEY WERE MALNOURISHED, OUTGUNNED, AND OUTNUMBERED, BUT THEY BATTLED THROUGHOUT THE NIGHT AND INTO THE NEXT DAY UNTIL THEIR ENEMIES WERE SLAIN.

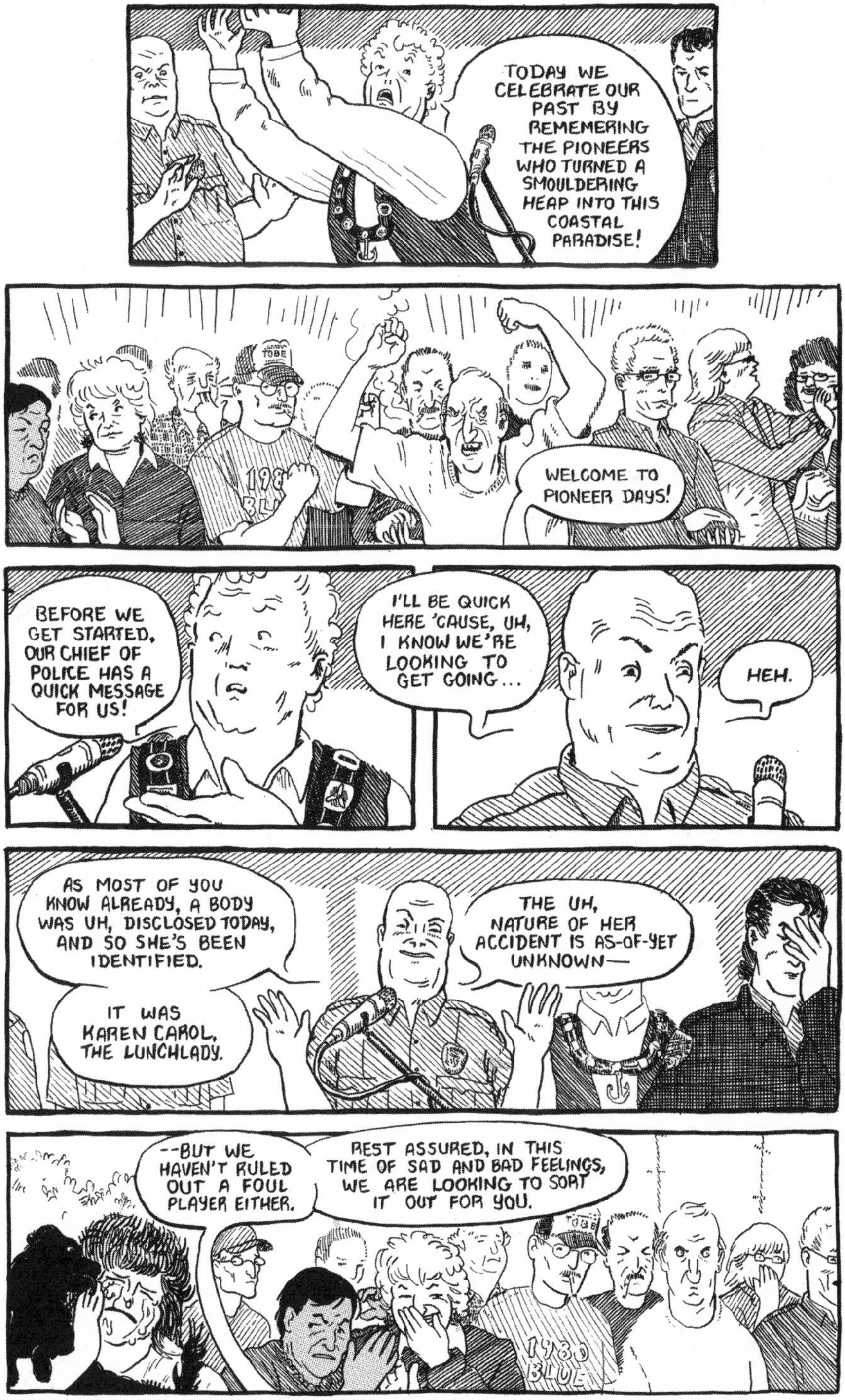
TODAY WE CELEBRATE OUR PAST BY REMEMERING THE PIONEERS WHO TURNED A SMOULDERING HEAP INTO THIS COASTAL PARADISE!
TOBE
1980 BLUE
WELCOME TO PIONEER DAYS!
BEFORE WE GET STARTED, OUR CHIEF OF POLICE HAS A QUICK MESSAGE FOR US!
I'LL BE QUICK HERE 'CAUSE, UH, I KNOW WE'RE LOOKING TO GET GOING...
HEH.
AS MOST OF YOU KNOW ALREADY, A BODY WAS UH, DISCLOSED TODAY, AND SO SHE'S BEEN IDENTIFIED.
IT WAS KAREN CAROL, THE LUNCHLADY.
THE UH, NATURE OF HER ACCIDENT IS AS-OF-YET UNKNOWN—
--BUT WE HAVEN'T RULED OUT A FOUL PLAYER EITHER.
REST ASSURED, IN THIS TIME OF SAD AND BAD FEELINGS, WE ARE LOOKING TO SORT IT OUT FOR YOU.
TOBE
1980 BLUE

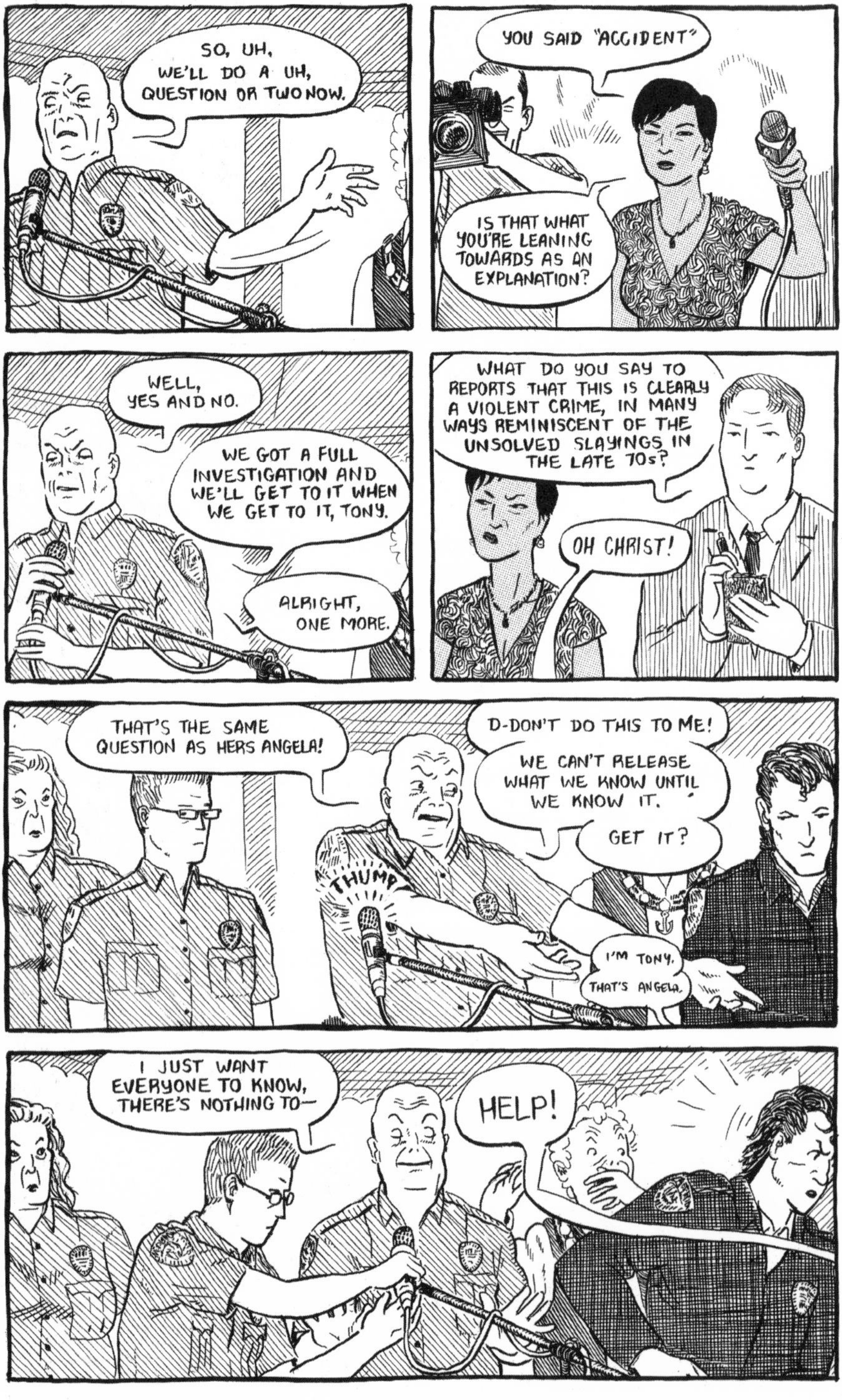
SO, UH, WE'LL DO A UH, QUESTION OR TWO NOW.
YOU SAID "ACCIDENT"
IS THAT WHAT YOU'RE LEANING TOWARDS AS AN EXPLANATION?
WELL, YES AND NO.
WE GOT A FULL INVESTIGATION AND WE'LL GET TO IT WHEN WE GET TO IT, TONY.
ALRIGHT, ONE MORE.
WHAT DO YOU SAY TO REPORTS THAT THIS IS CLEARLY A VIOLENT CRIME, IN MANY WAYS REMINISCENT OF THE UNSOLVED SLAYINGS IN THE LATE 70s?
OH CHRIST!
THAT'S THE SAME QUESTION AS HERS ANGELA!
D-DON'T DO THIS TO ME!
WE CAN'T RELEASE WHAT WE KNOW UNTIL WE KNOW IT.
GET IT?
THUMP
I'M TONY.
THAT'S ANGELA.
I JUST WANT EVERYONE TO KNOW, THERE'S NOTHING TO—
HELP!

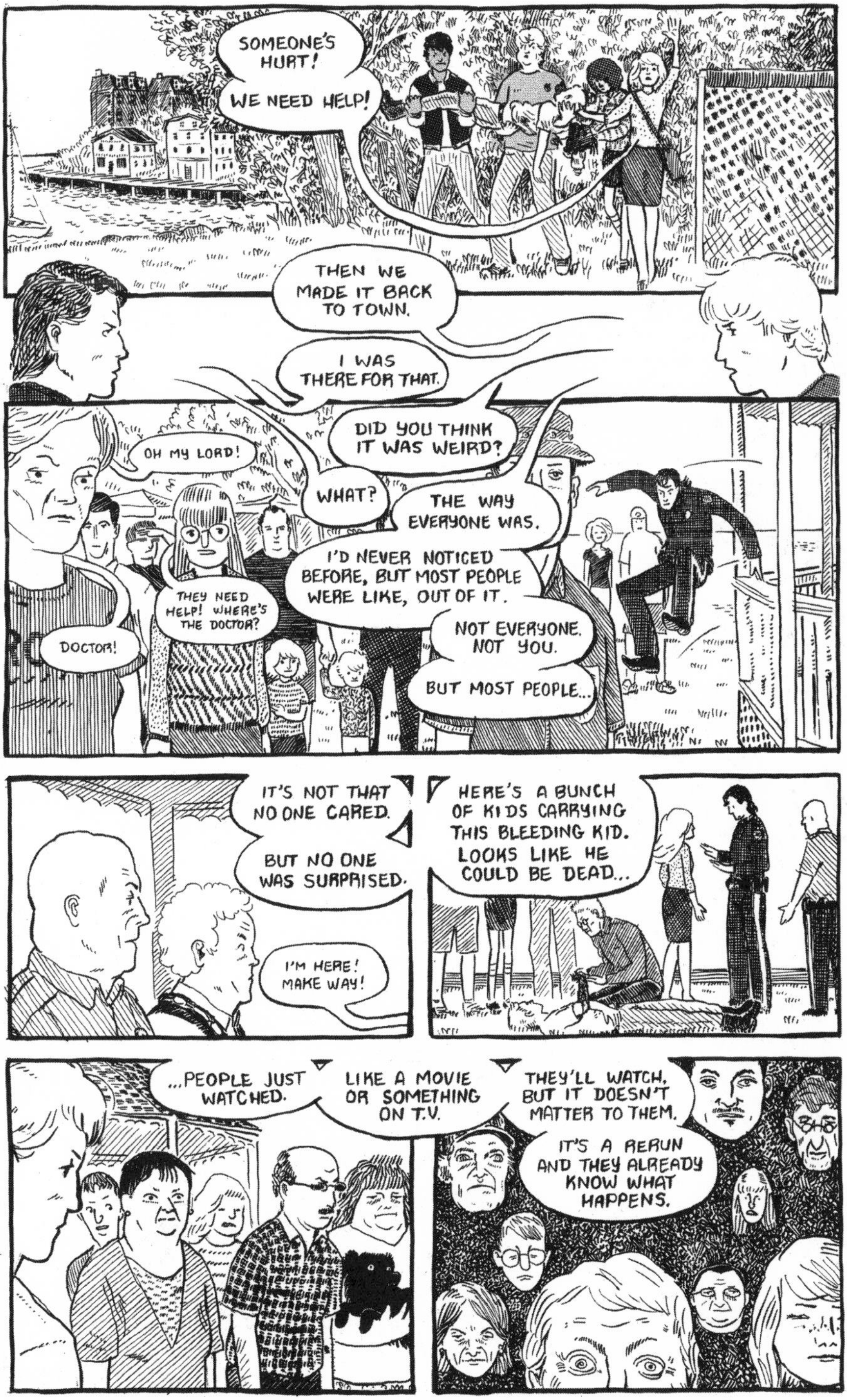
SOMEONE'S HURT!
WE NEED HELP!
THEN WE MADE IT BACK TO TOWN.
I WAS THERE FOR THAT.
DID YOU THINK IT WAS WEIRD?
OH MY LORD!
WHAT?
THE WAY EVERYONE WAS.
I'D NEVER NOTICED BEFORE, BUT MOST PEOPLE WERE LIKE, OUT OF IT.
THEY NEED HELP! WHERE'S THE DOCTOR?
DOCTOR!
NOT EVERYONE. NOT YOU.
BUT MOST PEOPLE...
IT'S NOT THAT NO ONE CARED.
BUT NO ONE WAS SURPRISED.
HERE'S A BUNCH OF KIDS CARRYING THIS BLEEDING KID. LOOKS LIKE HE COULD BE DEAD...
I'M HERE! MAKE WAY!
...PEOPLE JUST WATCHED.
LIKE A MOVIE OR SOMETHING ON T.V.
THEY'LL WATCH, BUT IT DOESN'T MATTER TO THEM.
IT'S A RERUN AND THEY ALREADY KNOW WHAT HAPPENS.

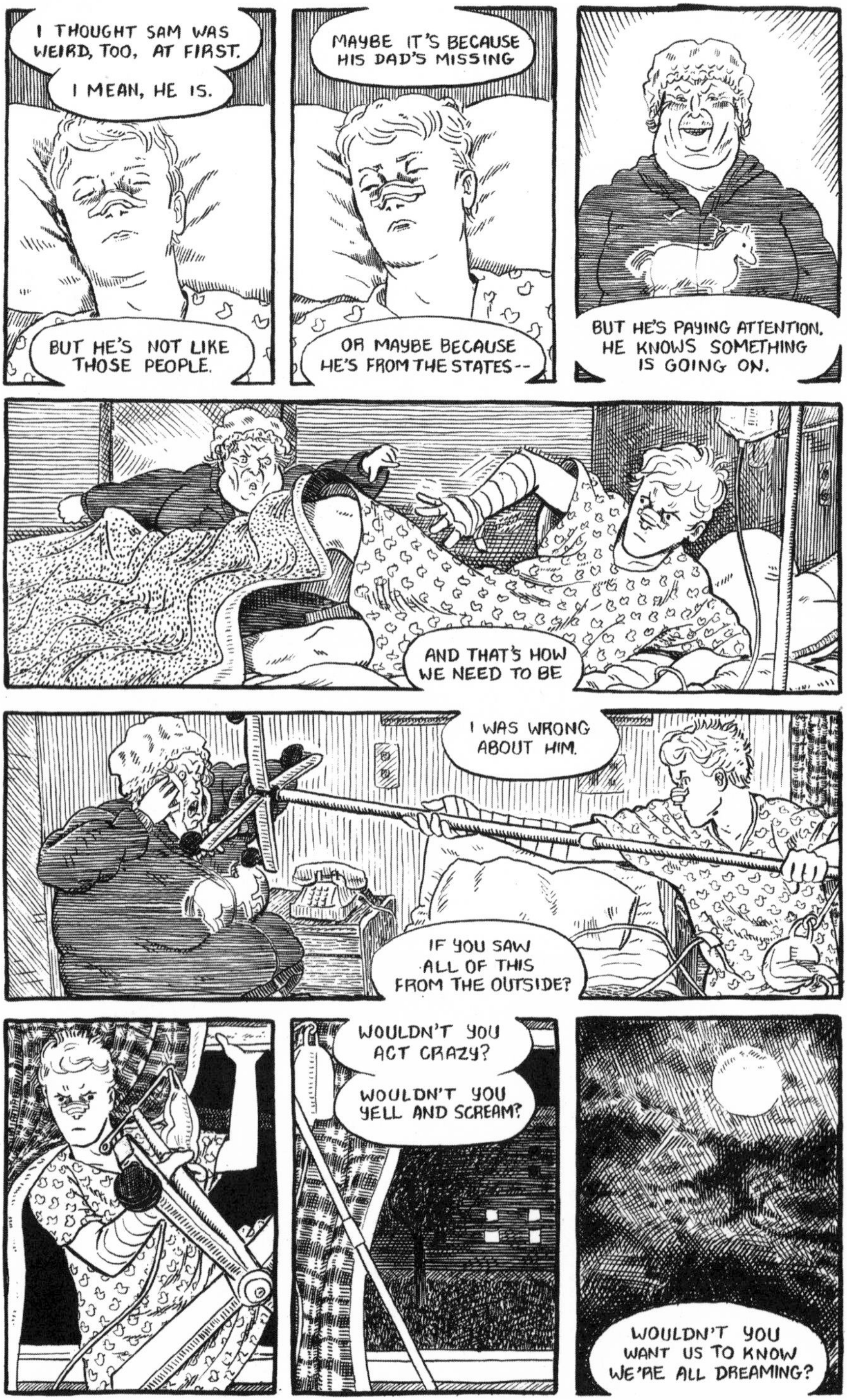

I THOUGHT SAM WAS WEIRD, TOO, AT FIRST.
I MEAN, HE IS.
BUT HE'S NOT LIKE THOSE PEOPLE.
MAYBE IT'S BECAUSE HIS DAD'S MISSING
OR MAYBE BECAUSE HE'S FROM THE STATES--
BUT HE'S PAYING ATTENTION. HE KNOWS SOMETHING IS GOING ON.
AND THAT'S HOW WE NEED TO BE
I WAS WRONG ABOUT HIM.
IF YOU SAW ALL OF THIS FROM THE OUTSIDE?
WOULDN'T YOU ACT CRAZY?
WOULDN'T YOU YELL AND SCREAM?
WOULDN'T YOU WANT US TO KNOW WE'RE ALL DREAMING?

WELL

YOUR FRIEND DANA CALLED US AND REPORTED THAT BODY,

YOU KNOW THAT?

YOU PROBABLY DON'T KNOW WHAT WE FOUND OUT THERE.

WHAT?

NOTHING...

...NOT A BODY, ANYWAY...

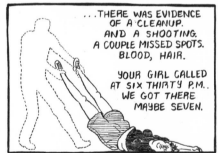

...THERE WAS EVIDENCE OF A CLEANUP. AND A SHOOTING. A COUPLE MISSED SPOTS. BLOOD, HAIR.

YOUR GIRL CALLED AT SIX THIRTY P.M.. WE GOT THERE MAYBE SEVEN.

YOUR FRIEND SAM WAS IN THE HOSPITAL AT THE POINT.

OR ... HE *WAS.* WHEN WE CHECKED, THEY HAD *LOST TRACK OF HIM.*

LAST SEEN IN HIS BED, JUST BEFORE DARK.

WHAT ARE YOU TRYING TO SAY?

YOU THINK SAM DID THIS?!

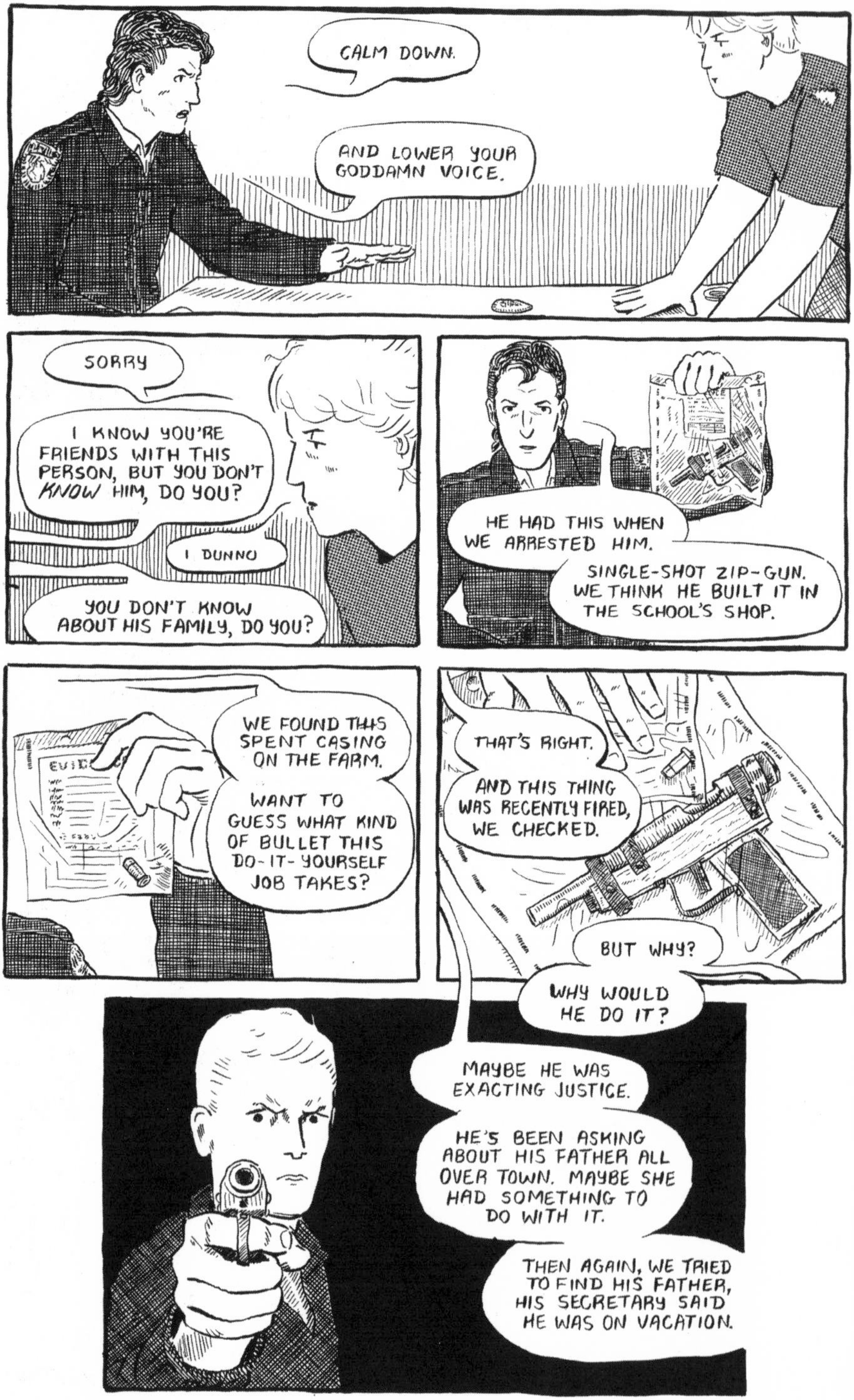
CALM DOWN.
AND LOWER YOUR GODDAMN VOICE.
SORRY
I KNOW YOU'RE FRIENDS WITH THIS PERSON, BUT YOU DON'T *KNOW* HIM, DO YOU?
I DUNNO
YOU DON'T KNOW ABOUT HIS FAMILY, DO YOU?
HE HAD THIS WHEN WE ARRESTED HIM.
SINGLE-SHOT ZIP-GUN. WE THINK HE BUILT IT IN THE SCHOOL'S SHOP.
WE FOUND THIS SPENT CASING ON THE FARM.
WANT TO GUESS WHAT KIND OF BULLET THIS DO-IT-YOURSELF JOB TAKES?
THAT'S RIGHT.
AND THIS THING WAS RECENTLY FIRED, WE CHECKED.
BUT WHY?
WHY WOULD HE DO IT?
MAYBE HE WAS EXACTING JUSTICE.
HE'S BEEN ASKING ABOUT HIS FATHER ALL OVER TOWN. MAYBE SHE HAD SOMETHING TO DO WITH IT.
THEN AGAIN, WE TRIED TO FIND HIS FATHER, HIS SECRETARY SAID HE WAS ON VACATION.

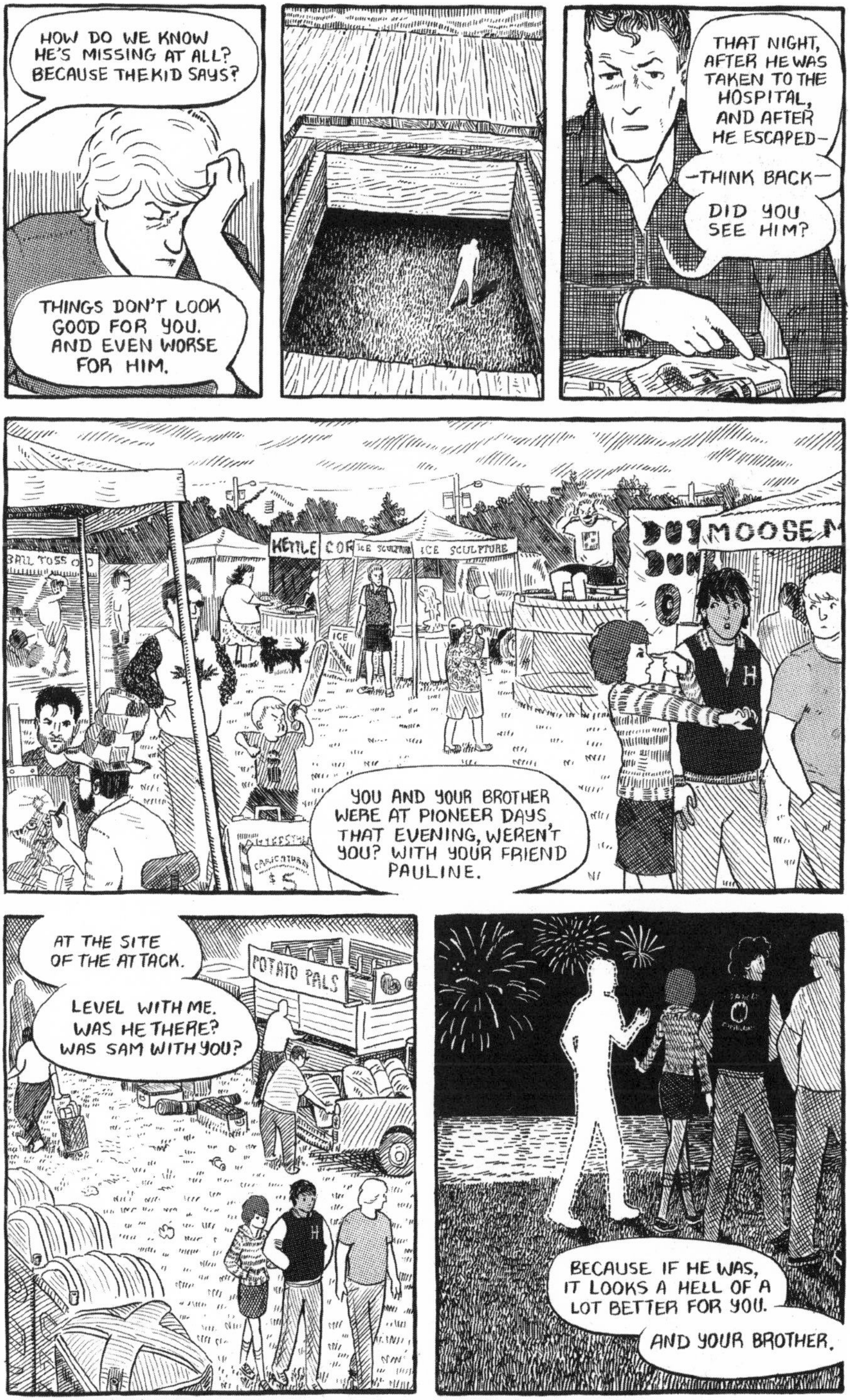
HOW DO WE KNOW HE'S MISSING AT ALL? BECAUSE THE KID SAYS?
THINGS DON'T LOOK GOOD FOR YOU. AND EVEN WORSE FOR HIM.
THAT NIGHT, AFTER HE WAS TAKEN TO THE HOSPITAL, AND AFTER HE ESCAPED—
—THINK BACK—
DID YOU SEE HIM?
BALL TOSS
KETTLE COR
ICE SCULPTURE
ICE SCULPTURE
ICE
MOOSE M
CARICATURES $5
YOU AND YOUR BROTHER WERE AT PIONEER DAYS, THAT EVENING, WEREN'T YOU? WITH YOUR FRIEND PAULINE.
AT THE SITE OF THE ATTACK.
POTATO PALS
LEVEL WITH ME. WAS HE THERE? WAS SAM WITH YOU?
BECAUSE IF HE WAS, IT LOOKS A HELL OF A LOT BETTER FOR YOU.
AND YOUR BROTHER.

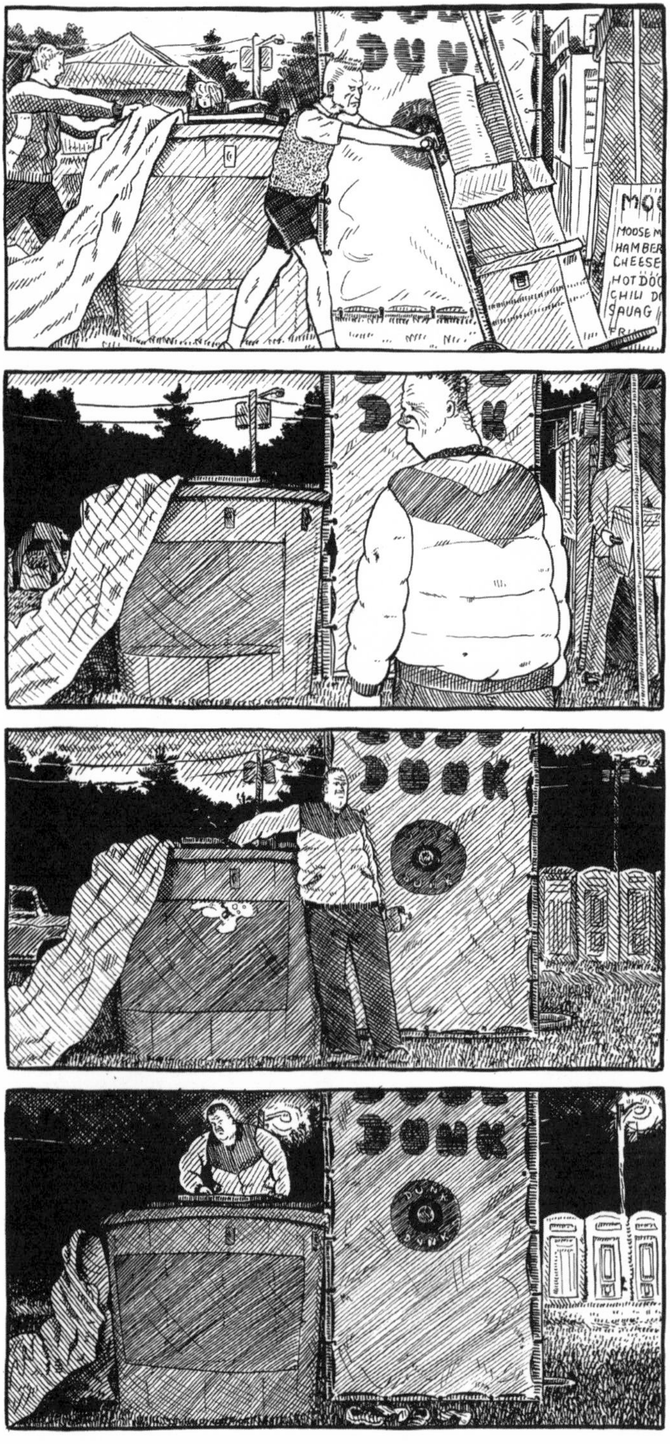
DUN
MOO
MOOSE M
HAMBER
CHEESE
HOT DOG
CHILI D
SAUAG
DUNK
DUNK
DUNK

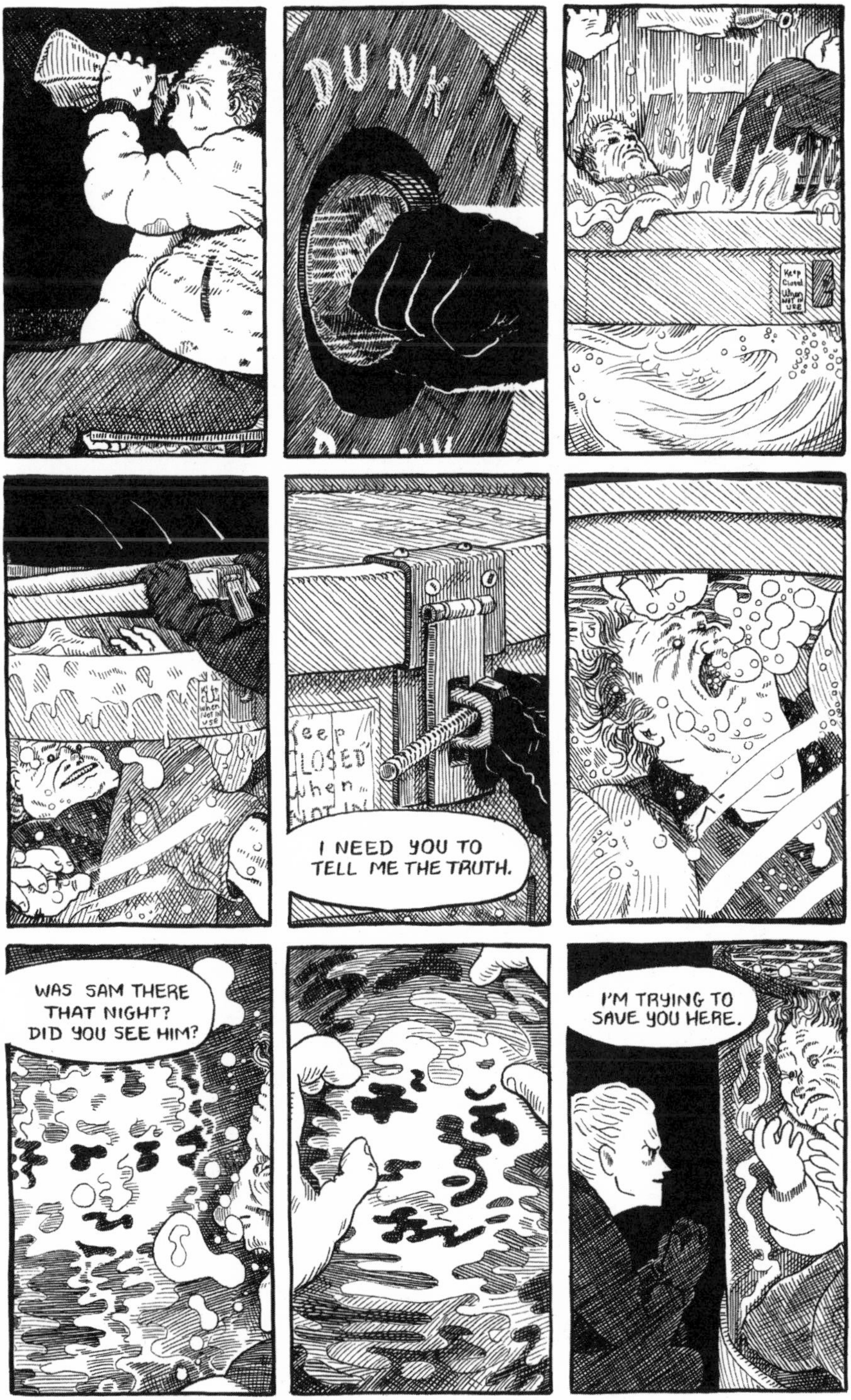
DUNK
Keep Closed When Not In Use
Keep CLOSED When
I NEED YOU TO TELL ME THE TRUTH.
WAS SAM THERE THAT NIGHT? DID YOU SEE HIM?
I'M TRYING TO SAVE YOU HERE.

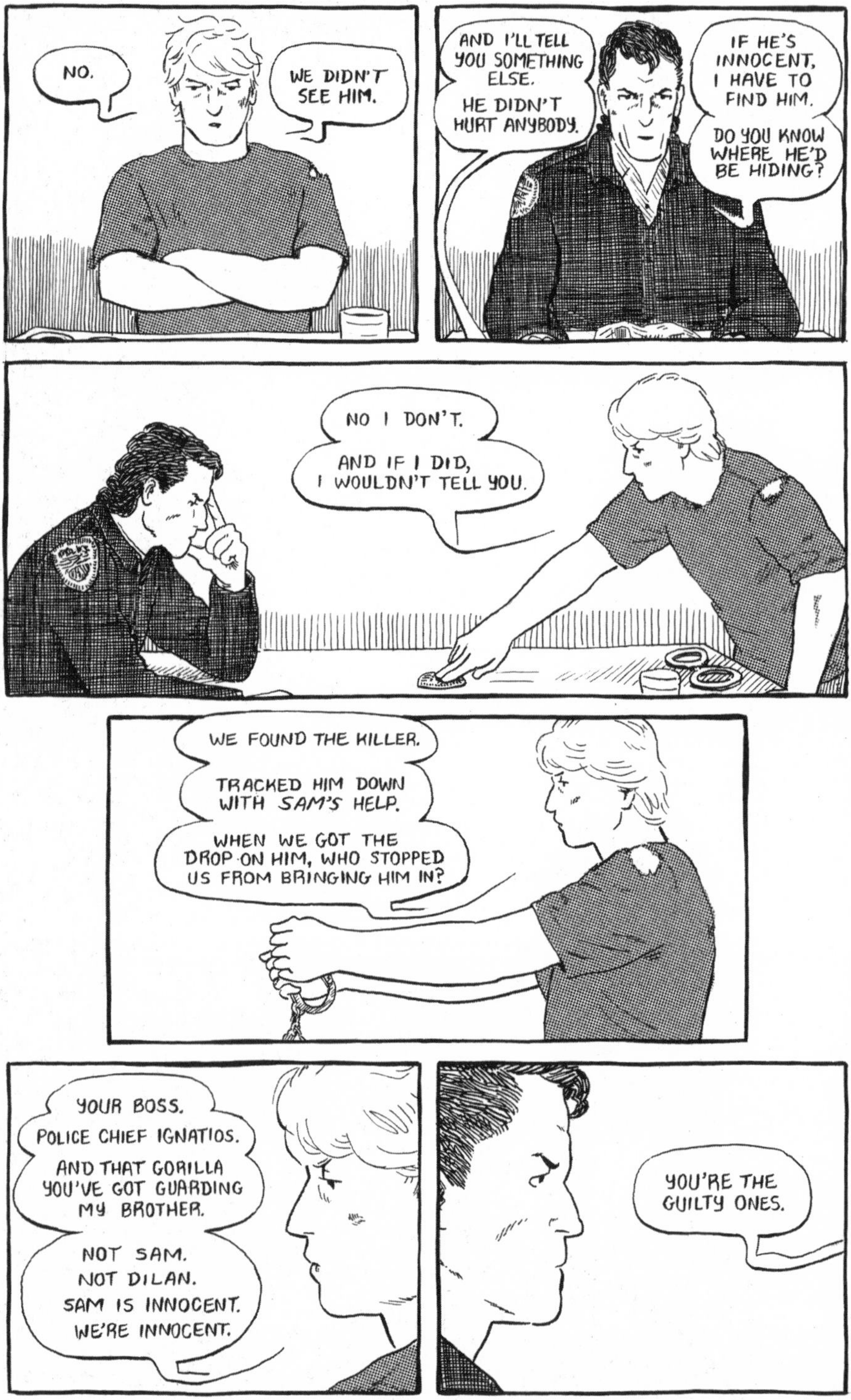
NO.
WE DIDN'T SEE HIM.
AND I'LL TELL YOU SOMETHING ELSE.
HE DIDN'T HURT ANYBODY.
IF HE'S INNOCENT, I HAVE TO FIND HIM.
DO YOU KNOW WHERE HE'D BE HIDING?
NO I DON'T.
AND IF I DID, I WOULDN'T TELL YOU.
WE FOUND THE KILLER.
TRACKED HIM DOWN WITH *SAM'S* HELP.
WHEN WE GOT THE DROP ON HIM, WHO STOPPED US FROM BRINGING HIM IN?
YOUR BOSS.
POLICE CHIEF IGNATIOS.
AND THAT GORILLA YOU'VE GOT GUARDING MY BROTHER.
NOT SAM.
NOT DILAN.
SAM IS INNOCENT.
WE'RE INNOCENT.
YOU'RE THE GUILTY ONES.

CHAPTER SEVEN

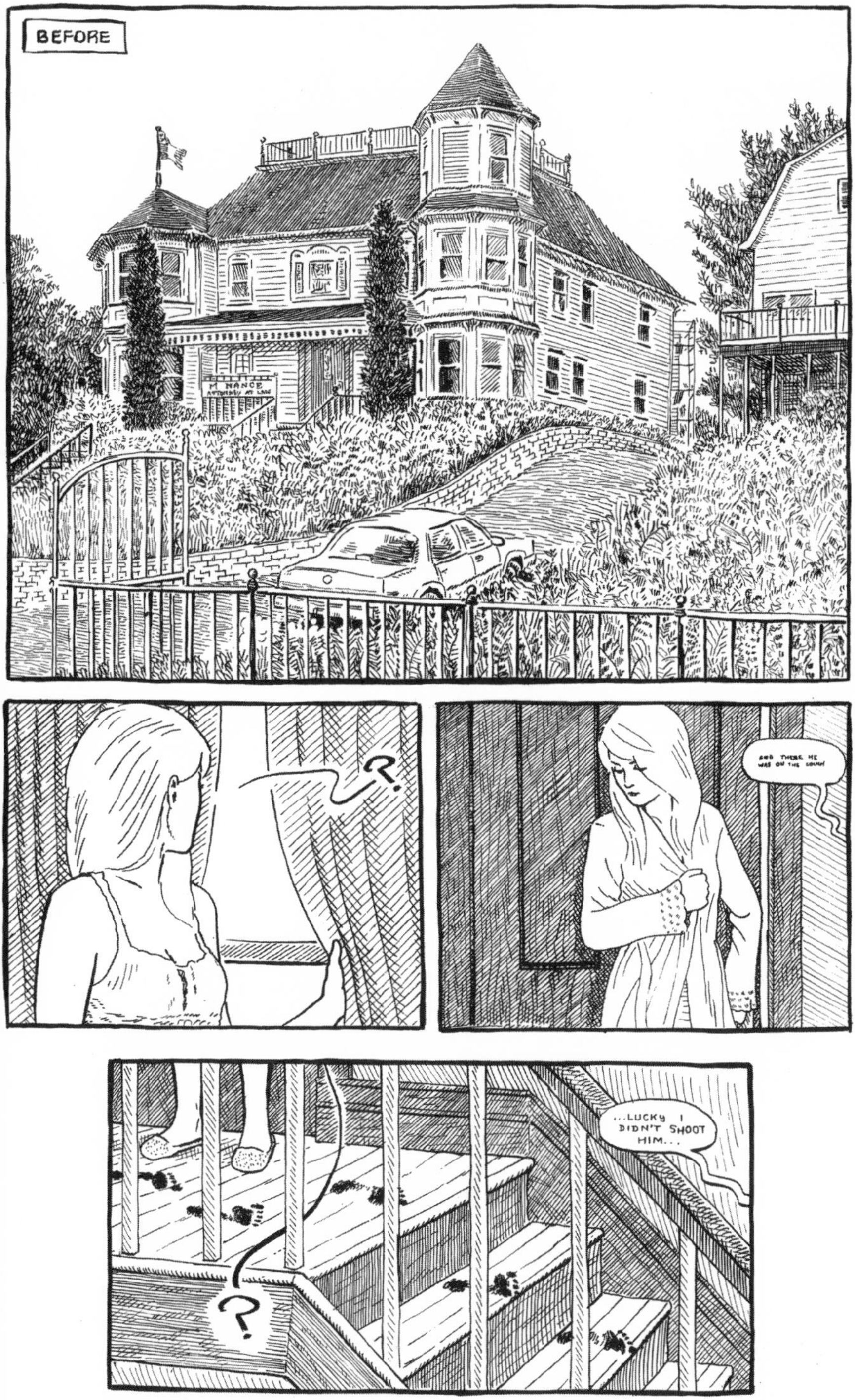
BEFORE
M NANCE
ATTORNEY AT LAW
?
AND THERE HE WAS ON THE COUCH
...LUCKY I DIDN'T SHOOT HIM...
?

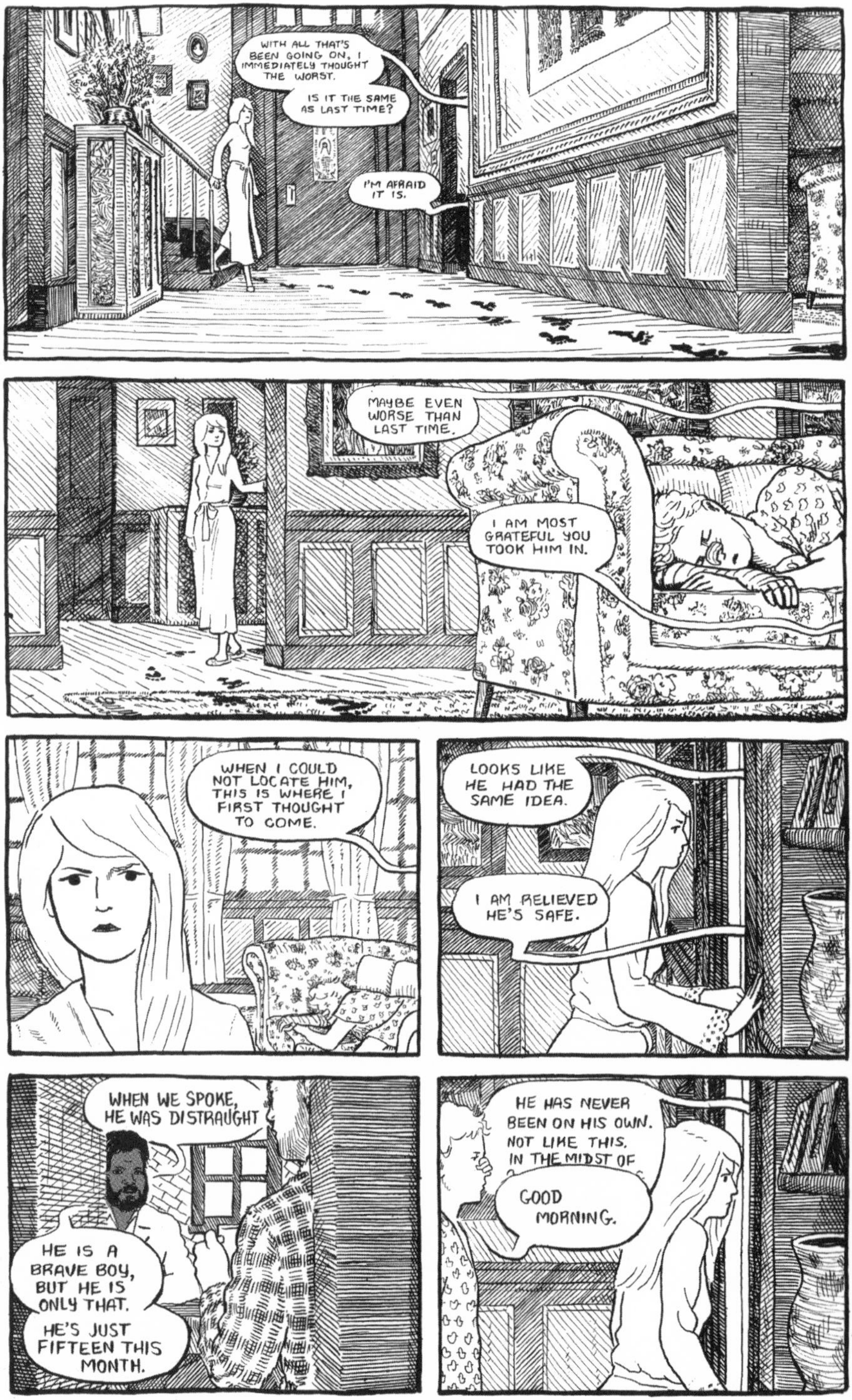
WITH ALL THAT'S BEEN GOING ON, I IMMEDIATELY THOUGHT THE WORST.
IS IT THE SAME AS LAST TIME?
I'M AFRAID IT IS.
MAYBE EVEN WORSE THAN LAST TIME.
I AM MOST GRATEFUL YOU TOOK HIM IN.
WHEN I COULD NOT LOCATE HIM, THIS IS WHERE I FIRST THOUGHT TO COME.
LOOKS LIKE HE HAD THE SAME IDEA.
I AM RELIEVED HE'S SAFE.
WHEN WE SPOKE, HE WAS DISTRAUGHT
HE IS A BRAVE BOY, BUT HE IS ONLY THAT.
HE'S JUST FIFTEEN THIS MONTH.
HE HAS NEVER BEEN ON HIS OWN. NOT LIKE THIS. IN THE MIDST OF
GOOD MORNING.

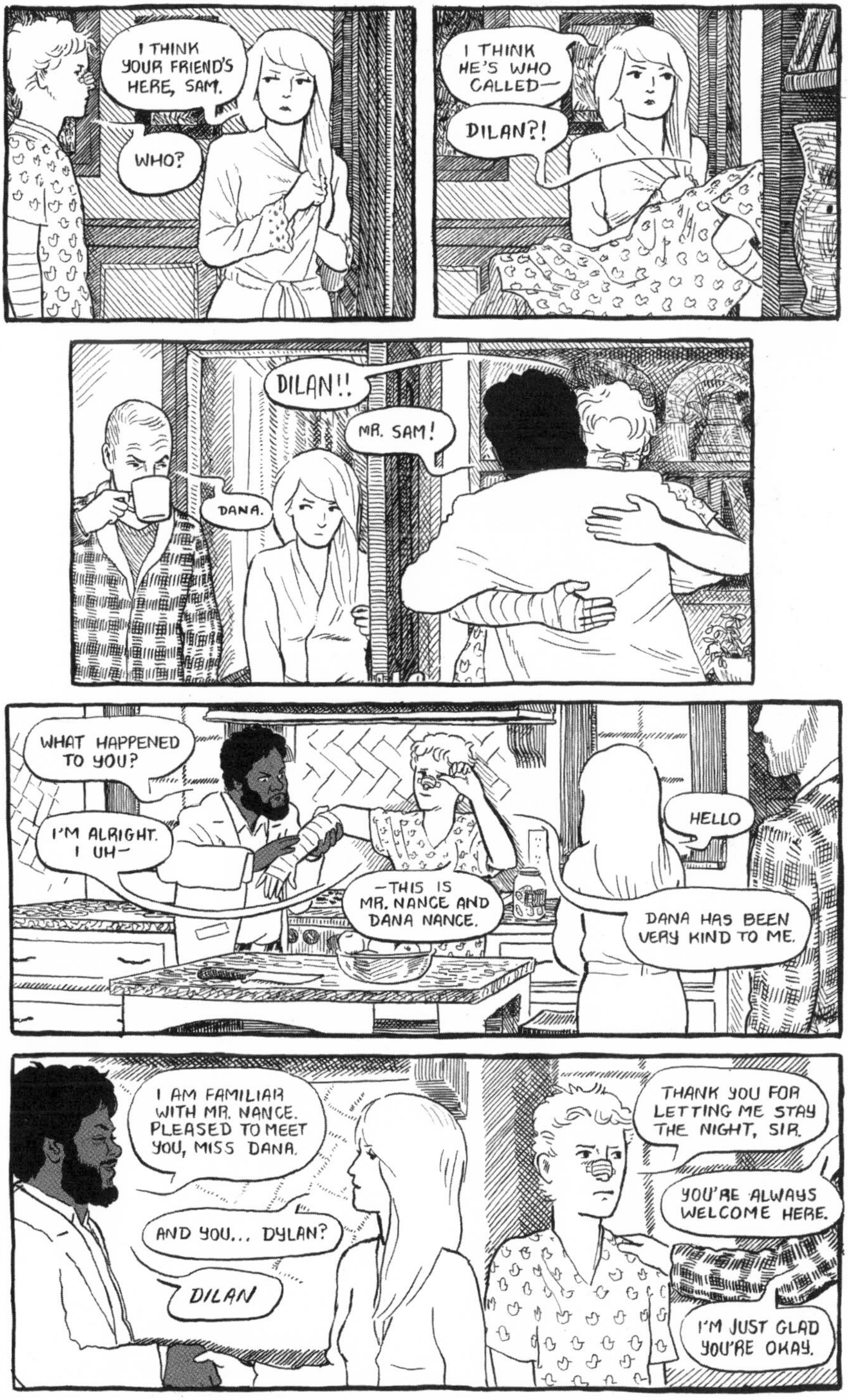

I THINK YOUR FRIEND'S HERE, SAM.
WHO?
I THINK HE'S WHO CALLED—
DILAN?!
DILAN!!
MR. SAM!
DANA.
WHAT HAPPENED TO YOU?
I'M ALRIGHT. I UH—
—THIS IS MR. NANCE AND DANA NANCE.
HELLO
DANA HAS BEEN VERY KIND TO ME.
I AM FAMILIAR WITH MR. NANCE. PLEASED TO MEET YOU, MISS DANA.
AND YOU... DYLAN?
DILAN
THANK YOU FOR LETTING ME STAY THE NIGHT, SIR.
YOU'RE ALWAYS WELCOME HERE.
I'M JUST GLAD YOU'RE OKAY.

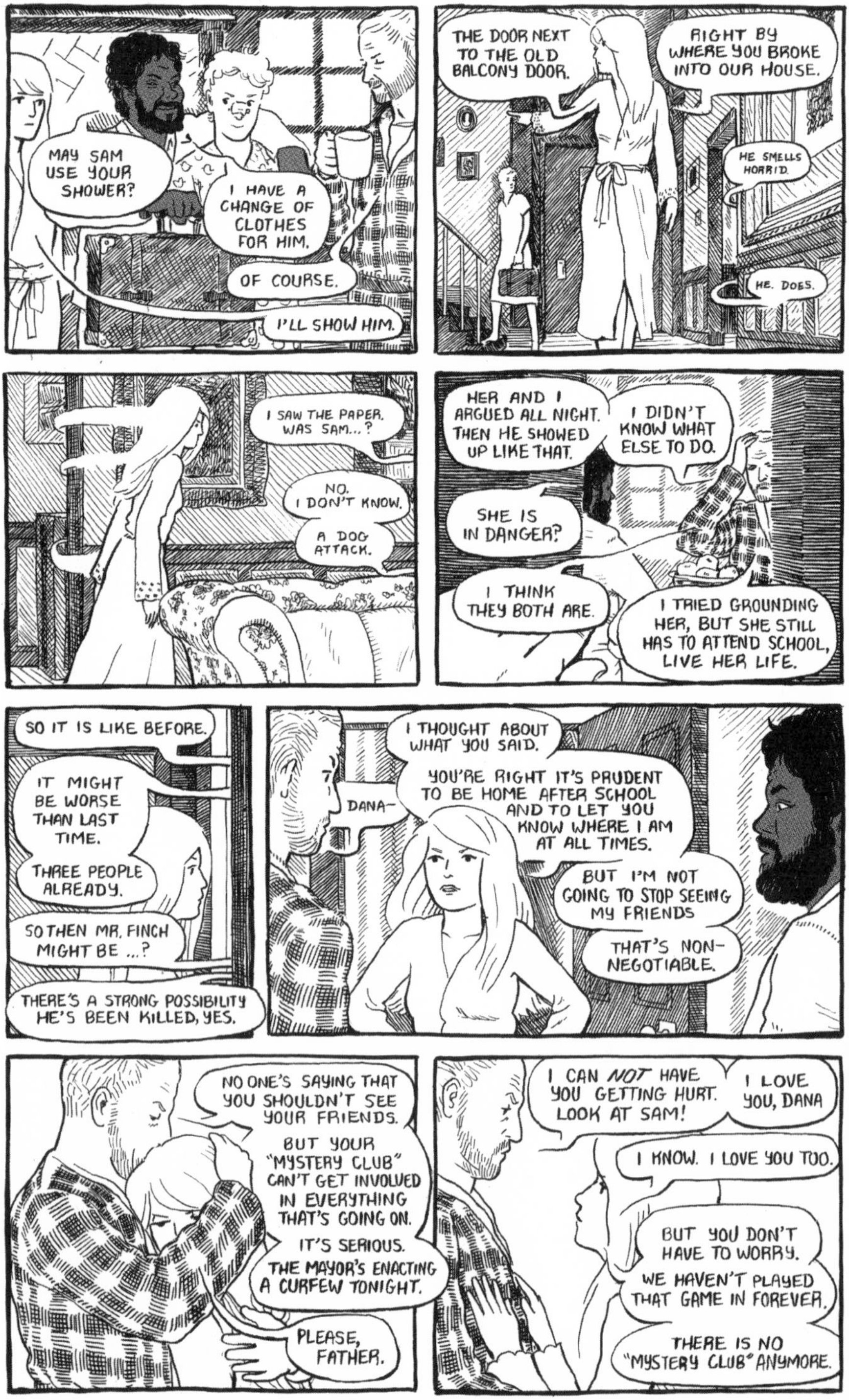
MAY SAM USE YOUR SHOWER?
I HAVE A CHANGE OF CLOTHES FOR HIM.
OF COURSE.
I'LL SHOW HIM.
THE DOOR NEXT TO THE OLD BALCONY DOOR.
RIGHT BY WHERE YOU BROKE INTO OUR HOUSE.
HE SMELLS HORRID.
HE. DOES.
I SAW THE PAPER. WAS SAM...?
NO. I DON'T KNOW.
A DOG ATTACK.
HER AND I ARGUED ALL NIGHT. THEN HE SHOWED UP LIKE THAT.
I DIDN'T KNOW WHAT ELSE TO DO.
SHE IS IN DANGER?
I THINK THEY BOTH ARE.
I TRIED GROUNDING HER, BUT SHE STILL HAS TO ATTEND SCHOOL, LIVE HER LIFE.
SO IT IS LIKE BEFORE.
IT MIGHT BE WORSE THAN LAST TIME.
THREE PEOPLE ALREADY.
SO THEN MR. FINCH MIGHT BE ...?
THERE'S A STRONG POSSIBILITY HE'S BEEN KILLED, YES.
DANA-
I THOUGHT ABOUT WHAT YOU SAID.
YOU'RE RIGHT IT'S PRUDENT TO BE HOME AFTER SCHOOL AND TO LET YOU KNOW WHERE I AM AT ALL TIMES.
BUT I'M NOT GOING TO STOP SEEING MY FRIENDS
THAT'S NON-NEGOTIABLE.
NO ONE'S SAYING THAT YOU SHOULDN'T SEE YOUR FRIENDS.
BUT YOUR "MYSTERY CLUB" CAN'T GET INVOLVED IN EVERYTHING THAT'S GOING ON.
IT'S SERIOUS.
THE MAYOR'S ENACTING A CURFEW TONIGHT.
PLEASE, FATHER.
I CAN *NOT* HAVE YOU GETTING HURT. LOOK AT SAM!
I LOVE YOU, DANA
I KNOW. I LOVE YOU TOO.
BUT YOU DON'T HAVE TO WORRY.
WE HAVEN'T PLAYED THAT GAME IN FOREVER.
THERE IS NO "MYSTERY CLUB" ANYMORE.

detective club
meeting
in theatre
erase this message

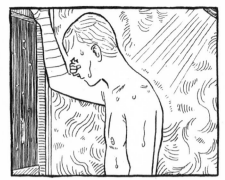

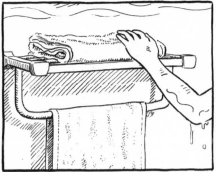

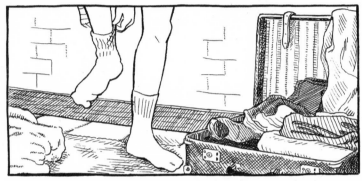

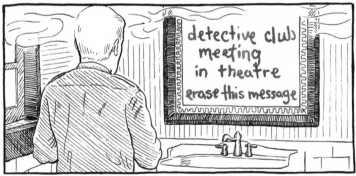

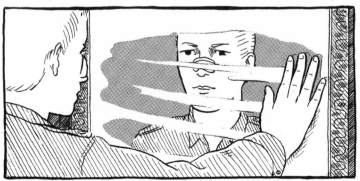

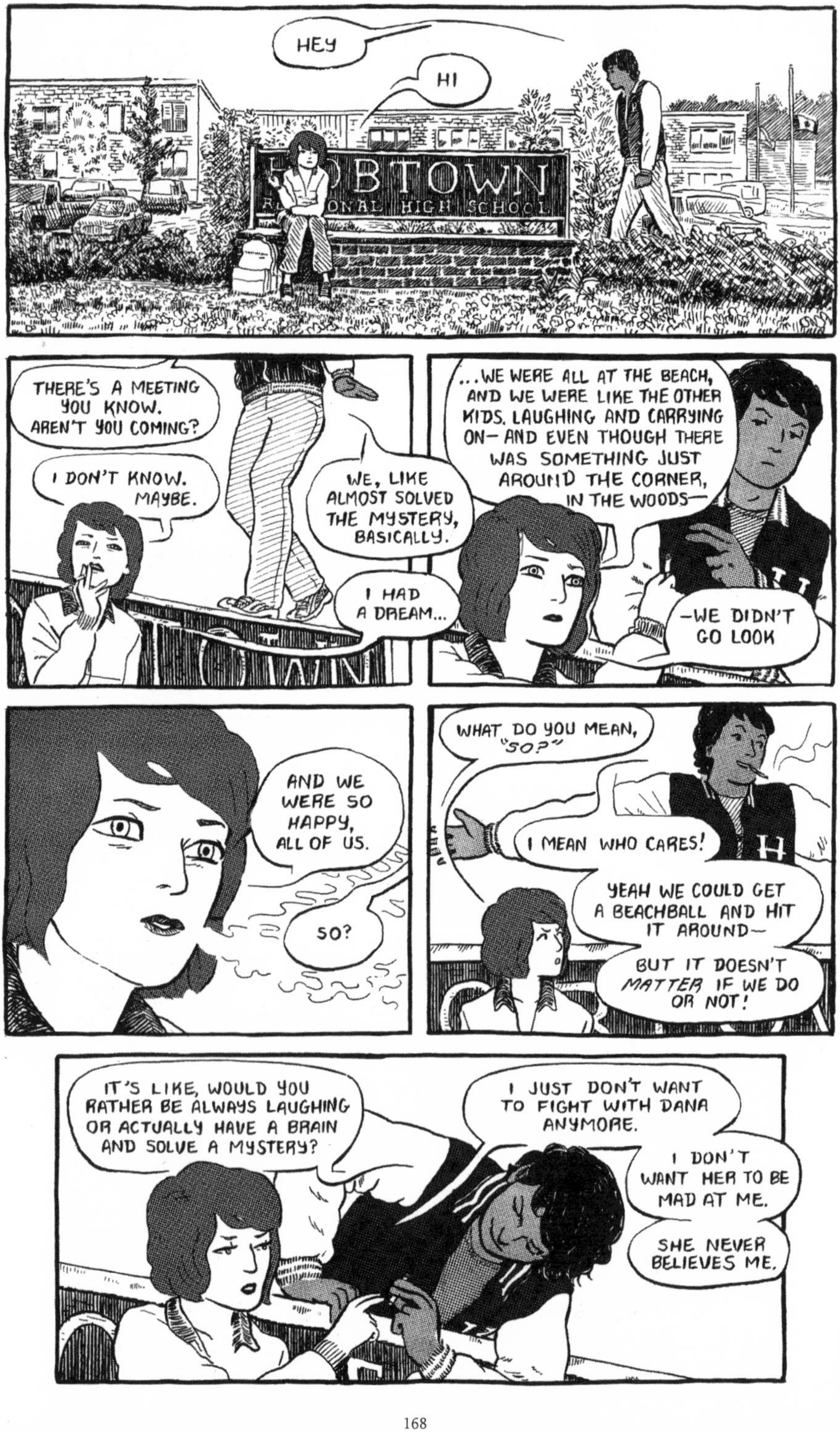
HEY
HI
OBTOWN
ONAL HIGH SCHOOL
THERE'S A MEETING YOU KNOW. AREN'T YOU COMING?
I DON'T KNOW. MAYBE.
WE, LIKE ALMOST SOLVED THE MYSTERY, BASICALLY.
I HAD A DREAM...
...WE WERE ALL AT THE BEACH, AND WE WERE LIKE THE OTHER KIDS, LAUGHING AND CARRYING ON— AND EVEN THOUGH THERE WAS SOMETHING JUST AROUND THE CORNER, IN THE WOODS—
—WE DIDN'T GO LOOK
AND WE WERE SO HAPPY, ALL OF US.
SO?
WHAT DO YOU MEAN, "SO?"
I MEAN WHO CARES!
YEAH WE COULD GET A BEACHBALL AND HIT IT AROUND—
BUT IT DOESN'T MATTER IF WE DO OR NOT!
IT'S LIKE, WOULD YOU RATHER BE ALWAYS LAUGHING OR ACTUALLY HAVE A BRAIN AND SOLVE A MYSTERY?
I JUST DON'T WANT TO FIGHT WITH DANA ANYMORE.
I DON'T WANT HER TO BE MAD AT ME.
SHE NEVER BELIEVES ME.

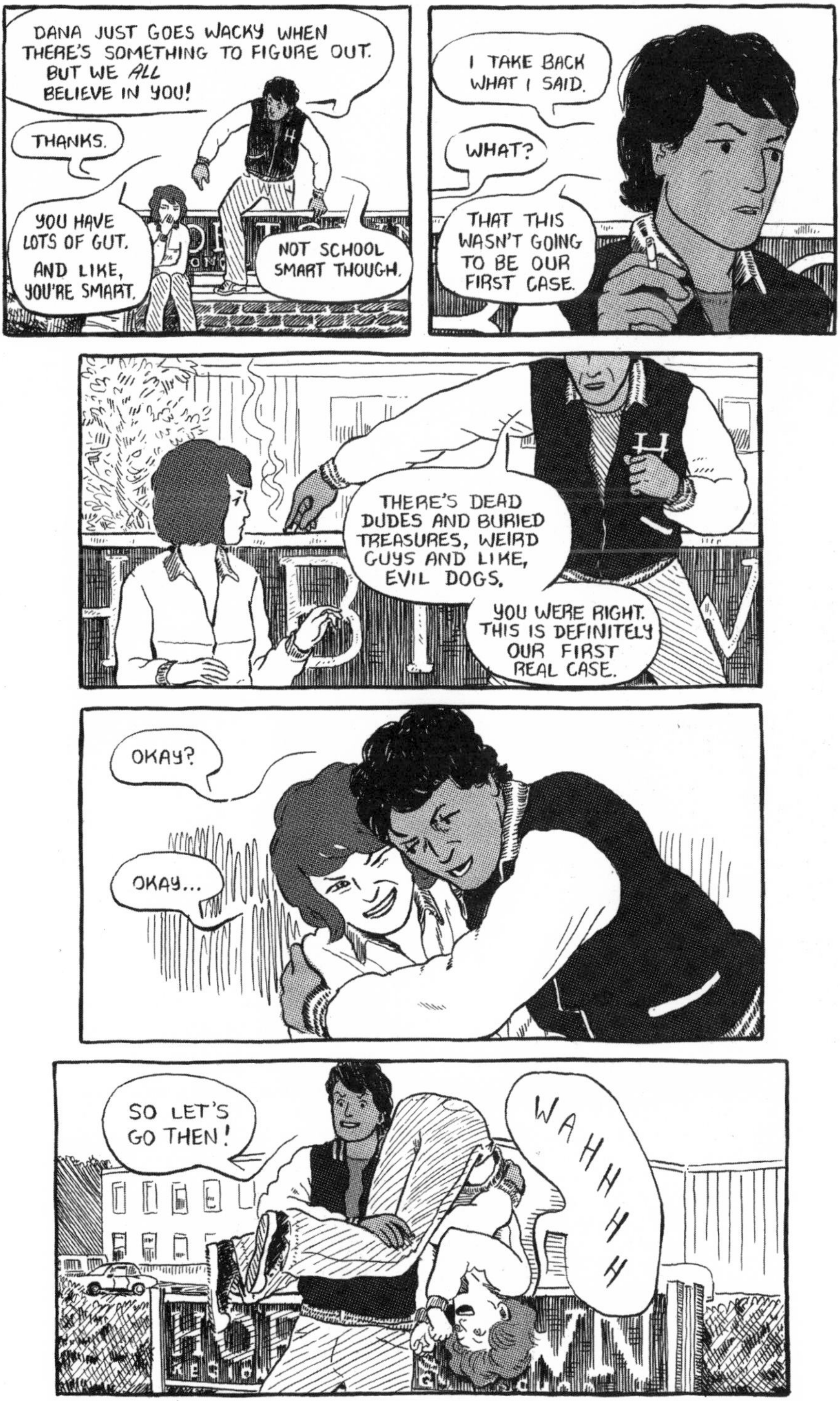
DANA JUST GOES WACKY WHEN THERE'S SOMETHING TO FIGURE OUT. BUT WE ALL BELIEVE IN YOU!
THANKS.
YOU HAVE LOTS OF GUT.
AND LIKE, YOU'RE SMART.
NOT SCHOOL SMART THOUGH.
I TAKE BACK WHAT I SAID.
WHAT?
THAT THIS WASN'T GOING TO BE OUR FIRST CASE.
THERE'S DEAD DUDES AND BURIED TREASURES, WEIRD GUYS AND LIKE, EVIL DOGS.
YOU WERE RIGHT. THIS IS DEFINITELY OUR FIRST REAL CASE.
OKAY?
OKAY...
SO LET'S GO THEN!
WAHHHHH

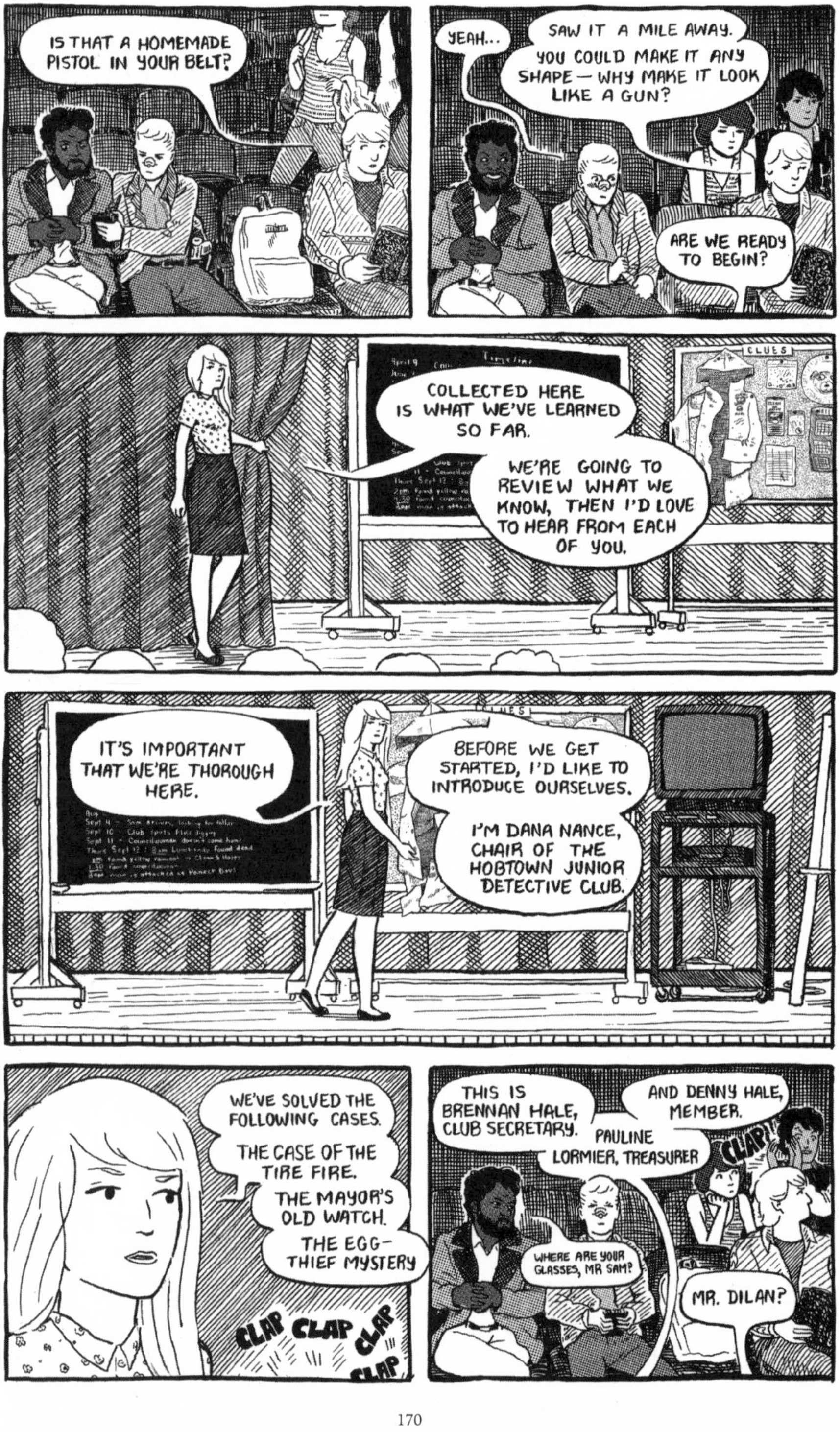
IS THAT A HOMEMADE PISTOL IN YOUR BELT?
YEAH...
SAW IT A MILE AWAY.
YOU COULD MAKE IT ANY SHAPE— WHY MAKE IT LOOK LIKE A GUN?
ARE WE READY TO BEGIN?
CLUES
COLLECTED HERE IS WHAT WE'VE LEARNED SO FAR.
WE'RE GOING TO REVIEW WHAT WE KNOW, THEN I'D LOVE TO HEAR FROM EACH OF YOU.
IT'S IMPORTANT THAT WE'RE THOROUGH HERE.
BEFORE WE GET STARTED, I'D LIKE TO INTRODUCE OURSELVES.
I'M DANA NANCE, CHAIR OF THE HOBTOWN JUNIOR DETECTIVE CLUB.
WE'VE SOLVED THE FOLLOWING CASES.
THE CASE OF THE TIRE FIRE.
THE MAYOR'S OLD WATCH.
THE EGG-THIEF MYSTERY
CLAP CLAP CLAP CLAP
THIS IS BRENNAN HALE, CLUB SECRETARY.
AND DENNY HALE, MEMBER.
PAULINE LORMIER, TREASURER
CLAP!
WHERE ARE YOUR GLASSES, MR SAM?
MR. DILAN?

YES, MY NAME IS DILAN SINHA, INTERNATIONAL OPERATIONS MANAGER, FINCH AVIATION.

THANK YOU FOR HAVING ME.

SAMUEL FINCH, ASSISTANT, FINCH AVIATION.

I'M PUTTING FORWARD A MOTION TO OFFER SAM AND MR. SINHA PROVISIONAL MEMBERSHIP.

ALL IN FAVOUR?

LET THE RECORD SHOW THE VOTE WAS UNANIMOUS.

THANK YOU, BRENNAN.

ONE LAST MOTION...

THIS CASE HAS GONE FROM A MISSING PERSON TO A MURDER. THINGS HAVE BECOME MUCH MORE SERIOUS, AND DANGEROUS.

ALL IN FAVOUR OF CEASING THIS INVESTIGATION.

Timeline

April 9 - Callie Birdman reported missing by church
June 30 - Dale Harper missing from church
July 28 - Farmhouse Job
July 29 -
Aug 1st - ...mer commits suicide
Aug 3rd - ...missing
Aug 10
Aug - Max Finch goes into
Sept - Sam arrives, looking for tw...
Sept 10 - Club spots Flice digging...
Sept 11 - Councilwoman doesn't com...
Thurs Sept 12 : 8am Lunchlady found dead
pm found yellow raincoat in Clean & Happy
1:30 found councilwoman
3pm man is attached at Pioneer Days

LET THE RECORD SAY, NO WAY, JOSE!

THANK YOU, DENNY.

OUR TIMELINE STARTS SIX MONTHS AGO WHEN THE FIRST CLEAN & HAPPY STAFF— CALLIE BIRDMAN—WENT MISSING, UP UNTIL TODAY.

I'VE JUST ADDED THESE: 58 YEAR-OLD COUNCILWOMAN COLLETTE JOUBERT REPORTED MISSING YESTERDAY.

AND: LOCAL MAN TERRY BAGGS WAS RESCUED FROM A DUNK TANK AFTER HE FELL IN AND BECAME TRAPPED.

BEFORE THAT, FLICE IS SPOTTED AT THE FARMHOUSE WITH THREE DOGS.

BEFORE THAT, LUNCHLADY IS FOUND DEAD.

BEFORE THAT, FLICE IS SPOTTED NEAR THE POINT.

MAX FINCH IS SPOTTED TALKING TO A MAN IN A YELLOW RAINCOAT TWO WEEKS BEFORE THAT, WHICH IS THE LAST TIME HE'S SEEN.

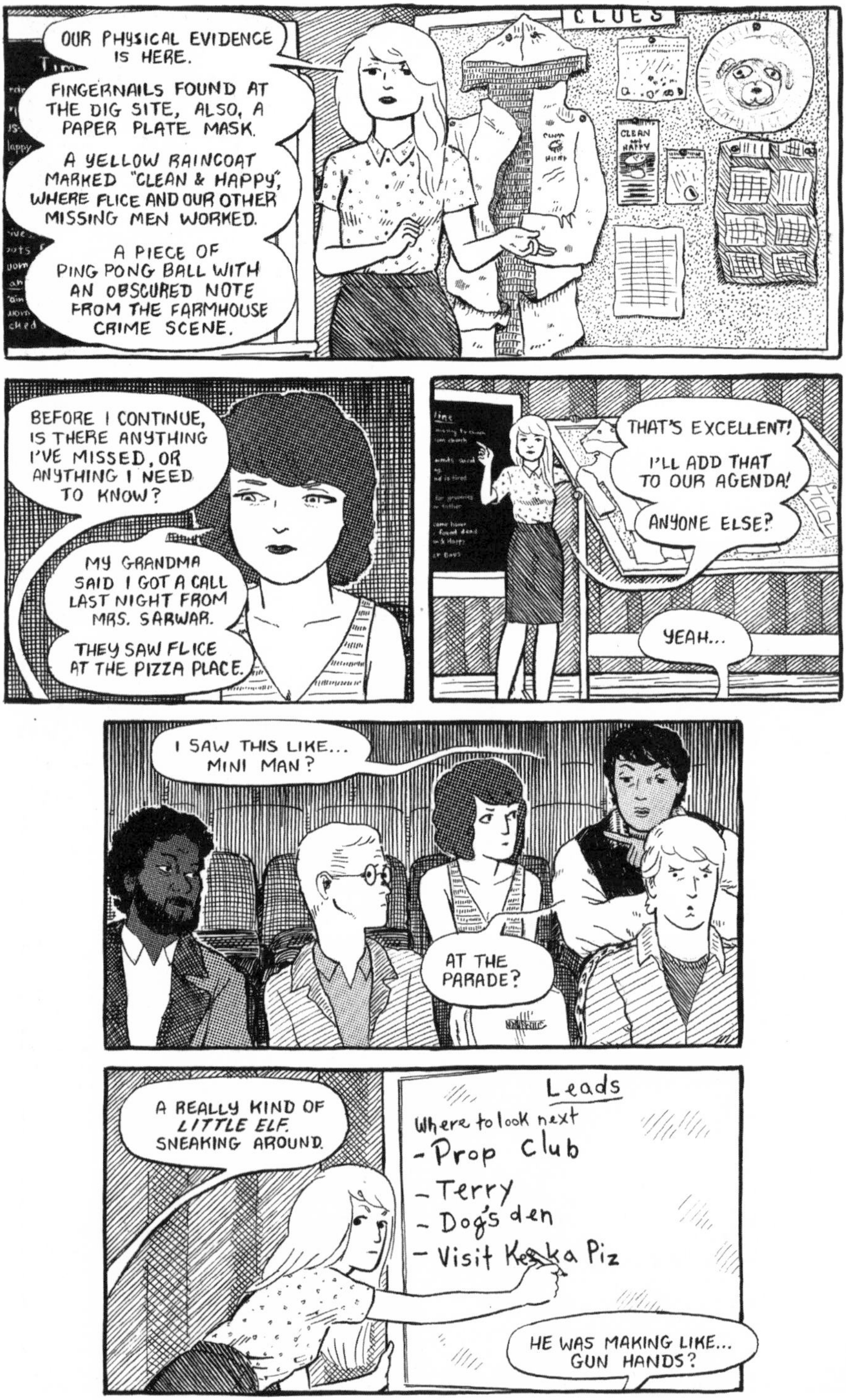
CLUES
OUR PHYSICAL EVIDENCE IS HERE.
FINGERNAILS FOUND AT THE DIG SITE, ALSO, A PAPER PLATE MASK.
A YELLOW RAINCOAT MARKED "CLEAN & HAPPY", WHERE FLICE AND OUR OTHER MISSING MEN WORKED.
A PIECE OF PING PONG BALL WITH AN OBSCURED NOTE FROM THE FARMHOUSE CRIME SCENE.
CLEAN HAPPY
BEFORE I CONTINUE, IS THERE ANYTHING I'VE MISSED, OR ANYTHING I NEED TO KNOW?
MY GRANDMA SAID I GOT A CALL LAST NIGHT FROM MRS. SARWAR.
THEY SAW FLICE AT THE PIZZA PLACE.
THAT'S EXCELLENT!
I'LL ADD THAT TO OUR AGENDA!
ANYONE ELSE?
YEAH...
I SAW THIS LIKE... MINI MAN?
AT THE PARADE?
A REALLY KIND OF *LITTLE ELF.* SNEAKING AROUND.
Leads
Where to look next
- Prop Club
- Terry
- Dog's den
- Visit Ke ka Piz
HE WAS MAKING LIKE... GUN HANDS?

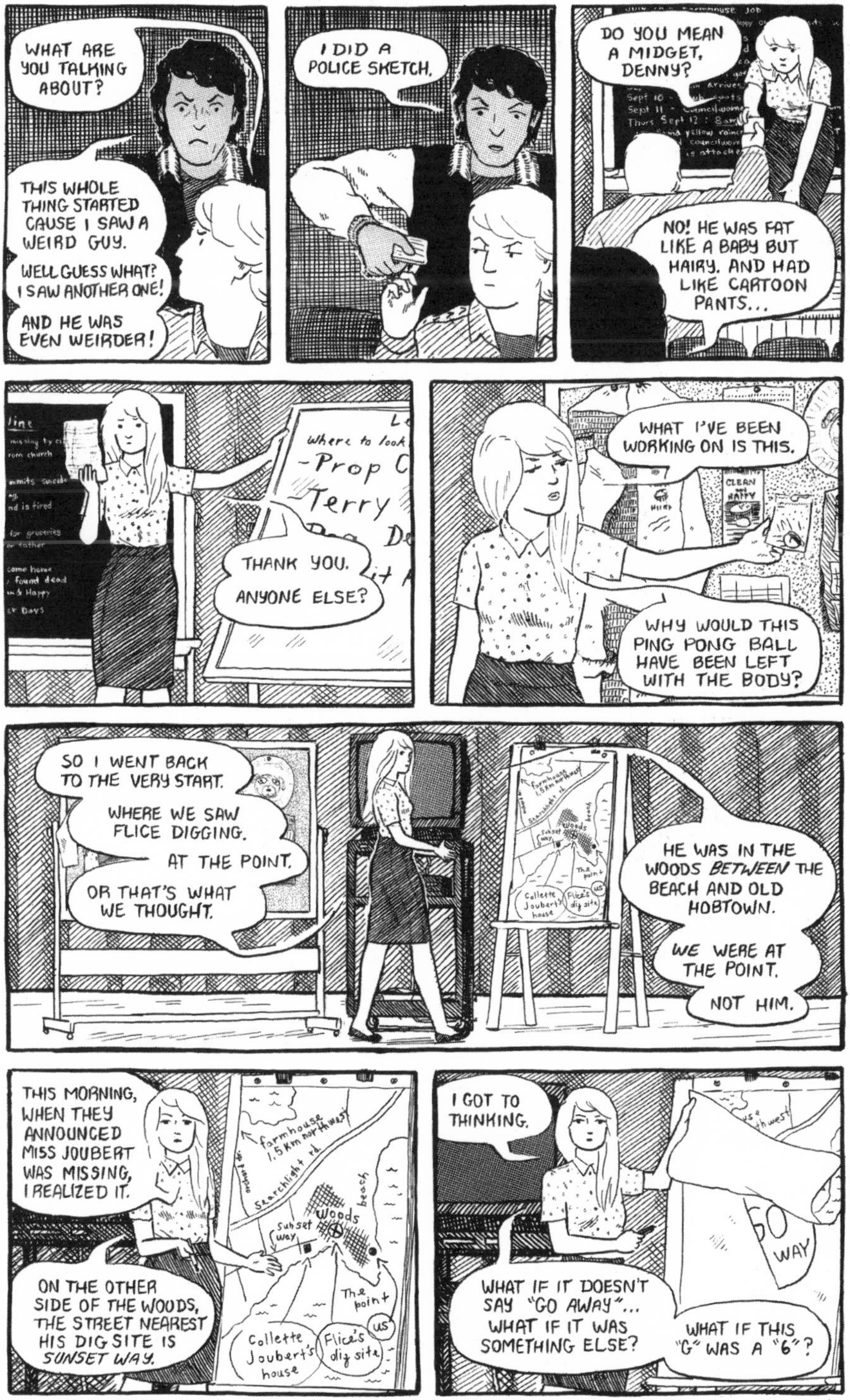

WHAT ARE YOU TALKING ABOUT?
THIS WHOLE THING STARTED CAUSE I SAW A WEIRD GUY.
WELL GUESS WHAT? I SAW ANOTHER ONE!
AND HE WAS EVEN WEIRDER!
I DID A POLICE SKETCH.
DO YOU MEAN A MIDGET, DENNY?
NO! HE WAS FAT LIKE A BABY BUT HAIRY. AND HAD LIKE CARTOON PANTS...
Where to look
THANK YOU.
ANYONE ELSE?
WHAT I'VE BEEN WORKING ON IS THIS.
WHY WOULD THIS PING PONG BALL HAVE BEEN LEFT WITH THE BODY?
SO I WENT BACK TO THE VERY START.
WHERE WE SAW FLICE DIGGING.
AT THE POINT.
OR THAT'S WHAT WE THOUGHT.
HE WAS IN THE WOODS *BETWEEN* THE BEACH AND OLD HOBTOWN.
WE WERE AT THE POINT.
NOT HIM.
THIS MORNING, WHEN THEY ANNOUNCED MISS JOUBERT WAS MISSING, I REALIZED IT.
farmhouse 1.5 Km northwest
Searchlight rd.
Woods
beach
Sunset way
The point
us
Collette Joubert's house
Flice's dig site
ON THE OTHER SIDE OF THE WOODS, THE STREET NEAREST HIS DIG SITE IS *SUNSET WAY.*
I GOT TO THINKING.
WHAT IF IT DOESN'T SAY "GO AWAY"... WHAT IF IT WAS SOMETHING ELSE?
WHAT IF THIS "G" WAS A "6"?

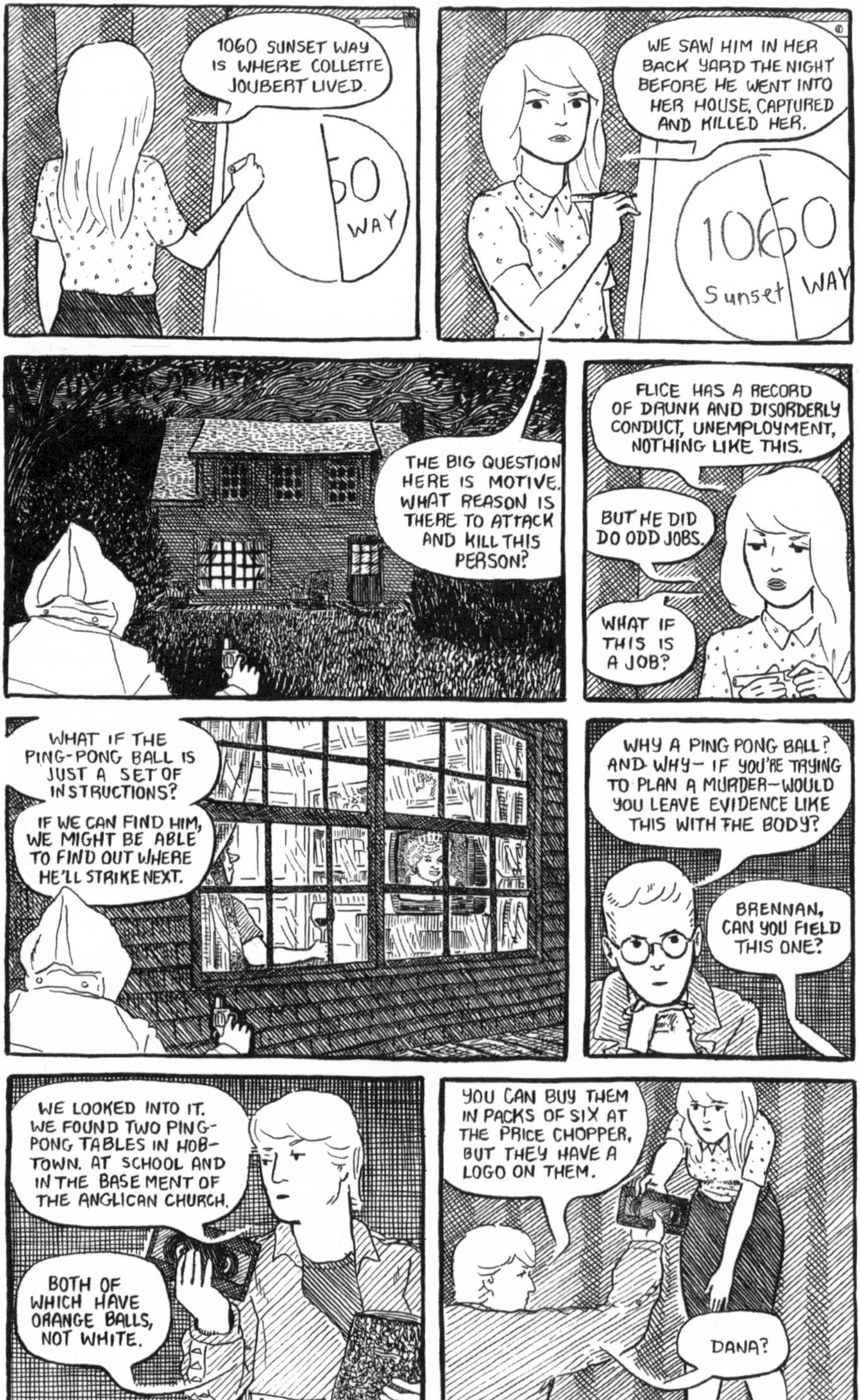
1060 SUNSET WAY IS WHERE COLLETTE JOUBERT LIVED.
60 WAY
WE SAW HIM IN HER BACK YARD THE NIGHT BEFORE HE WENT INTO HER HOUSE, CAPTURED AND KILLED HER.
1060 Sunset WAY
THE BIG QUESTION HERE IS MOTIVE. WHAT REASON IS THERE TO ATTACK AND KILL THIS PERSON?
FLICE HAS A RECORD OF DRUNK AND DISORDERLY CONDUCT, UNEMPLOYMENT, NOTHING LIKE THIS.
BUT HE DID DO ODD JOBS.
WHAT IF THIS IS A JOB?
WHAT IF THE PING-PONG BALL IS JUST A SET OF INSTRUCTIONS?
IF WE CAN FIND HIM, WE MIGHT BE ABLE TO FIND OUT WHERE HE'LL STRIKE NEXT.
WHY A PING PONG BALL? AND WHY– IF YOU'RE TRYING TO PLAN A MURDER–WOULD YOU LEAVE EVIDENCE LIKE THIS WITH THE BODY?
BRENNAN, CAN YOU FIELD THIS ONE?
WE LOOKED INTO IT. WE FOUND TWO PING-PONG TABLES IN HOB-TOWN. AT SCHOOL AND IN THE BASEMENT OF THE ANGLICAN CHURCH.
BOTH OF WHICH HAVE ORANGE BALLS, NOT WHITE.
YOU CAN BUY THEM IN PACKS OF SIX AT THE PRICE CHOPPER, BUT THEY HAVE A LOGO ON THEM.
DANA?

THANK YOU.

TO ANSWER YOUR QUESTION, SAM, WE NEED TO GO BACK TO THE CLEAN & HAPPY AND THAT RAINCOAT.

THE ONLY THING THAT CONNECTED YOUR FATHER TO THIS.

UNTIL NOW.

I WENT TO THE HALL OF RECORDS TO FIND OUT ABOUT THE CLEAN & HAPPY PROPERTY...

...IT WAS BOUGHT BY SOMETHING CALLED HOBTOWN COMMUNITY OUTREACH.

WARR~RRRRR

WHEN WE LEARNED THE PROPELLER CLUB GAMES ROOM ONCE HAD TABLE TENNIS, WE DECIDED TO LOOK INTO IT.

WE FOUND THIS AT THE LIBRARY.

HARD WORK. DEDICATION. TOGETHERNESS. FAMILY.

THESE ARE THE THINGS WE LOOK FOR IN OUR COMMUNITIES

MY NAME IS MAX FINCH OF AVIATION, FOUNDER OF THE PROPELLER CLUB.

THE PROPELLER CLUB IS...

IT SOUNDS SO FAMILIAR. SO IT'S A... SOCIAL CLUB HERE IN TOWN?

THIS MUST BE ONE OF HIS CHARITY ORGANIZATIONS.

WE HAVE TOO MANY TO COUNT.

YOUR DAD WAS GOING TO OPEN A FACTORY IN HOBTOWN.

THAT'S WHY HE STARTED IT.

HE NEVER WENT THROUGH WITH THE FACTORY, BUT THE CLUB IS STILL HERE.

HOBTOWN COMMUNITY OUTREACH IS FUNDED BY THE PROPELLER CLUB,

WHICH IS FUNDED BY MAX FINCH.

ALONG WITH PLENTY ELSE IN TOWN.

||PAUSE

CLICK

||PAUSE

THIS TAPE NAMES HOBTOWN POLICE AS A RECIPIENT OF SIGNIFICANT DONATIONS, TOO.

AND THERE'S ONE LAST THING. BRENNAN?

THANKS.

SO, UH, AFTER OUR MEETING AT THE TREEHOUSE, I HAD A STAKEOUT.

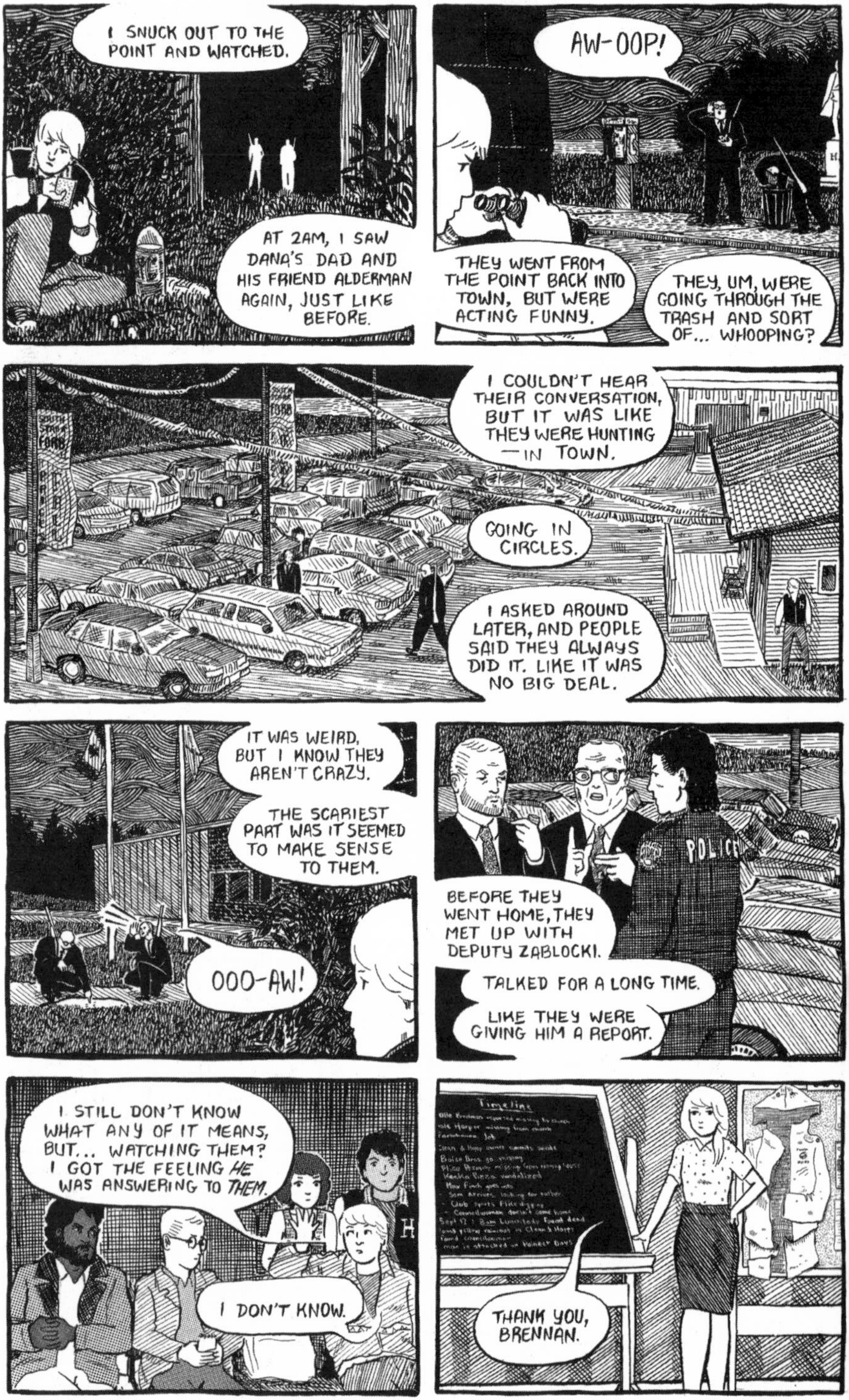
I SNUCK OUT TO THE POINT AND WATCHED.
AT 2AM, I SAW DANA'S DAD AND HIS FRIEND ALDERMAN AGAIN, JUST LIKE BEFORE.
AW-OOP!
THEY WENT FROM THE POINT BACK INTO TOWN, BUT WERE ACTING FUNNY.
THEY, UM, WERE GOING THROUGH THE TRASH AND SORT OF... WHOOPING?
I COULDN'T HEAR THEIR CONVERSATION, BUT IT WAS LIKE THEY WERE HUNTING —IN TOWN.
GOING IN CIRCLES.
I ASKED AROUND LATER, AND PEOPLE SAID THEY ALWAYS DID IT. LIKE IT WAS NO BIG DEAL.
IT WAS WEIRD, BUT I KNOW THEY AREN'T CRAZY.
THE SCARIEST PART WAS IT SEEMED TO MAKE SENSE TO THEM.
OOO-AW!
POLICE
BEFORE THEY WENT HOME, THEY MET UP WITH DEPUTY ZABLOCKI.
TALKED FOR A LONG TIME.
LIKE THEY WERE GIVING HIM A REPORT.
I STILL DON'T KNOW WHAT ANY OF IT MEANS, BUT... WATCHING THEM? I GOT THE FEELING HE WAS ANSWERING TO THEM.
I DON'T KNOW.
Timeline
THANK YOU, BRENNAN.

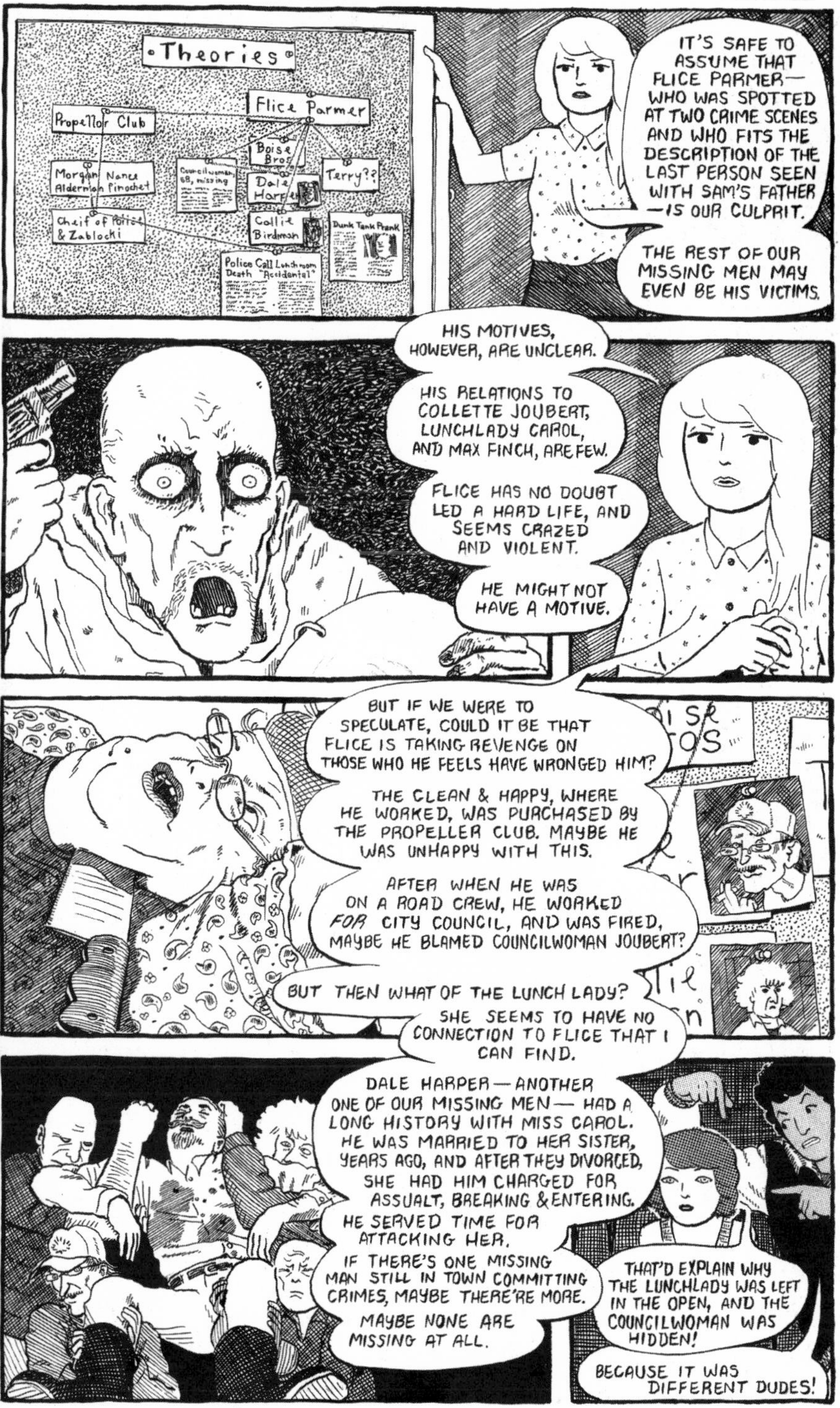

Theories
Propellor Club
Flice Parmer
Boise Bros
Morgan Nance
Alderman Pinochet
Councilwoman, 68, missing
Dale Harper
Terry??
Cheif of Police & Zablocki
Collie Birdman
Dunk Tank Frank
Police Call Lunchroom Death "Accidental"
IT'S SAFE TO ASSUME THAT FLICE PARMER— WHO WAS SPOTTED AT TWO CRIME SCENES AND WHO FITS THE DESCRIPTION OF THE LAST PERSON SEEN WITH SAM'S FATHER —IS OUR CULPRIT.
THE REST OF OUR MISSING MEN MAY EVEN BE HIS VICTIMS.
HIS MOTIVES, HOWEVER, ARE UNCLEAR.
HIS RELATIONS TO COLLETTE JOUBERT, LUNCHLADY CAROL, AND MAX FINCH, ARE FEW.
FLICE HAS NO DOUBT LED A HARD LIFE, AND SEEMS CRAZED AND VIOLENT.
HE MIGHT NOT HAVE A MOTIVE.
BUT IF WE WERE TO SPECULATE, COULD IT BE THAT FLICE IS TAKING REVENGE ON THOSE WHO HE FEELS HAVE WRONGED HIM?
THE CLEAN & HAPPY, WHERE HE WORKED, WAS PURCHASED BY THE PROPELLER CLUB. MAYBE HE WAS UNHAPPY WITH THIS.
AFTER WHEN HE WAS ON A ROAD CREW, HE WORKED FOR CITY COUNCIL, AND WAS FIRED, MAYBE HE BLAMED COUNCILWOMAN JOUBERT?
BUT THEN WHAT OF THE LUNCH LADY?
SHE SEEMS TO HAVE NO CONNECTION TO FLICE THAT I CAN FIND.
DALE HARPER— ANOTHER ONE OF OUR MISSING MEN— HAD A LONG HISTORY WITH MISS CAROL. HE WAS MARRIED TO HER SISTER, YEARS AGO, AND AFTER THEY DIVORCED, SHE HAD HIM CHARGED FOR ASSUALT, BREAKING & ENTERING.
HE SERVED TIME FOR ATTACKING HER.
IF THERE'S ONE MISSING MAN STILL IN TOWN COMMITTING CRIMES, MAYBE THERE'RE MORE.
MAYBE NONE ARE MISSING AT ALL.
THAT'D EXPLAIN WHY THE LUNCHLADY WAS LEFT IN THE OPEN, AND THE COUNCILWOMAN WAS HIDDEN!
BECAUSE IT WAS DIFFERENT DUDES!

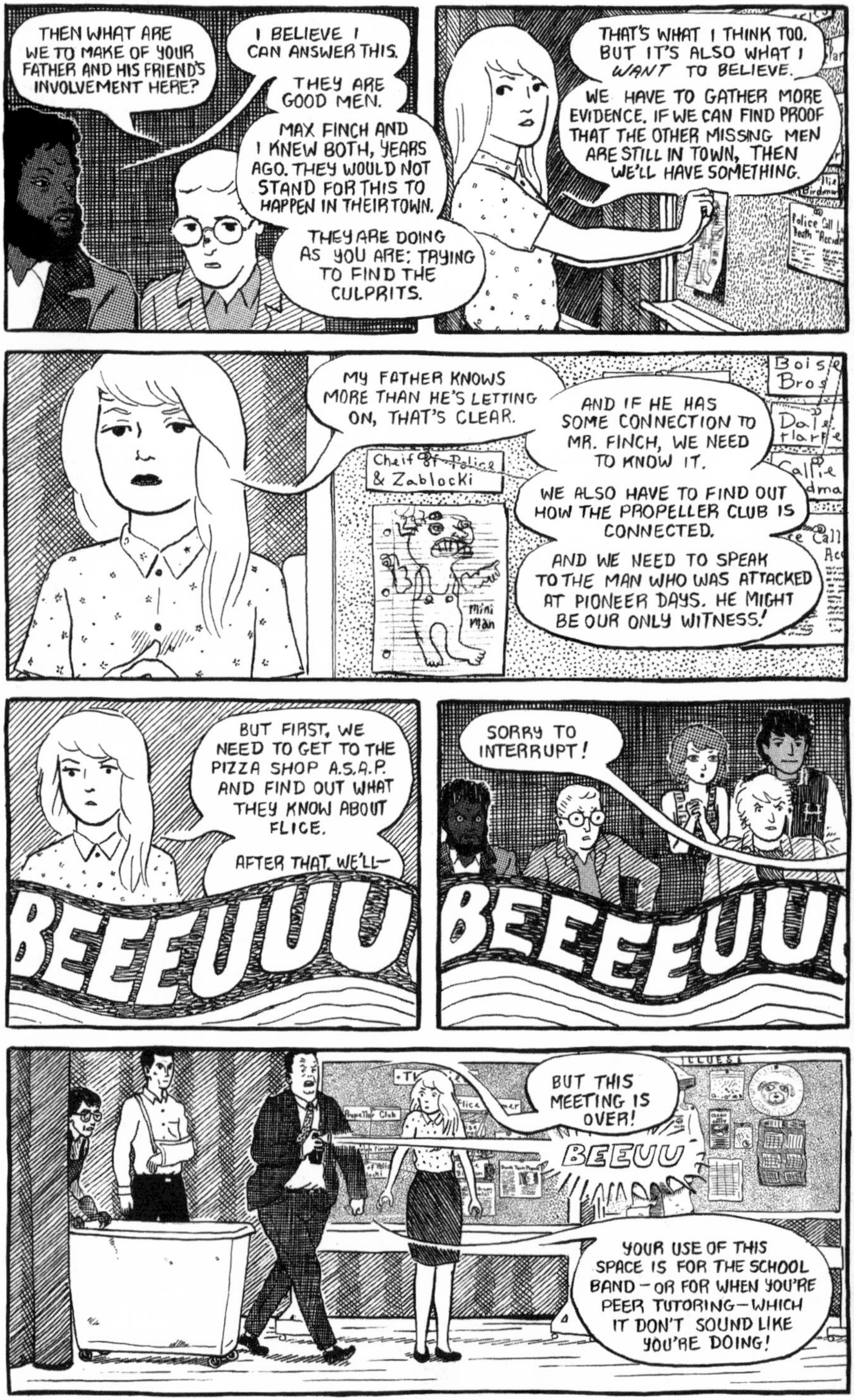
THEN WHAT ARE WE TO MAKE OF YOUR FATHER AND HIS FRIEND'S INVOLVEMENT HERE?
I BELIEVE I CAN ANSWER THIS.
THEY ARE GOOD MEN.
MAX FINCH AND I KNEW BOTH, YEARS AGO. THEY WOULD NOT STAND FOR THIS TO HAPPEN IN THEIR TOWN.
THEY ARE DOING AS YOU ARE: TRYING TO FIND THE CULPRITS.
THAT'S WHAT I THINK TOO. BUT IT'S ALSO WHAT I *WANT* TO BELIEVE.
WE HAVE TO GATHER MORE EVIDENCE. IF WE CAN FIND PROOF THAT THE OTHER MISSING MEN ARE STILL IN TOWN, THEN WE'LL HAVE SOMETHING.
MY FATHER KNOWS MORE THAN HE'S LETTING ON, THAT'S CLEAR.
AND IF HE HAS SOME CONNECTION TO MR. FINCH, WE NEED TO KNOW IT.
WE ALSO HAVE TO FIND OUT HOW THE PROPELLER CLUB IS CONNECTED.
AND WE NEED TO SPEAK TO THE MAN WHO WAS ATTACKED AT PIONEER DAYS. HE MIGHT BE OUR ONLY WITNESS!
Chief of Police & Zablocki
Mini Man
BUT FIRST, WE NEED TO GET TO THE PIZZA SHOP A.S.A.P. AND FIND OUT WHAT THEY KNOW ABOUT FLICE.
AFTER THAT, WE'LL—
BEEEUUU
SORRY TO INTERRUPT!
BEEEEEUUU
BUT THIS MEETING IS OVER!
BEEUU
YOUR USE OF THIS SPACE IS FOR THE SCHOOL BAND — OR FOR WHEN YOU'RE PEER TUTORING — WHICH IT DON'T SOUND LIKE YOU'RE DOING!

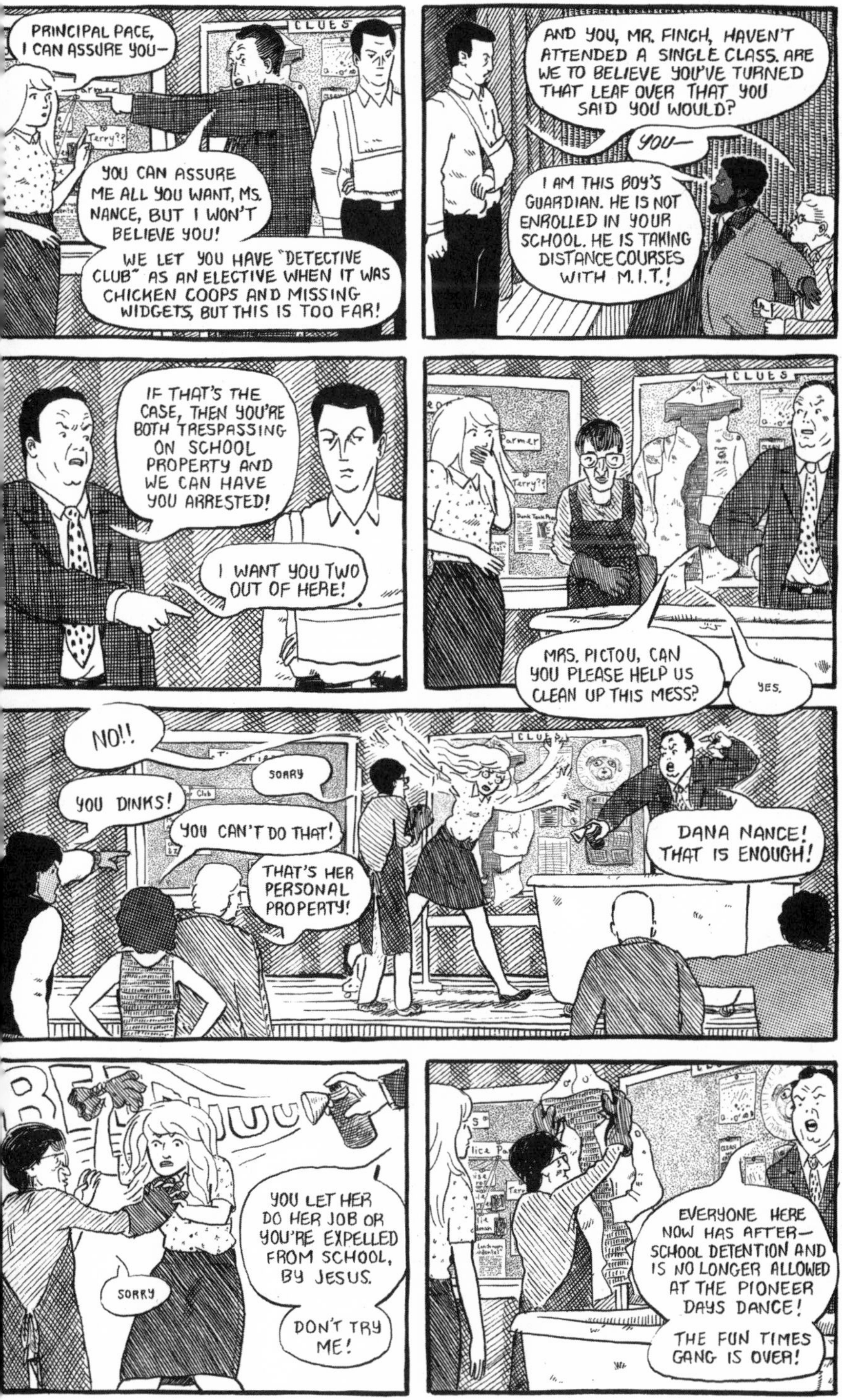
PRINCIPAL PACE, I CAN ASSURE YOU—
YOU CAN ASSURE ME ALL YOU WANT, MS. NANCE, BUT I WON'T BELIEVE YOU!
WE LET YOU HAVE "DETECTIVE CLUB" AS AN ELECTIVE WHEN IT WAS CHICKEN COOPS AND MISSING WIDGETS, BUT THIS IS TOO FAR!
AND YOU, MR. FINCH, HAVEN'T ATTENDED A SINGLE CLASS. ARE WE TO BELIEVE YOU'VE TURNED THAT LEAF OVER THAT YOU SAID YOU WOULD?
YOU—
I AM THIS BOY'S GUARDIAN. HE IS NOT ENROLLED IN YOUR SCHOOL. HE IS TAKING DISTANCE COURSES WITH M.I.T.!
IF THAT'S THE CASE, THEN YOU'RE BOTH TRESPASSING ON SCHOOL PROPERTY AND WE CAN HAVE YOU ARRESTED!
I WANT YOU TWO OUT OF HERE!
MRS. PICTOU, CAN YOU PLEASE HELP US CLEAN UP THIS MESS?
YES.
NO!!
SORRY
YOU DINKS!
YOU CAN'T DO THAT!
THAT'S HER PERSONAL PROPERTY!
DANA NANCE! THAT IS ENOUGH!
YOU LET HER DO HER JOB OR YOU'RE EXPELLED FROM SCHOOL, BY JESUS.
SORRY
DON'T TRY ME!
EVERYONE HERE NOW HAS AFTER-SCHOOL DETENTION AND IS NO LONGER ALLOWED AT THE PIONEER DAYS DANCE!
THE FUN TIMES GANG IS OVER!

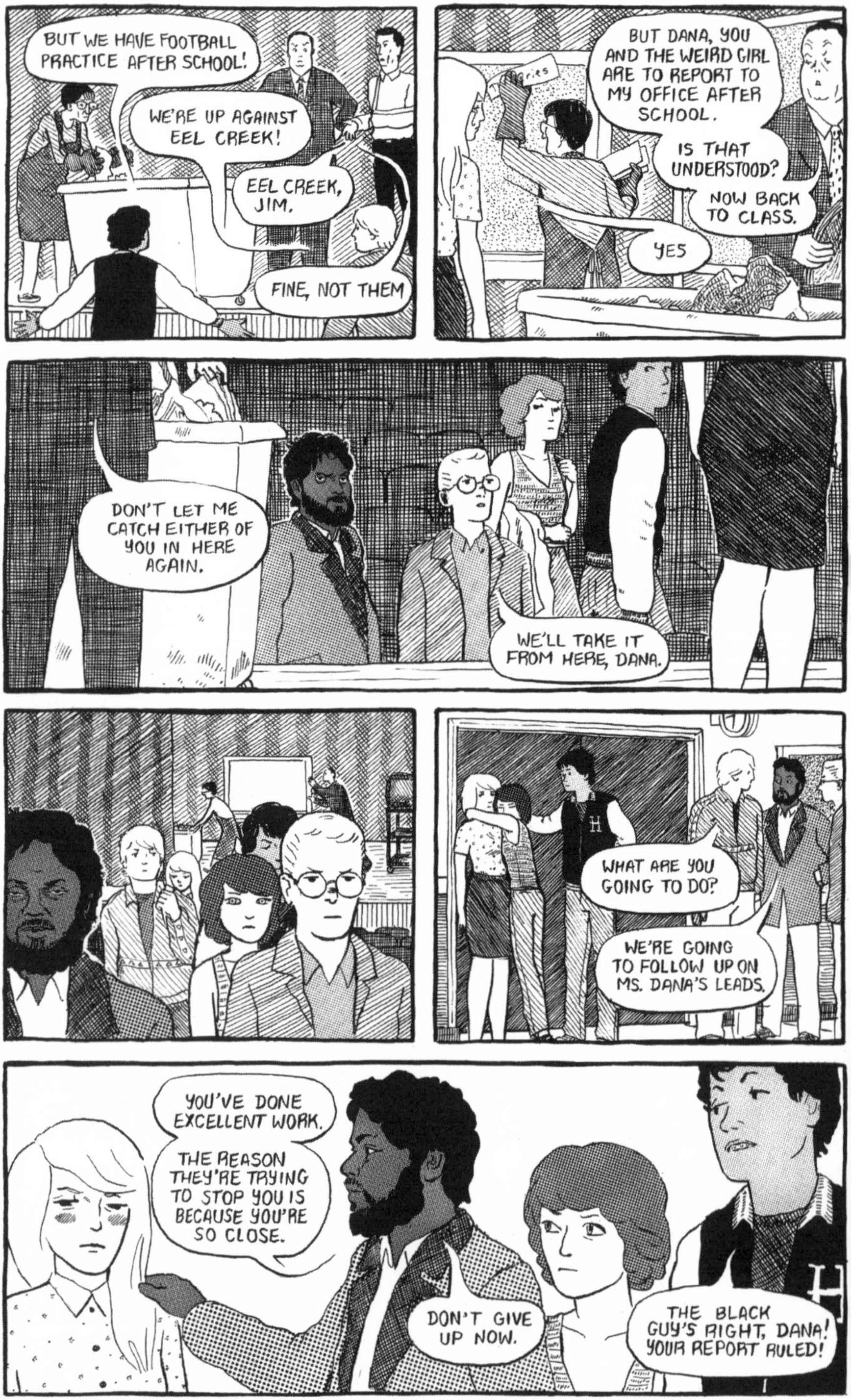
BUT WE HAVE FOOTBALL PRACTICE AFTER SCHOOL!
WE'RE UP AGAINST EEL CREEK!
EEL CREEK, JIM.
FINE, NOT THEM
BUT DANA, YOU AND THE WEIRD GIRL ARE TO REPORT TO MY OFFICE AFTER SCHOOL.
IS THAT UNDERSTOOD?
NOW BACK TO CLASS.
YES
DON'T LET ME CATCH EITHER OF YOU IN HERE AGAIN.
WE'LL TAKE IT FROM HERE, DANA.
WHAT ARE YOU GOING TO DO?
WE'RE GOING TO FOLLOW UP ON MS. DANA'S LEADS.
YOU'VE DONE EXCELLENT WORK.
THE REASON THEY'RE TRYING TO STOP YOU IS BECAUSE YOU'RE SO CLOSE.
DON'T GIVE UP NOW.
THE BLACK GUY'S RIGHT, DANA! YOUR REPORT RULED!

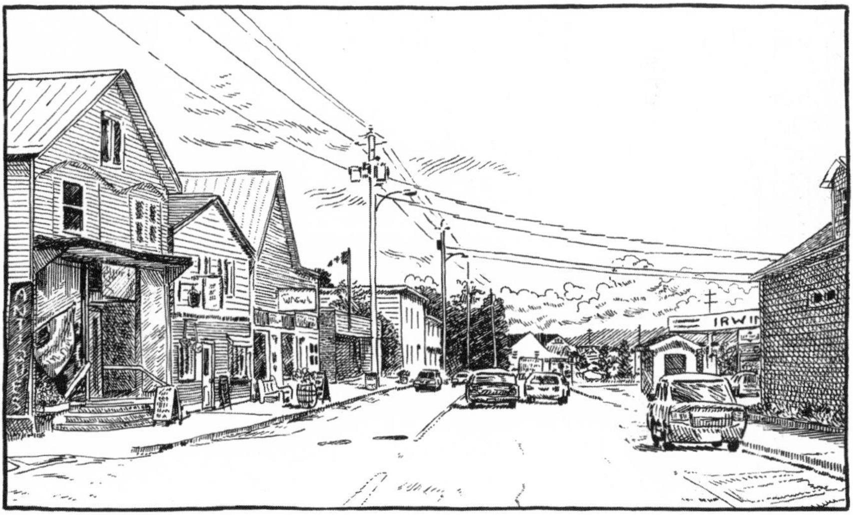
ANTIQUES
IRWI

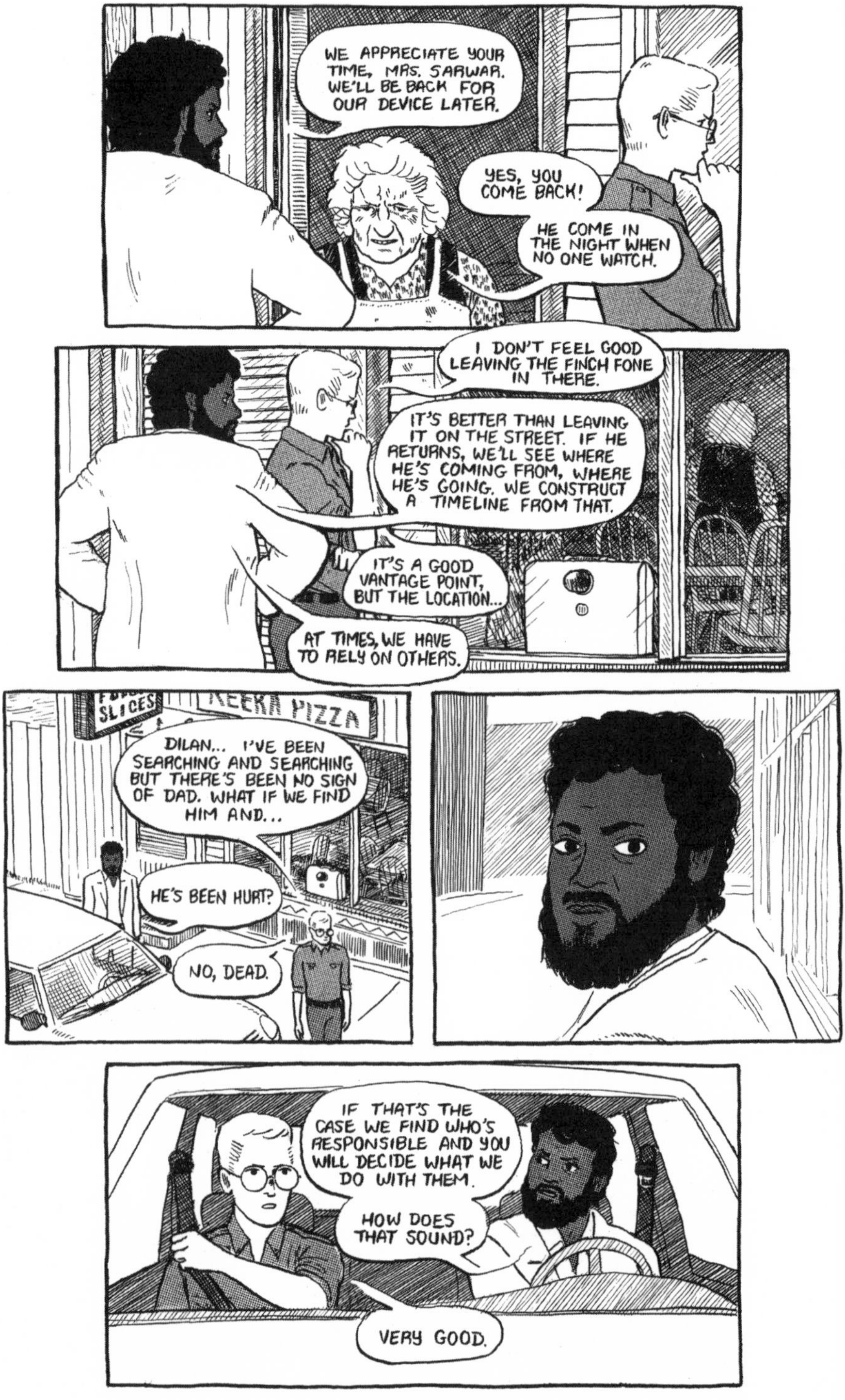

WE APPRECIATE YOUR TIME, MRS. SARWAR. WE'LL BE BACK FOR OUR DEVICE LATER.
YES, YOU COME BACK!
HE COME IN THE NIGHT WHEN NO ONE WATCH.
I DON'T FEEL GOOD LEAVING THE FINCH FONE IN THERE.
IT'S BETTER THAN LEAVING IT ON THE STREET. IF HE RETURNS, WE'LL SEE WHERE HE'S COMING FROM, WHERE HE'S GOING. WE CONSTRUCT A TIMELINE FROM THAT.
IT'S A GOOD VANTAGE POINT, BUT THE LOCATION...
AT TIMES, WE HAVE TO RELY ON OTHERS.
SLICES
DILAN... I'VE BEEN SEARCHING AND SEARCHING BUT THERE'S BEEN NO SIGN OF DAD. WHAT IF WE FIND HIM AND...
HE'S BEEN HURT?
NO, DEAD.
IF THAT'S THE CASE WE FIND WHO'S RESPONSIBLE AND YOU WILL DECIDE WHAT WE DO WITH THEM.
HOW DOES THAT SOUND?
VERY GOOD.

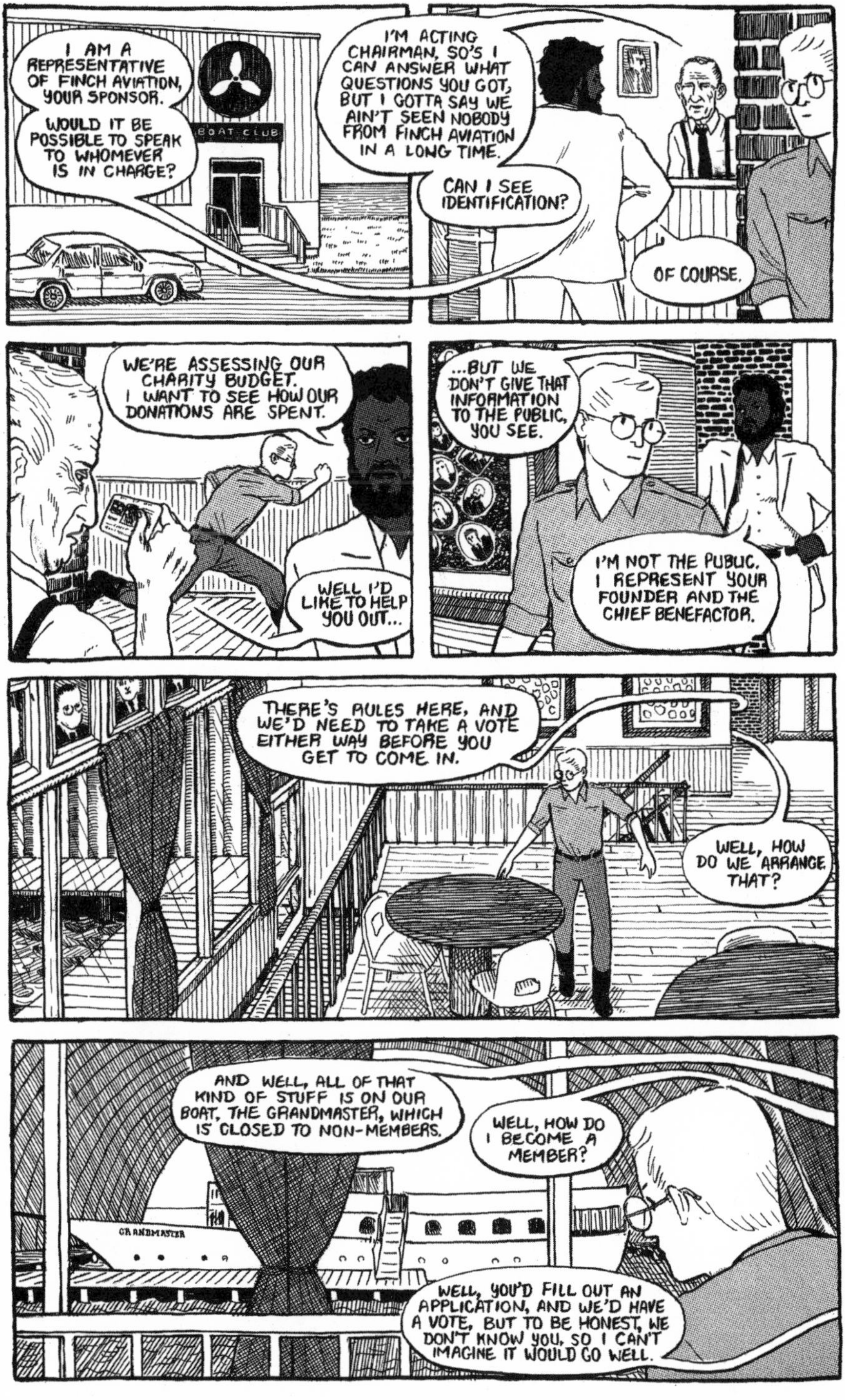
I AM A REPRESENTATIVE OF FINCH AVIATION, YOUR SPONSOR.
WOULD IT BE POSSIBLE TO SPEAK TO WHOMEVER IS IN CHARGE?
BOAT CLUB
I'M ACTING CHAIRMAN, SO'S I CAN ANSWER WHAT QUESTIONS YOU GOT, BUT I GOTTA SAY WE AIN'T SEEN NOBODY FROM FINCH AVIATION IN A LONG TIME.
CAN I SEE IDENTIFICATION?
OF COURSE.
WE'RE ASSESSING OUR CHARITY BUDGET. I WANT TO SEE HOW OUR DONATIONS ARE SPENT.
WELL I'D LIKE TO HELP YOU OUT...
...BUT WE DON'T GIVE THAT INFORMATION TO THE PUBLIC, YOU SEE.
I'M NOT THE PUBLIC. I REPRESENT YOUR FOUNDER AND THE CHIEF BENEFACTOR.
THERE'S RULES HERE, AND WE'D NEED TO TAKE A VOTE EITHER WAY BEFORE YOU GET TO COME IN.
WELL, HOW DO WE ARRANGE THAT?
AND WELL, ALL OF THAT KIND OF STUFF IS ON OUR BOAT, THE GRANDMASTER, WHICH IS CLOSED TO NON-MEMBERS.
WELL, HOW DO I BECOME A MEMBER?
GRANDMASTER
WELL, YOU'D FILL OUT AN APPLICATION, AND WE'D HAVE A VOTE, BUT TO BE HONEST, WE DON'T KNOW YOU, SO I CAN'T IMAGINE IT WOULD GO WELL.

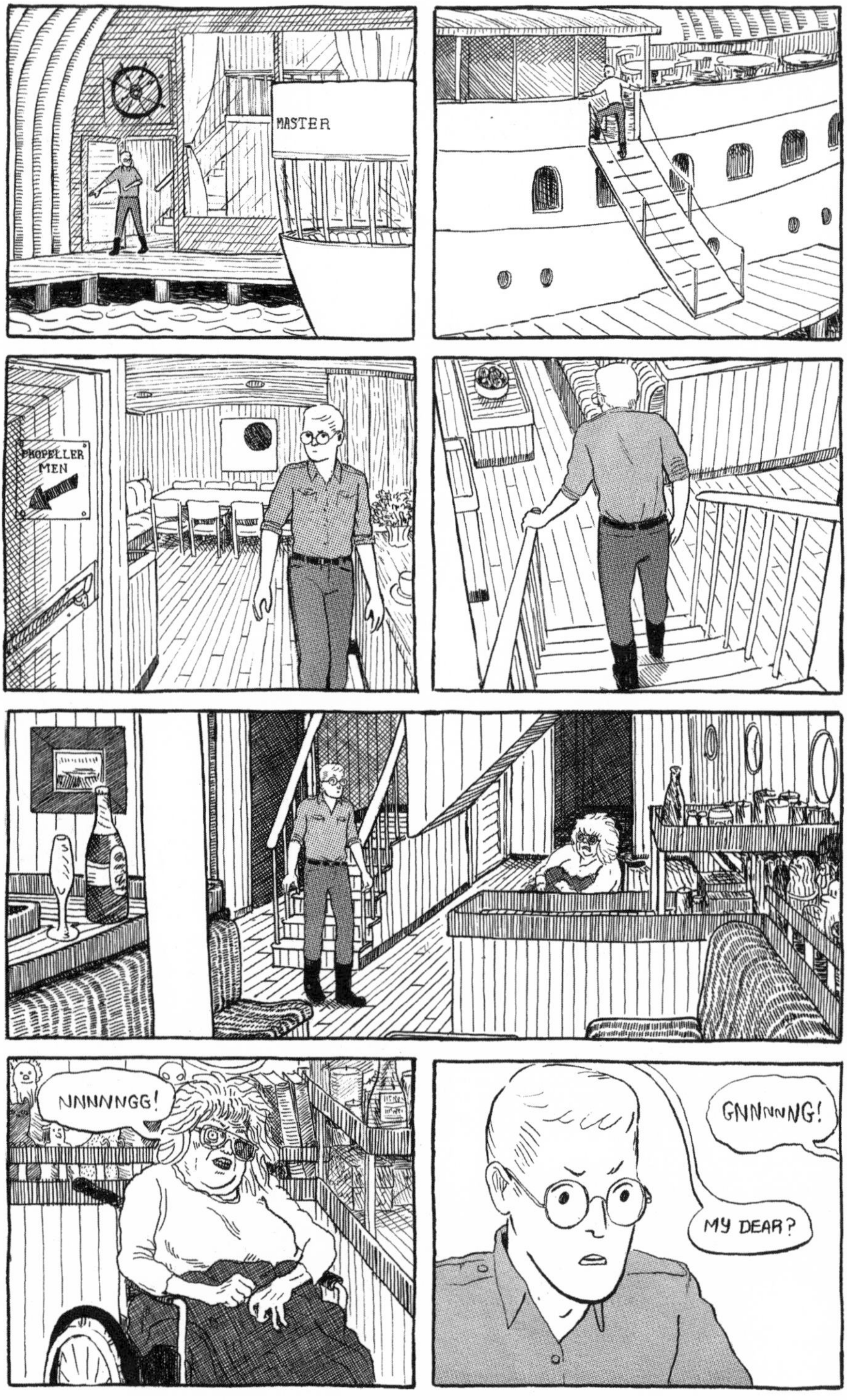
MASTER
PROPELLER MEN
NNNNNGG!
GNNNNNG!
MY DEAR?

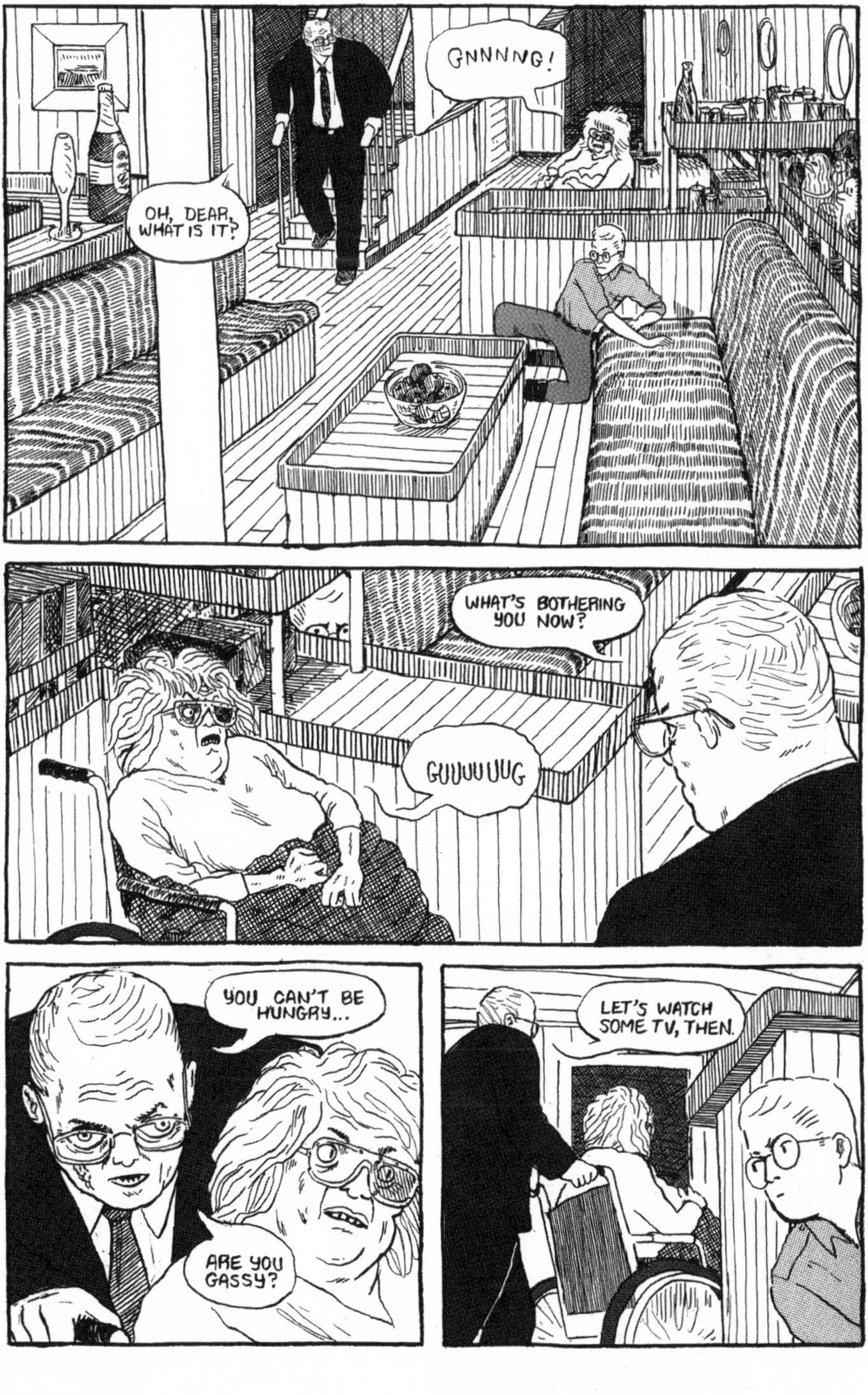
GNNNNG!
OH, DEAR, WHAT IS IT?
WHAT'S BOTHERING YOU NOW?
GUUUUUG
YOU CAN'T BE HUNGRY...
ARE YOU GASSY?
LET'S WATCH SOME TV, THEN.

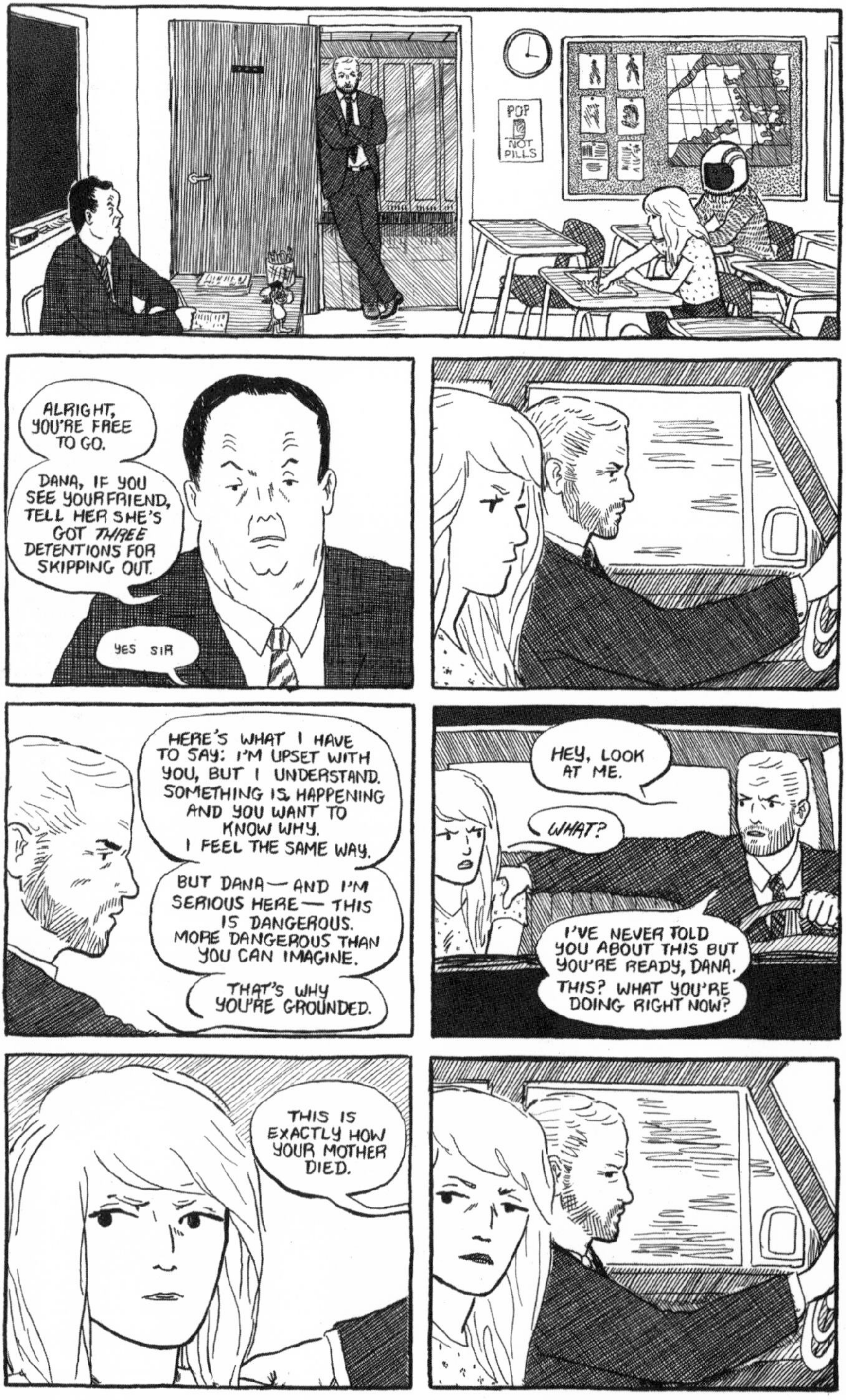
POP NOT PILLS
ALRIGHT, YOU'RE FREE TO GO.
DANA, IF YOU SEE YOUR FRIEND, TELL HER SHE'S GOT *THREE* DETENTIONS FOR SKIPPING OUT.
YES SIR
HERE'S WHAT I HAVE TO SAY: I'M UPSET WITH YOU, BUT I UNDERSTAND. SOMETHING IS HAPPENING AND YOU WANT TO KNOW WHY. I FEEL THE SAME WAY.
BUT DANA— AND I'M SERIOUS HERE— THIS IS DANGEROUS. MORE DANGEROUS THAN YOU CAN IMAGINE.
THAT'S WHY YOU'RE GROUNDED.
HEY, LOOK AT ME.
WHAT?
I'VE NEVER TOLD YOU ABOUT THIS BUT YOU'RE READY, DANA.
THIS? WHAT YOU'RE DOING RIGHT NOW?
THIS IS EXACTLY HOW YOUR MOTHER DIED.

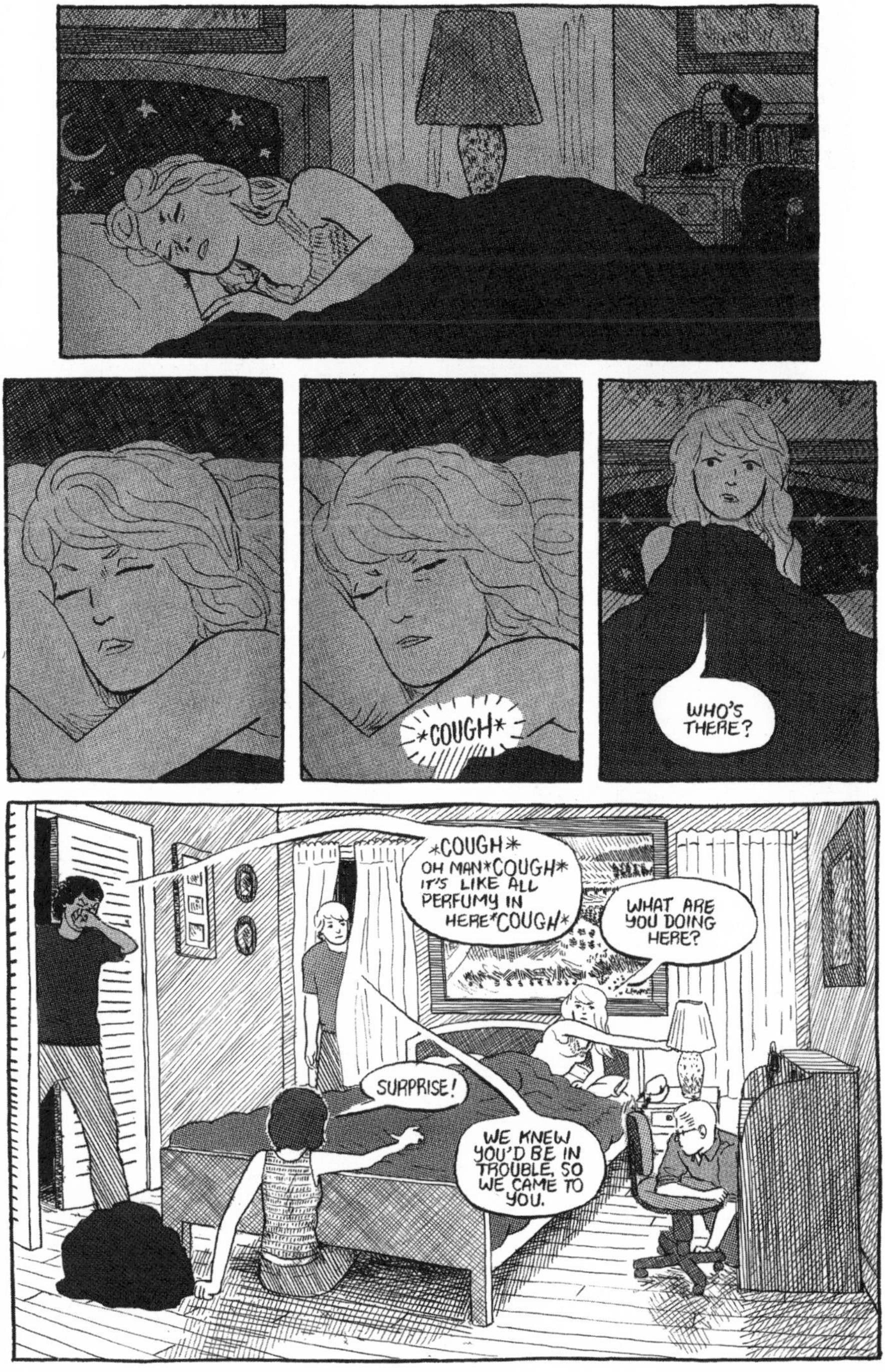
COUGH
WHO'S THERE?
COUGH OH MAN *COUGH* IT'S LIKE ALL PERFUMY IN HERE *COUGH*
WHAT ARE YOU DOING HERE?
SURPRISE!
WE KNEW YOU'D BE IN TROUBLE, SO WE CAME TO YOU.

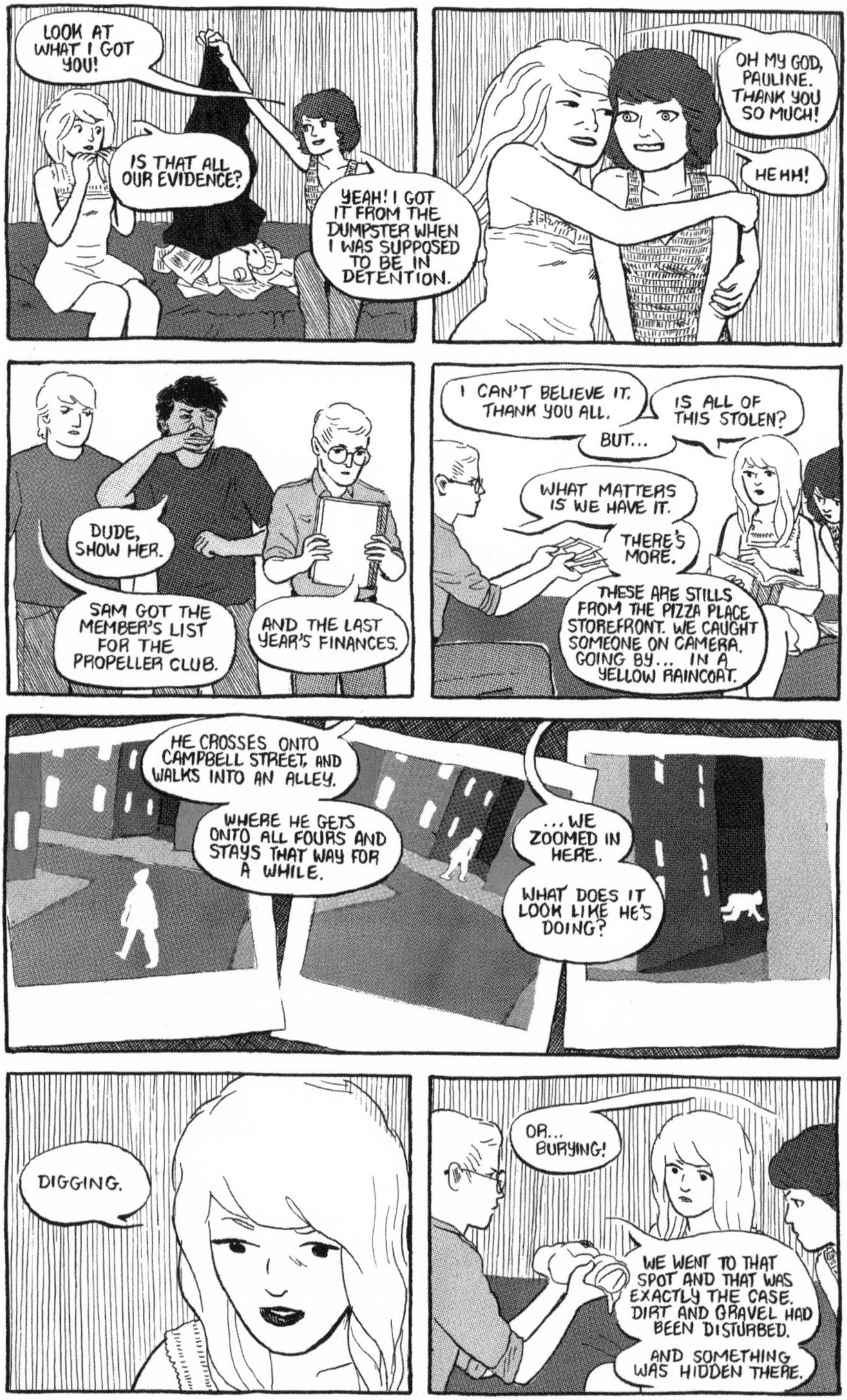
LOOK AT WHAT I GOT YOU!
IS THAT ALL OUR EVIDENCE?
YEAH! I GOT IT FROM THE DUMPSTER WHEN I WAS SUPPOSED TO BE IN DETENTION.
OH MY GOD, PAULINE. THANK YOU SO MUCH!
HEHH!
DUDE, SHOW HER.
SAM GOT THE MEMBER'S LIST FOR THE PROPELLER CLUB.
AND THE LAST YEAR'S FINANCES.
I CAN'T BELIEVE IT. THANK YOU ALL.
BUT...
IS ALL OF THIS STOLEN?
WHAT MATTERS IS WE HAVE IT.
THERE'S MORE.
THESE ARE STILLS FROM THE PIZZA PLACE STOREFRONT. WE CAUGHT SOMEONE ON CAMERA, GOING BY... IN A YELLOW RAINCOAT.
HE CROSSES ONTO CAMPBELL STREET, AND WALKS INTO AN ALLEY.
WHERE HE GETS ONTO ALL FOURS AND STAYS THAT WAY FOR A WHILE.
...WE ZOOMED IN HERE.
WHAT DOES IT LOOK LIKE HE'S DOING?
DIGGING.
OR... BURYING!
WE WENT TO THAT SPOT AND THAT WAS EXACTLY THE CASE. DIRT AND GRAVEL HAD BEEN DISTURBED.
AND SOMETHING WAS HIDDEN THERE.

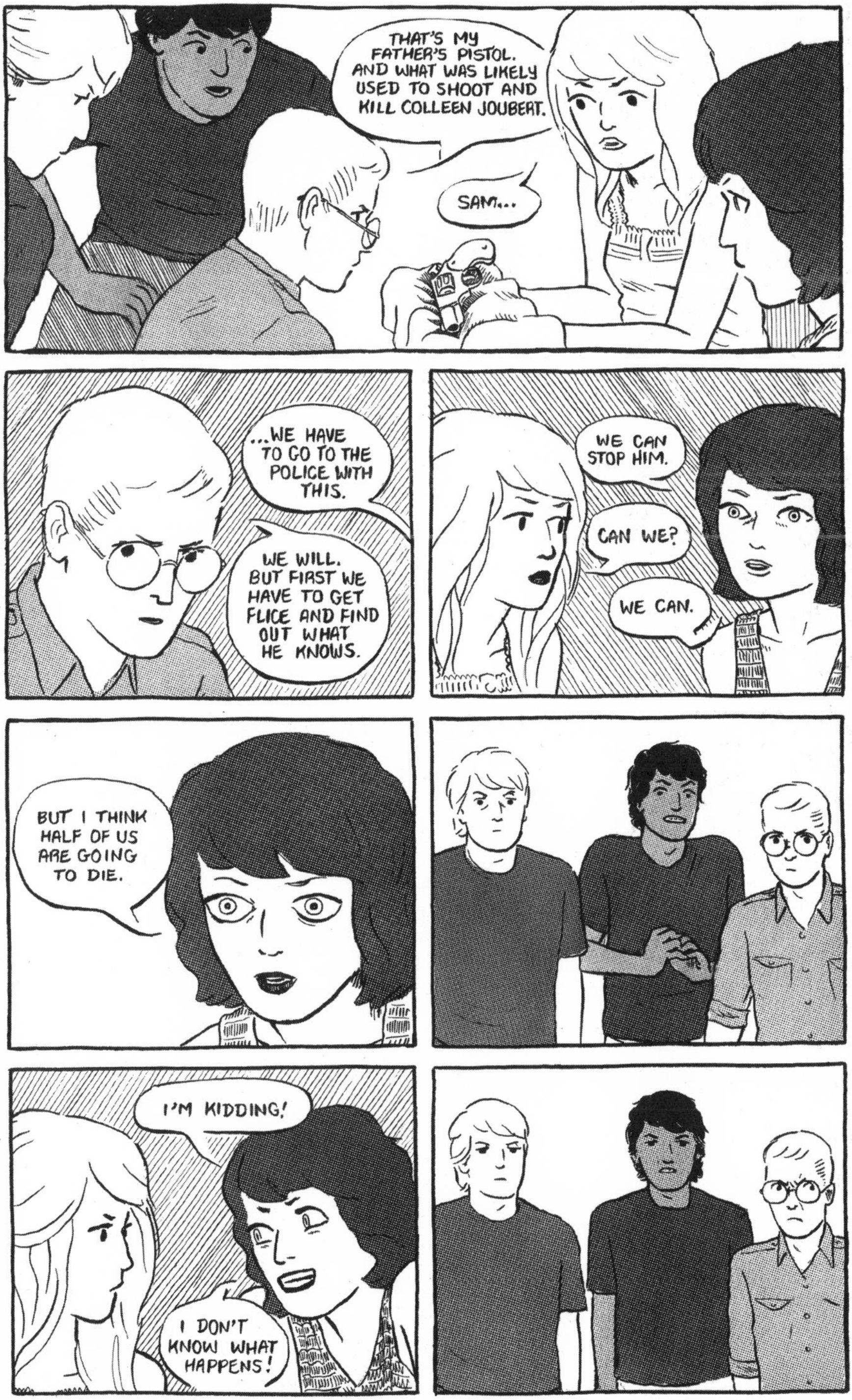
THAT'S MY FATHER'S PISTOL. AND WHAT WAS LIKELY USED TO SHOOT AND KILL COLLEEN JOUBERT.
SAM...
...WE HAVE TO GO TO THE POLICE WITH THIS.
WE WILL. BUT FIRST WE HAVE TO GET FLICE AND FIND OUT WHAT HE KNOWS.
WE CAN STOP HIM.
CAN WE?
WE CAN.
BUT I THINK HALF OF US ARE GOING TO DIE.
I'M KIDDING!
I DON'T KNOW WHAT HAPPENS!

CHAPTER
EIGHT

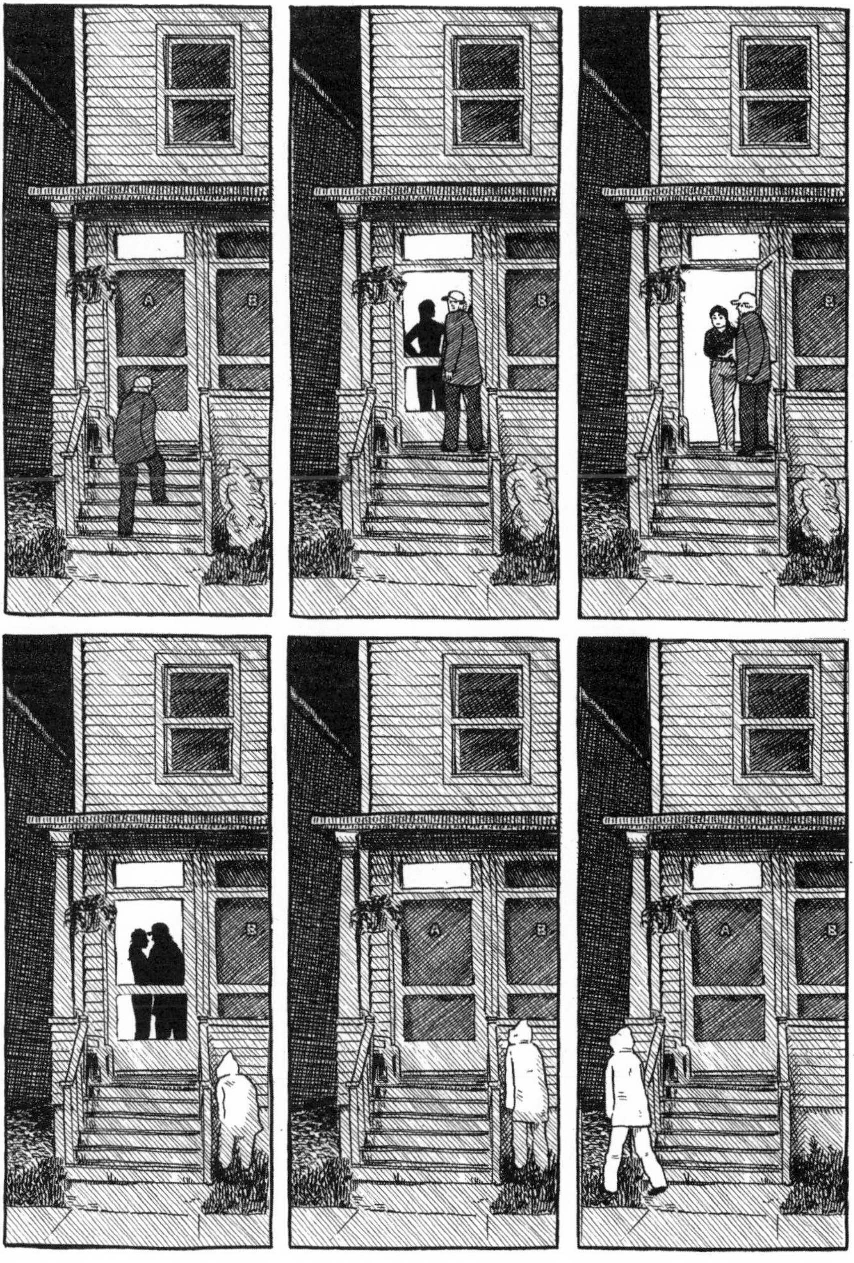

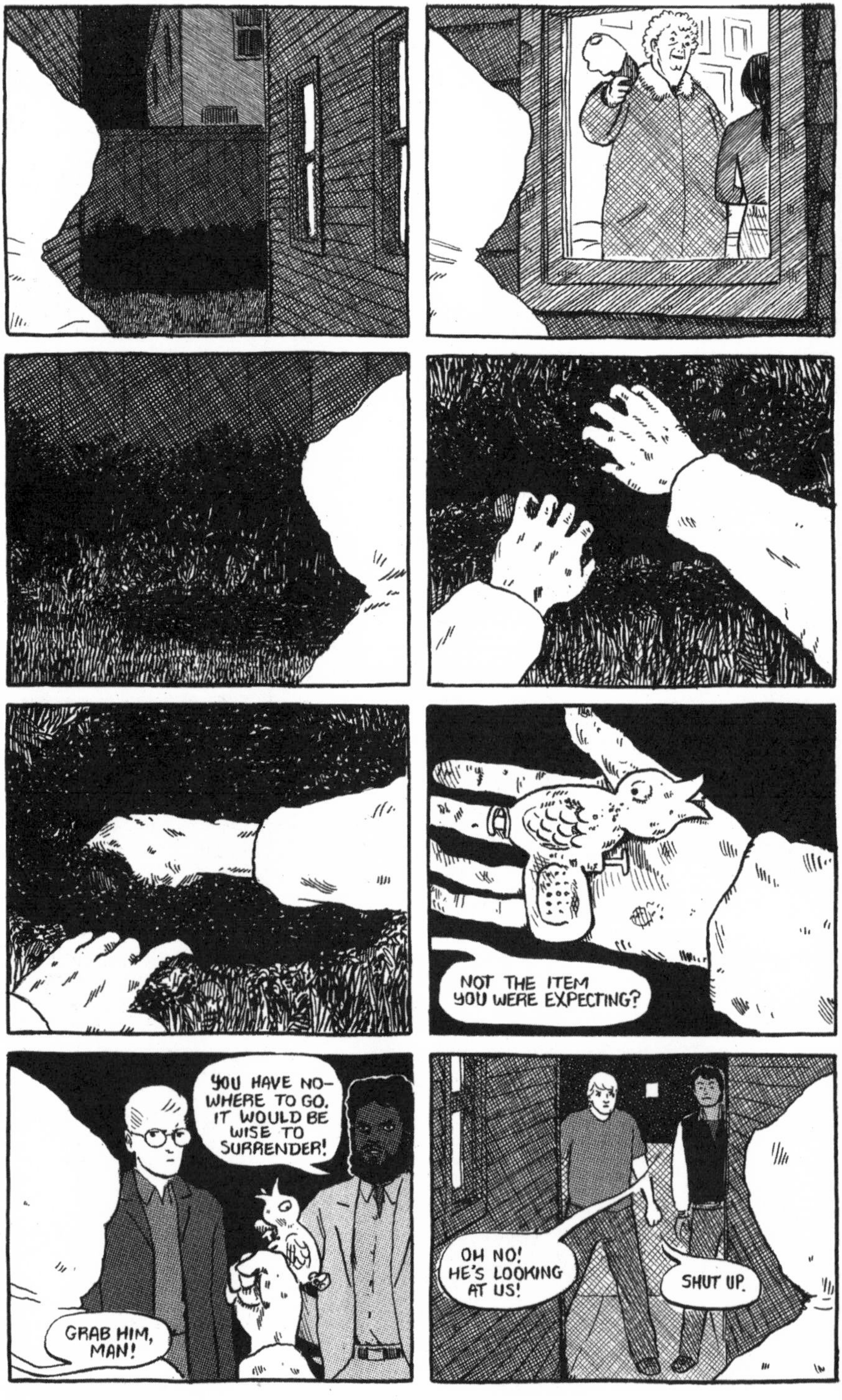
NOT THE ITEM
YOU WERE EXPECTING?
YOU HAVE NO-
WHERE TO GO.
IT WOULD BE
WISE TO
SURRENDER!
GRAB HIM,
MAN!
OH NO!
HE'S LOOKING
AT US!
SHUT UP.

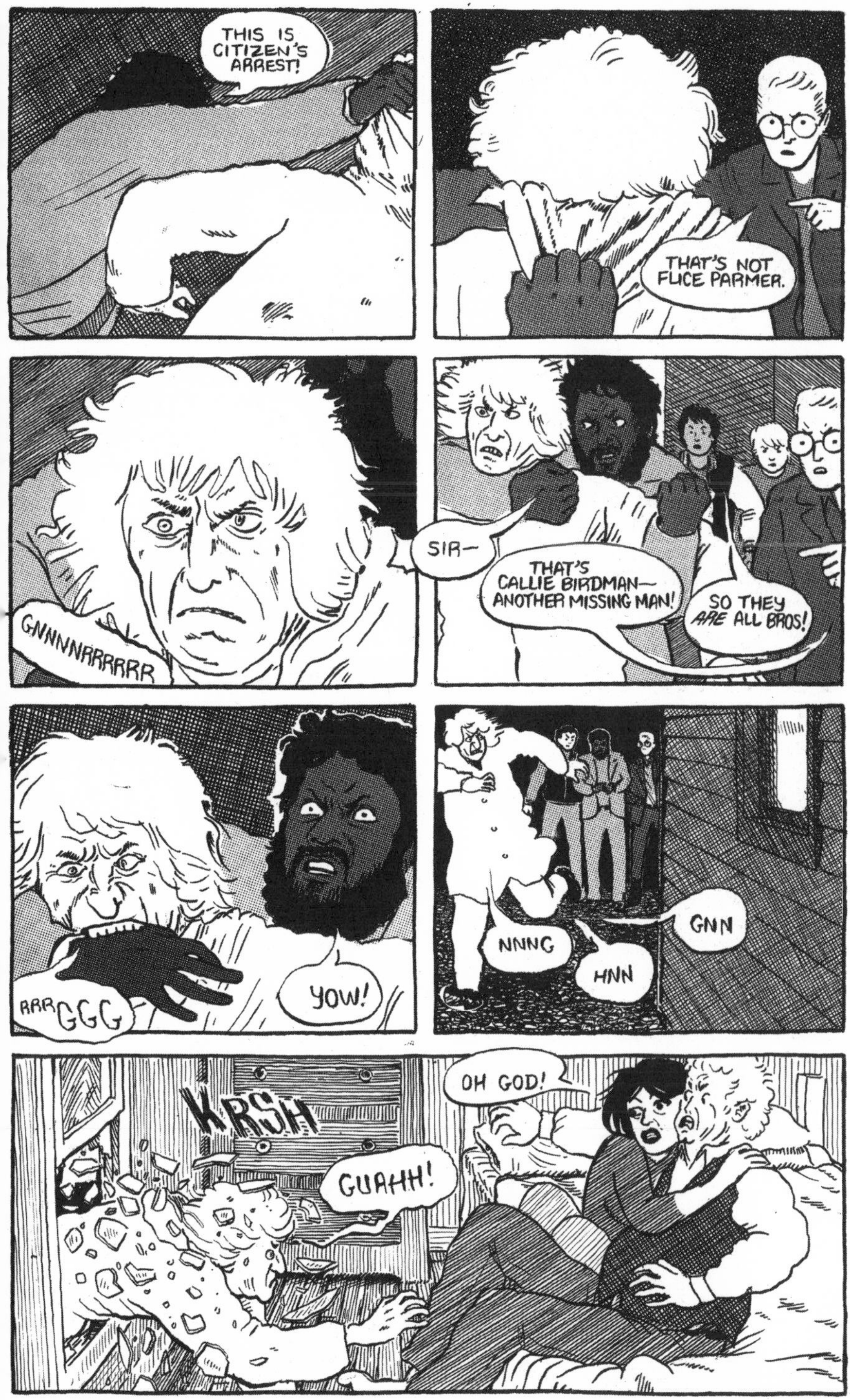
THIS IS CITIZEN'S ARREST!
THAT'S NOT FLICE PARMER.
GNNNNRRRRRR
SIR—
THAT'S CALLIE BIRDMAN— ANOTHER MISSING MAN!
SO THEY ARE ALL BROS!
RRRGGG
YOW!
NNNG
HNN
GNN
KRSH
GUAHH!
OH GOD!

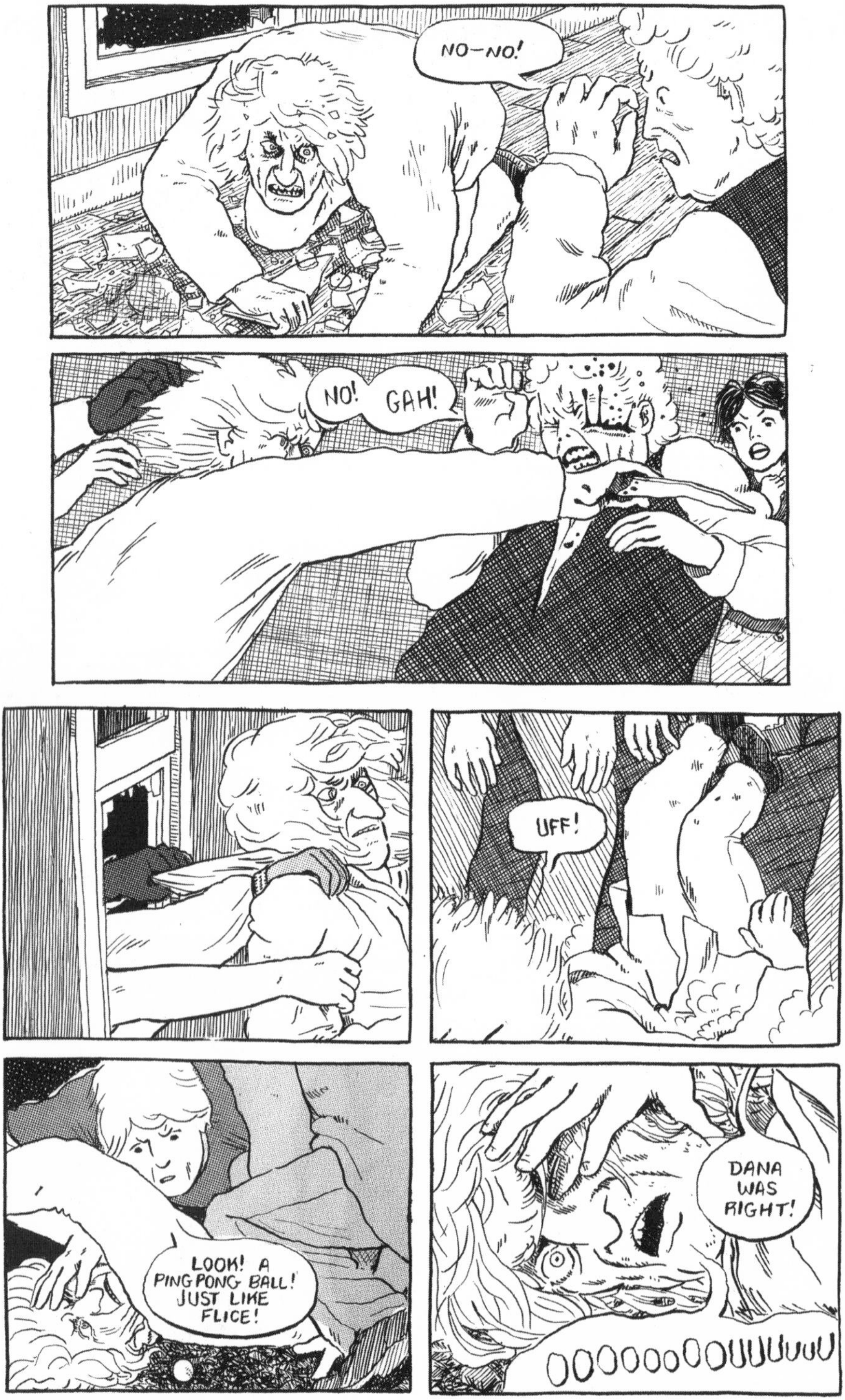
NO-NO!
NO!
GAH!
UFF!
LOOK! A PING PONG BALL! JUST LIKE FLICE!
DANA WAS RIGHT!
OOOOOOOOUUUUUU

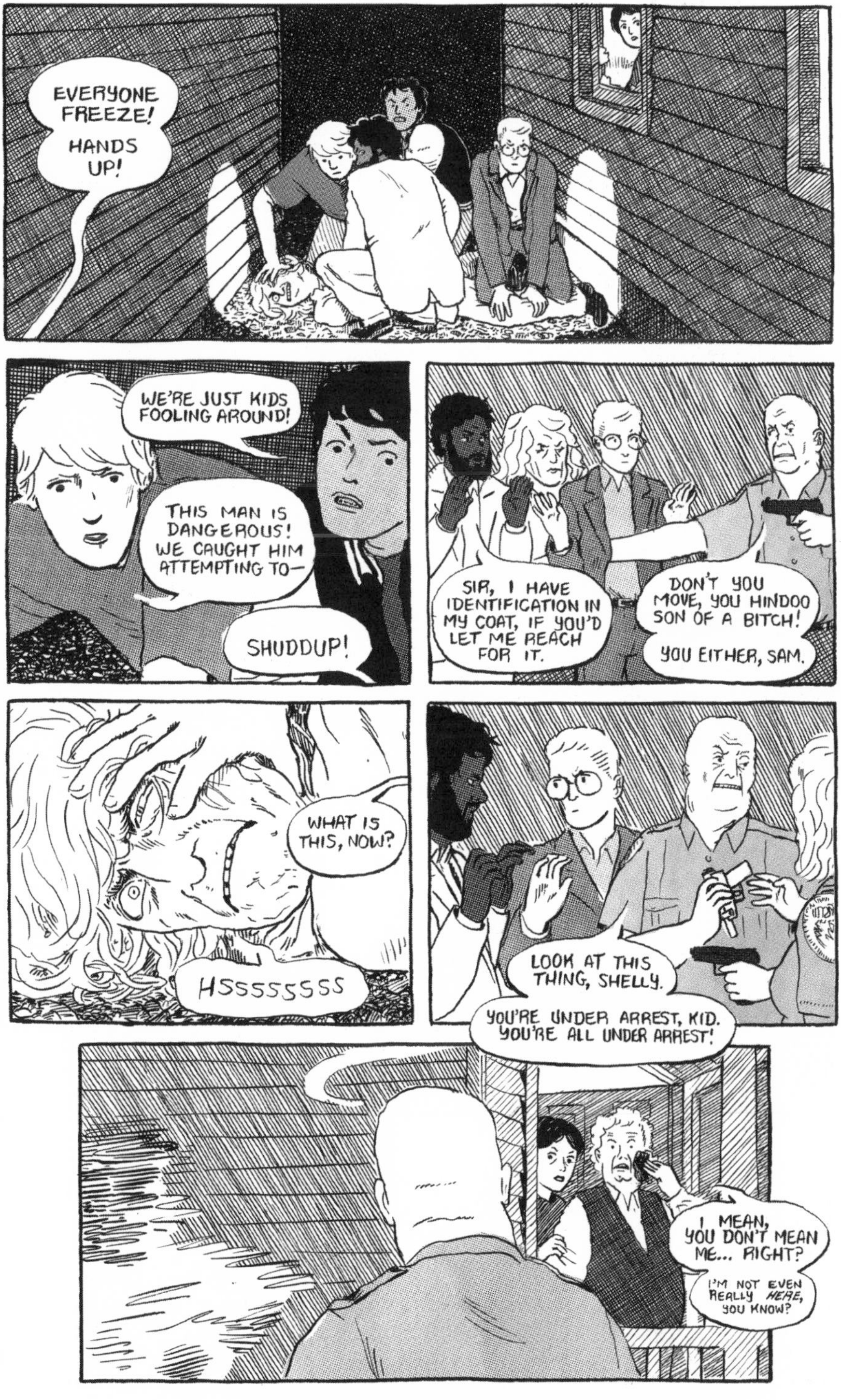

EVERYONE FREEZE!
HANDS UP!
WE'RE JUST KIDS FOOLING AROUND!
THIS MAN IS DANGEROUS! WE CAUGHT HIM ATTEMPTING TO—
SHUDDUP!
SIR, I HAVE IDENTIFICATION IN MY COAT, IF YOU'D LET ME REACH FOR IT.
DON'T YOU MOVE, YOU HINDOO SON OF A BITCH!
YOU EITHER, SAM.
WHAT IS THIS, NOW?
HSSSSSSSS
LOOK AT THIS THING, SHELLY.
YOU'RE UNDER ARREST, KID. YOU'RE ALL UNDER ARREST!
I MEAN, YOU DON'T MEAN ME... RIGHT?
I'M NOT EVEN REALLY HERE, YOU KNOW?

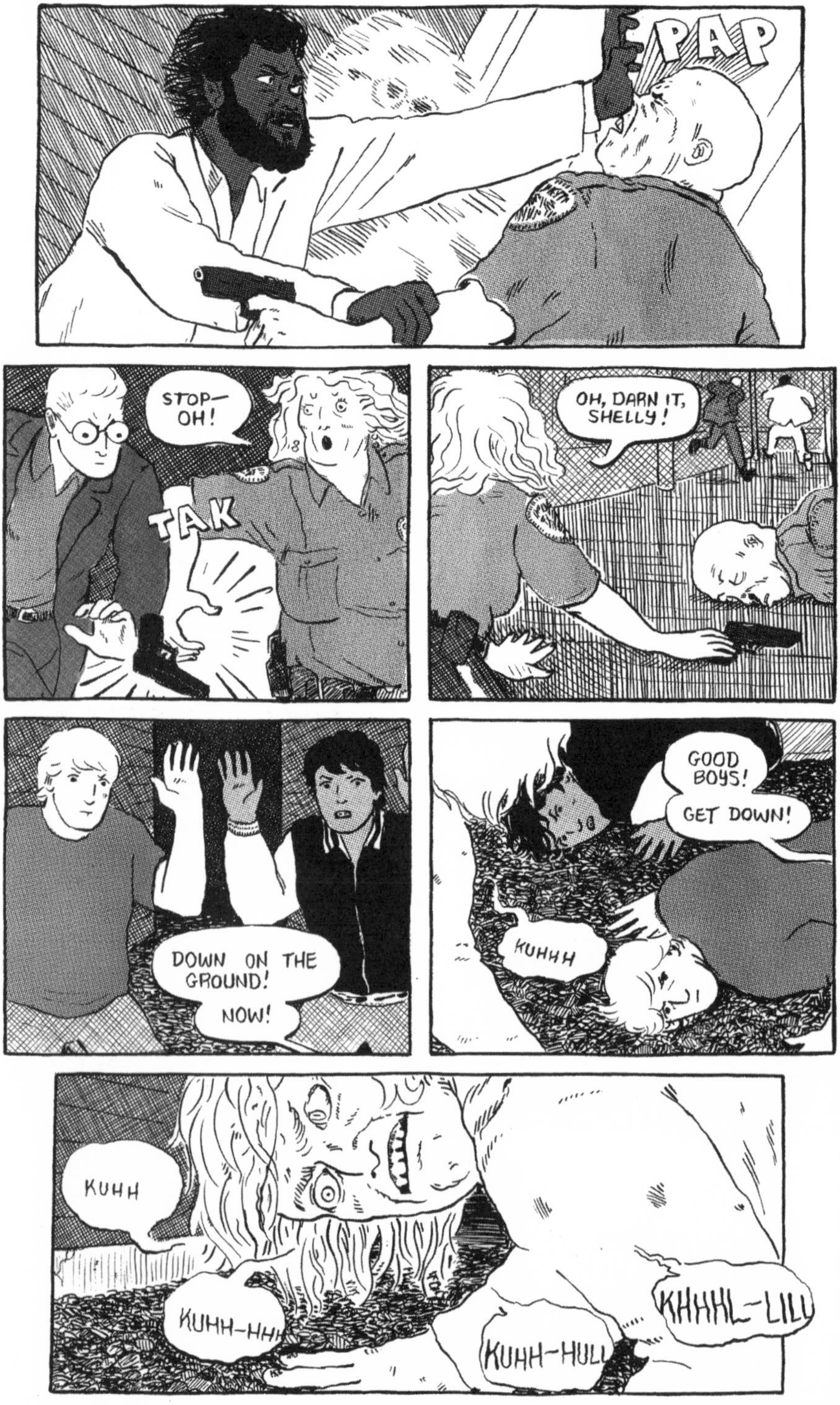
PAP
STOP—
OH!
TAK
OH, DARN IT, SHELLY!
DOWN ON THE GROUND!
NOW!
GOOD BOYS!
GET DOWN!
KUHHH
KUHH
KUHH-HHH
KUHH-HULL
KHHHL-LILL

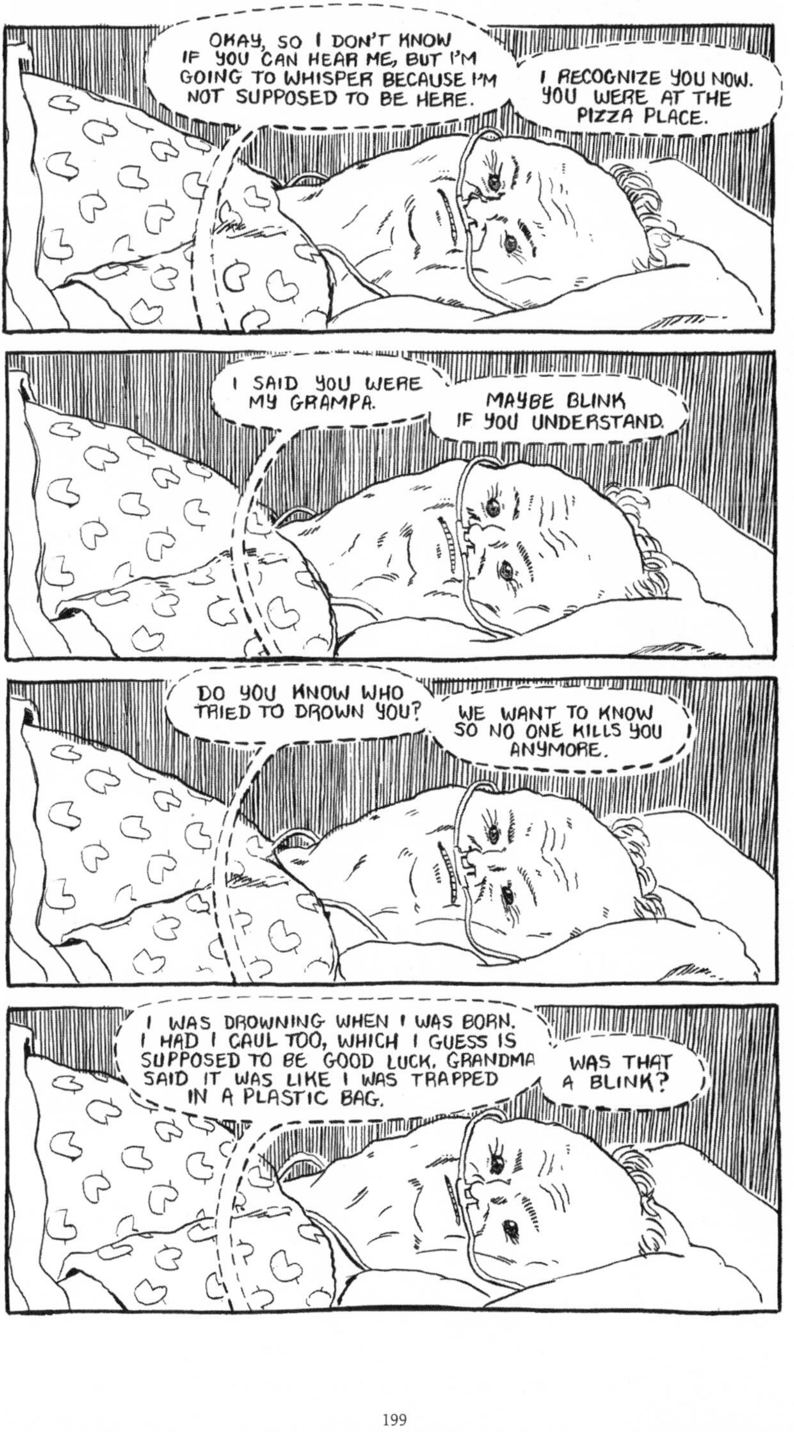
OKAY, SO I DON'T KNOW IF YOU CAN HEAR ME, BUT I'M GOING TO WHISPER BECAUSE I'M NOT SUPPOSED TO BE HERE.
I RECOGNIZE YOU NOW. YOU WERE AT THE PIZZA PLACE.
I SAID YOU WERE MY GRAMPA.
MAYBE BLINK IF YOU UNDERSTAND.
DO YOU KNOW WHO TRIED TO DROWN YOU?
WE WANT TO KNOW SO NO ONE KILLS YOU ANYMORE.
I WAS DROWNING WHEN I WAS BORN. I HAD I CAUL TOO, WHICH I GUESS IS SUPPOSED TO BE GOOD LUCK. GRANDMA SAID IT WAS LIKE I WAS TRAPPED IN A PLASTIC BAG.
WAS THAT A BLINK?

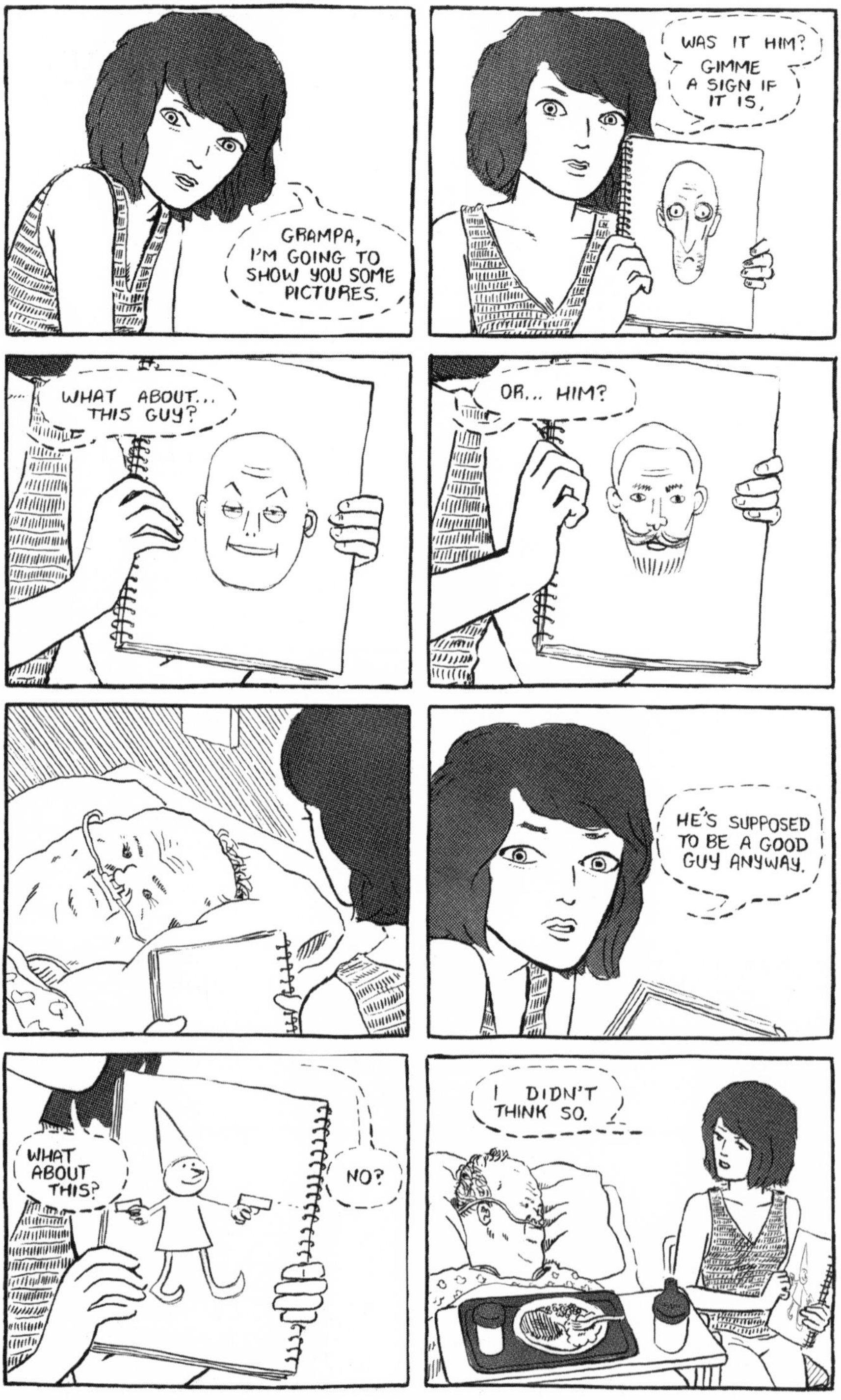
GRAMPA, I'M GOING TO SHOW YOU SOME PICTURES.
WAS IT HIM? GIMME A SIGN IF IT IS,
WHAT ABOUT... THIS GUY?
OR... HIM?
HE'S SUPPOSED TO BE A GOOD GUY ANYWAY.
WHAT ABOUT THIS?
NO?
I DIDN'T THINK SO.

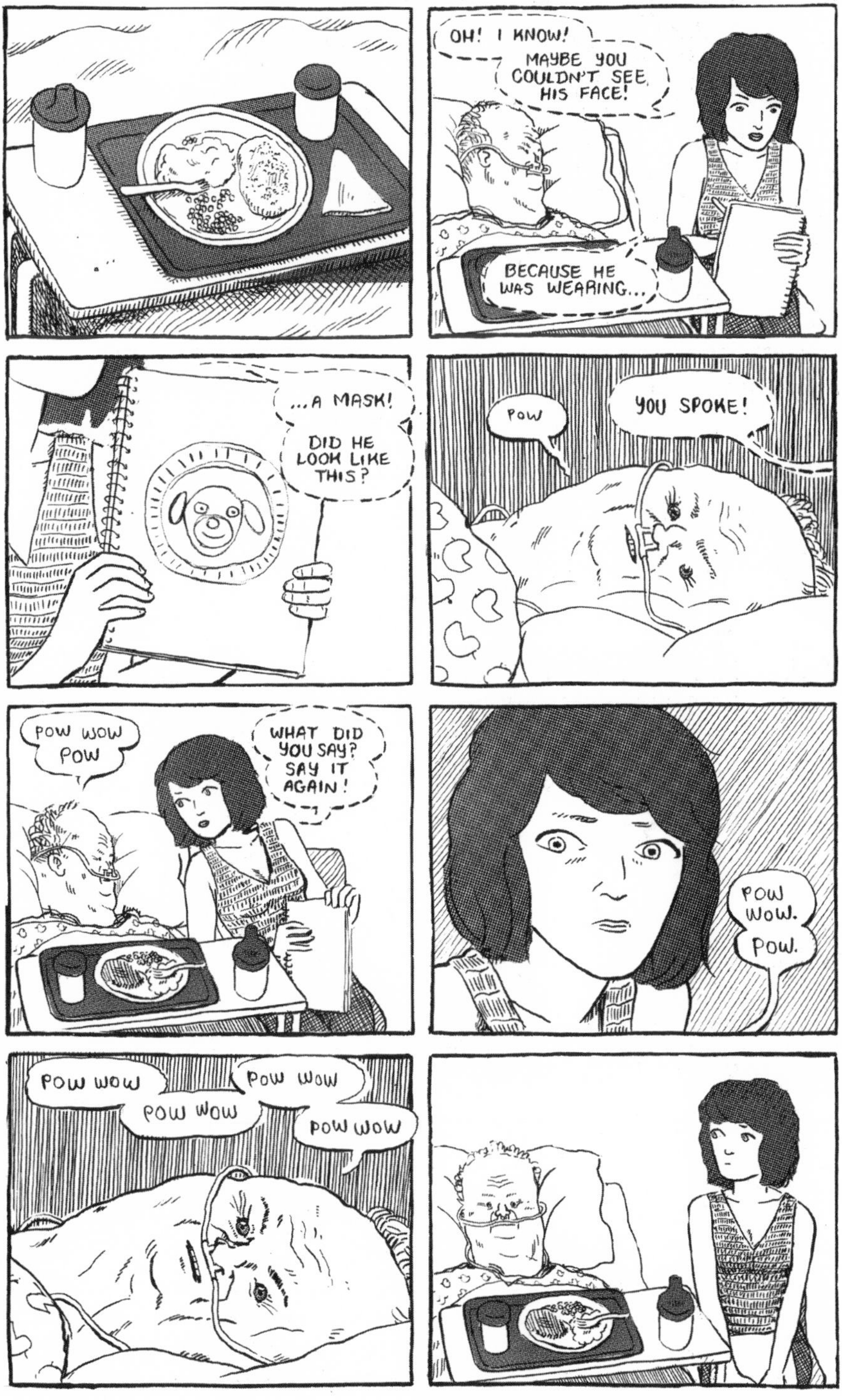
OH! I KNOW!
MAYBE YOU COULDN'T SEE HIS FACE!
BECAUSE HE WAS WEARING...
...A MASK!
DID HE LOOK LIKE THIS?
POW
YOU SPOKE!
POW WOW POW
WHAT DID YOU SAY? SAY IT AGAIN!
POW WOW. POW.
POW WOW
POW WOW
POW WOW
POW WOW

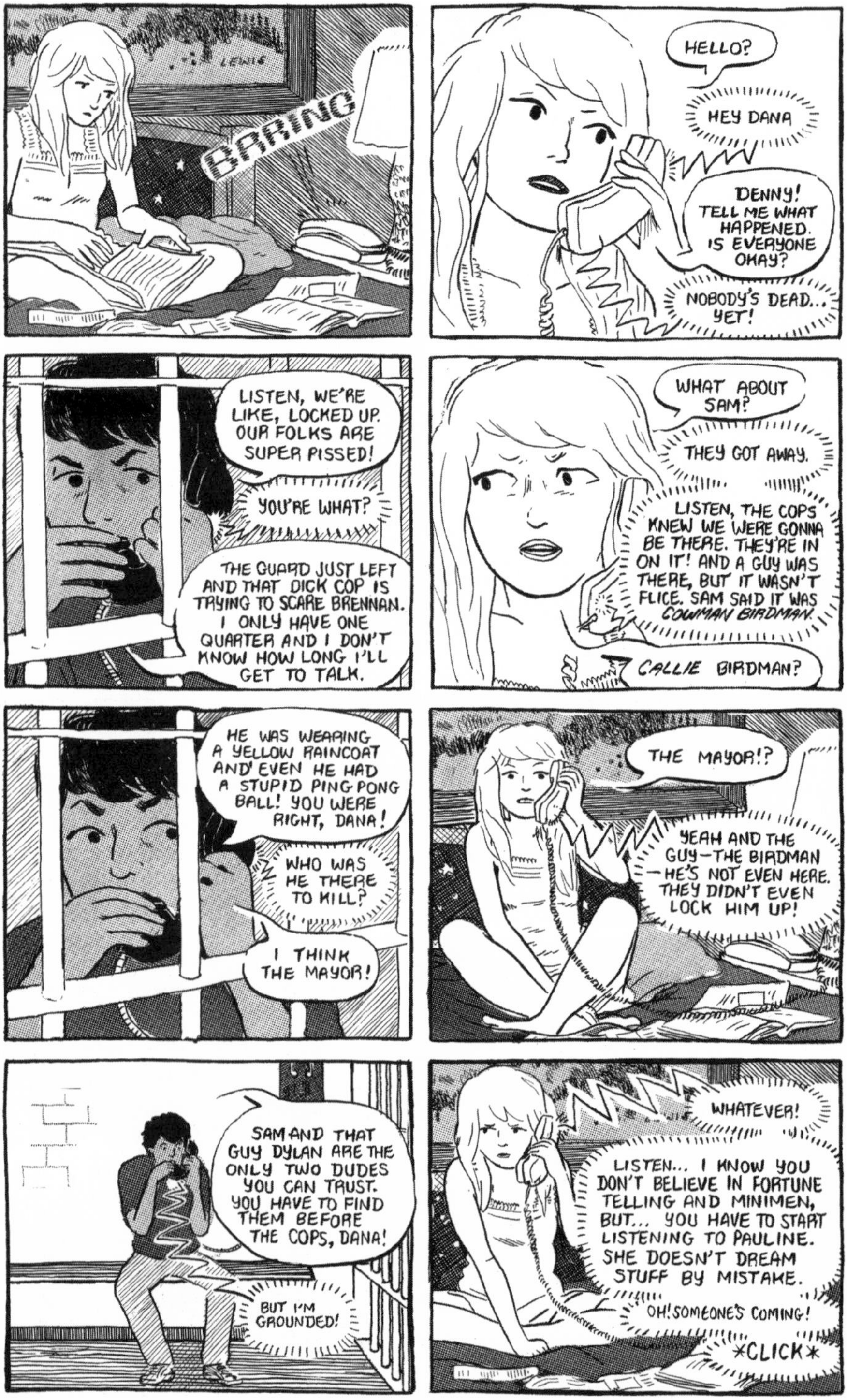
BRRING
HELLO?
HEY DANA
DENNY! TELL ME WHAT HAPPENED. IS EVERYONE OKAY?
NOBODY'S DEAD... YET!
LISTEN, WE'RE LIKE, LOCKED UP. OUR FOLKS ARE SUPER PISSED!
YOU'RE WHAT?
THE GUARD JUST LEFT AND THAT DICK COP IS TRYING TO SCARE BRENNAN. I ONLY HAVE ONE QUARTER AND I DON'T KNOW HOW LONG I'LL GET TO TALK.
WHAT ABOUT SAM?
THEY GOT AWAY.
LISTEN, THE COPS KNEW WE WERE GONNA BE THERE. THEY'RE IN ON IT! AND A GUY WAS THERE, BUT IT WASN'T FLICE. SAM SAID IT WAS COWMAN BIRDMAN.
CALLIE BIRDMAN?
HE WAS WEARING A YELLOW RAINCOAT AND EVEN HE HAD A STUPID PING PONG BALL! YOU WERE RIGHT, DANA!
WHO WAS HE THERE TO KILL?
I THINK THE MAYOR!
THE MAYOR!?
YEAH AND THE GUY—THE BIRDMAN —HE'S NOT EVEN HERE. THEY DIDN'T EVEN LOCK HIM UP!
SAM AND THAT GUY DYLAN ARE THE ONLY TWO DUDES YOU CAN TRUST. YOU HAVE TO FIND THEM BEFORE THE COPS, DANA!
BUT I'M GROUNDED!
WHATEVER!
LISTEN... I KNOW YOU DON'T BELIEVE IN FORTUNE TELLING AND MINIMEN, BUT... YOU HAVE TO START LISTENING TO PAULINE. SHE DOESN'T DREAM STUFF BY MISTAKE.
OH! SOMEONE'S COMING!
CLICK

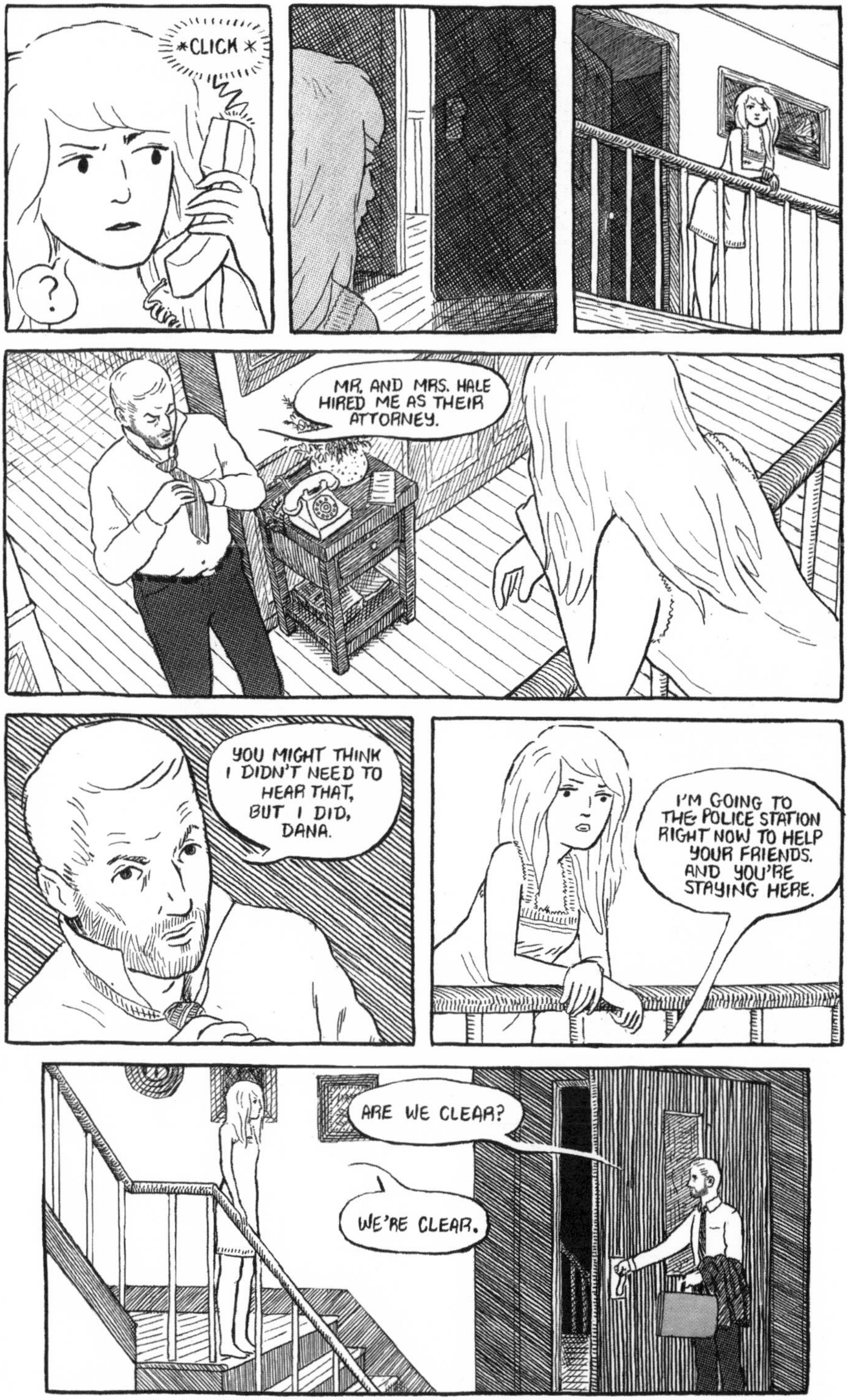
CLICK
?
MR. AND MRS. HALE HIRED ME AS THEIR ATTORNEY.
YOU MIGHT THINK I DIDN'T NEED TO HEAR THAT, BUT I DID, DANA.
I'M GOING TO THE POLICE STATION RIGHT NOW TO HELP YOUR FRIENDS. AND YOU'RE STAYING HERE.
ARE WE CLEAR?
WE'RE CLEAR.

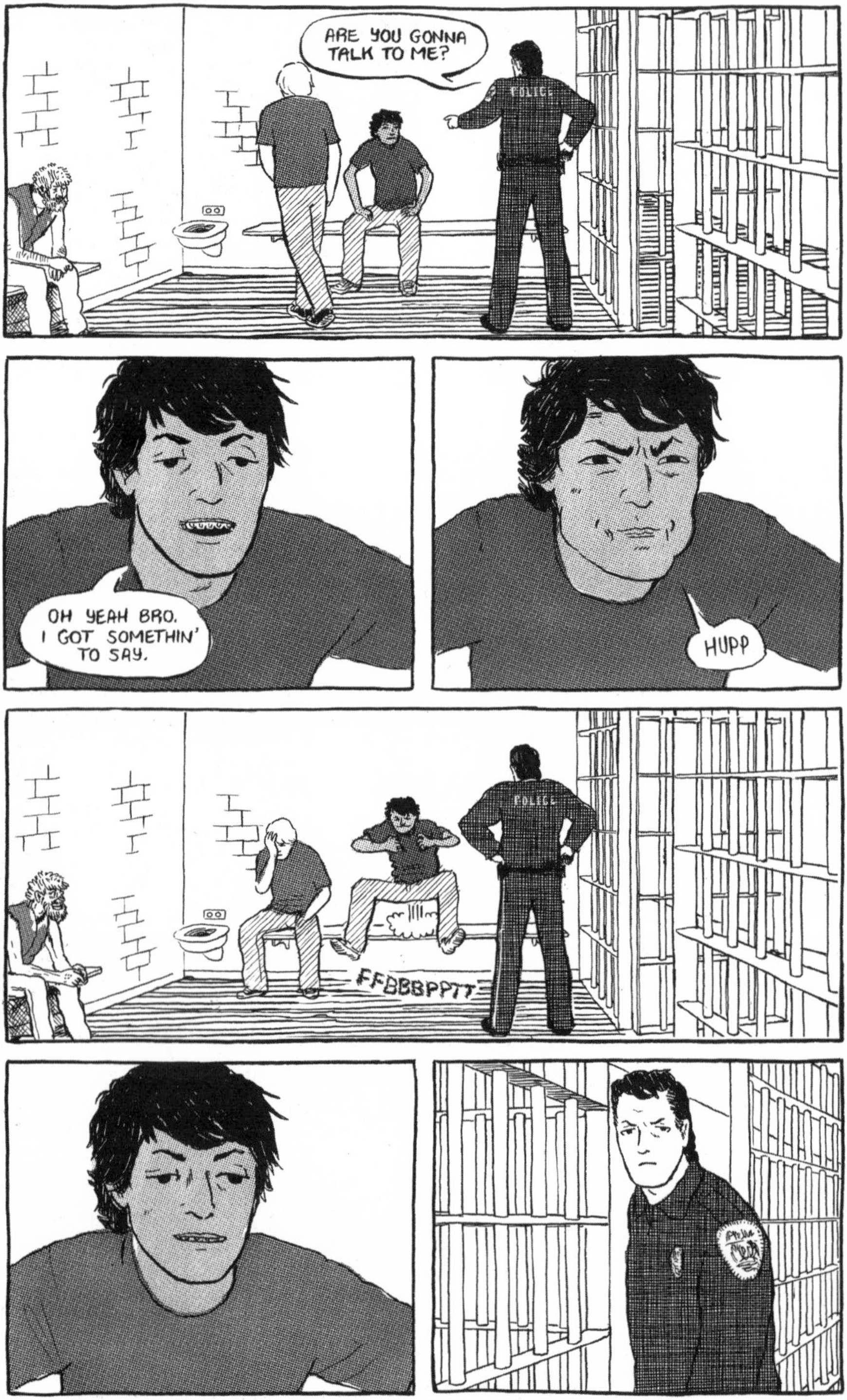
ARE YOU GONNA TALK TO ME?
POLICE
OH YEAH BRO. I GOT SOMETHIN' TO SAY.
HUPP
POLICE
FFBBBPPTT

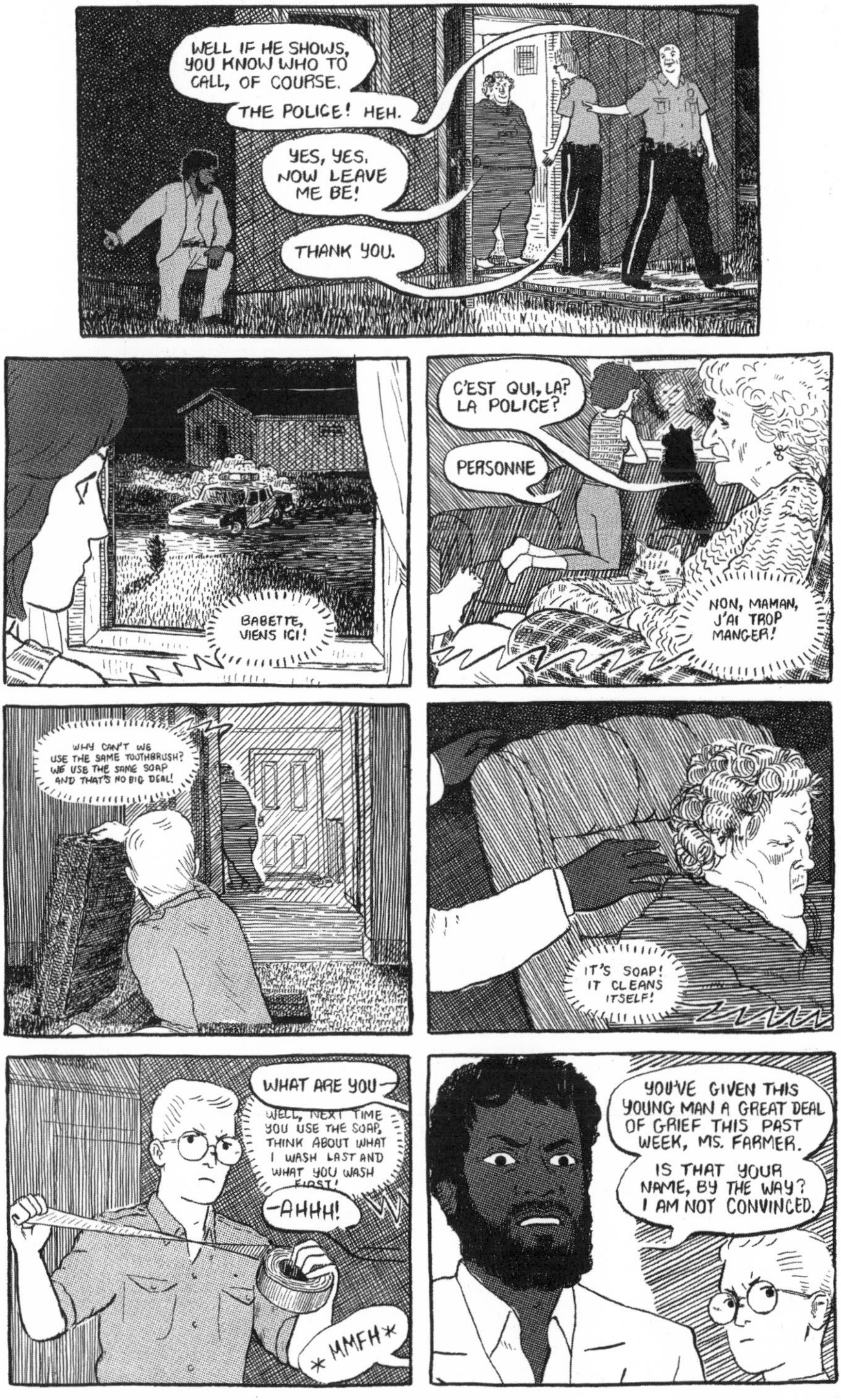
WELL IF HE SHOWS, YOU KNOW WHO TO CALL, OF COURSE.
THE POLICE! HEH.
YES, YES. NOW LEAVE ME BE!
THANK YOU.
BABETTE, VIENS ICI!
C'EST QUI, LA? LA POLICE?
PERSONNE
NON, MAMAN, J'AI TROP MANGER!
WHY CAN'T WE USE THE SAME TOOTHBRUSH? WE USE THE SAME SOAP AND THAT'S NO BIG DEAL!
IT'S SOAP! IT CLEANS ITSELF!
WHAT ARE YOU—
WELL, NEXT TIME YOU USE THE SOAP, THINK ABOUT WHAT I WASH LAST AND WHAT YOU WASH FIRST!
—AHHH!
MMFH
YOU'VE GIVEN THIS YOUNG MAN A GREAT DEAL OF GRIEF THIS PAST WEEK, MS. FARMER.
IS THAT YOUR NAME, BY THE WAY? I AM NOT CONVINCED.

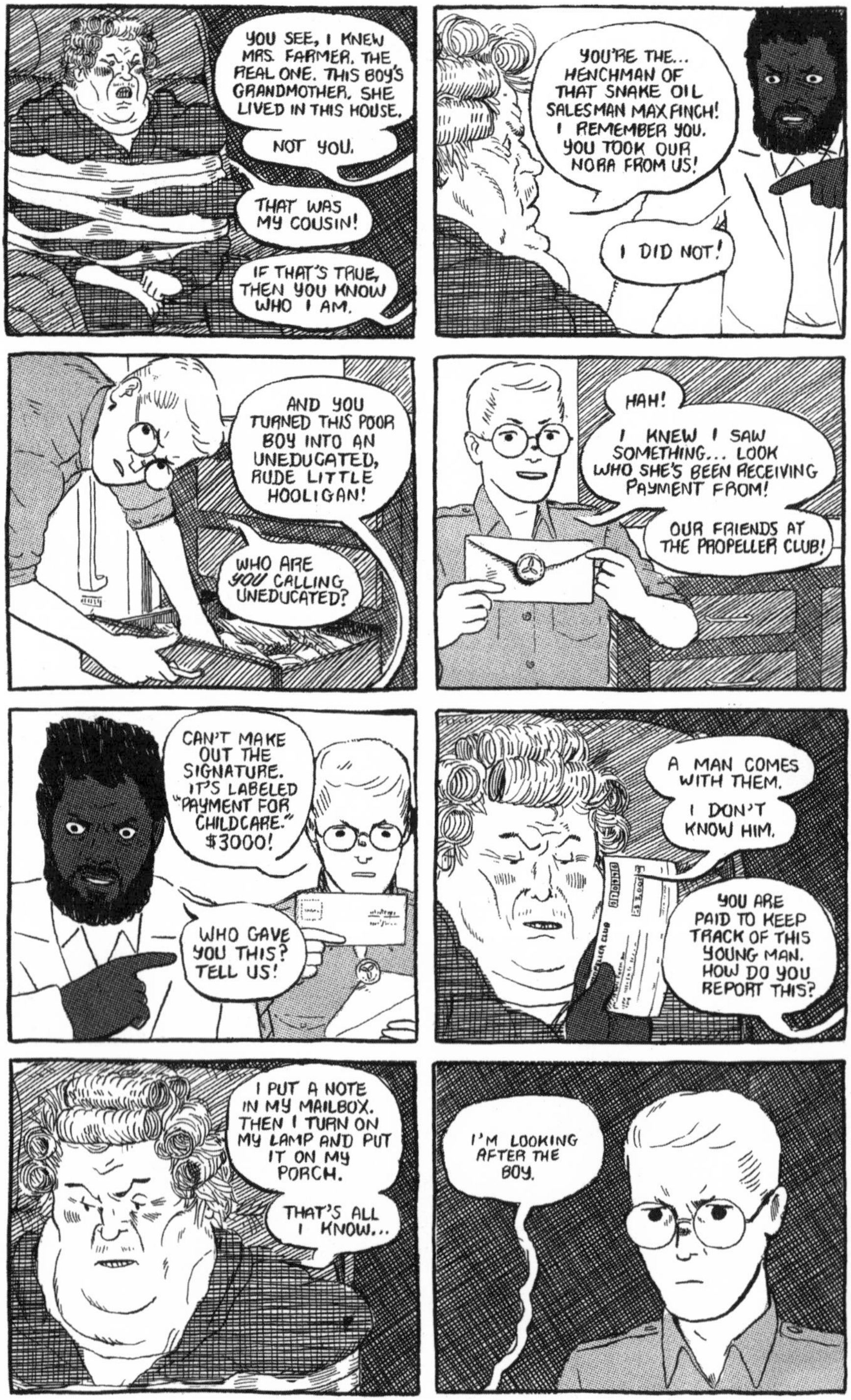
YOU SEE, I KNEW MRS. FARMER. THE REAL ONE. THIS BOY'S GRANDMOTHER. SHE LIVED IN THIS HOUSE.
NOT YOU.
THAT WAS MY COUSIN!
IF THAT'S TRUE, THEN YOU KNOW WHO I AM.
YOU'RE THE... HENCHMAN OF THAT SNAKE OIL SALESMAN MAX FINCH! I REMEMBER YOU. YOU TOOK OUR NORA FROM US!
I DID NOT!
AND YOU TURNED THIS POOR BOY INTO AN UNEDUCATED, RUDE LITTLE HOOLIGAN!
WHO ARE *YOU* CALLING UNEDUCATED?
HAH!
I KNEW I SAW SOMETHING... LOOK WHO SHE'S BEEN RECEIVING PAYMENT FROM!
OUR FRIENDS AT THE PROPELLER CLUB!
CAN'T MAKE OUT THE SIGNATURE. IT'S LABELED "PAYMENT FOR CHILDCARE." $3000!
WHO GAVE YOU THIS? TELL US!
A MAN COMES WITH THEM.
I DON'T KNOW HIM.
YOU ARE PAID TO KEEP TRACK OF THIS YOUNG MAN. HOW DO YOU REPORT THIS?
I PUT A NOTE IN MY MAILBOX. THEN I TURN ON MY LAMP AND PUT IT ON MY PORCH.
THAT'S ALL I KNOW...
I'M LOOKING AFTER THE BOY.

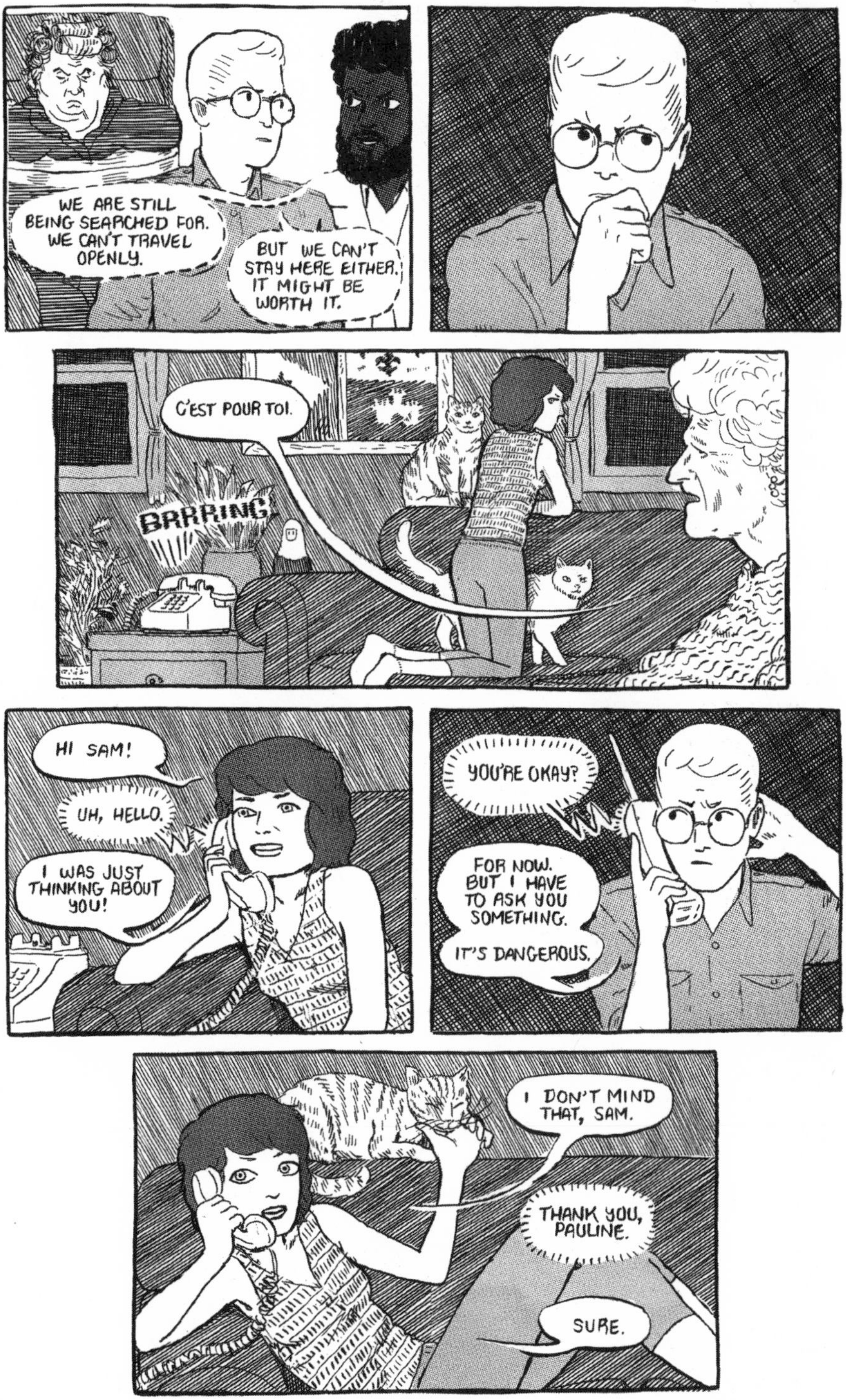
WE ARE STILL BEING SEARCHED FOR. WE CAN'T TRAVEL OPENLY.
BUT WE CAN'T STAY HERE EITHER. IT MIGHT BE WORTH IT.
C'EST POUR TOI.
BRRRING
HI SAM!
UH, HELLO.
I WAS JUST THINKING ABOUT YOU!
YOU'RE OKAY?
FOR NOW. BUT I HAVE TO ASK YOU SOMETHING.
IT'S DANGEROUS.
I DON'T MIND THAT, SAM.
THANK YOU, PAULINE.
SURE.

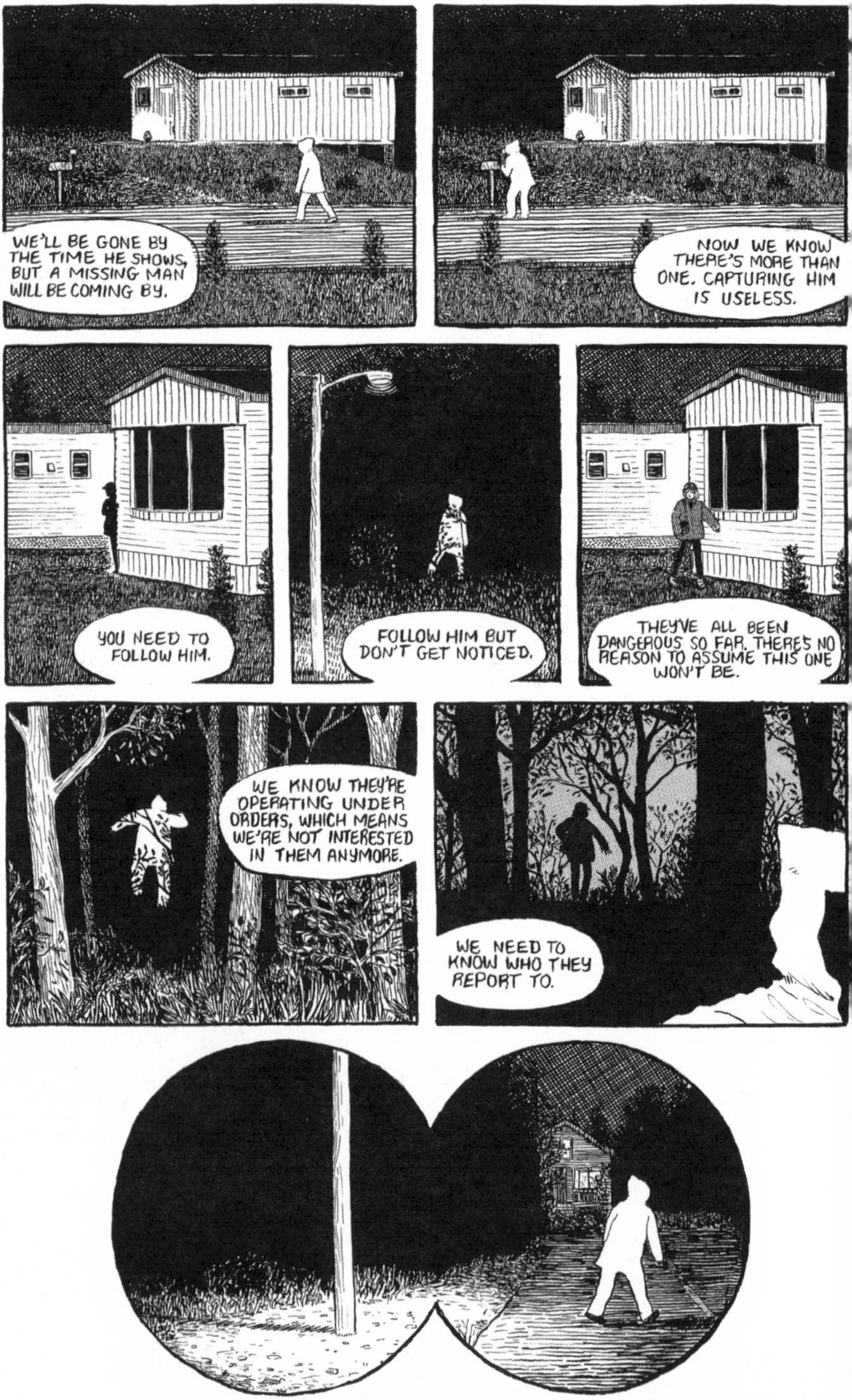

WE'LL BE GONE BY THE TIME HE SHOWS, BUT A MISSING MAN WILL BE COMING BY.
NOW WE KNOW THERE'S MORE THAN ONE. CAPTURING HIM IS USELESS.
YOU NEED TO FOLLOW HIM.
FOLLOW HIM BUT DON'T GET NOTICED.
THEY'VE ALL BEEN DANGEROUS SO FAR. THERE'S NO REASON TO ASSUME THIS ONE WON'T BE.
WE KNOW THEY'RE OPERATING UNDER ORDERS, WHICH MEANS WE'RE NOT INTERESTED IN THEM ANYMORE.
WE NEED TO KNOW WHO THEY REPORT TO.

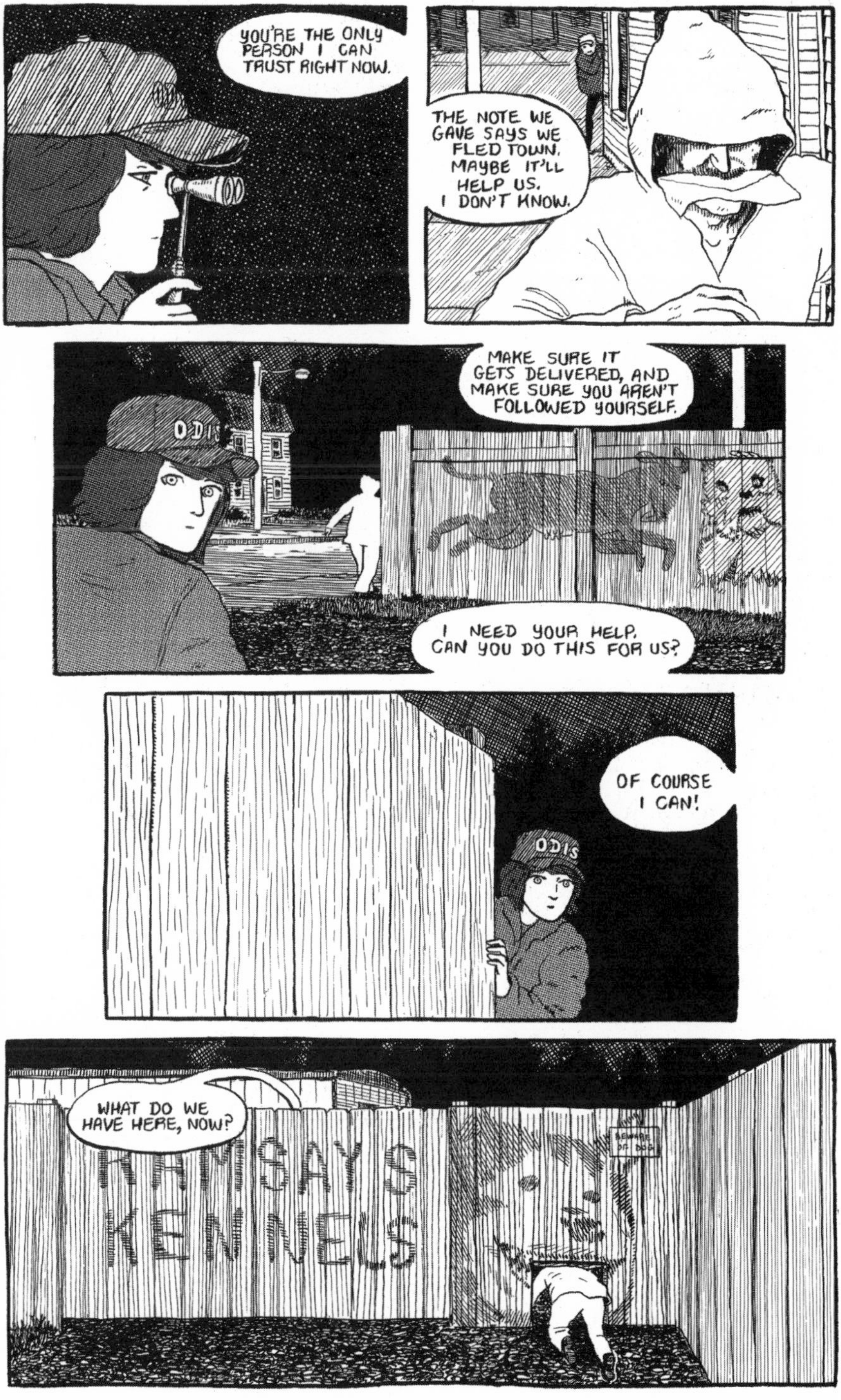
YOU'RE THE ONLY PERSON I CAN TRUST RIGHT NOW.
THE NOTE WE GAVE SAYS WE FLED TOWN. MAYBE IT'LL HELP US. I DON'T KNOW.
ODIS
MAKE SURE IT GETS DELIVERED, AND MAKE SURE YOU AREN'T FOLLOWED YOURSELF.
I NEED YOUR HELP. CAN YOU DO THIS FOR US?
ODIS
OF COURSE I CAN!
WHAT DO WE HAVE HERE, NOW?
RAMSAY'S KENNELS
BEWARE OF DOG

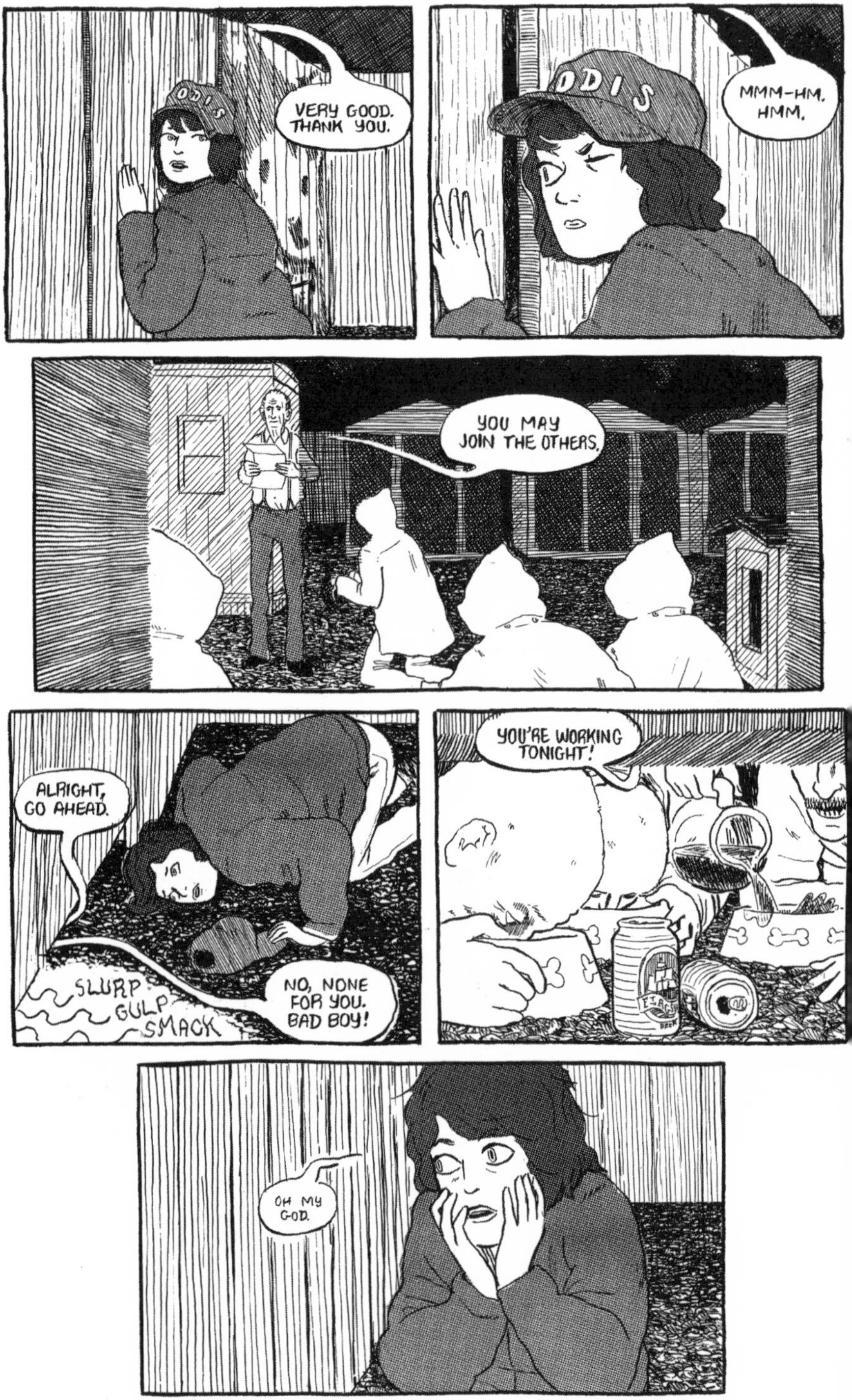
VERY GOOD. THANK YOU.
MMM-HM. HMM.
YOU MAY JOIN THE OTHERS.
ALRIGHT, GO AHEAD.
SLURP GULP SMACK
NO, NONE FOR YOU. BAD BOY!
YOU'RE WORKING TONIGHT!
OH MY GOD.

CHAPTER
NINE

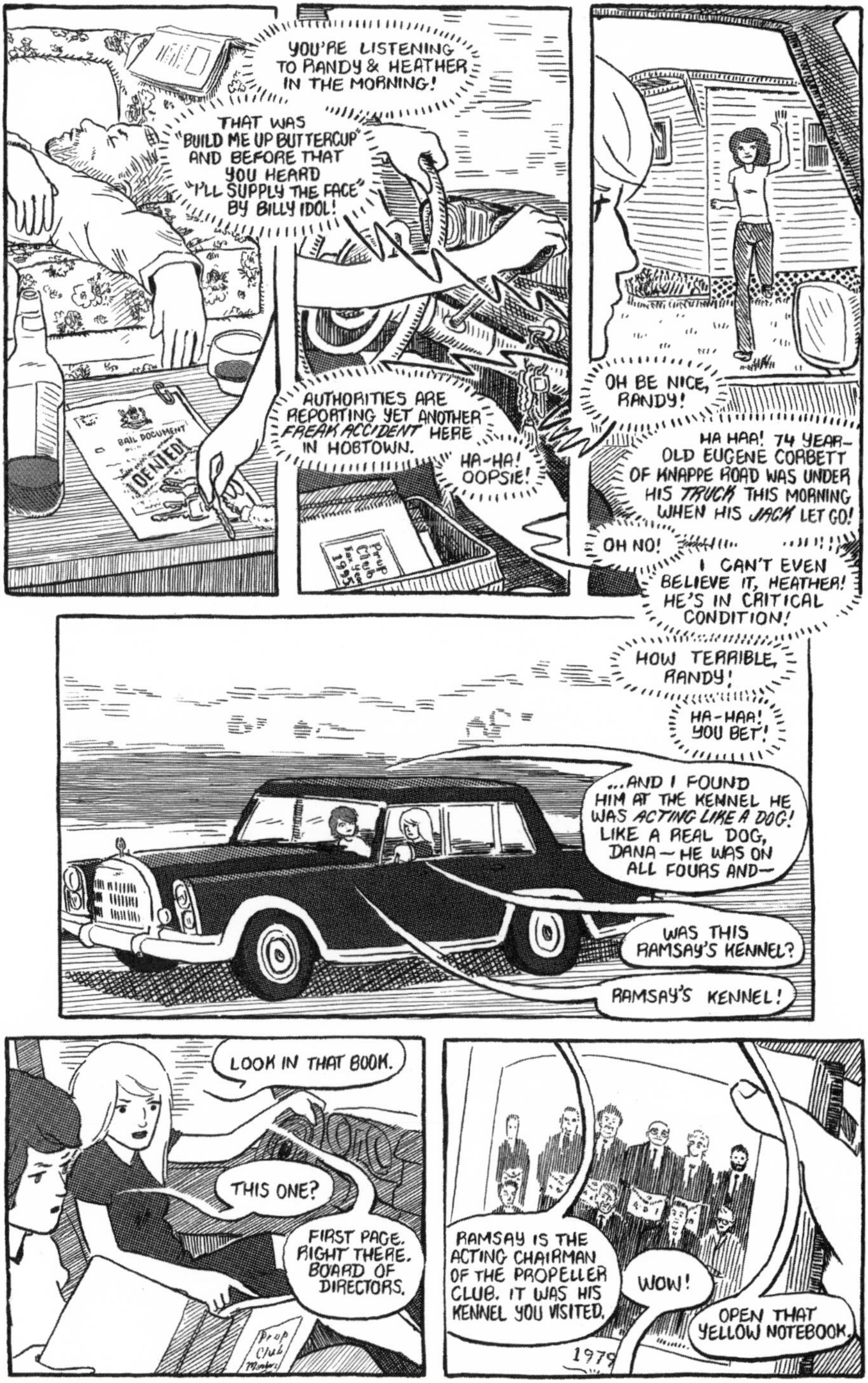
YOU'RE LISTENING TO RANDY & HEATHER IN THE MORNING!
THAT WAS "BUILD ME UP BUTTERCUP" AND BEFORE THAT YOU HEARD "I'LL SUPPLY THE FACE" BY BILLY IDOL!
BAIL DOCUMENT
DENIED!
AUTHORITIES ARE REPORTING YET ANOTHER FREAK ACCIDENT HERE IN HOBTOWN.
HA-HA! OOPSIE!
Prop Club Year 1995
OH BE NICE, RANDY!
HA HAA! 74 YEAR-OLD EUGENE CORBETT OF KNAPPE ROAD WAS UNDER HIS TRUCK THIS MORNING WHEN HIS JACK LET GO!
OH NO!
I CAN'T EVEN BELIEVE IT, HEATHER! HE'S IN CRITICAL CONDITION!
HOW TERRIBLE, RANDY!
HA-HAA! YOU BET!
...AND I FOUND HIM AT THE KENNEL HE WAS ACTING LIKE A DOG! LIKE A REAL DOG, DANA— HE WAS ON ALL FOURS AND—
WAS THIS RAMSAY'S KENNEL?
RAMSAY'S KENNEL!
LOOK IN THAT BOOK.
THIS ONE?
FIRST PAGE. RIGHT THERE. BOARD OF DIRECTORS.
Prop Club
RAMSAY IS THE ACTING CHAIRMAN OF THE PROPELLER CLUB. IT WAS HIS KENNEL YOU VISITED.
WOW!
OPEN THAT YELLOW NOTEBOOK.
1979

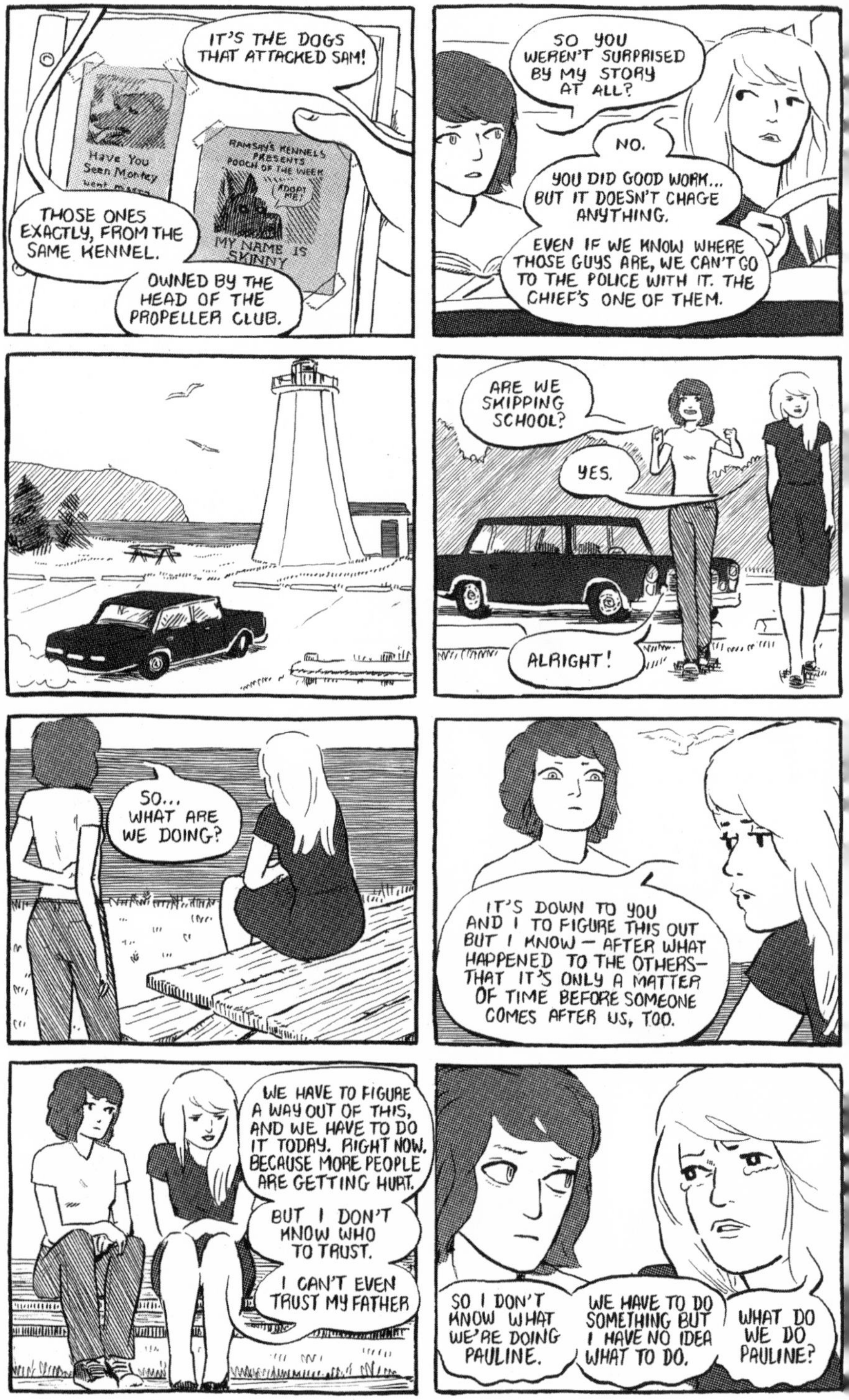
IT'S THE DOGS THAT ATTACKED SAM!
Have You Seen Montey
RAMSAY'S KENNELS PRESENTS POOCH OF THE WEEK
ADOPT ME!
MY NAME IS SKINNY
THOSE ONES EXACTLY, FROM THE SAME KENNEL.
OWNED BY THE HEAD OF THE PROPELLER CLUB.
SO YOU WEREN'T SURPRISED BY MY STORY AT ALL?
NO.
YOU DID GOOD WORK... BUT IT DOESN'T CHAGE ANYTHING.
EVEN IF WE KNOW WHERE THOSE GUYS ARE, WE CAN'T GO TO THE POLICE WITH IT. THE CHIEF'S ONE OF THEM.
ARE WE SKIPPING SCHOOL?
YES.
ALRIGHT!
SO... WHAT ARE WE DOING?
IT'S DOWN TO YOU AND I TO FIGURE THIS OUT BUT I KNOW — AFTER WHAT HAPPENED TO THE OTHERS— THAT IT'S ONLY A MATTER OF TIME BEFORE SOMEONE COMES AFTER US, TOO.
WE HAVE TO FIGURE A WAY OUT OF THIS, AND WE HAVE TO DO IT TODAY. RIGHT NOW. BECAUSE MORE PEOPLE ARE GETTING HURT.
BUT I DON'T KNOW WHO TO TRUST.
I CAN'T EVEN TRUST MY FATHER
SO I DON'T KNOW WHAT WE'RE DOING PAULINE.
WE HAVE TO DO SOMETHING BUT I HAVE NO IDEA WHAT TO DO.
WHAT DO WE DO PAULINE?

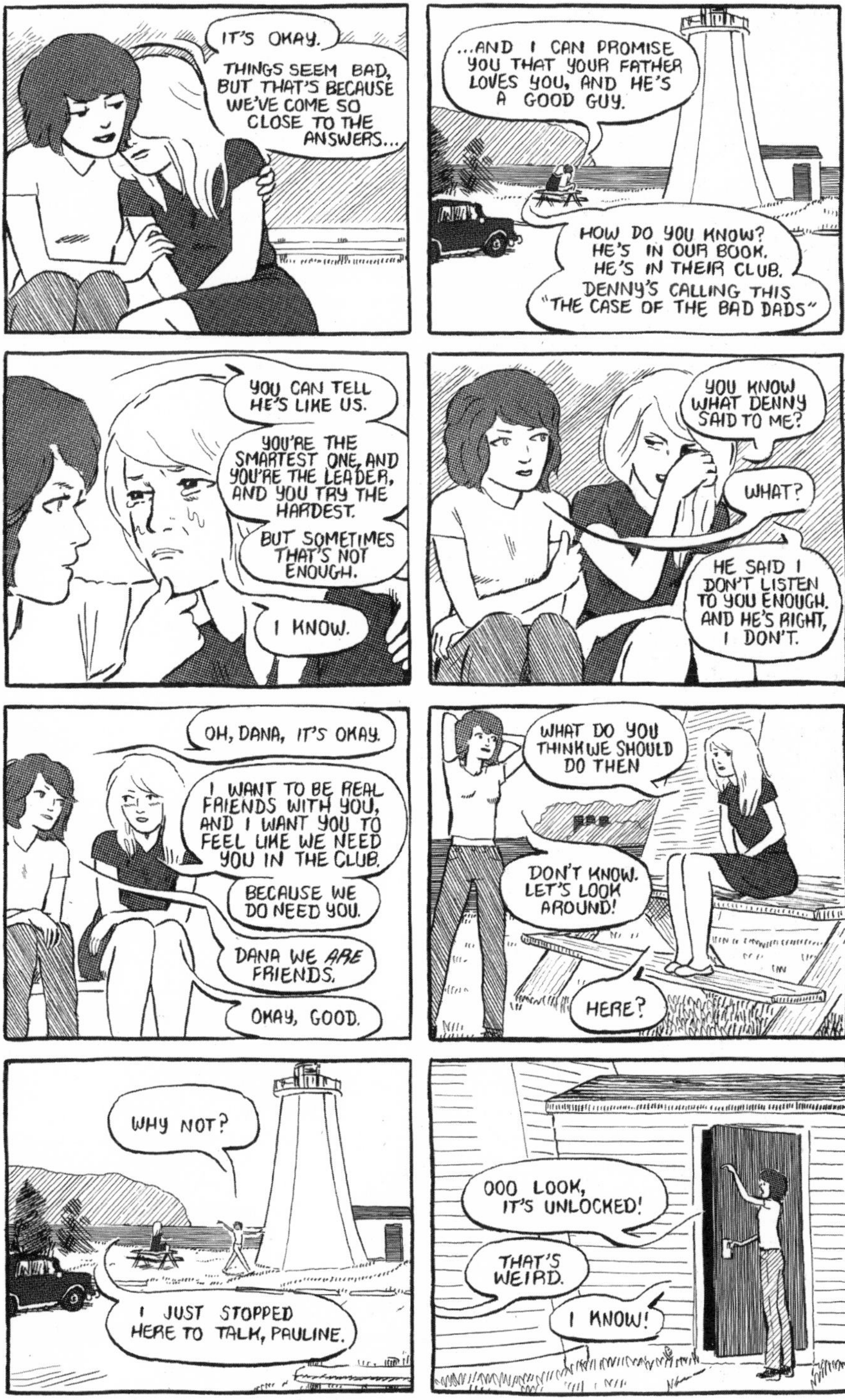
IT'S OKAY.
THINGS SEEM BAD, BUT THAT'S BECAUSE WE'VE COME SO CLOSE TO THE ANSWERS...
...AND I CAN PROMISE YOU THAT YOUR FATHER LOVES YOU, AND HE'S A GOOD GUY.
HOW DO YOU KNOW? HE'S IN OUR BOOK. HE'S IN THEIR CLUB. DENNY'S CALLING THIS "THE CASE OF THE BAD DADS"
YOU CAN TELL HE'S LIKE US.
YOU'RE THE SMARTEST ONE, AND YOU'RE THE LEADER, AND YOU TRY THE HARDEST.
BUT SOMETIMES THAT'S NOT ENOUGH.
I KNOW.
YOU KNOW WHAT DENNY SAID TO ME?
WHAT?
HE SAID I DON'T LISTEN TO YOU ENOUGH. AND HE'S RIGHT, I DON'T.
OH, DANA, IT'S OKAY.
I WANT TO BE REAL FRIENDS WITH YOU, AND I WANT YOU TO FEEL LIKE WE NEED YOU IN THE CLUB.
BECAUSE WE DO NEED YOU.
DANA WE *ARE* FRIENDS.
OKAY, GOOD.
WHAT DO YOU THINK WE SHOULD DO THEN
DON'T KNOW. LET'S LOOK AROUND!
HERE?
WHY NOT?
I JUST STOPPED HERE TO TALK, PAULINE.
OOO LOOK, IT'S UNLOCKED!
THAT'S WEIRD.
I KNOW!

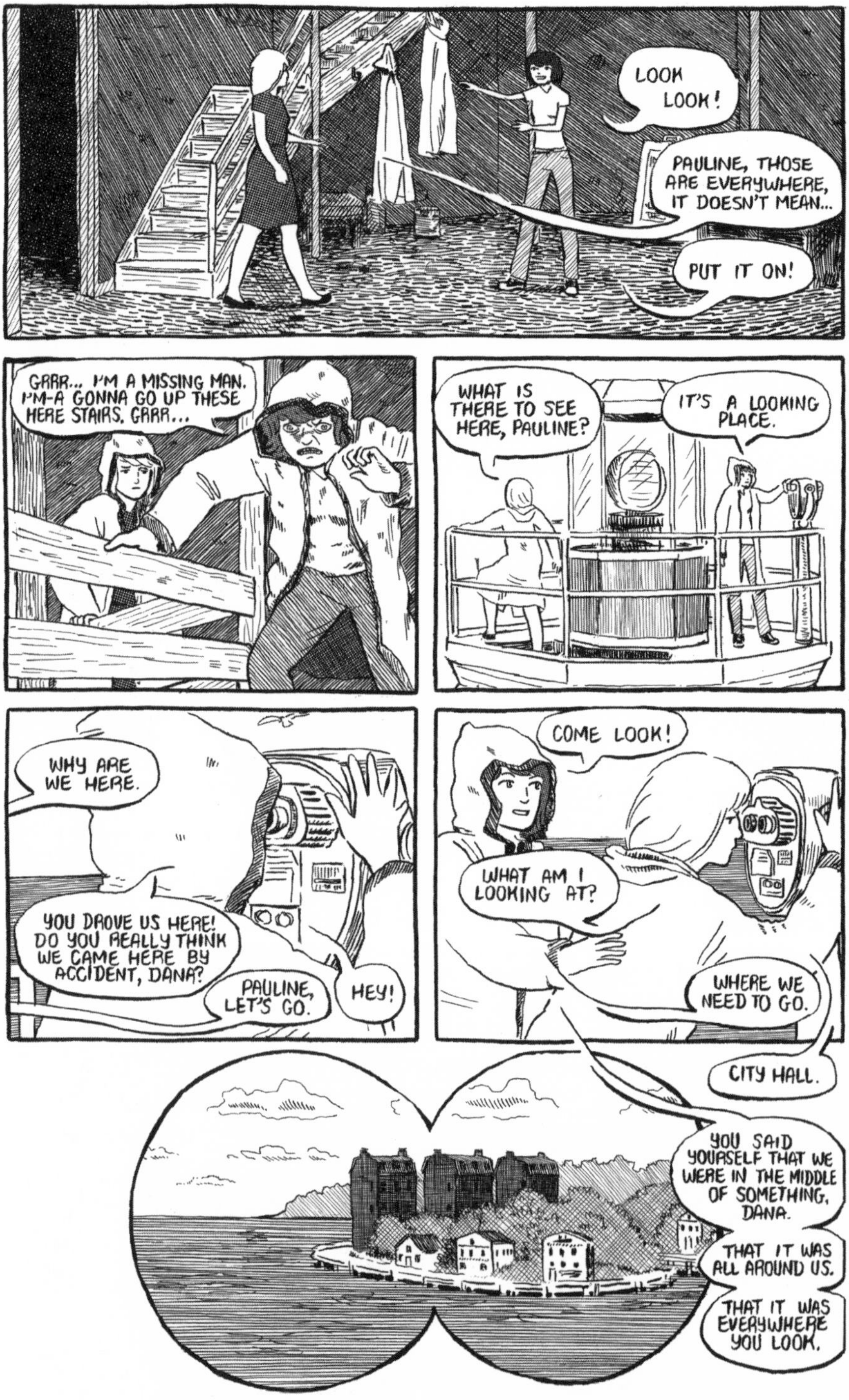
LOOK LOOK!
PAULINE, THOSE ARE EVERYWHERE, IT DOESN'T MEAN...
PUT IT ON!
GRRR... I'M A MISSING MAN. I'M-A GONNA GO UP THESE HERE STAIRS. GRRR...
WHAT IS THERE TO SEE HERE, PAULINE?
IT'S A LOOKING PLACE.
WHY ARE WE HERE.
YOU DROVE US HERE! DO YOU REALLY THINK WE CAME HERE BY ACCIDENT, DANA?
PAULINE, LET'S GO.
HEY!
COME LOOK!
WHAT AM I LOOKING AT?
WHERE WE NEED TO GO.
CITY HALL.
YOU SAID YOURSELF THAT WE WERE IN THE MIDDLE OF SOMETHING, DANA.
THAT IT WAS ALL AROUND US.
THAT IT WAS EVERYWHERE YOU LOOK.

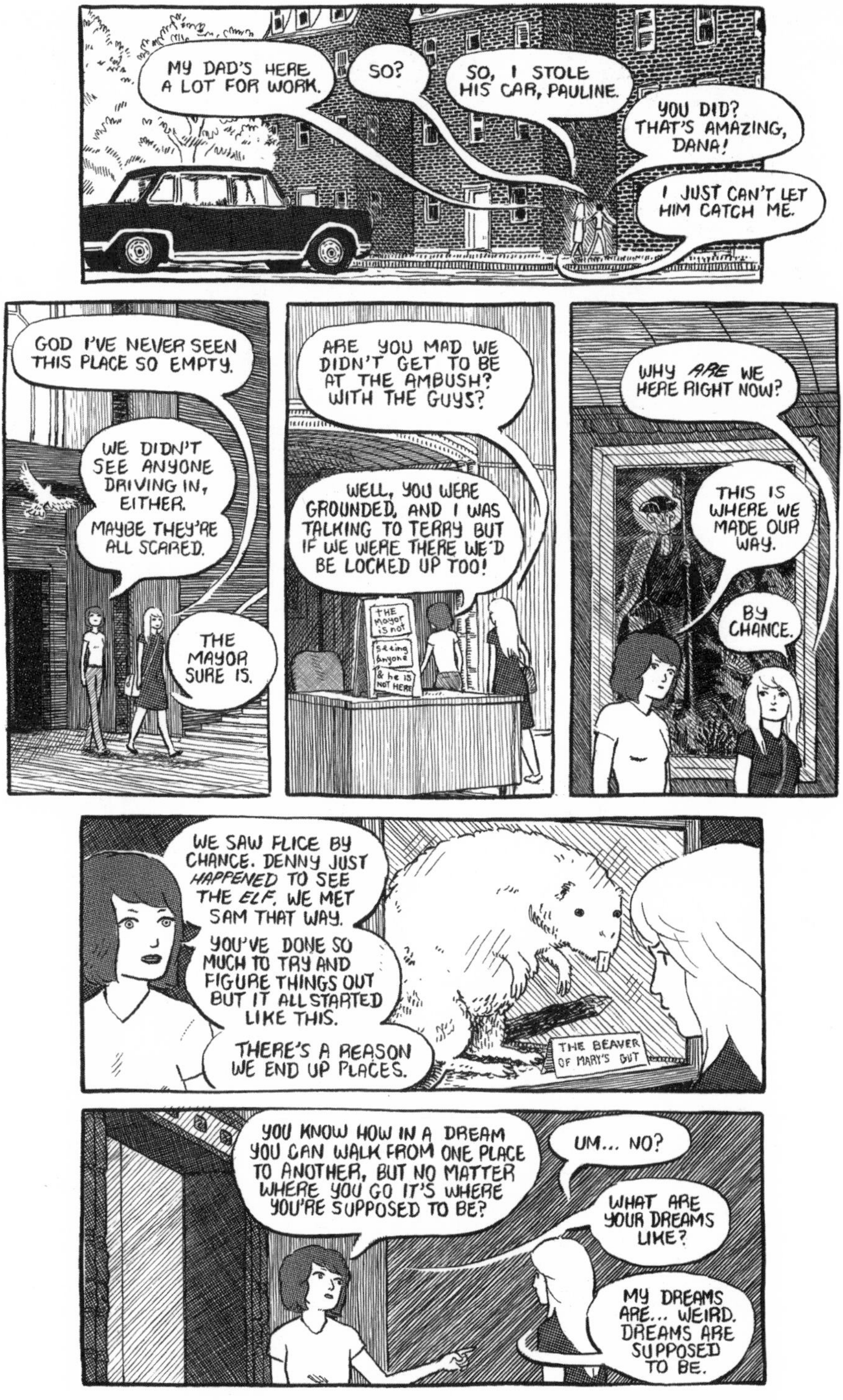

MY DAD'S HERE A LOT FOR WORK.
SO?
SO, I STOLE HIS CAR, PAULINE.
YOU DID? THAT'S AMAZING, DANA!
I JUST CAN'T LET HIM CATCH ME.
GOD I'VE NEVER SEEN THIS PLACE SO EMPTY.
WE DIDN'T SEE ANYONE DRIVING IN, EITHER.
MAYBE THEY'RE ALL SCARED.
THE MAYOR SURE IS.
ARE YOU MAD WE DIDN'T GET TO BE AT THE AMBUSH? WITH THE GUYS?
WELL, YOU WERE GROUNDED, AND I WAS TALKING TO TERRY BUT IF WE WERE THERE WE'D BE LOCKED UP TOO!
THE Mayor is not seeing Anyone & he is NOT HERE
WHY ARE WE HERE RIGHT NOW?
THIS IS WHERE WE MADE OUR WAY.
BY CHANCE.
WE SAW ALICE BY CHANCE. DENNY JUST HAPPENED TO SEE THE ELF. WE MET SAM THAT WAY.
YOU'VE DONE SO MUCH TO TRY AND FIGURE THINGS OUT BUT IT ALL STARTED LIKE THIS.
THERE'S A REASON WE END UP PLACES.
THE BEAVER OF MARY'S GUT
YOU KNOW HOW IN A DREAM YOU CAN WALK FROM ONE PLACE TO ANOTHER, BUT NO MATTER WHERE YOU GO IT'S WHERE YOU'RE SUPPOSED TO BE?
UM... NO?
WHAT ARE YOUR DREAMS LIKE?
MY DREAMS ARE... WEIRD. DREAMS ARE SUPPOSED TO BE.

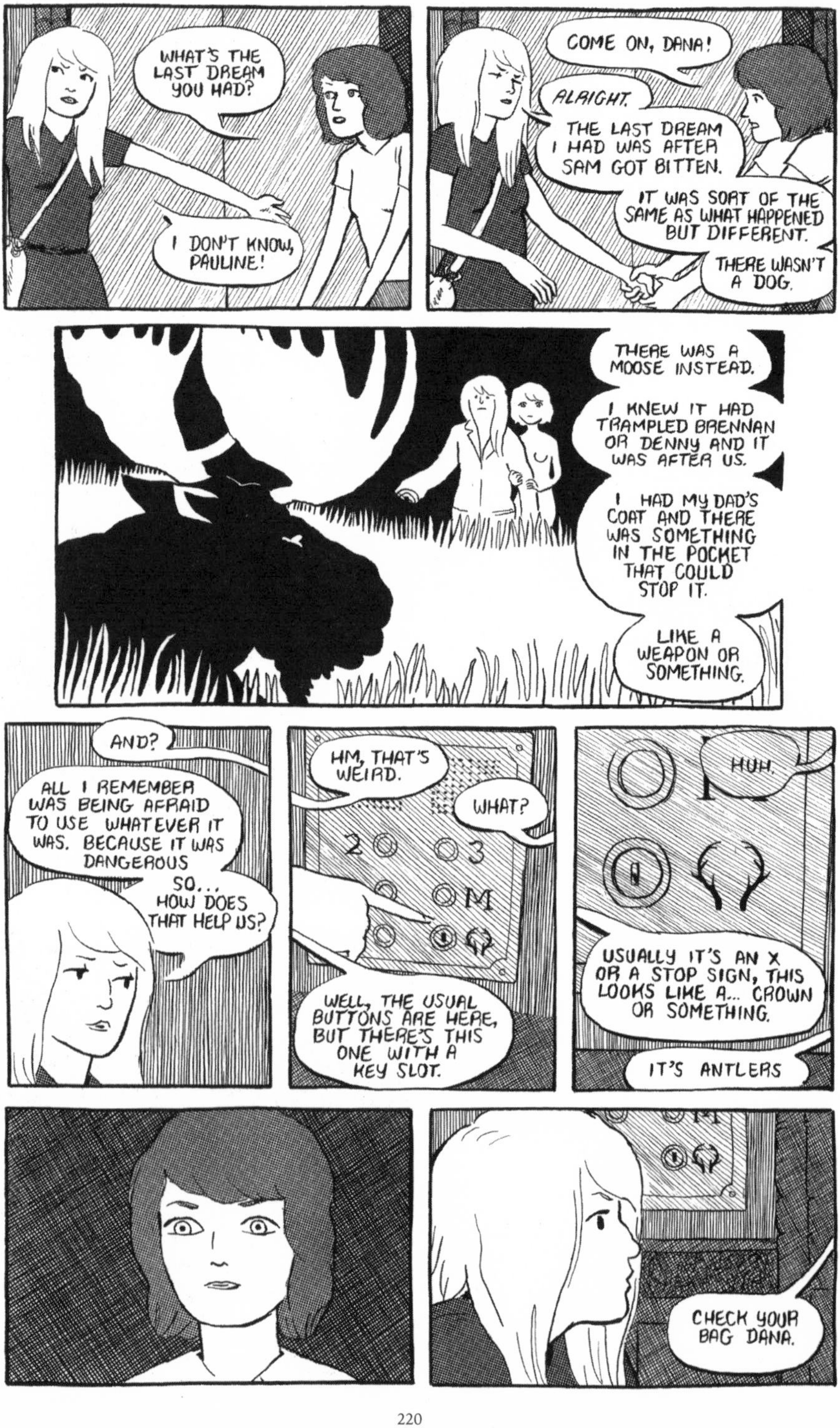

WHAT'S THE LAST DREAM YOU HAD?
I DON'T KNOW, PAULINE!
COME ON, DANA!
ALRIGHT.
THE LAST DREAM I HAD WAS AFTER SAM GOT BITTEN.
IT WAS SORT OF THE SAME AS WHAT HAPPENED BUT DIFFERENT.
THERE WASN'T A DOG.
THERE WAS A MOOSE INSTEAD.
I KNEW IT HAD TRAMPLED BRENNAN OR DENNY AND IT WAS AFTER US.
I HAD MY DAD'S COAT AND THERE WAS SOMETHING IN THE POCKET THAT COULD STOP IT.
LIKE A WEAPON OR SOMETHING.
AND?
ALL I REMEMBER WAS BEING AFRAID TO USE WHATEVER IT WAS. BECAUSE IT WAS DANGEROUS
SO... HOW DOES THAT HELP US?
HM, THAT'S WEIRD.
WHAT?
2
3
M
WELL, THE USUAL BUTTONS ARE HERE, BUT THERE'S THIS ONE WITH A KEY SLOT.
HUH.
USUALLY IT'S AN X OR A STOP SIGN, THIS LOOKS LIKE A... CROWN OR SOMETHING.
IT'S ANTLERS
CHECK YOUR BAG DANA.

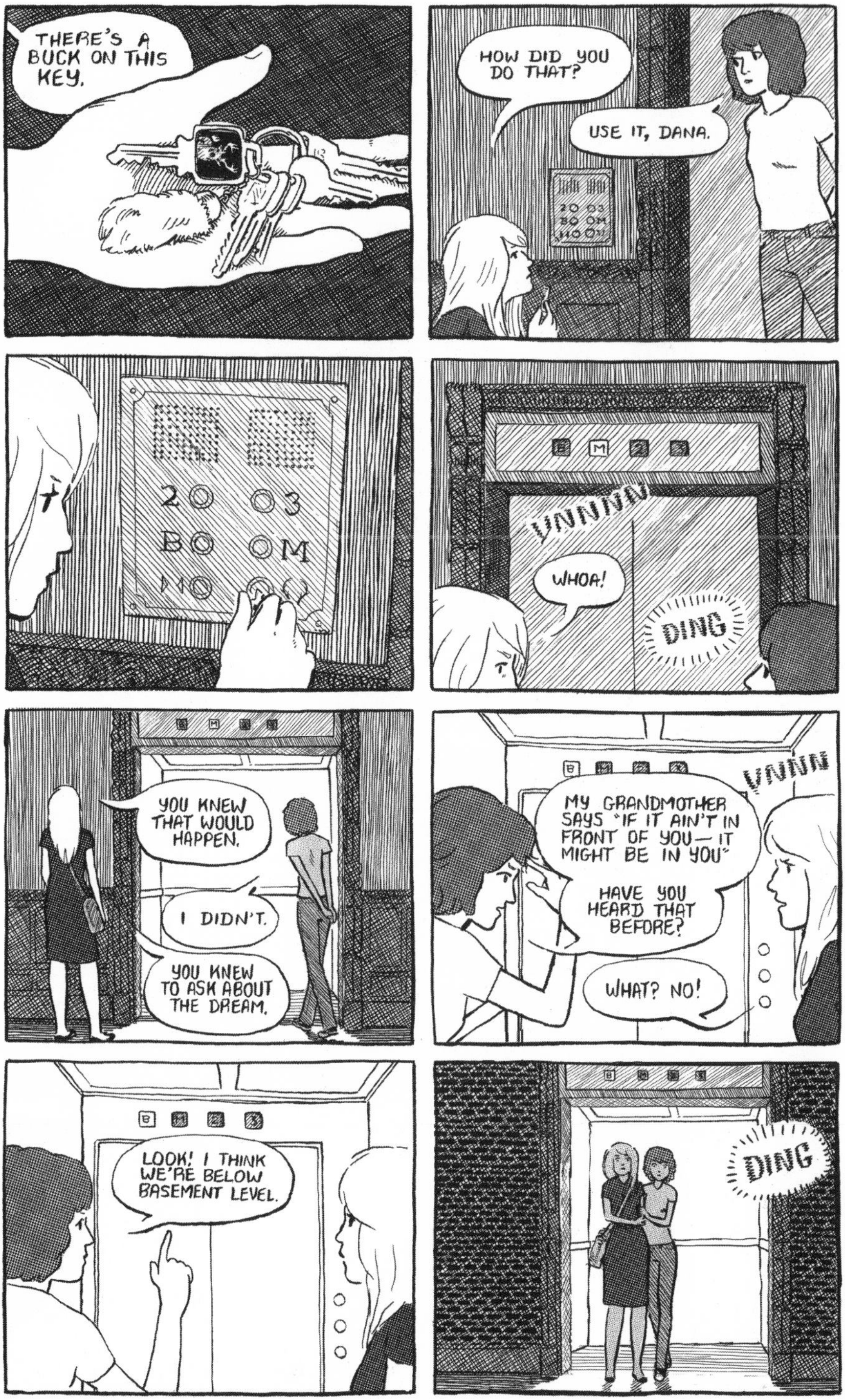
THERE'S A BUCK ON THIS KEY.
HOW DID YOU DO THAT?
USE IT, DANA.
VNNNN
WHOA!
DING
YOU KNEW THAT WOULD HAPPEN.
I DIDN'T.
YOU KNEW TO ASK ABOUT THE DREAM.
VNNN
MY GRANDMOTHER SAYS "IF IT AIN'T IN FRONT OF YOU— IT MIGHT BE IN YOU"
HAVE YOU HEARD THAT BEFORE?
WHAT? NO!
LOOK! I THINK WE'RE BELOW BASEMENT LEVEL.
DING

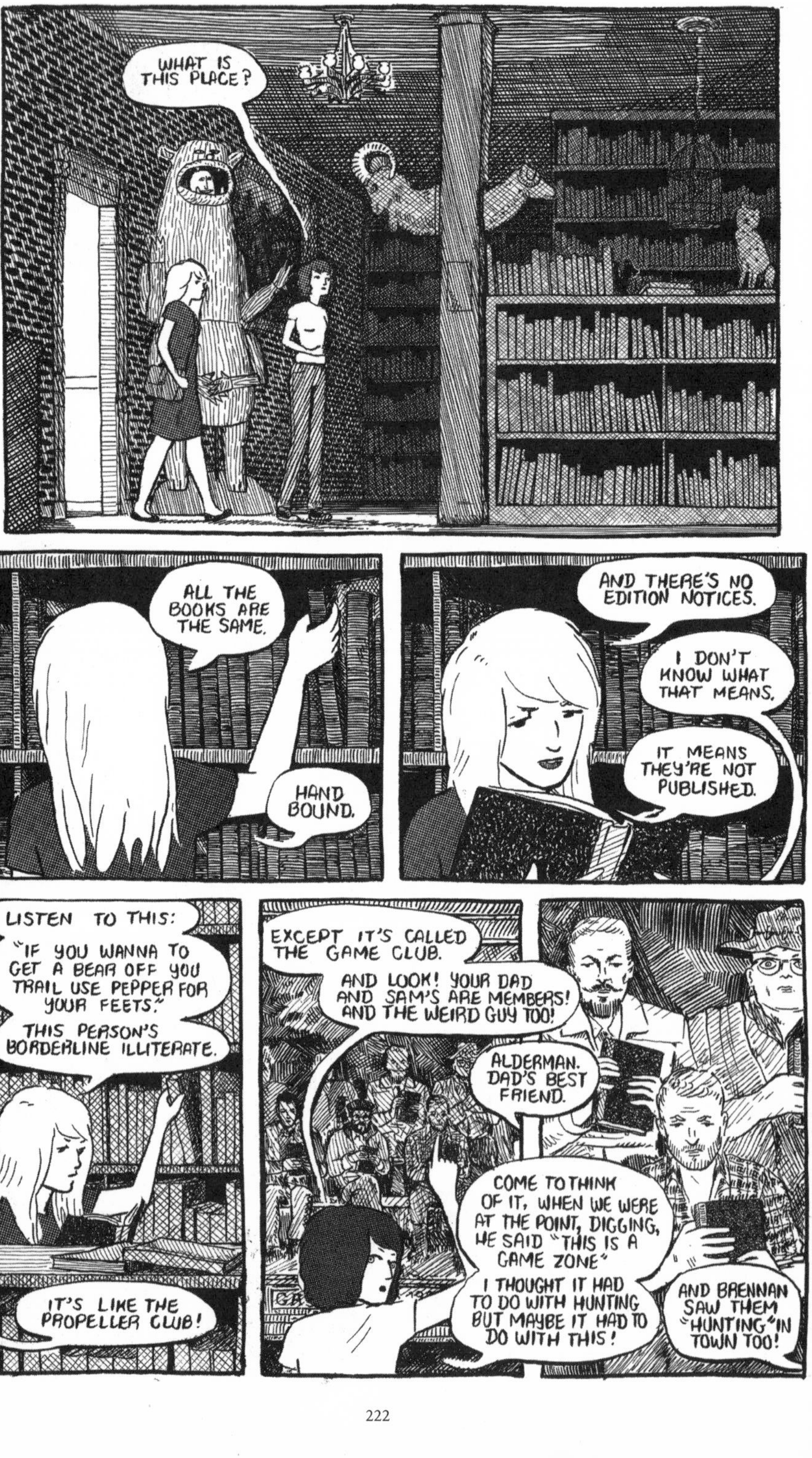
WHAT IS THIS PLACE?
ALL THE BOOKS ARE THE SAME.
HAND BOUND.
AND THERE'S NO EDITION NOTICES.
I DON'T KNOW WHAT THAT MEANS.
IT MEANS THEY'RE NOT PUBLISHED.
LISTEN TO THIS:
"IF YOU WANNA TO GET A BEAR OFF YOU TRAIL USE PEPPER FOR YOUR FEETS."
THIS PERSON'S BORDERLINE ILLITERATE.
IT'S LIKE THE PROPELLER CLUB!
EXCEPT IT'S CALLED THE GAME CLUB.
AND LOOK! YOUR DAD AND SAM'S ARE MEMBERS! AND THE WEIRD GUY TOO!
ALDERMAN. DAD'S BEST FRIEND.
COME TO THINK OF IT, WHEN WE WERE AT THE POINT, DIGGING, HE SAID "THIS IS A GAME ZONE"
I THOUGHT IT HAD TO DO WITH HUNTING BUT MAYBE IT HAD TO DO WITH THIS!
AND BRENNAN SAW THEM "HUNTING" IN TOWN TOO!

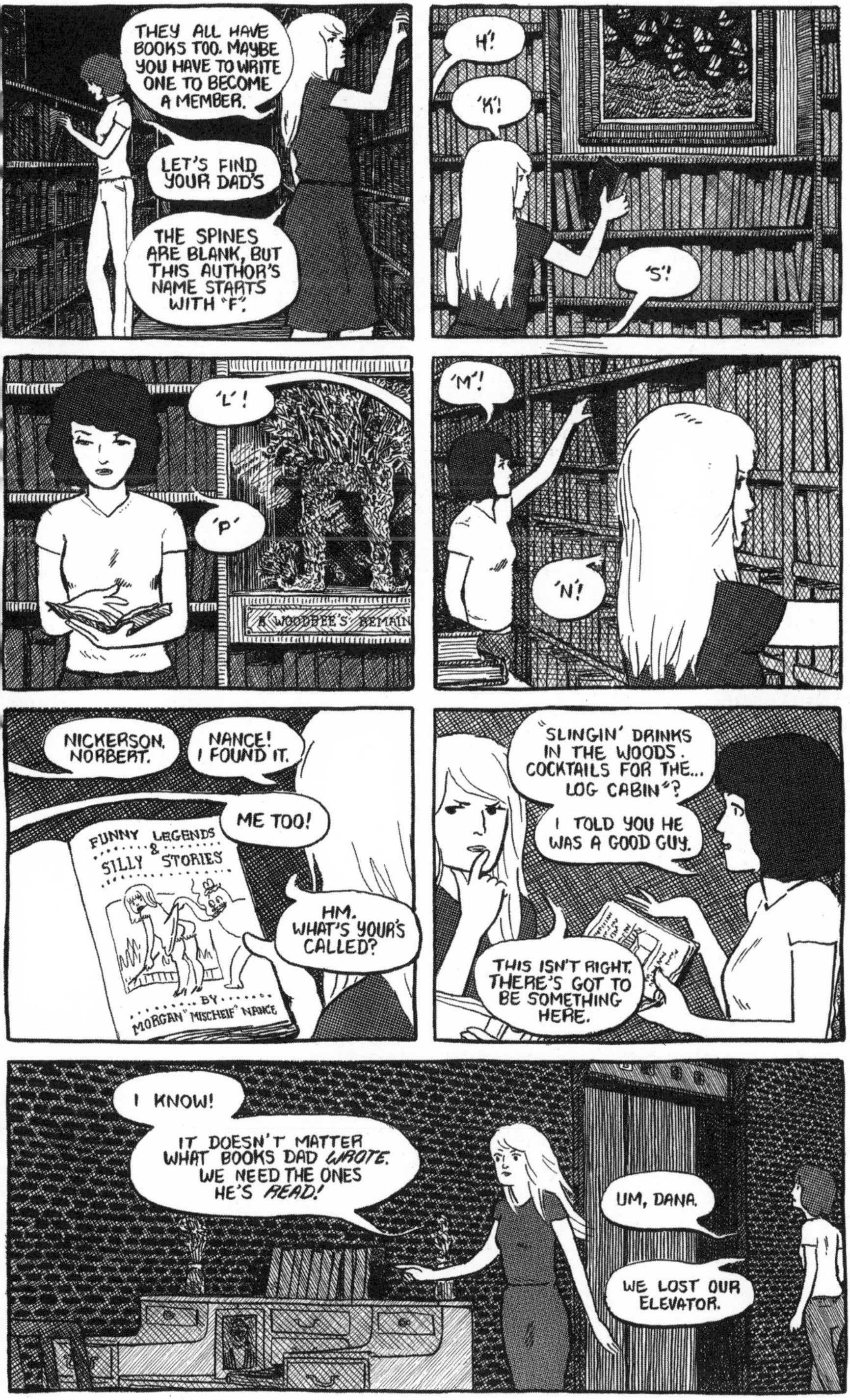

THEY ALL HAVE BOOKS TOO. MAYBE YOU HAVE TO WRITE ONE TO BECOME A MEMBER.
LET'S FIND YOUR DAD'S
THE SPINES ARE BLANK, BUT THIS AUTHOR'S NAME STARTS WITH "F".
'H'!
'K'!
'S'!
'L'!
'P'
A WOODBEE'S REMAIN
'M'!
'N'!
NICKERSON, NORBERT.
NANCE! I FOUND IT.
ME TOO!
FUNNY LEGENDS & SILLY STORIES
BY MORGAN "MISCHEIF" NANCE
HM. WHAT'S YOUR'S CALLED?
"SLINGIN' DRINKS IN THE WOODS. COCKTAILS FOR THE... LOG CABIN"?
I TOLD YOU HE WAS A GOOD GUY.
THIS ISN'T RIGHT. THERE'S GOT TO BE SOMETHING HERE.
I KNOW!
IT DOESN'T MATTER WHAT BOOKS DAD WROTE. WE NEED THE ONES HE'S READ!
UM, DANA.
WE LOST OUR ELEVATOR.

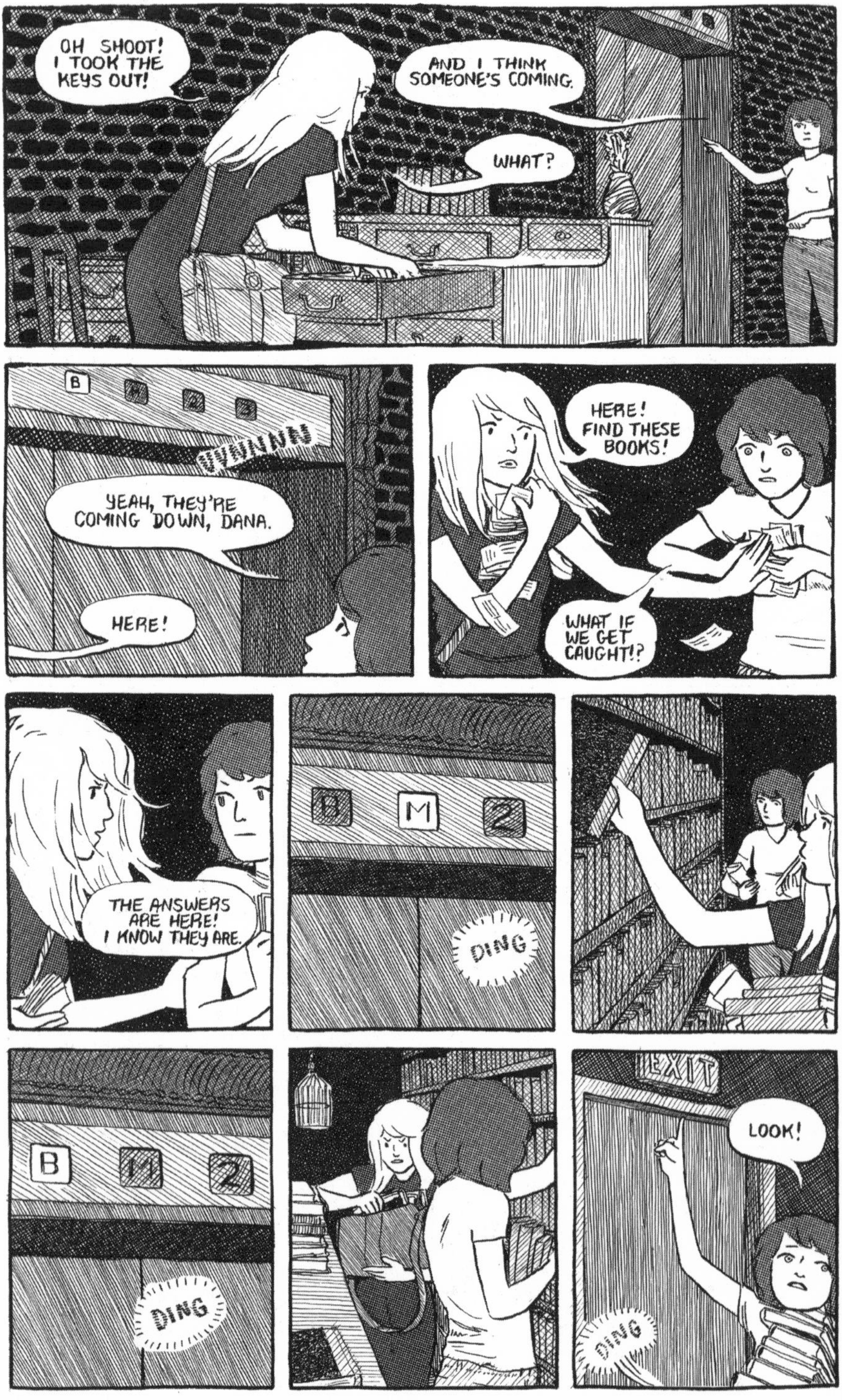
OH SHOOT! I TOOK THE KEYS OUT!
AND I THINK SOMEONE'S COMING.
WHAT?
B M 2 3
VVNNNN
YEAH, THEY'RE COMING DOWN, DANA.
HERE!
HERE! FIND THESE BOOKS!
WHAT IF WE GET CAUGHT!?
THE ANSWERS ARE HERE! I KNOW THEY ARE.
B M 2
DING
B M 2
DING
EXIT
LOOK!
DING

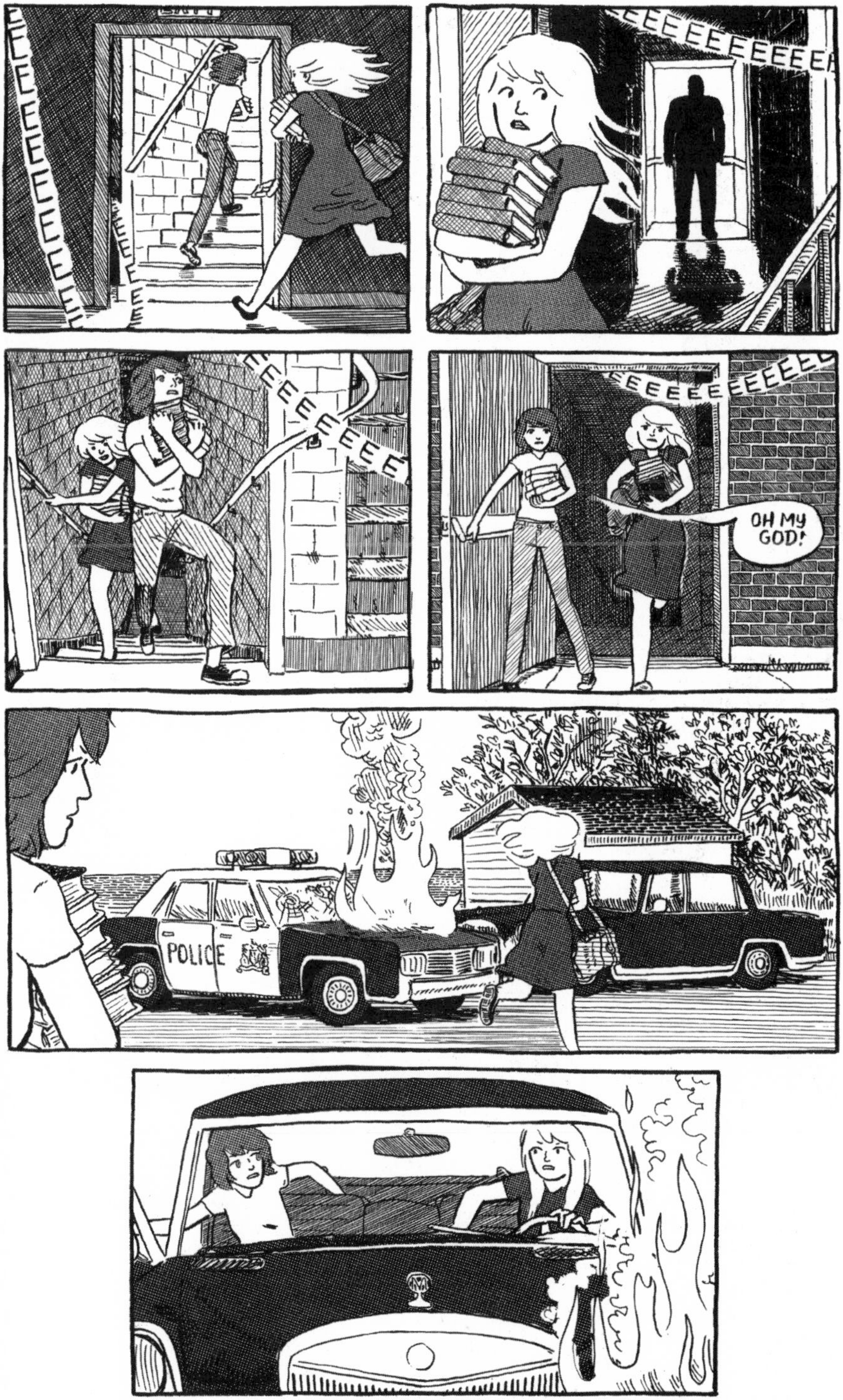
OH MY GOD!
POLICE

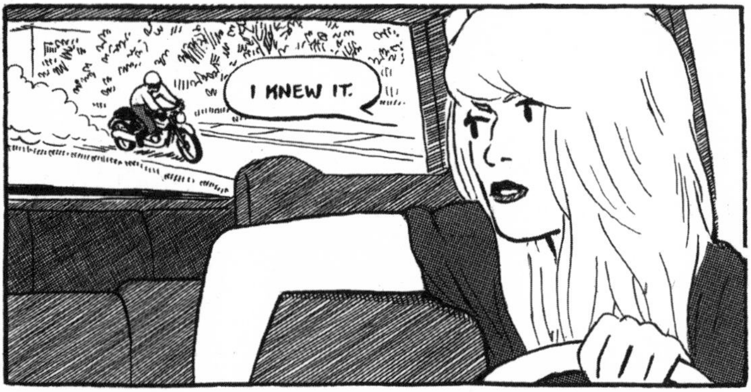
I KNEW IT.

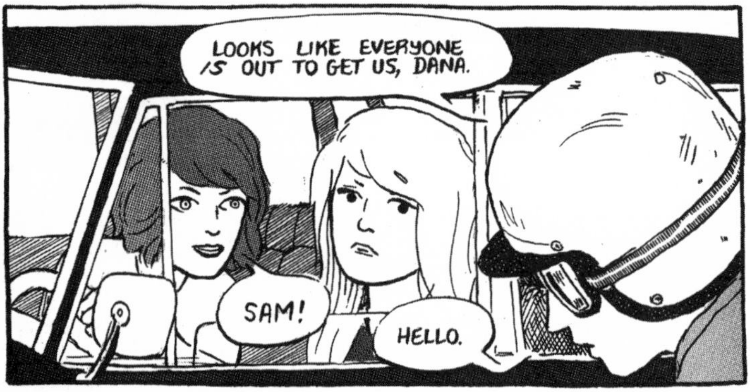
LOOKS LIKE EVERYONE IS OUT TO GET US, DANA.
SAM!
HELLO.

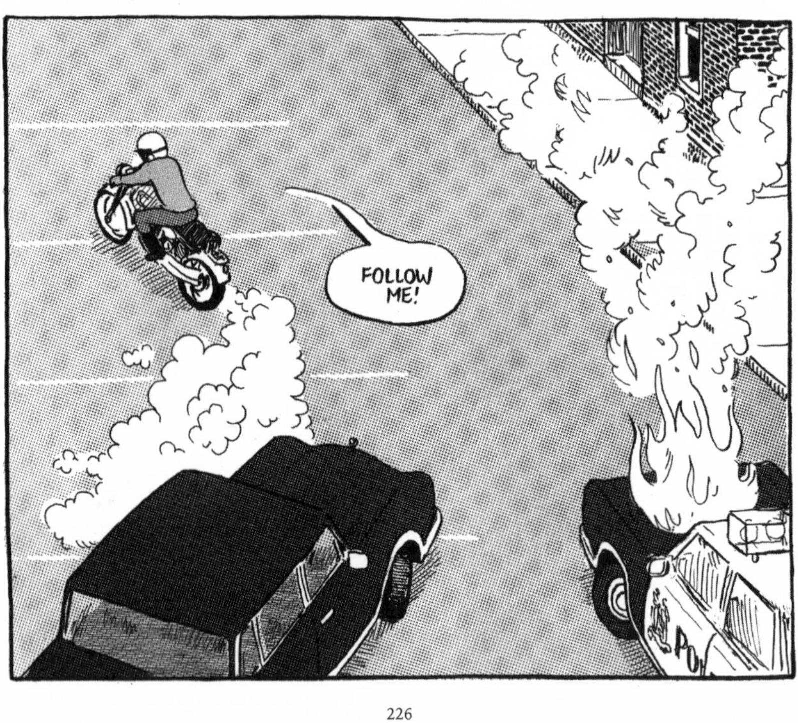
FOLLOW ME!

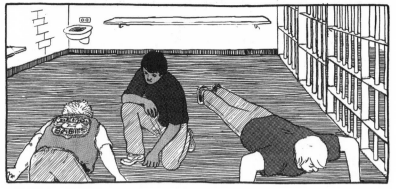

WHY'S HE BEING RELEASED?

HE'S THE KILLER, MAN!

I CAN'T BELIEVE THIS!

THEY CAN'T DO THIS. THESE ARE THE POLICE!

YOU GUYS ARE ALL DICKS!

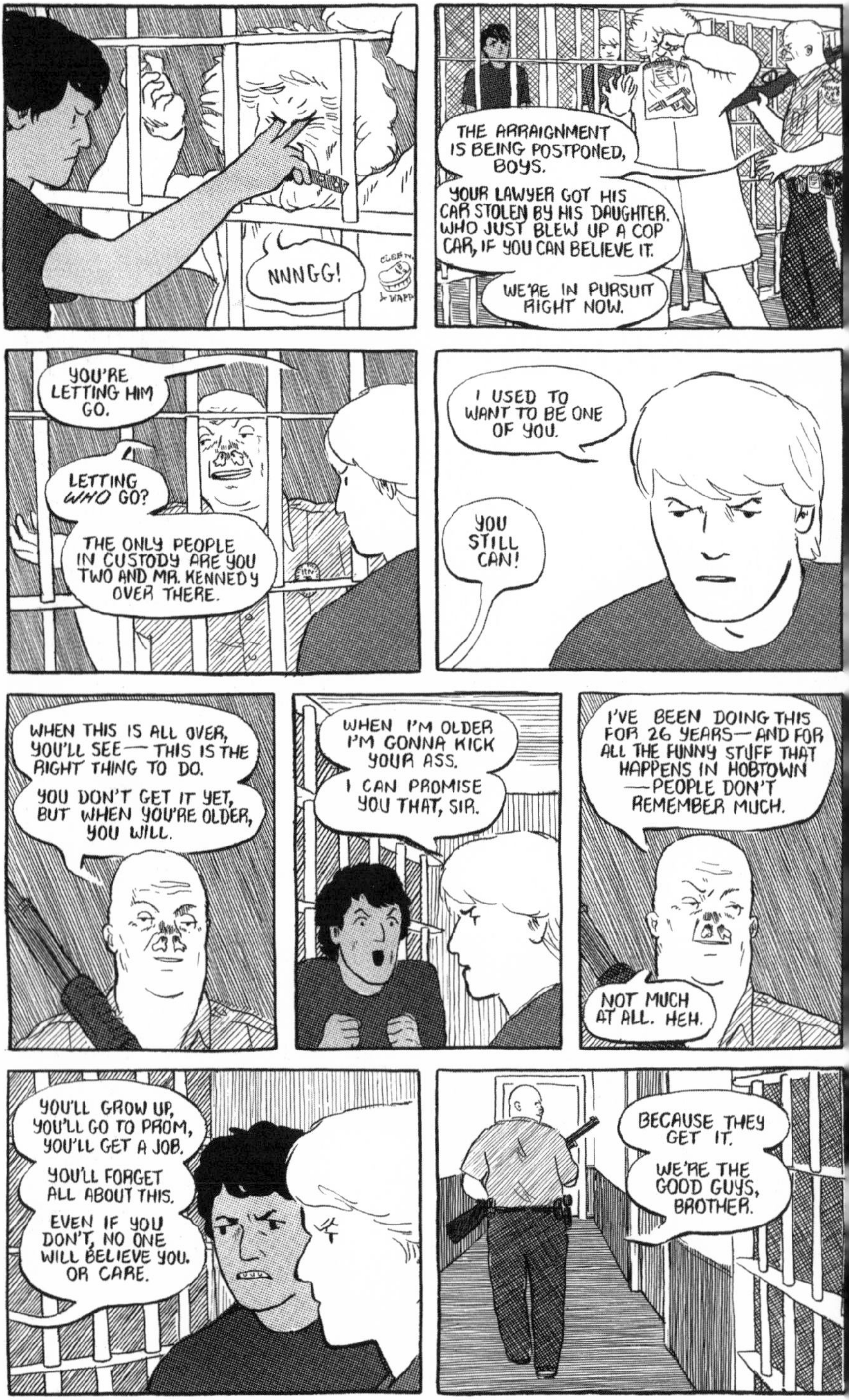
NNNGG!
THE ARRAIGNMENT IS BEING POSTPONED, BOYS.
YOUR LAWYER GOT HIS CAR STOLEN BY HIS DAUGHTER. WHO JUST BLEW UP A COP CAR, IF YOU CAN BELIEVE IT.
WE'RE IN PURSUIT RIGHT NOW.
YOU'RE LETTING HIM GO.
LETTING *WHO* GO?
THE ONLY PEOPLE IN CUSTODY ARE YOU TWO AND MR. KENNEDY OVER THERE.
I USED TO WANT TO BE ONE OF YOU.
YOU STILL CAN!
WHEN THIS IS ALL OVER, YOU'LL SEE— THIS IS THE RIGHT THING TO DO.
YOU DON'T GET IT YET, BUT WHEN YOU'RE OLDER, YOU WILL.
WHEN I'M OLDER I'M GONNA KICK YOUR ASS.
I CAN PROMISE YOU THAT, SIR.
I'VE BEEN DOING THIS FOR 26 YEARS— AND FOR ALL THE FUNNY STUFF THAT HAPPENS IN HOBTOWN —PEOPLE DON'T REMEMBER MUCH.
NOT MUCH AT ALL. HEH.
YOU'LL GROW UP, YOU'LL GO TO PROM, YOU'LL GET A JOB.
YOU'LL FORGET ALL ABOUT THIS.
EVEN IF YOU DON'T, NO ONE WILL BELIEVE YOU. OR CARE.
BECAUSE THEY GET IT.
WE'RE THE GOOD GUYS, BROTHER.

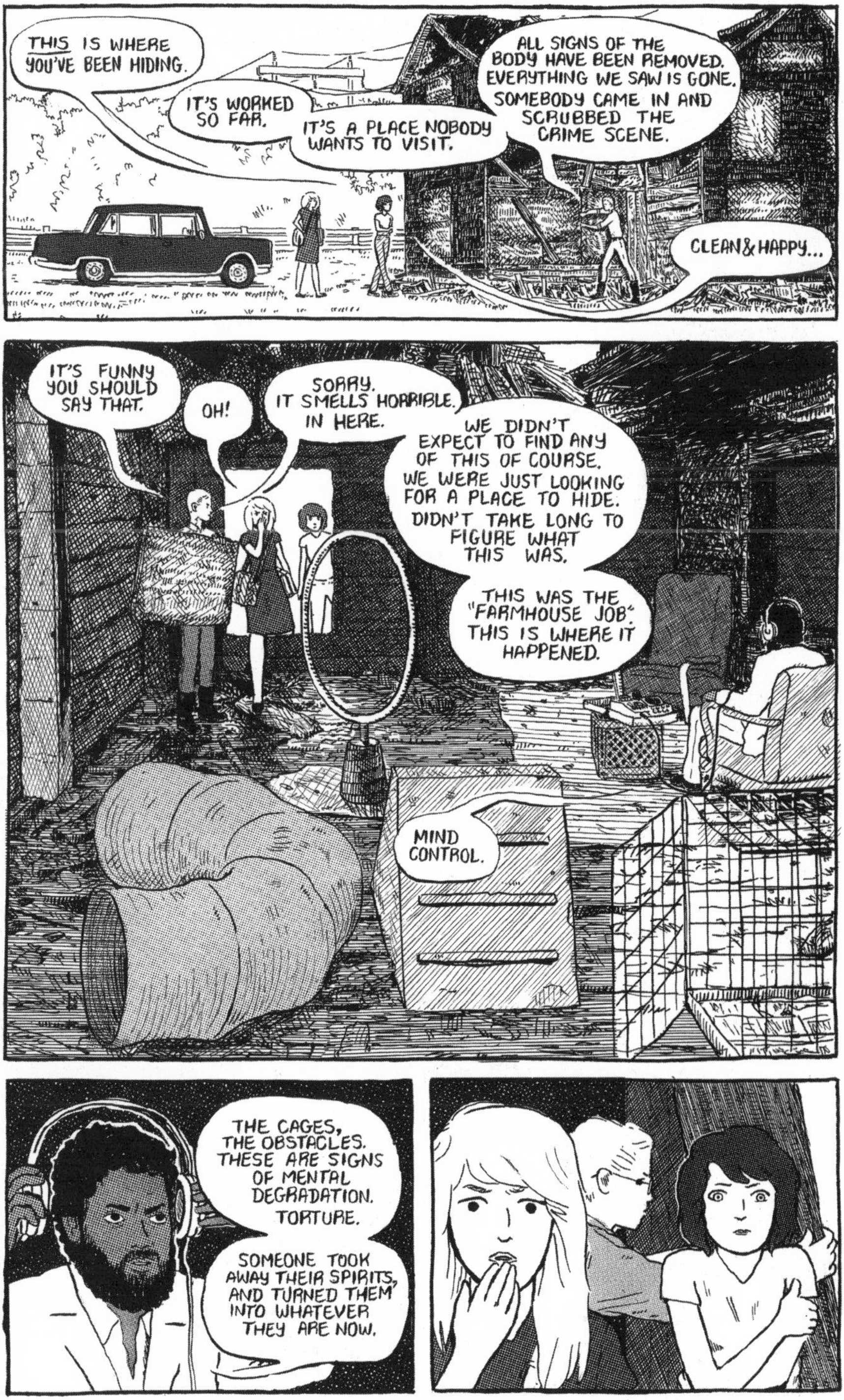
THIS IS WHERE YOU'VE BEEN HIDING.
IT'S WORKED SO FAR.
IT'S A PLACE NOBODY WANTS TO VISIT.
ALL SIGNS OF THE BODY HAVE BEEN REMOVED. EVERYTHING WE SAW IS GONE. SOMEBODY CAME IN AND SCRUBBED THE CRIME SCENE.
CLEAN & HAPPY...
IT'S FUNNY YOU SHOULD SAY THAT.
OH!
SORRY. IT SMELLS HORRIBLE. IN HERE.
WE DIDN'T EXPECT TO FIND ANY OF THIS OF COURSE. WE WERE JUST LOOKING FOR A PLACE TO HIDE. DIDN'T TAKE LONG TO FIGURE WHAT THIS WAS.
THIS WAS THE "FARMHOUSE JOB". THIS IS WHERE IT HAPPENED.
MIND CONTROL.
THE CAGES, THE OBSTACLES. THESE ARE SIGNS OF MENTAL DEGRADATION. TORTURE.
SOMEONE TOOK AWAY THEIR SPIRITS, AND TURNED THEM INTO WHATEVER THEY ARE NOW.

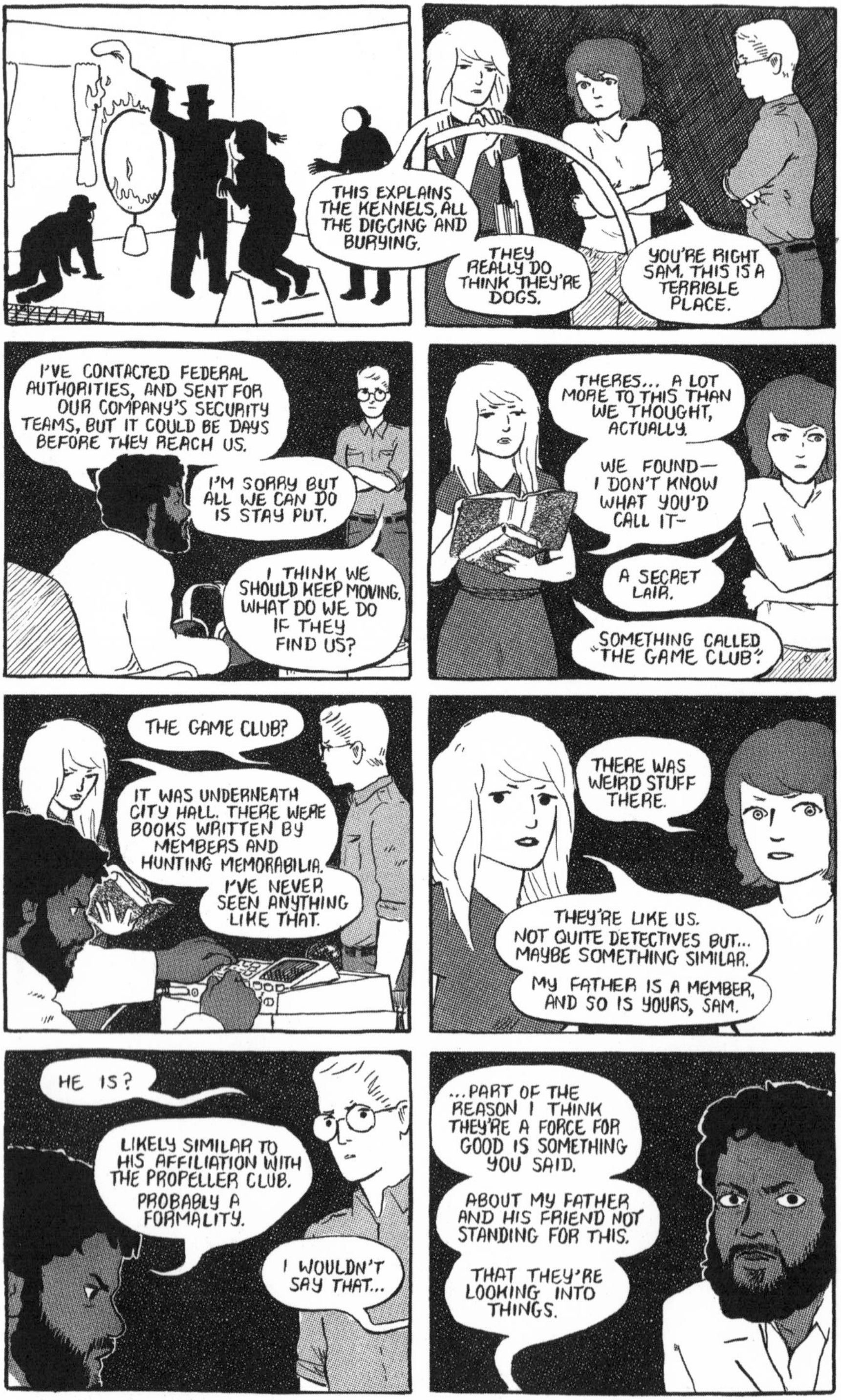
THIS EXPLAINS THE KENNELS, ALL THE DIGGING AND BURYING.
THEY REALLY DO THINK THEY'RE DOGS.
YOU'RE RIGHT SAM. THIS IS A TERRIBLE PLACE.
I'VE CONTACTED FEDERAL AUTHORITIES, AND SENT FOR OUR COMPANY'S SECURITY TEAMS, BUT IT COULD BE DAYS BEFORE THEY REACH US.
I'M SORRY BUT ALL WE CAN DO IS STAY PUT.
I THINK WE SHOULD KEEP MOVING. WHAT DO WE DO IF THEY FIND US?
THERES... A LOT MORE TO THIS THAN WE THOUGHT, ACTUALLY.
WE FOUND— I DON'T KNOW WHAT YOU'D CALL IT-
A SECRET LAIR.
SOMETHING CALLED "THE GAME CLUB".
THE GAME CLUB?
IT WAS UNDERNEATH CITY HALL. THERE WERE BOOKS WRITTEN BY MEMBERS AND HUNTING MEMORABILIA.
I'VE NEVER SEEN ANYTHING LIKE THAT.
THERE WAS WEIRD STUFF THERE.
THEY'RE LIKE US. NOT QUITE DETECTIVES BUT... MAYBE SOMETHING SIMILAR.
MY FATHER IS A MEMBER, AND SO IS YOURS, SAM.
HE IS?
LIKELY SIMILAR TO HIS AFFILIATION WITH THE PROPELLER CLUB.
PROBABLY A FORMALITY.
I WOULDN'T SAY THAT...
...PART OF THE REASON I THINK THEY'RE A FORCE FOR GOOD IS SOMETHING YOU SAID.
ABOUT MY FATHER AND HIS FRIEND NOT STANDING FOR THIS.
THAT THEY'RE LOOKING INTO THINGS.

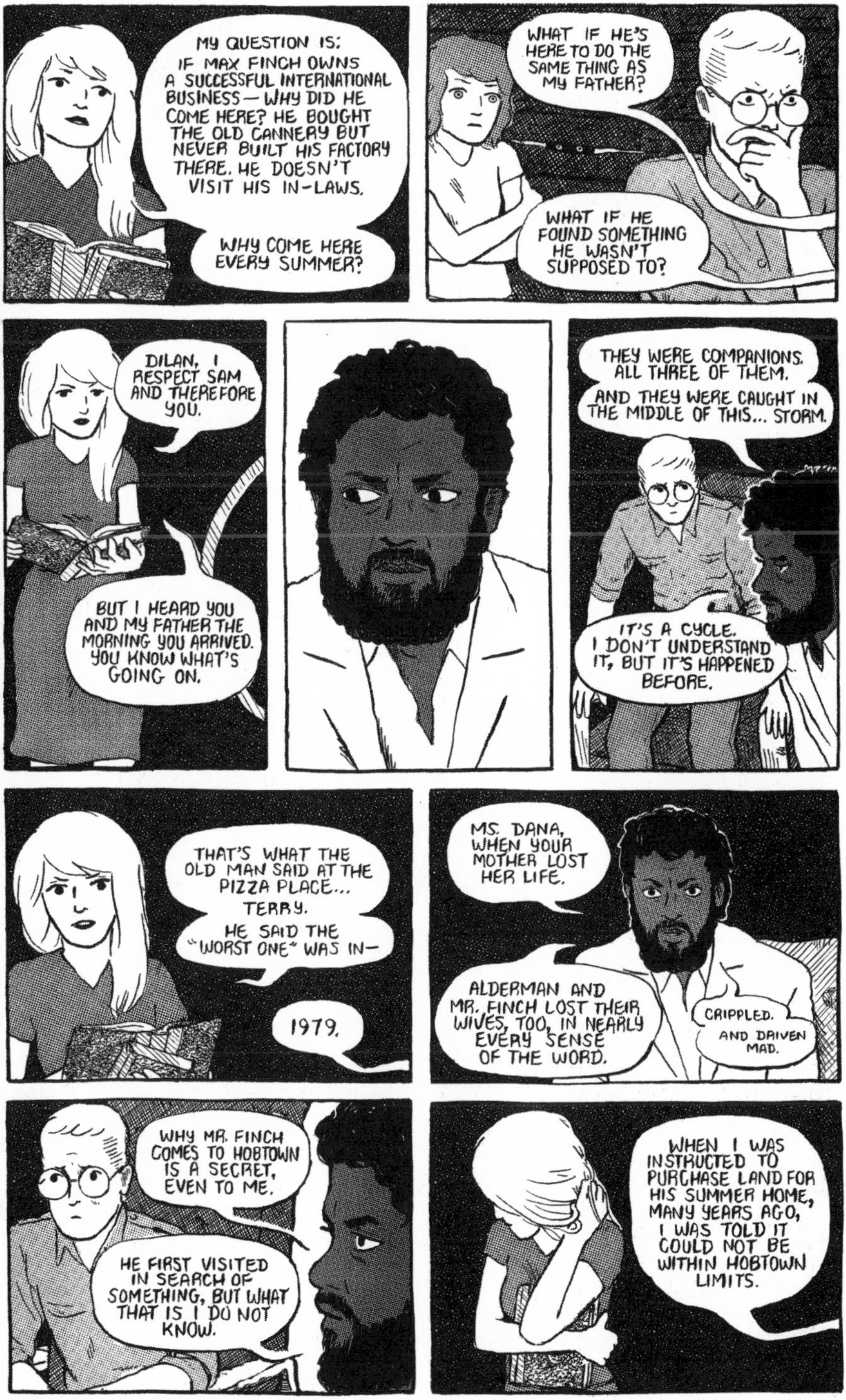
MY QUESTION IS: IF MAX FINCH OWNS A SUCCESSFUL INTERNATIONAL BUSINESS—WHY DID HE COME HERE? HE BOUGHT THE OLD CANNERY BUT NEVER BUILT HIS FACTORY THERE. HE DOESN'T VISIT HIS IN-LAWS.
WHY COME HERE EVERY SUMMER?
WHAT IF HE'S HERE TO DO THE SAME THING AS MY FATHER?
WHAT IF HE FOUND SOMETHING HE WASN'T SUPPOSED TO?
DILAN, I RESPECT SAM AND THEREFORE YOU.
BUT I HEARD YOU AND MY FATHER THE MORNING YOU ARRIVED. YOU KNOW WHAT'S GOING ON.
THEY WERE COMPANIONS. ALL THREE OF THEM.
AND THEY WERE CAUGHT IN THE MIDDLE OF THIS... STORM.
IT'S A CYCLE. I DON'T UNDERSTAND IT, BUT IT'S HAPPENED BEFORE.
THAT'S WHAT THE OLD MAN SAID AT THE PIZZA PLACE...
TERRY.
HE SAID THE "WORST ONE" WAS IN—
1979.
MS. DANA, WHEN YOUR MOTHER LOST HER LIFE.
ALDERMAN AND MR. FINCH LOST THEIR WIVES, TOO, IN NEARLY EVERY SENSE OF THE WORD.
CRIPPLED.
AND DRIVEN MAD.
WHY MR. FINCH COMES TO HOBTOWN IS A SECRET, EVEN TO ME.
HE FIRST VISITED IN SEARCH OF SOMETHING, BUT WHAT THAT IS I DO NOT KNOW.
WHEN I WAS INSTRUCTED TO PURCHASE LAND FOR HIS SUMMER HOME, MANY YEARS AGO, I WAS TOLD IT COULD NOT BE WITHIN HOBTOWN LIMITS.

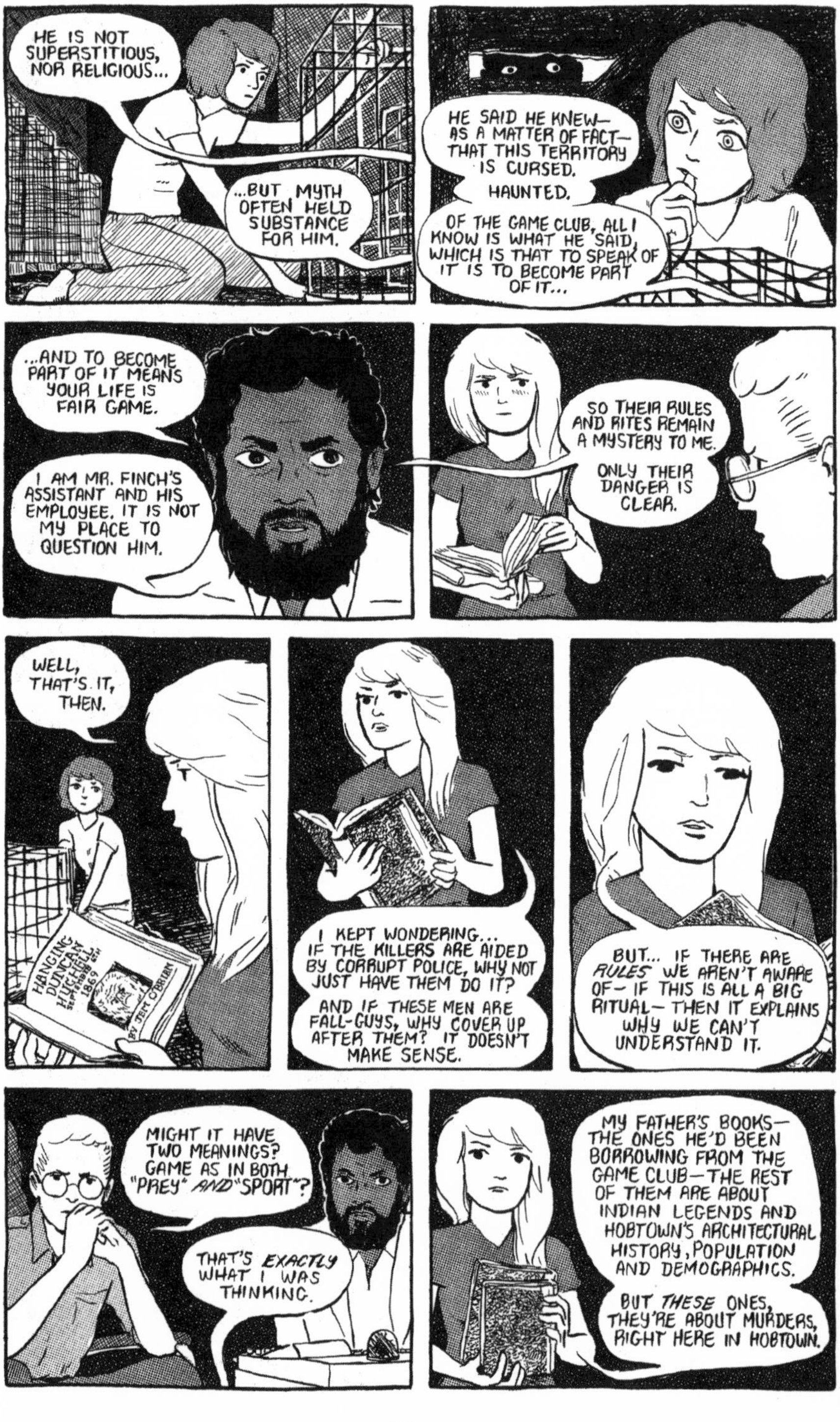
HE IS NOT SUPERSTITIOUS, NOR RELIGIOUS...
...BUT MYTH OFTEN HELD SUBSTANCE FOR HIM.
HE SAID HE KNEW— AS A MATTER OF FACT— THAT THIS TERRITORY IS CURSED.
HAUNTED.
OF THE GAME CLUB, ALL I KNOW IS WHAT HE SAID, WHICH IS THAT TO SPEAK OF IT IS TO BECOME PART OF IT...
...AND TO BECOME PART OF IT MEANS YOUR LIFE IS FAIR GAME.
I AM MR. FINCH'S ASSISTANT AND HIS EMPLOYEE. IT IS NOT MY PLACE TO QUESTION HIM.
SO THEIR RULES AND RITES REMAIN A MYSTERY TO ME.
ONLY THEIR DANGER IS CLEAR.
WELL, THAT'S IT, THEN.
HANGING DUNCAN HUGHELL SEPTEMBER 6TH 1869
BY JEFF O'BRIAN
I KEPT WONDERING... IF THE KILLERS ARE AIDED BY CORRUPT POLICE, WHY NOT JUST HAVE THEM DO IT?
AND IF THESE MEN ARE FALL-GUYS, WHY COVER UP AFTER THEM? IT DOESN'T MAKE SENSE.
BUT... IF THERE ARE *RULES* WE AREN'T AWARE OF— IF THIS IS ALL A BIG RITUAL— THEN IT EXPLAINS WHY WE CAN'T UNDERSTAND IT.
MIGHT IT HAVE TWO MEANINGS? GAME AS IN BOTH "PREY" *AND* "SPORT"?
THAT'S *EXACTLY* WHAT I WAS THINKING.
MY FATHER'S BOOKS— THE ONES HE'D BEEN BORROWING FROM THE GAME CLUB— THE REST OF THEM ARE ABOUT INDIAN LEGENDS AND HOBTOWN'S ARCHITECTURAL HISTORY, POPULATION AND DEMOGRAPHICS.
BUT *THESE* ONES, THEY'RE ABOUT MURDERS, RIGHT HERE IN HOBTOWN.

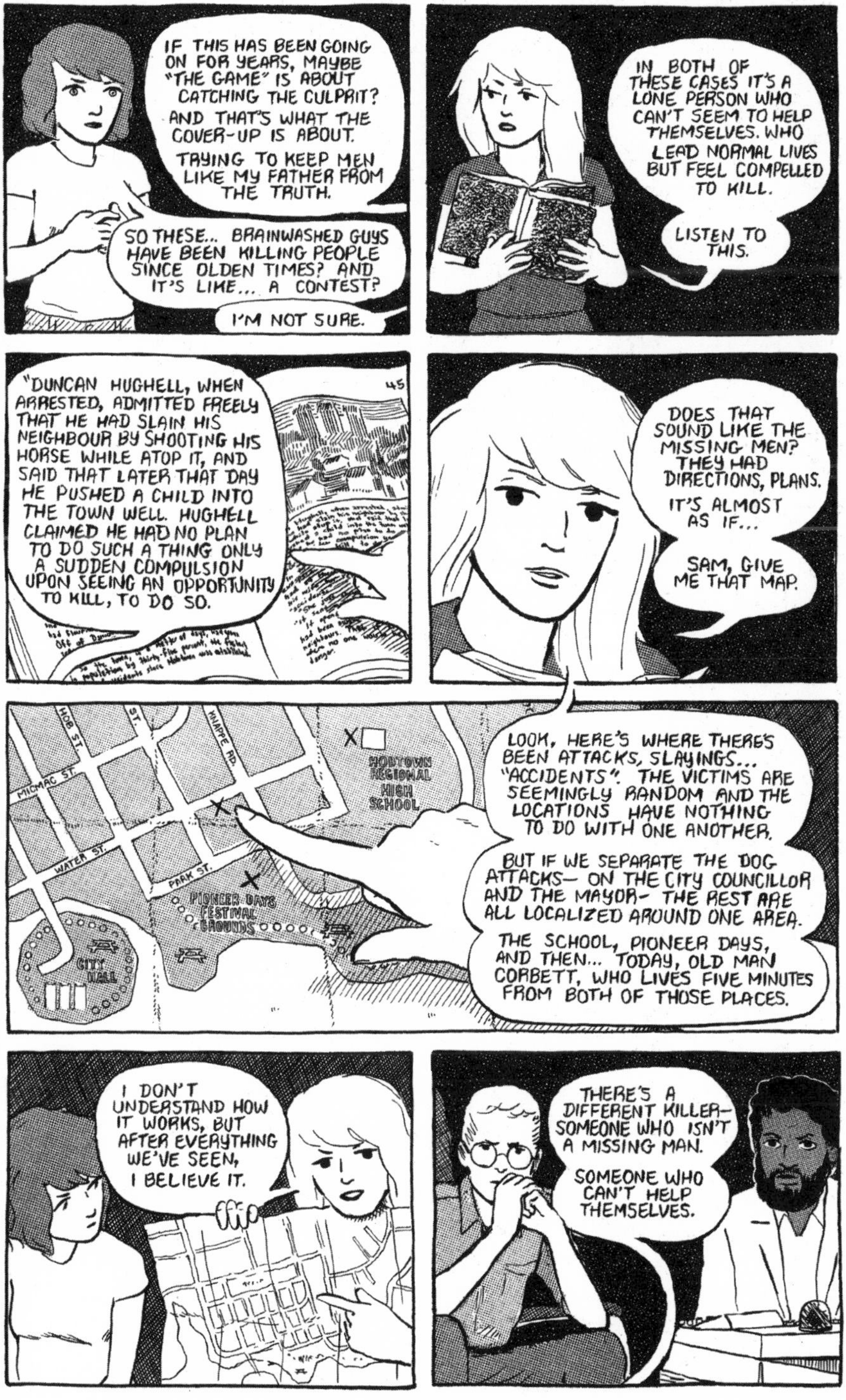
IF THIS HAS BEEN GOING ON FOR YEARS, MAYBE "THE GAME" IS ABOUT CATCHING THE CULPRIT?
AND THAT'S WHAT THE COVER-UP IS ABOUT.
TRYING TO KEEP MEN LIKE MY FATHER FROM THE TRUTH.
SO THESE... BRAINWASHED GUYS HAVE BEEN KILLING PEOPLE SINCE OLDEN TIMES? AND IT'S LIKE... A CONTEST?
I'M NOT SURE.
IN BOTH OF THESE CASES IT'S A LONE PERSON WHO CAN'T SEEM TO HELP THEMSELVES. WHO LEAD NORMAL LIVES BUT FEEL COMPELLED TO KILL.
LISTEN TO THIS.
"DUNCAN HUGHELL, WHEN ARRESTED, ADMITTED FREELY THAT HE HAD SLAIN HIS NEIGHBOUR BY SHOOTING HIS HORSE WHILE ATOP IT, AND SAID THAT LATER THAT DAY HE PUSHED A CHILD INTO THE TOWN WELL. HUGHELL CLAIMED HE HAD NO PLAN TO DO SUCH A THING ONLY A SUDDEN COMPULSION UPON SEEING AN OPPORTUNITY TO KILL, TO DO SO.
45
DOES THAT SOUND LIKE THE MISSING MEN? THEY HAD DIRECTIONS, PLANS.
IT'S ALMOST AS IF...
SAM, GIVE ME THAT MAP.
HOB ST.
ST.
KNAPPE RD.
MICMAC ST.
WATER ST.
PARK ST.
HOBTOWN REGIONAL HIGH SCHOOL
PIONEER DAYS FESTIVAL GROUNDS
CITY HALL
LOOK, HERE'S WHERE THERE'S BEEN ATTACKS, SLAYINGS... "ACCIDENTS". THE VICTIMS ARE SEEMINGLY RANDOM AND THE LOCATIONS HAVE NOTHING TO DO WITH ONE ANOTHER.
BUT IF WE SEPARATE THE DOG ATTACKS— ON THE CITY COUNCILLOR AND THE MAYOR— THE REST ARE ALL LOCALIZED AROUND ONE AREA.
THE SCHOOL, PIONEER DAYS, AND THEN... TODAY, OLD MAN CORBETT, WHO LIVES FIVE MINUTES FROM BOTH OF THOSE PLACES.
I DON'T UNDERSTAND HOW IT WORKS, BUT AFTER EVERYTHING WE'VE SEEN, I BELIEVE IT.
THERE'S A DIFFERENT KILLER— SOMEONE WHO ISN'T A MISSING MAN.
SOMEONE WHO CAN'T HELP THEMSELVES.

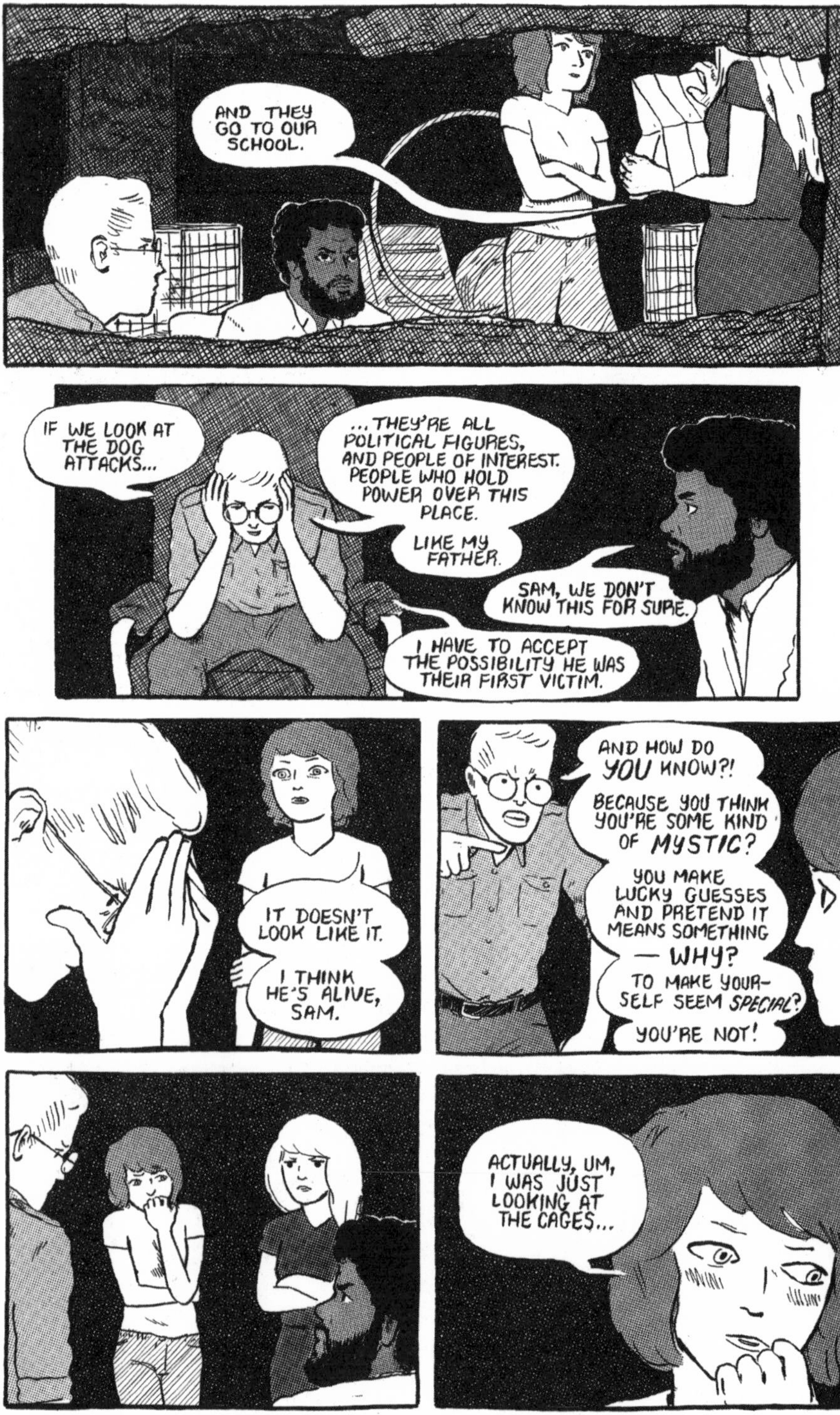

AND THEY GO TO OUR SCHOOL.
IF WE LOOK AT THE DOG ATTACKS...
...THEY'RE ALL POLITICAL FIGURES, AND PEOPLE OF INTEREST. PEOPLE WHO HOLD POWER OVER THIS PLACE.
LIKE MY FATHER.
SAM, WE DON'T KNOW THIS FOR SURE.
I HAVE TO ACCEPT THE POSSIBILITY HE WAS THEIR FIRST VICTIM.
IT DOESN'T LOOK LIKE IT.
I THINK HE'S ALIVE, SAM.
AND HOW DO YOU KNOW?!
BECAUSE YOU THINK YOU'RE SOME KIND OF MYSTIC?
YOU MAKE LUCKY GUESSES AND PRETEND IT MEANS SOMETHING — WHY?
TO MAKE YOURSELF SEEM SPECIAL?
YOU'RE NOT!
ACTUALLY, UM, I WAS JUST LOOKING AT THE CAGES...

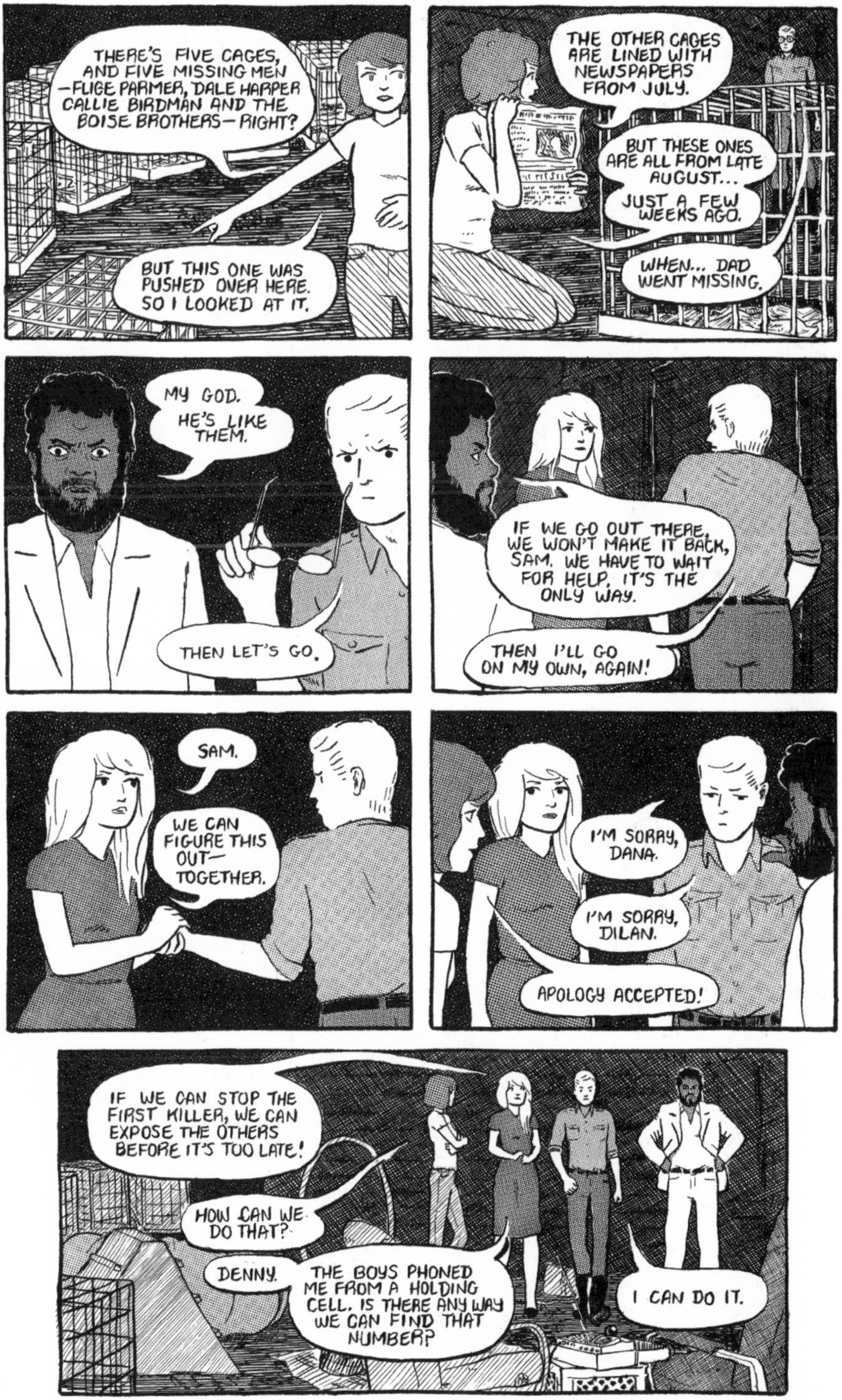
THERE'S FIVE CAGES, AND FIVE MISSING MEN —FLIGE PARMER, DALE HARPER CALLIE BIRDMAN AND THE BOISE BROTHERS— RIGHT?
BUT THIS ONE WAS PUSHED OVER HERE. SO I LOOKED AT IT.
THE OTHER CAGES ARE LINED WITH NEWSPAPERS FROM JULY.
BUT THESE ONES ARE ALL FROM LATE AUGUST...
JUST A FEW WEEKS AGO.
WHEN... DAD WENT MISSING.
MY GOD.
HE'S LIKE THEM.
THEN LET'S GO.
IF WE GO OUT THERE, WE WON'T MAKE IT BACK, SAM. WE HAVE TO WAIT FOR HELP. IT'S THE ONLY WAY.
THEN I'LL GO ON MY OWN, AGAIN!
SAM.
WE CAN FIGURE THIS OUT— TOGETHER.
I'M SORRY, DANA.
I'M SORRY, DILAN.
APOLOGY ACCEPTED!
IF WE CAN STOP THE FIRST KILLER, WE CAN EXPOSE THE OTHERS BEFORE IT'S TOO LATE!
HOW CAN WE DO THAT?
DENNY.
THE BOYS PHONED ME FROM A HOLDING CELL. IS THERE ANY WAY WE CAN FIND THAT NUMBER?
I CAN DO IT.

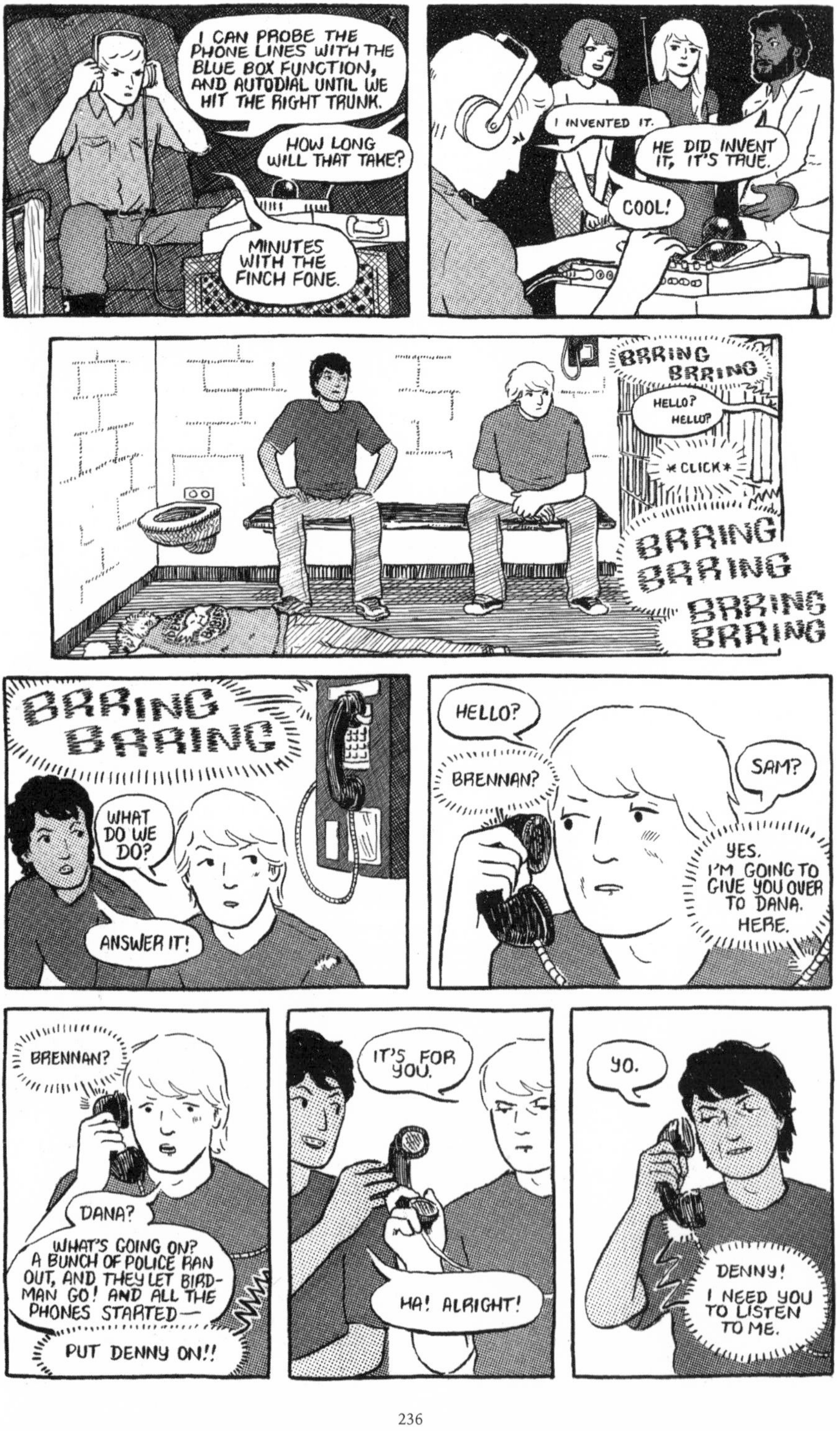

I CAN PROBE THE PHONE LINES WITH THE BLUE BOX FUNCTION, AND AUTODIAL UNTIL WE HIT THE RIGHT TRUNK.
HOW LONG WILL THAT TAKE?
MINUTES WITH THE FINCH FONE.
I INVENTED IT.
HE DID INVENT IT, IT'S TRUE.
COOL!
BRRING BRRING
HELLO? HELLO?
CLICK
BRRING BRRING
BRRING BRRING
BRRING BRRING
WHAT DO WE DO?
ANSWER IT!
HELLO?
BRENNAN?
SAM?
YES. I'M GOING TO GIVE YOU OVER TO DANA. HERE.
BRENNAN?
DANA?
WHAT'S GOING ON? A BUNCH OF POLICE RAN OUT, AND THEY LET BIRDMAN GO! AND ALL THE PHONES STARTED—
PUT DENNY ON!!
IT'S FOR YOU.
HA! ALRIGHT!
YO.
DENNY! I NEED YOU TO LISTEN TO ME.

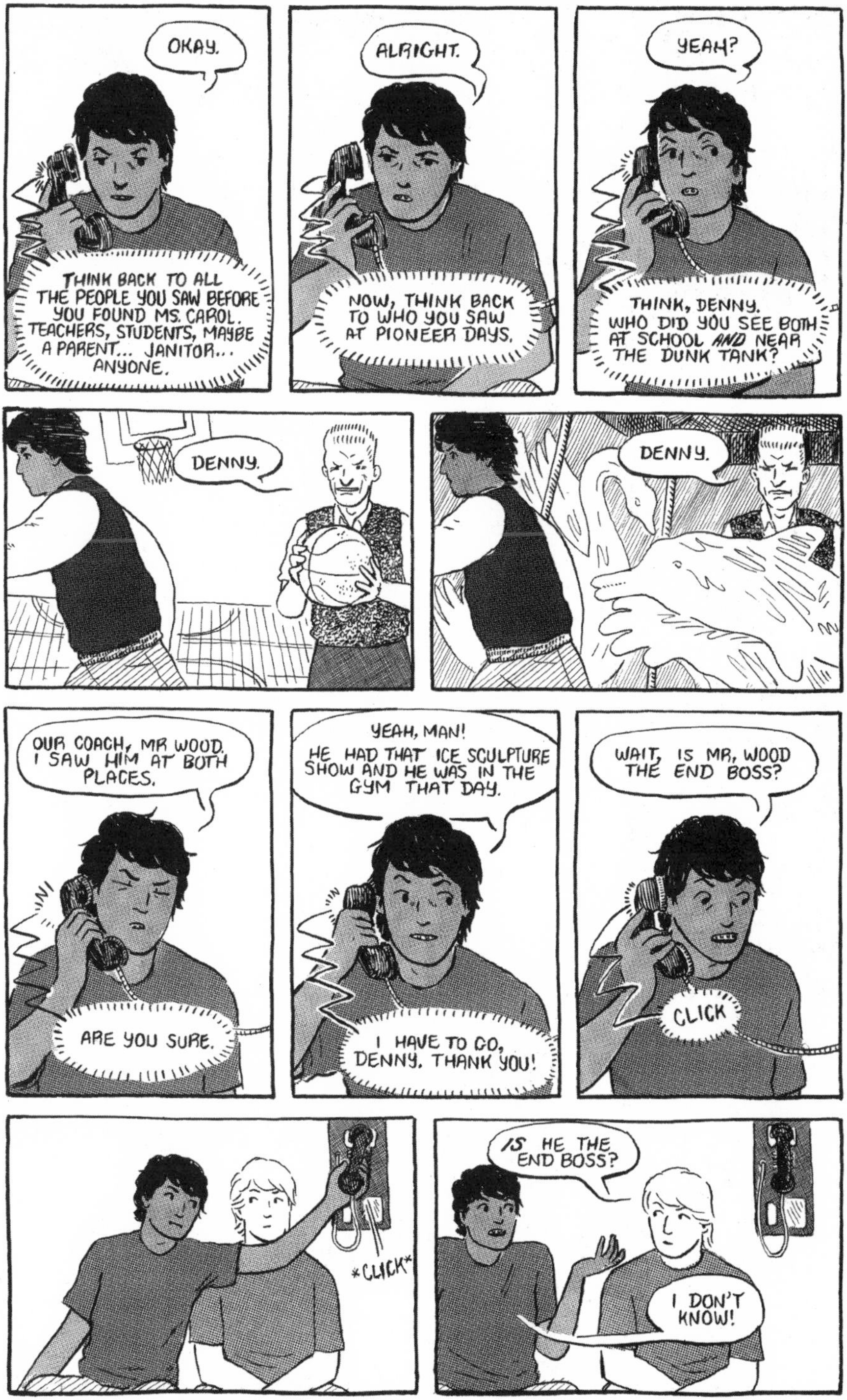
OKAY.
THINK BACK TO ALL THE PEOPLE YOU SAW BEFORE YOU FOUND MS. CAROL. TEACHERS, STUDENTS, MAYBE A PARENT... JANITOR... ANYONE.
ALRIGHT.
NOW, THINK BACK TO WHO YOU SAW AT PIONEER DAYS.
YEAH?
THINK, DENNY. WHO DID YOU SEE BOTH AT SCHOOL *AND* NEAR THE DUNK TANK?
DENNY.
DENNY.
OUR COACH, MR WOOD. I SAW HIM AT BOTH PLACES.
ARE YOU SURE.
YEAH, MAN! HE HAD THAT ICE SCULPTURE SHOW AND HE WAS IN THE GYM THAT DAY.
I HAVE TO GO, DENNY. THANK YOU!
WAIT, IS MR. WOOD THE END BOSS?
CLICK
CLICK
IS HE THE END BOSS?
I DON'T KNOW!

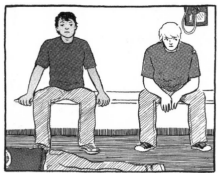

DID WE BEAT EEL CREEK?

SHE DIDN'T SAY.

HM

WE HAVE THE KILLER'S I.D.!

WHO IS IT?

I THINK IT'S MR. WOOD, THE GYM TEACHER.

SAM, YOUR MACHINE TAKES PHOTOS, RIGHT?

YES.

PHOTOGRAPH EVERYTHING HERE. WE'LL NEED IT LATER.

GOOD IDEA.

MS. DANA WHAT DO YOU PROPOSE TO DO HERE?

SNAP

WE STOP THE LUNCHROOM KILLER, THEN WE USE OUR EVIDENCE TO CONVICT THE PROPELLER CLUB FOR WHAT THEY'VE DONE.

SNAP

I SEE YOU CARE DEEPLY FOR YOUR FELLOW MAN, MS. DANA, BUT WHAT HAPPENS IF WE'RE CAUGHT BEFORE HELP ARRIVES?

OUR PROOF WILL BE DESTROYED MORE THAN LIKELY, AND WE'LL BE KILLED.

BUT WHAT'S THE ALTERNATIVE?

WE HAVE TO DO SOMETHING.

YOU KNOW IT'S THE RIGHT THING, DILAN.

SNAP

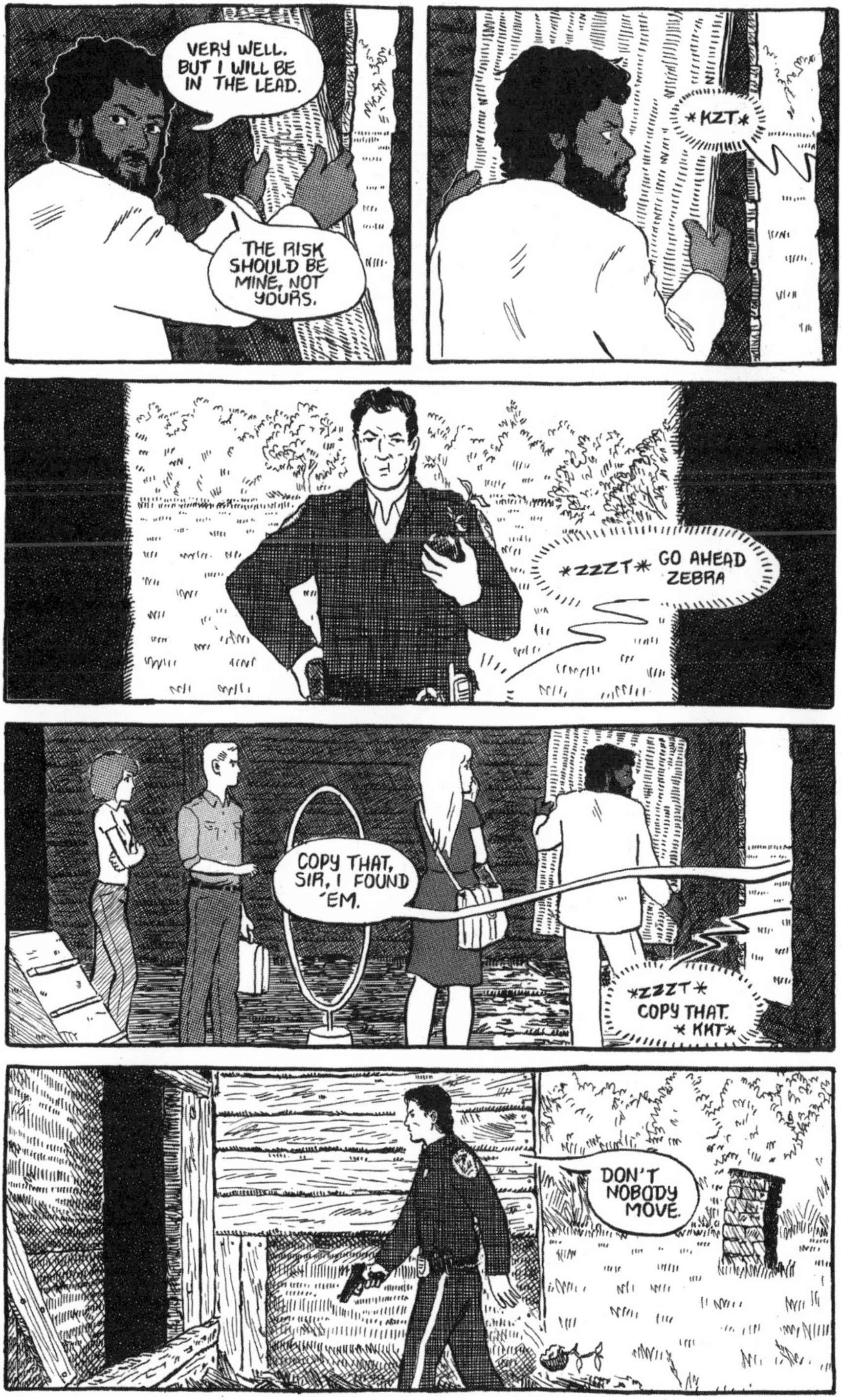
VERY WELL. BUT I WILL BE IN THE LEAD.
THE RISK SHOULD BE MINE, NOT YOURS.
KZT
ZZZT GO AHEAD ZEBRA
COPY THAT, SIR, I FOUND 'EM.
ZZZT COPY THAT. *KKT*
DON'T NOBODY MOVE.

CHAPTER TEN

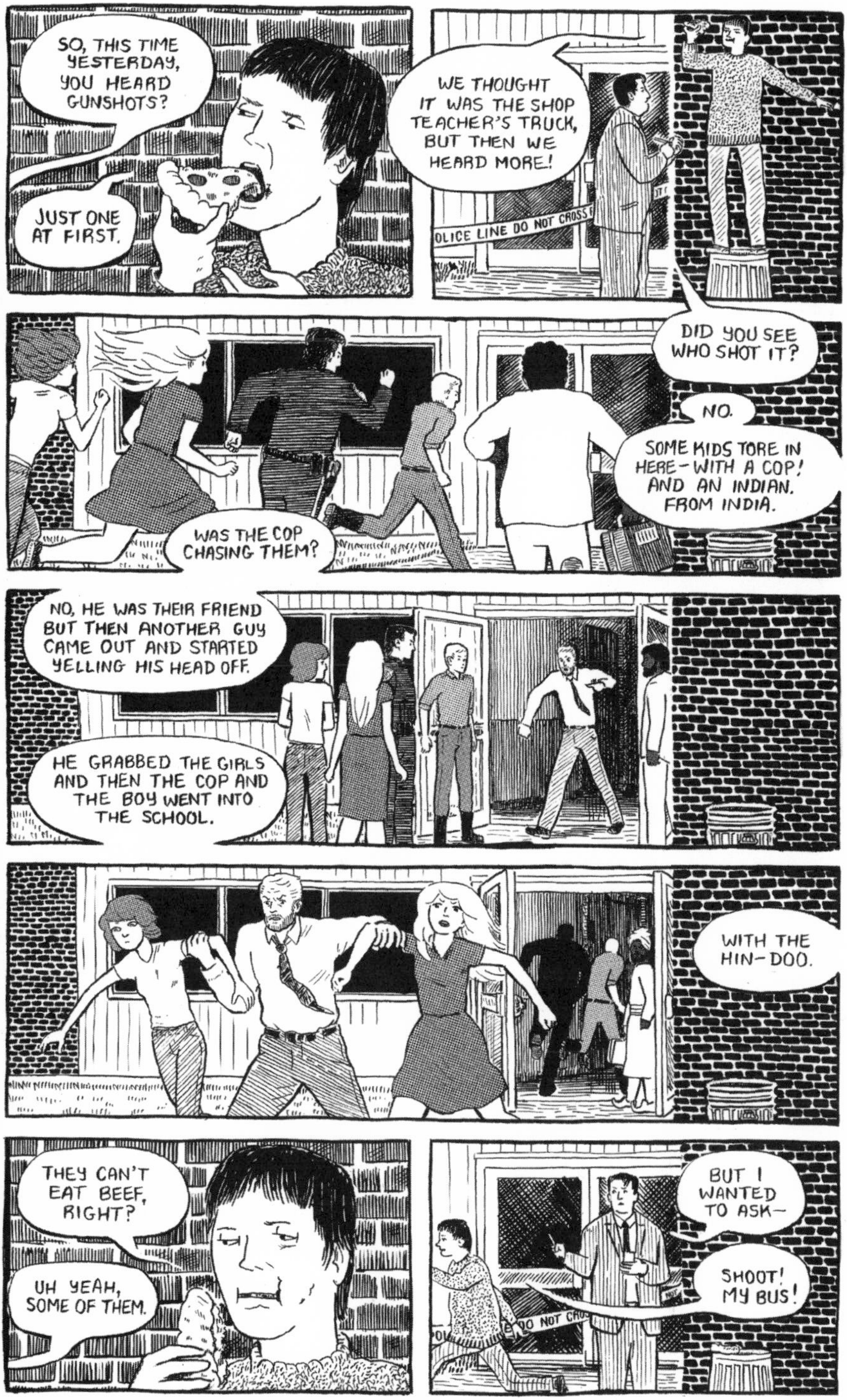
SO, THIS TIME YESTERDAY, YOU HEARD GUNSHOTS?
JUST ONE AT FIRST.
WE THOUGHT IT WAS THE SHOP TEACHER'S TRUCK, BUT THEN WE HEARD MORE!
OLICE LINE DO NOT CROSS
DID YOU SEE WHO SHOT IT?
NO.
SOME KIDS TORE IN HERE—WITH A COP! AND AN INDIAN. FROM INDIA.
WAS THE COP CHASING THEM?
NO, HE WAS THEIR FRIEND BUT THEN ANOTHER GUY CAME OUT AND STARTED YELLING HIS HEAD OFF.
HE GRABBED THE GIRLS AND THEN THE COP AND THE BOY WENT INTO THE SCHOOL.
WITH THE HIN-DOO.
THEY CAN'T EAT BEEF, RIGHT?
UH YEAH, SOME OF THEM.
BUT I WANTED TO ASK—
SHOOT! MY BUS!
DO NOT CRO

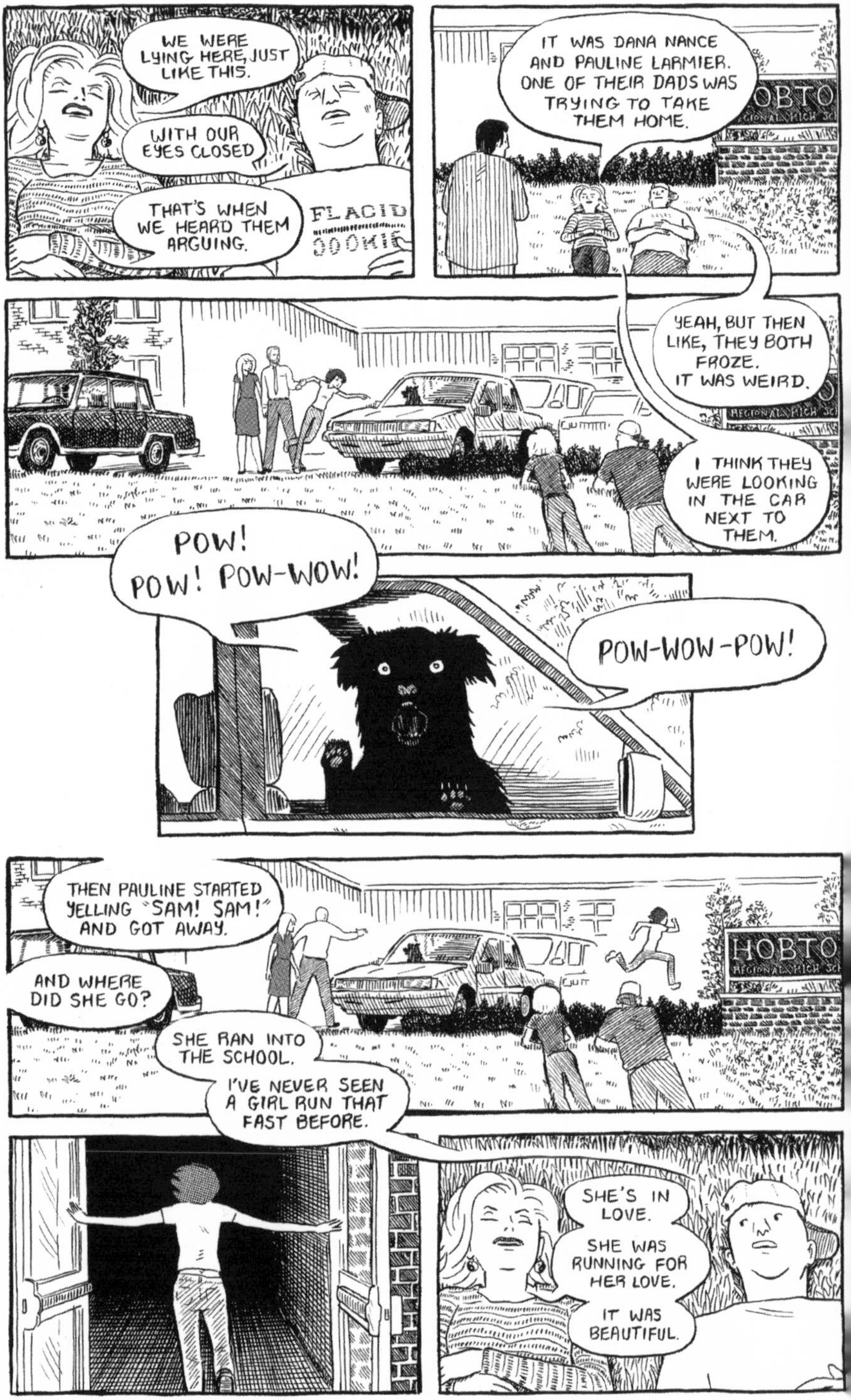
WE WERE LYING HERE, JUST LIKE THIS.
WITH OUR EYES CLOSED
THAT'S WHEN WE HEARD THEM ARGUING.
FLACID
IT WAS DANA NANCE AND PAULINE LARMIER. ONE OF THEIR DADS WAS TRYING TO TAKE THEM HOME.
HOBTO
YEAH, BUT THEN LIKE, THEY BOTH FROZE. IT WAS WEIRD.
I THINK THEY WERE LOOKING IN THE CAR NEXT TO THEM.
POW! POW! POW-WOW!
POW-WOW-POW!
THEN PAULINE STARTED YELLING "SAM! SAM!" AND GOT AWAY.
AND WHERE DID SHE GO?
SHE RAN INTO THE SCHOOL.
I'VE NEVER SEEN A GIRL RUN THAT FAST BEFORE.
HOBTO
SHE'S IN LOVE.
SHE WAS RUNNING FOR HER LOVE.
IT WAS BEAUTIFUL.

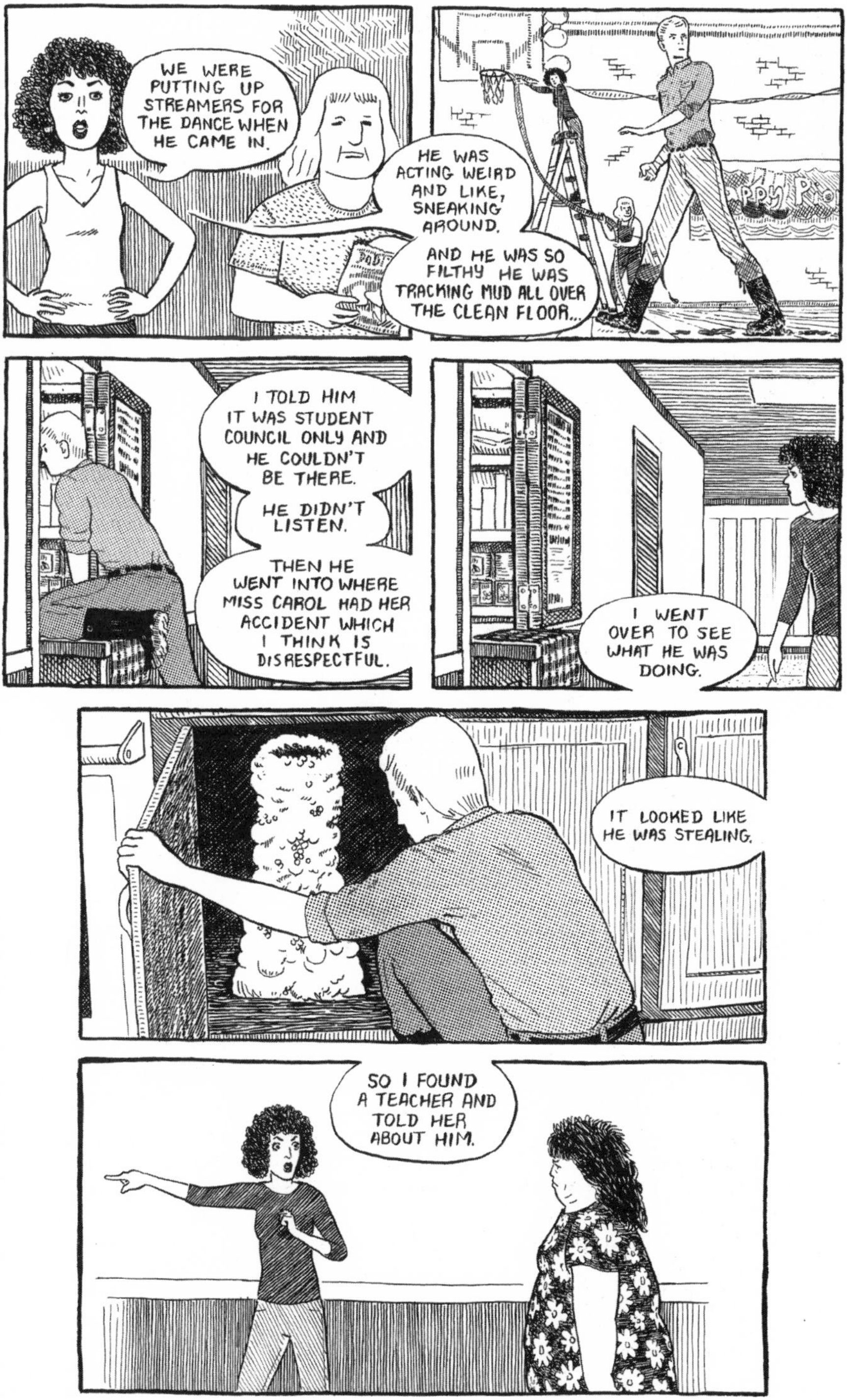
WE WERE PUTTING UP STREAMERS FOR THE DANCE WHEN HE CAME IN.
HE WAS ACTING WEIRD AND LIKE, SNEAKING AROUND.
AND HE WAS SO FILTHY HE WAS TRACKING MUD ALL OVER THE CLEAN FLOOR...
I TOLD HIM IT WAS STUDENT COUNCIL ONLY AND HE COULDN'T BE THERE.
HE DIDN'T LISTEN.
THEN HE WENT INTO WHERE MISS CAROL HAD HER ACCIDENT WHICH I THINK IS DISRESPECTFUL.
I WENT OVER TO SEE WHAT HE WAS DOING.
IT LOOKED LIKE HE WAS STEALING.
SO I FOUND A TEACHER AND TOLD HER ABOUT HIM.

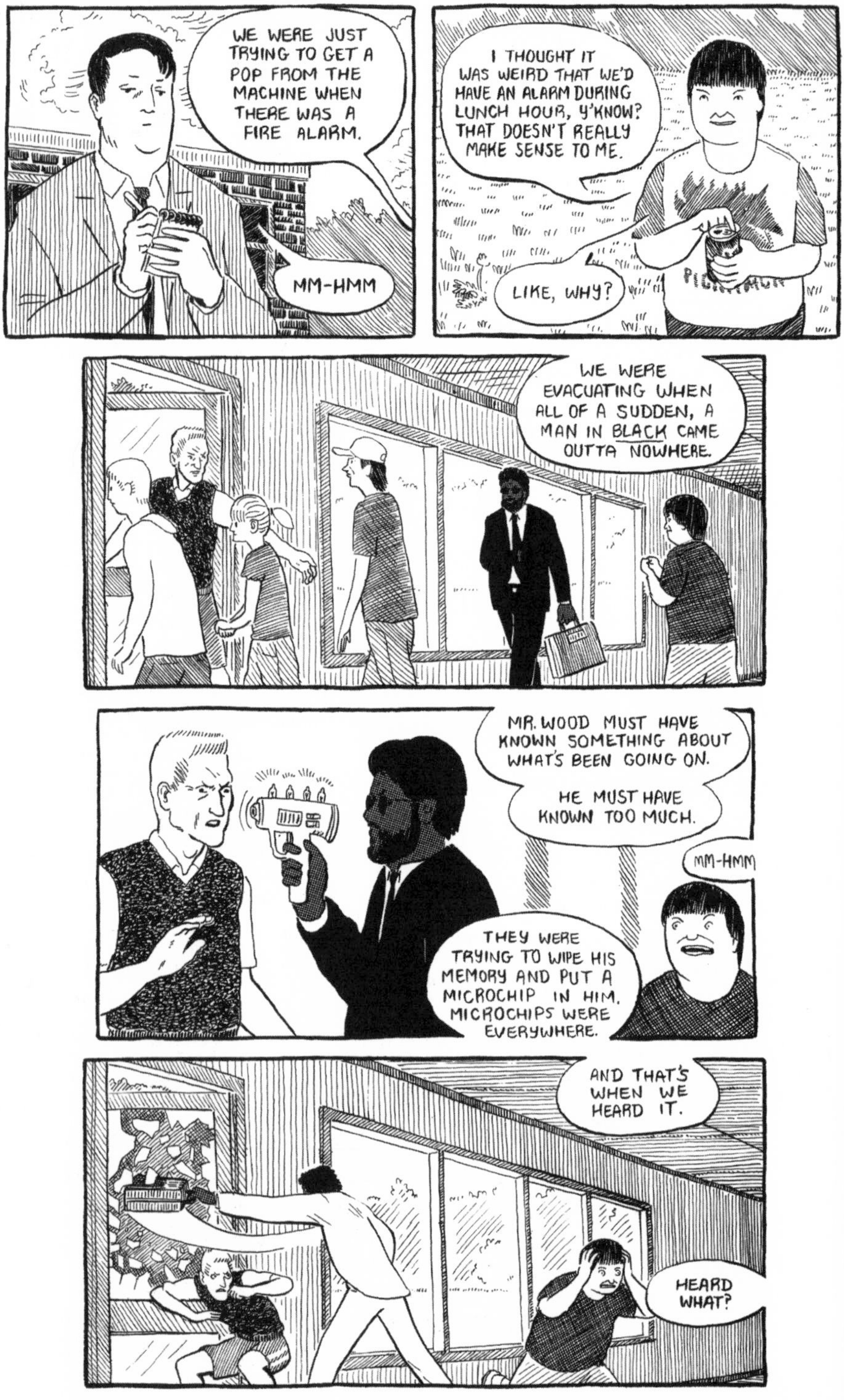

WE WERE JUST TRYING TO GET A POP FROM THE MACHINE WHEN THERE WAS A FIRE ALARM.
MM-HMM
I THOUGHT IT WAS WEIRD THAT WE'D HAVE AN ALARM DURING LUNCH HOUR, Y'KNOW? THAT DOESN'T REALLY MAKE SENSE TO ME.
LIKE, WHY?
WE WERE EVACUATING WHEN ALL OF A SUDDEN, A MAN IN BLACK CAME OUTTA NOWHERE.
MR. WOOD MUST HAVE KNOWN SOMETHING ABOUT WHAT'S BEEN GOING ON.
HE MUST HAVE KNOWN TOO MUCH.
MM-HMM
THEY WERE TRYING TO WIPE HIS MEMORY AND PUT A MICROCHIP IN HIM. MICROCHIPS WERE EVERYWHERE.
AND THAT'S WHEN WE HEARD IT.
HEARD WHAT?

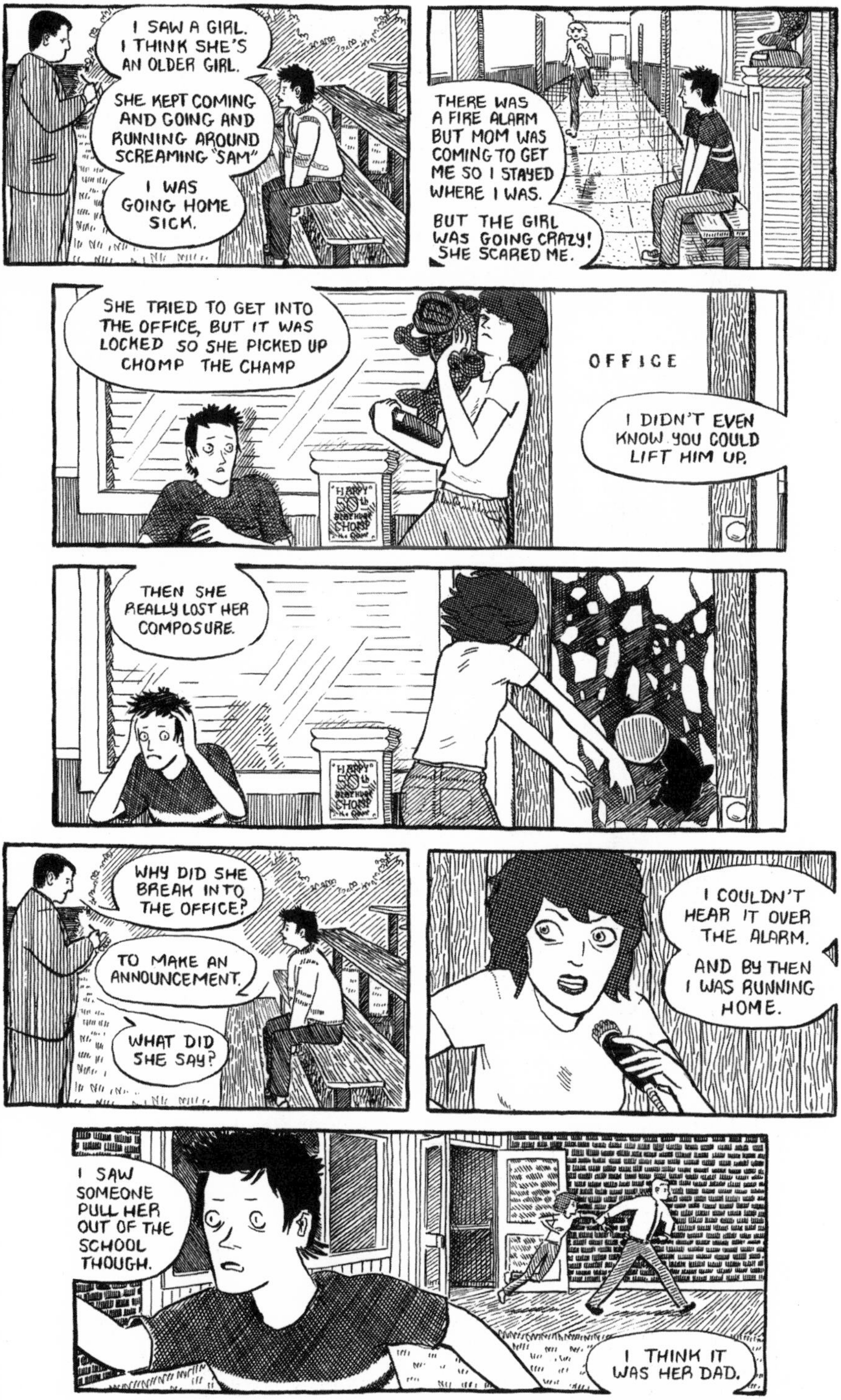
I SAW A GIRL. I THINK SHE'S AN OLDER GIRL.
SHE KEPT COMING AND GOING AND RUNNING AROUND SCREAMING "SAM"
I WAS GOING HOME SICK.
THERE WAS A FIRE ALARM BUT MOM WAS COMING TO GET ME SO I STAYED WHERE I WAS.
BUT THE GIRL WAS GOING CRAZY! SHE SCARED ME.
SHE TRIED TO GET INTO THE OFFICE, BUT IT WAS LOCKED SO SHE PICKED UP CHOMP THE CHAMP
OFFICE
I DIDN'T EVEN KNOW YOU COULD LIFT HIM UP.
THEN SHE REALLY LOST HER COMPOSURE.
WHY DID SHE BREAK INTO THE OFFICE?
TO MAKE AN ANNOUNCEMENT.
WHAT DID SHE SAY?
I COULDN'T HEAR IT OVER THE ALARM.
AND BY THEN I WAS RUNNING HOME.
I SAW SOMEONE PULL HER OUT OF THE SCHOOL THOUGH.
I THINK IT WAS HER DAD.

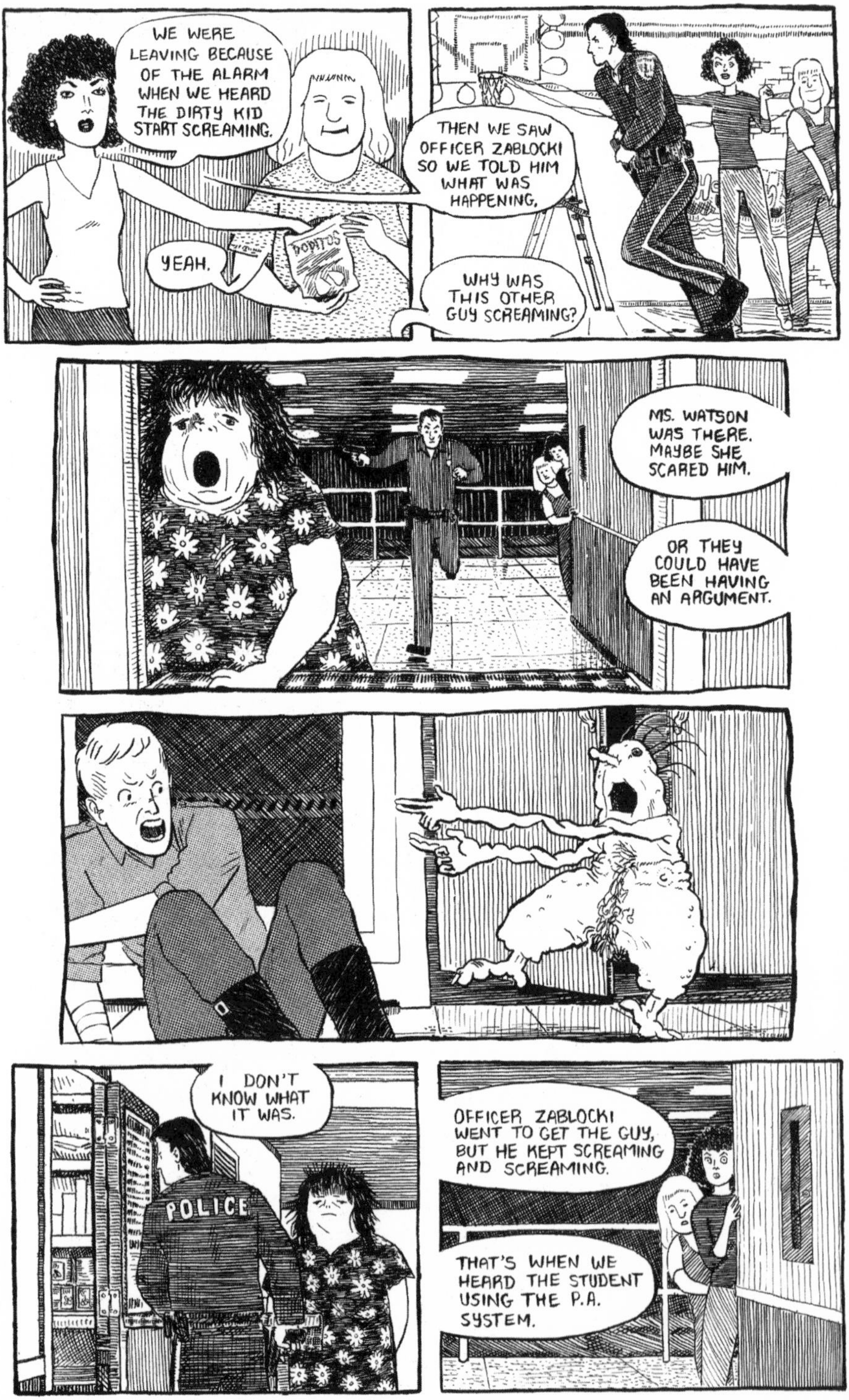
WE WERE LEAVING BECAUSE OF THE ALARM WHEN WE HEARD THE DIRTY KID START SCREAMING.
YEAH.
DORITOS
THEN WE SAW OFFICER ZABLOCKI SO WE TOLD HIM WHAT WAS HAPPENING.
WHY WAS THIS OTHER GUY SCREAMING?
MS. WATSON WAS THERE. MAYBE SHE SCARED HIM.
OR THEY COULD HAVE BEEN HAVING AN ARGUMENT.
I DON'T KNOW WHAT IT WAS.
POLICE
OFFICER ZABLOCKI WENT TO GET THE GUY, BUT HE KEPT SCREAMING AND SCREAMING.
THAT'S WHEN WE HEARD THE STUDENT USING THE P.A. SYSTEM.

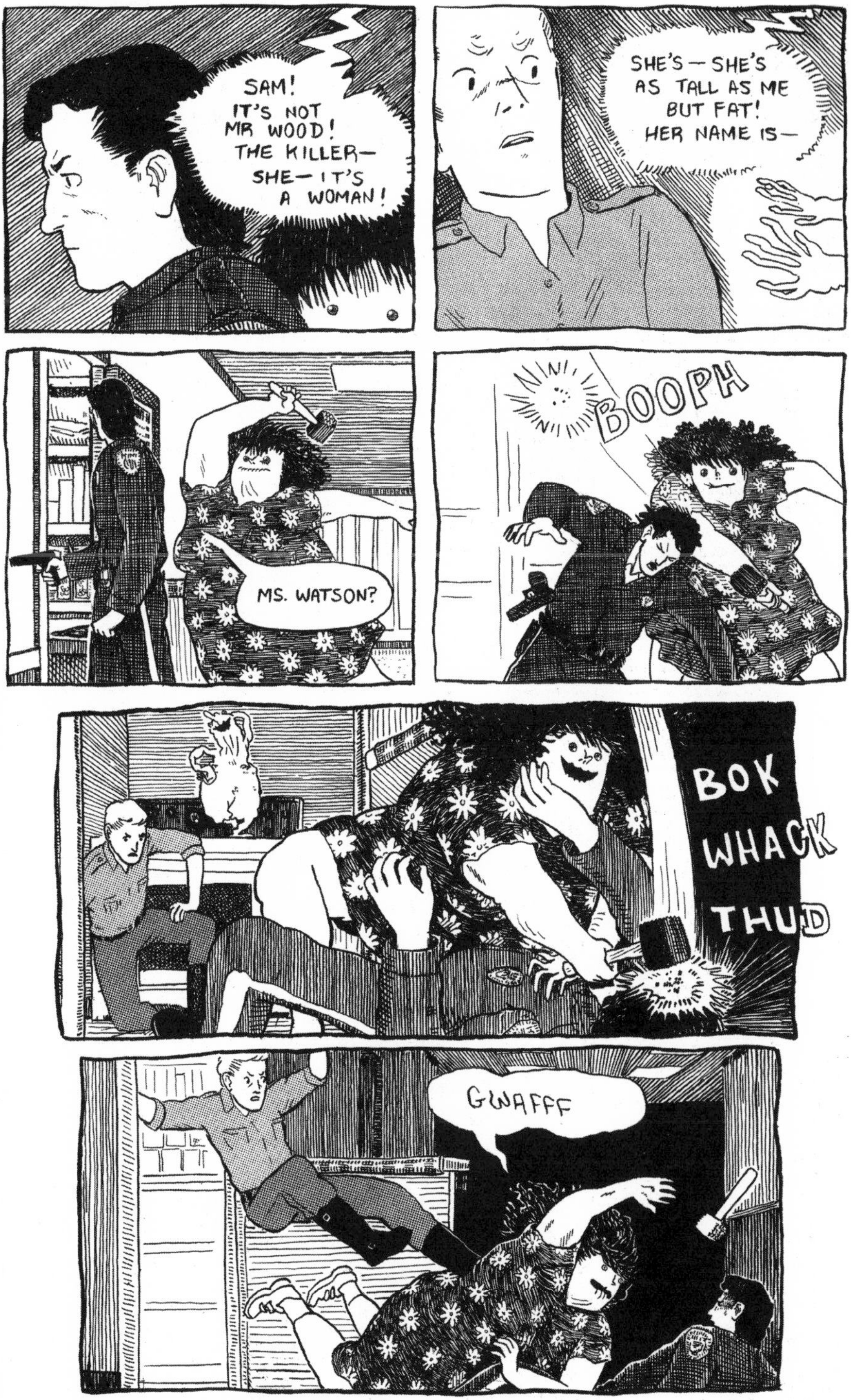
SAM! IT'S NOT MR WOOD! THE KILLER— SHE— IT'S A WOMAN!
SHE'S— SHE'S AS TALL AS ME BUT FAT! HER NAME IS—
MS. WATSON?
BOOPH
BOK
WHACK
THUD
GWAFFF

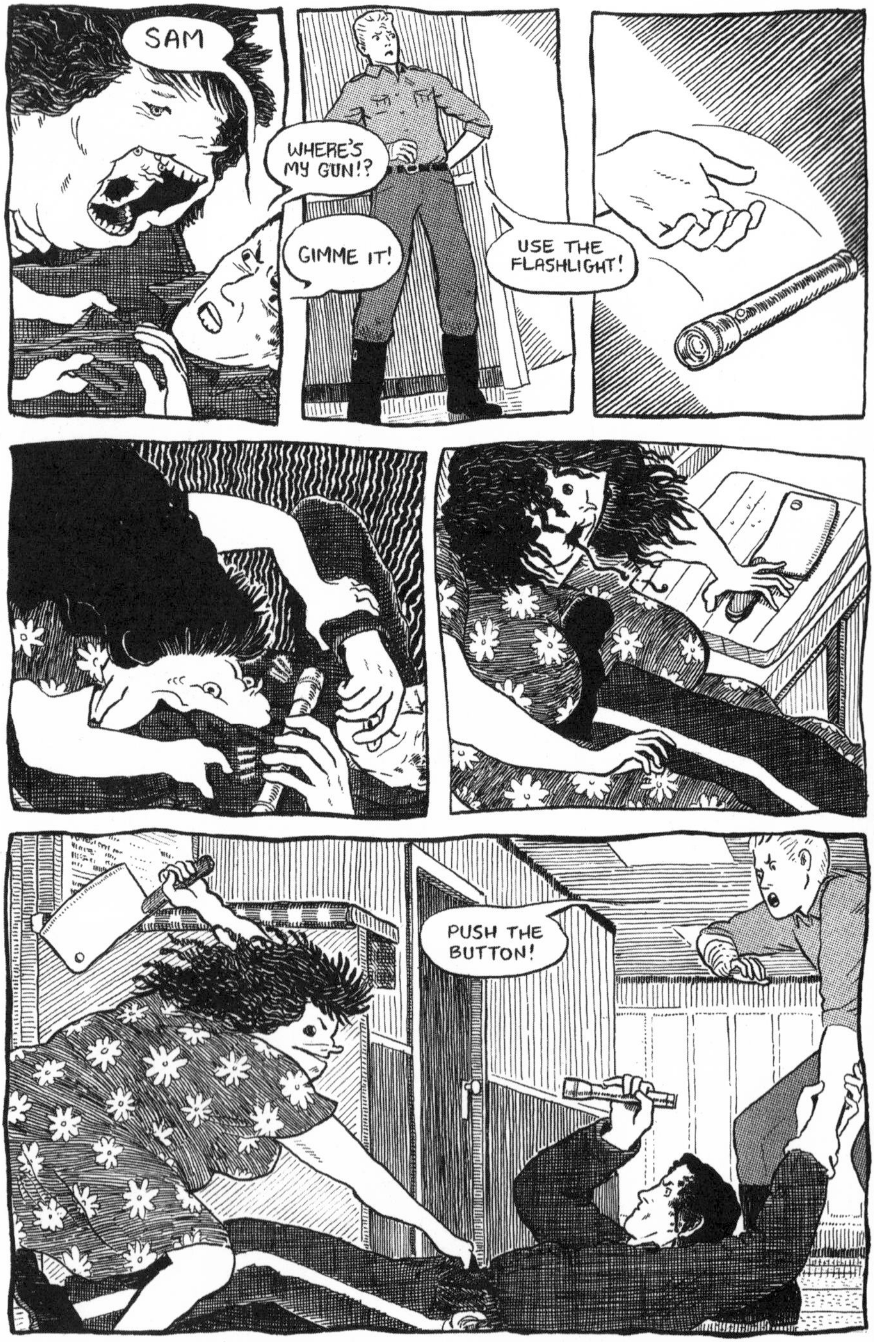
SAM
WHERE'S MY GUN!?
GIMME IT!
USE THE FLASHLIGHT!
PUSH THE BUTTON!

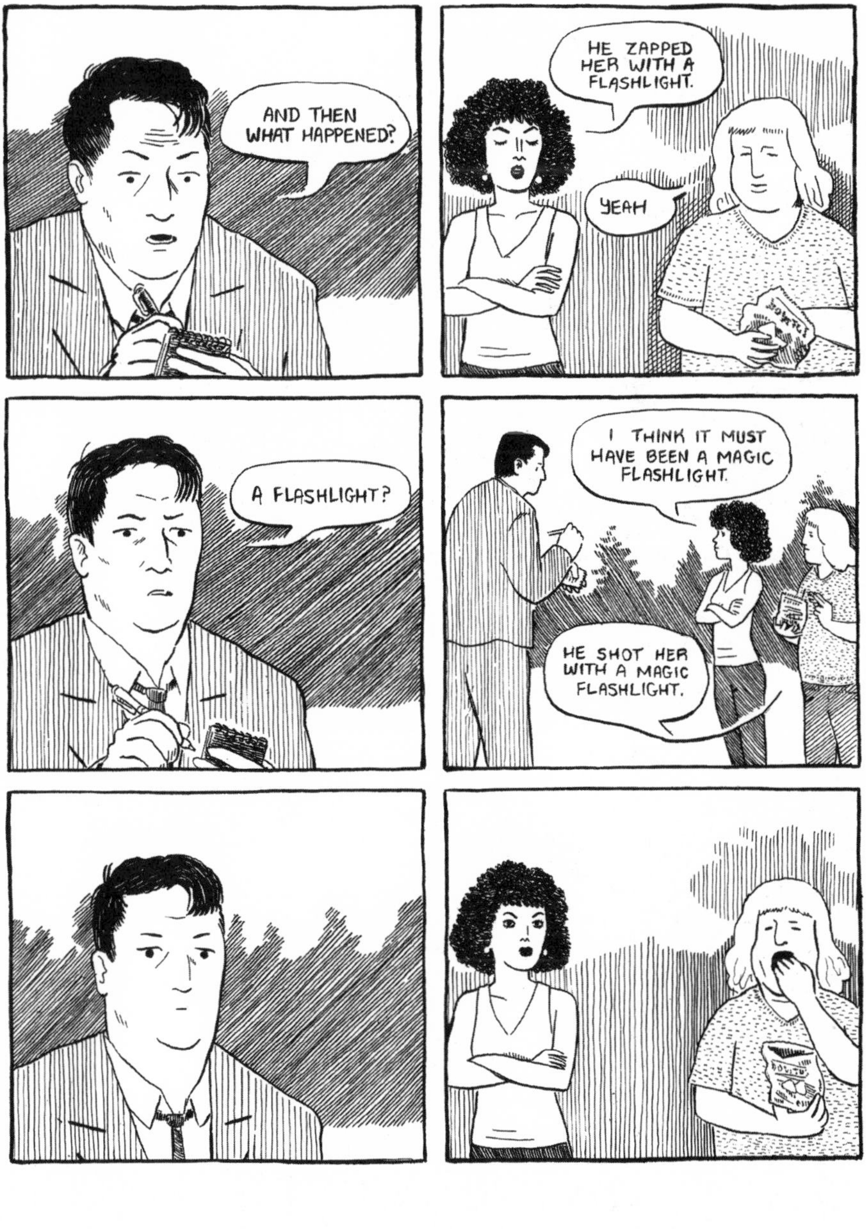
AND THEN WHAT HAPPENED?
HE ZAPPED HER WITH A FLASHLIGHT.
YEAH
A FLASHLIGHT?
I THINK IT MUST HAVE BEEN A MAGIC FLASHLIGHT.
HE SHOT HER WITH A MAGIC FLASHLIGHT.

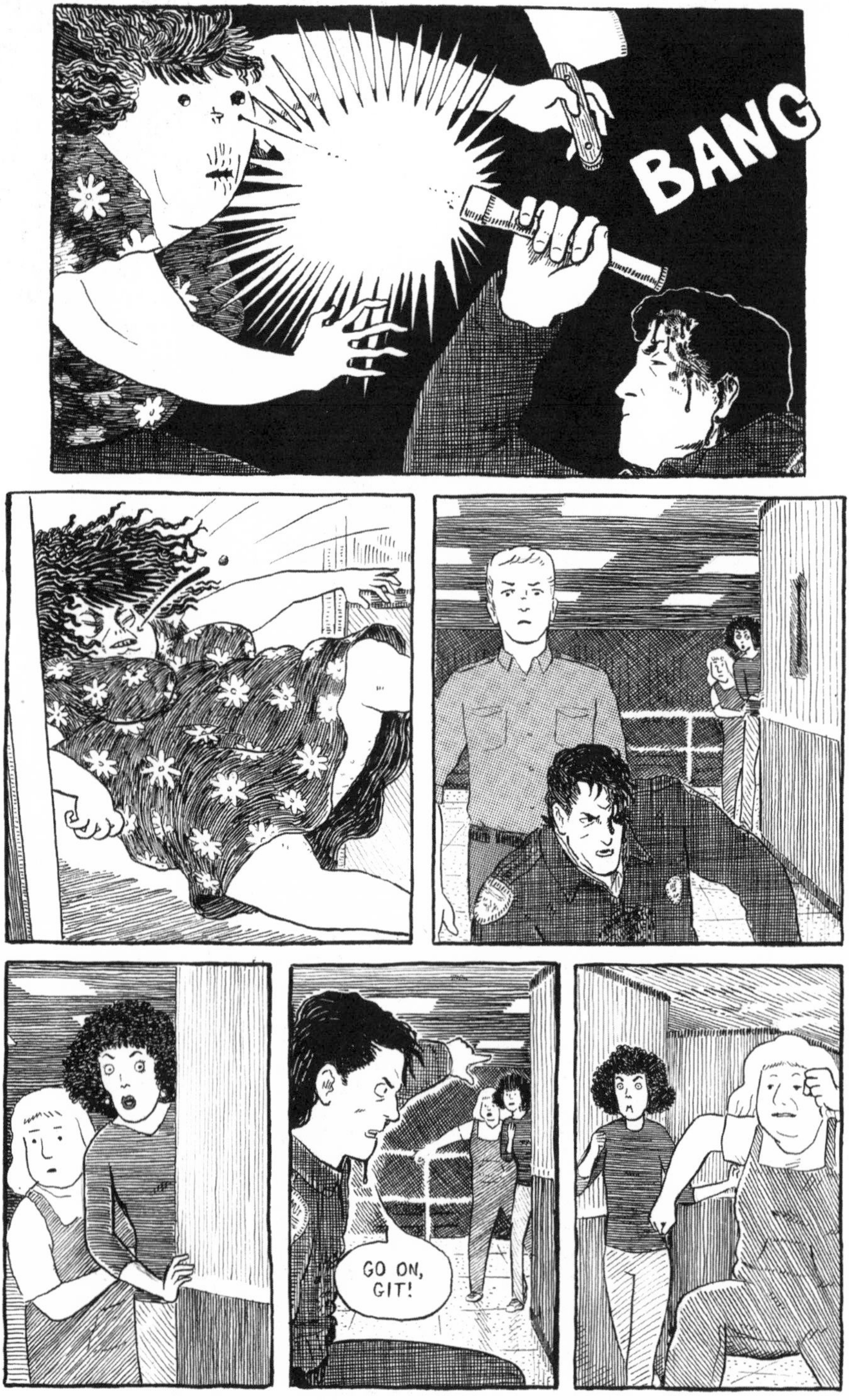
BANG
GO ON, GIT!

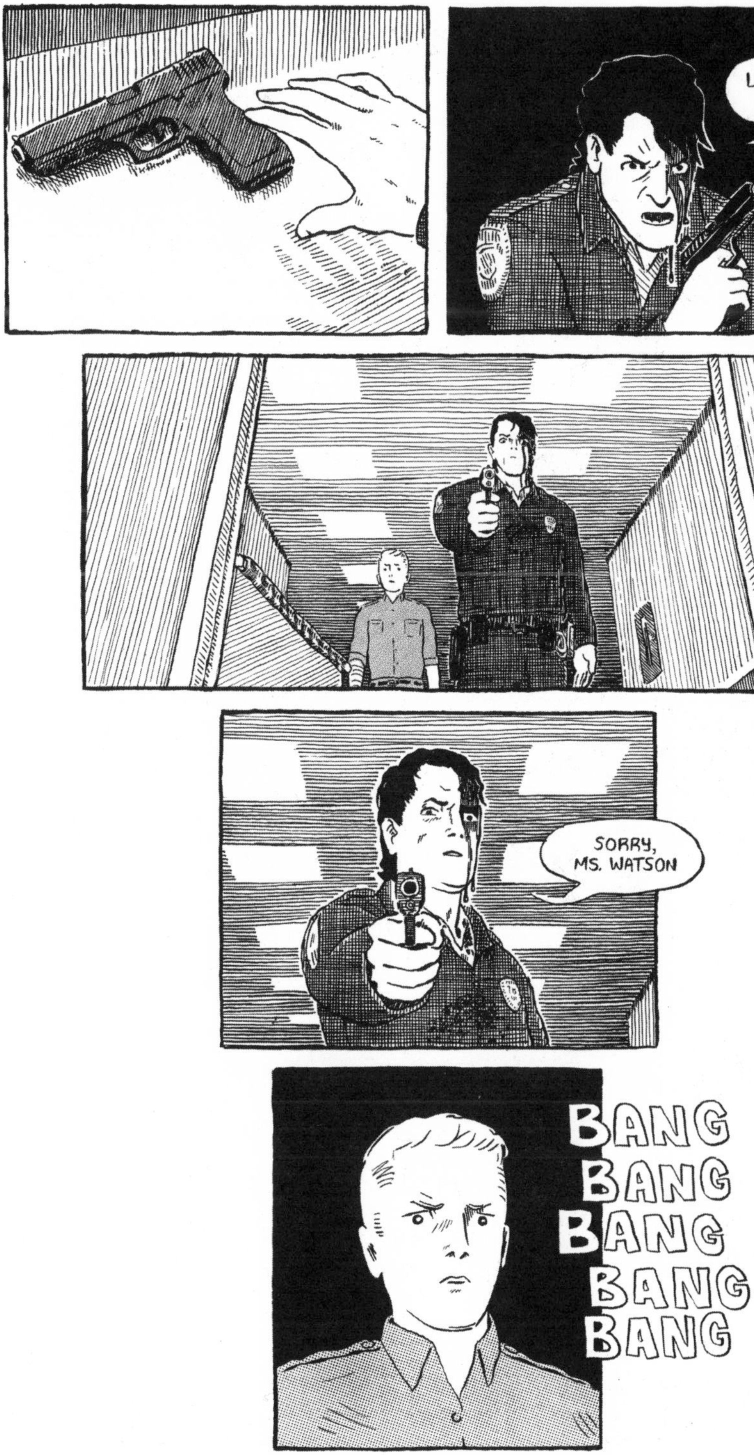
LOOK AWAY, SAM.
SORRY, MS. WATSON
BANG
BANG
BANG
BANG
BANG

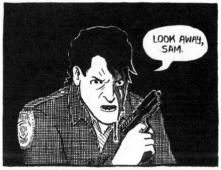

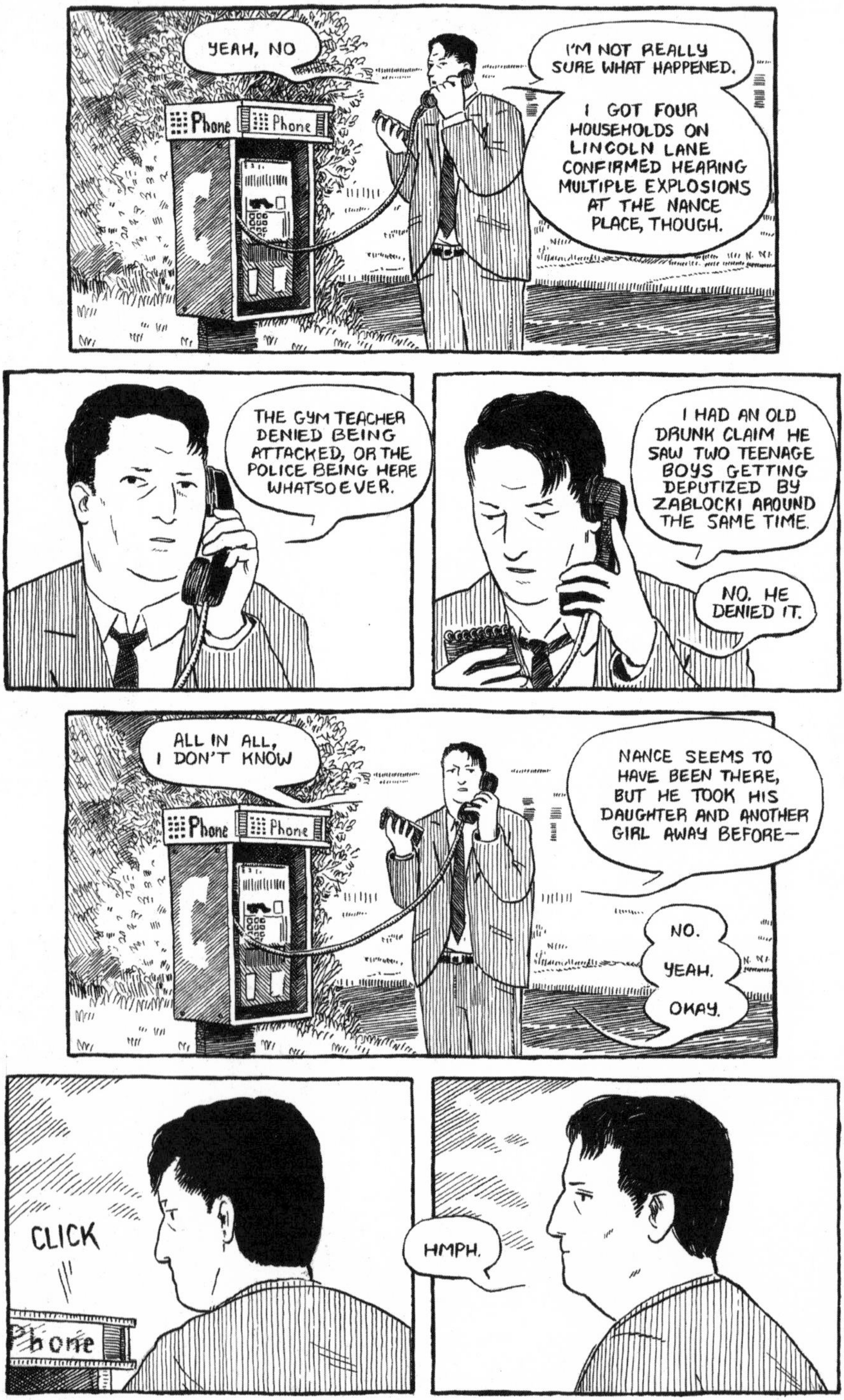
YEAH, NO
I'M NOT REALLY SURE WHAT HAPPENED.
I GOT FOUR HOUSEHOLDS ON LINCOLN LANE CONFIRMED HEARING MULTIPLE EXPLOSIONS AT THE NANCE PLACE, THOUGH.
Phone
Phone
THE GYM TEACHER DENIED BEING ATTACKED, OR THE POLICE BEING HERE WHATSOEVER.
I HAD AN OLD DRUNK CLAIM HE SAW TWO TEENAGE BOYS GETTING DEPUTIZED BY ZABLOCKI AROUND THE SAME TIME.
NO. HE DENIED IT.
ALL IN ALL, I DON'T KNOW
NANCE SEEMS TO HAVE BEEN THERE, BUT HE TOOK HIS DAUGHTER AND ANOTHER GIRL AWAY BEFORE—
Phone
Phone
NO.
YEAH.
OKAY.
CLICK
Phone
HMPH.

CHAPTER
ELEVEN

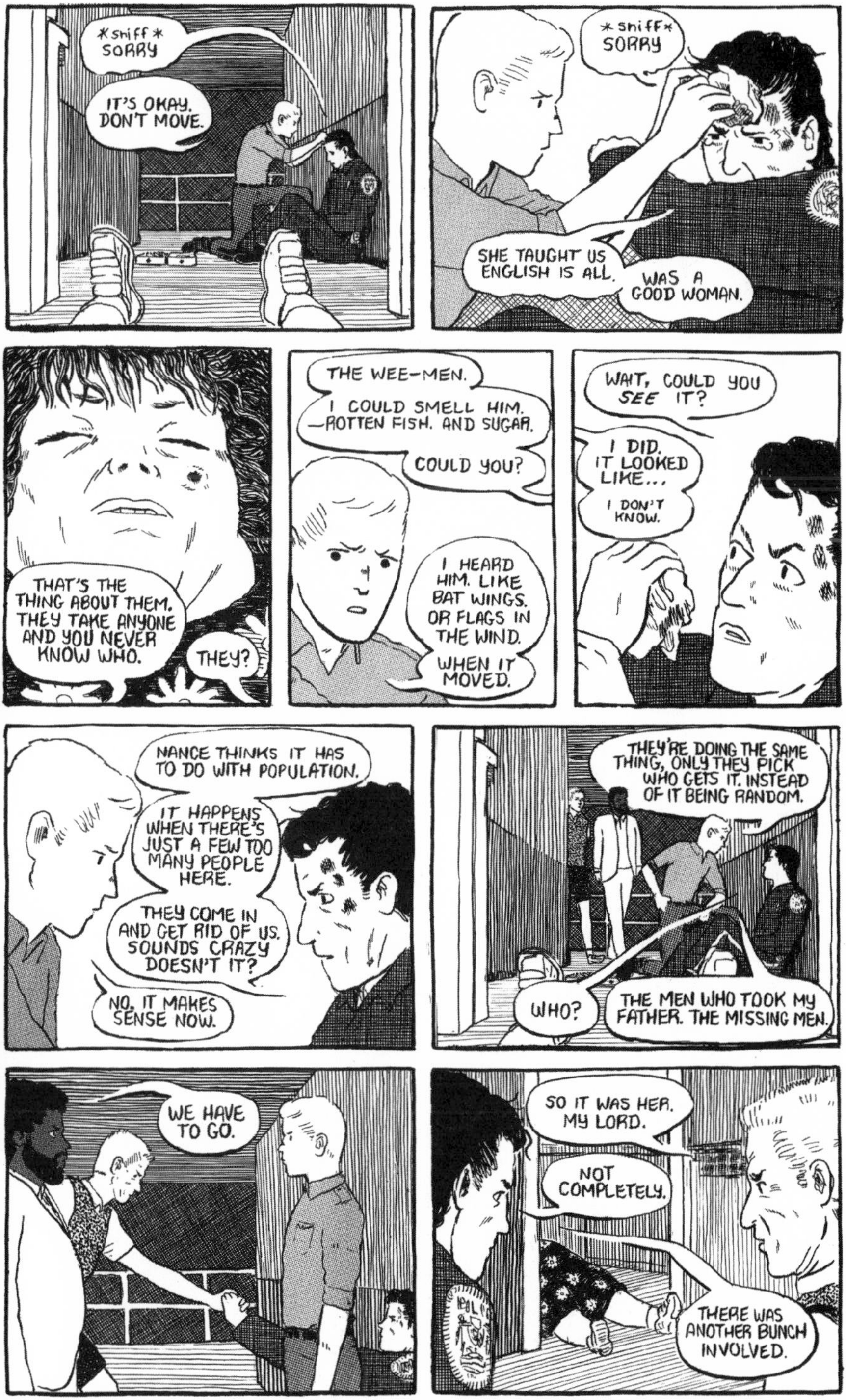
sniff SORRY
IT'S OKAY. DON'T MOVE.
sniff SORRY
SHE TAUGHT US ENGLISH IS ALL.
WAS A GOOD WOMAN.
THAT'S THE THING ABOUT THEM. THEY TAKE ANYONE AND YOU NEVER KNOW WHO.
THEY?
THE WEE-MEN.
I COULD SMELL HIM. —ROTTEN FISH. AND SUGAR.
COULD YOU?
I HEARD HIM. LIKE BAT WINGS. OR FLAGS IN THE WIND.
WHEN IT MOVED.
WAIT, COULD YOU SEE IT?
I DID. IT LOOKED LIKE...
I DON'T KNOW.
NANCE THINKS IT HAS TO DO WITH POPULATION.
IT HAPPENS WHEN THERE'S JUST A FEW TOO MANY PEOPLE HERE.
THEY COME IN AND GET RID OF US. SOUNDS CRAZY DOESN'T IT?
NO, IT MAKES SENSE NOW.
THEY'RE DOING THE SAME THING, ONLY THEY PICK WHO GETS IT. INSTEAD OF IT BEING RANDOM.
WHO?
THE MEN WHO TOOK MY FATHER. THE MISSING MEN.
WE HAVE TO GO.
SO IT WAS HER. MY LORD.
NOT COMPLETELY.
THERE WAS ANOTHER BUNCH INVOLVED.

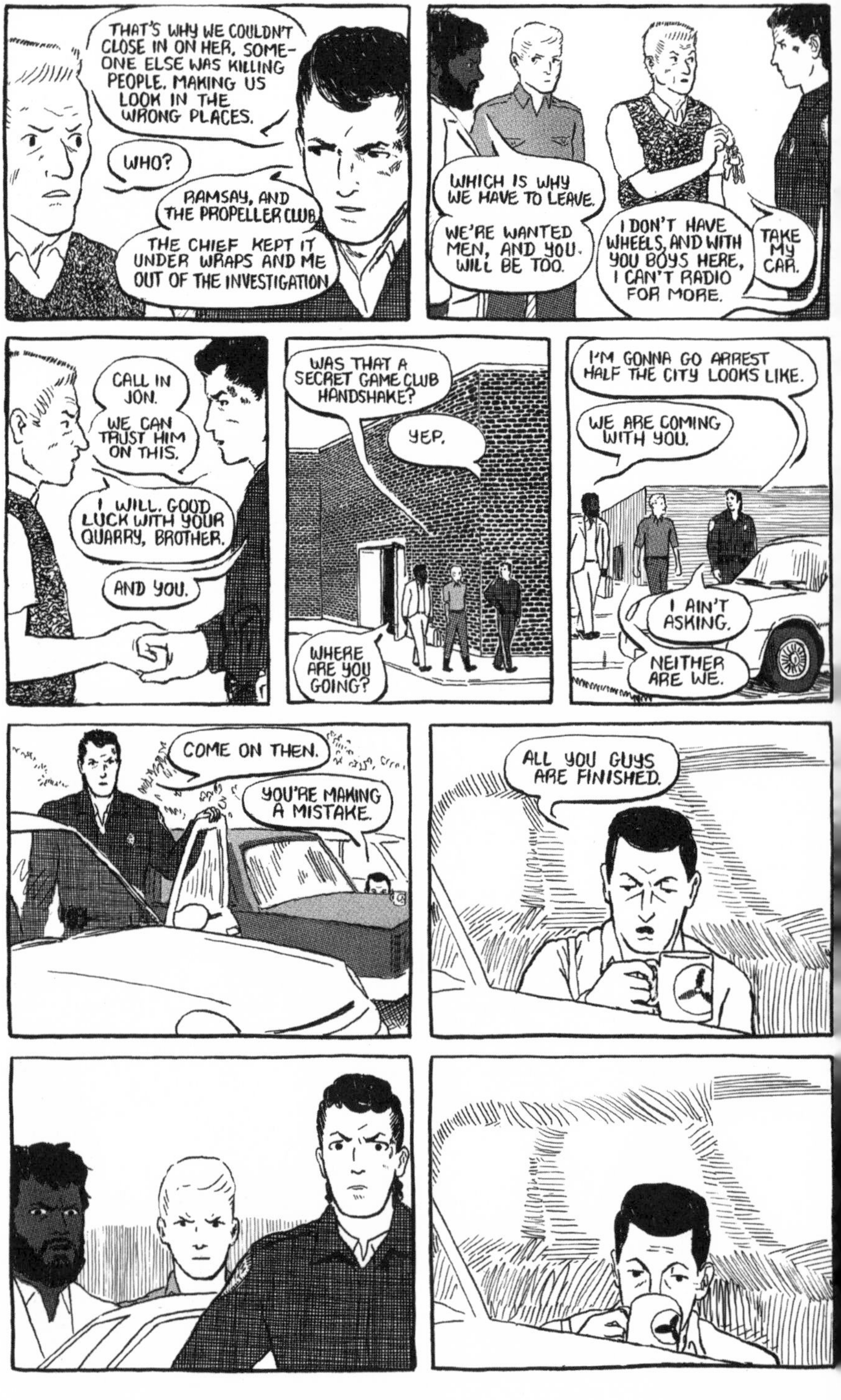
THAT'S WHY WE COULDN'T CLOSE IN ON HER, SOMEONE ELSE WAS KILLING PEOPLE, MAKING US LOOK IN THE WRONG PLACES.
WHO?
RAMSAY, AND THE PROPELLER CLUB
THE CHIEF KEPT IT UNDER WRAPS AND ME OUT OF THE INVESTIGATION
WHICH IS WHY WE HAVE TO LEAVE.
WE'RE WANTED MEN, AND YOU WILL BE TOO.
I DON'T HAVE WHEELS, AND WITH YOU BOYS HERE, I CAN'T RADIO FOR MORE.
TAKE MY CAR.
CALL IN JON.
WE CAN TRUST HIM ON THIS.
I WILL. GOOD LUCK WITH YOUR QUARRY, BROTHER.
AND YOU.
WAS THAT A SECRET GAME CLUB HANDSHAKE?
YEP.
WHERE ARE YOU GOING?
I'M GONNA GO ARREST HALF THE CITY LOOKS LIKE.
WE ARE COMING WITH YOU.
I AIN'T ASKING.
NEITHER ARE WE.
COME ON THEN.
YOU'RE MAKING A MISTAKE.
ALL YOU GUYS ARE FINISHED.

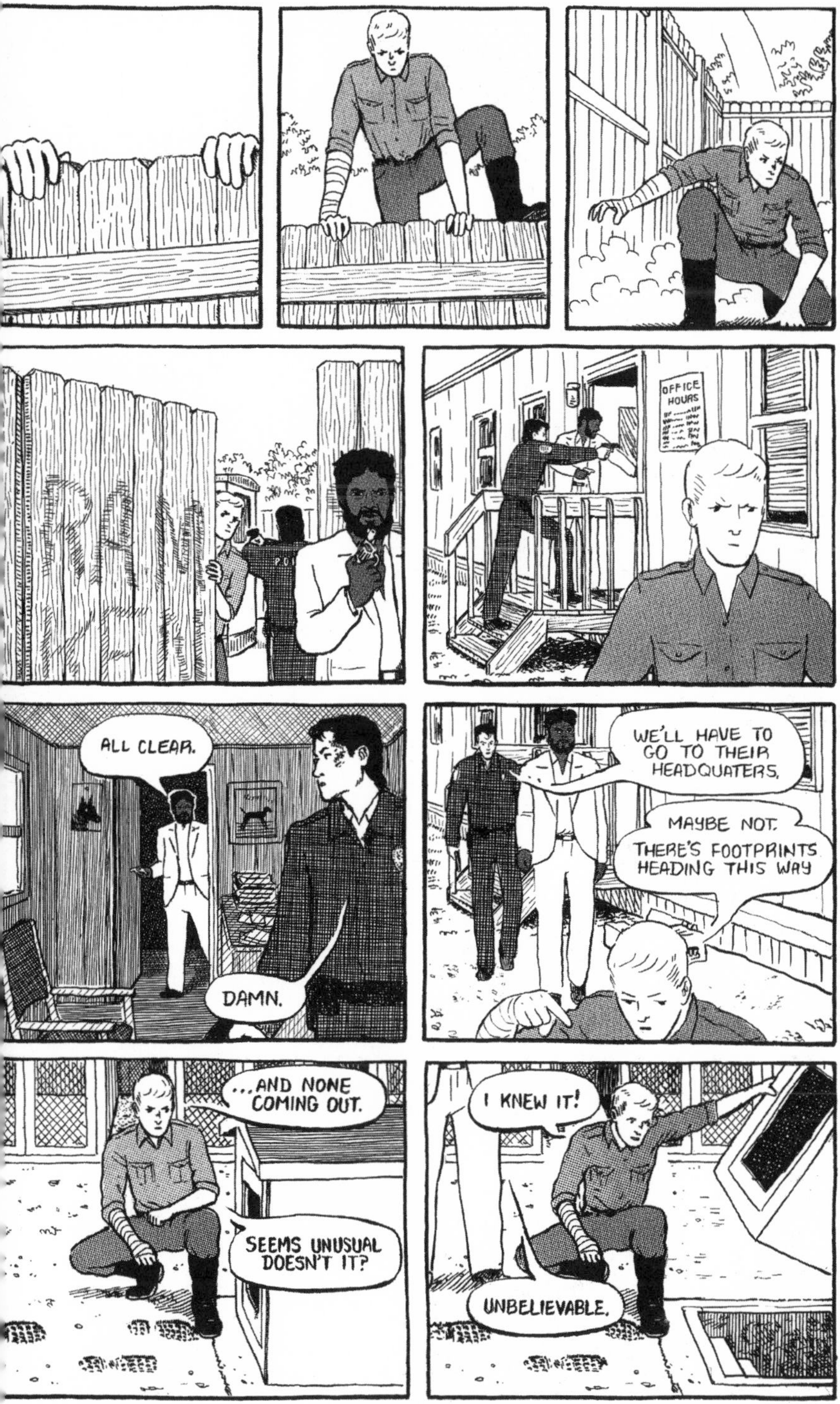
ALL CLEAR.
DAMN.
WE'LL HAVE TO GO TO THEIR HEADQUATERS.
MAYBE NOT. THERE'S FOOTPRINTS HEADING THIS WAY
...AND NONE COMING OUT.
SEEMS UNUSUAL DOESN'T IT?
I KNEW IT!
UNBELIEVABLE.

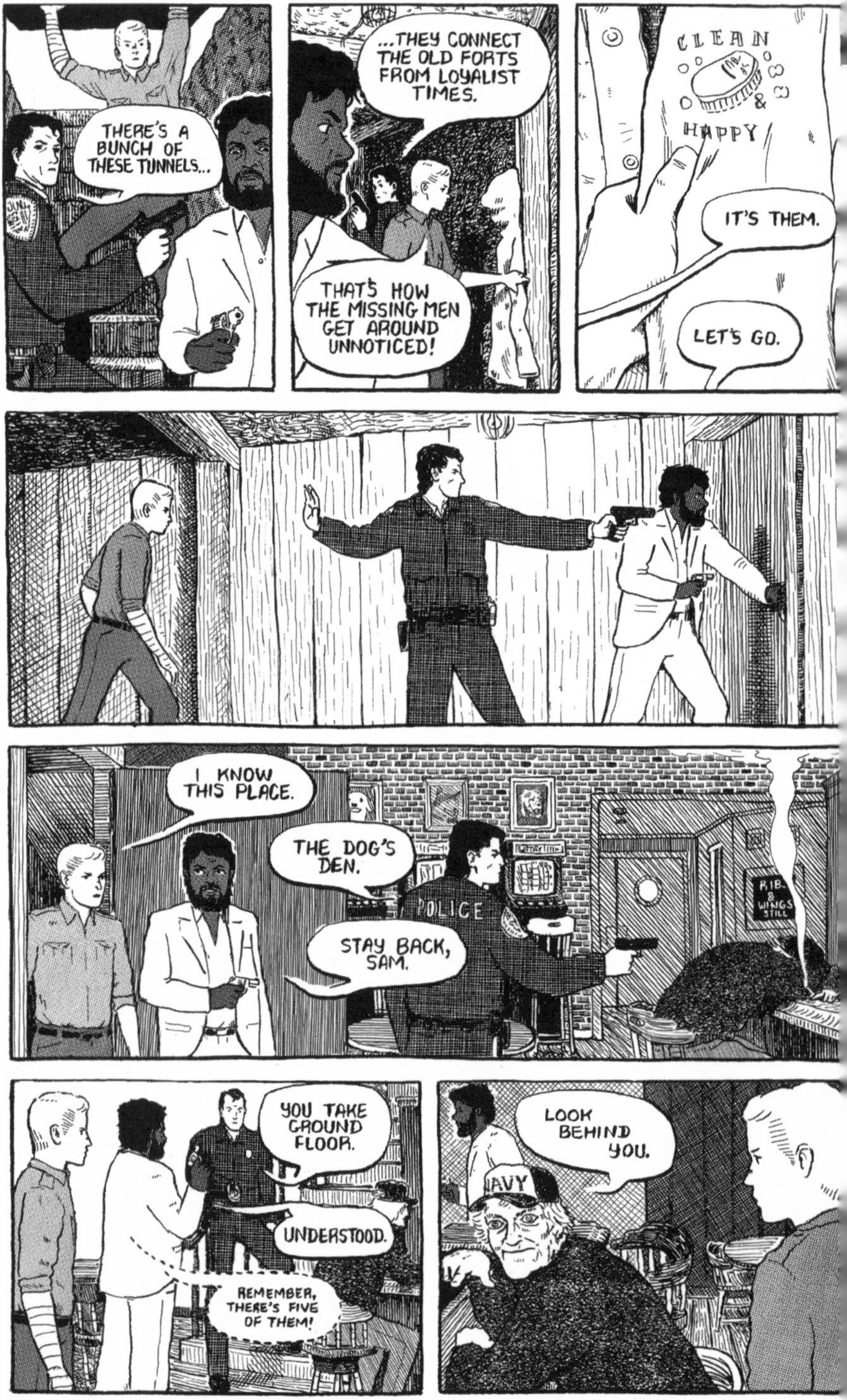
THERE'S A BUNCH OF THESE TUNNELS...
...THEY CONNECT THE OLD FORTS FROM LOYALIST TIMES.
THAT'S HOW THE MISSING MEN GET AROUND UNNOTICED!
CLEAN & HAPPY
IT'S THEM.
LET'S GO.
I KNOW THIS PLACE.
THE DOG'S DEN.
POLICE
STAY BACK, SAM.
RIBS & WINGS
YOU TAKE GROUND FLOOR.
UNDERSTOOD.
REMEMBER, THERE'S FIVE OF THEM!
LOOK BEHIND YOU.
NAVY

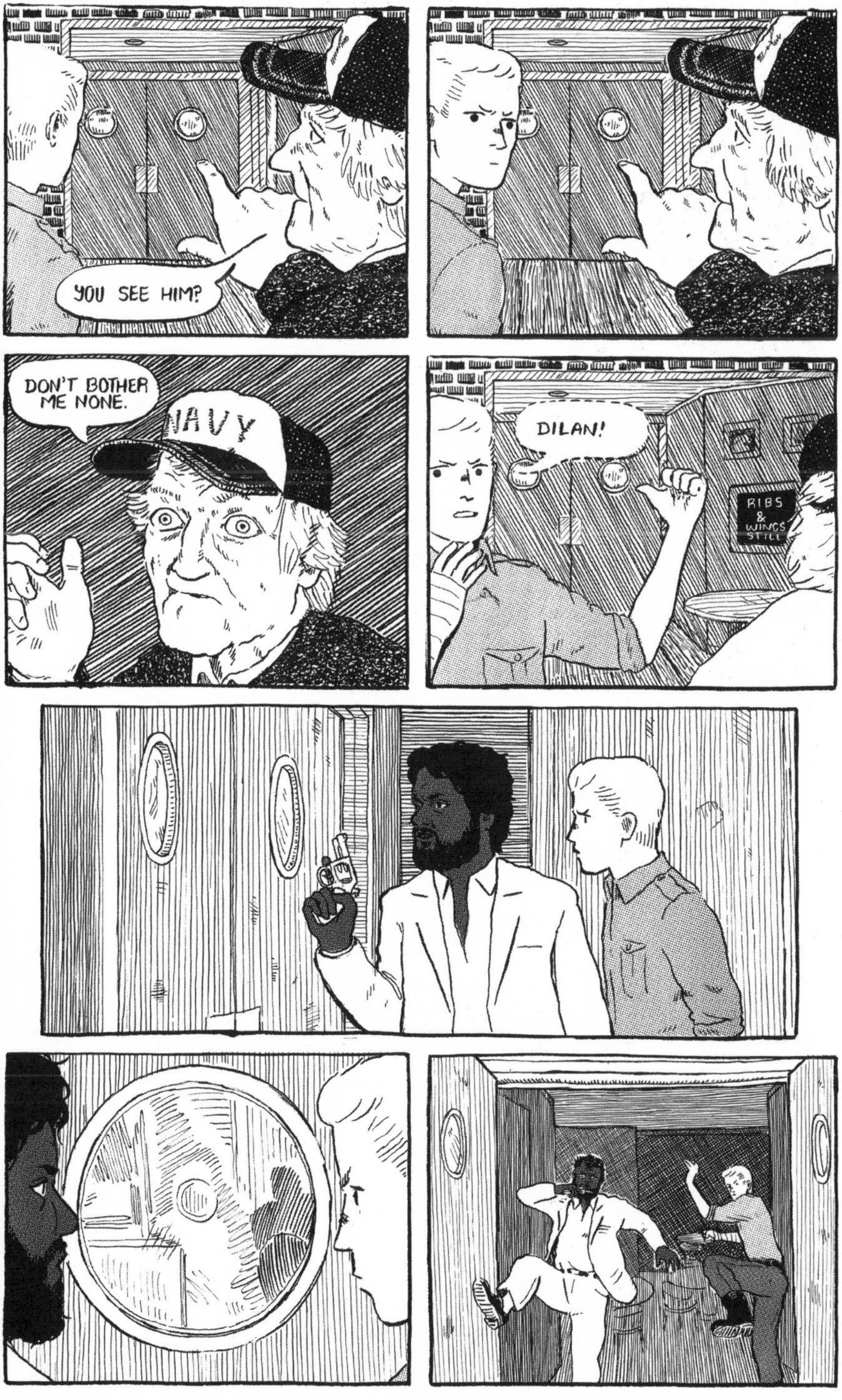
YOU SEE HIM?
DON'T BOTHER ME NONE.
NAVY
DILAN!
RIBS & WINGS STILL

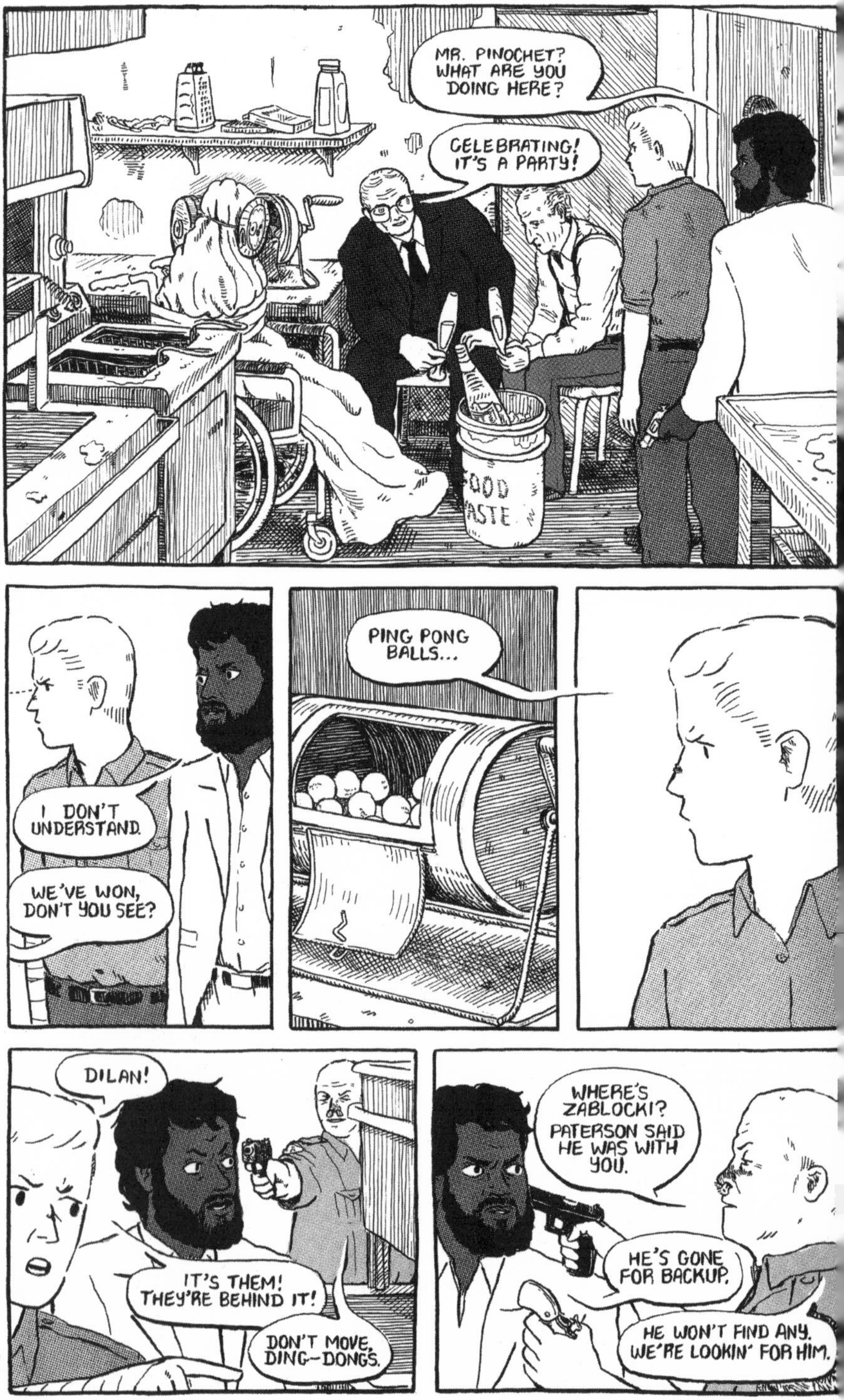
MR. PINOCHET? WHAT ARE YOU DOING HERE?
CELEBRATING! IT'S A PARTY!
FOOD WASTE
I DON'T UNDERSTAND.
WE'VE WON, DON'T YOU SEE?
PING PONG BALLS...
DILAN!
IT'S THEM! THEY'RE BEHIND IT!
DON'T MOVE, DING-DONGS.
WHERE'S ZABLOCKI? PATERSON SAID HE WAS WITH YOU.
HE'S GONE FOR BACKUP.
HE WON'T FIND ANY. WE'RE LOOKIN' FOR HIM.

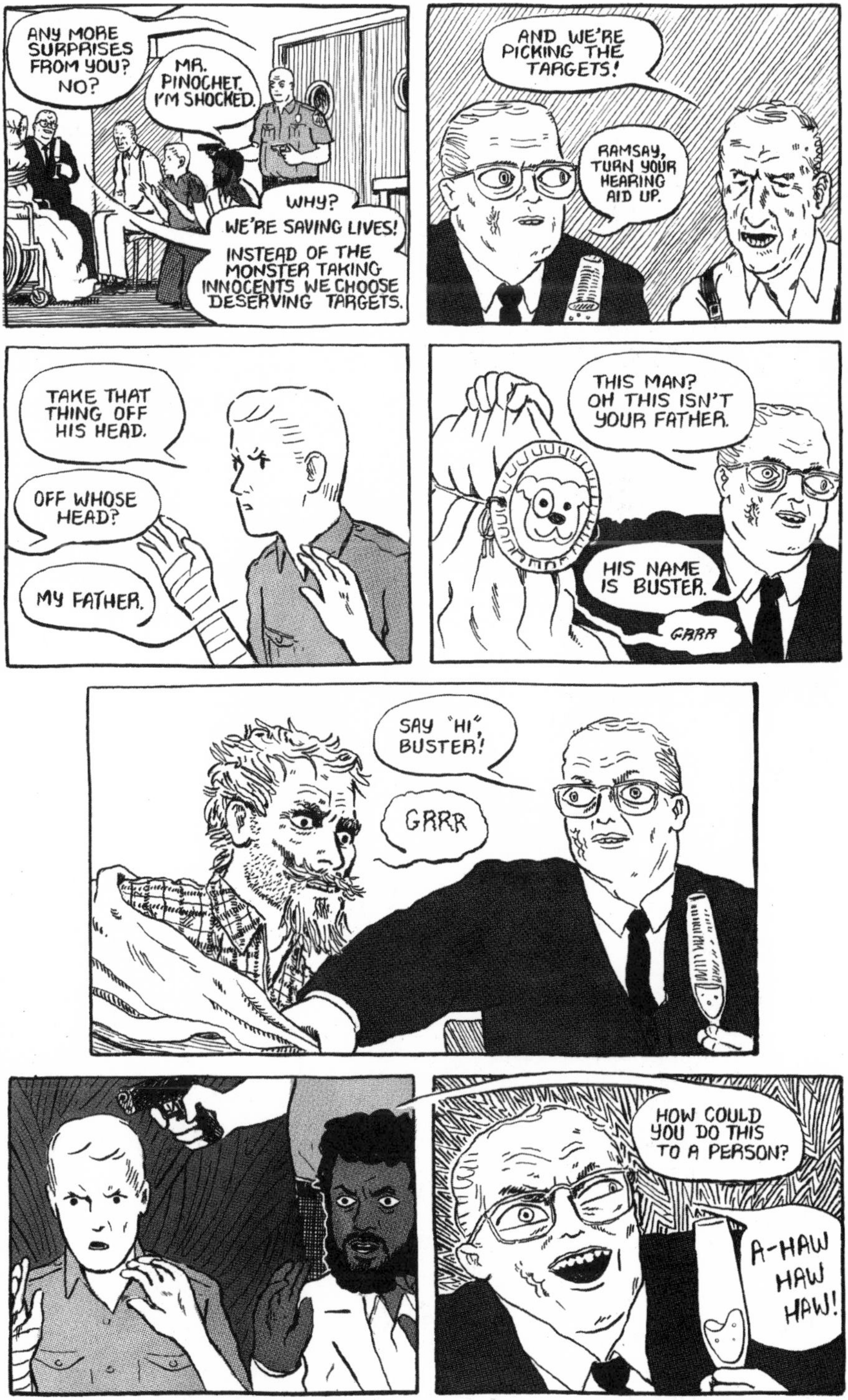
ANY MORE SURPRISES FROM YOU? NO?
MR. PINOCHET. I'M SHOCKED.
WHY?
WE'RE SAVING LIVES!
INSTEAD OF THE MONSTER TAKING INNOCENTS WE CHOOSE DESERVING TARGETS.
AND WE'RE PICKING THE TARGETS!
RAMSAY, TURN YOUR HEARING AID UP.
TAKE THAT THING OFF HIS HEAD.
OFF WHOSE HEAD?
MY FATHER.
THIS MAN? OH THIS ISN'T YOUR FATHER.
HIS NAME IS BUSTER.
GRRR
SAY "HI", BUSTER!
GRRR
HOW COULD YOU DO THIS TO A PERSON?
A-HAW HAW HAW!

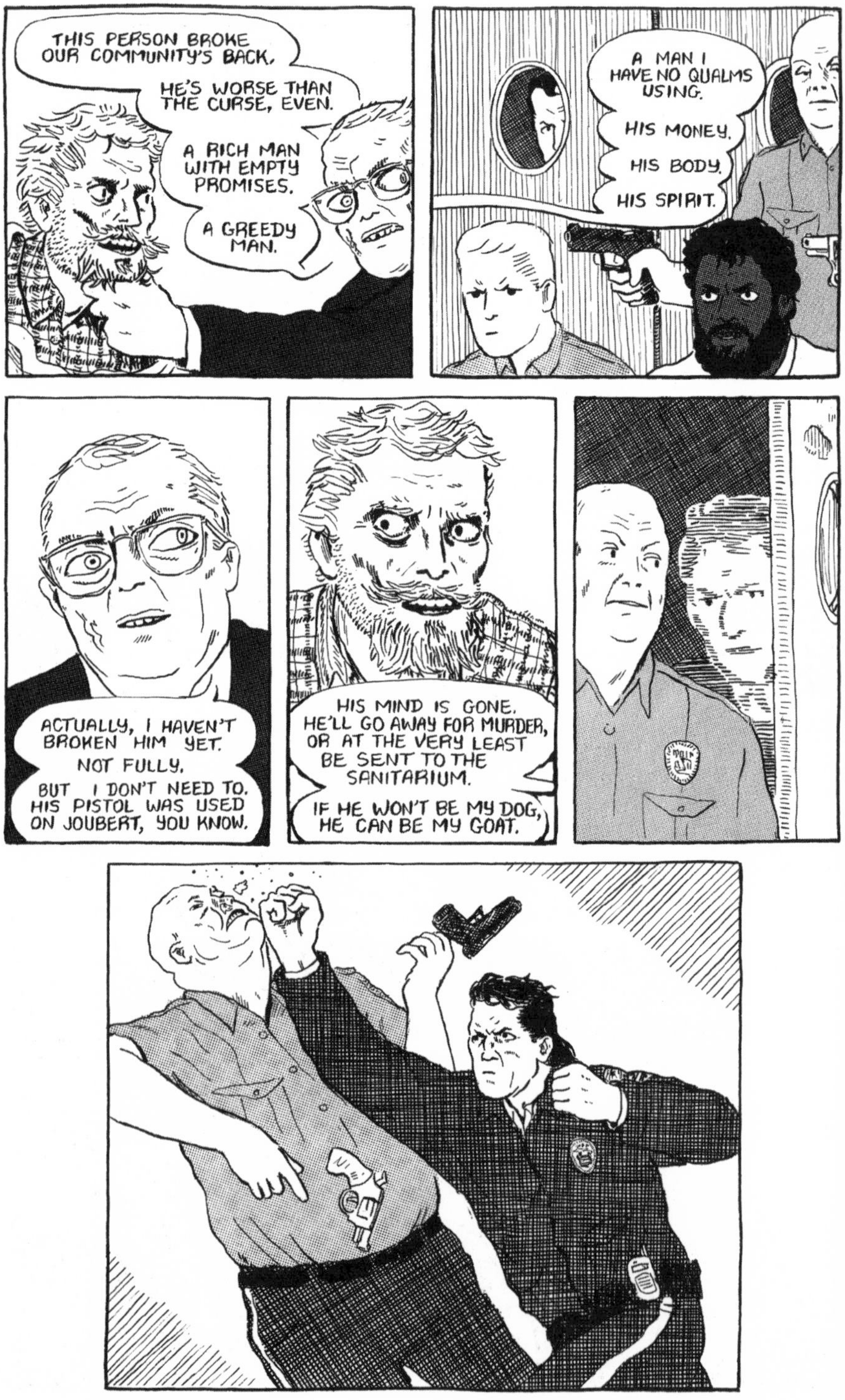
THIS PERSON BROKE OUR COMMUNITY'S BACK.
HE'S WORSE THAN THE CURSE, EVEN.
A RICH MAN WITH EMPTY PROMISES.
A GREEDY MAN.
A MAN I HAVE NO QUALMS USING.
HIS MONEY.
HIS BODY.
HIS SPIRIT.
ACTUALLY, I HAVEN'T BROKEN HIM YET.
NOT FULLY.
BUT I DON'T NEED TO. HIS PISTOL WAS USED ON JOUBERT, YOU KNOW.
HIS MIND IS GONE. HE'LL GO AWAY FOR MURDER, OR AT THE VERY LEAST BE SENT TO THE SANITARIUM.
IF HE WON'T BE MY DOG, HE CAN BE MY GOAT.

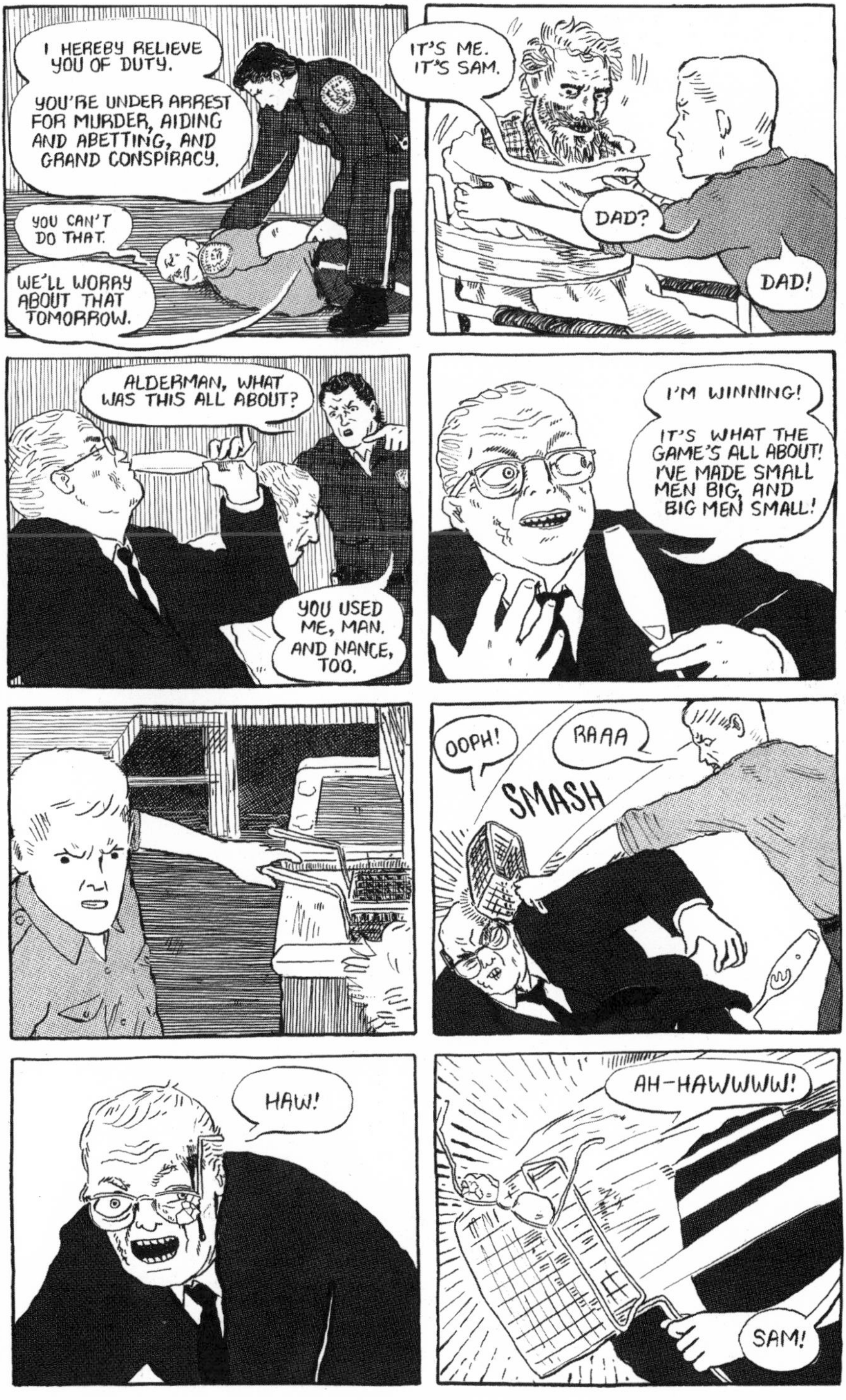
I HEREBY RELIEVE YOU OF DUTY.
YOU'RE UNDER ARREST FOR MURDER, AIDING AND ABETTING, AND GRAND CONSPIRACY.
YOU CAN'T DO THAT.
WE'LL WORRY ABOUT THAT TOMORROW.
IT'S ME. IT'S SAM.
DAD?
DAD!
ALDERMAN, WHAT WAS THIS ALL ABOUT?
YOU USED ME, MAN. AND NANCE, TOO.
I'M WINNING!
IT'S WHAT THE GAME'S ALL ABOUT! I'VE MADE SMALL MEN BIG, AND BIG MEN SMALL!
OOPH!
RAAA
SMASH
HAW!
AH-HAWWWW!
SAM!

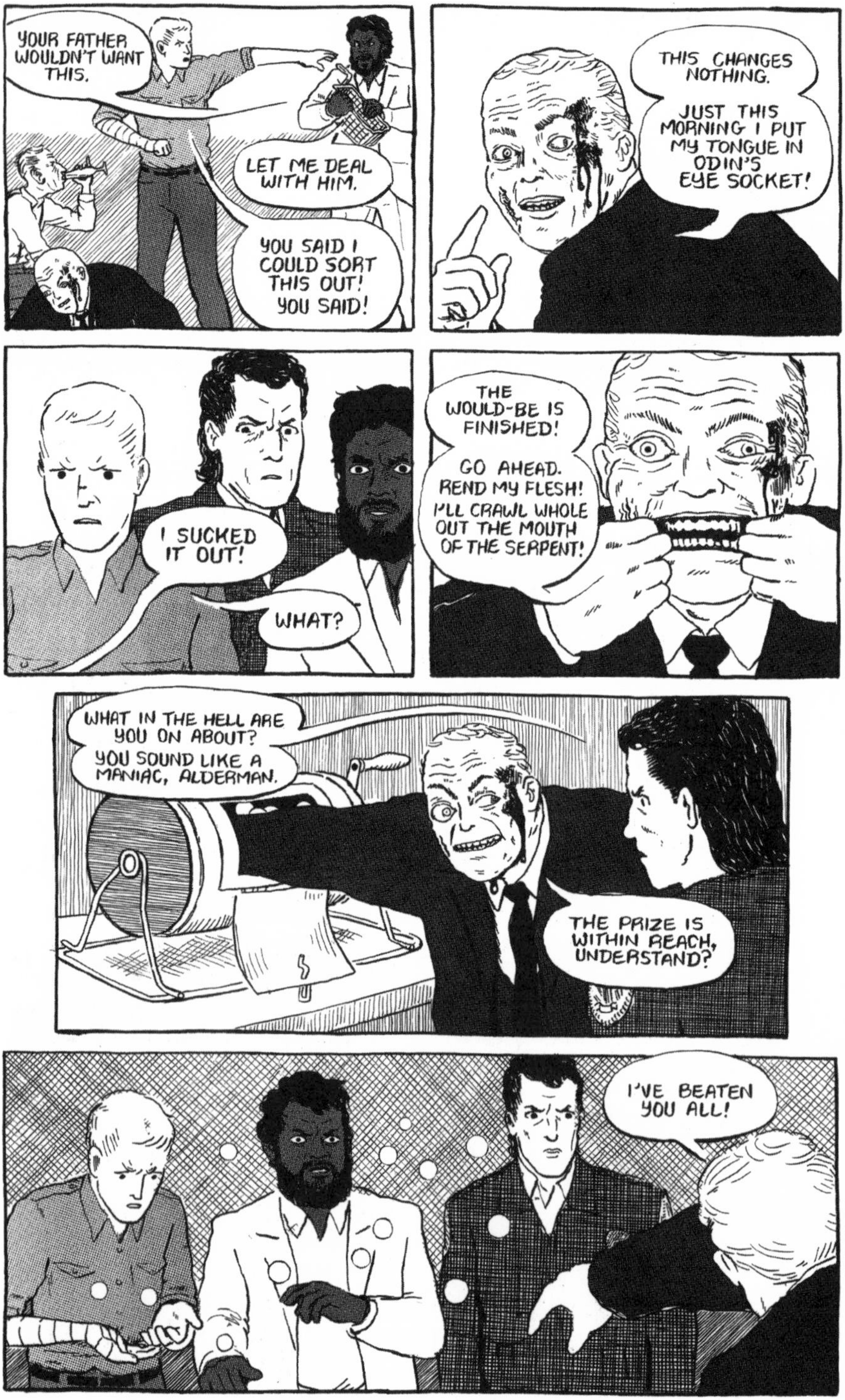
YOUR FATHER WOULDN'T WANT THIS.
LET ME DEAL WITH HIM.
YOU SAID I COULD SORT THIS OUT! YOU SAID!
THIS CHANGES NOTHING.
JUST THIS MORNING I PUT MY TONGUE IN ODIN'S EYE SOCKET!
I SUCKED IT OUT!
WHAT?
THE WOULD-BE IS FINISHED!
GO AHEAD. REND MY FLESH! I'LL CRAWL WHOLE OUT THE MOUTH OF THE SERPENT!
WHAT IN THE HELL ARE YOU ON ABOUT?
YOU SOUND LIKE A MANIAC, ALDERMAN.
THE PRIZE IS WITHIN REACH, UNDERSTAND?
I'VE BEATEN YOU ALL!

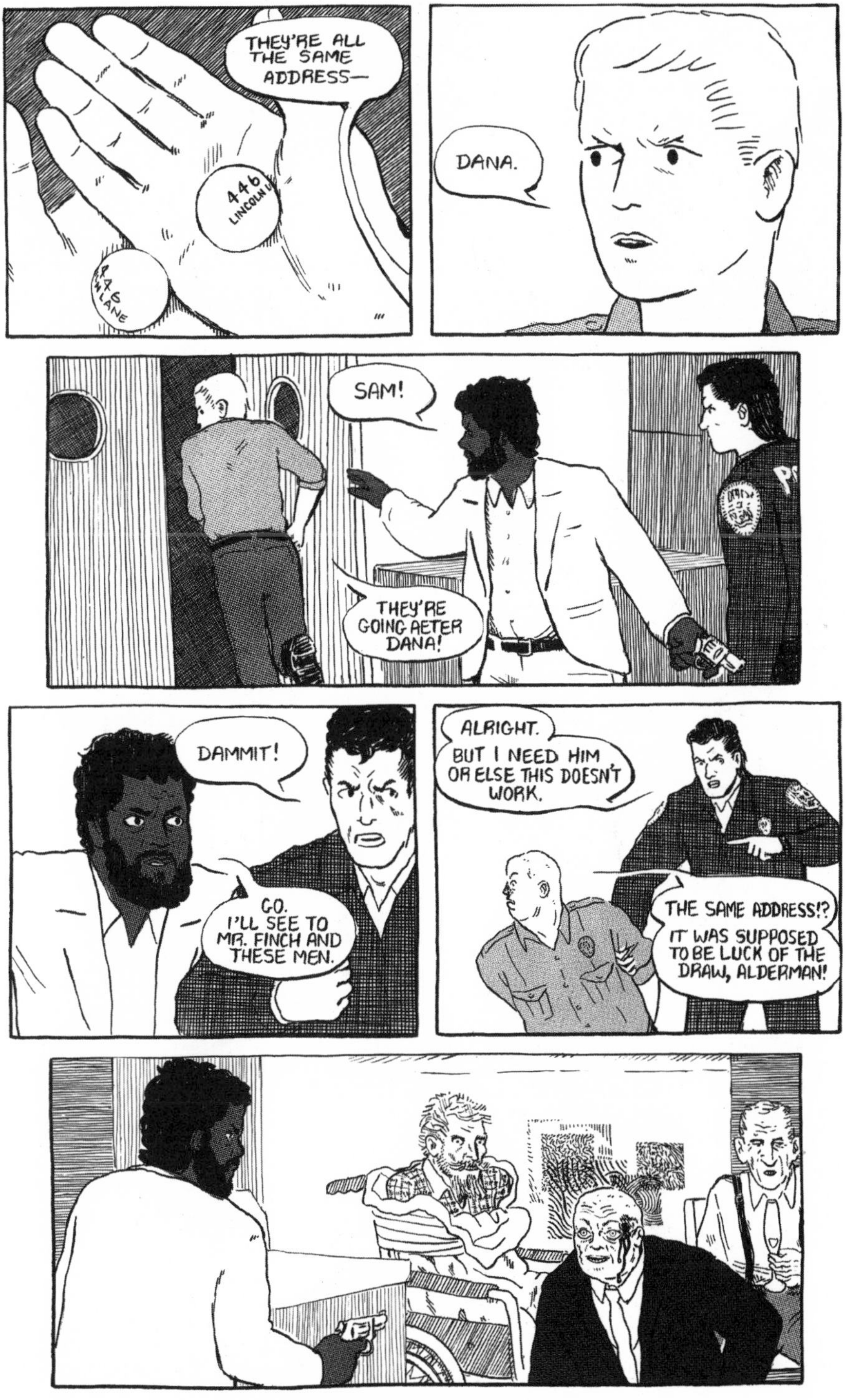
THEY'RE ALL THE SAME ADDRESS—
446 LINCOLN
446 LANE
DANA.
SAM!
THEY'RE GOING AFTER DANA!
DAMMIT!
GO. I'LL SEE TO MR. FINCH AND THESE MEN.
ALRIGHT.
BUT I NEED HIM OR ELSE THIS DOESN'T WORK.
THE SAME ADDRESS!?
IT WAS SUPPOSED TO BE LUCK OF THE DRAW, ALDERMAN!

DAD—
DON'T.
I DON'T WANT TO HEAR A WORD.
FROM EITHER OF YOU.
YOU DON'T KNOW WHAT YOU'VE GOTTEN INTO...

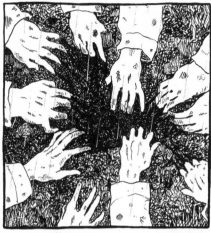

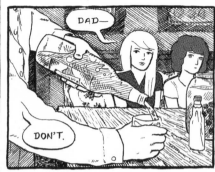

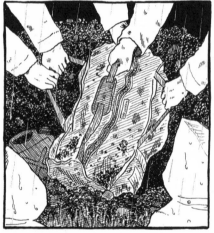

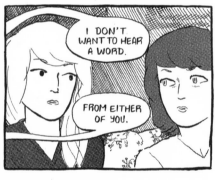

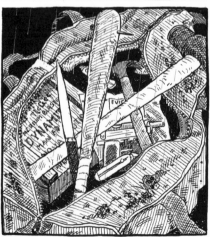

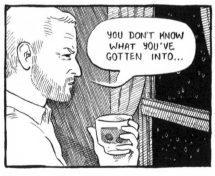

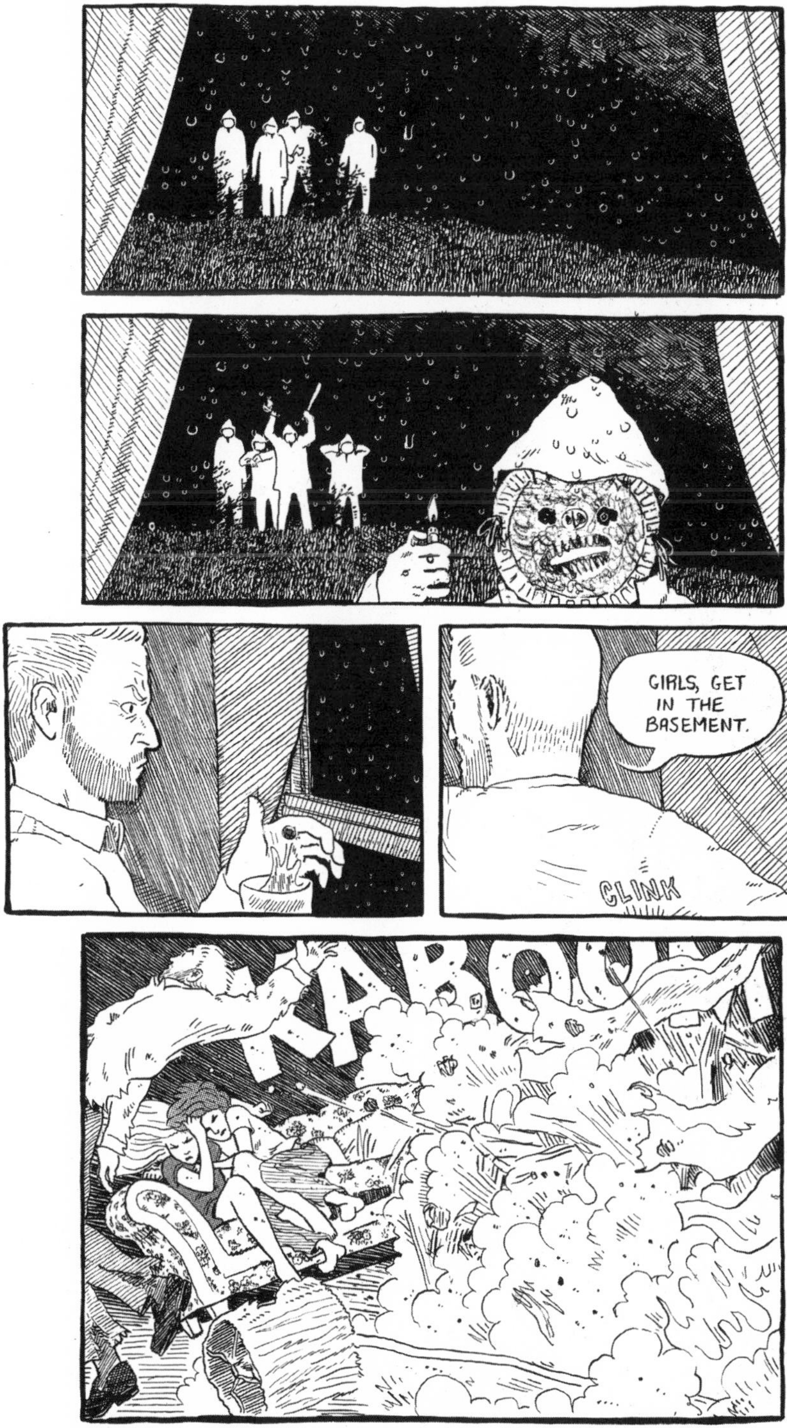
GIRLS, GET IN THE BASEMENT.
CLINK

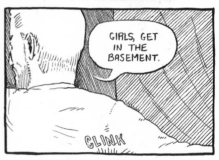

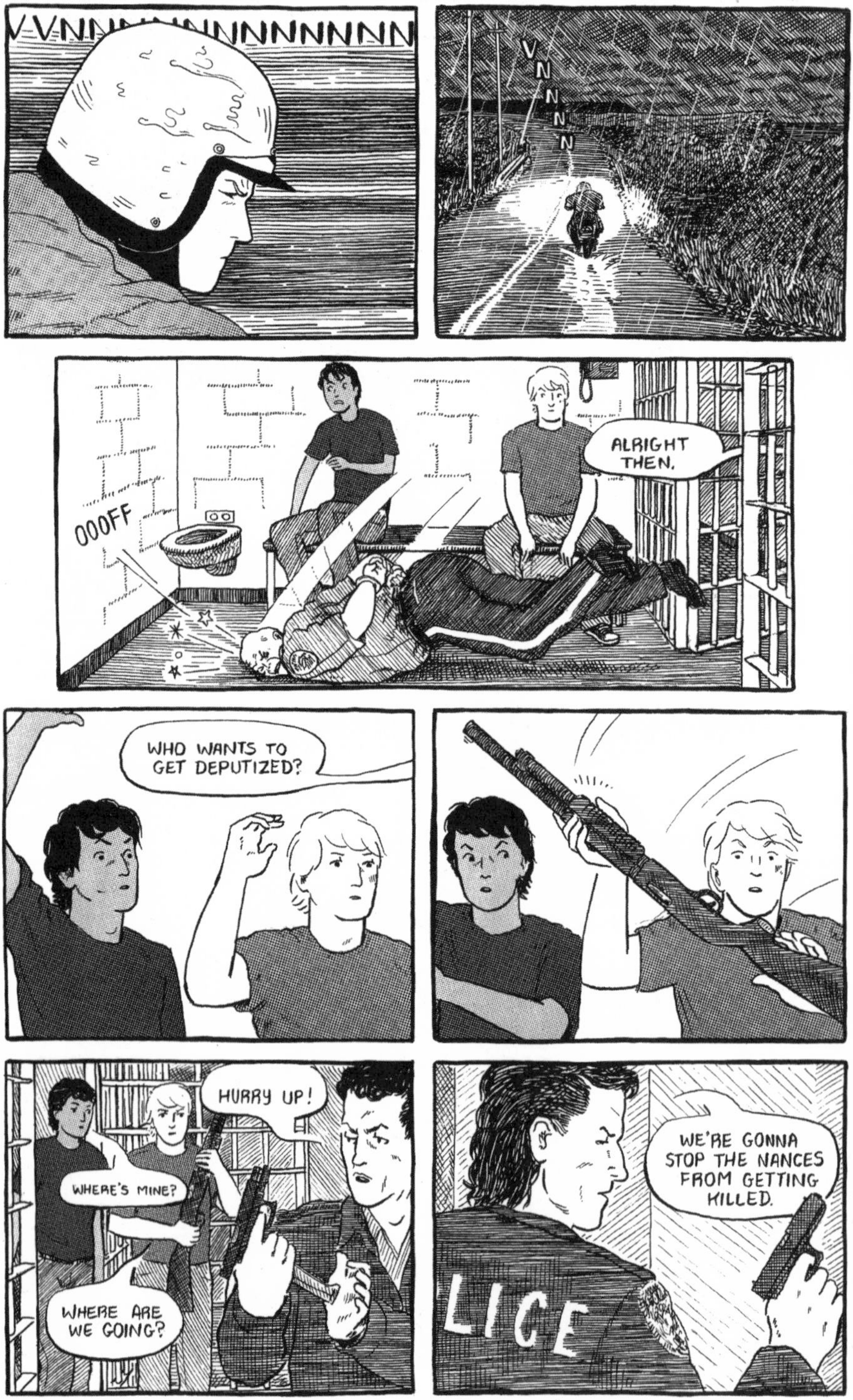
VVNNNNNNNNNNNNNN
VNNNN
OOOFF
ALRIGHT THEN.
WHO WANTS TO GET DEPUTIZED?
HURRY UP!
WHERE'S MINE?
WHERE ARE WE GOING?
WE'RE GONNA STOP THE NANCES FROM GETTING KILLED.
LICE

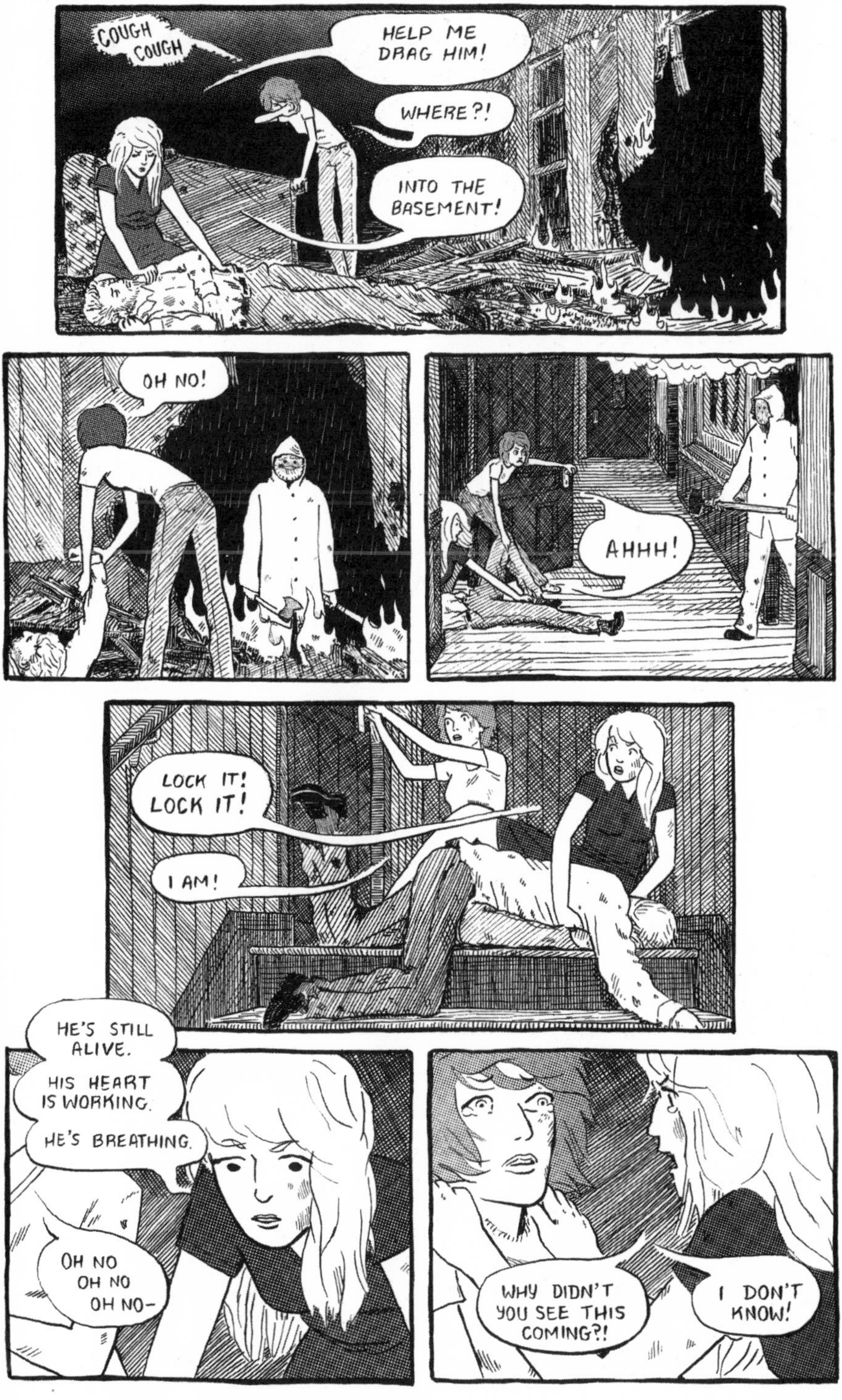
COUGH COUGH
HELP ME DRAG HIM!
WHERE?!
INTO THE BASEMENT!
OH NO!
AHHH!
LOCK IT! LOCK IT!
I AM!
HE'S STILL ALIVE.
HIS HEART IS WORKING.
HE'S BREATHING.
OH NO OH NO OH NO–
WHY DIDN'T YOU SEE THIS COMING?!
I DON'T KNOW!

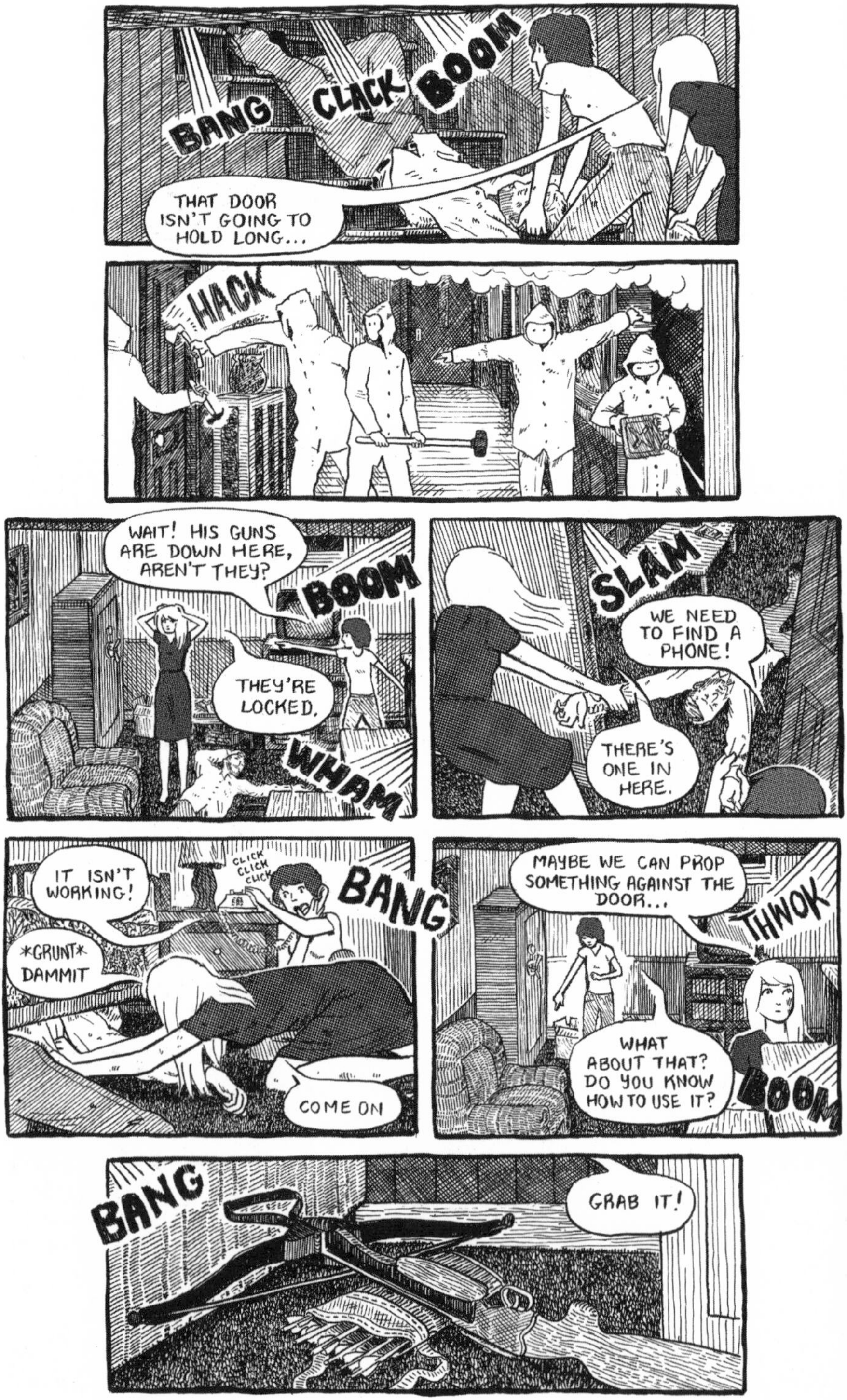
BANG
CLACK
BOOM
THAT DOOR ISN'T GOING TO HOLD LONG...
HACK
WAIT! HIS GUNS ARE DOWN HERE, AREN'T THEY?
BOOM
THEY'RE LOCKED.
WHAM
SLAM
WE NEED TO FIND A PHONE!
THERE'S ONE IN HERE.
IT ISN'T WORKING!
CLICK CLICK CLICK
BANG
GRUNT DAMMIT
COME ON
MAYBE WE CAN PROP SOMETHING AGAINST THE DOOR...
THWOK
WHAT ABOUT THAT? DO YOU KNOW HOW TO USE IT?
BOOM
BANG
GRAB IT!

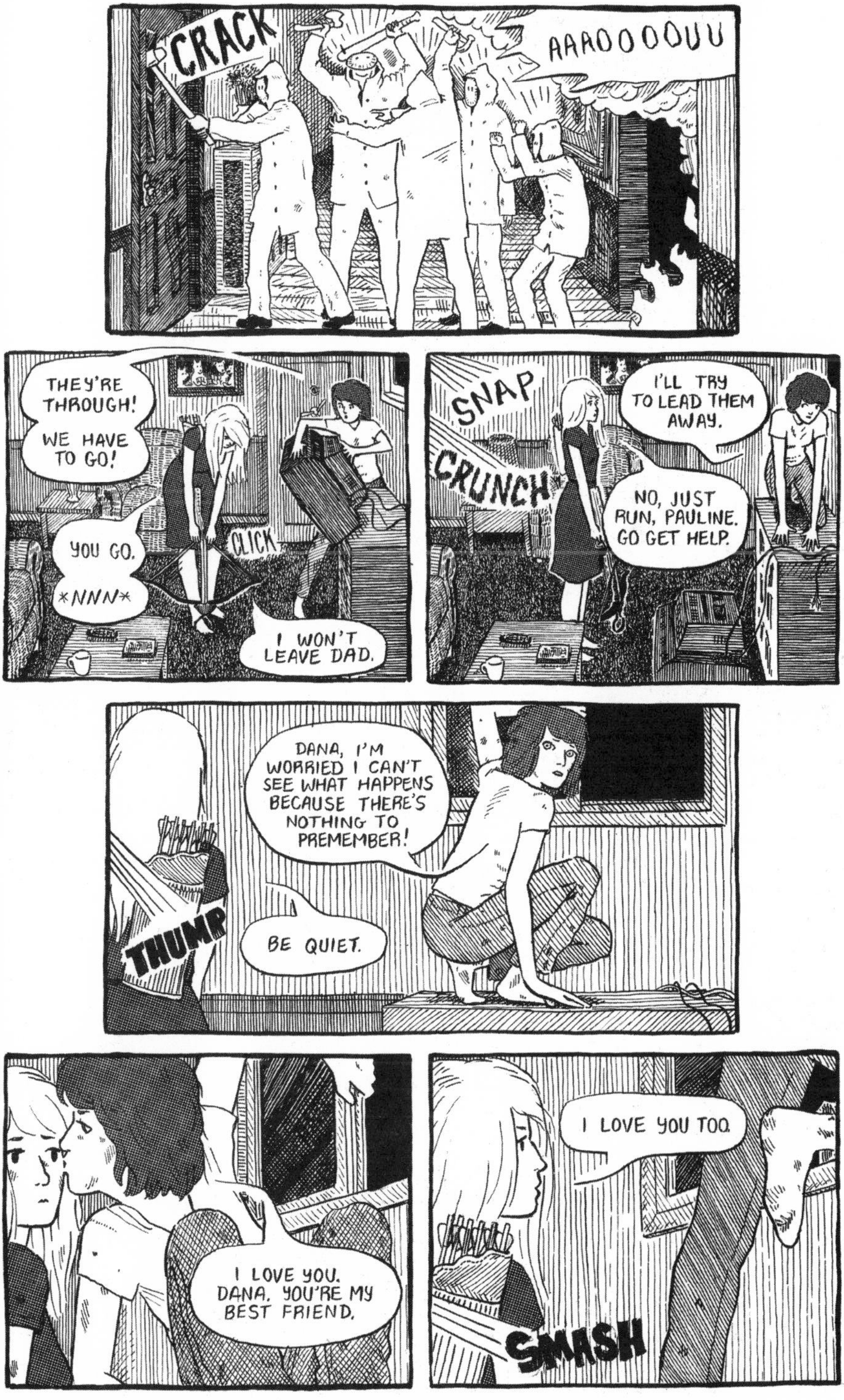
CRACK
AAAOOOOOUU
THEY'RE THROUGH!
WE HAVE TO GO!
YOU GO.
NNN
CLICK
I WON'T LEAVE DAD.
SNAP
CRUNCH
I'LL TRY TO LEAD THEM AWAY.
NO, JUST RUN, PAULINE. GO GET HELP.
DANA, I'M WORRIED I CAN'T SEE WHAT HAPPENS BECAUSE THERE'S NOTHING TO PREMEMBER!
THUMP
BE QUIET.
I LOVE YOU. DANA, YOU'RE MY BEST FRIEND.
I LOVE YOU TOO.
SMASH

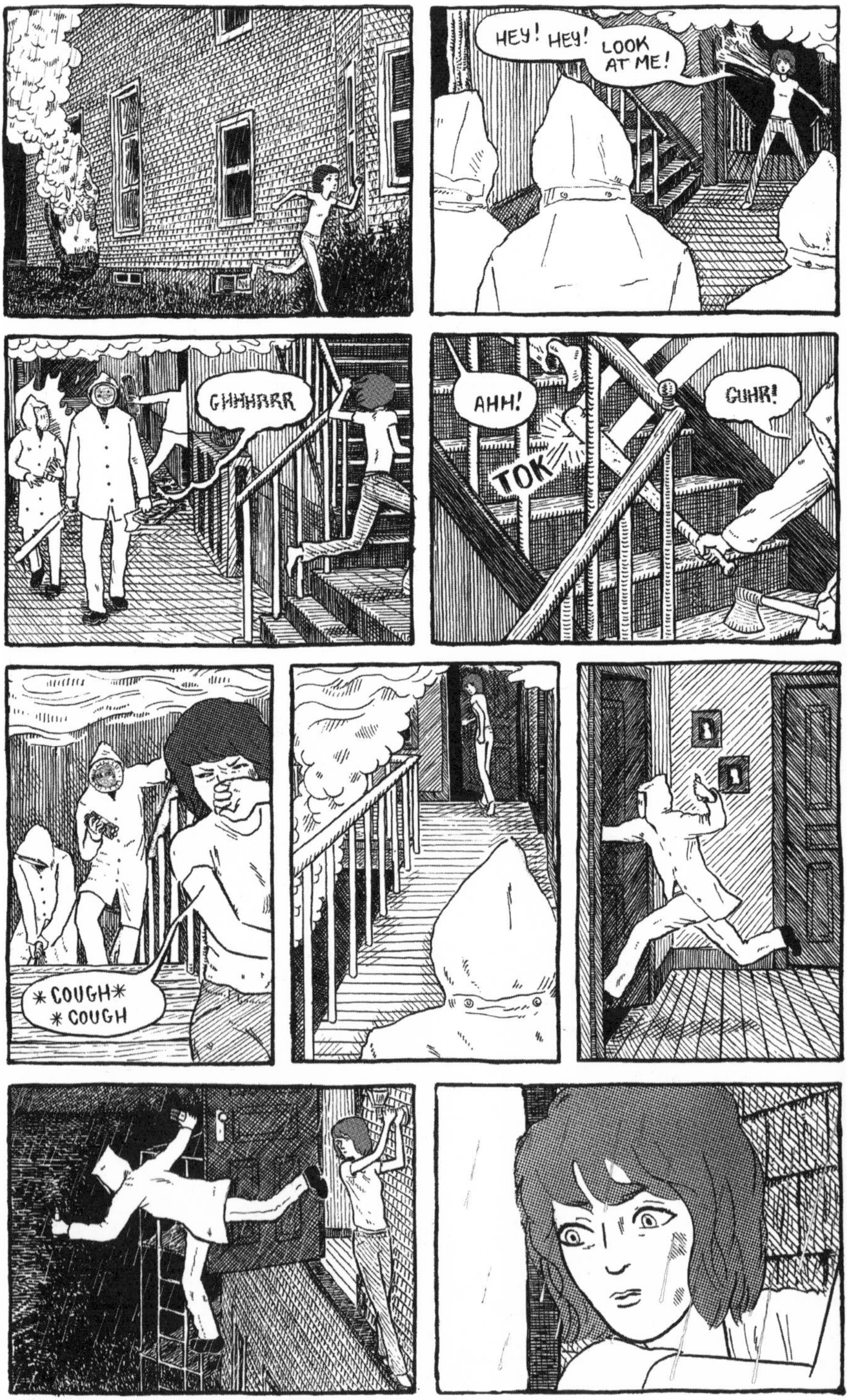
HEY! HEY!
LOOK AT ME!
GHHHRRR
AHH!
TOK
GUHR!
COUGH
*COUGH

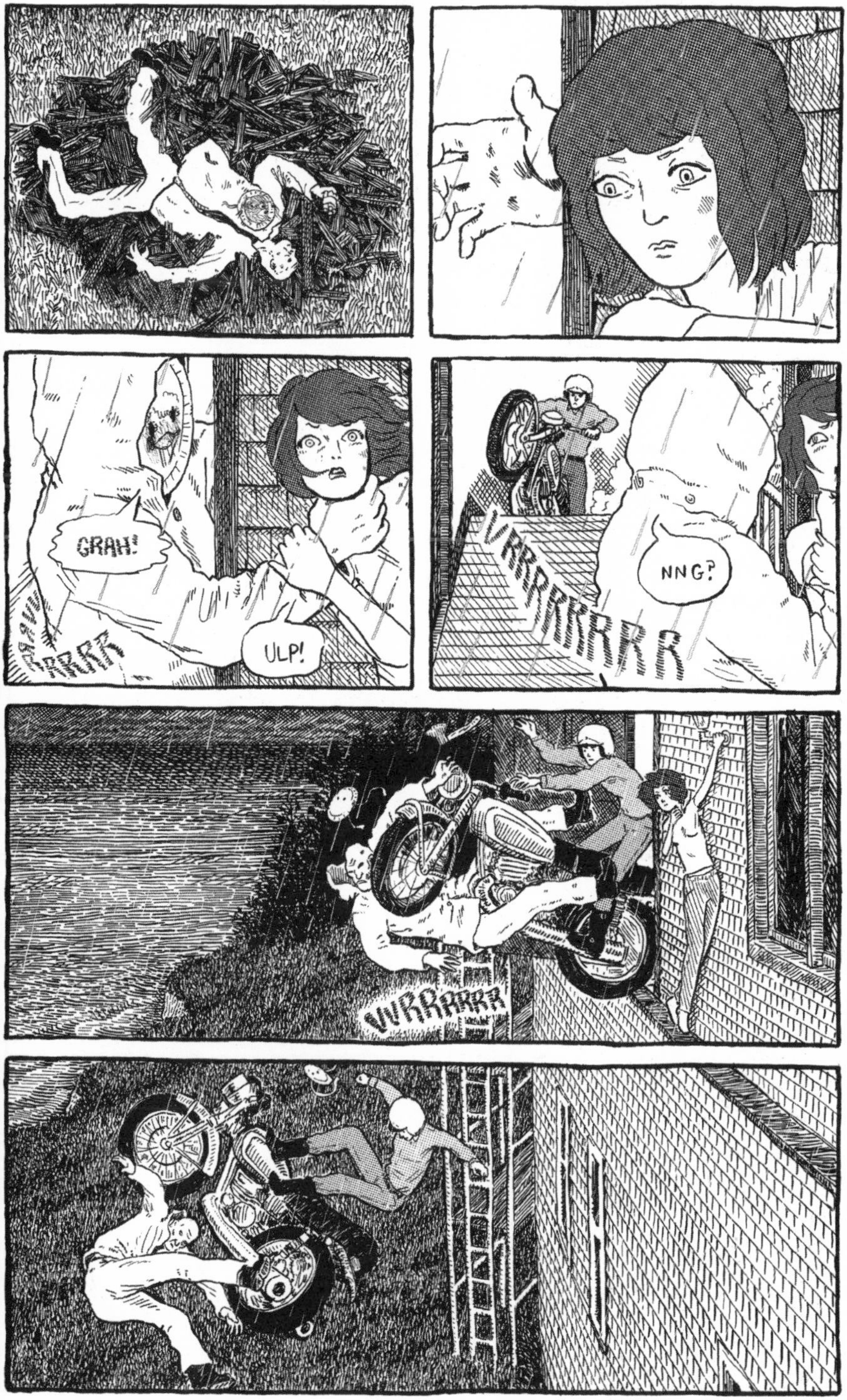
GRAH!
VRRRRRK
ULP!
VRRRRRRRRRR
NNG?
VVRRRRRR

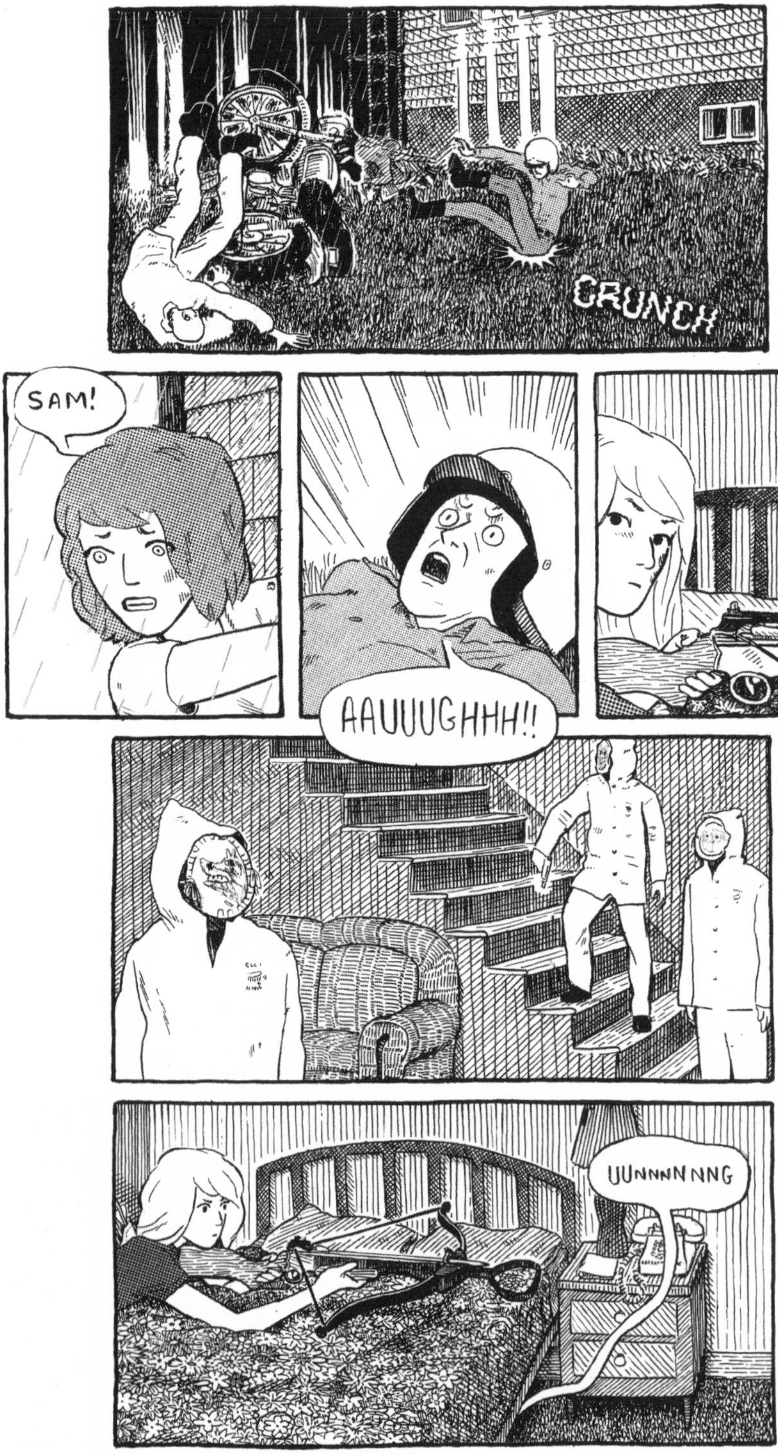
CRUNCH
SAM!
AAUUUGHHH!!
UUNNNNNNG

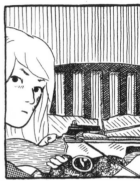

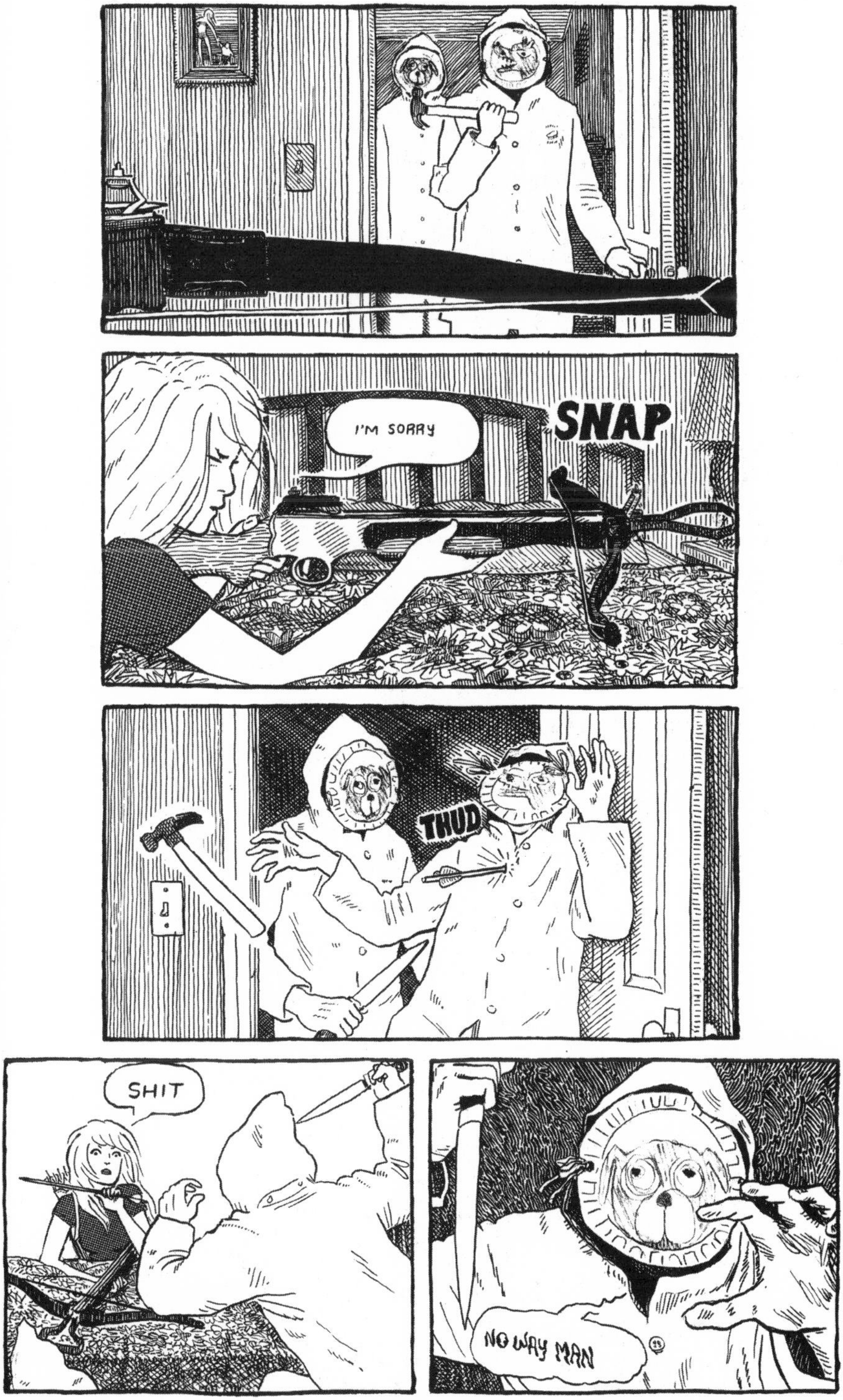
I'M SORRY
SNAP
THUD
SHIT
NO WAY MAN

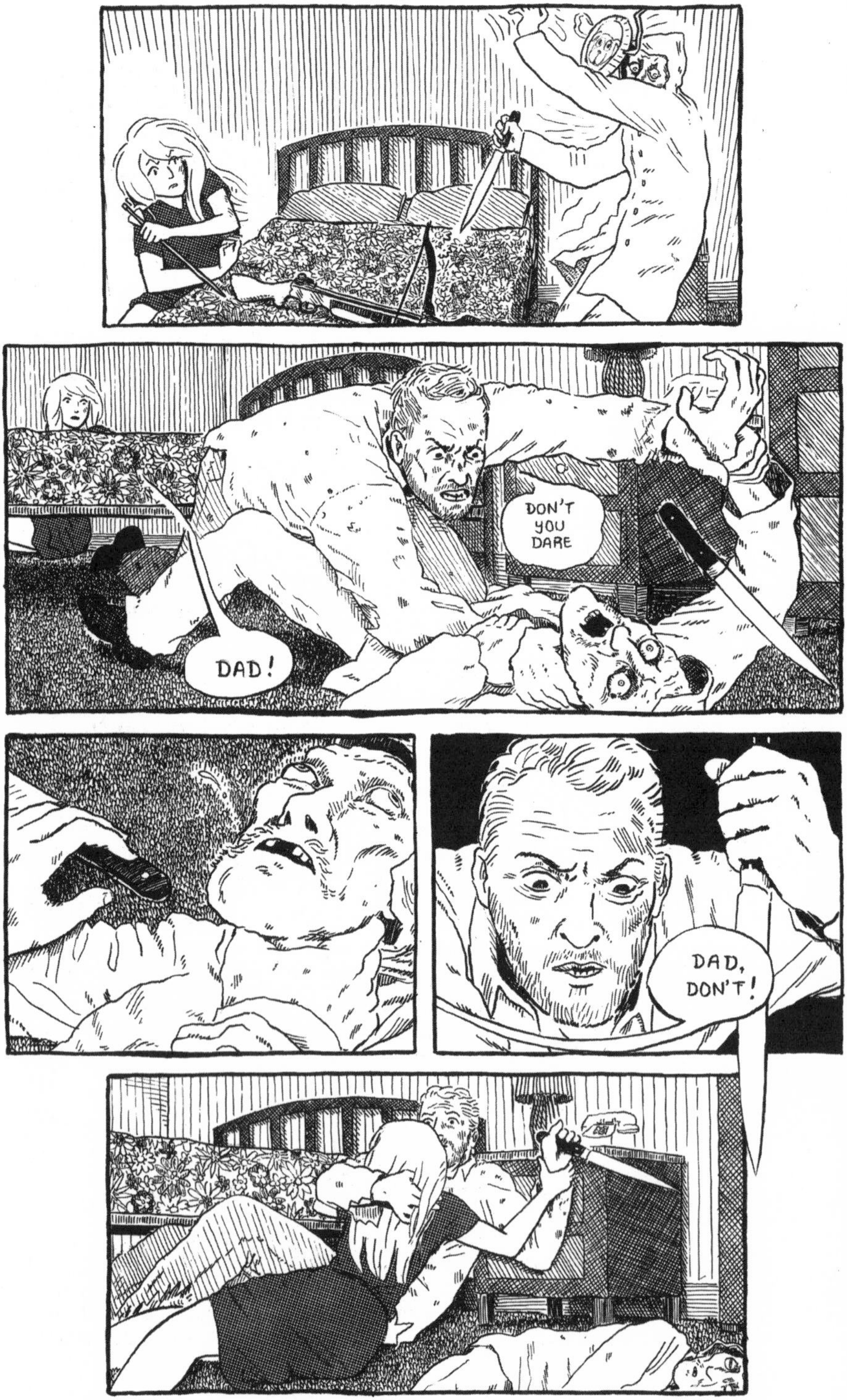
DON'T YOU DARE
DAD!
DAD, DON'T!

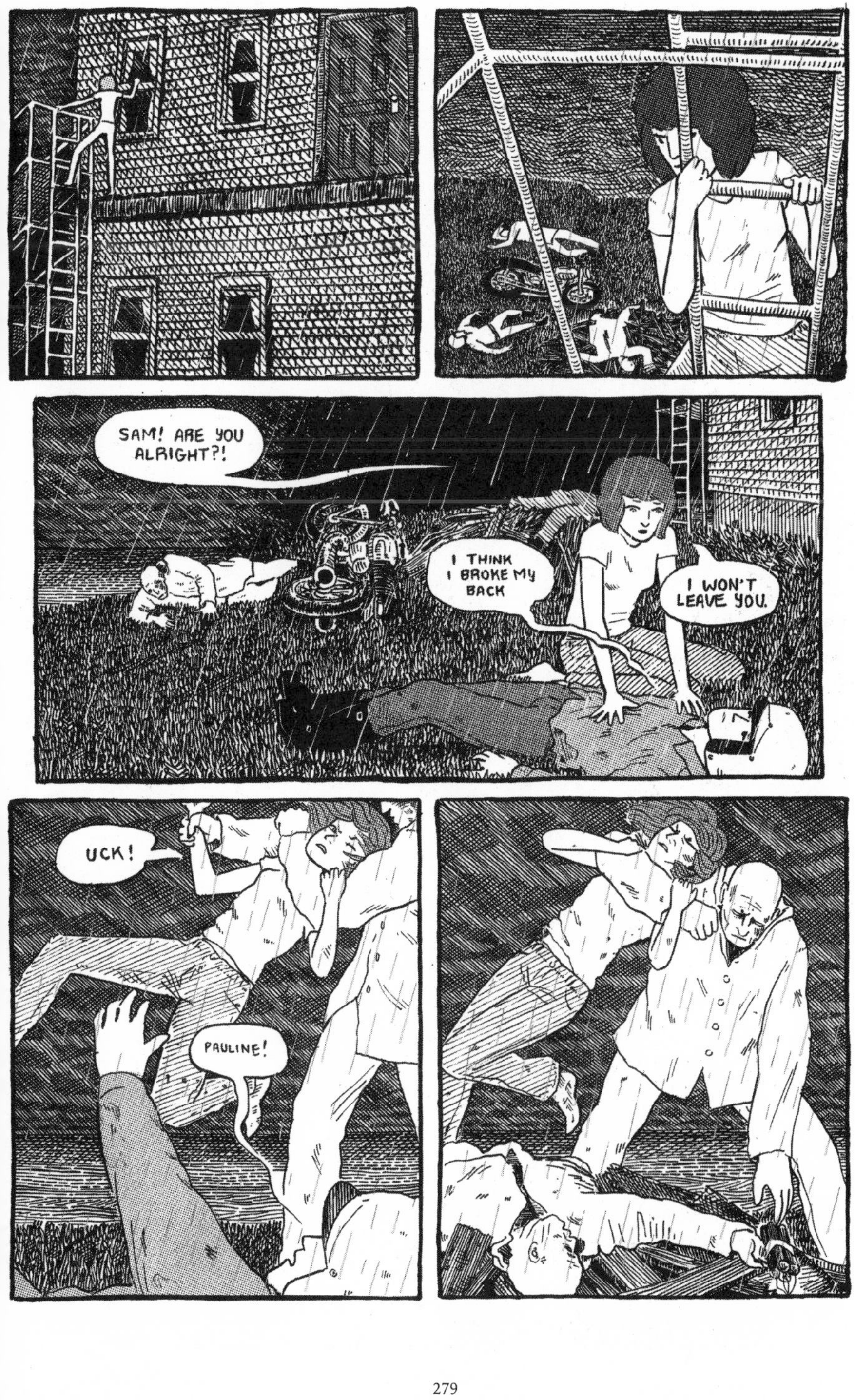
SAM! ARE YOU ALRIGHT?!
I THINK I BROKE MY BACK
I WON'T LEAVE YOU.
UCK!
PAULINE!

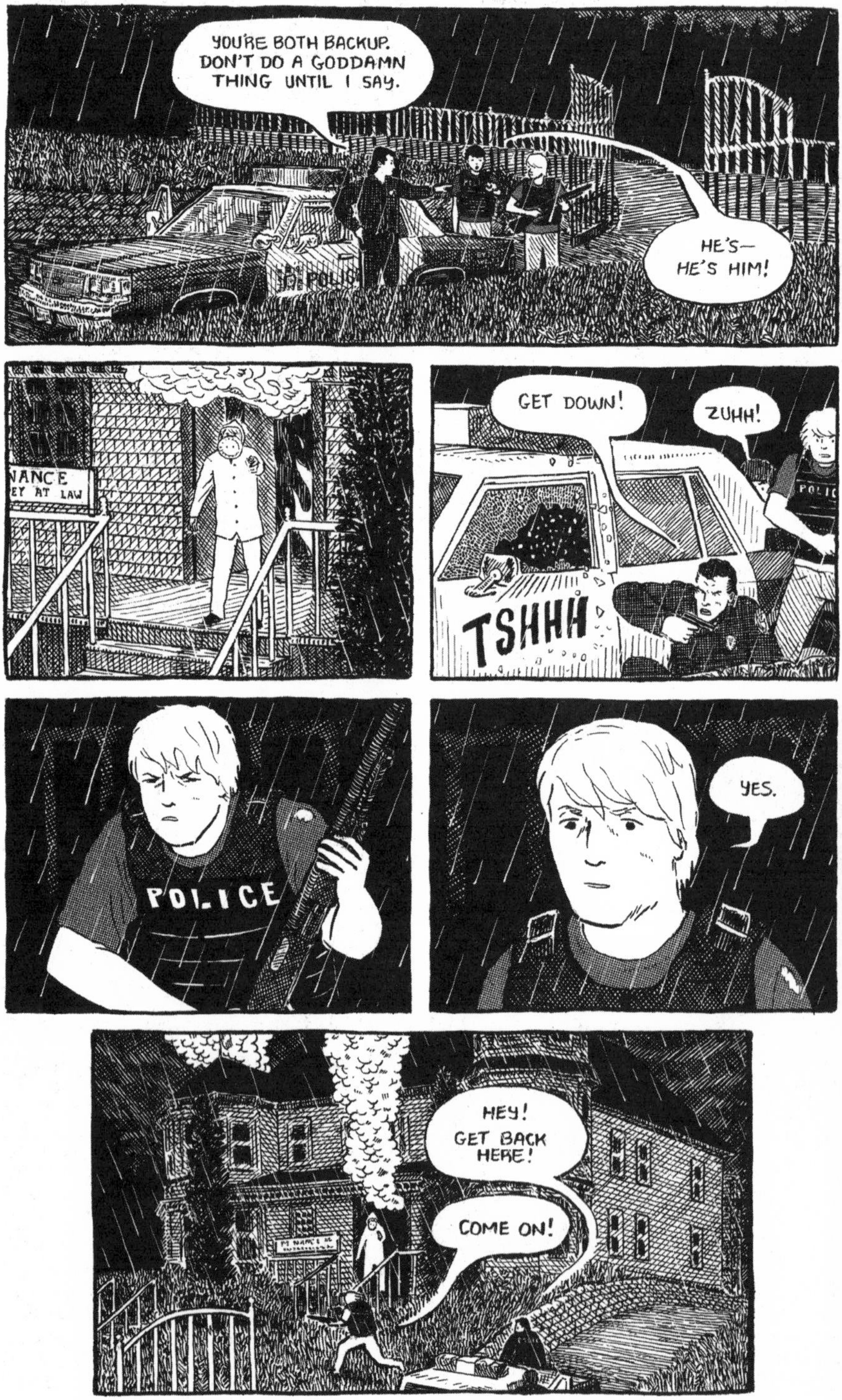
YOU'RE BOTH BACKUP. DON'T DO A GODDAMN THING UNTIL I SAY.
HE'S— HE'S HIM!
NANCE
EY AT LAW
GET DOWN!
ZUHH!
POLIC
TSHHH
POLICE
YES.
HEY! GET BACK HERE!
COME ON!

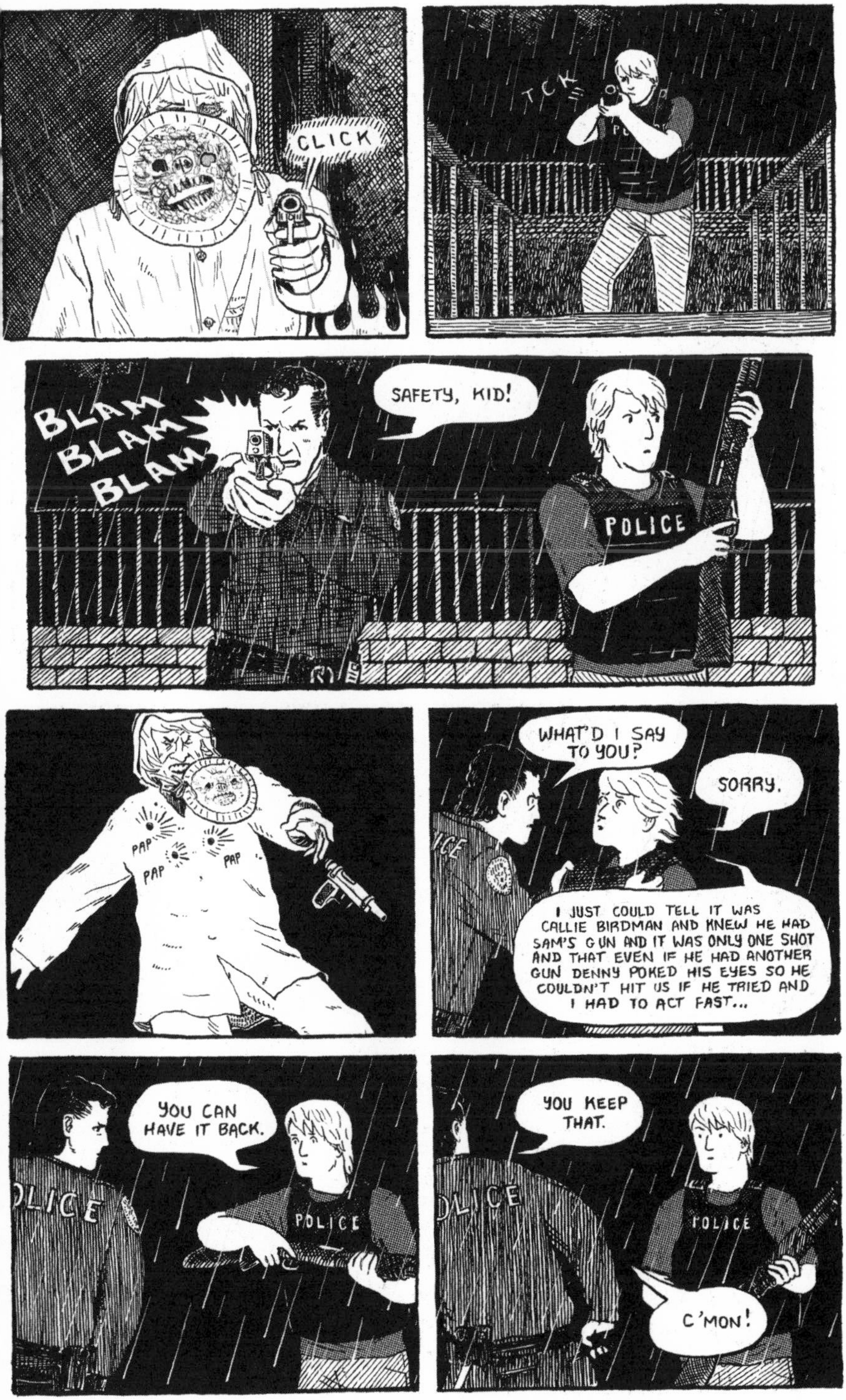

CLICK
TCK
BLAM BLAM BLAM
SAFETY, KID!
POLICE
PAP
PAP
PAP
WHAT'D I SAY TO YOU?
SORRY.
I JUST COULD TELL IT WAS CALLIE BIRDMAN AND KNEW HE HAD SAM'S GUN AND IT WAS ONLY ONE SHOT AND THAT EVEN IF HE HAD ANOTHER GUN DENNY POKED HIS EYES SO HE COULDN'T HIT US IF HE TRIED AND I HAD TO ACT FAST...
YOU CAN HAVE IT BACK.
POLICE
YOU KEEP THAT.
POLICE
C'MON!

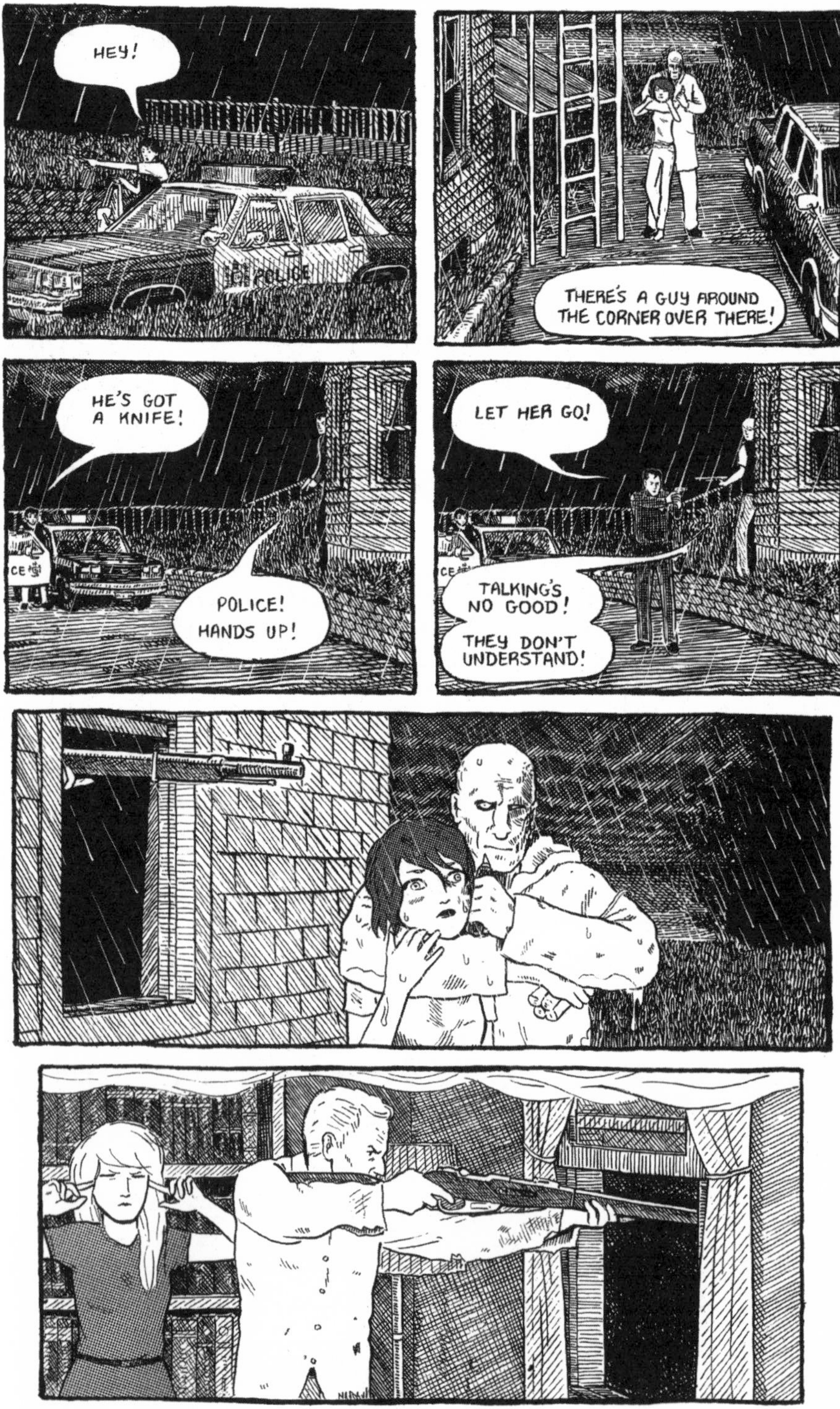
HEY!
THERE'S A GUY AROUND THE CORNER OVER THERE!
HE'S GOT A KNIFE!
POLICE! HANDS UP!
LET HER GO!
TALKING'S NO GOOD!
THEY DON'T UNDERSTAND!
POLICE

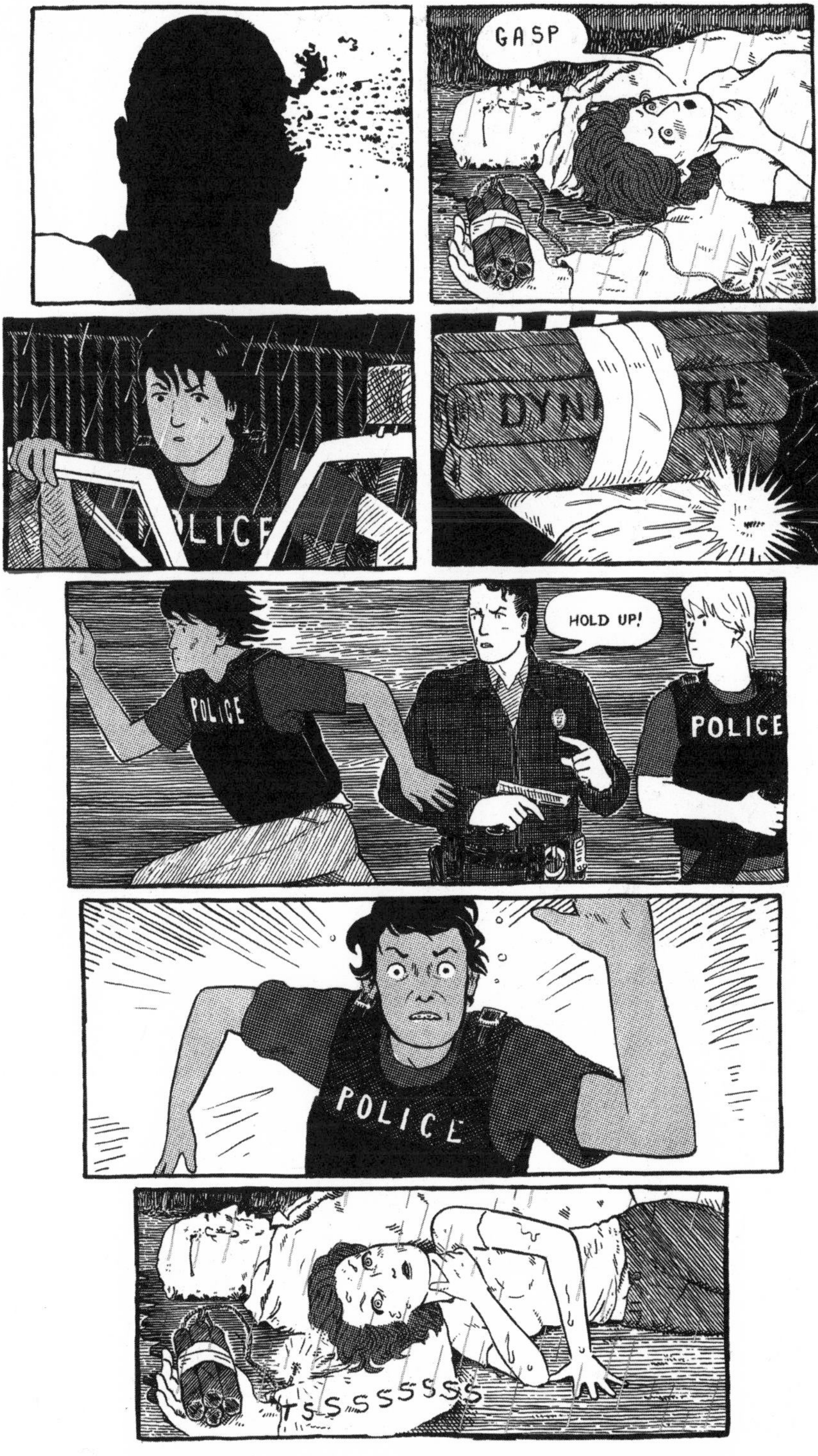
GASP
DYN TE
POLICE
POLICE
HOLD UP!
POLICE
POLICE
TSSSSSSSS

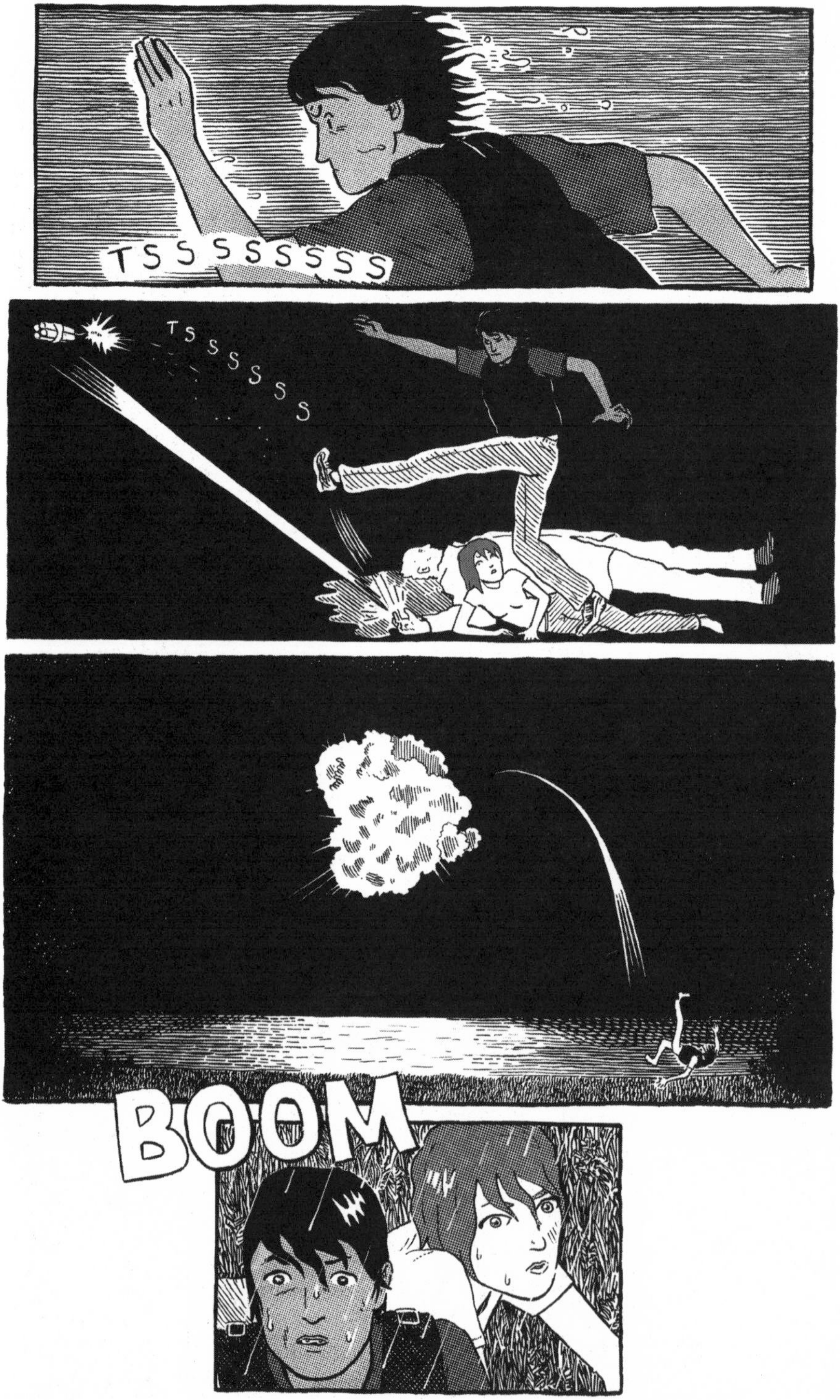
TSSSSSSSSS
TSSSSSSS
BOOM

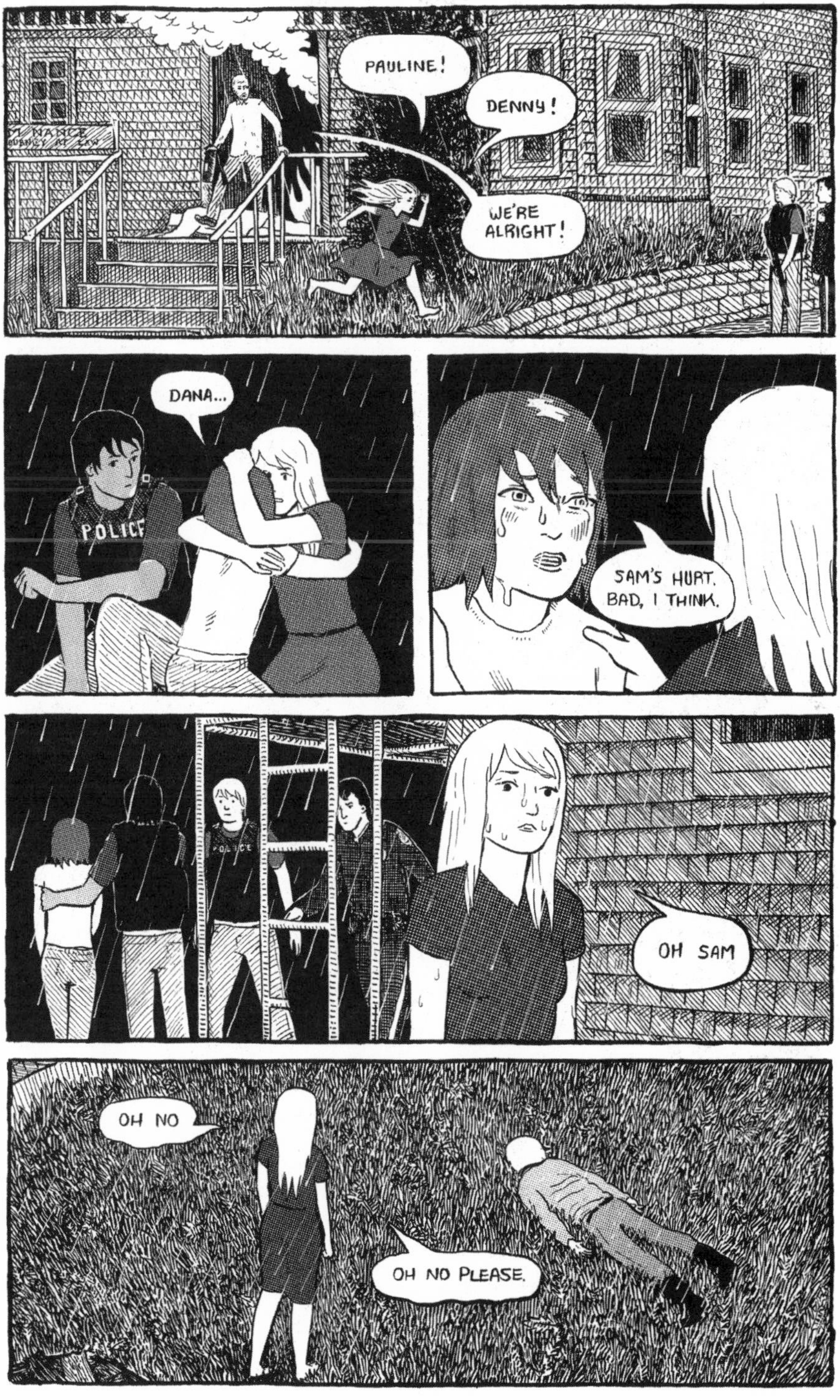
PAULINE!
DENNY!
WE'RE ALRIGHT!
DANA...
SAM'S HURT. BAD, I THINK.
OH SAM
OH NO
OH NO PLEASE.

EPILOGUE

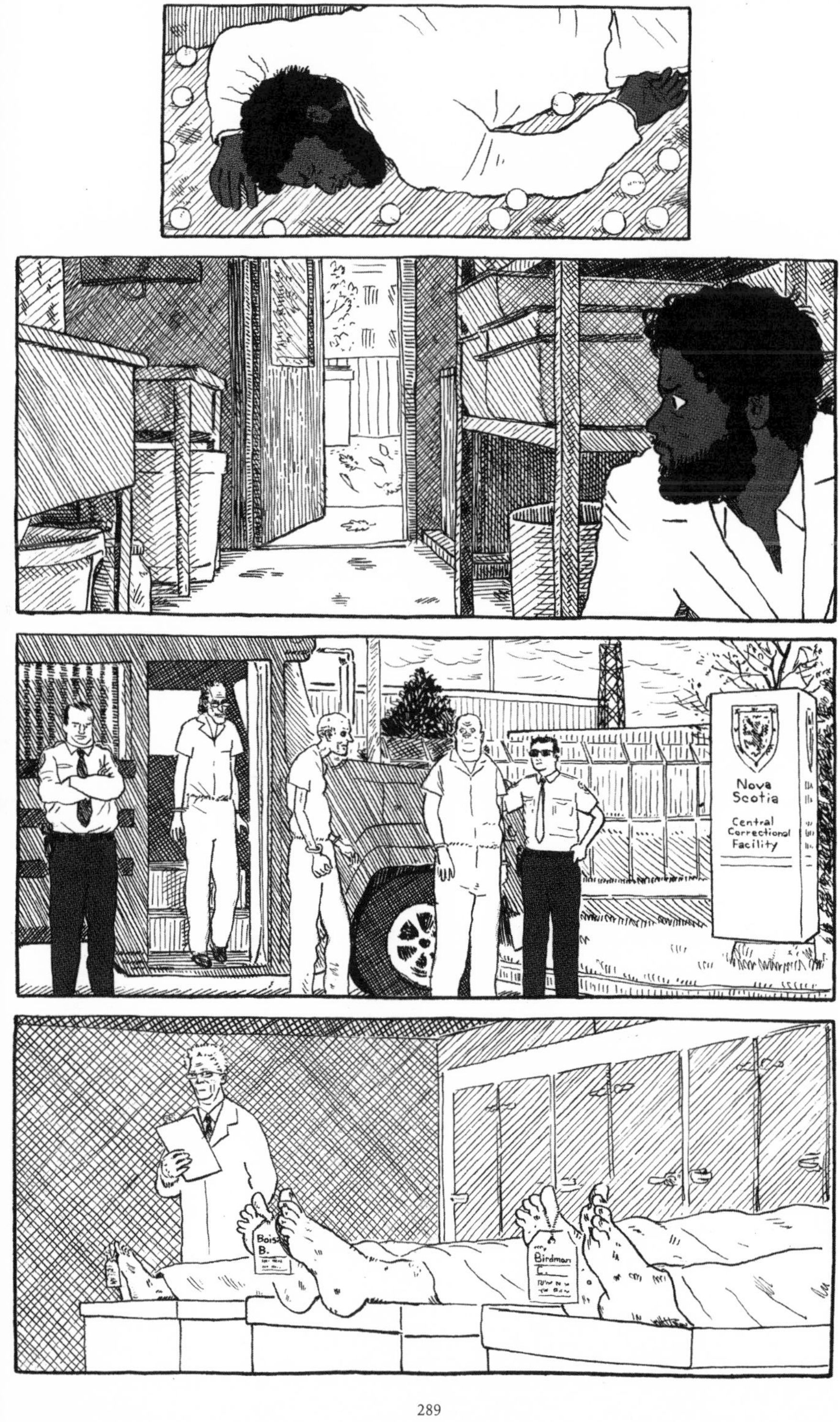
Nova Scotia
Central Correctional Facility
Birdman
C.

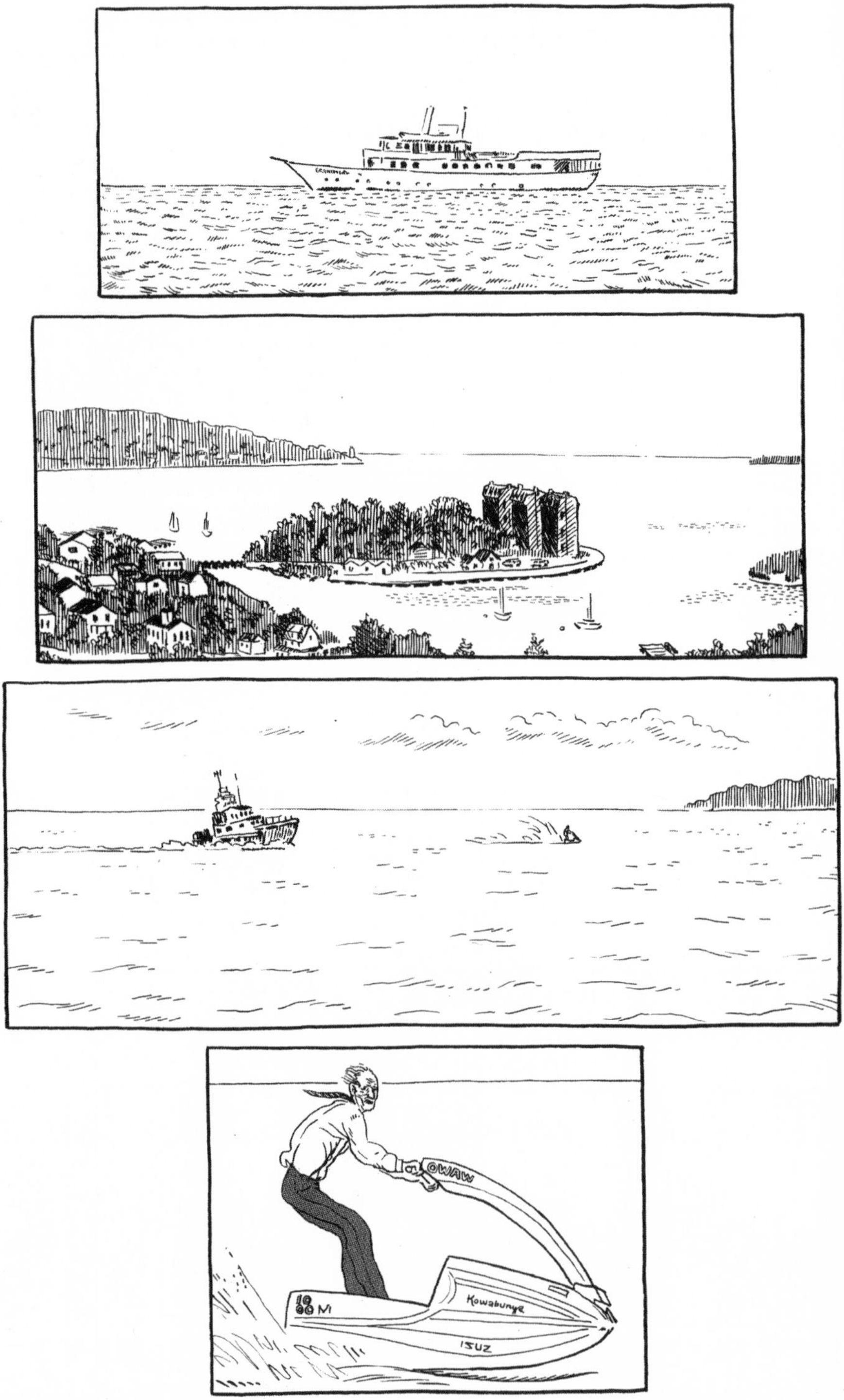
OWAW
Kowabunga
ISUZ

KRSSH

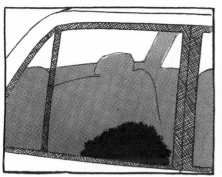

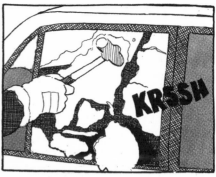

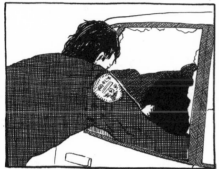

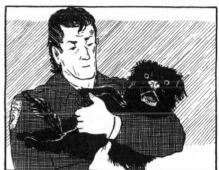

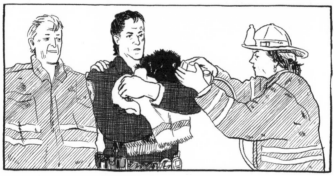

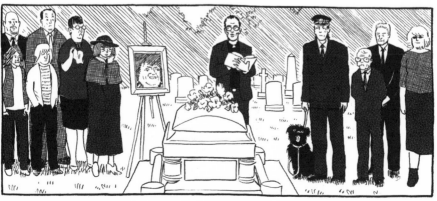

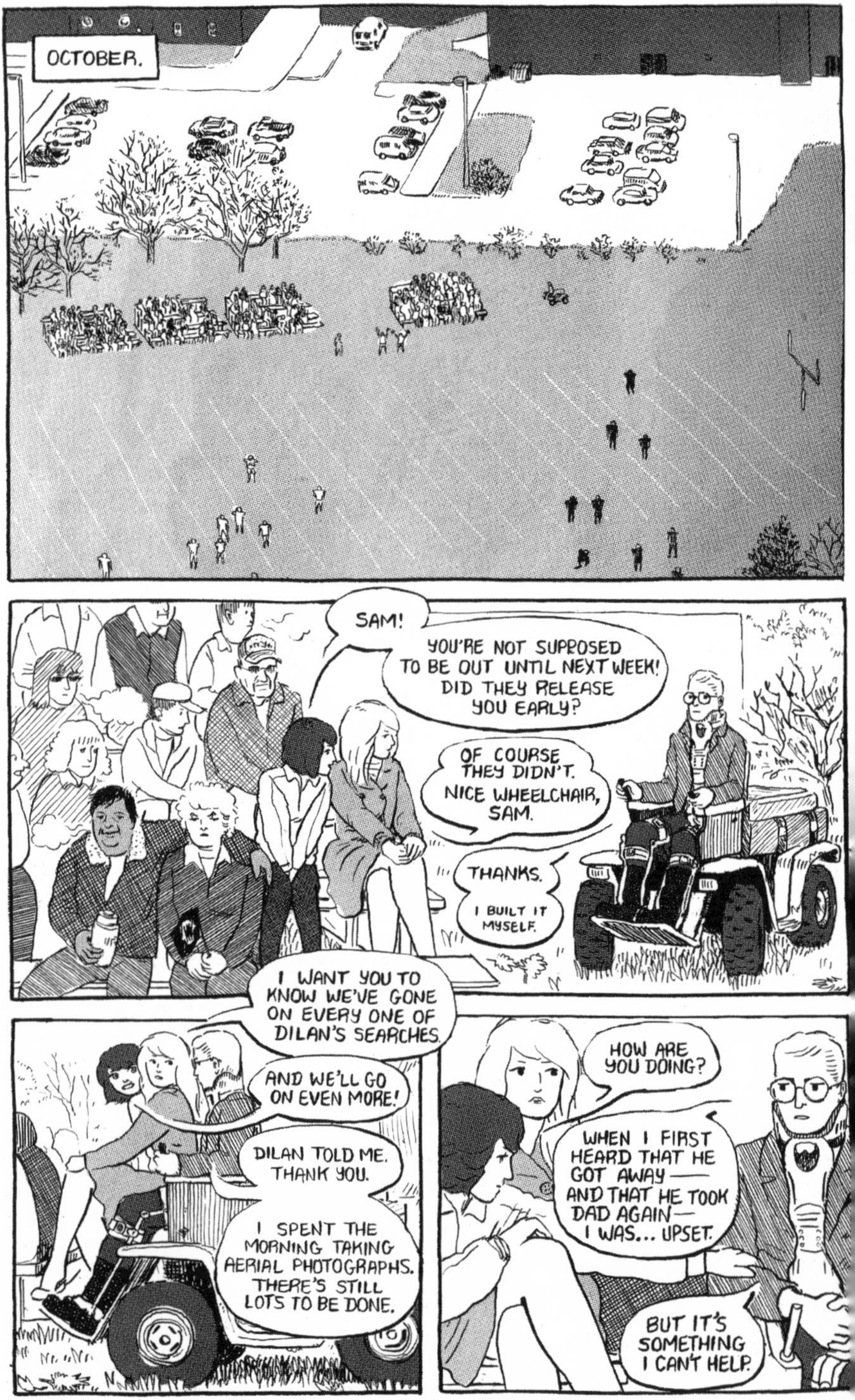
OCTOBER.
SAM!
YOU'RE NOT SUPROSED TO BE OUT UNTIL NEXT WEEK! DID THEY RELEASE YOU EARLY?
OF COURSE THEY DIDN'T. NICE WHEELCHAIR, SAM.
THANKS.
I BUILT IT MYSELF.
I WANT YOU TO KNOW WE'VE GONE ON EVERY ONE OF DILAN'S SEARCHES.
AND WE'LL GO ON EVEN MORE!
DILAN TOLD ME. THANK YOU.
I SPENT THE MORNING TAKING AERIAL PHOTOGRAPHS. THERE'S STILL LOTS TO BE DONE.
HOW ARE YOU DOING?
WHEN I FIRST HEARD THAT HE GOT AWAY — AND THAT HE TOOK DAD AGAIN — I WAS... UPSET.
BUT IT'S SOMETHING I CAN'T HELP.

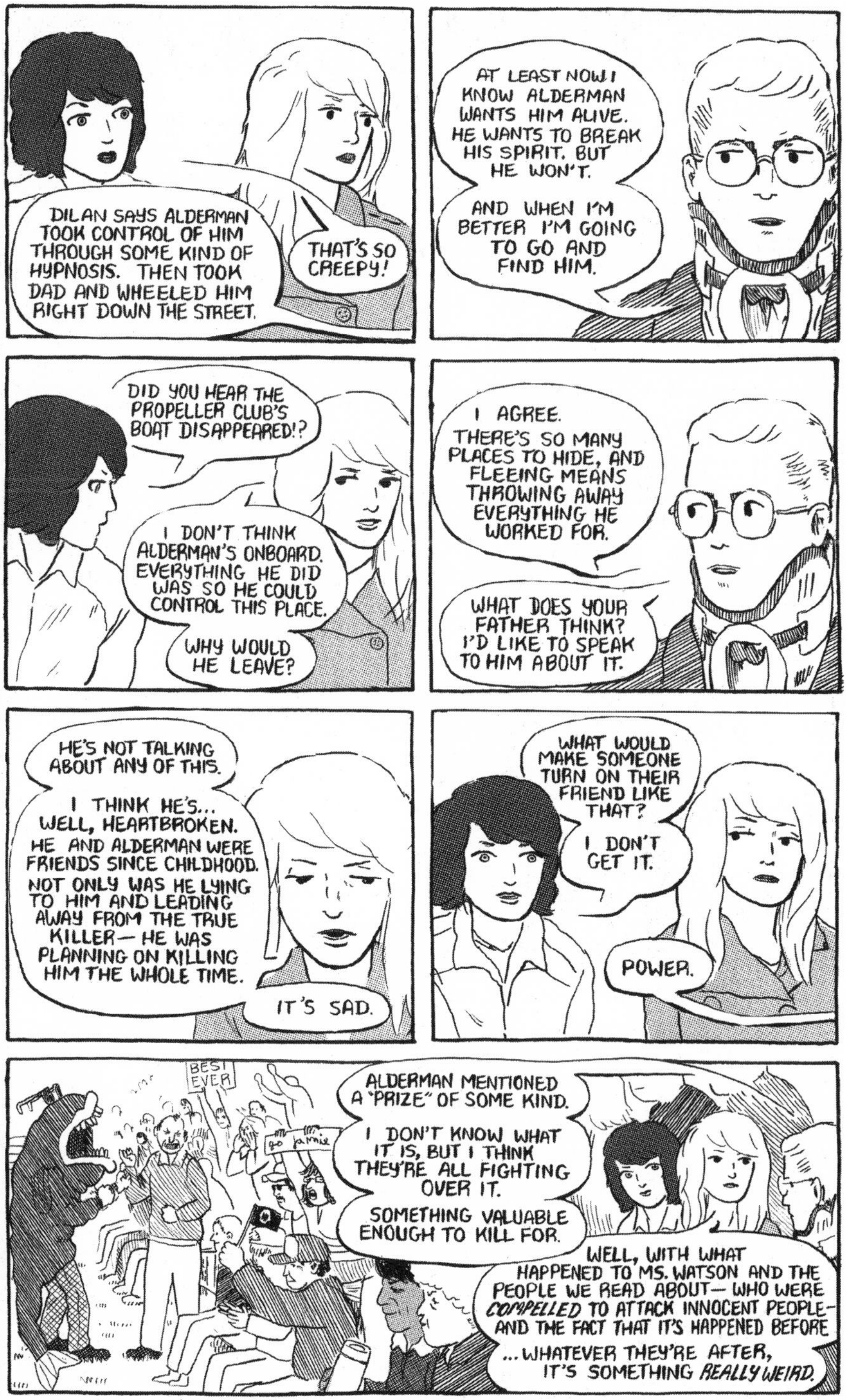
DILAN SAYS ALDERMAN TOOK CONTROL OF HIM THROUGH SOME KIND OF HYPNOSIS. THEN TOOK DAD AND WHEELED HIM RIGHT DOWN THE STREET.
THAT'S SO CREEPY!
AT LEAST NOW I KNOW ALDERMAN WANTS HIM ALIVE. HE WANTS TO BREAK HIS SPIRIT. BUT HE WON'T.
AND WHEN I'M BETTER I'M GOING TO GO AND FIND HIM.
DID YOU HEAR THE PROPELLER CLUB'S BOAT DISAPPEARED!?
I DON'T THINK ALDERMAN'S ONBOARD. EVERYTHING HE DID WAS SO HE COULD CONTROL THIS PLACE.
WHY WOULD HE LEAVE?
I AGREE.
THERE'S SO MANY PLACES TO HIDE, AND FLEEING MEANS THROWING AWAY EVERYTHING HE WORKED FOR.
WHAT DOES YOUR FATHER THINK? I'D LIKE TO SPEAK TO HIM ABOUT IT.
HE'S NOT TALKING ABOUT ANY OF THIS.
I THINK HE'S... WELL, HEARTBROKEN. HE AND ALDERMAN WERE FRIENDS SINCE CHILDHOOD. NOT ONLY WAS HE LYING TO HIM AND LEADING AWAY FROM THE TRUE KILLER— HE WAS PLANNING ON KILLING HIM THE WHOLE TIME.
IT'S SAD.
WHAT WOULD MAKE SOMEONE TURN ON THEIR FRIEND LIKE THAT?
I DON'T GET IT.
POWER.
BEST EVER
ALDERMAN MENTIONED A "PRIZE" OF SOME KIND.
I DON'T KNOW WHAT IT IS, BUT I THINK THEY'RE ALL FIGHTING OVER IT.
SOMETHING VALUABLE ENOUGH TO KILL FOR.
WELL, WITH WHAT HAPPENED TO MS. WATSON AND THE PEOPLE WE READ ABOUT— WHO WERE *COMPELLED* TO ATTACK INNOCENT PEOPLE— AND THE FACT THAT IT'S HAPPENED BEFORE
...WHATEVER THEY'RE AFTER, IT'S SOMETHING *REALLY WEIRD*.

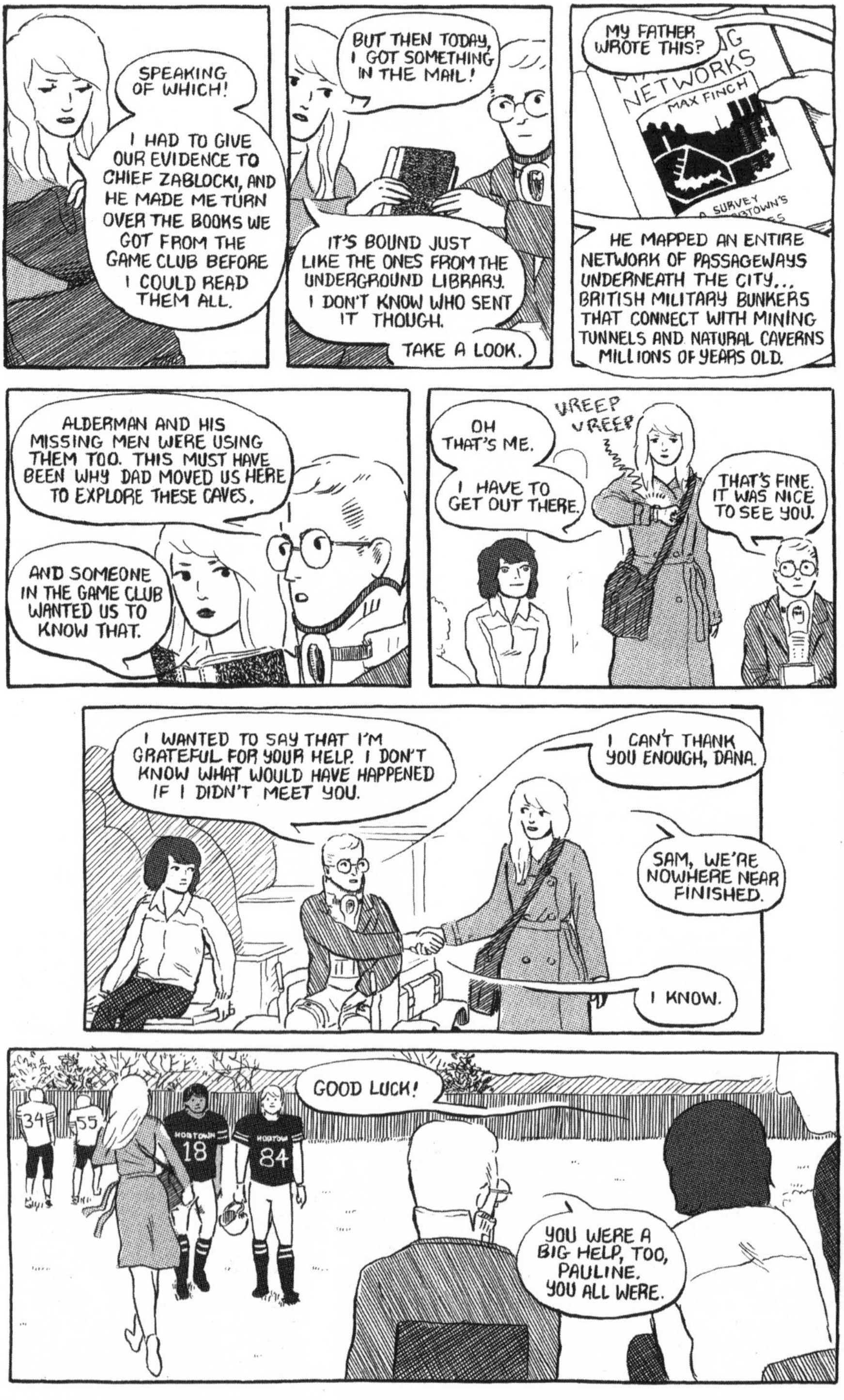
SPEAKING OF WHICH!
I HAD TO GIVE OUR EVIDENCE TO CHIEF ZABLOCKI, AND HE MADE ME TURN OVER THE BOOKS WE GOT FROM THE GAME CLUB BEFORE I COULD READ THEM ALL.
BUT THEN TODAY, I GOT SOMETHING IN THE MAIL!
IT'S BOUND JUST LIKE THE ONES FROM THE UNDERGROUND LIBRARY. I DON'T KNOW WHO SENT IT THOUGH.
TAKE A LOOK.
MY FATHER WROTE THIS?
NETWORKS
MAX FINCH
HE MAPPED AN ENTIRE NETWORK OF PASSAGEWAYS UNDERNEATH THE CITY... BRITISH MILITARY BUNKERS THAT CONNECT WITH MINING TUNNELS AND NATURAL CAVERNS MILLIONS OF YEARS OLD.
ALDERMAN AND HIS MISSING MEN WERE USING THEM TOO. THIS MUST HAVE BEEN WHY DAD MOVED US HERE TO EXPLORE THESE CAVES.
AND SOMEONE IN THE GAME CLUB WANTED US TO KNOW THAT.
VREEP VREEP
OH THAT'S ME.
I HAVE TO GET OUT THERE.
THAT'S FINE. IT WAS NICE TO SEE YOU.
I WANTED TO SAY THAT I'M GRATEFUL FOR YOUR HELP. I DON'T KNOW WHAT WOULD HAVE HAPPENED IF I DIDN'T MEET YOU.
I CAN'T THANK YOU ENOUGH, DANA.
SAM, WE'RE NOWHERE NEAR FINISHED.
I KNOW.
GOOD LUCK!
YOU WERE A BIG HELP, TOO, PAULINE. YOU ALL WERE.

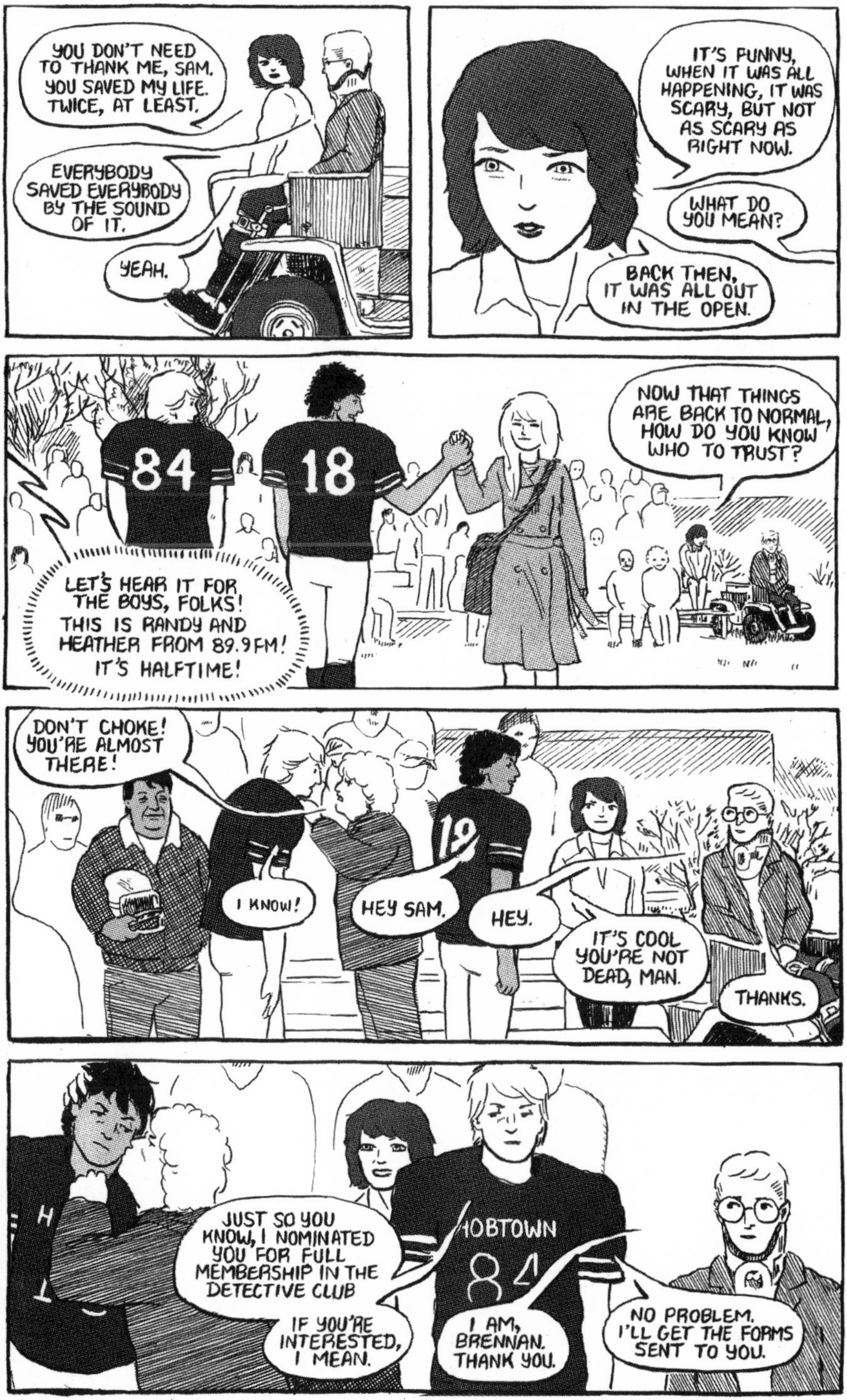

YOU DON'T NEED TO THANK ME, SAM. YOU SAVED MY LIFE. TWICE, AT LEAST.
EVERYBODY SAVED EVERYBODY BY THE SOUND OF IT.
YEAH.
IT'S FUNNY, WHEN IT WAS ALL HAPPENING, IT WAS SCARY, BUT NOT AS SCARY AS RIGHT NOW.
WHAT DO YOU MEAN?
BACK THEN, IT WAS ALL OUT IN THE OPEN.
84
18
NOW THAT THINGS ARE BACK TO NORMAL, HOW DO YOU KNOW WHO TO TRUST?
LET'S HEAR IT FOR THE BOYS, FOLKS! THIS IS RANDY AND HEATHER FROM 89.9 FM! IT'S HALFTIME!
DON'T CHOKE! YOU'RE ALMOST THERE!
I KNOW!
HEY SAM.
HEY.
IT'S COOL YOU'RE NOT DEAD, MAN.
THANKS.
HOBTOWN
84
JUST SO YOU KNOW, I NOMINATED YOU FOR FULL MEMBERSHIP IN THE DETECTIVE CLUB
IF YOU'RE INTERESTED, I MEAN.
I AM, BRENNAN. THANK YOU.
NO PROBLEM. I'LL GET THE FORMS SENT TO YOU.

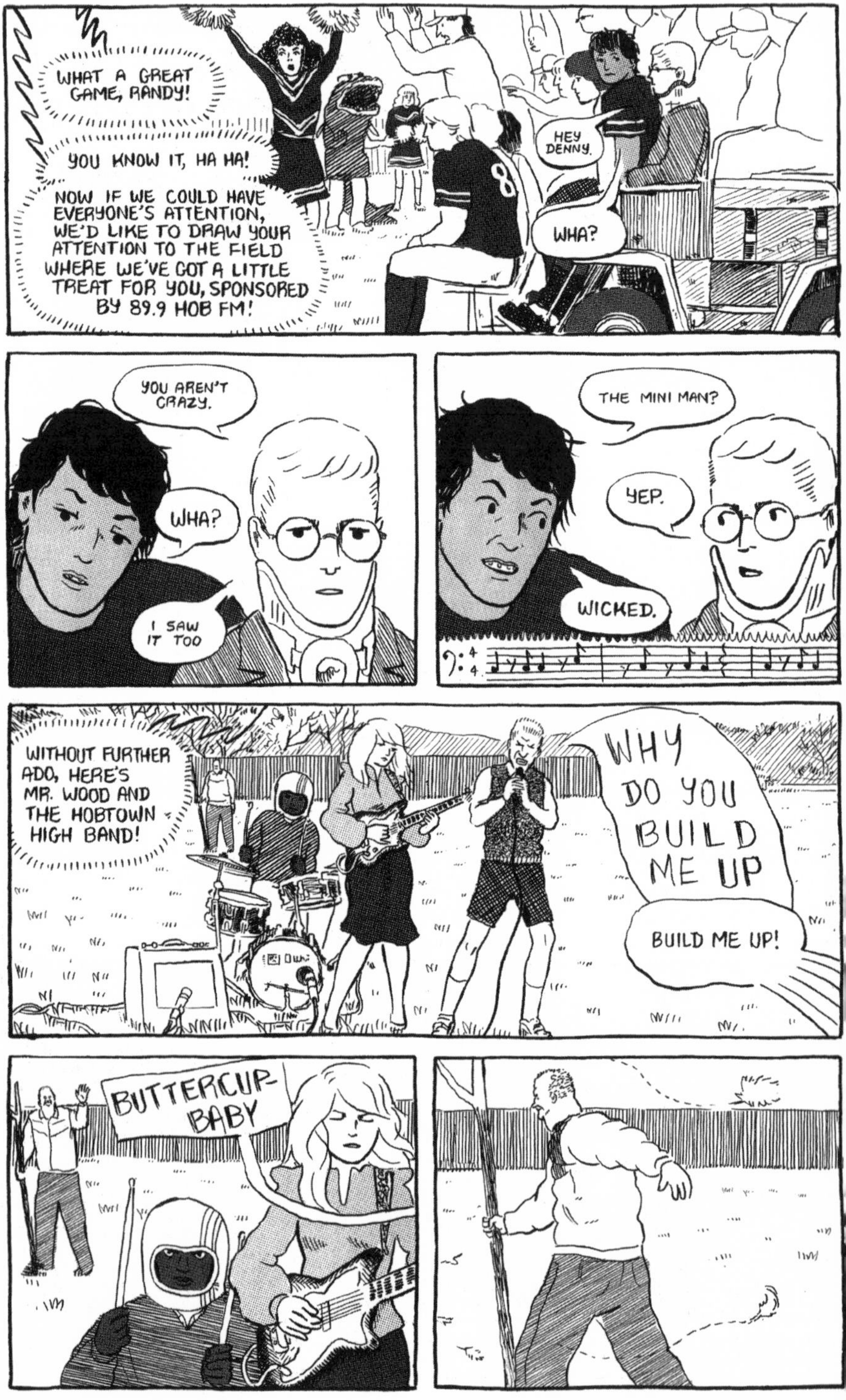

WHAT A GREAT GAME, RANDY!
YOU KNOW IT, HA HA!
NOW IF WE COULD HAVE EVERYONE'S ATTENTION, WE'D LIKE TO DRAW YOUR ATTENTION TO THE FIELD WHERE WE'VE GOT A LITTLE TREAT FOR YOU, SPONSORED BY 89.9 HOB FM!
HEY DENNY.
WHA?
YOU AREN'T CRAZY.
WHA?
I SAW IT TOO
THE MINI MAN?
YEP.
WICKED.
WITHOUT FURTHER ADO, HERE'S MR. WOOD AND THE HOBTOWN HIGH BAND!
WHY DO YOU BUILD ME UP
BUILD ME UP!
BUTTERCUP-BABY

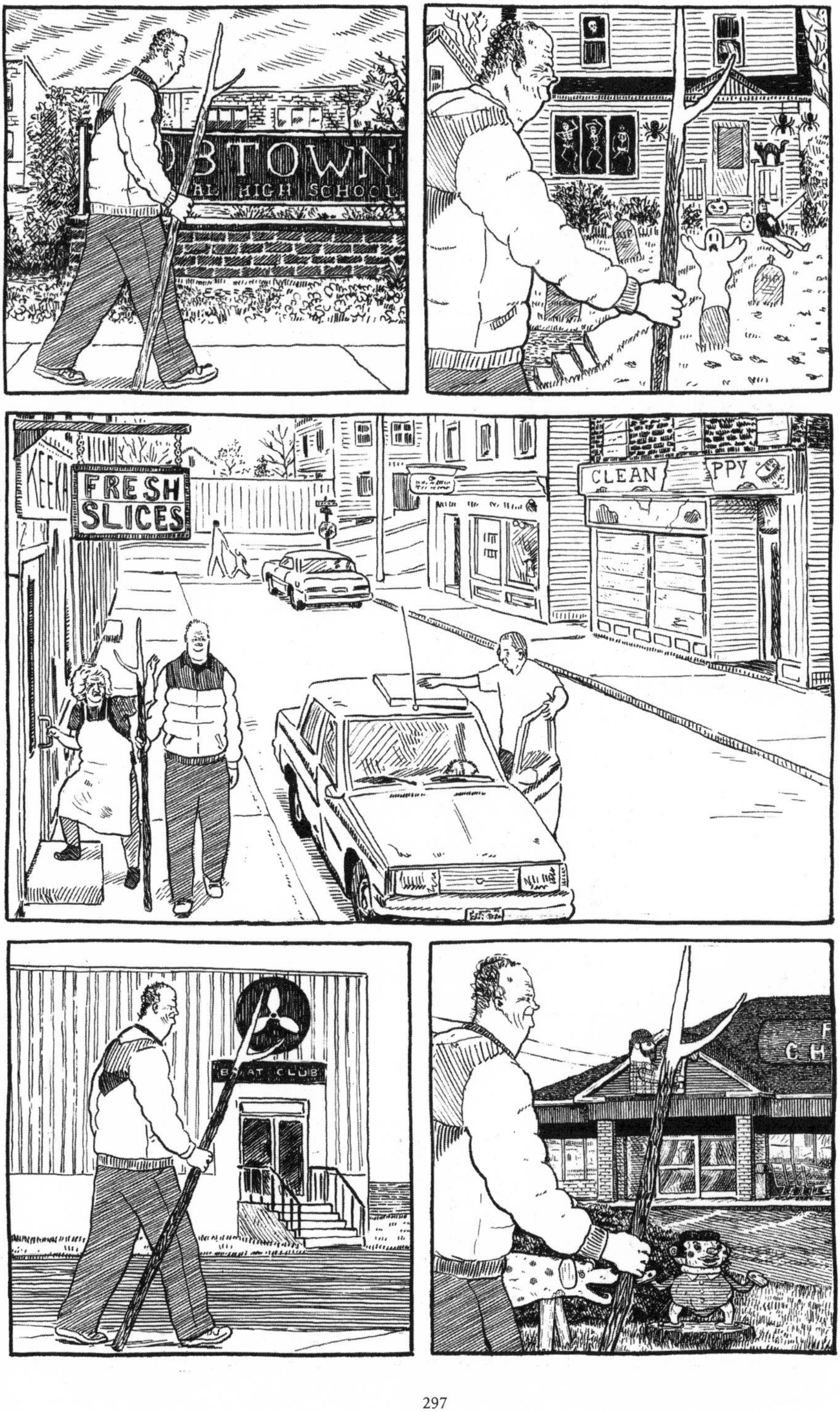
BTOWN
AL HIGH SCHOOL
FRESH SLICES
CLEAN
PPY

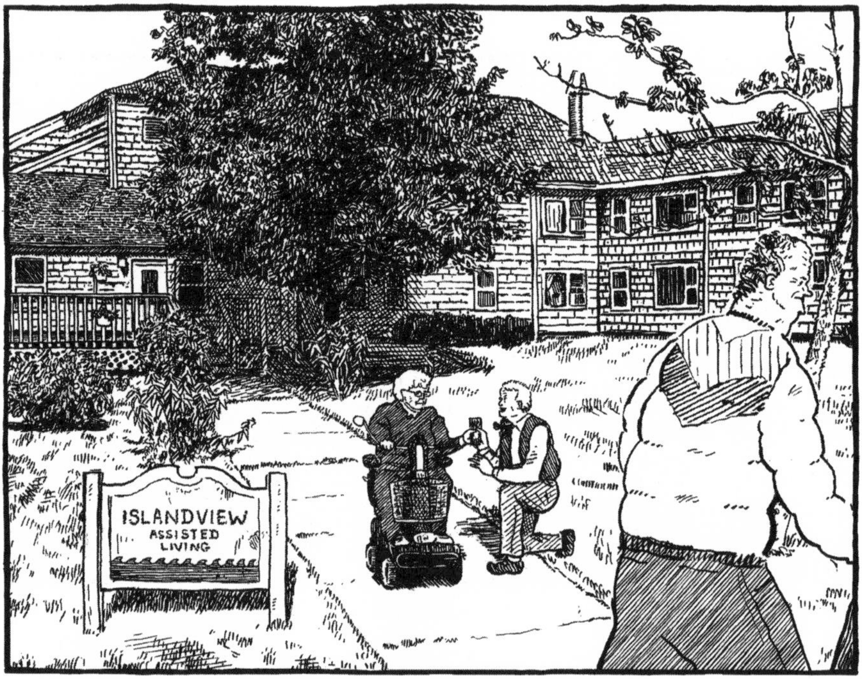
ISLANDVIEW
ASSISTED
LIVING

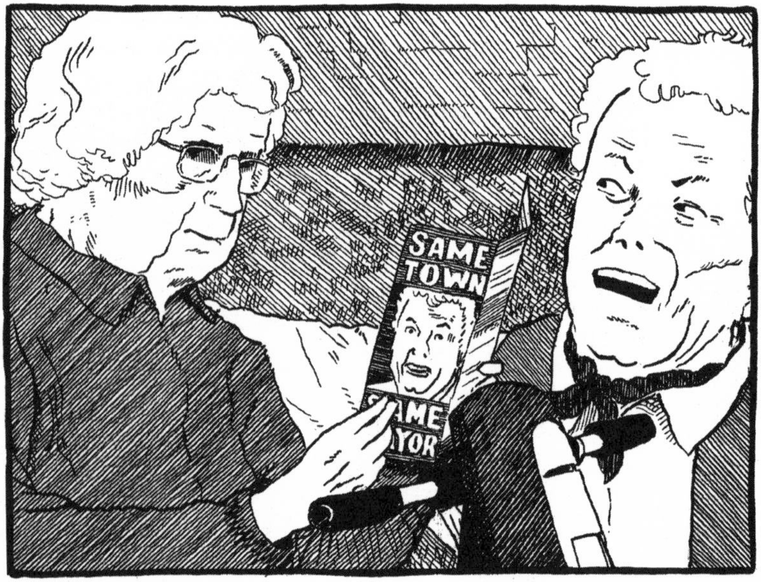
SAME
TOWN

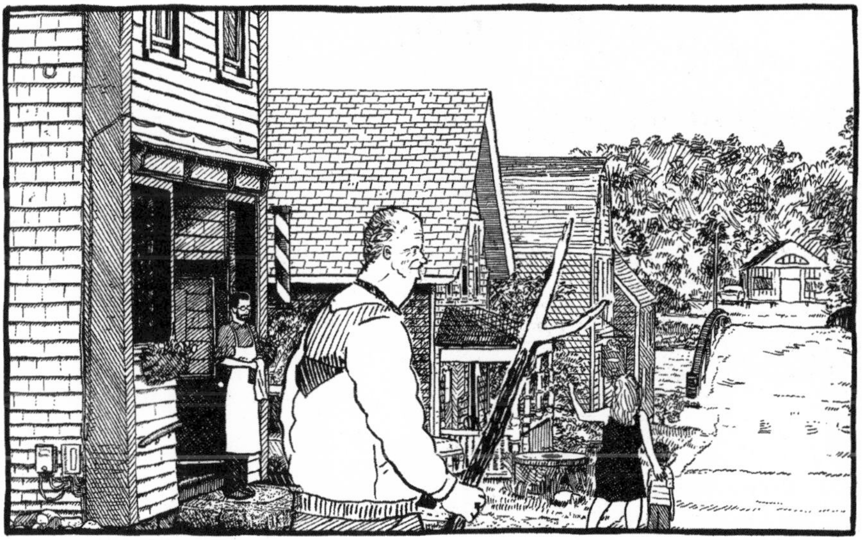

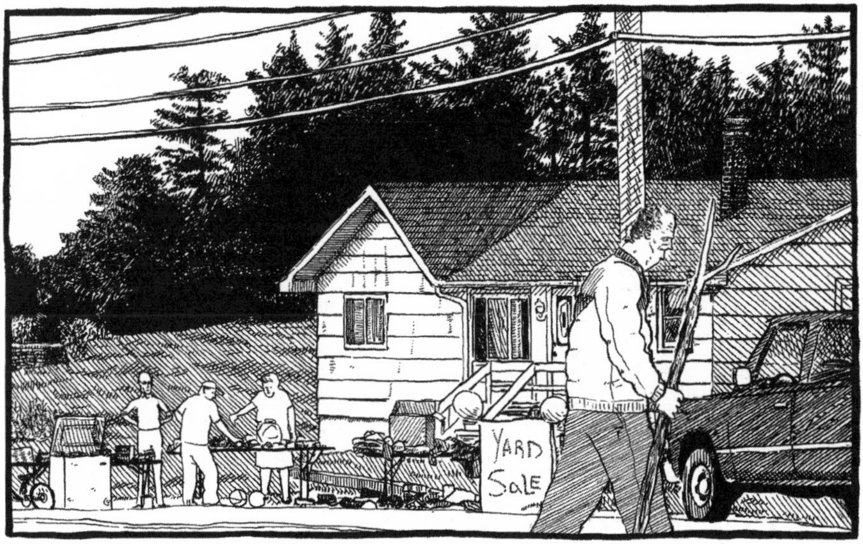
YARD
SALE

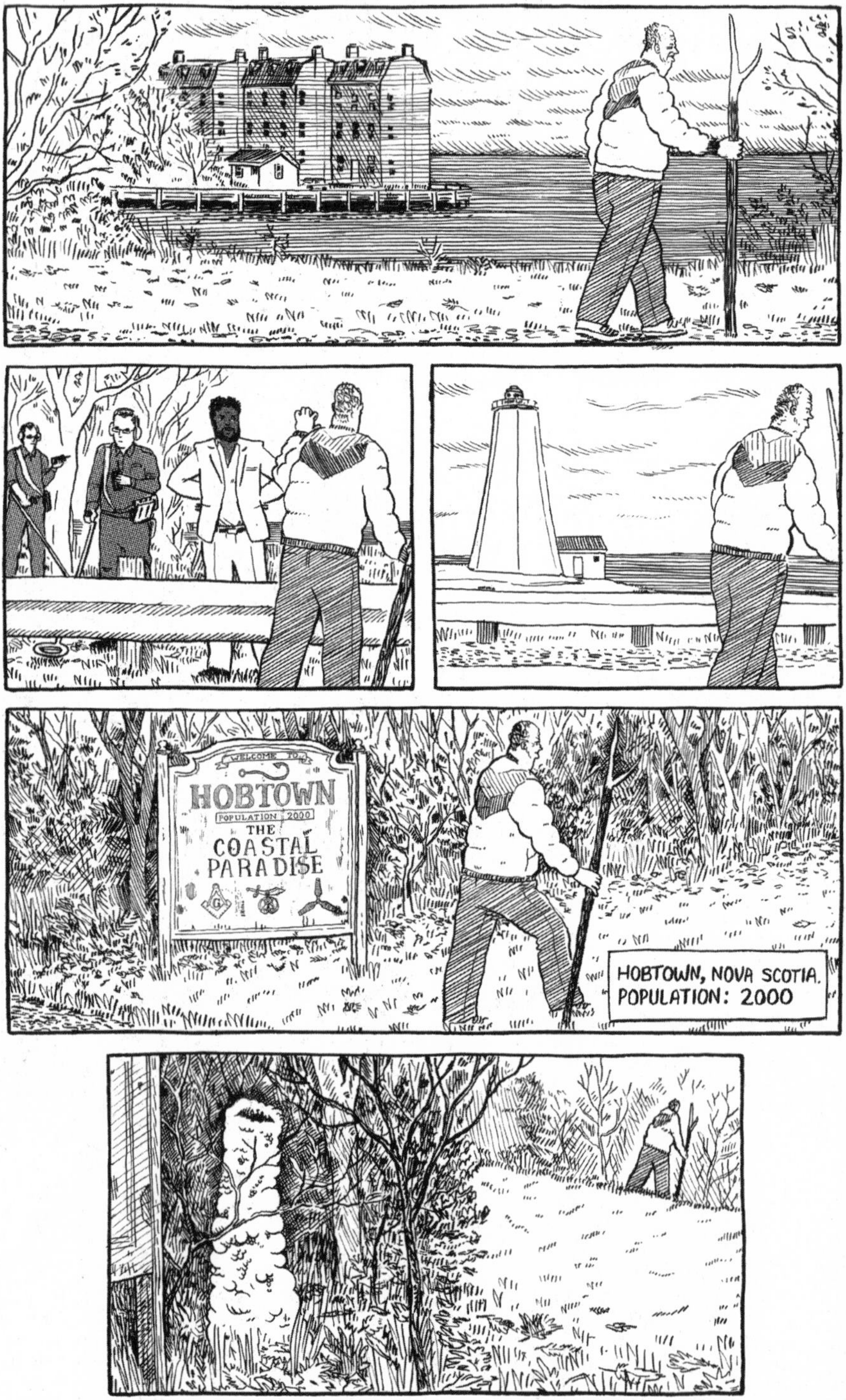
WELCOME TO
HOBTOWN
POPULATION 2000
THE
COASTAL
PARADISE
HOBTOWN, NOVA SCOTIA.
POPULATION: 2000

THE
END

We would like to thank our families, friends, and most of all, our patient and loving wives, Ashley and Rebecca, for their help, inspiration, and encouragement on this multi-year project. A very big thank you to John Forbes, Andy and Christy Ann, Alexander MacLeod, Dan Wells, Calum Johnston, and Bearly's staff and regulars. Thanks to all of our early readers, peekers, and well-wishers: Ryan Paterson, Naben and Rudrapriya, James and Gina, Trish Forbes, Nathan Boone, Amy Jones and all the Andrews, Kevin and Will, Grant Munroe, and Jason Canam. Lastly, thank you to Tony Von Richter, who first encouraged us to become friends and draw pictures together, way back in the first grade.

The Case of the Missing Men
A Hobtown Mystery #1

© 2017, Kris Bertin / Alexander Forbes

First Edition

Printed by Gauvin in Gatineau, Quebec

Library and Archives Canada Cataloguing in Publication

Bertin, Kris, author
    The case of the missing men / Kris Bertin, Alexander
Forbes.

ISBN 978-1-77262-016-0 (softcover)

    1. Graphic novels. I. Forbes, Alexander, 1985-, illustrator
II. Title.

PN6733.B48C37 2017   741.5'971   C2017-904617-9

Conundrum Press
Wolfville, Nova Scotia, Canada
www.conundrumpress.com

This is a work of fiction. Names, characters, businesses, events and incidents are the products of the author's imagination.

Conundrum Press acknowledges the financial assistance of the Canada Council for the Arts, the Government of Canada, and the Nova Scotia Creative Industries Fund toward this publication.

Canada Council   Conseil des Arts
for the Arts   du Canada

NOVA SCOTIA   Canadä